VISUAL CULTURE
IN THE BUILT
ENVIRONMENT

fb

VISUAL CULTURE IN THE BUILT ENVIRONMENT

A GLOBAL PERSPECTIVE

Susan M. Winchip

Professor Emerita, Illinois State University
PhD, LEED AP, IDEC

FAIRCHILD BOOKS

NEW YORK

Executive Editor: Olga T. Kontzias

Assistant Acquisitions Editor: Amanda Breccia

Editorial Development Director: Jennifer Crane

Associate Art Director: Erin Fitzsimmons

Production Director: Ginger Hillman

Senior Production Editor: Elizabeth Marotta

Cover Design: Erin Fitzsimmons

Cover Art: © Iain Masterton/Alamy

Text Design: Alicia Freile

Library of Congress Catalog Card Number: 2009931524

ISBN: 978-1-56367-679-6

GST R 133004424

Printed in the United States

TP08

CONTENTS

EXTENDED CONTENTS

Chapter 8 Emphasis: The 1960s 257

PREFACE

Visual Culture in the Built Environment: A Global Perspective was written for those seeking to understand and discuss the recent history of the global built environment by engaging in a contextual analysis of a particular time period from a visual culture perspective. The Visual Culture Center at the University of Wisconsin–Madison (2007) explains the emerging academic discipline, "Visual Culture Studies looks at the production and consumption of images, objects, and events from diverse cultures, across national boundaries, and within a global context" (p. 1). Numerous colleges and universities throughout the world are developing courses, programs, centers, and majors in visual culture, including Chinese University of Hong Kong, University of London, University of Art and Design Helsinki School of Visual Culture, University of Copenhagen, University of Wisconsin–Madison, and several institutions associated with the University of California (Irvine, San Diego, Santa Cruz). New international academic journals are specifically for articles pertaining to visual culture, such as *Journal of Visual Culture*, *Invisible Culture* (an electronic journal for visual culture), *Visual Culture and Gender*, and *Visual Studies Journal*.

This book was written as an introductory textbook for students studying interior design, architecture, and visual culture; however, the content and nontraditional format should prove interesting to anyone who enjoys learning about history and the built environment. The text and illustrations are presented to *explain* selected global styles and movements in the context of their development. Thus, in addition to describing characteristics and designers of a particular style, the book is written to explain *what* impacted and influenced the built environment and *why*. The book also addresses several student learning expectations listed in the

2009 *Professional Standards* of the Council for Interior Design Accreditation (CIDA). For more information on the CIDA standards, please visit their Web site at www.accredit-id.org.

Obviously, the current built environment is the result of hundreds of generations of humans and required the efforts of people from diverse disciplines across millennia. Every aspect of the built environment has been affected by countless events, conditions, and developments caused by nature or by people. As with visual culture studies, this book analyzes the recent history of the built environment within the context of these global events, conditions, and developments. Rather than simply stipulating what was designed by whom and when, this book discusses designs within the context of their evolution. For example, to understand how and why the Viceroy's House (1912–1931) in New Delhi, India, was designed, the section begins with a description of Great Britain's existence as a colonial power. To fully understand how and why public housing in the United States and Australia was built requires an explanation of social issues in the 1970s. To fully understand how and why Joe Colombo designed the *Universale* chair (1965) requires an explanation of space exploration and the development of plastic technologies. This narrative format should aid retention, encourage discussions, enhance critical thinking skills, and develop an understanding of the relationships between events and the built environment.

In addition to reviewing commonly known built environments are contextual discussions on topics such as low-income housing, apartheid, air terrorism, recent excavations, commerce, photonic textiles, fashion, influenza pandemic, and nuclear disasters. The book also addresses the built environment in places such as Lhasa, Tibet; Mali, Africa; Uruguay; Argentina; Bangladesh; Saudi Arabia; New Caledonia; Slovenia; Guadalajara, Mexico; and Algeria. Every chapter discusses how global interior environments and architecture were impacted by current events, developments, and conditions. These occurrences serve as the causal actions for understanding how and why interior environments and architecture developed from predominantly the 19th century to the 2000s. The description of events also provides a rich potpourri of information. For example, in Chapter 3 one can read about the built environment within the context of the 1911 Chinese Revolution, the 1917 Russian Revolution, archeological discoveries, World War I, the building of the Panama Canal, Formica, Elsie de Wolfe, Frank Parsons, the 1918 Influenza Pandemic, and the flourishing of Ballets Russe.

The textbook divides the prescribed timeline into 11 chapters, with some topics overlapping decades. Except for the first and last chapters, each chapter emphasizes a decade in the 20th century. The first chapter provides an overview of the global events and conditions that affected designs predominantly in the 19th century, providing the context for understanding the deveopments that occurred in the 20th and 21st centuries. The last chapter includes the 1990s and the 2000s. Each chapter reviews a time period within the global context of six areas: (1) politics and government, (2) the effects and conditions of the natural environmental conditions, (3) technological developments, (4) life and work styles, (5) visual and performing arts, and (6) business and economics.

To identify the topics for each area, the author conducted an extensive review of global historical events. Concurrently, an extensive analysis was conducted of significant developments during corresponding periods. Each section in a chapter reflects an integration of global events and developments. For example, one section in Chapter 9 examines the way the Vietnam War affected architecture and interior design. The text provides a brief description of the Vietnam War, followed by a discussion of how and why the war affected various types of dwellings in South Vietnam. Similarly, a section in Chapter 10 discusses the impact of religion with regard to the architecture and design of mosques. The section begins with a brief description of Morocco's history and the Islam religion, which provides the basis for the discussion of the Hassan II Mosque in Morocco and the Hajj Terminal in Saudi Arabia. The descriptions give an understanding of how and why historical events affected the design of the built environment. Merely identifying an event is not sufficient for understanding design within the context of the cultural, sociological, and political conditions, and for recognizing the relationships between events and the built environment.

Connections, such as Colombo's *Universale* chair (1965) and plastic technologies, are identified as a way to stimulate discussions regarding the causes and effects of the built environment. Other individuals may contend, for example, that Colombo's designs were primarily influenced by other topics, such as Italian lifestyles. This book was written to encourage these various perspectives and their subsequent discussions. Every example cited has a multitude of influences, thus stimulating perspectives that present alternative arguments, such as analyses that involve multiple decades. For example, projects from Le Corbusier's long career are identified in several chapters. Individuals could therefore discuss how Le Corbusier's oeuvre changed over the decades, as well as the events, conditions, and developments that elicited Le Corbusier's respective designs. Examining technology across several decades is another approach that could be explored using the content provided throughout the book. Hopefully, by exploring and discussing the built environment in a broader context of its development, the reader will gain an understanding of past designs, and the book's pedagogical approach will stimulate perspectives regarding expectations for future interior environments and architecture.

ACKNOWLEDGMENTS

This textbook is the fourth book the author has written for Fairchild Publications. A great deal of gratitude is extended to Olga Kontzias, who years ago gave me the opportunity to become an author. I am very appreciative for the thoughtful analysis and suggestions provided by the reviewers, including S. J. Normand, Algonquin College; Douglas Stewart, O'More College of Design; and Philip E. Smith, Art Institute of York—Pennsylvania. Thank you also to all of the talented and professional Fairchild Books staff, including Jennifer Crane, Erin Fitzsimmons, Alicia Freile, Elizabeth Marotta, account managers, and the other individuals in editorial development, design, and production. Warm appreciation is extended to my children, parents, grandmother, siblings, and friends for their years of encouragement. As always, I am deeply thankful for my husband, Galen, and his unending support and patience. This book is dedicated to my dear father, Harry Tabel, who passed away months before publication, and my first grandchild, Christian Samuel Harshbarger, whose sweet smile provides all the inspiration an author ever needs.

INTRODUCTION

UNDERSTANDING THE BOOK'S PREMISE AND ITS IMPLICATIONS TO READERS

Visual Culture in the Built Environment: A Global Perspective is not a traditional approach to the history of interior environments and architecture. The book was written to broaden an understanding of Western and non-Western interior environments and architecture by exploring the built environment within the *global* context of the arts, business, education, engineering, humanities, medicine, technology, the sciences, and social sciences. This interdisciplinary global approach reflects the perspectives of "visual culture" studies, an emerging international academic discipline. The University of Wisconsin–Madison (2007) provides a definition:

> *[Visual culture] is concerned with everything we see, have seen, or may visualize—paintings, sculptures, movies, television, photographs, furniture, utensils, gardens, dance, buildings, artifacts, landscape, toys, advertising, jewelry, apparel, light, graphs, maps, websites, dreams— in short, all aspects of culture that communicate through visual means. We draw on methodologies from the arts, humanities, sciences, and social sciences. We focus on production and on reception, on intention and on deployment. We consider institutional, economic, political, social, ideological, and market factors. (p. 1)*

As mentioned in the Preface, the book's approach and content are in concert with several student learning expectations in *Council for Interior Design Accreditation (CIDA) Professional Standards 2009*, such as "Standard 2. Global Context for Design"; "Standard 3. Human Behavior"; "Standard 5. Collaboration"; "Standard 7. Professionalism and Business Practice"; "Standard 8. History"; and "Standard 11. Furniture, Fixtures, Equipment, and Finish Materials." In reflecting CIDA's standards and visual culture studies, this textbook expands on traditional approaches to studying the history of the built environment by presenting content within the global interdisciplinary context of (1) politics and government, (2) the effects and conditions of the natural environment, (3) technological developments, (4) life and work styles, (5) visual and performing arts, and (6) business and economics. The reader will note that chapters are presented in chronological order and each chapter has examples of these categories. The reader has the opportunity to read each chapter in chronological order or to select an architect, interior designer, or category, such as technological developments, and explore how this person or topic affected the built environment over several decades. For more information on the CIDA standards, please visit their Web site at www.accredit-id.org.

An important point for the reader to understand is that examples of the built environment provided for each category were based on the author's discretion with the understanding that the multifaceted aspects of visual culture can be approached from several perspectives. Thus, the reader has the opportunity to debate that a particular interior environment or architecture discussed within the context of "politics and government" could also be reviewed within the context of "life and work styles" or "business and economics."

Another issue related to cause and effect is whether an event influenced a style or a style affected an event. Often the answer to the "chicken or the egg" argument is both. The reader has the option to reanalyze a topic from opposing perspectives. Dates are another topic for discussion. For the most part topics for each chapter were determined by the date of an event. However, due to the fluidity of events, and the potentially long period of time from developing the design of a building to occupancy, the reader will note dates and topics that overlap chapters. In differing from the book's presentation readers may discuss reasons why a topic could be explored within the context of another decade's events. The author welcomes and encourages these debates, analyses, and interactive experiences.

To explore interior environments and architecture within the context of visual culture studies requires an explanation of why material was selected for this textbook as well as what the author wanted the reader to gain from the discussions, including broadening the reader's view and understanding of: (1) the design profession; (2) how global events and conditions affect the built environment; (3) history and cultures; (4) non-Western built environments; (5) definitions of a dwelling; (6) how a variety of structures affect people; and (7) criteria that should be considered when designing the built environment. Criteria for the textbook's content focused on visual representations that were illustrative of:

- Global interior environments and architecture that include examples from Africa, Asia, Europe, North America, South America, and Oceania (islands in the central and western Pacific Ocean—Australia, Melanesia, Micronesia, New Zealand, and Polynesia).
- A wide range of socioeconomic perspectives ranging from the elite to the homeless.
- A town, region, or nation's historical and cultural heritage.
- World-renowned and lesser-known interior environments and architecture.

- Traditional and nontraditional (e.g., boats, ghettos, concentration camps) dwellings.
- Objects, products, materials, and technology associated with the built environment.
- Contributions to the world's cultural, architectural, or design heritage via international recognition (United Nations Educational, Scientific, and Cultural Organization's World Heritage List; The Pritzker Architecture Prize; Aga Khan Award for Architecture; and peer-reviewed inclusion in *The Phaidon Atlas of Contemporary Architecture*).
- The changing roles and responsibilities of the design profession related to ethics, society, humanitarianism, sustainable development, public health, life safety, welfare, and universal design.

Within the context of these criteria, the reader will notice nontraditional content as well as atypical approaches to presenting a contemporary history of the built environment. For example, to understand the culture of a country, as well as an event or condition that may have affected the built environment, design-related topics may be accompanied by considerable content related to history, technological developments, or lifestyles. In the 21st-century era of globalization, these discussions are included to help understand a culture as well as other nontraditional topics that are excluded from most traditional history formats. Stating or illustrating in a timeline that a building was constructed at the same time as World War II is not enough to demonstrate the connections between an event and the built environment. To have contextual understanding rather than memorized facts, a reader needs a narrative that discusses the causes and effects of visual culture. At times, the reader may expect to see more details about nontraditional materials, furniture, or architecture. Often these occurrences were based on difficulties associated with acquiring details of the built environment from remote locations, buildings located in a communist state, or atypical examples, such as residences established by Mother Teresa.

Within the context of a contemporary timeline, the reader might be surprised to see examples of historic interiors or architecture, such as the Temple of Heaven (15th century) in Beijing, China, or traditional Korean ceramics. Their inclusion is based on various reasons, including rediscoveries and public access that occurred in the 20th century, as well as reflecting the essence of material and visual culture; "all parts of the human made world are cultural documents that provide us insight into the past and present" (University of Wisconsin–Madison, 2007, p. 1). In addition to acquiring a better understanding of global cultures, discussing historical built environments within the context of their rediscoveries, or public access, captures events that occurred at a given point in time and helps to explain their subsequent influence on contemporary designs. The author invites you to enjoy the "stories" associated with events, developments, and conditions, and appreciate learning about the built environment from the perspective of visual culture.

VISUAL CULTURE IN THE BUILT ENVIRONMENT

CHAPTER 1

THE ERA OF EUROPEAN COLONIZATION AND INDUSTRIAL TECHNOLOGY DEVELOPMENTS

OBJECTIVES

After reading this chapter, you should be able to describe and analyze:

■ How selected 19th-century global political events, such as wars, revolutions, and the colonization in India and Africa by Western European countries, affected interior environments and architecture.

■ How selected 19th-century excavations (Angkor Wat and Temple of Borobudur) and global environmental disasters, such as the cholera outbreak of 1817 and the 1871 Chicago fire as well as natural resources that allowed production of the popular Chinese porcelain and Indian textiles, affected interior environments and architecture.

■ How selected 19th-century global technologies and materials affected interior environments and architecture as evident by London's Crystal Palace, advancements in the textile industry, Thonet's bentwood furniture, and railroad stations.

■ How selected 19th-century global work styles and lifestyles affected interior environments and architecture as evident by the development of *modern* homes, slum tenements, the Arts and Crafts movement, and Native American settlements.

■ How selected 19th-century global visual arts and performing arts affected interior environments and architecture as evident by fine and decorative art museums, Japan's Meiji Restoration, the Paris Opéra, and the Bolshoi Theater.

■ How selected 19th-century global business developments and economics affected interior environments and architecture as evident by Bon Marché, Sears Roebuck and Company, and the development of Art Nouveau.

■ How to compare and contrast selected 19th-century interior environments and architecture of the Americas, Asia/Oceania, Europe, and the Middle East/Africa.

*V*isual Culture in the Built Environment begins with the 19th century because of the extent of globalization during the century and provides a foundation for understanding how and why these developments impacted 20th- and 21st-century interior environments and architecture. For thousands of years, people have designed interior environments. However, an understanding of how people throughout the world have designed interior environments is relatively recent. Early civilizations were geographically isolated from each other; consequently, each community designed interior environments and architecture to accommodate the needs of its people within the unique conditions of their environment. Exploration and trade accelerated rapidly in the 19th century. Developments such as the steam locomotive, steamships, suspension bridges, the electric telegraph, and the opening of the Suez Canal facilitated the global exchange of ideas, inventions, products, and materials. Technologies enabled millions of people, rather than the few initial explorers and officials, to experience and live in various locations throughout the world (Figure 1.1).

GLOBAL POLITICS AND GOVERNMENT

A comparison of world maps at the beginning and end of the 19th century illustrates the dramatic political changes that occurred during that 100-year span. At the beginning of the 19th century, many European countries had colonies in various parts of the world, including the Americas, India, and islands in the Pacific and Indian oceans. At the end of the 19th century, Britain possessed approximately one-quarter of the territory in the world by colonizing India, Australia, New Zealand, Canada, islands in the Pacific Ocean, and regions in Africa, South America, and the Caribbean. The Russian Empire had expanded, and the Netherlands possessed the Dutch East Indies (modern Indonesia). The Ottoman Empire, one of the most powerful empires in the history of the world, still had possession of areas in Northern Africa, the Middle East, and Europe.

Figure 1.1 Map of the world.
Source: Illustration by Steven Stankiewicz.

China was the most populated country in the world and was considered the most advanced. The Chinese Qing empires possessed large areas of land in Asia and Eastern Europe. Dramatic changes occurred in the Americas and Africa during the 19th century. The extensive areas Spain and Portugal possessed in the southwest region in North America, Mexico, and South America were relinquished via revolutions and conflicts. Africa was nearly totally dominated by numerous European countries, including France, Britain, Spain, Italy, and Germany.

In the 19th century, some of the most important impacts on interior environments and architecture were a result of colonization, revolutions, wars, and declarations of independence. Nineteenth-century architecture can be seen as a symbol of conquest. Significant cultural interactions and influences resulted from Great Britain's colonization of India, Australia, New Zealand, Canada, and regions of China and Africa. Numerous revolutions affected previous colonization in South America and Mexico and altered political boundaries in North America and Central and Eastern Europe. Wars of the 19th century that impacted the design of architecture and interiors included an Opium War (1839–1842), the war between Mexico and the United States (1846–1848), the Crimean War (1853–1856), the American Civil War (1861–1865), the Franco-Prussian War (1870–1871), and a Boer War (1899–1902).

Colonization: Cultural Exchanges Between the East and West

Territorial conflicts and possessions of the 19th century had a significant impact on architecture and interior environments. When a country explored and subsequently colonized a foreign territory, people were exposed to different concepts, architectural styles, furniture designs, technologies, and decorative arts. For example, numerous cultural exchanges occurred as a result of Britain's colonization of India. Britain's expansion in India began with the development of the East India Company (EIC) in 1600. Queen Elizabeth I chartered the EIC to encourage trade between Britain and India. Europeans were very interested in purchasing luxury products—such as silk lacquerware, porcelain, spices, tea, and **calico,** the small patterned cotton textile from India—from the East. EIC's profits were tremendous due to the low prices the company paid people in Asia and the high prices it charged Europeans. To protect profits, India had become a British colony by the end of the 19th century.

At the same time that Europeans were culturally affected by imports from Asia, India was impacted by Britain's domination of that country. To monitor and govern its new territory, Britain constructed public buildings and residences for British officials. Some buildings, such as the Calcutta High Court in India, had Western architectural and interior styles. Some buildings had a combination of Western and Indian styles. An example of this can be seen in Figure 1.2, a painting of an interior in India with Western attributes, including portraits on the walls, sash windows, a round-headed archway window, gas fixtures, and an apparent sofa. In comparison, Figure 1.3 is an example of an Indian interior in 1807 without the Western influences. Some of the Indian details include the series of **Islamic**-inspired horseshoe arches with cusps and surface decoration, and the railings with jalis, pierced wooden screens. Notice also the lack of furniture, the fact that there are no portraits hanging on the walls, and the use of textiles to cover the doorway. The amount of furniture in interiors increased as India became more populated with British officials and citizens.

Islamic art and architecture is derived from the religious faith of the Muslim Empire. Most notable are the Islam mosques and palaces with spectacular interior ornamentation. In the 8th century, the Muslim Empire included India, Spain, North Africa, Egypt, central Asia, Arabia, Iran, and Iraq. The Islamic style evolved by blending the native traditions of the countries the Muslims ruled with specific decorative themes, such as

Figure 1.2 Painting of a 19th-century interior in India with Western attributes, such as portraits on the walls, sash windows, a round-headed archway window, gas fixtures, and what appears to be a sofa.
Source: Werner Forman/Art Resource, NY.

Figure 1.3 Painting of a 19th-century Indian interior without the influences of westernization. Some of the Indian details include the series of Islamic-inspired horseshoe arches with cusps and surface decoration, and railings with jalis, pierced wooden screens.
Source: HIP/Art Resource, NY.

calligraphy, stylized figures, plant motifs, **arabesque,** and geometric patterns. Visually stylized people and animals were based on the Islamic faith, which prohibits true representation of figures in religious art and architecture. The arabesque, or Arabian style, developed into an ornamentation of intertwining vines with flowers and geometrical forms.

The rugs in Figures 1.2 and 1.3 illustrate the design of Islamic-inspired rugs. The rugs in each room have borders with a floral arabesque pattern. The fields, or centers of the rugs, feature geometric patterns comprised of stylized flowers. Figure 1.2 is an excellent example of blending Islamic forms by inserting floral representations inside the eight-pointed star. Within each star, flowers are arranged using radial symmetry

by having eight flowers radiating from the red flower in the center of the arrangement. Islamic-inspired decorative themes are also evident in the textiles used for cushions, coverlets, and wall hangings. For example, the orange textile in Figure 1.2 has a repetitive motif of stylistic flowers and blooms.

Colonization of India and other Asian countries also had an affect on interior environments and architecture in the West. Europeans valued art and materials from Asia and appreciated owning possessions from "exotic" places (as well as the sense of status some felt it bestowed). An excellent example of exoticism is the Royal Pavilion (1815–1822) in Brighton on Britain's southern coast. To create a royal residence, Prince Regent, who later became King George IV, commissioned the architect John Nash to enlarge and redesign the prince's country home. Nash and interior designers Frederick Crace and Robert Jones designed the palace with an eclectic composition of Indian, Chinese, and Gothic characteristics. Inspired by Indian Mughal architecture, the Pavilion has onion domes, jalis, horseshoe arches with cusps, minarets, and pinnacles. Gothic revival influences include pointed arches, towers, and decorative tracery. **Chinoiserie** dominated the interior decorations. For example, the banqueting room illustrates Jones's interpretation of the Chinese style (Figure 1.4) by using dragons, bamboo, and painted Chinese scenes. An enormous mythical dragon is holding the large **gasolier** in the center of the room, and dragons also hold the gasolier's glass lotus flower bowls. Gilded

dragons are mounted on the rosewood **sideboards** and also appear on the eight standard lamps surrounding the perimeter of the room.

It is important to note that the banqueting room reflects a Western interpretation of the Chinese style. In the early 19th century, Westerners' understanding of Asian interiors and architecture was often based on writings, drawings, and paintings of people who traveled to the East. Jones's impressions of Chinese designs were derived from *Oriental Scenery* (1816), which included drawings of Asian landscapes by Thomas and William Daniell. Thus, the Chinese-inspired interior that Jones designed reflects his interpretation of the "exotic" Orient. The windows have swag and cascade drapery treatment inspired from the West (i.e.,

Figure 1.4 The banqueting room at the Royal Pavilion at Brighton illustrates Jones's *interpretation* of the Chinese style by using dragons, bamboo, and painted Chinese scenes. A mythical dragon holds the large central gasolier and its glass lotus flower bowls. Compare this room to the interior in Figure 1.5.

Source: Private Collection/Bridgeman Art Library.

Figure 1.5 Painting of a 19th-century Chinese interior in subtropical Canton (modern Guangzhou) area. Compare this room to the interior in Figure 1.4. Note the differences in the style of furniture, the type of lighting, the use of bamboo, the approach to the outdoors, and the subject matter of the paintings.

Source: © 2009 The British Library.

Europe), and the stained glass used in the clerestories reflects the Gothic style. The furniture and light fixtures have Chinese motifs, but the forms and designs were derived from styles and customs of the West. For example, in the late 18th century, English designers created the sideboard (without dragons) for the purpose of storing dishes and utensils required for dining. The designs of the luminaires, or light fixtures, were similar to chandeliers designed for magnificent European palaces, such as Versailles in France.

Figure 1.5 provides a comparative example for analyzing differences between an authentic 19th-century Chinese interior and Robert Jones's Chinoiserie interpretation. In comparing the two interiors, it is important to note the differences in the style of furniture, type of lighting, use of bamboo, approach to the outdoors, and subject matter of the paintings. The rosewood chairs in the interior in China are simple, without upholstery or cushions. The wood side table is hand carved and lacks gilded mounts. Daylight provides illumination during the day, and the colorful lanterns softly light the room in the evening. The room in China does not have any window treatments; this allows for unobstructed views of the garden and maximizes daylight. In lieu of painted bamboo and Chinese scenes, the authentic room in China has a latticework pattern made from wood and paintings without representations of Chinese figures. The simple ceiling is in strong contrast to the highly decorated dome in the Pavilion. The room in Figure 1.5 also demonstrates the common Chinese practice of designing buildings in groups with shared courtyards. Courtyard-style residences enabled generations to live together, but in separate buildings.

Another example of cross-cultural influences resulting from colonization is in Africa. Discoveries of gold and diamonds precipitated an extensive colonization of Africa in the late 19th century. The "scramble for Africa" involved Britain, France, Germany, Italy, Portugal, and Belgium. Each country sought to control regions in Africa via trade agreements. However, because the European concept of owning land was not familiar to many Africans, they did not always understand the arrangements. Battles ensued when Africans refused to agree with European trade arrangements, but Europeans easily won the conflicts because their weapons were superior to the Africans' spears and knives. The quest for colonization became so complicated and competitive that in 1884 European countries convened in Berlin to formulate a strategy for dividing Africa. The agreement gave each European country various regions, involving most of the continent.

As is the case everywhere, Africa's geographical and climatic conditions influenced its built environment. Africans who lived in dry regions used collapsible housing, which allowed them to easily move to areas experiencing rainfall. And, as was the case in other regions that were colonized, the diversity of colonization affected African interior environments and architecture in a variety of ways. Generally, any construction or amenities were built to accommodate the financial, political, and religious interests of the ruling European country. For example, roads were constructed to ease and quicken the travel required to mine diamonds, gold, copper, and coal. Within each colonized territory, Europeans constructed residences and governmental buildings in the style of their own architectural traditions. Some Europeans were involved in building schools and churches in order to convert the Africans to Christianity. The architectural and interior elements of these buildings often disregarded native customs and traditions. For example, Figure 1.6 is a drawing of a German missionary school in Namibia, a territory controlled by the Germans in Southwest Africa.

Every detail and element in the room is derived from German traditions, including the children's garments. The desk, chairs, benches, bookshelves, European portrait, world map, casement windows, and wall finishes are all Western designs. The furniture arrangement reflects the European custom of having the instructor in the front of the classroom and the students in rows facing the teacher.

The German classroom interior lacks the acknowledgment of the indigenous peoples, as was present in the British residence in India (see Figure 1.2). There are many ways the German classroom could have included motifs, colors, patterns, and materials that reflected African designs. Inspiration could have been derived from African textiles, headdresses, masks, stools, baskets, or brass containers. For example, the headdress, or *ci wara*, a mythical animal-human figure made by the Bamana people, could have inspired the use of geometric motifs in the form of a sunburst (Figure 1.7). Textiles could have provided the inspiration for colors and patterns on walls or floors. Floor mats, which children were accustomed to using, could have been used in lieu of benches. Classroom furniture could have been crafted in the typical African woodworking manner by carving an object from a single piece of wood.

Figure 1.6 A 19th-century drawing by Bernhard Mühlig of a German missionary school in Namibia. Every detail and element in the room is derived from German traditions, including the children's garments. Compare this drawing with Figure 1.8.
Source: Bildarchiv Preussischer Kulturbesitz/Art Resource, NY.

Figure 1.7 A headdress, or *ci wara*, a mythical animal-human figure, made by the Bamana peoples has an inspirational sunburst form.

Source: Image copyright © The Metropolitan Museum of Art/Art Resource, NY.

Teaching outdoors also could have been an option in an African village. In many African regions, structures served to protect people from the elements. However, most activities occurred outdoors in cool breezes and in the shade of trees, textiles, or animal hides (Figure 1.8). The 19th-century African dwelling illustrated in Figure 1.8 could have inspired the architecture for the school. The walls of these round residences were made from mud bricks covered with layers of plaster on the interior and exterior. The thatched roof resting on poles and reeds extends beyond the exterior walls to protect the exterior surface from rain. Floors were often decorated by carving patterns into the surface. The most common African patterns were geometric, animal, human, and floral. Animals were selected based on desirable characteristics, such as "the elephant for its

size and strength, the leopard for its lethal cleverness," and geometric patterns would "often impart proverbial or symbolic meanings" (Smithsonian, 2009, p. 1).

Revolutions and Wars: Destruction and Renovation of Buildings and Hospicio Cabañas (1810) in Guadalajara, Mexico

Revolutions and war impact interior environments and architecture in a variety of ways, including the destruction of buildings, the altering of buildings to accommodate the war effort, and providing the inspiration for the development of new architectural concepts. Wars and revolutions obviously result in the loss of lives and property and the destruction of buildings, but the type of building destroyed is sometimes actually determined by the cause—war or revolution (discounting, of course, for unintended collateral damage / destruction). Generally, buildings targeted for destruction during a war are the structures that will weaken the enemy and lead to an effective occupation. A revolution often prompts the selective destruction of buildings that are associated with the hated ruler or the contested government.

For example, specific buildings were destroyed in Europe in 1848 to make a statement to regimes. Many countries experienced revolutions around that time because of food shortages, recessions, opposition to monarchies, and the rising interest in nationalism. In addition to these conditions, *The Communist Manifesto*, written by Germans Karl Marx and Friedrich Engels, influenced the views of the revolutionaries. The *Manifesto* contended that the low wages of the working class and poverty of the masses were forms of slavery that must be abolished. Anti-capitalism declarations spurred numerous social revolutions in the 19th and 20th centuries. In opposition to the authorities, French revolutionaries in 1848 tried to destroy buildings associated with royalty, including the Louvre and the Palais Royal (a former royal family residence in Paris). Palais Royal was attacked again during the 1871 French revolution.

Figure 1.8 A 19th-century African dwellings that are designed with local materials to protect people from the elements. Compare this figure with the drawing in Figure 1.6.
Source: Bildarchiv Preussischer Kulturbesitz, Art Resource, NY.

The strategy of targeting architecture in wartime was also employed in the Americas. Provoked by numerous economic reasons in the War of 1812 (1812–1815) between Britain and the United States, the British burned the White House in Washington, D.C., considered to be the seat of power in the United States. The **Palladian**-style White House was designed by architect James Hoban; its first residents were President John Adams and family in 1800. The Palladian style is based on the work of the 16th-century Italian Renaissance architect Andrea Palladio. In using the classical orders and harmonic proportions, the Palladian style is similar to the **neoclassical** style, whose elements include a strict symmetry, columns, capitals, and pediments. The neoclassical style was a popular style in the early 19th century because it symbolized the achievements of Rome and Greece.

Several decades later, revolutionaries in India used the same tactic against the British as the British troops had used on the Americans. Cultural clashes and loss of property due to the excessive EIC tax collection system resulted in a revolt against the rulers in 1857. To clearly show their attitude about British dominance in their country, the Indian revolutionaries destroyed buildings in the neoclassical style.

Interior environments and architecture were also affected by revolutions and wars in the 19th century through the adaptation of buildings for the purpose of serving the needs of battles. As can be imagined, converting secular or religious architecture into military strongholds had devastating consequences to the interiors (as well as the environment those interiors had created). Some rooms were cleared of furniture and were transformed into torture chambers, jail cells, and horse stables. Buildings suffered assaults from the enemy; theft and substantial destruction of furniture and art also occurred. Military sites were selected for their inherent advantageous and fortification characteristics, such as being located on mountainous peaks with commanding views of waterways, a town, or the countryside. Buildings on these sites were converted to administrative headquarters, forts, and prisons. For example, high above the city of Salzburg, Austria, the Hohensalzburg Castle, a previous residence of archbishops, was transformed into a prison and military barracks during the Napoleonic wars at the end of the 18th and early 19th centuries. In Greece, on a perilous cliff overlooking the Aegean Sea, the monasteries of Mount Athos became the headquarters for military involved with the Greek independence movement. (Mount Athos was inscribed on the United Nations Educational, Scientific and Cultural Organization's [UNESCO's] World Heritage List in 1988.) According to UNESCO (2009), "to be included on the World Heritage List, sites must be of outstanding universal value and meet at least one out of ten selection criteria." The criteria include exhibiting "an important interchange of human values, over a span of time or within a cultural area of the world, on developments in architecture or technology, monumental arts, town-planning or landscape design; and to be an outstanding example of a type of building, architectural or technological ensemble or landscape which illustrates (a) significant stage(s) in human history" (UNESCO, 2009, p. 1). Other religious structures were also used for military purposes in the 19th century. On a small French island, the Benedictine abbey of Mont Saint-Michel was used as a prison beginning during the French Revolution in 1789–1799 and lasting until 1863. The initial church was constructed during the 8th century in the Romanesque style, but the abbey is well known for its group of Gothic buildings that were constructed in the 12th century. Known as the "Merveille" (Marvel), the soaring pointed arches of the structural composition echo the formation of the nearby cliffs. The flamboyant arches of the Gothic style are in contrast to the heavy masonry semicircular forms of the Romanesque style. The most elusive phenomenon of Mont Saint-Michel is derived from an element controlled by nature. During high tide, the abbey and its surrounding small village are on an island, but when the tides recede, they are accessible by land. Mont Saint-Michel and its bay were inscribed on UNESCO's World Heritage List in 1979.

War and revolutions also occurred in the Americas during the 19th century. Influenced by the French and American revolutions, Simón Bolívar of Venezuela led South American revolutionaries to fight for their independence from Spain. Battles from 1810 until 1826 resulted in South America becoming fully independent from Spain and Portugal. The quest for independence spread to Mexico in 1810, where the revolution was led by a priest, Miguel Hidalgo y Costilla. The Mexicans were victorious, and in 1824 Mexico was declared a republic. As in other parts of the world, secular and religious buildings were transformed to accommodate the military in Mexico. A noteworthy example is the Hospicio Cabañas in Guadalajara. The overall size of the complex is 538 feet (164 meters) by 476 feet (145 meters) and includes a chapel and several other buildings (UNESCO 1997, p. 69).

Hospicio Cabañas was built in the late 18th and early 19th centuries for the purpose of providing a home for the elderly, invalids, and abandoned children. The European-influenced architecture is evident in the neoclassical style, complete with a portico, ionic columns, multiple courtyards, and an imposing dome. Hospicio Cabañas opened in 1810, the year of the start of the Mexican Revolution. Consequently, the home was transformed into a prison and military headquarters, and was used by both the insurgents and the royalists. By 1824, Mexico had successfully thrown off Spain's dominance and was declared a republic. After the war, the building was used for its intended purpose except during a brief military occupation in 1858.

The architect, Manuel Tolsá, and his assistant, José Gutiérrez, exhibited incredible foresight in the details of Hospicio Cabañas by incorporating principles associated with **Universal Design** and **sustainable design** (these two principles are further explained in examples throughout the book). In understanding that Hospicio Cabañas would serve the needs of children, the elderly, and people with disabilities, Tolsá and Gutiérrez purposely designed the building to be accessible, and to be conducive to the health and well-being of its occupants. For example, with the exception of the chapel and the kitchen, the entire building is on one level without stairways. Facilities used by all of the occupants, such as the classrooms, kitchen, and chapel, are centralized for easy access with a minimum of walking. Sustainable designs "reflect a respectful interaction between people and the earth by conserving resources for current and future generations. Criteria focus on developing designs that sustain societies, the environment, and the economy" (Winchip, 2007, p. 343). Important aspects of sustaining societies are air quality and individuals' ability to interact with nature.

Every space in Hospicio Cabañas faced 1 of 23 courtyards. This layout provided people with the benefits of fresh air, sunlight, and interaction with nature.

Hospicio Cabañas was inscribed on UNESCO's World Heritage List in 1997. Today Hospicio Cabañas is well known for its extensive **frescoes** painted by José Clemente Orozco in 1937–1939. The series of murals painted on the walls throughout the interior of the main chapel illustrate the history of Mexico, including the country's quest for independence in the 19th century (Figure 1.9). Orozco artistically communicates the importance of the writings of Karl Marx by placing him in the center of the mural. The figures surrounding Marx depict the essence of his writing and its subsequent outcomes. The working class "slaves" form a sunburst shape around Marx, and the faces of the ethnically diverse Mexican people show their determination to fight for liberty and reform.

Revolutions and Wars: Monuments and Victoria Terminus in Bombay (1888) and Urban Planning in Russia and Paris

As reflected in the murals of José Clemente Orozco, a spirit of national pride is a common reaction following triumphs in war. To celebrate victories, officials frequently called for the construction of monuments and buildings. One of the most famous landmarks in the world, the Arc de Triomphe de l'Étoile in Paris, is a monument constructed to celebrate victorious battles. In 1806, self-proclaimed Emperor Napoleon I ordered Jean-François-Thérèse Chalgrin to design the neoclassical arch to commemorate his victories. Britain's victory in suppressing the attempted Indian Revolution (1857–1859) resulted in buildings in India being constructed with elements associated with English or Victorian **Gothic Revival.** The British government had determined that the style, with its Tudor influences, was unique to Britain. Thus, to demonstrate and project Britain's power and world dominance, governmental buildings had to be designed in this style. This

was the basis for the architectural style of the rebuilt Westminster Palace (1835–1852). As the home for London's Houses of Parliament, Westminster Palace was the perfect structure to showcase the British Empire and to establish an architectural style that would be associated with Britain. This style influenced many buildings constructed in the late 19th century, including new construction in Britain's colonies.

Following Britain's victory in India, some architecture resulted in an eclectic blend of Gothic Revival and traditional Indian styles. This was the result of the mind-set described above and an interest in indigenous art and craftsmanship in the late 19th century. An excellent example is the Victoria Terminus (1878–1888) in Bombay (modern Chhatrapati Shivaji Terminus in Mumbai) (Figure 1.10). The railroad station illustrates Gothic Revival characteristics, such as the pointed arches, extensive decoration, and towers. Traditional Indian architectural elements include the Taj Mahal–inspired onion domes, spinnerets, and turrets. To incorporate indigenous arts and crafts, students at the School of Art in Bombay were commissioned to create

Figure 1.9 Hospicio Cabañas is well known for its extensive frescoes painted by José Clemente Orozco in 1937–1939. The series of murals painted on the walls throughout the interior of the main chapel illustrate the history of Mexico, including their quest for independence in the 19th century.

Source: Schalkwijk, Art Resource, NY.

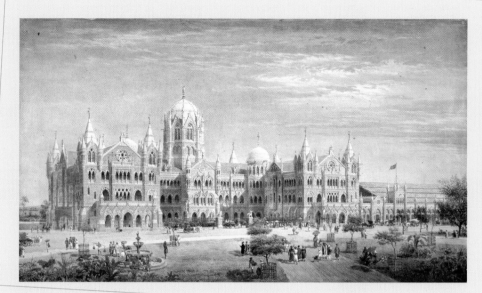

Figure 1.10 Victoria Terminus in Bombay (modern Chhatrapati Shivaji Terminus in Mumbai). Completed in 1888. The railroad station illustrates Gothic Revival characteristics, such as the pointed arches, extensive decoration, and towers.
Source: HIP/Art Resource, NY.

some of the interior ornamentation, such as decorative tiles, wood carvings, and metal railings.

The aftermath of the revolutions and wars in the 19th century also resulted in new urban plans and buildings. St. Petersburg, Russia, and Paris are two excellent examples of these extensive undertakings. In a quest to control the European continent, Napoleon I invaded Russia in 1812. The harsh winter and lack of supplies resulted in the deaths of most of Napoleon's army and its subsequent retreat from Moscow. The Russian victory had a significant impact on Europe and the world's impression of Russia's power. The defeat of France also resulted in the eventual exile of Napoleon and the loss of many of his territorial conquests, which included most of Europe. Inspired by the Russian victory, Alexander I sought to create a city in Russia that would be the envy of Europe. To accomplish his vision, Alexander I formed a central planning committee in St. Petersburg. This committee was charged with the task of transforming the city by creating new buildings, street patterns, squares, canals, and bridges.

One of the most beautiful structures built during this ambitious program was the Greek Orthodox cathedral of St. Isaac of Dalmatia (1818–1858) (Figure 1.11). The French architect Auguste Ricard de Montferrand was commissioned to design the cathedral. Ironically,

Montferrand had been a soldier in Napoleon's army. Montferrand not only designed the cathedral, but his work also included a solid granite monument celebrating the defeat of Napoleon: the Alexander Column (1830–1832) located in St. Petersburg's Palace square. Montferrand designed the neoclassical cathedral of St. Isaac in the shape of a Greek cross with a magnificent gold-gilded dome. The interior reflects the Russian appreciation for highly decorative surfaces. Marble, granite, lapis, gold, silver, bronze, and malachite are used throughout. The walls and ceiling are covered with gold-gilded religious carvings, paintings, murals, and mosaics. Some of the many artists who decorated the interior were painter Karl Bryullov, stained-glass artist M. E. Ainmiller, and sculptors Ivan Vitali, Peter Klodt, Josef Hermann, and Nikolay Pimenov.

Not long after the revolution in France in 1848, Napoleon III ordered Georges-Eugène Haussmann, the chief administrative officer of the Department of the Seine River, to completely redesign the city of Paris. In addition to needing a city plan that could support the city's rapidly growing population, Napoleon wanted a street layout that could easily accommodate his army if there were another attempted uprising or revolution. During the previous revolutions, the revolutionaries took advantage of the crooked and narrow street

Figure 1.11 The Greek Orthodox cathedral of St. Isaac of Dalmatia (1818–1858) designed by the French architect Auguste Ricard de Montferrand, and a bronze equestrian statue of Peter the Great in St. Petersburg, Russia.
Source: Adoc-photos/Art Resource, NY.

patterns of the old city and blockaded certain areas, which gave them a tactical advantage. Thus, Napoleon wanted large, *open* areas and *wide* boulevards that were *straight*. Napoleon also wanted a city plan that reflected the glory and power of France by adding more civic buildings, parks, gardens, and modern amenities, such as gas lighting, underground sewers, and adequate healthy water. To accomplish this vision, Haussmann designed the city plan that Paris is well known for today, including the *wide* and *straight* boulevard the Champs-Elysées, the parks Bois de Boulogne and Bois de Vincennes, and a redesigned Place de la Concorde with a substantial amount of *open* space. Sadly, the renovation of the city required the destruction of thousands of Paris' historical houses and streets, but Haussmann's innovative city plan, which was constructed in just 17 years (1853–1870), inspired the planning of many cities in the 19th century, including Washington, D.C., Vienna, Rome, and Mexico City.

Nineteenth-century revolutions stimulated a democratic philosophy, which was translated into new types of buildings. There was a philosophical change from the aristocratic-based thinking of the past: Buildings should be designed for citizens, not subjects. Government by monarchy was over, and the aristocracy had lost a significant amount of its ruling power. A proliferation of buildings constructed during this period—including town halls, courthouses, and national museums—embodied the newfound principles. An impetus of this transformation was the laws embedded in the Napoleonic Code created by Napoleon I in 1804, which influenced laws in many countries. The code's fundamental principles focused on freedom of person, contract, and property. To accommodate the implementation of the laws, new public and civic buildings had to be constructed. Town halls were constructed to enable public discourse. Courthouses were built to conduct trials, and to store property and civil records. Government buildings, such as the neoclassical Capitol Building (1793–1874) in Washington, D.C., were constructed as the workplaces for elected officials.

To demonstrate national pride and to sustain a country's cultural heritage, numerous national and regional museums were built throughout the world. Europeans established museums in their colonies, such as the Indian museum in Calcutta and the Central Museum of Indonesian Culture in Jakarta, Indonesia. Many national museums were founded in Eastern Europe, such as Hungary, Poland, Austria, and Germany. Other locations included Canada, Egypt, Australia, India,

Russia, South Africa, and Thailand. Collections funded by private and public sources focused on promoting indigenous arts, cultural objects, architecture, music, books, documents, science, history, and industry.

EFFECTS AND CONDITIONS OF THE NATURAL ENVIRONMENT

As is the case with every other period, the 19th century included various examples of how natural environmental conditions affected interior environments and architecture. The following discussion focuses on the effects of climate, geographical features, natural disasters, and excavations during that 100-year period. This section begins by addressing how climate and geographical features affect interior environments. Environmental conditions can destroy buildings and objects; however, in contrast, the world has been able to excavate ancient civilizations because their remains were preserved by environmental conditions. Submerged under rocks, sand, and earth, ancient civilizations have been protected from the various elements that destroy materials, such as light, moisture, pollution, high temperatures, and fluctuations in humidity. Thus, "protective" environmental conditions have preserved historical architecture, interiors, furniture, and decorative arts. Some of the natural disasters and excavations that occurred in the 19th century are reviewed in this book because of their impact on interior environments and architecture in the 19th, 20th, and 21st centuries. For the purpose of this discussion, a natural disaster includes fires, floods, hurricanes, tornadoes, epidemics, volcanic eruptions, and earthquakes.

Climate and Geography: Chinese Porcelain, Indian Textiles, and the Silkworm Crisis

Interior designers have always understood how natural environmental factors affect the development of interior environments and architecture. For example, the composition of many decorative objects is based on local materials—a necessity in remote communities whose members have limited travel options due to technology or geography. An interesting way to analyze this occurrence is to examine production processes for some of the most *popular* decorative arts and materials of the 19th century, such as porcelain, cotton, and silk. The Chinese, Koreans, and Japanese understood how to use their local natural resources to create porcelain. The Chinese invented porcelain during the Tang Dynasty in the 6th to 7th centuries. However, Europeans did not become aware of porcelain until the 14th century and were unable to manufacture true, or hard-paste, porcelain until the late 18th century. Some of this delay was due to a critical ingredient, kaolin clay, which was found in the mountains of China. Kaolin is required for high-fired temperatures. Higher firing temperatures result in the desired qualities of hard-paste porcelain, such as its purity, durability, white translucence, and inherent ability to resist dirt without a glaze. An illustration painted in the 19th century shows Chinese people carrying kaolin clay from the Gaoling granite mountain range in southern China (Figure 1.12). Formed over the ages, the unique environmental attributes of the Gaoling Mountains are required for the kaolin clay. Alterations to the environment, such as temperature changes, mineral depletions, or pollution, can affect the quality and quantity of kaolin clay.

Westerners did not discover local kaolin deposits in Europe until the late 18th century. Prior to the discovery in France, Europeans created artificial porcelains, including soft-paste and bone china. Soft-paste porcelain is comprised of clay and glass fragments. The addition of calcified animal bones to soft-paste porcelain created bone china. As demand for porcelain grew, new forms were created that accommodated customs that were unique to Westerners, such as soup tureens, cups with saucers, and candlestick holders. Porcelain even played a role in the nationalism movement by featuring the portraits of historical figures—such as Napoleon, royal family members, and George Washington—on table service pieces.

Another example of how the existence of specific natural resources fosters the development of unique arts and crafts is in India. During the 19th century, India became widely known for its hand-woven cotton, and Indians gained recognition for their mastery of dyeing techniques. Indians developed expertise in working with cotton because the fiber was in great demand due to that country's hot and humid climate. Additionally, the country's environmental conditions were ideal for growing cotton, which has unique growing conditions that include maintaining temperatures above freezing for approximately 4 months. The lack of cotton production in the United States during the Civil War (1861–1865) resulted in huge demand for Indian cotton.

This precipitated a profusion of new cotton mills in India and extensive international exports. At the end of the 19th century, India was one of the leading textile producers in the world and currently is one of India's primary manufacturing industries.

Obviously, the temporary lack of U.S. production was not the only reason for the high demand for cotton in the 19th century. Europeans valued India's cotton textiles because of the material's softness, ease of laundering, low costs, and color-fastness properties. During this period, textiles with these attributes were remarkable because Europeans were accustomed to textiles such as wool, which were hot, rough, and difficult to launder. Cotton textiles, such as sheer muslin, were ideal for clothing in hot weather, and the fabric's ease in draping was ideal for many interior applications. The highly skilled native Hindu weavers were experts at weaving lightweight cotton fabric. Europeans produced curtains, valances, wall hangings, quilts, cushions, and coverlets from Indian calico and **chintz,** a large-scaled, printed cotton textile that usually had a glazed finish.

Figure 1.12 A 19th-century painting of Chinese people carrying kaolin clay from the Gaoling granite mountain range in southern China.

Source: Réunion des Musées Nationaux/Art Resource, NY.

Cotton's ability to retain color after repeated laundering underscored the beauty of Indian dyes and techniques. Indians' mastery of working with natural dyes was the result of an understanding about how to use chemicals that adhere a dye to fibers. **Mordants,** a substance used to set dyes, created colorfast textiles by retaining bright colors. The use of natural dyes is another example of how an environment affects interior materials. Natural dyes are derived from minerals, plants, and animals. India has a rich collection of plants and minerals for natural dyes, such as the indigo plant for an intense blue and the madder plant for red (see Figure 1.2). The availability of local cotton, natural dyes, and talented weavers resulted in innovative textile designs, such as **batik, tie-dyeing,** and **ikat.** With origins in Java, batik, a **resist-dyeing** process, involves applying wax in a pattern on the cloth. Wax prevents the absorption of dyes. After the application of the dyes, the wax is removed and a crackle pattern emerges. Common colors of batik textiles are blue, brown, or red.

Another resist process, tie-dyeing, is created by gathering and tying various areas of a cloth followed by an immersion in a dye bath. The tied areas do not absorb the dye, thus creating the pattern. This process is usually repeated with a variety of colors to create an array of patterns. Ikat is a complex weaving and resist-dyeing process that requires tying threads before they are dyed and woven (Figure 1.13). The process results in a pattern that has a water-stained appearance. Resist-dyeing processes have been an important folk art in China, Southeast Asia, Indonesia, and Africa.

In addition to beautiful weaves and dyes, Indian textiles have been known for their unique motifs, patterns, embroideries, and needlework. Islamic-inspired motifs used in Indian textiles include birds, animals, and flowers. Common motifs are elephants, conch shells, mythical birds, mangos, forest scenes, and geometric shapes. The most famous Indian motif is the **paisley.** The shape, which resembles an apostrophe, was based on the outline of an elongated floral bouquet. In the

Figure 1.13 An example of ikat, a complex weaving and dyeing resist process that requires tying threads before they are dyed and woven (1860–1870).

Source: © V&A Images, Victoria and Albert Museum.

19th century, Indians used the paisley motif in cashmere shawls. Once exported to Britain, the shawls were immensely popular, which also encouraged the production of shawls in the town of Paisley, Scotland. Another very popular pattern derived from India is the **palampore.** The palampore design consists of a *tree of life* filled with intertwining vines, flowers, and blooms. The pattern was often used for cotton coverlets and wall hangings. Indians also decorated the surface of textiles by adding hand-stitched embroidery and needlework. Some threadwork was done with gold or silver threads and supplemented with sequins and small mirrors.

Natural disasters in the 19th century also affected the subsequent designs of cities, interior environments, and architecture. This section examines three disasters that had a significant impact on interior environments. These events also demonstrate the necessity of practicing the principles of sustainability. The international cholera outbreak in 1817 and the silkworm crisis in Europe beginning in the 1840s are directly related to the importance of monitoring and preserving the planet's natural resources. The Chicago fire in 1871 illustrates how human action can destroy people, property, and natural resources. Fortunately, all three disasters resulted in changes that improved interior environments.

As briefly mentioned earlier, silk imported from China was highly valued in the West in the 19th century. To capitalize on the demand for silk, Europeans and others wanted to produce the fiber. But learning how to produce silk was not easy. The painting in Figure 1.14 illustrates Chinese people sorting cocoons, one stage of the complex process. In addition to showing the cocoon-sorting process, the painting is an excellent resource for understanding Chinese interiors, architecture, and landscapes. The decorated wooden **frieze** and pierced screens illustrate China's mastery of relief and openwork carving. The few wooden furniture pieces depict elements of the Chinese style, which could have been constructed from zitan, a dense hardwood in the rosewood family that was popular during the Qing (1644–1911) Dynasty and grows in southern China. The Chinese kept the silk-production process a secret for thousands of years, until silkworms were smuggled out of China in the 3rd and 4th centuries. The luxuriousness of the fiber made it the perfect textile for royalty; thus by the mid-15th century, the French became very successful at producing silk.

Silk production in France was nearly destroyed after a disease infected silkworms, beginning in the 1840s. In 1865, the French government charged scientist Louis Pasteur with the task of solving the problem. After years of research Pasteur was successful in developing a solution (based on killing germs that were attacking silkworm eggs) that saved silk production in France. His work also produced an unexpected outcome. Pasteur's chemical experiments resulted in the creation of the first manmade fiber: rayon. The only fibers that were available for clothing and furnishings until this time were flax, cotton, wool, and silk. Rayon is a regenerated cellulose fiber that was inexpensive to produce yet had a luster that resembled silk. Rayon was easy to dye but was highly flammable. Based on initial positive public reactions, France began producing textiles made with rayon—an inexpensive substitute for silk—in the late 19th century. Pasteur's discovery that it was possible to create fibers stimulated the development of synthetic fibers, which forever changed the properties of textiles used in interior environments.

Natural Disasters: The 1871 Chicago Fire and the 1817 Cholera Outbreak

Fires destroy lives and property. From an interior design perspective, it is critical to study the causes and characteristics of specific fire events in order to learn how to design interiors that lessen the potential of a fire and reduce the loss of life when a fire is unavoidable. Two of the world's most famous fires occurred approximately 200 years apart in London (in 1666) and Chicago (in 1871). Actions following London's fire (September 2–4, 1666), which included the establishment of fire departments, fire and building codes, structures that were made of stone and brick, and insurance policies that included coverage for losses due to fire, significantly helped to prevent fires—or limit their tragic effects—in the future.

Some fire-prevention initiatives existed in Chicago when the 1871 fire started, but many other conditions fueled the flames that destroyed the city in roughly 30 hours. The ample availability of forests in the Midwest resulted in the construction of wooden buildings, sidewalks, streets, bridges, barns, and ships. In 1871, approximately two-thirds of the buildings in Chicago were constructed from wood, and some of the buildings that appeared to be masonry actually had wood structures. In the fast growth of the city, buildings had been located close together and constructed quickly. Factories with flammable substances, such as furniture-finishing manufacturers, were close to wooden buildings that stored hay for horses and wood for heating. Thus, a combination of compacted wooden structures, high winds, and a hot, dry summer provided the formula for an extensive, uncontrollable fire. The fire lasted 3 days (October 8–10), and once the flames subsided, more

Figure 1.14 The sorting cocoon process performed in producing silk. The painting (early 19th-century gouache) is an excellent resource for understanding Chinese interiors, architecture, and landscapes.

Source: Réunion des Musées Nationaux.

than 20,000 acres had been destroyed. Remarkably, however, it has been estimated that only 300 of the 300,000 people in the area died as a result of the fire.

At the time of the fire, Chicago was one of the fastest growing cities in the world. The 1871 fire destroyed all of buildings that were part of that rise, including residences, churches, banks, courthouses, hotels, theaters, offices, restaurants, schools, stores, fire departments, and the city's water supply. But in retrospect, the timing of the fire, which coincided with developments of the 19th century, was fortuitous. The city and its loyal residents had established a commercial foundation that was strong enough to withstand the tragedy and begin to move beyond it. To help rebuild, people from around the world sent money, food, and supplies. The thousands of books that Britain sent to Chicago became the foundation for the Chicago Public Library. In the spirit of victory over devastation, city officials and business leaders were determined to rebuild the city using the most advanced technologies. This set the stage for the development of modern architecture, the **Chicago School**, and skyscrapers.

New materials and technologies included steel frames, improvements in glass manufacturing, and the

elevator, or "lift." Tall structures became a more feasible proposition from one perspective when Elisha Graves Otis invented the elevator in the mid-1850s. While working in a bed frame factory in New Jersey, Otis created a safety device that prevented platforms that were connected to ropes from freefalling to the ground. This device enabled people to safely ride on what became elevators. The invention of electricity in the late 1880s improved the speed of elevators by the installation of electric motors and push-button controls.

In the aftermath of the fire, architects were drawn to Chicago to compete for hundreds of commissions. Among these were William Le Baron Jenney, Louis Sullivan, Dankmar Adler, Daniel H. Burnham, John W. Root, Charles B. Atwood, Henry Hobson Richardson, Frank Lloyd Wright, and the firm McKim, Meade, and White. Land prices escalated. Bankers and business leaders were interested in buildings that maximized their profits. An excellent solution was to reduce land costs by minimizing the **building's footprint.** However, to ensure profits, especially from rent, buildings had to be designed to maximize vertical space. Jenney, founder of the Chicago School (architecture), is credited with accomplishing this by helping to create the world's first steel-frame skyscraper. The Home Insurance Building (1884–1885, demolished 1931) in Chicago had 11 stories, which were supported by a skeletal frame of steel and wrought iron. This **curtain wall** construction method enabled the exterior walls to be non–load bearing. The transfer in building loads allowed for new designs on the interiors and exteriors, such as the extensive use of glass. As an architect in the firm of Burnham and Root, Atwood brilliantly interpreted this new architectural style in the 14-story Reliance Building (1894–1895) in Chicago (Figure 1.15). The curtain wall terracotta façade of the building elegantly displays the skeletal frame by contrasting the vertical piers with wide bay windows. These innovations, which were stimulated by the building boom, rebuked traditional architectural styles and ushered in the modern movement in architecture.

The technological advances represented by skyscrapers provide a sharp contrast to the setbacks that occurred in human health throughout the world during the 19th century. An unfortunate consequence of the accelerated rate of world travel was the spread of disease. Compared to 18th-century horse-drawn vehicles, which were slow and time consuming, the new fast and efficient railway networks enabled people with a range of economical means to travel quickly. This was how cholera killed tens of thousands of people in several epidemics throughout the 19th century, starting in 1817. People in every major city and country in the world—including India, China, Japan, Russia, United States, and major population centers in Europe, Africa, and South America—died from this condition. Cholera, which continues to kill people today, is an intestinal disease that causes its victims severe pain, diarrhea, and a significant loss of body fluids. Death is rapid: a person who has contracted cholera can become ill in the morning and be dead by the evening. Greek historical records show that cholera existed in ancient times, but the disease became an international crisis when large numbers

of people started to journey and migrate to all parts of the world. Initially, physicians believed that people contracted cholera by breathing contaminated airborne particles. In 1854, Dr. John Snow traced the source of a cholera outbreak in London, discovering that cholera was contracted through unhealthy drinking water.

Snow determined this by studying the areas in England that had the highest number of deaths from the disease; he found that these were the overcrowded, filthy slums where the poor lived. Unsanitary housing conditions resulted in sewage being dumped into rivers, the source of a town's water supply. Public water pumps contained the microorganism that was responsible for cholera. When authorities finally believed Snow's observations, public pumps were shut off and cholera subsided in those areas. Serious changes in water and

Figure 1.15 Atwood interpreted a new architectural style in the 14-story Reliance Building (1894–1895) in Chicago. The curtain wall terracotta façade of the building displays the skeletal frame by contrasting the vertical piers with wide bay windows.
Source: Chicago History Museum.

sanitation systems did not occur until scientist Robert Koch supported Snow's research with additional data in the late 1800s.

In the quest to eradicate cholera, cities developed separate systems that prevented sewage from entering the drinking water supply. Edwin Chadwick became well known for his 1842 publication, *Report on the Sanitary Conditions of the Labouring Population of Great Britain*, which specified how the country should enact hygiene and sanitation standards. Chadwick's recommendations were based on the far superior water and sewage systems developed by the ancient Romans. This report eventually affected building codes, ordinances, and the design of plumbing systems in buildings. Knowledge of how an environment could cause and spread a disease prompted cities to take responsibility for municipal services—such as sewer systems, water supplies, utilities, transportation, and streets—that affected all inhabitants.

Natural Environmental Conditions: Angkor Wat (Rediscovered 1860) and Buddhist Temple of Borobudur (Rediscovered 1814)

Excavating the built environment in the 19th century provided new knowledge about how previous civilizations designed and constructed buildings. In the quest to travel and explore all regions of the planet, people discovered, rediscovered, or began excavating several sites, including Angkor Wat in Angkor (modern Cambodia); Temple of Borobudur in Java, Indonesia; Treasury of Petra in Jordan; Pompeii in Italy; Temples of Ramesses and Nefertari in Abu Simbel, Egypt; Palace of Knossós, Crete; Mesa Verde in Colorado; and Moai statues on Easter Island in the South Pacific. Several Greek sites were excavated, including the Theater and Temple of Apollo in Delphi, Greece, as well as ancient Olympia, the site of the first Olympic Games. Frequently these discoveries provided new ideas and concepts for designing interior environments and architecture. For example,

the official excavations of Pompeii in the 1860s by the archeologist Giuseppe Fiorelli inspired a resurgence of Roman architecture, motifs, styles, colors, and decorative arts in Europe. Technological advances in the 19th century, including the steam-powered printing press, telegraph, and photography, helped to disseminate images and descriptions of the sites that had been recorded by the people working onsite.

The photograph in Figure 1.16, taken after Frenchman explorer Henri Mouhot rediscovered Angkor Wat in 1860, illustrates the challenges archeologists face. After approximately 400 years of neglect, Angkor Wat had suffered abuse from its environment: overgrown vegetation, excessive rain, and insect infestation. The photograph is an excellent example of how the interactions between architecture and the environment can be disastrous.

The rediscovery of Angkor Wat by French travelers provided the world with an awareness, understanding, and appreciation of the art, architecture, and engineering of one of Southeast Asia's greatest civilizations. As a dominant power in Southeast Asia (9th–15th centuries), the Khmer Empire was responsible for the temples in Angkor, which include the Angkor Wat complex. King Suryavarman II built the complex in the 12th century as a funerary temple using drystone, or without mortar, construction techniques. The terraced complex, surrounded by a moat, has a temple in the center with a central tower and four shorter towers at each corner. The towers resemble the lotus flower, which has spiritual significance in the Buddhist faith due to the belief that a god was born in the flower. The temple is known for its thousands of feet of **bas-reliefs** that depict everyday life, battles, dancers, and mythical scenes from Hindu poems. The scenes carved in large blocks of stone illustrate in superb detail the elaborate headdresses, jewelry, and textiles of the Khmer Empire. Another remarkable aspect of the complex from an engineering perspective is the sophisticated irrigation and water-control system that was developed via reservoirs, canals, and ditches.

Figure 1.16 Photograph taken after the Frenchman Henri Mouhot rediscovered Angkor Wat in 1860 illustrates the challenges archeologists undertake to restore a project.

Source: Adoc-photos/Art Resource, NY.

Figure 1.17 King Suryavarman II built the Angkor Wat complex in the 12th century as a funerary temple using drystone, or without mortar, construction techniques.

Source: Adoc-photos/Art Resource, NY.

In 1898 the French École Française d'Extrême Orient (French School of the Far East) initiated an ongoing extensive research and restoration project of the city and its temples, art, architecture, and reservoirs (Figure 1.17). This work has been invaluable in understanding and preserving the accomplishments of the Khmer Empire. In more recent satellite images, it appears that more structures of the complex remain to be discovered. Unfortunately, due to theft, damage from war, and neglect, in 1992 UNESCO added Angkor Wat to its list of "World Heritage in Danger"; however, due to "numerous conservation and restoration activities coordinated by UNESCO," in 2004, the site was removed from the list (UNESCO, 2009).

The life and religious beliefs of the people of the island of Java are depicted in the architecture and carvings of the Buddhist temple of Borobudor (Figure 1.18). In 1814, while exploring the islands of the South Pacific, Sir Thomas Stamford Raffles, a British official, rediscovered the temple. Folklore had described the magnificent temple, but its existence did not become a reality until Raffles and a team of workers removed the volcanic rock that had buried the area 1,000 years earlier. Influenced by methods derived from India, the temple was constructed by the Sailendra Dynasty in the 8th–10th centuries. The pyramid form of the temple, resembling the lotus flower, symbolically reflects beliefs of Buddhism. The square shape of the temple's base represents earth, and the circular forms at the top of the structure depict heaven. Hand carved out of volcanic rock, the five square terraces have hundreds of bas-reliefs that depict the history of Java and the life and teachings of Buddha ("He who understands"). Seated, meditating Buddha are located in numerous niches of the terraces and are under the pierced openings of the 72 large bell-shaped **stupas,** which are reliquaries containing the ashes of religious figures.

At the peak of the temple is the largest stupa, which represents nirvana and infinity. To serve instructional purposes, the layout of the temple was coordinated with the originally painted bas-reliefs. The lessons, derived from the teachings of Buddha, begin at the base of the temple and progress in the same path as the sun, a clockwise direction, as one ascends the hill. The teachings of the bas-reliefs begin with scenes of everyday life of the Java people, transition to the lives of Buddha, and conclude at the pinnacle of the temple with enlightenment. Volcanic rock had preserved the temple for 1,000 years. Unfortunately, after Raffles exposed the temple of Borobudur, the site was left unsecured and unprotected. Approximately 100 years elapsed before restoration efforts began on the structure. As with Angkor Wat, vegetation, rain, humidity, and theft caused destruction of the site. Fortunately, the temple is now undergoing extensive restoration, but the original elements that were destroyed are irreplaceable losses of the Javanese culture. Borobudur Temple

Figure 1.18 The life and religious beliefs of the Java people are depicted in the architecture and carvings of the Buddhist Temple of Borobudor. Photograph is from after the restoration.

Source: Werner Forman/Art Resource, NY.

and its compounds were inscribed on UNESCO's World Heritage List in 1991. According to UNESCO, "Borobudur is a principal monument of the Buddhist patrimony" and "the complex forms a characteristic ensemble of Buddhist art in Java" (1991, p. 12).

GLOBAL TECHNOLOGICAL DEVELOPMENTS

The Industrial Revolution began in the 18th century. It has changed innumerable facets of life (including architecture and interior design) during the past 200-plus years and will continue to do so far into the future. This section focuses on some of the most important technological innovations, processes, and products of the 19th century that affected interior environments and the interior design profession. Mechanization stimulated and helped to establish many of the industries that are critical to the work of interior designers today, including textiles, wallcoverings, flooring, and furniture.

Technologies and Materials: Crystal Palace (1851) in London, UK, by Joseph Paxton

The Industrial Revolution began in Britain and spread to Western Europe and the United States. The initial phases of Westernization in Asia fostered industrialization in India, China, and Japan. Developments in the late 18th and 19th centuries created new machinery, materials, energy sources, manufacturing processes, transportation, and communication. These technological changes affected the production of textiles, carpet, wallcoverings, and furniture. As previously described, new materials, such as cast iron and steel, radically changed the ways buildings could be constructed and transformed architectural concepts. These new materials were initially used for structures designed by engineers, such as bridges and canals. The Iron Bridge in England (1779), Brooklyn Bridge in New York City (1883), and Forth Bridge in Scotland (1890) are excellent examples of the use of cast iron, steel, and galvanized steel wire, respectively. The interest in using iron and steel in architecture prompted partnerships between engineers and architects, a situation that was used in the designing and building of the Eiffel Tower (1887–1889) in Paris. To improve the aesthetics of the steel and wrought iron structure, the French civil engineer Gustave Eiffel sought the assistance of architect Stephen Sauvestre.

Joseph Paxton is an excellent example of an architect who demonstrated the vision for understanding how to use the new materials and for developing new methods that were employed to fabricate structures. Paxton, known for his greenhouses, designed the Crystal Palace for London's 1851 Great Exhibition (Figure 1.19). The purpose of the exhibition was to showcase Britain's escalating world power, which was derived from the rising number of colonial territories and the country's enormous success with industrialization. Other countries were invited to exhibit their products, but the overall emphasis focused on showcasing British products, machines, and materials. Paxton's design for the building that housed the exhibits was ideal for promoting Britain. The unprecedented use of iron and glass for the walls and vaulted ceilings projected a modern image and demonstrated extraordinary engineering expertise.

More than six million visitors experienced the Crystal Palace, a building that had the soaring features of the grandest Gothic cathedrals without the enormous stone columns and thick walls. In working with new materials and a 6-month timeline, Paxton developed an innovative prefabricated construction method. Materials were delivered to the building site ready to be assembled using clips and fasteners. Another

19th-century development that made the Crystal Palace possible was the ability to produce clear-plate glass at reasonable prices. The French had mastered the technique, and Paxton established glassmaking factories in England with French employees. From an interior design perspective, the Crystal Palace represents a dramatic transformation in the conceptualization of space. Large open areas without intrusive columns provided designers with new space-planning opportunities. Once delegated to cathedrals, the inspirational psychological effects derived from voluminous spaces could now be applied to secular architecture.

Technologies and Furnishings: Mechanization, the Textile Industry, and Thonet's Bentwood Furniture

New sources of power drove the development of new machinery and the concept of factories. Improvements in the steam engine enabled machines to manufacture products with speed and efficiency. Products that had been made by people were manufactured by power-driven machinery in large factories. This obviously affected the production of items related to interior design, such as textiles, wallpaper, furniture, carpet, and decorative arts. Mechanization enabled consumers to purchase an assortment of interior furnishings at reasonable prices. New technologies revolutionized the textile industry by increasing the speed of the weaving process, and altering its appearance by producing textiles with fewer flaws and a more consistent pattern to the weave. Power looms and the spinning jenny, a device that permitted multiple threads to be spun at one time, mechanized the weaving process. These and other technologies enabled manufacturers to produce large quantities of textiles at low costs. Nineteenth-century mechanization also affected the types of floor coverings that were available at reasonable prices. Power looms were used to produce carpet beginning in 1839, and patterned carpets with multiple colors were produced after the invention of the Axminster loom in 1876. **Linoleum,** a resilient floor covering that possesses sustainability characteristics, was invented in 1860. Originally manufactured in only solid colors, linoleum is made from a mixture of linseed oil derived from flaxseed and other natural substances.

In addition to weaving textiles faster, new technologies from the Industrial Revolution enabled machinery to produce materials that had complex patterns and colors. Complicated designs, such as tapestries, had previously been created by hand, a very time-intensive process. The invention of the Jacquard attachment by the French inventor Joseph-Marie Jacquard in 1804–1805 mechanized the production of textiles with complicated patterns and multiple colors. Mounted on a loom, the Jacquard attachment uses perforated cards to control the warp, or the lengthwise threads, of the textile's pattern. This manipulation and control creates textiles with large, all-over figured patterns, such as damasks, brocades, and tapestries—fabrics often used for upholstery, draperies, and table linens. The production of lace, another traditionally handmade textile, also became mechanized in the 19th century. The increase in the production of textiles coincided with the invention of the sewing machine in 1846 by Elias Howe.

Patterns and colors of textiles and wallpapers were altered by the invention of industrialized roller-printing machines and synthetic dyes discovered by William Henry Perkin in 1856. In the mid-19th century, the first machine-printed wallpapers were manufactured in Britain. Similar to processes used to print newspapers, roller-printing machines enable patterns to be printed on surfaces quickly and at very low cost. However, inexpensive textiles and wallpapers would not have been possible without the invention of synthetic dyes. The time and expense associated with the production of natural dyes would not have been economically feasible for the mass production of textiles and wallpapers. To capitalize on the demand for interior furnishings, many businesses were started, such as Britain's Liberty of London (founded in 1875); some are still selling furnishings today.

The construction and production of furniture was also impacted by the steam engine and new machinery. New band saws and assembly-line production methods

Figure 1.19 Joseph Paxton, known for his greenhouses, designed the Crystal Palace for London's 1851 Great Exhibition. The purpose of the Exhibition was to showcase Britain's escalating world power.

Source: Victoria & Albert Museum, London/Art Resource, NY.

were used to produce furniture. Most furniture was poorly constructed and lacked good design, but prices were reasonable. The development of the furniture industry can be illustrated to some degree by the example of Michael Thonet, whose company was established in 1819. Thonet, a German-Austrian cabinetmaker, developed the process for using heated steam to bend wooden rods. Thonet's **bentwood** furniture of laminated veneers was strong, lightweight, durable, and very inexpensive. Mechanization and factory production lines had an important impact on the price of bentwood furniture. Thonet used the new technologies to produce bentwood furniture in extraordinary volumes. His most popular pieces were café chairs, hat racks, and rocking chairs (Figure 1.20). In the mid-19th century, Thonet opened factories in several locations, including Hungary, Vienna, and Moravia. He had the business savvy to take advantage of the accelerating global market by advertising, printing product catalogues, and opening showrooms throughout the world.

The early international appeal of Thonet's furniture is evident in the photograph of Pyotr I. Tchaikovsky's bedroom in Klin, Russia (see Figure 1.20). Tchaikovsky, the renowned Russian composer of ballets, including *Swan Lake*, *The Nutcracker*, and *Sleeping Beauty*, died of cholera in 1893 at the age of 53. The chair in the room is one of Thonet's most popular items, no. 14, with a plywood seat. In addition to illustrating bentwood furniture, this photo of Tchaikovsky's bedroom provides a glimpse of a middle-class Russian interior in the 19th century. Some noteworthy items are the unique profile in the crown molding, the sparse amount of furniture, and the bed made from the new material, wrought iron. The patterns, colors, and use of textiles are also informative. Every textile, including Tchaikovsky's morning gown, is patterned with various shades of red, a favorite Russian color. Textiles were used as a wall hanging, coverlet, fringed table linen on the bedside cabinet, and small Oriental rug.

Tchaikovsky's room also has a kerosene wall bracket, one of the lighting technologies invented in the 19th century. Kerosene was an efficient light source that provided considerable illumination for reasonable costs. By the early 19th century, the French and English had developed the means to use natural gas for illumination. However, complexities associated with transporting natural gas and installing gas pipes primarily restricted its use to urban areas. The limited availability of natural gas and high installation costs could explain Tchaikovsky's use of kerosene lighting. Both of these technologies were usurped by the inventions of electricity and the incandescent lamp in the late 1800s.

As a new source of energy, electricity transformed people's lives, work styles, technologies, interior environments, and architecture. Physicists, especially Nikola Tesla, developed the technologies to convert mechanical energy into electric power and devised a means to transport the energy to buildings. The carbon-arc lamp, invented by Sir Humphry Davy, initiated the technology for electrical lighting. However, a practical

Figure 1.20 Tchaikovsky's bedroom with Thonet's café chair.

Source: Bildarchiv Preussischer Kulturbesitz/Art Resource, NY.

form of interior illumination was not developed until the Englishman Joseph W. Swan and Thomas Edison in the United States invented the incandescent lamp in 1880.

Transportation and Communication: Railroad Stations, Hotels, Printing, and Photography

The development of steam power also revolutionized transportation because it allowed for the invention of steam locomotives and steamships. Railroads played a critical role in providing consumers with interior furnishings. They were essential to the delivery of raw materials to factories and to the distribution of large quantities of manufactured products. Railroads also provided the means to transport building materials to multiple locations at great distances. This convenience had a tremendous impact on architecture; previously, materials and supplies selected for a project were determined by what was available within a limited distance from the building site.

Some entrepreneurs noted how railroads and steamships could be used for pleasure travel. For the first time in history, people could travel easily and relatively quickly on railroads and ocean liners. To accommodate travelers, new railroad stations had to be constructed throughout the world, but most stations were constructed at the start of the 20th century. Buildings that provide a new function in society require considerable conceptualization. Urban planners designed extraordinary railroad stations to stress their city's importance and impress visitors. Consequently, the waiting rooms in many of the world's finest railroad stations feature interiors and architecture that resemble awe-inspiring buildings such as Gothic cathedrals or the Pantheon in Rome. In the 19th century, buildings were often designed in an eclectic manner by combining neoclassicism, Gothic Revival, and the new rational style (see Figure 1.10). Eventually, the ability to travel had a tremendous impact on the growth of hotels and restaurants. Early

hotels were located close to railroad stations; some were even connected to the station. As the number of travelers increased, more hotels were built close to the heart of a city. A few of the spectacular hotels built at the end of the 19th century were the Savoy in London and the Raffles in Singapore (named for the explorer Sir Thomas Stamford Raffles, previously mentioned in the discussion of the Buddhist temple of Borobudor). The Savoy was the first large hotel to install electrical lighting.

Efficient means of communication were also developed in the 19th century. The electric telegraph and telephone were invented, and advances in the printing process significantly impacted mass communication. The Chinese invented printing in the 2nd century, but the ability to print quickly and economically did not occur until the late 1800s. As with other technologies developed during this century, steam power enabled mechanization of the printing process. Other critical inventions related to printed communication were the linotype, a typesetting machine that mechanized the composition process, and a mechanism for reproducing illustrations (the latter is crucial in showing details related to architecture and interior design). Printing advances helped to establish the publishing industry, which included newspapers, magazines, journals, and catalogues. The newly established factories and railroads provided the means for the mass circulation of publications. New publications were ideal for educating people about topics such as architecture, interior furnishings, and new equipment. People became even more knowledgeable about the availability of new technologies and interior furnishings when advertisements were added to publications in the late 19th century.

Another important invention that affected interior environments was photography. In 1837, the French artist and scientist Louis Daguerre developed the first form of photography, the daguerreotype. The process involved exposing an iodized silver-coated plate. The first photographic negatives and the Kodak box camera followed Daguerre's invention. The importance of photography to the interior design profession cannot be overstated. Prior to photography, exposure to interiors was limited. The only way someone could see an interior was by invitation to a private residence or viewing a painting of a room, which most often was in a private collection. The lack of public buildings also restricted exposures to interior environments. The ability to photograph an interior, print the illustration, and then distribute the publication revolutionized interior environments and architecture. Initially, photographs were taken to document events, as illustrated in Figure 1.16, but the medium was quickly adapted to both create and inform visual art.

GLOBAL LIFE AND WORK STYLES

An unprecedented population increase occurred during the 19th century. The number of people on the planet had almost doubled in 100 years, from nearly one billion people in 1800 to almost two billion in 1900. Some of the increase was due to improvements in hygiene and sanitation and developments from the Industrial Revolution. Increases in population affected the availability of adequate housing, affected lifestyles, and contributed to the rise of social reformists. Some architects and interior designers responded to societal issues by advocating designs that avoided mechanization and encouraged handcrafted furnishings.

The Industrial Revolution: Modern Homes, Tenement Slums, and Hospitals

The Industrial Revolution obviously resulted in conditions that were both positive and negative. Transportation improvements facilitated immigration to various parts of the world, including the Americas. Larger cities created the demand for public transportation within a city.

London responded to this need by starting construction of the first passenger underground transportation system, "the Tube," in 1868. Employment in factories resulted in a major shift from agrarian to urban lifestyles and a redistribution of wealth. A significant number of previously poor people became the newly established middle class. In addition to factory work, industrialization spawned other employment opportunities, including management and clerical positions. Office employees were needed to manage records and process orders for a company's products. The development of the typewriter, stencil duplicator (mimeograph), and file cabinets facilitated business processes. Eventually, buildings had to be designed that would accommodate large numbers of office workers. Thus, the Industrial Revolution helped to establish the origins of the modern office building, which is explored in many future chapters of this book.

Substantial incomes and an exposure to comfortable living standards created demands for amenities associated with a modern world. Therefore, in the late 1800s, some interiors in Western societies featured an eclectic assortment of furnishings and decorative arts. People could buy numerous pieces of interior furnishings because factories made products that were relatively inexpensive. Some people saw it as prestigious to own "exotic" decorative arts from Asia. Thus, the residences of such people included Oriental rugs, porcelain, and carved wooden objects. Comfort was essential, which reestablished the ancient Romans' technology of central heating. Emitted through room radiators, steam was used as the energy source for central heating systems.

A focus on desirable living standards also manifested in an interest in urban parks. Prior to the 19th century, the concept of enjoying beautiful gardens, forests, and natural-looking lakes was primarily limited to royalty and the aristocracy. Revolutions transformed this practice by converting some private estates to public entities. In addition, new urban planning projects, such as the previously discussed plan for Paris by Haussmann, specifically designated areas for public parks and gardens. Consequently, some of the world's most famous public parks were developed in the 1800s, including Central Park in New York City, St. James Park adjoining Buckingham Palace in London, and Ueno Park in Tokyo. Public parks had a dramatic effect on the lifestyles of people and also impacted the world of architectural design. Parks contributed to health by conveniently enabling people to enjoy fresh air and exercise. In the 19th century, public parks were also a popular location for socializing, playing games, and enjoying live music, activities that continue today. The desirability of having access to the outdoors and the enjoyment of beautiful views influenced the development of buildings that surrounded public parks. For example, to maximize the use of Central Park, most of the land area facing the park was dedicated to residential rather than commercial buildings. Moreover, window placements, interior floor plans, and furniture arrangements were designed to maximize views of the park.

Unfortunately, the Industrial Revolution also had a terrible impact on the quality of life for many people, especially women and children. The rapid increase in the number of people drawn to cities resulted in severe housing shortages, poverty, and rampant illnesses such as cholera, tuberculosis, and small pox. In an attempt to house people, many cities in Western Europe and the United States created **tenement buildings.** Generally, tenements were created by dividing an existing building into several apartments, which were then shared by many people.

The squalid conditions prompted many writers, such as the English novelist Charles Dickens, to publish articles and stories that described the deplorable environments and demanded reform. Women and children were in high demand in the textile factories because their small hands could easily repair broken threads and they worked for less money than men. The work conditions were miserable, and they were required to work an unreasonable number of hours. In response to public pressure to the abuses, the British government was forced to create several child labor laws that mandated minimum ages for employment and maximum number of hours in a 6-day workweek. The first laws mandated that the minimum employment age be *9 years*, and the maximum amount of time per day that children younger than age 16 could work was *12 hours*.

The initial attitude about working conditions was also applied to the type of housing that was constructed for workers. Many factories were built away from urban areas in order to take advantage of rivers for waterpower and railroads for transportation. Manufacturers were in need of employees, but the remote locations were barren. Thus, manufacturers quickly built housing that was poorly constructed, small, and of "cookie-cutter" design to economize on production costs. Houses were built very close together and lacked sewage systems and fresh water. After living in one of the factory towns, Friedrich Engels (co-author of the *Communist Manifesto*) wrote about these deplorable conditions in *The Condition of the Working Class in England* in 1845. His writings and the efforts of many other social reformists helped to improve the living conditions of the poor.

One solution developed by conscientious business leaders was to build model communities for their workers. These "company towns" were located next to a factory, and the owners built everything that was needed for a community, including all of the housing, stores, hospitals, schools, fire stations, and churches. Housing was stratified according to employment status. Management had large, single-family houses, and factory workers lived in small, multi-dwelling units. Employees paid rent to the employer. Pullman, Illinois, is an example of a company town of 12,000 people that was built at the end of the 19th century by George M. Pullman, the founder of the Pullman sleeping car for passenger railcars.

In addition to spawning deplorable living conditions, factories also polluted the air, water, and land, degrading the overall environment of people living nearby. Life-threatening pollutants were emitted from factory stacks, chimneys, and gaslights. The atmosphere was filled with soot, smoke, and toxic substances. People were poisoned by coal and gas emissions, and they suffered infections from the lack of sanitation and enormous rat populations. Escalating diseases, illnesses, and war injuries focused attention on the lack of quality hospital care. In the mid-1800s, approximately half of the patients died in hospitals, primarily through poor hygiene and the lack of knowledge regarding the spread of infection from bacteria on hands, medical instruments and supplies, and linens.

As illustrated in Figure 1.21, large numbers of patients grouped together in one room created an ideal environment for the spread of bacteria. The layout allowed for overcrowding, and doctors could easily move from bed to bed without washing their hands or changing their garments. The situation was made worse by the lack of clean linens, shared bedding, minimum fresh water supplies, and inadequate human waste disposal. Bazille's painting of the French Impressionist painter Claude Monet in a hospital bed illustrates the unsanitary hospital conditions, including his exposed wounded leg, and the open pail and bowl for human waste (Figure 1.22).

In the mid-1800s, English nurse Florence Nightingale witnessed the appalling conditions of urban hospitals and the British army's barracks hospitals in the Crimean War (1853–1856). She worked with the British govern-ment to reform hospital standards, improve hygiene, and initiate the nursing profession in 1856. Her work reduced the number of deaths and dramatically improved the design of hospital interiors by focusing on her "'Six D's' that were most likely to cause disease: dirt, drink (impure water), diet, damp, draughts, and drains (improper drainage and sewage removal)" (Dossey, Selanders, Beck, & Attewell, 2005, p. 110). To improve the design of hospitals, Nightingale proposed hygiene procedures, including "floorplans for lying-in wards with more sinks than usual for use with delivery and cleaning the lying-in room with lime wash" (Dossey, Selanders, Beck, & Attewell, 2005, p. 112). Nightingale wrote, "Sinks and W.C. sinks must be everywhere conveniently situated" (1871, p. 81).

Concerns for the basic welfare of people generated the founding of several new social organizations, including the international Red Cross in Switzerland in 1863 and the Salvation Army in Britain in 1865. In addition, a number of "settlement houses" were established in communities to provide shelter and food for the needy. Residences were converted into housing for the homeless, especially new immigrants. To help individuals acquire employment and adjust to urban life, settlement houses were staffed with college-educated people. The concept and need was so great that settlement houses were built in Chicago, Japan, New York City, Southeast Asia, and Western Europe.

Figure 1.21 Large numbers of patients grouped together in one room created an ideal environment for the spread of bacteria. The layout encouraged overcrowding and doctors could easily move from bed to bed without washing their hands or changing their garments.

Source: Bildarchiv Preussischer Kulturbesitz/Art Resource, NY.

Figure 1.22 Painting by Frederic Bazille of the French impressionist painter Claude Monet in a hospital bed, which illustrates unsanitary procedures, including his exposed wounded leg and the open pail and bowl for human waste.

Source: Erich Lessing/Art Resource, NY.

Philosophy and Literature: Arts and Crafts Movement

Social reform philosophies also existed in the work of architects, interior designers, and artists associated with the **Arts and Crafts movement.** The writings of the English philosopher John Ruskin examined the effects of mechanization on the lives and morality of people and society. A social and art critic, Ruskin is known for his books *The Seven Lamps of Architecture* (1848) and *The Stones of Venice* (1851–1853). Ruskin's philosophy influenced the English designer and socialist William Morris. Both men were adamantly opposed to the material excesses associated with the fashionable Victorian consumerism. Their perspectives were very influential in forming the philosophy of the Arts and Crafts movement.

The name of the movement was derived from the Arts and Crafts Society, founded in 1887. Initiated in Great Britain, the Arts and Crafts movement spread to Western Europe, the United States, and Asia with the Mingei (Folk Crafts) movement in Japan. Guided by the premise that capitalism and greed were destroying the moral fabric of society, those involved with the movement reverted to traditional skills, craftsmanship, quality, and indigenous materials. Their source of inspiration was the craftsmen's guilds of medieval artists, furni-

ture-makers, and masons. Their intent was to create honest, functional, and simplistic designs that would transform society. Furniture in the Arts and Crafts style is known for being handcrafted, having exposed construction techniques, using hand-hammered hardware, and emphasizing the natural beauty of oak graining. To reach a larger number of people, Morris established a business, Morris, Marshall, Faulkner and Company (Morris & Co.), to manufacture textiles, furniture, tiles, stained glass, and wallpaper. These products are still available today.

Morris & Co. developed interior furnishings that were true to their materials, used stylized floral patterns, and showcased the art of handcrafted skills. These attributes are illustrated in the photograph of the drawing room of Kelmscott House in Hammersmith, a residence of Morris and his family from 1878 to 1896 (Figure 1.23). The walls are draped with a woven textile in the pattern known as "Bird," one of his most famous designs. This and many other patterns designed by Morris resemble tapestries from the Middle Ages, and the installation on the walls imitates the medieval practice of lining walls with textiles to prevent drafts. Another reference to medieval customs is evident in the wooden **settle,** designed by Morris & Co. Close inspection of Morris's reclining chair reveals joints that are

Figure 1.23 The north wall of the drawing room of Kelmscott House in Hammersmith, a residence of Morris and his family from 1878 to 1896.

Source: William Morris Gallery, London Borough of Waltham Forest.

solid and secure. A typical characteristic of furniture constructed in the Arts and Crafts style is that the art of joinery is exposed, and **dovetail,** or **mortise and tenon joints,** are used for wood furniture. The chair's turned spindle sides and stretchers are exposed to emphasize craftsmanship. The decorative arts in the room reflect folk crafts from around the world, including rugs from Persia, Eastern brassware, lusterware plates decorated with metallic pigments from Spain, and a Moorish-inspired side table inlaid with mother-of-pearl.

Simplistic Values: Shakers, Native Americans, and Russian Wooden Architecture

As previously discussed, the Industrial Revolution had a major impact on millions of people during the 19th century, but that figure is actually dwarfed by the number of people in the world who were *not* affected by mechanization. The Shakers, a Christian religious community in the Northeast United States, believed in an austere lifestyle that was reflected in the simple, bare interiors of their homes and other buildings. Furniture was utilitarian, revealed fine craftsmanship, and had simple forms without any ornamentation. The most well-known pieces are the **ladder-back** rocking chairs

with caned or woven taped seats and the cupboard with turned wooden knobs. The Shaker interior was distinctive for its sparse furniture, box stove, and white walls with pegboards, which were used to hang clothes (and also the chairs while the floor was being cleaned). Shaker communities no longer exist due to their celibate lifestyle, but their furniture and interiors provide instructional value for understanding how to implement principles of sustainable design. The Shakers' use of local materials, minimal furnishings, energy conservation, maximization of daylight, and focus on maintaining rather than replacing structures and furnishings reflect sustainable design principles.

Another group in the United States with a relatively simple lifestyle was Native Americans. In the 16th century, Spanish explorers started to discover areas where Native Americans were living in what is now the Southwest United States, but the 19th century dramatically affected their lives. In a quest for territory acquisition, Europeans and U.S. troops frequently used violence (including slaughter) to force Native Americans from their homes and communities until they were relegated to living on reservations. One of the worst examples of this policy occurred after the U.S. Congress passed the Indian Removal Act in 1830. President Andrew Jackson ordered the removal of Cherokees east of the Mississippi River. Referred to as "The Trail of Tears," the journey from the East Coast to modern-day Oklahoma took 6 months during the winter of 1838–1839. With a minimum number of shoes and few clothes, more than 4,000 Cherokees died during the relocation. After this tragedy, many battles were fought between the U.S. government and Native Americans. By the end of the 19th century, the U.S. government subdued any uprisings and most Native Americans were living on reservations.

Many Native American communities have UNESCO registration, including Mesa Verde in Colorado, the Pueblo in Taos, New Mexico, and the Chaco Culture National Historical Park in New Mexico. These

Figure 1.24 A Pueblo residence illustrates the principles associated with sustainable design. The thick walls helped to keep the dwelling cool in the summer and warm in the winter.

Source: Picture Collection, The New York Public Library, Astor, Lenox and Tilden Foundations.

settlements provide important insights into the lifestyles and arts and crafts of the first Americans in the Southwest. Many of the Pueblo's construction techniques provide excellent examples of sustainable design. For example, houses were built from local materials. Structures were made from adobe bricks and covered with a plaster made from mud. In the heat of the desert, the structures dried quickly and became very strong. The thick walls helped keep the dwelling cool in the summer and warm in the winter. One entered a dwelling by climbing an outdoor ladder to the rooftop and proceeding through the opening in the roof (Figure 1.24). The rooftop also provided an ideal location to dry chili pepper and plants used to produce natural dyes. As shown in the drawing of the 19th century, interior rooms were heated with a corner fireplace and ceilings were supported with wooden beams. Because the custom was to use the floor for sitting and sleeping, rooms were sparsely furnished, but woven textiles, pottery, and dried vegetables provided vibrant colors and patterns. Native Americans create beautiful handcrafted pottery, woven textiles, sand paintings, jewelry, baskets, and leatherwork. Many of these arts and crafts are important in religious ceremonies and rituals, and thus colors and patterns have symbolic meanings. For example, red can represent lightning, yellow is sunlight, and wavy lines are water or rain.

Vernacular, or local traditions, was also evident in Russia in the 19th century. Due to their extensive forested zones, for centuries the Russians constructed magnificent wooden architecture. Even though architecture in St. Petersburg and Moscow was influenced by Western styles, including the use of stone as a building material and classical columns (see Figure 1.11), most of the Russian residences were wooden. In the 19th century, Russia was a vast territory with a population that included more than 200 different nationalities. In an attempt to establish some unity within the provinces, people turned to the unique traditional craftsmanship associated with Russian wooden architecture. The provincial practices provide another example of sustainable design. The extensive timber forests in northern Russia provided the construction materials for housing, churches, and farm buildings. The local availability of considerable timber also fostered the development of exceptional woodworking skills among some members of the population.

The 19th-century Oshevnev house in Figure 1.25 is an outstanding example of the fundamental traditions of the peasant's vernacular architecture. The house also reflects the principles of sustainability through its use of local materials and design features that helped to contend with the cold weather

Figure 1.25 The 19th-century Oshevnev house on Kizhi Island is an outstanding example of the fundamental traditions of the peasant's vernacular architecture. The log building was constructed with joints without using nails.

Source: Erich Lessing/Art Resource, NY.

GLOBAL VISUAL AND PERFORMING ARTS

Advances in the visual and performing arts in the 19th century had a tremendous impact on interior environments and architecture. The development of public museums enhanced education, and transformed the way people learned about fine and decorative arts. Aspects of the visual arts world in the 19th century that strongly impacted interior environments and architecture were Realism, Japanese woodblock prints (ukiyo-e), and Impressionism. Music created by renowned composers during the 19th century helped the world of performing arts influence the design and construction of new buildings for the enjoyment of opera and ballet.

Fine and Decorative Art Museums

The modern concept of a museum was formed in the 19th century. The development of fine and decorative art museums had a dramatic affect on interior environments, architecture, education, and preservation. For the first time the public was exposed to fine art, decorative arts, and the interiors of some of the world's most elaborate palaces. Previously, art collections resided with a church or in the palaces and residences of royalty and aristocrats. Technically, the first time the general public could view art collections was in the 18th century with the openings of the British Museum in London and the Louvre in Paris. However, during this period, access was either restricted or offered at very limited hours. Opening these museums initiated the concept and led to the construction of numerous fine and decorative arts museums throughout the world. The impact of allowing people to experience fine and decorative arts in museums cannot be overstated. Displays, models, or re-creations of unique spaces are invaluable to understanding

conditions. Logs were cut and joined with a precision that did not require nails or filler substances, such as mud wedged between the cracks. Windows were small to protect the interior in harsh winters but were highly decorated to provide ornamentation to the exterior and the illusion of larger openings. Another source of ornamentation was the end boards, which were carved or sawn in folk art motifs (see Figure 1.25). To conserve heat in the coldest climates, living areas were adjacent to stalls with animals that generated heat and the structures were elevated to help avoid snowdrifts. Other design elements employed to protect the structure from climatic conditions were the deep eaves made from extended logs and the steep pitched roof, which helped prevent the buildup of snow. Wood craftsmanship was also evident in every detail in the interior, including the utensils, flooring, walls, ceiling, and furniture. Interiors were designed to maximize heat by locating the massive stone fireplace in the center of the structure.

interior environments. These experiences not only inform the profession of interior design, but they educate and inspire members of the public, some of whom buy interior design products and services.

Since most of the fine art was from royal collections, the obvious display site was the monarchs' palaces. This perspective had benefits and drawbacks. From a positive viewpoint, people not only had the opportunity to study collections, but they could view the art in the context of the original setting. People also could learn how interiors were designed by examining the interior furnishings, room configurations, and lighting techniques. Another benefit was that the artwork did not have to be moved over any significant distance, which eliminated the possibility of travel-related damage. Public museums also helped to protect and preserve collections for future generations.

However, the creation of museums did result in some ill effects, many of which were the result of inadequate planning. Serious forethought about the consequences of thousands of people walking through fragile environments would have revealed potential abuses, such as damaged or stolen art pieces, ruined finishes from display installations, and basic wear and tear on materials and surfaces. An unforeseen outcome of using palaces as art museums was that architects and interior designers developed the mind-set that the layout and spaces in palaces were appropriate and ideal for new buildings. Therefore, establishing museums in palaces potentially hindered the creativity related to newly constructed art museums. Many early museums resemble palaces with respect to the architecture, interior plans, use of daylight, and dimensions of the spaces. Walking through these museums is similar to walking through the adjoined rooms of palaces.

Visual Arts: Movements, Styles, and Japan's Meiji Restoration

The history of art in the 19th century is extensive and diverse. Western art started with remnants of the 18th century Enlightenment philosophy, which embodied the "Age of Reason" and neoclassicism. Breaking away from classical perspectives favored in the 1700s, various forms of artistic and intellectual expression in the 19th century progressed to Romanticism in the arts, literature, and philosophy. The period of Romanticism in art (1800–1850) encouraged architectural and interior styles that reinforced nationalism, such as the U.S. Capitol. With an emphasis on action, sentiment, and emotion, Romanticism was important in advocating for the causes of the revolutionaries, including Eugene Delacroix's *Liberty Leading the People* (1830) and Francisco Goya's *The Third of May 1808* (1814). Both of these paintings dramatically depict the horrors of war and the perseverance of the common people in seeking freedom.

Realism (1840–1880) was an important artistic movement because it helped improve the living conditions of people in poverty. In response to the horrific affects of the Industrial Revolution on some people, artists painted the reality of everyday living conditions. For example, in paintings and graphics, Honoré Daumier attempted to improve the lives of common people by illustrating the realities of living in poverty, while criticizing the government and rich bourgeoisie.

At the end of the 19th century, many artists in Paris were involved with developing the movement that became known as Impressionism. A critic of the first Impressionists' exhibition in 1874 identified the name from the Claude Monet painting *Impression—Sunrise*. After several exhibitions, Impressionist art finally became accepted and successful. Many of the developments discussed in this chapter demonstrate the interactions between Impressionist art and technology, interior environments, architecture, lifestyles, and urban planning. For example, Impressionist artists such as Gustave Caillebotte and Camille Pissarro often painted the new Parisian architecture and urban planning designed by Haussmann. In several paintings, Monet romanticized the iron structure of the railroad shed of the new Saint-Lazare railroad station in Paris. Pierre-Auguste Renoir painted people engaged in leisure activities in the new public parks in Paris. Edgar Degas was intrigued with painting the dancers at the new Opera in Paris (discussed below). In capturing despondent expressions on the faces of patrons in cafés, Henri de Toulouse-Lautrec communicated the realities of everyday people.

Impressionist artists were experts at painting fleeting moments or *impressions,* even when the elusive sunlight, sky, or clouds complicated the details of a landscape, architecture, or people. The reframing of the way the Impressionist artists viewed the world stimulated architects and interior designers in the 20th century to reevaluate how color and light affect interior environments and architecture. This analysis was especially helpful for understanding how to use the new invention, electrical lighting.

The increasing international travel and trade with Japan also had a significant effect on artists, interior designers, and architects. Japan's self-imposed seclusion from most Western cultures ended when Commodore Matthew Perry of the U.S. Navy forced the Japanese to open trade with the United States in 1853. As an aspect of Japan's Meiji restoration, Japanese fine art, decorative arts, and crafts were displayed in international exhibitions and museums. Europeans' attraction to the Japanese culture stimulated an interest in collecting and displaying decorative arts in their residences, such as porcelain, woodblock prints, lacquer, fans, and folding screens.

Exported in large quantities, most notably to Great Britain and France, Japanese woodblock prints were important sources for understanding Japanese interior environments, architecture, and textile patterns and colors. Many of the prints illustrate Japanese people engaged in activities in their homes or in public buildings (Figure 1.26). These prints provide excellent information regarding Japanese 19th-century interior environments, such as their space-planning techniques, **shoji** panels with rice paper, stone floors, and use of sliding panels as a means to integrate interiors with courtyard gardens. The prints also illustrate the Japanese use of interior furnishings and accessories, such as **tatami mats,** paper lanterns, bamboo shades, black lacquer, and baskets.

In the latter decades of the 19th century, common motifs in Japanese paintings, such as insects, peacock feathers, birds, and stylized flowers, were used in Western textiles, furniture inlays, and wall decorations. Peacocks became the theme in a dining room painted and designed by the American James McNeill Whistler and the architect Thomas Jeckyll (Figure 1.27) in 1876. Originally located at the residence of the ship-owner F. R. Leyland in London, the *Peacock Room* was moved in 1919 to the Freer Gallery of Art in Washington, D.C. Japanese paintings on gold leaf on paper also influenced numerous Western interiors. For example, in the *Green Dining Room* (1866–1867)

Figure 1.26 Japanese woodblock prints provide excellent information regarding Japanese 19th-century interior environments, such as their space planning techniques, shoji panels with rice paper, stone floors, and sliding panels. This print (1857) by Utagawa Kunisada illustrates processes of print-making.

Source: Victoria & Albert Museum, London/Art Resource, NY.

in the South Kensington Museum (modern Victoria and Albert), designed by William Morris and Philip Webb, furniture and panels have gold leaf with paintings of figures, fruit, vines, and flowers (Figure 1.28).

At the end of the 19th century, many Western European artists, architects, and interior designers favored the elegant Japanese designs. The simplicity, openness, quality craftsmanship, and integrity of materials reflected in Japanese art and culture were especially appealing to the designers associated with the Arts and Crafts movement and people involved with the **Aesthetic movement.** As a movement that shared many of the beliefs associated with Arts and Crafts, the Aesthetic philosophy was in opposition to machine-created furniture as well as the clutter in Victorian interiors. The Aesthetic movement's most important premise was "art for art's sake," or appreciating the beauty of the arts. The *Peacock Room* incorporates many of the stylistic motifs associated with the Aesthetic movement, including the peacock, blue and white porcelain, sunflowers (see fireplace andirons in Figure 1.27), and intense colors. To enhance the owner's porcelain collection, Whistler painted feather patterns on the ceiling and rich blues and greens on the walls. The Aesthetic movement also favored "ebonized" black-painted furniture, an imitation of Japanese black lacquer. Inspired by Japanese art, in the late 19th century E. W. Godwin was known for designing ebonized **Anglo-Japanese** furniture with simple geometric forms.

Japanese interiors were influenced by the West, but for very different reasons. When the Japanese were forced to open trade with the United States, they feared becoming another colony. Therefore, to avoid colonization, the Japanese focused on building military strength, industrializing, and adopting Western customs. The woodblock print in Figure 1.29 illustrates how the Japanese were trying to convince Western societies that the country had modernized by using Western musical instruments, clothing, and interior furnishings. As a consequence of Japan's willingness to comply with

Figure 1.27 Peacocks became the theme in a dining room painted and designed by the American James McNeill Whistler and the architect Thomas Jeckyll in 1876. The *Peacock Room* was moved in 1919 to the Freer Gallery of Art in Washington, DC.

Source: Freer Gallery of Art Smithsonian Institution, Washington, D.C.: Gift of Charles Lang Freer, F1904.61.

Figure 1.28 The *Green Dining Room* (1866–1867) in the South Kensington Museum (modern Victoria and Albert) designed by William Morris and Philip Webb.

Source: Victoria & Albert Museum, London/Art Resource, NY.

Westernization, people in the West had very positive images of the country. These attitudes contributed to greater demands for Japanese-inspired art, interior environments, and architecture.

Figure 1.29 A woodblock print that illustrates how the Japanese were trying to convince Western societies that Japan had modernized by using Western musical instruments, clothing, and interior furnishings.

Source: Photograph © 2009 Museum of Fine Arts, Boston.

Performing Arts: Paris Opéra (modern Opéra Garnier or Palais Garnier) (1861–1875) by Jean-Louis-Charles Garnier and the Bolshoi Theater (Third Building 1850s) in Moscow, Russia, by Albert Kavos

Music and the performing arts flourished in the 19th century. A number of gifted composers, many from Eastern Europe, were writing compelling music, such as the Polish composer Frédéric Chopin; Hungarian Franz Liszt; Austrian Johann Strauss II; Russian Pyotr Ilyich Tchaikovsky; Czech Antonin Dvorak; Frenchman Hector Berlioz; Italian Giacomo Puccini; and German composers Johannes Brahms, Richard Wagner, and Felix Mendelssohn. Appreciating the incredible music required appropriate settings that could accommodate large numbers of people. As an outcome of the Industrial Revolution, the emergence of the new middle class with money and leisure time contributed to a strong demand for entertainment. This resulted in new theaters, opera houses, music halls, and bandstands in public parks. The origins of theater date back to ancient Greece,

but today's concept of theaters for the performing arts was developed in the 18th and 19th centuries.

The Paris Opéra (modern Opéra Garnier or Palais Garnier) (1861–1875), designed by the French architect Jean-Louis-Charles Garnier, was used as a model for many theaters built in the 19th and early 20th centuries. Opéra Garnier was an important design element in Haussmann's plan for Paris. In creating dramatic vistas along broad boulevards, Haussmann wanted a powerful monumental statement at the end of Avenue de l'Opéra. Garnier accomplished this goal by designing a façade that has become an icon of the city. To enhance the vista and emphasize the façade, Haussmann created an open public square in front of Opéra Garnier and commissioned architects to design architecture for the surrounding buildings that would complement the Opéra.

The façade and interior environment of Opéra Garnier reflect the eclecticism that was prevalent in the late 19th century. Garnier's education at the French École des Beaux-Arts provided the background for the Opéra's blend of traditional classicism, baroque, and

Renaissance architecture. For example, the façade's elevated ground floor and double columns resemble the east front of the Louvre in Paris, designed by Louis Le Vau (1631–1670). The Opéra's classical forms are decorated with elaborately carved members and gilded statuary. Richly decorated columns and statues are found in the grand staircase and the arcaded galleries.

Garnier understood the importance of addressing contemporary conditions. He created an interior environment that is an informative example of how to design for the users of a space and their activities. He designed the interiors to reflect the drama and prestige of attending opera and ballet performances. Because the theater was considered an important emerging social setting, Garnier created a highly ornamented "stage" for the theatergoers. Innovative concepts included a grand foyer as an entrance to the auditorium; arcaded galleries; and separate entrances for the general public, Emperor Napoleon III, and season ticket subscribers. Garnier's design accommodated society's desire to use theater as a social salon by dedicating more space for the attendees than the auditorium. The grand staircase and voluminous space created the perfect setting to observe people and their elaborate dress. The surrounding arcaded galleries provided a perfect view of the "stage" and an ideal area to socialize. Garnier's "set design" for the dramatic entrance features the finest materials and artistic techniques, including marble, paintings, mosaics, and elaborate candelabras.

Even though the structure was still being constructed, Opéra Garnier is an example of a building that was temporarily converted for military purposes: During the 1871 French Revolution, the construction site was seized by the revolutionaries and used as a hospital and military barracks.

Interest in the performing arts and a setting for socializing stimulated the construction of opera houses in many other cities, including Moscow. After the extensive destruction of Moscow by the French in the War of 1812, the city was engaged in a comprehensive rebuilding program. One of the areas targeted for restoration was Theater Square. The program included a new building for the original neoclassical Bolshoi Theater, which was destroyed in a fire during the late 18th century. This theater, designed by Osip Bove and Andrei Mikhailov, also burned down in 1853. Albert Kavos was commissioned to design the third Bolshoi Theater in the 1850s. Kavos based the design on the original building by Bove and Mikhailov, but with revisions. The theater experience was improved by enhancing acoustics, redesigning the stage to allow for multiple backdrops, and providing larger and grander areas for socializing. In following the prevailing eclectic style, the architecture combines neoclassical with references to the Renaissance. The Bolshoi Theater shares some of the same features of Opéra Garnier, including lyre motifs; decorative sculptures of Apollo, the god of music and sun; magnificent staircases; a grand foyer for socializing; paintings of muses; and an auditorium ornamented with gilding and draped red velvet. The Bolshoi Theater has a well-known reputation for its elaborate set designs; innovative costumes; and performances featuring some of the world's finest ballet dancers, musicians, and composers.

GLOBAL BUSINESS AND ECONOMICS

As discussed in this section, huge profits and greed incited the explosion of international trade in the 19th century. The technological advances in transportation, manufacturing, and communication facilitated profitable trade. Some trade was mutually beneficial to each country, but in other instances, to ensure substantial profits under colonial rule, new European empires forced nations to indoctrinate Western products, customs, religions, languages, and legal systems. For example, when India was a colony of Great Britain, the British mandated Indians to import textiles that were manufactured in Great Britain, even though compared to Indian textiles the materials were more expensive and lower quality. Importing British textiles to India helped advance Britain's economical conditions by bolstering employment and maximizing their investments in mechanization associated with the Industrial Revolution.

International Trade and Expositions

The Asian market represented large profits to Western countries because of the high demand for many products used in interiors, such as porcelain, cotton, silk, textiles, bamboo, ivory, and lacquer. Profits escalated when transporting products became easier, faster, and cheaper because of the thousands of miles of railroad tracks that were constructed and improvements in water travel. In addition to the invention of the steamship, the opening of the Suez Canal in 1869 significantly shortened the distance between Europe and Asia. Rather than navigating around the tip of Africa, the Suez Canal enabled ships to sail directly from the Mediterranean Sea to the Red Sea.

International expositions and exhibitions were a perfect forum for stimulating the demand for new merchandise and thereby increasing profits. London's 1851 "Great Exhibition of the Works of Industry of all Nations" at the Crystal Palace featured more than 100,000 exhibits from around the world (Kersten, 2004) (Figure 1.30). Most of the exhibitors displayed merchandise for residences, including furniture, stained glass, textiles, Gothic-style metal stoves, heating stoves capped by a suit of armor, sculptures, rugs, light fixtures, and decorative arts. Exhibitors featured dark wood furniture that was stained black to imitate the popular Japanese lacquer. The dark wood furniture had fine craftsmanship, but the designs were overly large with unappealing proportions and excessive ornamentation with carvings of flowers, animals, creatures, scrolls, vines, and fruit. Six million people attended the exhibition in approximately 6 months (Kersten, 2004). Exhibits at the Crystal Palace, and at many subsequent exhibitions, had a significant effect on interior environments by motivating people to acquire the new furnishings and stimulating new business ventures. Manufacturing companies were founded to produce the new merchandise, and merchants opened retail establishments to display and sell their products.

Figure 1.30 London's 1851 "Great Exhibition of the Works of Industry of all Nations," the *Crystal Palace*, had over 100,000 exhibits from around the world. Most of the exhibitors had merchandise for residences, including furniture, stained glass, textiles, and gothic-style metal stoves.

Source: © The Metropolitan Museum of Art/Art Resource, NY.

CHAPTER 2

EMPHASIS: 1900 TO 1910

OBJECTIVES

After reading this chapter, you should be able to describe and analyze:

■ How selected global political events from 1900 to 1910 affected interior environments and architecture as evident by cultural exchanges between Africa and Western Europe as well as public access to Potala Palace in Lhasa, Tibet, and the Palace of the Captains General in Havana, Cuba.

■ How the natural environment and disasters from 1900 to 1910 affected selected global interior environments and architecture as evident by the excavation of Chichén Itzá in 1904, the destruction of buildings caused by San Francisco's 1906 earthquake and fires, and Chicago's Iroquois Theater fire.

■ How selected global technologies and materials from 1900 to 1910 affected interior environments and architecture as evident by Frank Lloyd Wright's Larkin Building, the Purkersdorf Sanatorium by Josef Hoffmann, and the Mosque at Djenné in Mali, Africa.

■ How selected work styles and lifestyles from 1900 to 1910 affected interior environments and architecture as evident by the main building on Ellis Island, Prairie Houses, and the Deutscher Werkbund.

■ How selected global visual arts and performing arts from 1900 to 1910 affected interior environments and architecture as evident by Wiener Werkstätte, and the designs of Charles Rennie Mackintosh and Antoni Gaudí.

■ How selected global business developments and economics from 1900 to 1910 affected interior environments and architecture as evident by Louis Sullivan's Midwestern banks, Peter Behrens' AEG Building, and the American Arts and Crafts Movement.

■ How to compare and contrast selected interior environments and architecture of the Americas, Asia/Oceania, Europe, and the Middle East/Africa from 1900 to 1910.

The new century stimulated people to create a modern world that dissolved allegiances with historical traditions. Mechanization, transportation, and communication developments of the 19th century served as the basis for establishing the new modern world. The political dominance of the industrial powers resulted in the spread of Westernization by either mandate or choice. When a colony decided to adopt Westernization practices, its people often believed this was the only way their country would be economically solvent and have a strong military. Wars in the 1900s strengthened the imperial powers of Britain, Japan, and the United States, while weakening China, Africa, Korea, and the Philippines. Significant increases in the world's population mandated mechanization of products and materials. Western designers were still involved with the Arts and Crafts movement and Art Nouveau, but these styles evolved into very expensive handcrafted industries for the elite. Interior designers and architects had to identify the best approach for using machines to manufacture interior furnishings and create products that were aesthetically pleasing. This required creative solutions for working with iron, steel, and electricity. The end of this decade was also the eve of World War I, which radically transformed perceptions of mechanization and demonstrated negative consequences of global interactions.

GLOBAL POLITICS AND GOVERNMENT

At the turn of the century, the British Empire controlled approximately one-quarter of the world by ruling colonies in India, Canada, Australia, New Zealand, some islands in the South Pacific, several regions in Africa, and areas in South America and the Middle East. France also dominated many regions in the world, including parts of Africa, Southeast Asia, South America, and South Pacific islands. Mechanization, a strong military force, and wealth accumulated from profitable international trade contributed to the dominance of Western European powers over much of the world. Even though most of South America and Mexico had won their independence in the 19th century, the economic strength of the former rulers had a significant impact on living standards in those areas.

British Expansionary Conquests: Potala Palace (Public Access 1904) in Lhasa, Tibet

The consequences of Europeans' quest for domination of China continued into the 20th century. At the beginning of the 19th century, China was the most populated and advanced country in the world. For centuries the Chinese had excelled in engineering, technical skills, architecture, literature, pottery, painting, textiles, bronze work, lacquer, and the performing arts. At the end of the century, the Qing Empire was severely weakened by the expansionary conquests of Europe, Russia, and Japan.

In the quest for more power, territories, and a strategic military post, Britain pursued control of Tibet. The small country is located in the mountains of Central Asia, with India to the south, China to the north, and Russia to the northwest. At the time, Tibet had warm relations with Russia, and Britain perceived this location as an important military site that could be used to prevent the Russians from invading British India. In 1904 the British army overcame Tibetan forces and required Tibet to sign a treaty that prevented foreign control. The violence forced the 13th Dalai Lama, the head of state and the spiritual leader of the country, to flee the country and his palace, the Potala, in Tibet's capital city of Lhasa. The British invasion of Tibet in 1904 gave the world the chance to learn about the spectacular beauty and engineering feat of the Potala Palace (Figure 2.1). The palace was built hundreds of

Figure 2.1 The British invasion of Tibet presented the opportunity for the world to experience the spectacular beauty and engineering feat of the Potala Palace in Lhasa, Tibet.

Source: Erich Lessing/Art Resource, NY.

years ago, but due to its remote location and its secular purpose, very few people were aware of its existence or the interior's magnificent decoration. Known as the "pearl on the roof of the world," the palace is located on the top of the Red Mountain (Marpo Ri) and is surrounded by the Himalayan Mountains. For centuries the mountains and the palace's fortification deterred travelers and invasions.

This isolated location was further protected by the private purpose of the palace. Songtsen Gampo, the ruler of Tibet from 629 to 650 CE, first constructed the Potala Palace in the 7th century for his wife, Princess Wencheng of China's Tang Dynasty. Potala Palace includes a building that is known as the White Palace and the Red Palace, a structure that forms the central area of the entire complex. The palace had nearly 1,000 rooms and several defensive walls. In the 9th century it was used for religious purposes, but it was deteriorating from years of neglect. After destruction by the Chinese, the 5th Dalai Lama began to reconstruct the palace in 1645. It was to serve as the Dalai Lama's religious and administrative complex. For political reasons and to protect the Dalai Lama, the palace was designed with defensive walls, bastions, a hidden entrance, and a maze of switchback ramps leading to the top of the hill. The palace's land area is 1.4 million square feet (130,064 square meters) with a height of over 360 feet (110 meters). To withstand earthquakes, the structure of the palace is embedded with copper. The complex has a rich combination of flat roofs and Chinese-inspired gilded roofs with turned-up corners. Windows have black wooden frames, and some buildings have golden Buddhas embossed on cornices. The exterior has gilded lions mounted on the corners of buildings and gilded pinnacles encircled with bells.

Completed in three years, the White Palace and its surrounding administrative buildings were used for official ceremonies, offices, and storage. The top level of the White Palace (Phodrang Karpo), named for its white-painted walls, was for the private use of the Dalai Lama, who lived in rooms that were known as the East and West Sunshine Apartments. The rooms were filled with sunlight and highly ornamented interior furnishings. The adjoining 13-story Red Palace (1690–1694) was built for religious purposes and to contain tombs and stupas for the Dalai Lamas. The Chapels of the 5th and 13th Dalai Lamas contain the funerary stupas that are covered with gold and precious stones. The Buddha statue in Figure 2.2 is in the Grotto of Meditation, from the original 7th-century palace. This statue and tens of thousands of other sculptures, paintings, murals, carpets, porcelain, jade pieces, and paintings on silk demonstrate the exceptional artistic skills of the Tibetan people. Most murals and paintings have a religious subject, such as Buddhist teachings and the lives of Dalai Lamas. The Potala Palace was registered on the UNESCO World Heritage List in 1994 for its significant contribution to Tibetan architecture, metalwork, sculptures, and wall paintings and its association with important Tibetan political and religious figures.

African Colonization: Cultural Exchanges Between Africa and Western Europe; and Spanish Colonization: The Palace of the Captains General in Havana, Cuba (1902)

By the end of the 19th century, Africa was nearly entirely controlled by several Western European countries. In the 17th century, Dutch Boers (farmers) occupied South Africa's Cape of Good Hope. Many residences were constructed in a single-storied Cape Dutch style with a central front door flanked by symmetrical windows. Residences were painted white and had thatched roofs made from local straw or reeds. Common roofs were the **Dutch gambrel** with two flat surfaces on either side of the ridge; these often had **crow-stepped gables** at the ends of the pitched roofs. When the Congress of Vienna declared that South Africa was a British colony in 1815, the Boers moved to the Transvaal and the Orange Free State. These republics became a battlefield at the end of the century, when gold and diamonds were discovered in the region. The Boer War (1899–1902) between Britain and the Boers ended with a British victory. To emphasize British imperialism, the government commissioned the English architect Herbert Baker to design monumental buildings in the capital city of Pretoria. Baker designed the Union Building in 1909 to serve the city's administrative functions.

Baker's inspiration for the design of the Union Building was European classicism (Figure 2.3). The Union Building features two identical blocks that are connected by a curved colonnade. In a similar format to European palaces, the building overlooks terraced formal gardens, including fountains, sculptures, and ponds. Baker used the classical style to emphasize the presumed power of Western Europe. One block was for the British, and the other block was for the Dutch. The colonnade section connecting the two blocks, or "countries," represented the union between the Dutch and the British. Some indigenous materials were used to construct the building and to finish the interior, such as sandstone, teak, and granite. However, the use of local materials appears to be the building's only connection to the history and traditions of the South African people.

In contrast to the British officials who were interested in architecture that promoted their political agendas, some European artists were inspired by African art. Two photographs taken in the early 20th

Figure 2.2 The Chapels of the 5th and 13th Dalai Lamas contain the funerary stupas that are covered with gold and precious stones. The Buddha statue is in the *Grotto of Meditation*, which remains from the original 7th-century palace.

Source: Erich Lessing/Art Resource, NY.

century illustrate the impact of African and Oceanic art on European artists (Figures 2.4 and 2.5). The photograph of Herbert Ward's studio provides insight into his interest in African art and weapons. Ward was a British artist and sculptor involved with the journeys of explorer Henry Stanley in the late 19th century. Stanley is known for being the first European to explore and navigate the Congo River in the 1870s and for finding the lost explorer Dr. David Livingstone in Zanzibar. Stanley greeted Livingstone by asking the question, "Dr. Livingstone, I presume?" Ward's studio reveals numerous artifacts that appear to have been collected while he was traveling with Stanley. The walls are covered with African spears and knives, and African animals are represented as well, including a wall-mounted elephant head and a leopard-skin area rug.

Pablo Picasso's studio in Bateau-Lavoir, France, reveals his interest in **primitive** or tribal **art.** Some of the artifacts in the room appear to be from Africa, and the male and female statues are from New Caledonia, a group of islands in the southwest Pacific. In addition to personal collections, Picasso studied primitive art in the new ethnographic museums in Paris. Picasso's intrigue with African masks and sculpture is best depicted in his painting *Les Demoiselles D'Avignon* (1907). The painting is considered a masterpiece and prompted Picasso and

George Braque to develop **Cubism.** In opposition to traditional values and pictorial representations, Picasso painted prostitutes using angular forms and multiple views. Colors and contours of African masks inspired the faces of two of the women; the others resemble Iberian sculptures. As the century progressed, Cubism and tribal art had a significant impact on interior environments and architecture. For example, the flat, two-dimensional emphasis of the Cubist style influenced architects in the early 20th century, such as Le Corbusier and Walter Gropius. Cubism and tribal art influenced colors and patterns used in Art Deco (1910–1939).

Spanish colonization influenced Cuba's interior environments and architecture. Cuba's central location in the Gulf of Mexico and the Caribbean Sea played an important role when Spain possessed multiple colonies in the Americas. To oversee their Empire, the Spanish army and government officials were stationed in Cuba and could easily travel to the United States, Mexico, or South America. In the 16th century, Havana was identified as Spain's governmental seat because the city had a natural harbor that was easy to defend with surrounding fortifications, such as Morro Castle (Castillo del Morro) and La Punta Fortress (Castillo de la Punta). To facilitate the responsibilities of the Spanish government, several

Figure 2.3 Baker's inspiration for the design of the Union Building was European classicism. In a similar format to European palaces, the building overlooks terraced formal gardens, including fountains, sculptures, and ponds.
Source: © Dennis Cox/Alamy.

buildings were constructed in Havana in the 18th century. In a location close to the harbor, the Spanish constructed the Plaza de Armas, which included a council hall, a jail, and the Palace of the Captains General (1776–1792). The palace was used as the home of the Spanish colonial governors until Cuba gained independence in 1899. In contrast to many other governmental buildings that were heavily damaged or destroyed during revolutions, the palace was left intact. When Spanish rule ended, the Palace of the Captains General became the seat of the new Republic of Cuba in 1902. This provided an opportunity for people to experience the exceptional beauty of the palace.

The ornate palace is an excellent example of how Spanish colonization affected interior environments and architecture in Cuba's tropical setting. The colonial baroque mansion has many elements used in Spanish architecture, such as a central courtyard, columns, arcades, and porticoes, and wrought-iron balconies, railings, screens, and grills. The palace has attributes that are unique to Cuban architecture, such as floors with embedded coral fossils. Large doorways and windows help provide excellent ventilation in Havana's tropical environment. The luxurious interior has tall ceilings, elaborate chandeliers, Venetian mirrors, gold gilding, and stone floors.

Currently, the palace is the Museum of the City of Havana (Museo de la Ciudad). The exhibits focus on the history of Havana, including memorabilia from the wars of independence and artifacts from the colonial period, including pottery, silverware, glass, porcelain, paintings, and furniture. The central courtyard is filled with color; peacocks roam throughout the space, which includes a statute of Christopher Columbus, the first European to see Cuba. In 1982, "Old Havana and its Fortifications" were declared a UNESCO World Heritage Site for their unique urban pattern, complex of 17th–19th-century buildings, and the "historic fortunes of Havana" due to its bay's location for a maritime route to the New World (UNESCO, 1981, pp. 1–2).

Figure 2.4 This photograph and Figure 2.5 taken in the early 20th century illustrate the impact of African and Oceanic art on European artists. Herbert Ward's studio provides insight regarding his interest in African art and weapons.

Source: Adoc-photos/Art Resource, NY.

Figure 2.5 Pablo Picasso's studio in Bateau-Lavoir, France, reveals his interest in primitive or tribal art. This photograph and Figure 2.4 taken in the early 20th century illustrate the impact of African and Oceanic art on European artists.

Source: Reunion des Musees Nationaux/Art Resource, NY.

EFFECTS AND CONDITIONS OF THE NATURAL ENVIRONMENT

Several natural disasters occurred at the turn of the century that resulted in the deaths of thousands of people and the destruction of buildings, bridges, and transportation networks. The disasters included a sleeping sickness epidemic in Uganda, an avalanche in Canada, and earthquakes in San Francisco and Messina. Events and conditions that caused the tragedies can provide excellent information for preventing future fatalities and destruction of property. Lessons learned from disasters can lead to the development of improved construction methods, ordinances, building codes, and urban planning.

Also at the start of the new century, explorers and archeologists rediscovered the architectural remains of several civilizations, which provided more in-depth understanding of global traditions, customs, and lifestyles. These discoveries provided invaluable inspiration for new conceptualizations of interior environments and architecture.

Natural Disasters: San Francisco's 1906 Earthquake and Fires and Chicago's Iroquois Theater Fire in 1903

The world witnessed Chicago's devastating fire in 1871 and observed how the city rebuilt with an attitude of defiance. In the spring of 1906, another tragic fire occurred in a major city. In the early hours of April 18, a fire erupted after a strong earthquake shook San Francisco. The city had already experienced three significant earthquakes since the mid-19th century, but the 1906 earthquake and subsequent fires resulted in the deaths of thousands of people, thousands more left homeless, and the destruction

of the city's entire business district, along with factories, hotels, and residential communities. After completing an inspection of the damaged city, Victor H. Metcalf, the U.S. Secretary of Labor and Commerce, sent a telegram to President Theodore Roosevelt on April 26, 1906, summarizing the conditions:

> *In my judgment it will be impossible to determine the exact number of deaths, but conservative estimates place the number not to exceed three hundred [subsequently, estimates were approximately 3,000]. There are about one thousand sufferers in local hospitals, and not over four hundred are seriously injured. No necessity exists at the present time for nurses or doctors, and they should not be sent except on recommendation of General Greeley or Dr. Devine.*
>
> *As regards industrial and commercial losses, the conditions are appalling; figures and distances convey slight conceptions or realities. Not only have the business and industrial houses and establishments [with] one-half million people disappeared, [the conditions are] leaving them destitute financially and their means of livelihood temporarily gone. . . .*
>
> *Three hundred thousand people were rendered homeless, and their ordinary methods of providing themselves with food, clothing, and shelter, being entirely destroyed, their feeding and sheltering demanded extraordinary action and engrossed the attention of every one as soon as the ravages of the fire were checked.* (Metcalf, 1906)

San Francisco's natural disaster in 1906 had a dramatic impact on interior environments and architecture immediately after the event, during the rebuilding period, and years later. To accommodate the hundreds of thousands of people who had been left homeless, the U.S. Army erected tents in parks throughout the city, including Golden Gate Park (Figure 2.6).

To restore confidence in the viability of living and working in a city prone to earthquakes, many businessmen believed it would be better to minimize attention to the earthquake and instead focus the discussion on other causes of the disaster. Many reports blamed the extensive damage on the fires, which would have been perceived as more preventable than earthquakes. This perspective had perceived public support as a result of the recent successful rebuilding of Chicago after its devastating fires. A special *New San Francisco Emergency Edition* of *Sunset Magazine* published in May 1906 intentionally downplayed the effects of the earthquake by focusing on other factors: "The part destruction of several large buildings, including the City Hall, churches and other public edifices is evidence of its severity; and yet undoubtedly to some extent faulty construction was a factor in the loss. Many of the older houses erected by the pioneers and early citizens withstood the shock unharmed. Aside from the flimsier tenements and time-worn houses of cheap construction, the residence district presents no general evidence of earthquake damage save fallen chimneys" (Harriman, 1906, p. 2). The destruction of City Hall from San Francisco's disaster was extensive; however, in

Figure 2.6 San Francisco's natural disaster in 1906 had a dramatic impact on people and the built environment. To accommodate the hundreds of thousands of people who were homeless, the U.S. Army erected tents in parks throughout the city, including Golden Gate Park.

Source: San Francisco History Center, San Francisco Public Library.

contrast to Harriman's suggestion, subsequent studies found that the building had sound construction.

Unfortunately, denying the potential of earthquakes became the prevailing attitude in San Francisco until Santa Barbara experienced an earthquake in 1925 (Maher, 1965). Rather than focusing on rebuilding the city to minimize the destruction from earthquakes *and* fires, the city established new laws that emphasized fire prevention. For example, in 1906 Harriman provided fire prevention suggestions in *Sunset Magazine,* writing, "The heights of buildings may be limited to one and one half times the width of the street and avenues surely shall be widened. The city is not only to be beautiful, but enabled to isolate fires and to provide clearer avenues of intercommunication" (Harriman, p. 2).

Developing new building codes that help prevent fires and require sound construction methods is essential; however, to design buildings that are as safe as possible, all conditions and factors within an environment must be accounted for in architectural solutions. Seismographs, instruments that record waves caused by earthquakes, were available to city officials in 1906. Originally invented by a Chinese scholar in the 1st century, modern seismographs were designed in Japan at the end of the 19th century. As mentioned earlier in this chapter, earthquake-resistant technologies were included in the Potala Palace in the 7th century.

Hopefully, every disaster results in improvements in the safety of interior environments and architecture. The Chicago fire of 1871 led to extensive improvements in the safety of buildings and fire-prevention precautions. In addition, as a result of many theater fires in other cities and countries, many fire-prevention regulations were developed specifically for theaters. Fire-prevention standards were supposed to be used in the design of the new "fireproof" Iroquois Theater in Chicago, which opened in November 1903. Unfortunately, 1 month later, numerous preventable conditions led to the deaths of nearly 600 people, mostly women and children. Even though firemen extinguished the fire in just 30 minutes,

Figure 2.7 Iroquois Theater in Chicago. Even though firemen extinguished the fire in just 30 minutes, hundreds of people in the audience died in the first 15 minutes.
Source: AP Photo.

hundreds of people in the audience died in the first 15 minutes (Figure 2.7). Due to this extraordinarily high number of deaths from burns, gaseous fumes, and being trampled, the Iroquois Theater fire has been recorded as one of the deadliest in the world. Nearly all of the problems were the result of management's failure to follow fire regulations and safety procedures. The fire started on stage when one of the canvas scenery backdrops with highly flammable oil paint was too close to the extremely hot stage lights. The fire then spread to the velvet curtains. The stage fireman tried to extinguish the fire with a fire-suppressant material, Kilfyres, but soon it was out of control. Stage crew and actors started to evacuate the building through the rear exits. The airflow created an updraft that caused the fire to explode in the auditorium. People in the front rows were immediately killed, and the rest of the audience panicked and caused a stampede while trying to exit the building. Many people were killed in the stampede or died when they jumped from the balconies.

The extent of the tragedy could have been avoided if management had complied with theater fire regulations.

To prevent stage fires, which were very common in the early years of electrical stage lighting, theaters were required to employ a fireman on stage, and have fire hoses and extinguishers. The stage was supposed to have an asbestos curtain that would prevent a fire from reaching the audience. Exit doors were supposed to be operable, and ushers were expected to know how to help people exit the theater safely. As reported in a series of articles in the *Chicago Daily Tribune* during January 1904, these regulations were not enacted the afternoon of the 1903 matinee performance. The stage fireman had only two tubes of Kilfyres; the emergency curtain was not fireproof and failed to come down; some exit doors were locked or screened with iron gates; and the ushers had no training in evacuation procedures.

This tragedy prompted theaters in cities around the world to stop performances while they inspected their fire-prevention equipment, and reviewed the related policies and procedures. To ensure laws were enforced, increased pressure was applied to city building inspectors. New regulations were enacted that required regular inspections of water hoses, fire extinguishers, and operable exit doors. Stage equipment and materials, such as scenery backdrops, curtains, and props, had to be fireproof. To facilitate evacuation procedures, regulations required that theaters have wider hallways, trained ushers in uniforms, and out-swinging exit doors. Exit doors in the Iroquois Theater swung *into* the building, which slowed or prevented people from escaping. Consequently, stipulating that exit doors in commercial buildings must swing *out* changed many previous regulations. The basically undamaged theater reopened the following year and was eventually closed for demolition in 1925.

Environmental Conditions: Chichén Itzá in Mexico (Excavation 1904)

Chichén Itzá is an ancient Mayan city located on the Yucatán Peninsula in Mexico. The civilization existed in the pre-Columbian period, which is the era before Spain's discovery of the region in the 16th century. The

Mexican government's excavation of the city in the mid-19th century (UNESCO, 1987) and the purchase of the site by an American, Edward Herbert Thompson, the United States Consul to Yucatán, in 1904 enabled the world to study, research, and appreciate an extremely advanced civilization. A discussion of Chichén Itzá can help reinforce ideas about the importance of relationships between the environment and humans.

The foundation of the Yucatán Peninsula is made from limestone without substantial sources for potable water. Sinkholes in the formation of limestone create natural wells, or cenotes. Thus, to have adequate water for drinking and farming, communities were established close to the cenotes. For the Mayan people living in Chichén Itzá, the cenotes also served an important role in religious ceremonies. As a sacrifice to the gods and to connect with the kingdom of the underworld, people, animals, and precious metals were thrown into the wells. This ceremonial practice and other customs of the Mayan people are revealed in the city's architecture, sculptures, and bas-reliefs.

The abundance of local limestone had a significant impact on the area's architecture, art, and activities. More than 50 limestone temples and palaces were constructed in two phases. The first phase was in the late 7th century until the early 10th century. During this classical era, five major temples were constructed in the Puuc style, including the Red House group and the Casa de la Monjas (The Nunnery House). Characteristics of the Puuc style include stone veneers with carved geometric patterns, **corbelled vaults,** and **roof-combs,** a unit on the top of buildings decorated in pierced stone. The assemblage of stones with rubble filling the cracks created an interesting mosaic pattern to façades. Corners of some buildings had profiles of the masks of gods with long, curled noses and ornamented large circles surrounding the eyes. The second phase, the post-classical period, did not begin until approximately 1000 CE and ended in the 13th century. The reasons for the civilization's demise at two different eras are unknown, but

speculation focuses on the possibility of droughts in the arid climate, famines, or perhaps military conquests.

By studying the architecture, statues, and stone carvings, researchers have discovered that the Mayan people were experts at mathematics, astronomy, writing, and the solar calendar. The circular Caracol was an astronomical observatory that enabled the Mayans to study the stars and astronomical occurrences. They used this information to develop a solar calendar for agricultural, social, and religious purposes. The Pyramid of Kukulcán is an excellent example of their engineering expertise and their astronomical knowledge (Figure 2.8).

The pyramidal temple has four sides; each side has a staircase with 91 steps. By adding the step at the summit of the temple, the total number of steps equals 365, the number of days in a solar calendar. The height and position of the temple was planned to make it appear that during the sunrise and sunset of the spring and autumn equinoxes, the sun's movement casts shadows on the steps that resemble a snake slithering along the edges of the pyramid. Plumed serpents, eagles, and jaguars were common decorative motifs used on the temples of the Chichén Itzá. Sculptures, bas-reliefs, and mosaics depict the importance of religious ceremonies in the lives of the Mayan people. To please the gods,

Figure 2.8 The Pyramid of Kukulcán is an excellent example of Mayans' engineering expertise and their astronomical knowledge. The pyramidal temple has four sides, and each side has a staircase with 91 steps.
Source: © Sola/parasola.net/Alamy.

a common depiction in stone carvings was decapitation or a row of skulls of people who had been killed. In recognition of the "fusion of Mayan construction techniques with new elements from central Mexico," Chichén Itzá was registered on the UNESCO World Heritage Site List in 1988.

GLOBAL TECHNOLOGICAL DEVELOPMENTS

Several technological research and initiatives from the 19th century came to fruition at the turn of the century, including two new modes of transportation. Henry Ford sold his first inexpensive automobile in 1903, followed by the first Model T in 1908. The year 1903 was also important for another monumental advance in transportation: the first flight in a powered airplane—by Wilbur and Orville Wright at Kitty Hawk, North Carolina. By 1909, the Wright brothers had created an airplane with a powerful engine and a passenger seat. The 19th-century modes of transportation, including railroads and subways, continued to improve in tandem with these modern innovations. Additionally, advances in understanding about electricity and new building materials manifested in modern approaches to the design of commercial and residential interiors.

Technologies: Larkin Building (1902–1906) in Buffalo, New York, by Frank Lloyd Wright (Demolished 1950)

Often viewed as the first building of the **Modern movement,** Wright's Larkin building in Buffalo, New York, has many attributes that changed the conceptualization and design of office environments. Prominent in the transformational process were technological advances in electrical lighting, fire precautions, and mechanical systems. These technologies enabled Wright to design the Larkin building in the center of a polluted industrial area. The extremely successful Larkin Company manufactured soap and was a premium-based mail-order business. The company's founder, John D. Larkin, commissioned Wright to design an administrative building for executives, department managers, and approximately 1,800 clerical workers. To facilitate administrative activities, including correspondence to customers, Larkin wanted a building that was bright and clean, and addressed the needs of employees. These characteristics were especially important to entice intelligent people to work in a building that was located on a dismal industrial site. To project the proper image to its customers, Larkin wanted smart clerical workers who could write prompt and effective responses; offices, therefore, had to be clean to ensure that letters did not have soil or stains.

To accommodate the needs of the Larkin Company, Wright designed a building that blocked the industrial views and prevented soot and smoke from entering the structure. Daylight was provided by skylights in the central atrium and by perimeter windows located close to ceilings and above eye level (Figure 2.9). To maximize daylight, Wright designed one of the first **open-plan offices** and pioneered the concept of using glass doors surrounded by windows for commercial entrances. Open-plan offices have altered how people work in an office and have an impact on noise levels, security, and perceptions of privacy and personal space. Wright also employed an example of sustainability by integrating the use of daylight with electrical fixtures (which were mounted on ceilings, walls, and floors). Electrical lighting was essential to provide adequate illumination on the first floor in the building's five-story atrium and in areas far away from windows. Another important sustainability solution was the creation of adequate ventilation and quality indoor air. To accomplish this, Wright designed one of the world's first buildings to consider indoor air quality by having *conditioned air*. In a 1956 interview, the architect explained, "I had, already, in the Larkin Building in Buffalo, put in air conditioning because the building was down on the railroad tracks and gas from the engines and all that was around it all day long. So the Larkin Building was the first air-conditioned building in the world" (Meehan, 1984).

In addition to technological advancements, the Larkin Building is an excellent example of a building designed to accommodate the needs of a client and the users of the space. In addition to conditioned air, Wright developed several solutions to Larkin's demand for a clean environment. In a building with a lot of illumination, dirty floors, surfaces, and furniture are very

Figure 2.9 To accommodate the needs of the Larkin Company, Wright designed a building that blocked the industrial views and prevented soot and smoke from entering the structure. Daylight was provided by skylights in the central atrium and by perimeter windows located close to ceilings and above eye levels.

Source: The Frank Lloyd Wright Foundation, AZ/Art Resource, NY.

noticeable. Wright therefore designed furniture and equipment that enabled the maintenance staff to clean the floors easily. For example, custom keyhole desks had chairs that were mounted to the front of the desk and were not supported with a base (Figure 2.10). The chair could be pivoted to fold neatly under the desk. In the bathrooms, Wright designed wall-mounted lavatories and water closets (W.C.). The partitions used in restroom stalls were suspended above the floor and were attached to a single pole at the front of the partition and the wall behind the W.C. Metal furniture was easy to clean and helped address Larkin's concern regarding fires. As a witness to Chicago's fire in 1871, he was adamant that his new building be "fireproof." In addition to the steel-framed, clad-brick structure, a fireproof material—magnetite—was applied to floors and furniture.

To create a setting conducive to employees, the Larkin Building had a library; classroom; conservatory; roof terrace; locker areas; restaurant; kitchen; and lounge with a fireplace, leather reclining chairs, and piano. Unfortunately, after internal strife and significant losses in the mail-order business, the Larkin Building was converted into an unsuccessful department store, followed by bankruptcy. Due to unpaid taxes, the City of Buffalo took ownership of the building and sold the property to be demolished for a truck terminal in 1950.

Technologies and Materials: Purkersdorf Sanatorium (1904–1906) in Vienna, Austria, by Josef Hoffmann and Mosque at Djenné (Rebuilt 1906–1907) in Mali, Africa

Technologies and materials had a significant effect on the design of the Purkersdorf Sanatorium, which was located outside of Vienna. As a forerunner to the International Style, the Purkersdorf demonstrated the advanced techniques for constructing buildings with reinforced concrete and flat roofs. A new material from the late 19th century, reinforced concrete enabled the architect and designer, Josef Hoffmann, to design a structure that emphasized forms and had plain surfaces

Figure 2.10 Wright designed furniture and equipment that enabled the maintenance staff at the Larkin Building to easily clean the floor. Custom keyhole desks had chairs that were mounted to the front of the desk and were not supported with a base. When not in use, the chair could pivot and fold neatly under the desk.

Source: The Frank Lloyd Wright Foundation, AZ/Art Resource, NY.

(Figure 2.11). Reinforced concrete made it possible for Hoffmann to create a rational design by emphasizing utility, form, and structure. To underscore the geometric forms created by the concrete, the exterior of Purkersdorf lacks cornices, projections, or roof angles. Hoffmann used a very subtle form of ornamentation on the exterior by outlining windows, doors, and the edges of the building with small blue and white square tiles. The white color of concrete was ideal in presenting a "sanitized" appearance to the clients of the health retreat. Furthermore, concrete surfaces are easy to clean and maintain, which enabled the building to sustain a sanitary appearance over the years.

Technology also played a role in the design of the interior. Hoffmann and Koloman Moser had to design the interior environment to accommodate new medical technologies, hygiene standards, and hydro treatments. They included several rooms for recreational therapy, including music, writing, billiards, reading, and cards.

One of Hoffmann's most important designs provided comfort for the clients at the Purkersdorf Sanatorium. The *sitzmaschine* (machine for sitting) was made of stained beechwood or bentwood, and used ball brackets to lock the back in several reclined positions. Fresh air, daylight, cleanliness, and nutritious foods were considered essential for good health. Therefore, the Purkersdorf had numerous large operable windows and balconies. Daylight penetration was maximized by white walls, ceilings, and glazing on doors (Figure 2.12). In addition, an abundance of natural daylight presented the impression that the environment was clean and healthy. To help keep the interior clean, Hoffmann selected materials that were easy to maintain, such as ceramic tile for floors and walls. Furniture was designed to be easy to maintain by reducing or eliminating ornamentation and using materials that could be wiped clean, such as lacquer finishes and wickerwork for upholstery (see Figure 2.12).

The importance of healthy food was evident by the extraordinarily large dining room, with one long dining table that could seat more than 60 people. As proponents of **Wiener Werkstätte's** *Gesamtkunstwerk* (total artwork), Hoffmann and Moser designed all of the interior furnishings to harmonize with the exterior. For example, the small squares on the exterior were repeated in the interior (see Figure 2.12) on chair seats, floor patterns, tile walls, the *sitzmaschine,* and wooden panels on furniture, walls, and doors. Even the round cutouts on the back of the dining room chairs appeared to be a series of squares. Hoffmann became renowned for small squares, especially his grid-patterned metalwork designs for baskets, flower vases, and tableware. Nearly all of the interior furnishings and decorative arts designed by Hoffmann and Moser were fabricated in the Wiener Werkstätte (Vienna Workshops). The Wiener Werkstätte and Hoffmann and Moser's involvement with its founding are discussed later in this chapter.

Within a broad context, "technology" includes a wide range of materials, tools, and techniques. The

Mosque at Djenné is an outstanding example of constructing and maintaining a building with technologies that do not require the power of electricity or the consumption of nonrenewable resources, such as oil or natural gas. Located close to the Niger River in northwest Africa (present-day Mali), Djenné was founded in the late 13th century as an important city for the trans-Saharan gold trade. The king of Djenné converted to Islam and ordered the construction of the mosque on the site of his previous palace (Figure 2.13). Religious officials (*muezzin*) climb the stairs to the top of the three rectangular-shaped minarets to call worshippers for daily prayers. The mosque's three main areas for prayer are the outdoor courtyard, the covered archway surrounding the courtyard, and the prayer hall. The prayer hall (*musalla*) has a sand floor, a wooden ceiling, and no furniture and is fairly dark due to its small apertures. After many years of neglect, the mosque was in ruins by the end of the 19th century. The Mosque was rebuilt in 1906–1907 and has been maintained to the present day.

The architectural style of the mosque has sculptural beauty and is an excellent application of the principles of sustainability. Its design incorporated concepts and technologies that would prevent its destruction from floods, sun, heat, and wind. Located on the flood plain of the Niger and Bani rivers, the mosque was built on a base that was higher than flood levels. It is made from sun-baked mud bricks (adobes), which are covered with mud plaster. Using locally available mud is ideal for withstanding climatic conditions, and it reduces the consumption of fuel that would be required to transport materials from another location. The Mali region has become well known for using mud to create **bogolan** (mud cloth). The very dark brown color of the bogolan textile is derived from minerals in the mud and is often emphasized by a geometric pattern in a contrasting color.

The mosque features other examples of sustainability, including its construction techniques, maintenance procedures, and sources of illumination, cooling, heating, and ventilation. Over centuries local masons perfected a technology for forming the bricks by hand and mixing the mud with their feet. Bare hands and special trowels are used to "sculpt" surfaces and forms. The palm beams protruding from the sides of the mosque are another local material and demonstrate an innovative approach to using multifunctional technologies. The beams both help to support the structure and are used for scaffolding when the mosque has to be restored every spring due to the seasonal floods. Windows and numerous openings in the roof supply daylight and natural ventilation. When it rains, locally

Figure 2.11 As a forerunner to the International Style, the Purkersdorf demonstrated the advanced techniques for constructing buildings with reinforced concrete and flat roofs. Reinforced concrete enabled Josef Hoffmann to design a structure that emphasized forms and had plain surfaces.

Source: Wikimedia Commons.

Figure 2.12 Purkersdorf has numerous large operable windows and balconies. Daylight penetration is maximized by white walls, ceilings, and glazing on doors.

Source: WOKA Lamps Vienna, Wolfgang Karolinsky.

crafted terracotta conical units are used to cover the apertures in the roof. The thick walls provide insulation in warm or cool weather. In proclaiming that Djenné was a premier example of a "typical African city," UNESCO included the mosque and its surrounding landscape on the World Heritage List in 1988.

GLOBAL LIFE AND WORK STYLES

The earliest years of the 20th century produced changes in where and how people lived and worked. Transportation advances made it much easier to move to locations with perceived better opportunities.

People continued to immigrate to the "New World" (North America) and to urban settings. The population increases in cities fostered the development of urban planning as an academic discipline, beginning in 1909 at the University of Liverpool. Formalized city planning occurred in the New World, Europe, and European-dominated colonies, including India and Africa. To facilitate the exchange of knowledge, concepts, and ideas, many countries focused efforts on establishing educational institutions and professional societies, among other ventures. Cultural exchanges that naturally occur as a result of immigration and educational interactions can have significant effects on people, interior environments, and architecture, as described below.

Immigration and Emigration: Ellis Island (Rebuilt 1900), Upper New York Bay

From 1892 until 1954, Ellis Island served as the U.S. immigration processing station. People from every country in the world came to the United States during that period. Historians have estimated that approximately 15 million people passed through the station. Immigration peaked in 1907; more than one million people, most notably from Italy, Austria, Hungary, and Greece, were processed through Ellis Island. These staggering numbers represent the largest relocation of people in world history. Immigration and emigration obviously result in cultural exchanges, and from a design perspective, that sometimes results in a transfer of concepts, skills, and techniques that can be used to improve interior environments and architecture. The New World gained from the expertise accumulated from centuries of experience, and people in the "Old World" learned of innovations in the United States via communication or when immigrants returned to their homeland. Serving as the processing station, Ellis Island symbolized these global cultural exchanges. To celebrate the cultural assimilation that was occurring in New York City, Israel Zangwill wrote the play *Melting Pot* in 1908. From the playwright's perspective, the blending of cultures and ethnicities should be viewed as a "stew."

Figure 2.13 The king of Djenné converted to Islam and ordered the construction of the Mosque on the site of his previous palace. Religious officials (*muezzin*) climb the stairs to the top of the three rectangular-shaped minarets to call the worshippers for daily prayers.

Source: Werner Forman/Art Resource, NY.

Each ingredient used to make a stew is enhanced when the flavors interact with each other in the pot. Likewise, the quality of life improved when people from disparate lands melted together in a city.

The events that occurred in the main building on Ellis Island can be viewed as the initial phase in a chain of events that affected the lives of people, the design of interior environments, and architectural styles throughout the world. The Station building was designed to "process" individuals and families. The main building (now a museum) was the third structure used as a processing station. The replacement building was the small "Castle Garden," which had to be replaced to accommodate the escalating number of immigrants. The new building was destroyed by fire in 1897, and the reconstructed Station, designed by Edward Lippincott Tilton and William Boring, opened in 1900.

There are many ways the Station directly and indirectly affected people. When third-class immigrants, who made up the largest group on a ship, arrived at the Station, they were exhausted and hungry and had not bathed during the 3-week journey. Due to the processing of first- and second-class passengers, sometimes the third-class passengers had to wait for days to be ferried to Ellis Island. When they finally arrived at the Station, they were even more tired, and upon entering the Station, they often became confused and frightened. Most of the immigrants did not know English, and there was very little assistance from interpreters.

The Station was designed so that the first space the immigrants entered was the baggage room. They were immediately required to leave all of their belongings in this room, baggage that often was never recovered due to loss or theft. The next stage in the process was to walk up the staircase to the imposing Main Hall. The scale of the room was intimidating, and the numerous aisles separated by iron bars resembled the layout of stockyards. Perched on the second-floor balconies were U.S. officials who scrutinized the crowd for anyone who appeared to be ill, disabled, or mentally challenged. To identify these people for a thorough medical examination, the U.S. officials drew a letter on their back in chalk. For example, an "H" represented a potential heart problem and an "X" represented mental concerns. Physical exams were given in an open medical examination area in the Main Hall. Anyone with a disease or disability was denied entry into the country. Children were separated from their family when a relative was forced to return to his or her homeland because of a physical or mental disability. The volumetric proportions and the poor acoustical properties of the Main Hall magnified the screams, cries, and groans of frightened and panicked immigrants.

Once people passed the medical and psychological examinations and successfully responded to the questions from officials, they could take a ferry to New York City or buy a train ticket to other cities in the United States. Immigrants tended to be restricted to living in cities that were easily accessible from Ellis Island. These are the cities that benefited most directly from the experience, skills, and knowledge of the immigrants. Among other things, their abilities helped improve the techniques used to create architecture, furniture, and the fine and decorative arts. The hard physical labor that immigrants were willing to do affected these communities by the efficient manufacturing of interior furnishings, and the construction of buildings, bridges, and transportation networks.

Life and Work Styles: The Prairie House and Deutscher Werkbund (1907)

Immigrants were able to easily take a train from New York City to Chicago and the Midwest. One of the immigrants was a little girl from Wales, Anna Lloyd Jones, who was to become Frank Lloyd Wright's mother. Wright was born and raised on the Wisconsin prairie but moved to Chicago to become an architect during the building boom that resulted from the fire there in 1871. At the time, Chicago was one of the fastest growing cities in the world. By 1900, the city's population was 2.2 million and the land area had quadrupled. Bounded on the east by Lake Michigan, the city's crescent-shaped expansion was to the north, west, and south. The expansion was facilitated by electrified railway transportation, new utilities, and paved roads. Rapid public transportation enabled people to live in newly formed suburbs and commute into the city to work. Residences became a refuge from the congestion of the city and were perceived as an important place for feeling safe.

This new way of living had an enormous impact on interior environments and architecture. The high prices for land in the cities fundamentally forced the creation of residences in high-rise buildings. Moving to areas with much cheaper land enabled people to have residences that were spread out with surrounding green space. This was the lifestyle that Wright experienced when he lived in Oak Park, a suburb 8 miles (13 kilometers) west of downtown Chicago. In 1889 he designed his Oak Park residence in a wooded community with ample prairie

and in close proximity to the Des Plaines River. Oak Park was one of the few suburbs that had rapid transit access at the time, and thus Wright was able to easily commute to his office in downtown Chicago.

In 1893 Wright launched his architectural firm, and Chicago hosted the World's Columbian Exposition. The simultaneous occurrences of Wright's need to acquire commissions, people wanting homes in the suburbs, and the Japanese *Ho-o-Den* exhibit at the Exposition all influenced the design of Wright's **Prairie Houses.** The Prairie House is one of Wright's most important architectural achievements, and its conceptual design required the land area and landscaping of suburbia.

The conceptual origins of the Prairie House can be traced to articles Wright wrote for the *Ladies' Home Journal* in February and July of 1901. Edward Bok, the president of the company that published the *Journal*, was interested in encouraging Americans to build well-designed residences. Bok solicited designs and working drawings from architects, which he published in the magazine. Wright submitted two Prairie House designs that were published in the *Journal* (Figure 2.14). The first design was priced at $7,000, and the other model was $5,800. Both models illustrate many of the defining characteristics of the Prairie House. In the February issue, "A Home in a Prairie Town," Wright explained the need for adequate land area for a prairie community, stating, "A city man going to the country puts too much in his house and too little in his ground" (Wright, 1901, p. 17). He also noted that the exterior of his design "recognizes the influence of the prairie, is firmly and broadly associated with the site, and makes a feature of its quiet level. The low terraces and broad eaves are designed to accentuate that quiet level and complete the harmonious relationship" (Wright, 1901, p. 17).

In the July issue, "A Small House with 'Lots of Room in it,'" Wright discussed other attributes associated with living in the suburbs, noting, "The plan disregards somewhat the economical limit in compact planning to take advantage of light, air, and prospect, the enjoyable things one goes to the suburbs to secure" (Wright, 1901, p. 15).

As explained by Wright, the Prairie House was created to establish an architectural style that was unique to the landscape of the Midwest. The region's low hills, forests, rivers, and prairies influenced architectural directional lines, textures, patterns, and colors. In echoing the undulating hills of the prairie, horizontal lines dominated the exterior and manipulated the flow of interior space. To have a low-lying profile, roofs had very deep overhangs and were either flattened hips or broad gables. Bands of casement windows wrapping around the structure further emphasized the horizontal direction. In lieu of the square shape that was conducive to high-rises on city lots, many plans of the Prairie House were elongated rectangles with rooms projecting from the central core, as in the library and dining room in Figure 2.14. The design of roofs and fireplaces played critical roles in conveying a feeling that Prairie Houses provided shelter from the elements. The low-lying roof appeared to embrace the interior, and the broad chimney gave the impression that substantial heat would radiate from its central location and fill the home with warmth.

The horizontal line and ecological references were repeated in the interior of the Prairie House. In reflecting societal lifestyle changes, Wright eliminated the "parlor" and created an open living area by combining the new "living room," dining room, and a library (see Figure 2.14). Eliminating interior partitions reinforced the horizontal line and helped to improve ventilation and the dispersion of daylight. The expansive fireplace became the focal point of the interior and symbolically served as the heart of family life. The dark beams on the ceiling reinforced a sense of the roof providing shelter from the elements. References to the prairie were reflected in the prominent use of oak and the natural colors green, brown, gold, and rust.

Integration with nature and many other characteristics of the Prairie House reflect attributes of Japanese architecture that Wright had studied at the 1893 Exposition in Chicago. He was very familiar with those exhibits because he worked with Louis Sullivan and Dankmar Adler in designing its Transportation building. On the Exposition's "Wooded Isle," the *Ho-o-Den* was constructed as a scaled model of the Fujiwara family temple near Kyoto, Japan. Some characteristics of Japanese architecture found in the Prairie House are the low-lying roof lines, deep eaves, high blank walls, and windows and doorways that encouraged interaction with nature. Both styles have simplified interiors by removing partitions and using plain surfaces, minimal furniture, and few, but discriminating, decorative arts.

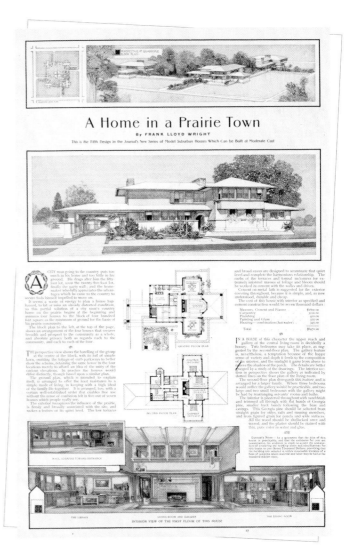

Figure 2.14 Wright submitted two Prairie House designs that were published in the *Journal*. Both models illustrate many of the defining characteristics of the Prairie House.

Source: © The Frank Lloyd Wright Foundation, AZ/Art Resource, NY.

The simplicity and adaptability of the style resulted in hundreds of Prairie Houses constructed in a variety of sizes and price ranges from 1900 until the early 1910s. Some important examples of Prairie Houses designed by Wright include the Bradley House (1900) in Kankakee, Illinois; Willits House (1902–1903) in Highland Park, Illinois; Dana House (1902–1904), in Springfield, Illinois; Coonley House (1906–1909) in Riverside, Illinois; and the Robie House (1908–1910) on the south side of Chicago.

Initially, Germany lagged behind the progressive industrialization that occurred in other countries, such as Britain and the United States. However, German industry made significant strides in the late 19th and early 20th centuries, which transformed its military power and manufacturing output. These advances prompted the development of social and cultural changes that would transform the way people worked and the products they purchased.

At the core of the effort was the quest to identify a means for compromise between the individualistic perspective of artists and the standardization that was required for the manufacturing industry. To provide an appropriate structure that would encourage artists and industrialists to communicate with each other, Prussian architect Hermann Muthesius and Belgian artist and designer Henry Van de Velde formed the **Deutscher Werkbund** (DWB) (German Work Federation) in 1907. DWB was a professional organization whose membership included artists, architects, interior designers, craftsmen, manufacturers, and industrial designers. The DWB was founded on the premise that a formalized forum for communication and education was necessary to foster cultural and social reforms. Industry-wide transformation would then improve the quality of German products and the country's subsequent economic position in the world.

To facilitate the transformation process, DWB sponsored symposia, conferences, exhibitions, and various publications, including *Yearbooks*. The DWB influenced design education by developing curriculum that focused on multiple philosophical perspectives, such as the Arts and Crafts movement, Art Nouveau, and Functionalists. The association also examined how to design products with new materials and techniques. The DWB organization helped to improve workshop training and the overall quality of working in factories. The high standards of design developed by members of the DWB resulted in quality objects that were manufactured using standardized processes. An ability to produce well-designed objects using mass-production methods influenced the Modern movement and the industrial design profession. The success of the DWB prompted other countries to establish professional organizations, including Austria, Sweden, Switzerland, and Britain, where the Design and Industries Association was founded.

GLOBAL VISUAL AND PERFORMING ARTS

Numerous artists influenced the design of interior environments and architecture in the first decade of the 20th century. Via informal conversations in coffee or teahouses, artists, interior designers, and architects shared and debated perspectives that would provide the vocabulary for the Modern movement. Artists influenced aesthetics, production methods, applied arts, and the importance of a *Gesamtkunstwerk*. Opera performances, such as Puccini's *Madama Butterfly* (1904) in Milan, were another source of influence in the development of a *Gesamtkunstwerk*. Total artwork is evident in an opera performance by the artistic way that the elements on a stage present a unified composition. Costumes, choreography, stage sets, music, lighting, drama, and makeup are harmoniously designed to create a *Gesamtkunstwerk*.

Visual Arts: Wiener Werkstätte (Vienna Workshops) (1903) and Charles Rennie Mackintosh

A number of artists in Vienna at the turn of the century were interested in creating art for modern living. To break from traditional art, several artists formed an organization, the Secession, in 1897. Led by a highly influential artist of the times, Gustav Klimt, the Secessionists intended to transform the applied arts. In the first issue of the group's publication, *Ver Sacrum* (Sacred Spring), they proclaimed a primary purpose of their new organization: "We know no distinction between 'high art' and 'handicraft.'" In stating this premise, the Secessionists were expressing their intention of designing interior environments that were in harmony with art objects. To exhibit their work, architect Joseph Maria Olbrich designed the 1898 Secession Building. The structure featured a prominent dome, which became known as the *Golden Cabbage* due to the gilded leaves of the dome and the building's close proximity to a vegetable market (Figure 2.15).

After a successful exhibit at the 8th Exhibition of the Secession, two of its founders, Josef Hoffmann and painter and graphic artist Kolo Moser, furthered the organization's cause by creating the Wiener Werkstätte in 1903. To create a *Gesamtkunstwerk,* Secessionists believed that artists and craftspeople needed to work together and they needed oversight of production methods, materials, and administration processes. With funding from a wealthy textile manufacturer, Fritz Wäerndorfer, Wiener Werkstätte was created to provide a studio for artists and craftspeople. To fuse "high art" with "handicraft," the studio environment encouraged exchanges between artists, craftspeople, architects, and designers.

Artists and craftspeople learned from each other and applied their education to a range of objects for interior environments. To emphasize the importance of each person's contribution to objects created in the workshop, the organization developed a protocol for marks and monograms. Pieces were stamped with the organization's trademark, WW, and also the artist's or craftsman's monogram. Craftsmen included goldsmiths, silversmiths, joiners, metal workers, bookbinders, leather workers, varnishers, and painters. The variety of products created in the Wiener Werkstätte is astounding. From its inception until the workshop closed in 1932, artists and craftspeople had an impact on both interior environments and fashion by creating paintings, sculpture, furniture, ceramics, light fixtures, glass, wallpaper, textiles, vases, carpets, silver services, jewelry, handbags, dresses, coats, millinery, theater costumes, postcards, and posters.

The residence that best demonstrates the *Gesamtkunstwerk* and the artistic talents of the Wiener Werkstätte is the Palais Stoclet (1906–1911) in Brussels, designed by Josef Hoffmann. As with Hoffmann's design for the Purkersdorf Sanatorium, the exterior of

Figure 2.15 To exhibit their work, Joseph Maria Olbrich designed the 1898 Secession building with its prominent dome, which became known as the *Golden Cabbage*.
Source: Erich Lessing/Art Resource, NY.

Palais Stoclet has plain surfaces that emphasize architectural forms. With unlimited funds from its owner, the wealthy Belgian industrialist Adolphe Stoclet, the residence has extremely expensive art, objects, and interior furnishings. The dining room is renowned for its rare variegated marble walls, furniture made from exotic woods, and friezes painted by Klimt with gold and jewels (Figure 2.16).

The Scottish artist, designer, and architect Charles Rennie Mackintosh was very much involved with the artists at the Wiener Werkstätte. Mackintosh and three of his close friends, who were also artists, had an exhibition at the 8th Exhibition of the Secession. The Exhibition was important for introducing modernist designers. This exposure and Mackintosh's subsequent commission to design a music room for Fritz Wäerndorfer, businessman and art lover, initiated a collaborative relationship with the artists of the Wiener Werkstätte.

Mackintosh was working during the Arts and Crafts movement and the Art Nouveau era, but he had a unique style that was viewed as modern and embraced by the Viennese designers. Fine and applied arts had a significant impact on Mackintosh's interior environments and

architecture. Mackintosh was professionally trained as an artist at the Glasgow School of Art, and there were several artists and artistic movements that influenced his designs, including James McNeill Whistler, Aubrey Beardsley, the Pre-Raphaelites, Jan Theodoor Toorop, ancient Celts, and Japanese woodblock prints. Mackintosh's career started with his professional and personal relationships with three other artists, Herbert MacNair and Frances and Margaret Macdonald, two sisters. In 1899, MacNair married Frances, and in 1900, Mackintosh married Margaret. Known as "The Four," they exhibited their work in various international exhibitions, but their partnerships ended when MacNair and Frances moved to an educational appointment in England.

Mackintosh and Margaret collaborated on projects until the early 1920s, when their few clients significantly reduced commissions of their expensive designs. For approximately 20 years, the couple designed extraordinary "total designed" interiors that were so exquisitely detailed that each space appeared to be a painting. Mackintosh is well known for his redesign of the Glasgow School of Art (1897–1899; 1907–1909) with its regional ornamental motifs, exquisite decorative metalwork, and abundance of natural daylight. However, influences from the visual and performing arts are most evident in their residential interiors and in the tearooms commissioned by patron Catherine Cranston. For example, in 1901, the couple entered a contest to design a *Haus eines Kunstfreundes* (House for an Art Lover). The Mackintoshes' designs were disqualified due to their late entry; however, they were given a special prize from the judges because of "their pronounced personal quality, their novel and austere form and the uniform configuration of interior and exterior" (www.houseforanartlover.co.uk). Eventually, a collaborative effort between the Glasgow City Council and the Glasgow School of Art resulted in the construction of the House (1989–1994) in Bellahouston Park in Glasgow. Influence from the visual arts is evident in

Figure 2.16 The dining room of Palais Stoclet is renowned for its rare variegated marble walls, furniture made from exotic woods, and friezes painted by Klimt with gold and jewels.

Source: Foto Marburg/Art Resource, NY.

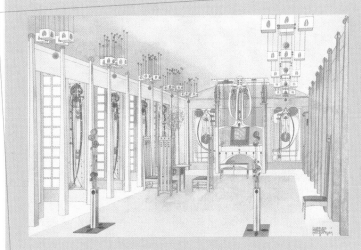

Figure 2.17 A collaborative effort between the Glasgow City Council and the Glasgow School of Art resulted in the construction of the House (1989–1994) in Bellahouston Park in Glasgow. Influence from the visual arts is evident in the artistic composition of the lounge and music hall room and in Mackintosh's mastery of perspective drawings.

Source: Victoria & Albert Museum, London/Art Resource, NY.

the artistic composition of each room and in their mastery of perspective drawings (Figure 2.17).

The visual and the performing arts influenced the design of their interiors. In referencing Japanese art, Mackintosh carefully positioned two vases with sparse flowers in the *ikebana* style. As in many of Mackintosh's interiors, the stylized pink roses arranged in the vases are repeated throughout the room. The influence of the performing arts is evident in the designer's repeated use of very thin lines that resemble the strings of an instrument. Strings can be found on the high back of the piano, lanterns suspended from the ceiling, and wall decorations. The suspended lanterns are pierced with pink glass in a shape that resembles the quarter note in music.

The music room has many examples of Mackintosh's preferred architectural features, colors, ornamentation, illumination strategies, and furniture designs (see Figure 2.17). The music room is filled with daylight due to the expansive bow windows with a southern exposure and the reflectance from the white surfaces. Mackintosh often enveloped a room with white surfaces, textiles, and furniture. White was an excellent color for maximizing daylight, which was critical for Scottish interiors. Scotland's northern latitude results in just 8 (or fewer) daylight hours in the winter, and the climate is cold and damp.

White was also important for providing the contrast to Mackintosh's familiar black geometric forms, as in his iniquitous high-back chair designed for Hill House and the tall curved back chair for the Willow Tea Rooms (Figure 2.18). The music room's white high-backed chairs and tables help to brighten the room and are artistically positioned to harmonize with the placement of the bow windows and suspended fixtures.

Other outstanding examples of the Mackintoshes' artistic approach to designing interior environments include the magnificent Hill House (1902–1903), the interiors of 14 Kingsborough Gardens (1901–1902), the Room de Luxe in the Willow Tea Rooms (1903–1904), and the couple's home at 6 Florentine Terrace 9 (1906).

Visual Arts: Antoni Gaudí

Mackintosh's stylized pink rose even had an impact on Antoni Gaudí, as evident by its presence in Gaudí's designs. Incorporating Mackintosh's rose in decorative ornamentation is only one example of how the visual arts affected the interior environments and architecture of Gaudí. The visual arts and many of the unique confluences of being a Catalan formed the essence of Gaudí's designs. Gaudí lived most of his life in the province of Catalonia, a small area in the northeast section of Spain. To the east of Catalonia is the Mediterranean

Sea, and to the north are the Pyrenees Mountains, which separate the Spanish province from France. Catalonia is close to Italy and Africa. Thus, Gaudí's sources of inspiration were the sea, mountains, and visual arts of France, Italy, Spain, and North Africa. As with other Spanish designers Gaudí was influenced by Islamic designs of the North African Moors, who controlled Spain from the 8th to the 15th century. Gaudí was especially inspired by the connectedness to bright sunlight that the Catalonians shared with the Italians. Bright sunlight influenced Gaudí's colors and textures, and, most important, the sculptural qualities of his interior environments and architecture. To emphasize the three-dimensional forms and voids of sculpture requires a direct and intense light source. Details of

Figure 2.18 White was important for providing contrast to Mackintosh's familiar black geometric forms, as in his iniquitous high-back chair.

Source: Art and Architecture Collection, Miriam and Ira D. Wallach Division of Art, Prints and Photographs, The New York Public Library, Astor, Lenox and Tilden Foundations.

a sculpture are enhanced by extremes of light, shade, and shadows. Sunlight is ideal because of its high level of illumination, and the sun's continuous movement results in a constantly changing design.

In thinking like a sculptor, Gaudí used nonrepresentational forms inspired by nature and the sea to create architecture, furniture, and decorative ornamentation. A sculptor's perspective was essential in creating Gaudí's architectural façades, interior spaces, decorative objects, tactile qualities, and, perhaps most important, desire to evoke emotional responses. An outstanding example of Gaudí's sculptural architecture is Casa Milà (1905–1910) in Catalonia's capital, Barcelona (Figure 2.19).

Known as La Pedrera (The Quarry), its stone façade appears to replicate the undulating forms of a Catalonian mountain, the Montserrat (sacred mountain). Blocks of stone were carved and modeled to create the façade's relief sculpture. On the rooftop of Casa Milà, the sculpted chimneys, staircase exits, and ventilation towers resemble the peaks of Montserrat. The surfaces of these "peaks" are decorated using mosaic art. The wrought iron balcony balustrades handcrafted by José and Luis Badia illustrate another artistic element of Casa Milà. The artists used recycled metal in creating a three-dimensional composition that is unique for each balustrade. In another example of sustainability, Gaudí used recycled ceramic fragments that were rejected by local workshops. Artistic qualities are repeated in the interior's spatial sculpture. The interior of the apartment building does not have any straight lines or angles. Corners disappear as walls blend with ceilings, columns, and staircases.

Gaudí had the remarkable ability to simultaneously apply artistic techniques to his interior environments and architecture, and to design extraordinarily complex structural engineering systems. He used parabolic arches as both a flowing dynamic form and for structural support of walls, entrances, domes, and corridors. Nature's structural design of trees was used to engineer components of buildings. Gaudí used this technique

Figure 2.19 An outstanding example of Gaudí's sculptural architecture is Casa Milà (1905–1910) in Catalonia's capital, Barcelona. Known as La Pedrera (The Quarry), its stone façade appears to replicate the undulating forms of the Catalonian Mountains.

Source: Vanni/Art Resource, NY.

in the cathedral of the Sagrada Familia (Holy Family) (1883–1926; construction continues) in Barcelona (Figure 2.20). When Gaudí completed Casa Milà, he was involved with the owner of the apartment building in a dispute regarding fees. Consequently, Gaudí never accepted another private commission and devoted the rest of his life to the work of Sagrada Familia. In 1926 he left the building site and was killed by a streetcar. The project was unfinished, but construction continues with the aspiration that Gaudí's dream will be completed on the 100th anniversary of his death in 2026.

Support for the structure is derived from a "forest" of columns that resemble trees, including their trunks, branches, and leaves. The relief sculpture of the cathedral's façade has many statues depicting Christian beliefs, such as the crowning of the Virgin Mary, the birth of Christ, and the presentation of gifts from the Three Wise Men. Gaudí designed the cathedral with 12 bell towers, one for each apostle. Each façade has four towers, or pinnacles. The overall profile of the pinnacles, their sandy-appearing texture, and their sculptural qualities resemble the architecture of the Mosque at Djenné (see Figure 2.13). Gaudí could have been influenced by the mosque's use of dried mud to sculpt architecture

when he visited Africa early in his career. His unique approach to architecture, technology, sculpture, and decorative arts contributed to UNESCO's decision to register many of his properties. In 1984, Parque Güell, Palacio Güell, and Casa Milà were registered, followed by nine other properties in 2005, including Sagrada Familia. UNESCO summarized that Gaudí's work "may be seen as truly universal in view of the diverse cultural sources that inspired them. They represent an eclectic as well as a very personal style which was given free reign not only in the field of architecture but also in the design of gardens, sculpture and all forms of decorative arts" (UNESCO, 2004, p. 169).

GLOBAL BUSINESS AND ECONOMICS

At the turn of the century, the number of new manufacturers of interior furnishings continued to increase in selected regions, as well as other companies that wanted to project a modern and progressive image. New technologies and materials, such as iron, steel, and glass, provided the source for modern interior environments and architecture. Business initiatives and economics had a significant impact on the development of Arts and Crafts, especially in the United States. The examples discussed in this section demonstrate the reciprocal effects that can occur between business and the design of buildings and interiors.

Goals of Business: Louis H. Sullivan and AEG (1908–1909) by Peter Behrens

While Gaudí was creating artistic masterpieces in Spain, architect Louis Henry Sullivan was designing numerous commercial buildings in the United States. As

Figure 2.20 The relief sculpture of Gaudí's Sagrada Familia Cathedral's façade has many statues depicting Christian beliefs, such as the crowning of the Virgin Mary, the birth of Christ, and the presentation of gifts from the Three Wise Men.

Source: Vanni/Art Resource, NY.

represented in Sullivan's renowned statement, "Form follows function," both of these architects were committed to using ornamentation to emphasize the structural features of buildings. Frank Lloyd Wright referred to Sullivan as his "lieber meister" (beloved master). In following the path of many architects, Sullivan came to Chicago a few years after the city's 1871 fire. He started working for the architect Dankmar Adler, and then in the late 19th century he was associated with the Chicago School of architects and engineers, including Daniel Burnham, William Le Baron Jenney, and John Root. During this period, Sullivan and Adler received international recognition for Chicago's

Auditorium Building (1886–1889), the Wainwright Building (1890–1892) in St. Louis; Chicago's Schiller Building (1891–1893); the Transportation Building at the World's Columbian Exposition (1893); the Chicago Stock Exchange (1892–1893); and the Guaranty Building (1894–1895) in Buffalo, New York. The construction of the Schlesinger & Mayer (later Carson Pirie Scott) department store in Chicago started at the end of the 19th century; the actual store opened in 1903. This building is an outstanding example of work associated with the Chicago School and demonstrates how the goals of a client (in this case, a retailer) affected Sullivan's design of the interior environments and architecture.

In the early 1900s, State Street in Chicago was a premier location for large department (dry good) stores, such as Marshall Fields, The Fair, and Schlesinger & Mayer. State Street was also a major cable car route, which connected the business district to the populated residential areas on the south side of the city. The flurry of commercial activity drew shoppers to the area, but the intense competition required retailers to find ways to attract consumers to their stores. Schlesinger's strategy focused on identifying the ideal location, commissioning the famous Louis Sullivan, and constructing a new, grand building complete with all of the modern amenities. To attract attention to the store from the north, south, and west, the store was relocated to the corner of State and Madison streets. Subsequently, this corner location became one of the most defining architectural details associated with the store.

The design of the exterior and interior of the building had to incorporate important attributes of a department store in the early 20th century. The architecture had to present an image of success, and the size had to be massive to give the impression to shoppers that they could view and touch large quantities of merchandise. To entice people to come into the store, Sullivan developed several solutions. For example, to emphasize the store's corner location, he designed a tall and highly ornate circular entrance (Figure 2.21).

At street level, attraction to the store was derived from multiple contrasts. The filigree ornamentation made from bronze-plated cast iron contrasted with the smooth plate-glass display windows. The dark metal also contrasted with the upper structure's white glazed terracotta cladding. Sullivan designed the first level two stories high in order to attract attention to the displays in the bay windows and to create a majestic setting for the premier merchandise that was sold on the first floor.

Schlesinger requested an interior that was efficient for employees and customers and would present the impression that the store had first-class merchandise for their fashionable female clientele. Sullivan met Schlesinger's objectives by specifying wide aisles, including a main aisle that was 16 feet (4.88 meters) wide and large glass display cases at a convenient height for viewing merchandise. Due to the building's steel skeleton construction, Sullivan was able to eliminate many interior walls and decorated the capitals of the support columns with ornamental plasterwork. This openness let shoppers see an enormous amount of merchandise from one location.

To reinforce a glamorous experience, Sullivan used mahogany, marble, and intricate metalwork throughout the store, including the stairways, elevator grilles, light fixtures, and hot air grilles. At this time, women did nearly all of the shopping. Women appreciated Sullivan's filigree ornamentation; the store also had several "distinctive features" designed to attract women, including the Paris millinery salon, a French lingerie room, the great fabric room, and an exhibition of Paris hats and gowns.

The store's distinctive features also included areas that reflected Schlesinger's interest in portraying his civic responsibility to the people and city of Chicago. Thus, Sullivan designed rooms that the general public could use, such as reading rooms, writing rooms, rest rooms, an emergency medical aid room, art galleries, and telephone booths.

This cultural condition at the turn of the century affected retailers and other businesspersons, including bankers. Sullivan became involved with several projects that required facilities for general use by the community and had to accommodate the goals of the banking industry. At the end of the 19th century, the banking industry had a terrible reputation. Many people thought bankers were robbers because they received high profits from other people's money and restricted the amount of money that was available for loans. Therefore, at the beginning of the 20th century, bankers wanted to improve their image and create a credible profession. This was especially important in the Midwest because of the many farmers who had had negative experiences with bankers. Thus, for several years Sullivan was commissioned to design many small-town banks in the Midwest. He was selected for a variety of reasons that basically focused on his reputation for designing progressive and modern architecture in big cities. This

Figure 2.21 The Schlesinger & Mayer (modern Carson Pirie Scott) department store in Chicago. To emphasize the store's corner location, Sullivan designed a tall and highly ornate circular entrance.

Source: City of Chicago, Commission on Chicago Landmarks.

appealed to bankers because they wanted their banks to present a progressive image to people living in the community and to individuals or corporations who wanted to invest in the town. Bankers hoped that, as the center of the community, they could foster the success that was required to build another large city, like New York, Philadelphia, or Chicago.

Sullivan was commissioned to design the National Farmers' Bank (1907–1908) in Owatonna, Minnesota. The goals of the banking business in Owatonna affected how Sullivan designed the interior environment and architecture. To present an image of stability and security, Sullivan designed a formidable brick-and-stone structure. The strength displayed by the exterior was reinforced with the repetitive use of his famous arch from the 1893 Transportation Building in Chicago, brick walls, stone, and ornamental details in the bank's interior (Figure 2.22). Progressive attributes are evident by the decorative ornamentation that Sullivan had also used in Chicago's successful Schlesinger & Mayer store and in the Chicago Stock Exchange (1892–1893; demolished in 1972; Trading Room installed in the Chicago Art Institute). For the bank, filigree ornamentation was applied to the exterior, interior arches, entry, and light fixtures.

The large glass areas within the two main arches communicated to the community that the bank was open to those who lived there. The interior's open plan enabled people to watch the bank employees. This gave people the impression that bankers were not hiding how they were handling money. To help build trust and long-term relationships, Sullivan designed facilities for community-sponsored functions, display areas to showcase local accomplishments, and ladies' waiting rooms. Waiting rooms for women were especially important because at this time, all banking transactions were supposed to be conducted only by men. Women were attracted to National Farmers' Bank's progressive approach to providing private space for them, as well as Sullivan's filigree ornamentation. His success in fulfilling the needs of the banking industry became evident by numerous other commissions he received throughout the Midwest.

Certain members of the electric industry were also challenged with creating an appropriate image. Specifically, in the early 20th century, AEG (Allgemeine Elektricitäts Gesellschaft), the German electrical manufacturing company, was interested in developing a progressive image for mass-produced electrical products. AEG had to overcome any negative public perceptions

Figure 2.22 The decorative interior of the National Farmers' Bank (1907–1908) in Owatonna, Minnesota, by L. Sullivan.

Source: Minnesota Historical Society.

Figure 2.23 AEG was interested in developing a progressive image of mass-produced electrical products. Designed by Peter Behrens, the AEG turbine factory has extensive use of modern glass and excellent daylight for the workers.

Source: Foto Marburg/Art Resource, NY.

appearance of the factory and provided excellent daylight for workers (Figure 2.23). The turbine factory is a model example of the Modern movement's emphasis on form and function. The shape of the structure was dictated by the function of the space. The width, height, and length of the factory were specifically designed to accommodate the size of the turbines and the manufacturing process. To facilitate the production process, the configuration of the building conformed to the large overhead cranes that moved on rails along the length of the building.

To create a positive image of AEG and the electrical industry, Behrens applied the identical conceptual process to the design of small appliances, including irons, kettles, and fans. The artistic approach to these mundane products transformed expectations regarding the appearance of utilitarian items. His considerable influence on the development of industrial design is evident in his design for the electric kettle. He not only designed an aesthetically pleasing appliance, but he created a design that could be easily mass-produced in a variety of appearances. Behrens' electric kettle was available in three different shapes, finishes, and materials (copper-plated, nickel-plated, and brass). This approach to AEG's electric kettle demonstrated to customers that a mass-produced item could still be available with the uniqueness that was associated with handcrafted products. The kettle's woven cane handle hinted at the aesthetics associated with the Arts and Crafts movement, and functionally fulfilled the requirement of being able to handle a hot unit. Behrens' design solutions for AEG resulted in transforming engineering aesthetics; they also prompted efficient, simple designs for the Modern movement.

associated with manufactured products, and they had to persuade customers that electricity, the newly invented technology, was safe for domestic use. In alignment with the goals of the Deutscher Werkbund, AEG's president, Emil Rathenau, hired designer and architect Peter Behrens as the company's design advisor (1907–1914). Rathenau's vision in hiring Behrens to enhance the electric products industry had a significant impact on interior environments, architecture, industrial design, and corporate identities. As the design advisor, Behrens had control over how and what reflected the new modern image of AEG. To create a unified identity, Behrens designed AEG's factories, showrooms, domestic electrical appliances, advertising materials, stationery, furniture, light fixtures, and worker housing.

The progressive and efficient image that Behrens created for AEG is best illustrated in the AEG turbine factory and the company's domestic electrical appliances. Designing a modern factory using new materials and technologies was a perfect strategy for reforming the public perception that factories were dark, dingy places. The extensive use of glass modernized the

Business Initiatives: American Arts and Crafts Movement (1895–1920)

Behrens' progressive designs for AEG reflect how European architects and designers were transitioning away from the Arts and Crafts movement. However, in the United States, several designers and manufacturers were interested in capitalizing on the popularity of the Arts and Crafts movement by developing designs that could be mass produced. Philosophically, the American Arts and Crafts movement had ties to its English counterpart, but often designs in the United States were influenced by business initiatives and advances in manufacturing processes. The transformation to an acceptance of using machines to create interior furnishings and decorative arts could be attributed to Frank Lloyd Wright's lecture "The Art and Craft of the Machine" in 1901. In speaking to the Arts and Crafts Society in Chicago, Wright acknowledged the essence of William Morris's values, but he advocated for designs that were appropriate for machine production techniques. Chicago's Arts and Crafts Society was one of numerous related organizations that had developed throughout the United States. The large number of members in the Arts and Crafts Societies reflected the country's considerable interest in the movement.

To profit from this popularity, numerous entrepreneurs established businesses to manufacture products in the Arts and Crafts style. These initiatives had a significant impact on interior environments. The proliferation of manufacturers increased the quantity and diversity of interior furnishings, and the substantial quantities that were manufactured resulted in better prices.

During this time, many of the businesses were established in manufacturing regions of New York, Massachusetts, Ohio, and Michigan. Products included furniture, enamels, leaded glass, textiles, pottery, light fixtures, and metalwork in silver and copper. To capitalize on the popularity of Arts and Crafts, a vast assortment of items—such as inkwells, cigar boxes, bowls, boxes, pen trays, book stands, candleholders, books, folding screens, wall plaques, bookends, smoking sets, trays, picture frames, vases, manicure cases, hatpins, and wastebaskets—were manufactured in the style. Some of the most noteworthy companies that created these products included Tiffany Studios, New York; Rookwood Pottery, Cincinnati, Ohio; Roycrofters, East Aurora, New York; Grueby Faience and Pottery, Boston; Stickley Brothers, Grand Rapids, Michigan; and Chelsea Keramic Art Works, Chelsea, Massachusetts.

Gustav Stickley is a classic example of an entrepreneur who became very successful selling numerous Arts and Crafts interior furnishings, including furniture, light fixtures, clocks, textiles, copper hardware,

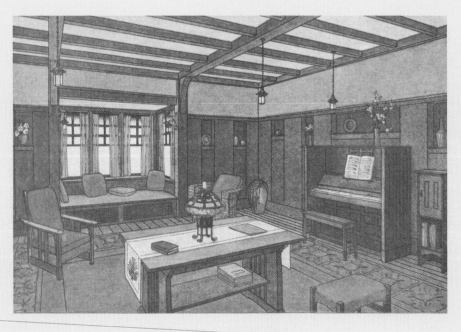

Figure 2.24 *The Craftsman* (1901–1916) magazine advertised Stickley's products and advocated for the Arts and Crafts Movement.
Source: Art and Architecture Collection, Miriam and Ira D. Wallach Division of Art, Prints and Photographs, The New York Public Library, Astor, Lenox and Tilden Foundations.

hammered metalwork, and pottery. Stickley started in the late 1880s as a furniture maker in a small town near Syracuse, New York. His furniture designs were simple. They were made of wood and had clean lines and exposed joinery. The motto for Stickley's *The Craftsman* magazine, which he founded in 1901, was the Flemish saying *Als ik kan* (to the best of my ability), which was written in the arch of a joiner's compass. Public attention was drawn to Stickley's work at the 1901 Pan-American International Exposition in Buffalo, New York, and through his monthly publication, *The Craftsman* (1901–1916). The magazine advertised Stickley's products, advocated for the Arts and Crafts movement, and attempted to educate the public about how to design residential interiors that were simple, comfortable, and unified in their composition (Figure 2.24).

Stickley had enormous success, as evident by his catalogue sales, publications, showrooms in major U.S. cities, and displays in prestigious department stores. Two architects working in California, Charles S. Greene and Henry M. Greene, were exposed to *The Craftsman* and incorporated many of the principles associated with the Arts and Crafts movement in their work. However, in contrast to the simple rooms illustrated in *The Craftsman*, Greene and Greene designed residences for very affluent clients, such as David Gamble of the Proctor and Gamble Company. The Gamble House (1908) in Pasadena, California, is an outstanding example of craftsmanship (Figure 2.25). Wood was used extensively in the interior of the Gamble House. All of the interior furnishings were custom designed and handcrafted by numerous Scandinavian woodworkers. In addition to harmonious interiors, the Gamble House has other characteristics that reflect the American version of the Arts and Crafts style, including international influences and the installation of new technologies.

Figure 2.25 The Gamble House (1908) in Pasadena, California, is an outstanding example of craftsmanship.
Source: Tim Street-Porter Studio.

The Greene brothers were first exposed to Japanese architecture at the 1893 Columbian Exposition in Chicago. Consequently, Japanese architecture had an impact on the design of the Gamble House, as evident by the low-profile roof, deep eaves, use of natural materials, exquisite craftsmanship, and integration between the interior and exterior. To accommodate Southern California's climate, the Greene brothers developed an architectural style that has become known as the California **bungalow.** Other than size, the Gamble House has the typical characteristics of the bungalow. A bungalow is a small, single-story residence with a low-pitched roof, deep eaves, and a front veranda. Westerners became aware of the bungalow style when Britain colonized India. The American Arts and Crafts style was also influenced by businesses that were developing new technologies, including electricity and the telephone. Many American residences in the Arts and Crafts style were designed to accommodate wiring for electrical and telephone service, and custom-designed electrical fixtures.

SUMMARY

Developments and discoveries of the 19th century transformed life at the turn of the century. The British Empire's domination of one-quarter of the world affected lifestyles, mechanization, interior environments, and architecture. In 1904 the British army overcame Tibetan forces and required Tibet to sign a treaty that prevented foreign control. The British invasion of Tibet presented the opportunity for the world to experience the spectacular beauty and engineering feat of the Potala Palace. The quest for colonies affected Central Asia, South Africa, and many other areas around the globe. The Boer War (1899–1902) between Britain and the Boers ended with a British victory. To emphasize British imperialism, the government commissioned the English architect Herbert Baker to design monumental buildings in the capital city of Pretoria. Cubism and tribal art had a significant impact on the built environment. For example, the flat, two-dimensional emphasis of the Cubist style influenced architects in the early 20th century, such as Le Corbusier and Walter Gropius. Spanish colonization influenced Cuba's interior environments and architecture.

Earthquakes and fires at the start of the 20th century, such as the 1906 disaster in San Francisco and Chicago's Iroquois Theater Fire in 1903, resulted in the deaths of hundreds of people and significant property damage. These types of disasters continue to inform the work of some architects, engineers, and interior designers, helping them to create safer buildings. Excavations continued to reveal the rich history of lost civilizations, including Chichén Itzá on the Yucatán Peninsula in Mexico.

Technological developments affected the quality of the work environment and the materials used to construct buildings. Often viewed as the first building of the Modern movement, Wright's Larkin Building in Buffalo, New York, has many attributes that changed the conceptualization and design of office environments. Prominent in the transformational process were technological advances in electrical lighting, fire precautions, and mechanical systems. Technologies and materials had a significant effect on the design of the Purkersdorf Sanatorium, which was located outside of Vienna. As a forerunner to the International Style, the Purkersdorf demonstrated the advanced techniques for constructing buildings with reinforced concrete and flat roofs. As shown with the Mosque at Djenné, within the context of "modern" technologies and methods, ancient processes used to construct and maintain buildings still play an important role in sustainable design.

Improved modes of transportation transformed immigration patterns, expanding the possibilities of where people were able to work and live. Ellis Island, the immigration processing site in the United States at the turn of the century, served as the station for cultural exchanges that have continued to impact global relations and developments. The Prairie House, designed by architect Frank Lloyd Wright, fundamentally changed the design of domestic architecture and helped make suburban living an attractive option to life in the city. Professional organizations improved interactions between industry and designers. To provide an appropriate structure that would encourage artists and industrialists to communicate with each other, Prussian architect Hermann Muthesius and Belgian artist and designer Henry Van de Velde formed the Deutscher Werkbund (DWB) (German Work Federation) in 1907.

The visual and performing arts influenced workshops, interior environments, and architecture. Secessionists believed that artists and craftspeople needed to work together and they needed oversight of production methods, materials, and administration processes. With funding from a wealthy textile manufacturer, Fritz Wäerndorfer, Wiener Werkstätte was created to provide a studio for artists and craftspeople. Charles Rennie Mackintosh is well known for his redesign of the Glasgow School of Art with its regional ornamental motifs, exquisite decorative metalwork, and abundance of natural daylight. Influences from the visual and performing arts are most evident in their residential interiors and in the tearooms commissioned by patron Catherine Cranston. As the construction of Sagrada Familia continues, Antoni Gaudí's architecture will maintain a dialogue that focuses on his sculptural interpretations.

Interior designers and architects responded to the aspirations of businesses by designing commercial buildings that both accommodated industry goals and served the interests of consumers. Louis Sullivan's Schlesinger & Mayer (later Carson Pirie Scott) department store in Chicago opened in 1903. This building is an outstanding example of work associated with the Chicago School and demonstrates how the goals of a client (in this case, a retailer) affected Sullivan's design of the interior environments and architecture. Certain members of the electric industry were also challenged with creating an appropriate image. Specifically, in the early 20th century, AEG, the German electrical manufacturing company, was interested in developing a progressive image for mass-produced electrical products. In alignment with the goals of the Deutscher Werkbund, AEG's president, Emil Rathenau, hired designer and architect Peter Behrens as the company's design advisor. Behrens' progressive designs for AEG reflect how European architects and designers were transitioning away from the Arts and Crafts movement.

However, in the United States, several designers and manufacturers were interested in capitalizing on the popularity of the Arts and Crafts movement by developing designs that could be mass produced. In reviewing the events and developments that occurred at the turn of the century, this chapter emphasized global perspectives by describing and explaining interior environments and architecture of cultures living in China, Africa, Mexico, Germany, Austria, Cuba, Scotland, Spain, Belgium, and the United States. The next chapter examines how World War I, among other events and conditions of the decade between approximately 1910 and 1920, affected global interior environments and architecture.

KEY TERMS

bogolan

bungalow

corbelled vault

crow-stepped gables

Cubism

Deutscher Werkbund

Dutch gambrel

Gesamtkunstwerk

Modern movement

open-plan office

Prairie House

primitive art

roof-combs

Wiener Werkstätte

EXERCISES

1. Research Design Project. The world has experienced many deadly fires, such as the Iroquois Theater in Chicago and the devastation in San Francisco after that city's 1906 earthquake. Research local state laws and regulations affecting fire safety. Select a local commercial interior and provide suggestions for fire prevention and safe evacuation procedures. Write a report that could include drawings, sketches, and photographs. The report could include information from local firefighters.

2. Philosophy and Design Project. As proponents of *Gesamtkunstwerk* (total artwork), Hoffmann and Moser designed all of the interior furnishings to harmonize with the exterior. Research examples of non-Western interior environments that demonstrate *Gesamtkunstwerk*. In a written report (including illustrations), summarize your findings and provide suggestions for an oral presentation. In a team with other students, prepare a presentation that is supported with visual materials.

3. Human Factors Research Project. Frank Lloyd Wright's Larkin Building incorporated many features that were designed to facilitate the work of employees. An excellent way to recognize ideal design solutions is to engage in observations. Identify a public space and observe how people use the interior environment. Record activities, characteristics of people, and the interior elements that are effective, as well as any design features that are hindrances. Write a report that summarizes your observations and include recommendations for future practice. The report could include sketches, drawings, or photographs.

CHAPTER 3

EMPHASIS: THE 1910S

OBJECTIVES

After reading this chapter, you should be able to describe and analyze:

■ How selected global political events in the 1910s affected interior environments and architecture as evident by public access to the Temple of Heaven in Beijing; the establishment of Palais des Nations; and the destruction and closure of Russian palaces, cathedrals, and churches.

■ How natural environmental conditions affected selected global interior environments and architecture in the 1910s as evident by the discovery of Machu Picchu in Peru and the excavation of Stupa I in Sanchi, Central India.

■ How selected global technologies and materials in the 1910s affected interior environments and architecture as evident by the impact of the construction of the Panama Canal and the development of Formica.

■ Describe and analyze how selected global work styles and lifestyles in the 1910s, such as the writings of designers Elsie de Wolfe and Frank A. Parsons as well as the 1918 influenza pandemic, affected interior environments and architecture.

■ How selected global visual arts and performing arts in the 1910s affected interior environments and architecture as evident by designs inspired by the Ballets Russes and the designs of Louis Comfort Tiffany.

■ How selected global business developments and economics in the 1910s affected interior environments and architecture as evident by Bruno Taut's *Glashaus*, the founding of Steelcase, and designs based upon Frederick W. Taylor's management philosophy.

■ How to compare and contrast selected interior environments and architecture of the Americas, Asia/Oceania, Europe, and the Middle East/Africa from the 1910s.

The seemingly calm initial years of the 20th century changed dramatically in the 1910s. The decade was dominated by World War I, which started in 1914 and ended in 1918. For the first time in history, countries from multiple continents were engaged in battle. The war involved 30 nations on five continents. Advances in 19th-century mechanization enabled the development of sophisticated military equipment. Consequently, the war resulted in millions of casualties and immense physical damage to the environment, both built and natural. Activities related to technological developments primarily focused on the war effort; most building construction stopped until the war ended. The primary concern for many people in the warring countries was finding enough food, basic shelter, and clothing. However, some advances occurred in the production of automobiles, building materials, and interior furnishings.

Major manufacturers and organizations were founded in the 1910s, some of which have improved the life and work styles of people throughout the world. Explorers were still discovering, rediscovering, and excavating the ruins of ancient civilizations—one very important discovery was Machu Picchu in South America.

During the 1910s, artists, musicians, and choreographers continued to create, and the future of the performing arts world changed when Thomas Edison demonstrated the first talking motion pictures. Some artists during the decade were creating paintings that challenged traditional forms, colors, and angles of perspective, and these radical perspectives would eventually transfer to the way interior environments and architecture were designed in the 1920s and 1930s.

GLOBAL POLITICS AND GOVERNMENT

Numerous wars and revolutions caused a tremendous amount of bloodshed and destruction throughout the world during the period from 1910 to 1920. Mexico

Figure 3.1 The Hall of Prayers for Abundant Harvests has several cosmological references.

Source: Vanni/Art Resource, NY.

experienced an entire decade of civil wars and revolutions that resulted in the deaths of thousands of people and the destruction of communities. A significant number of schools were also destroyed before the revolution ended in 1920. The unrest in Southeastern Europe due to the Balkan wars in 1912 and 1913 helped set the stage for World War I, which obviously had a dramatic effect on people who had to endure the casualties and horrific conditions. During this decade, revolutions in China and Russia resulted in the demise of dynasties and the rise of new political structures based on socialist principles. The following discussion examines how the revolutions and wars during the 1910s affected interior environments and architecture.

The 1911 Chinese Revolution: The Temple of Heaven (15th Century, Public Access 1918) in Beijing, China

A series of events in the 19th century significantly reduced the sovereignty of the Manchu Dynasty in China. The country was involved in two Opium Wars with Britain and the Sino-Japanese War of 1894–1895. China's defeat in each successive war had a profound impact on the country's economic stability and territorial possessions. For example, China's economy was affected by losing Korea and Taiwan, and the Chinese island of Hong Kong became a possession of the United Kingdom. This situation prompted an anti-foreigner sentiment and stimulated the Boxer Rebellion of 1900. To protect their economic interests and newly acquired territories, Western armies and Japan came to the defense of the Chinese government. The Boxers (anti-foreign revolutionaries) were defeated, but their anger and discontent continued.

The revolutionaries' unrest manifested again in 1911. Revolutionaries were distraught with concessions that the Manchu Empress Dowager, Tz'u-hsi, had afforded the Western powers and Japan, such as paying a large indemnity and allowing foreign troops in China. Furthermore, people were devastated by a series of disasters that had occurred in 1911, including famine and the deaths of 100,000 people due to a flood in Chang Jiang. Another outbreak of revolution that began in Wuchang on October 10, 1911, culminated in the demise of the Manchu (Qing) Dynasty and revolutionary leader Sun Yat-sen declaring the establishment of the Republic of China on January 1, 1912.

One of the outcomes of the 1911 Chinese revolution was the government's order to cease ceremonial sacrifices. This mandate affected the Temple of Heaven (Tiantan) in Beijing, the complex finished in 1420 CE as a place to offer sacrifices to heaven. China's shift from a dynastic empire to a republic also changed the rules regarding access to buildings of the Chinese dynasties. In 1918, the Ming-Qing Temple (Altar) of Heaven was opened to the public after centuries of access that was restricted to Chinese emperors. The Ming Emperor Yongle started construction of the complex in early 1406, and its structures have been revised, rebuilt, and repaired over the millennia. The complex is a magnificent example of Chinese architecture, exceptional woodworking skills, and centuries of cultural tradition. To demonstrate the connection between people and nature, the complex is surrounded by gardens and is located in a forest of cypress trees. The two main buildings are the Hall of Prayers for Abundant Harvests (Qiniandian) and the Imperial Vault of Heaven (Figure 3.1). The Echo Wall, which surrounds the Imperial Vault of Heaven and has a circumference of approximately 633 feet (193 meters), is known for its unique ability to transfer a whisper from one end to another. The Red Stairway Bridge connects these structures. On the north end of the north-south axis is the open-air sacrificial Circular Mound Altar.

As an imperial sacrificial altar, the complex is embedded with symbols of heaven and earth that represent ancient Chinese beliefs. For example, reflecting the Chinese belief that "Heaven is round, earth is square," the *round* Temple of Heaven is surrounded by a *square* wall. The Circular Mound Altar also has a square-shaped wall that encompasses the ceremonial site. As an auspicious symbol for the Chinese Empire, the number nine (or multiples of it) is used in various contexts, such as the number of steps or posts or the height of a structure. The complex includes the color red to represent the Emperor, blue for heaven, and green for nature. The Hall of Prayers for Abundant Harvests features several cosmological references. The balustrades of the hall's three-level marble base have a post for each of the 360 days of the Chinese lunar year. The interior has four centrally located pillars that represent the seasons (see Figure 3.1). Each of the 12 exterior pillars represents a month of the year, and the 12 upper-level pillars signify the two 12-hour periods of the day.

The construction and the decoration of the Hall of Prayers for Abundant Harvests illustrate the exceptional design skills of the Chinese people. The hall is a timber frame that was assembled without nails or hardware. The precise interlocking joints are ideal for the expansion and contraction that occurs in wood when temperatures and humidity levels change. The broad eaves of the blue-tiled roofs help to protect the wooden structure from the weather.

The emperor's throne, painted decorations, and an astonishing **conical dome** dominate the interior of the hall. The painted surfaces help to protect the wood and illustrate the Chinese tradition of using primary and secondary colors. Other examples of traditional ornamentation are the windows' **fretwork** inserts, paintings of natural flowers, and floral designs interwoven with geometric patterns. The center of the conical dome has a painting of a dragon and a phoenix. The dragon represents the emperor and denotes wisdom and strength. The phoenix is for the empress and is believed to bring happiness and good fortune. In 1998, the Temple of Heaven complex was added to UNESCO's World Heritage List based on several criteria, including recognition that the architecture and landscape are a "masterpiece" and that the site illustrates the "evolution of one of the world's great civilizations" (UNESCO, 1997, p. 83).

World War I: Palais des Nations (Established 1919, Completed 1938) in Geneva, Switzerland, by a Team of International Architects

World War I created an unprecedented number of dead and wounded soldiers. Nearly 9 million soldiers and approximately 10 million civilians were killed, and more than 21 million people were forever changed by the war as a result of being wounded or gassed or suffering from trauma. The industrial progress of the 18th and 19th centuries had resulted in new forms of weapons that caused widespread and instantaneous destruction. For the first time in history, battles involved machine guns, poisonous gas, tanks, submarines, and biplanes. The entire world was affected by the Great War, as it was then called, even countries that remained neutral.

The causes of World War I can be traced to a long series of diplomatic clashes and tangled alliances among European nations. Economic and imperial competition and fear of war prompted military alliances and an arms race—armies and navies were greatly expanded—which further escalated the tensions contributing to the outbreak of war. The trigger for the start of World War I was the assassination of the heir to the Austrian-Hungarian throne, Archduke Francis Ferdinand, and his wife by a Serbian nationalist in Sarajevo, Bosnia, on June 28, 1914. Austria-Hungary declared war on Serbia; Russia, bound by treaty to Serbia, announced it would mobilize forces in her defense, and Germany, an ally of Austria-Hungary, followed by declaring war on Russia and France (an ally of Russia through treaty).

Soon the Allies in the war were Britain, France, and Russia. Eventually, the Allies also included Japan, Italy in 1915, and the United States in 1917. Initially the Central Powers were Germany and Austria-Hungary, and they were ultimately joined by the Ottoman Empire and Bulgaria. By the conclusion of the war, powerful and enduring empires had been dissolved, including the Habsburg Empire (1278–1918), Ottoman Empire

(1299–1923), and, indirectly, the Romanov Dynasty (1613–1918), following the Russian Revolution. At the end of the war, all of the European countries that had fought were close to bankruptcy and had acquired substantial debt.

Most of the land battles occurred on the Western and Eastern fronts. The Western Front was an imaginary line that started in northern Belgium, traveled between France and Germany, and ended in the north central area of Switzerland. The Eastern Front stretched from the Baltic Sea in the north to the Black Sea in Southeastern Europe. Trenches for the soldiers were constructed along the two fronts. Soldiers fought from the trenches; offensives were thus contained to these areas, and millions of civilians and thousands of communities were spared the destruction of war. None of the participating countries were prepared for a lengthy war because of their assumed military power. But the toll on every country was devastating.

In 1918, Russia signed a peace treaty with Germany after the Bolsheviks, the Russian Social-Democratic Workers' Party led by Lenin, had seized control in the Russian Revolution of 1917, overthrowing Czar Nicholas II. Then, as the British, French, and American armies advanced toward Germany in late 1918, the alliance between the Central Powers began to collapse. Armistice was signed on November 11, 1918, followed by the Treaty of Versailles on June 28, 1919. As the designated initiator of the war, Germany was forced to make numerous concessions, including reducing its army, paying the Allies for damages, and relinquishing substantial territories and colonies. Although the Covenant (constitution) establishing the League of Nations was part of the Treaty of Versailles, it did not formally come into existence until January 10, 1920. The League was the first international organization created to maintain peace by arbitrating disputes through open diplomacy. The League of Nations dissolved in 1946, its responsibilities and assets transferred to the newly formed United Nations.

Given its magnitude and extent, the war's most obvious impact on interior design and architecture was the damage done to communities, and the various building industries halted both during and immediately after the war. To support the war effort, many manufacturers of building materials and products converted their equipment to producing goods for the war.

One positive outcome of the war, however, was the establishment of the previously mentioned League of Nations. To accommodate the organization's goals, a new building was required with a very special design—the Palais des Nations. Architecturally, the Palais des Nations may not be widely acclaimed; however, the building is an outstanding example of how to design for *international* communication. From its conception, design considerations centered on creating an environment that was neutral and conducive to amicable discussions. Selecting Geneva, Switzerland, the "city of peace," was ideal for a neutral location, and the city's beautiful natural surroundings on a lake bounded by the Swiss Alps provided a perfect, tranquil setting. The international competition requirements stated, "The Palais, whose construction is the object of the competition, is intended to house all the organs of the League of Nations in Geneva. It should be designed in such a way as to allow these organs to work, to preside, and to hold discussions, independently and easily in the calm atmosphere which should prevail when dealing with problems of international dimension" (www.unog.ch). The competition for the design of the Palais des Nations drew 377 entries, but the jury did not declare a single winning design. In a collaborative spirit, the jury selected the five top designs and commissioned the architects to work together on the final design. The team of architects consisted of Carlo Broggi (Italy), Julien Flegenheimer (Switzerland), Joseph Vago (Hungary), and Camille Lefèvre and Henri-Paul Nénot (France).

The team of architects designed the Palais des Nations for international discussions in a "calm atmosphere." Originally, the main areas of the Palais were the Council Chamber, Assembly Hall, and Library.

Two extensions were added in 1952 and 1973. The Salle des Pas Perdus (Hall of Lost Steps) is a passageway that connects the original structure with the new conference rooms and offices. The simple and elegant architecture presents a soothing appearance and a "neutral" style.

The refined beauty of the exterior is also reflected in the interior. The smooth, refined furnishings help provide a calm, serene environment. Fundamentally, the only interior colors or patterns are derived from the donated art collection from a variety of countries. The serenity is further enhanced by the magnificent views of Lake Geneva and the Swiss Alps. Perhaps the organizers of the project felt that the spectacular display of nature would be a subtle reminder of the importance of peace when those in attendance were working on difficult negotiations.

Other subtle messages regarding peace, health, and harmony are evident in the artwork that was selected for the Palais. Most notable are José María Sert's gold and sepia murals, which cover the ceiling and walls of the Council Chamber (Figure 3.2). The murals illustrate human progress in health, technology, freedom, and peace. The ceiling has a painting of five figures, one for each continent, holding hands in triumph. To promote neutrality, semicircular desks substitute for podiums and monograms interlace the initials of the League of Nations in two languages. Moreover, the Assembly Hall is recognized as the first conference room in the world to have simultaneous language interpretation. Currently, the Palais des Nations is used for the work of the United Nations Office at Geneva, including the Human Rights Council.

The 1917 Russian Revolution: Russian Palaces, Cathedrals, and Churches

The decade between 1910 and 1920 saw Russia undergo a series of revolutions in addition to a sense of demoralization from the country's defeats and eventual withdrawal from World War I. The major turning point was the Russian Revolution in 1917. Russian peasants and factory workers were depressed and exhausted from the hardships imposed by the war. People were hungry and unemployed, and lacked adequate clothing and shelter. Russian peasants were seeking social reforms, localized political control, rights of land ownership, and economic stability. To inspire people to revolt, Vladimir

Figure 3.2 José María Sert's gold and sepia murals cover the ceiling and walls of the Council Chamber in the Palais des Nations in Geneva.
Source: © Bettmann/CORBIS.

Lenin, founder of Russian communism, promised "peace, bread, and land." The 1917 revolution, led by Lenin, started in St. Petersburg (at that time, Petrograd), where Czar Nicholas II and his family were living in the Winter Palace. The czar was overthrown in battles supported by soldiers who refused to shoot the revolutionary Bolsheviks. Lenin became the leader of the Communist party and, as the head of Russia, immediately negotiated a peace treaty with Germany in 1918. The treaty ended Russia's involvement in World War I at a high cost by relinquishing substantial territory, including Ukraine, Finland, and provinces in Poland and the Balkans. Concessions of the treaty caused a furor in Russia. The reaction was so severe that a civil war erupted in 1918. The "Red" Bolsheviks fought the opponents of Lenin, the "Whites," for 2 years. The Great Civil War resulted in 15 million people being killed, which was more than the number of Russia's casualties in World War I. The Bolsheviks were victorious, and Lenin was empowered to establish the Union of Soviet Socialist Republics (USSR) in 1922.

The Soviet rule affected interior environments and architecture by the destruction and closure of cathedrals, churches, and a monastery and the suppression of Russia's *kustar* (peasant handcraftsmanship) art industries. Lenin also proclaimed that individuals could no longer own real estate in the cities, and the state took control of many institutions. St. Petersburg and Moscow were significantly affected by this change. St. Petersburg had been the capital of Russia's provisional government at the start of the Bolshevik revolution. To gain control of Russia, the Bolsheviks raided the government's headquarters at the Fourth Winter Palace (1754–1764) on October 25, 1917 (Figure 3.3).

The architect of the Court, Bartolomeo Francesco Rastrelli, had designed the 18th-century Baroque palace. The magnificent palace is an excellent example of how the czars directed architects and designers to create a unique architectural style for Russia that fused Western elements with a sense of grandeur they felt befitted the

Figure 3.3 After the siege of the Winter Palace, painted by Vladimir Serov.

Source: Adoc-photos/Art Resource, NY.

Figure 3.4 To honor Ivan the Terrible's conquest of Kazan in 1552, the Cathedral of Saint Basil the Blessed was constructed between 1555–1561. The cathedral opened as a military museum in 1923. Compare the architectural shapes and profiles with the church in Figure 3.5.

Source: Adoc-photos/Art Resource, NY.

Russian culture. Western inspiration is evident in the columns, statuary, ornamental vases, and balustrade. The green pastel color of the exterior walls and the elaborate white trim are reflective of Russian architecture. The palace's 700 rooms are detailed with the finest luxurious materials, such as crystal chandeliers and silk textiles, and attest to Russia's sense of grandeur (see Figure 3.3). Some walls and ceilings are covered with gilding, and the palace is filled with hundreds of pieces from the royal art collection. To display the enormous royal collection, Catherine the Great commissioned two additional buildings, the Small Hermitage and the Large (Old) Hermitage. Aligned along the bank of the Neva River, the Winter Palace and the Hermitages were declared state museums in 1917. The museums currently house over 3 million pieces of art and were registered with other historic monuments in St. Petersburg as a UNESCO World Heritage Site in 1990.

Lenin changed the Russian capital to Moscow in 1918, which affected the buildings in the Kremlin and Red Square. Specifically, numerous Russian Orthodox churches (such as the Cathedral of the Annunciation and the Cathedral of Saint Basil the Blessed, also known as the Cathedral of the Intercession) were closed or services were prohibited. Accompanying the closure of churches was state control of paintings and sculpture. As reflected by their inclusion on UNESCO's World Heritage List, all of the buildings in the Kremlin, Red Square, and Monastery are important for their unique contributions to Russian architecture, history, and culture. For example, as the site of coronations and royal burials, the Cathedral of the Annunciation is important to Russia's heritage. The Cathedral of Saint Basil the Blessed (1555–1561) and the Monastery were involved with previous Russian conquests and battles (Figure 3.4).

The multiple towers and walls that are defining attributes of the Kremlin and the Monastery were originally designed as fortifications. The Kremlin has 20 towers, which include four major entrance towers and large corner towers. The Monastery has a bell tower and 11 fortress towers. Each tower has a unique design that contributes to Russia's architectural heritage. Many of the towers have a large square base that supports several levels in diminishing size up to the crowning **tent roof.** The buildings at the Kremlin, Red Square, and Monastery have other elements that are important expressions of Russian design; many of these attributes are derived from the country's extraordinary wooden architecture. For example, wooden churches and the cathedrals have faceted surfaces, **onion domes,** tent roofs, **drums** that support **cupolas,** and multiple towers (Figure 3.5). The concentric semicircle and **ogive-shaped projections** (kokoshniki) on the towers of St. Basil resemble the **bochka** used in the wooden churches. Positioning windows close to St. Basil's domes maximizes daylight by

Figure 3.5 Transfiguration Church on Kizhi Island is an example of Russia's extraordinary wooden architecture. Wooden churches have faceted surfaces, onion domes, tent roofs, drums that support cupolas, and multiple towers. Compare the architectural forms and shapes of this church with the cathedral in Figure 3.4.

Source: Erich Lessing/Art Resource, NY.

reflecting the gold gilding that covers the interior of the cupolas. An abundance of daylight is especially important for Russia's cold, long, and dark winters.

EFFECTS AND CONDITIONS OF THE NATURAL ENVIRONMENT

Improvements and advances in transportation, including the automobile and air travel, resulted in the ability of people to travel to remote locations around the globe and search for lost civilizations. During the 1910s, two important developments occurred that enabled the world to study and attempt to understand the daily life, art, and architecture of amazing ancient civilizations. In 1911, a professor of history and politics from the United States, Hiram Bingham, discovered Machu Picchu in the Peruvian Andes. The Buddhist site, the Great Stupa

in Sanchi, Central India, was rediscovered in the 19th century, but the excavation of the site from 1912 to 1919 revealed the beauty of the architecture. Both of these sites are important in understanding global architecture, interior environments, and cultural heritages.

Environmental Conditions: Machu Picchu (Discovered 1911) in Peru

Machu Picchu (Old Peak), located high in the cloud-enveloped Andes Mountains, was a royal estate of the Inca emperor Pachacútec Inca Yupanqui (Figure 3.6). The ancient Incan city was built in a saddle between two steep peaks, the Huayna Picchu (New Peak) and the Machu Picchu, at nearly 8,000 feet (2,438 meters) above sea level. The city was constructed in the 15th century during the zenith of the Inca Empire but was abandoned when the Spanish conquistadors invaded Peru in the early 1500s. In contrast to other South American cities, Machu Picchu was not damaged or looted because the Spaniards never found the city. Therefore, when Bingham discovered Machu Picchu in 1911, the city was in its 15th-century condition (aside from rampant vegetation).

Machu Picchu, which seems to have been utilized by the Inca as a secret ceremonial city, is an engineering

Figure 3.6 Machu Picchu (Old Peak), located high in the clouds of the Andes Mountains, was a royal estate of the Inca Emperor, Pachacútec Inca Yupanqui.
Source: Nick Saunders/Barbara Heller Photo Library, London/Art Resource, NY.

and architectural masterpiece that illustrates the importance of integrating structure and nature. The city's remote location required the use of local materials. The sacred mountain's granite provided the stone that was used to construct buildings, stairways, ramps, terraces, aqueducts, and religious artifacts. Engineers today can only hypothesize how the Incans were able to mine the granite and then work with stones weighing several tons without the use of iron tools, wheels, or strong animals. Apparently, the stonemasons used stones to cut large boulders into smaller blocks of granite. The blocks of stone were pounded into shapes that enabled the sides to mold to each other. Amazingly, mortar was not necessary because the space between stones was so small that even a knife could not pass through an opening. This was especially difficult when stones had polygonal shapes.

Over the centuries the stone structures have withstood storms, frigid conditions, earthquakes, and extreme vegetation. Religious buildings had the most exquisite masonry craftsmanship. For example, the walls of the Temple of the Sun are very smooth from extensive pounding, and part of the structure has a semicircular tower, an extremely difficult shape to create from stone. A ceremonial sundial, the Intihuatana (Hitching Post of the Sun), was carved from one large boulder and was critical to identifying the ideal time for planting crops. Several of the most amazing structures were built by carving the mountainside to form walls or staircases. Some staircases were built by blending hand-tooled blocks with the contour of the mountain.

Machu Picchu's remote location obviously required the city population of approximately 1,000 to be self-sufficient. The city's main areas were the religious ceremonial sites, royal residences, urban cottages, workshops, and stone-terraced agricultural fields. The primary religious structures adorned with bas-reliefs are the Temple of the Sun, the Three Window Temple, and the Royal Temple. Most of the urban homes were two-story buildings with thatched roofs and

Figure 3.7 The Incas were very artistic and created beautiful objects from gold, silver, clay, wool, and exotic bird feathers. This illustration is a quipu, a sophisticated accounting method. Many of these skills were recorded by illustrations drawn by the Spaniards.

Source: Nick Saunders/Barbara Heller Photo Library, London/Art Resource, NY.

trapezoid-shaped windows and doorways. Water was supplied from natural springs and thawing ice from the mountain peaks. The Incas created a sophisticated aqueduct system that used gravity to distribute water to fountains, troughs, and irrigation. When Bingham discovered Machu Picchu, he found utilitarian objects, such as pottery and tools. However, the Incas were also very artistic and created beautiful objects from gold, silver, clay, wool, and exotic bird feathers. Many of these skills were later recorded by illustrations drawn by the Spanish conquistadors (Figure 3.7). Beautiful textiles were woven from cotton, vegetal fibers, and the wool from llamas and alpacas. Expert weaving skills were also evident by bridges that were woven with vegetable fibers and the complex *quipu*. The Incas did not have money or a written language; therefore, to keep records they created *quipus,* a sophisticated accounting method that involved a series of multicolored ropes and knots (see Figure 3.7). The master "accountant" used colors, lengths, and various knots to record demographic and financial statistics, such as a community's population, the number of hours someone worked, or the quantity of crops produced by a farmer. Without written records, scholars are still searching for answers to how the "accountant" understood the complex weaving system, as well as many of the other remarkable achievements of the Inca civilization. Machu Picchu was inscribed on UNESCO's World Heritage List in 1983 for its "absolute master piece of architecture" and for the archeological site's "unique testimony to the Inca civilization" (UNESCO, 1982, p. 2).

Environmental Conditions: Stupa I (Excavation 1912–1919) in Sanchi, Central India

Built in the 1st and 2nd centuries BCE, the Buddhist monuments at Sanchi, Central India, were rediscovered in the early 19th century, but serious excavation of the site did not occur until 1912. Unfortunately, the time between the rediscovery and the excavation resulted in looting and damage to the site. Analyses of the monuments are therefore derived from the conditions uncovered in the 1910s. Approximately 50 monuments were excavated at Sanchi, including three stupas, an assembly hall, a monastery, palaces, and temples. The Great Stupa I is revered as one of the world's oldest and most complete Buddhist monuments (Figure 3.8). As depositories of Buddha relics, the stupa evolved from a grassy rounded mound of earth to the elaborate terraces of Borobudur at Java (described in Chapter 1). Stupa I at Sanchi began as a simple structure with a base covered by a dome and was transformed into its current sophisticated form by the ruler Ásoka in the 2nd century BCE.

Stupa I at Sanchi is a solid-brick structure built on a round base and is surrounded by two **vedikás** (balustrades). The **egg-shaped dome** is flattened at the top to serve as a base for the **harmika,** a square-shaped railing and the three umbrellas (Figure 3.9). Scholars believe that originally the dome was covered with a very thick layer of stucco; however, there is disagreement

Figure 3.8 Built in the 1st and 2nd centuries BCE, approximately 50 monuments were excavated at Sanchi. The Great Stupa I is revered as one of the world's oldest and most complete Buddhist monuments.

Source: Borromeo/Art Resource, NY.

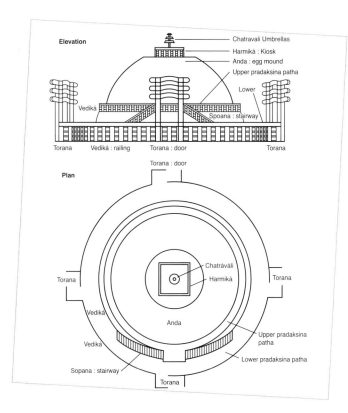

Figure 3.9 Stupa I at Sanchi is a solid brick structure built on a round base and is surrounded by two vedikás. The egg-shaped dome is flattened at the top to serve as a base for the harmika, a square-shaped railing and the three umbrellas.

Source: Tomoty, E. (1982). *A history of fine arts in India and the west.* Bombay: Orient Longman. Illustration by Steven Stankiewicz.

regarding how the stucco was finished. Adequate evidence does not exist that the stucco was painted or gilded, but there appears to be consensus that during religious festivities, the dome was decorated with flowers and fabrics. The vedikás are aligned with pathways that are used for processional worship in the clockwise direction. The exterior vediká has four **toranas** (gateways) facing each of the cardinal points. Each torana has square posts and three curved horizontal architraves. When the site was first excavated, the only standing toranas were the northern and southern structures. The eastern and western toranas had to be restored from ruins scattered on the ground. A remarkable attribute of Sanchi I's vediká and the toranas is that their construction method reflects the transition

from wood to stone. Assemblage of the units reflects joinery methods used in wood construction, such as mortise and tenon joints. For example, the horizontal rails of the vedikás are inserted in the square pillars and a tenon is used to join the stone cap.

As magnificent examples of Indian art, the bas-reliefs and friezes of the toranas are the most important features of Stupa I (Figure 3.10). The stone surfaces were carved by those skilled in working with ivory and wood. The carved people, flora, and fauna on the fronts and backs of the toranas depict the life and teachings of Buddha. Scholars believe that each torana was a gift presented to Ásoka. The northern torana is considered the most elaborate and artistic. Square pillars and elephant capitals support the torana. Each **architrave** has exquisitely carved statues, bas-relief, and friezes. Depicting the life of a Buddha, the carvings have domestic and processional themes that include women, lotus flowers, jars, vases, four-horse chariots, winged lions, and various species of trees that were worshipped. The scrolls at the end of the architraves resemble rolls of paper,

Figure 3.10 Stupa I's toranas are considered elaborate and artistic. The carved people, flora, and fauna on the fronts and backs of the toranas depict the life and teachings of Buddha.

Source: Borromeo/Art Resource, NY.

symbolizing the stories that are illustrated in the ornamental carvings. The Buddhist monuments at Sanchi were inscribed on UNESCO's World Heritage List in 1989 for many reasons, including "the perfection of its proportions and the richness of the sculptured decorative work on its four gateways" and "Sanchi's role as intermediary for the spread of cultures" (UNESCO, 1989, p. 19).

GLOBAL TECHNOLOGICAL DEVELOPMENTS

A significant amount of the global technological advances in the 1910s occurred in the area of transportation. More railroad stations were constructed, including New York City's Grand Central Station (1913), and Henry Ford's assembly line manufacturing methods resulted in the annual production of over one million Model T automobiles. Progress was made in the development of air travel, and more people were taking pleasure trips on ocean liners. But negative consequences soon became associated with both modes of transportation. For the first time in history, battles could be fought from the air (this new era was demonstrated in World War I), and in 1912 the *Titanic* sunk in the Atlantic Ocean, killing over 1,500 people. The Panama Canal, a different facet of transportation, employed construction technology that was complex and innovative and connected the world in a manner that altered international commerce.

Scientists and engineers also developed new materials and products during the decade, which resulted in items used in 21st-century life, including zippers, neon lamps, **Formica,** and the industrially produced plywood.

Technologies and Transportation: Panama Canal (1914)

Centuries after the construction of Machu Picchu, another amazing engineering feat occurred in the Americas. The Panama Canal, one of the world's greatest engineering achievements, opened in August of 1914 (the outbreak of World War I understandably subdued the celebration). The creation of the Panama Canal had both an indirect and a direct impact on the world of interior environments and architecture. The opening of the facility resulted in an unprecedented trade of international commerce. Cultural exchanges of materials, products, equipment, and supplies could occur more frequently and at lower costs. This was its indirect influence. The construction of the Panama Canal helped educate people about how to design buildings that would deter the spread of mosquito-borne disease. An awareness of the construction conditions also helped provide a basis for understanding the scope of international building projects. Finally, segregation that was mandated during the construction period demonstrated how buildings can be used to promote social injustices. The positive and negative results associated with the Panama Canal help to inform contemporary professional interior design practice.

Prior to the Canal, the Isthmus of Panama was the narrowest area of land that separated the Pacific and Atlantic oceans. To save thousands of miles of travel, engineers had to create a 50-mile (80.47-kilometer) canal (Figure 3.11). In the late 19th century, this project did not seem difficult to the French, because under the direction of engineer Ferdinand de Lesseps, they had successfully completed the 105-mile (168.98-kilometer) Suez Canal. For 8 years (1881–1889), the French attempted to construct the Panama Canal, but bankruptcy and the region's tropics and diseases precluded success. To strengthen the U.S. Navy's ability to navigate between the Pacific and Atlantic oceans, President Roosevelt became interested in taking over the construction of the Panama Canal. The United States used

Figure 3.11 Prior to the Canal, the Isthmus of Panama was the narrowest area of land that separated the Pacific and Atlantic oceans. To save thousands of miles of travel, engineers created a 50-mile (80.47-kilometer) canal.

Source: Snark/Art Resource, NY.

a veritable army of resources to build the canal in only 10 years. Unfortunately, to obtain the rights to construct the canal, the United States created significant political problems by signing a treaty with the Republic of Panama that violated a previous treaty with Colombia. The treaty gave America control of the Panama Canal and the Canal Zone, a 5-mile (8-kilometer) tract of land on each bank of the canal. A treaty signed by President Carter transferred the Panama Canal and the Canal Zone back to the Panamanians in 1999.

The first challenge of constructing the Panama Canal was the inhospitable natural environment. Panama is a lush tropical region; however, the isthmus also featured torrential rainfalls, deep mud, alligators, jaguars, venomous snakes, mountains, raging rivers, and disease-carrying mosquitoes. During this period, Panama was overcome with mosquitoes that carried malaria and yellow fever. People were still learning that insects carried the diseases. Thousands of the French people who had worked on the canal died from malaria and yellow fever. In 1914, the U.S. government made Dr. Gorgas, a member of the U.S. Army Medical Corps, Surgeon General of the Army to help eliminate the diseases. Gorgas's prior success in Cuba worked in the Panama Canal region. By eliminating standing water, using screens over windows, and spraying insecticides, Panama's incidence of yellow fever and malaria was reduced by 90 percent. Engineers controlled the raging Chagres River by building the Gatun Dam and used dynamite charges to create Culebra Cut, a canyon through the Cordillera Mountains. The dense mountainous area was miles higher than the sea levels at each end of the canal. The French had learned it was impossible to remove enough rock and earth for the canal to be at sea level. Therefore, engineers developed lock canals that enabled ships to move up or down, one level at a time. Lock canals have been constructed at other waterways; however, the Panama Canal locks were built with concrete and were powered by electricity.

In addition to the environmental and engineering challenges, U.S. administrators of the project experienced the complexity of construction in a foreign country and employing people from more than 60 countries. Some local Panamanians were hired for the project, but nearly all of the manual workers were immigrants. Most of the employees were from

Barbados, Jamaica, Martinique, Italy, and Spain. U.S. citizens were given supervisory or professional responsibilities, such as teaching, medicine, or engineering. Administrators had to create entire communities for the employees. Officials learned that to retain employees in a foreign country they had to provide educational and recreational activities, such as dancing, night school, billiards, and "moving pictures." Towns became complete communities with new housing, schools, churches, post offices, libraries, medical facilities, hotels, and ballparks. A government commissary provided food, clothing, and other items at reduced prices.

The U.S. government gave an official order that called for white and black people to be segregated. This affected housing, food, pay, schools, churches, and every public building. White employees were "gold" and black individuals were "silver"; therefore, separate entrances of public buildings or restrooms were marked "gold" and "silver." White U.S. citizens had the highest pay, free furnished housing, paid utilities, free maintenance, dining privileges, social clubs, and competent schools and medical care. Depending upon a white employee's position, housing was either a spacious private residence or a house that was shared with two or four families. These homes had verandas to help temper the hot weather and screens on the windows to prevent mosquitoes. Black employees did manual labor; had the lowest pay; had minimal health care; attended crowded schools; and lived in tenements, shacks, huts, 72-person barracks, or boxcars (Figure 3.12). Rent and meals were deducted from their pay. A quote associated with the opening of the Panama Canal was "The Land Divided—The World United." It is disheartening that administrators divided people as they were dividing the land, but the Panama Canal has subsequently facilitated international cultural exchanges, which may contribute to a "World United." When the canal opened in 1914, however, the human and financial costs were staggering. By combining the French and U.S. operations, over 25,000 people lost their lives at a financial cost of more than $650 million in early 20th-century dollars.

Technologies and Materials: Formica (1913)

An emphasis on industrial technologies that were used to construct the Panama Canal is also evident in the

Figure 3.12 Black employees building the Panama Canal did manual labor; had the lowest pay; minimal health care; attended crowded schools; and lived in tenements, shacks, huts, 72-room barracks, or boxcars.
Source: Snark/Art Resource, NY.

invention of Formica in 1913. Formica has had a dramatic impact on interior environments. Since the Formica Corporation has been in existence through most of the 20th century, the history of the product provides insight regarding the effects of war on manufacturing, prevailing 20th-century fashions, global expansion, and attitudes regarding domestic lifestyles. Formica's success is fundamentally derived from the product's durability, low cost, ease in fabrication, range of colors, creative advertising, and resistance to scratches and moisture.

Two engineers in the United States, Daniel O'Conor and Herbert Faber, invented Formica and founded the international corporation that became synonymous with synthetic surfaces. **Bakelite** was the first synthetic resin, created in 1907; however, Formica's success resulted in Bakelite merging with the Formica Corporation in 1919 in Cincinnati, Ohio. Formica was invented during the early stages of electricity and electrical lighting. To convince consumers that electricity was a safe technology, engineers were constantly pursuing products that would improve the reliability and safety of electrical installations. O'Conor's solution was to insulate electrical equipment with a laminated material. At this time, mica was the insulating material; O'Conor and Faber therefore named their new material "for mica."

In the 1910s, the company made products for electric motor parts, and sales escalated for materials that were needed to fight World War I. After the war, engineers focused on improving Formica by creating "cigarette-proof" finishes, more colors, and decorative wood-grain and marble-surfaced laminates. The development of melamine, an organic compound often combined with formaldehyde to produce the fire-resistant and heat-tolerant melamine resin, in the 1930s resulted in extensive improvements in Formica's durability and resistance to moisture. The high demand for machinery and aircraft during World War II was a phenomenal boost for the Formica Corporation. Jubilation from the ending of the war and significant population

Figure 3.13 Advertisements in newspapers and magazines presented the message to women that to have a modern home required plastic in flattering colors.
Source: Formica Corporation.

increases caused a building boom in the United States. Soon after the war, the Formica Corporation ended their production of industrial laminates and focused exclusively on residential and commercial applications.

Advertising was an important part of their success. Advertisements in newspapers and magazines presented the message to women that to have a modern home required plastic in flattering colors (Figure 3.13). An ad showing a woman in a "modern" kitchen included the line "Some colors bring out the best features in a gal and others do less than nothing for her." In addition to glorifying women's housework, advertisements focused on the importance of having an impeccably clean kitchen, which, it was implied, was attainable with Formica's "wipe-clean" surface.

GLOBAL LIFE AND WORK STYLES

Prior to World War I, books and articles were published that formulated the "modern" approach to interiors. Designers Elsie de Wolfe and Frank A. Parsons each wrote books that detailed a profile of the modern home. However, the development of the modern home was postponed because of World War I. To reserve every resource for the war effort, everyday needs—including food, clothing, and fuel—were rationed. Women started to be employed with jobs that previously were only available to men. To the disappointment of many women, most of them lost their jobs when men returned from the war. At the end of the war, countries were bankrupt and their people exhausted and disillusioned. One of the consequences of this weakened physical condition was the deadly "Spanish" influenza that spread throughout the world and killed more than six million people in 1918. Scientists still do not have a cure for the disease even though people have tried to eliminate the flu by altering lifestyles and interior environments.

Philosophies of Interior Designers: Elsie de Wolfe (1913) and Frank A. Parsons (1915)

In the early 1910s, two interior designers working in New York City wrote books that presented their perspectives of the "Modern House." Both books included numerous photographs of interiors that illustrated concepts and principles (Figures 3.14 and 3.15). Elsie de Wolfe's book *The House in Good Taste* was a compilation of writings that had been published in various publications from 1911 until 1913. Frank A. Parsons wrote *Interior Decoration: Its Principles and Practice* in 1915 when he was the president of the New York School of Fine and Applied

Figure 3.14 A perspective of the "Modern House" in Elsie de Wolfe's 1913 book, *The House in Good Taste.* Compare the design of the "modern" room to the space in Figure 3.15.

Source: Art and Architecture Collection, Miriam and Ira D. Wallach Division of Art, Prints and Photographs, The New York Public Library, Astor, Lenox and Tilden Foundations.

Figure 3.15 A perspective of the "Modern House" in Frank A. Parsons' 1915 book *Interior Decoration: Its Principles and Practice.* Compare this "modern" interior to the bedroom in Figure 3.14.

Source: Art and Architecture Collection, Miriam and Ira D. Wallach Division of Art, Prints and Photographs, The New York Public Library, Astor, Lenox and Tilden Foundations.

Art (modern Parsons The New School for Design). Parsons's delineation of the elements and principles of design has had a profound influence on the interior design profession.

Both authors focused on the importance of creating an environment that was conducive to an individual's lifestyle and aesthetics. They also advocated for simplicity, "suitability," and eliminating all of the Victorian period's clutter, excessive furniture, and dark spaces. However, each author had a distinctive approach to stipulating how to design the interior of a house. Most notable were their views regarding which gender was responsible for the development of the modern house. For example, de Wolfe explains, "I do wish to trace briefly the development of the modern house, the woman's house, to show you that all that is intimate and charming in the home as we know it has come through the unmeasured influence of women. Man conceived the great house with its parade rooms, its *grands appartements* but woman found eternal parade tiresome, and planned for herself little retreats, rooms small enough for comfort and intimacy. In short, man made the house: woman went him one better and made it a home" (de Wolfe, 1913, p. 9).

In the Foreword of Parsons's book, he notes

MUCH *confusion exists at the present time as to the artistic essentials of a modern house. A great deal has been written—perhaps more has been said—about this subject, and still it is vague to most of us. This vagueness is partly because we have not realized fully that a house is but the normal expression of one's intellectual concept of fitness and his aesthetic ideal of what is beautiful. The house is but the externalized man; himself expressed in colour, form, line and texture. To be sure, he is usually limited in means, hampered by a contrary and penurious landlord or by family heirlooms, and often he cannot find just what he wants in the trade; but still the house is his house. It is* **he.**
(Parsons, 1915, p. vii)

Each book includes a chapter dedicated to the "Modern House." Not only does an analysis of how each designer approached the topic reveal his or her perspective on the subject, but the writings also provide insight into how Western interior designers were grappling with transitioning from "period" to "modern" interiors. The authors viewed period interiors as rooms that were designed in one historical style, such as Louis XVI or French Renaissance. Parsons explained that he included chapters on historic periods in order to "show the qualities for which they stand and our need to assimilate these qualities."

The word "Development" in the title of de Wolfe's chapter "Development of the Modern House" is important to understanding her definition of the modern house. De Wolfe contended that the modern house has been evolving since the 1496 "studio-like apartment of Isabella d'Este, the Marchioness of Mantua." But she explains that Madame de Rambouillet's hôtel is the "earliest modern house" because she expressed herself "in her house, her awakened consciousness of beauty and reserve, of simplicity and suitability." In contrast to the fashion of French 17th-century interiors, Madame de Rambouillet created a house that reflected her personality. As described by de Wolfe, Madame had a "light and gracefully curving stairway leading to her salon." Madame also grouped rooms that had a "diversity of size and purpose" and provided her bedroom with an "alcove, boudoir, antechamber, and even its bath." According to de Wolfe, Madame also reflected her personal aesthetics on the choice of color, "her famous silver-blue," rather than the prevailing red and yellow.

De Wolfe concluded this analysis by noting that the concept of the modern house was developed by the 18th century and subsequent endeavors, such as the "search for beauty" and the "magic-making of convenience and ingenuity of the 19th century" could not fundamentally make a difference. The 20th century could "only add material comforts and an expression of our personality." Elsie de Wolfe worked as a professional interior designer in Europe and the United States most of her adult life, except when she served in a French hospital during World War I. For her commendable effort helping soldiers inflicted with poisonous gas burns, she received the Croix de Guerre and the Legion of Honour.

To describe his vision for the 20th century, Parsons titled the chapter simply "The Modern House." His portrayal of the modern house focused on "functional and artistic phases" and noted that the environment can be a means to a "higher state of aesthetic appreciation in the generation that is to follow." He also contended that an artistic home was not a "luxury" and "should be regarded as a duty to the cause of civilization as well as a response to the normal desires inspired by the aesthetic sense" (Parsons, 1915, p. 227).

To advance the cause of aesthetic environments, Parsons identified several "stumbling blocks" he had encountered while working with clients and provided solutions. Some of the stumbling blocks were associated with the assumption that a person could not "afford to buy good things" or that a client must always display heirlooms even when the piece was a bad design. Parsons suggested that when money was a limitation, the best approach was to first invest in the background of the room by focusing on the woodwork, walls, ceiling, and floor. The next most important items were hangings and rugs. The last *gradual* additions to the interior environment were furniture and decorative materials. Landlords were also stumbling blocks, as were clients' perceptions that good designs were not available in their city. Parsons's concluding recommendation was "to investigate the fundamental principles which govern form and decoration, and to use these principles daily in our selections and in our arrangements" (Parsons, 1915, p. 237).

Disease: 1918 Influenza Pandemic

Parsons and de Wolfe acknowledged the importance of "sanitation" in the modern house but elected to not discuss the topic because they contended that it was covered in many other publications. However, sanitation,

suitable living conditions, and "unhealthy" public buildings were critical topics in 1918 throughout the world. The 1918 influenza pandemic, referred to as the Spanish Influenza due to misinformation regarding the origins of the disease, was the most deadly pandemic in the history of civilization. In a little over a year, it has been estimated that more than *50 million* people died from the disease and more than *two billion* had become infected by the virus. Scientists today believe that it began in rural Kansas and rapidly spread to every continent in the world and countless locations, including Japan, India, China, New Zealand, the Philippines, Russia, Artic Eskimo villages, and remote islands in the South Pacific. Isolated communities were severely affected because people did not have immunity from previous epidemics. Influenza, or the flu, is caused by the influenza virus and is highly contagious. The symptoms of the disease include headaches, high fever, cough, sore throat, and extreme fatigue. Influenza has several strains that are constantly mutating. Thus, scientists must develop a new vaccine every year. Influenza is easily spread by coughing and sneezing, and can afflict people of any age or health condition.

The cause of the devastating 1918 influenza was not discovered until 1932. However, it was clear that many of the technological advances of the late 19th and early 20th centuries contributed to both the rapid spread of the disease and the severity of the epidemic. Improvements in transportation significantly increased the number of people affected by the condition. Shortened travel durations resulted in more people traveling around the world at greater frequency. Improved travel times meant that contagious travelers arrived at their destinations faster and could spread the disease to people at the destination.

The rapid spread was also caused by the significant increase in the number of people living in small and crowded tenement buildings. For example, greater London's population was approximately 6.5 million people in 1900, and by the end of the 1930s the city's population was 8.6 million. People did not take precautionary measures because the germ theory still was not considered viable, and there was a false sense of security due to significant advances in medicine, such as the elimination of malaria and yellow fever in the Panama Canal region. World War I also affected the spread and severity of the pandemic. Contagious soldiers were sent to various parts of Europe, thus passing along the disease to civilians and fellow combatants. The confined, dark quarters of the trenches provided ideal conditions to spread the influenza. It has been estimated that half of the American soldiers who died from disease in World War I were infected with the flu (Barry, 2004). Soldiers were not only in close contact with each other, but were also susceptible to the disease because they were exhausted and malnourished. Physicians from the United States saw more than 500 patients a day (Barry, 2004).

The 1918 influenza pandemic had a significant impact on interior environments of public buildings. The extraordinarily large number of people who were infected and the speed at which they became ill caused overcrowding in hospitals, morgues, and cemeteries. City officials ordered makeshift hospitals from tents, closed public buildings, and established ordinances that prohibited coughing and sneezing in public (Figure 3.16).

People were fined or jailed for not complying with the laws. Public facilities, buildings, and transportation systems were disinfected on a regular basis. Public buildings were required to post warnings from health officials. For example, a sign posted in a Chicago theater read:

> *Influenza frequently complicated with pneumonia is prevalent at this time throughout America. This Theatre is cooperating with the Department of Health. YOU MUST DO THE SAME IF YOU HAVE A COLD AND ARE COUGHING AND SNEEZING. DO NOT ENTER THE THEATRE. GO HOME AND GO TO BED UNTIL YOU ARE WELL. Coughing, Sneezing, or Spitting Will Not Be Permitted In The Theatre. In case you must Cough or Sneeze, do so in your own handkerchief and if the Coughing or Sneezing Persists Leave The Theatre At Once.*

The severity of the 1918 pandemic was overlooked by some because of its seemingly benign symptoms and the jubilation caused by the end of the war. However, as previously noted, this was the most deadly pandemic in world history—and there is still no cure for influenza. It is anticipated that another outbreak could be far more

Figure 3.16 To combat Spanish Influenza, city officials ordered makeshift hospitals from tents, closed public buildings, and established ordinances that prohibited coughing and sneezing in public.
Source: Getty Images.

serious because of the millions of people who travel on a daily basis and the many people who have immune systems weakened by medical treatments such as chemotherapy and transplants. Furthermore, scientists today are making analogies between the 1918 influenza pandemic, and contemporary biological weapons and bioterrorism. As designers of health-care facilities, interior designers should be cognizant of the seriousness of contagious diseases and strategize how to create makeshift hospital rooms that isolate patients from healthy individuals. Information can be obtained from the World Health Organization (WHO), a sponsor of programs presented at the Palais des Nations in Geneva. The WHO is responsible for monitoring worldwide endemics, and for organizing vaccination and eradication efforts if an outbreak occurs.

GLOBAL VISUAL AND PERFORMING ARTS

World War I also affected visual and performing arts. There were important creative endeavors prior to the war, but many activities were halted during the most intense years of fighting. The war can also help to explain the lag time between the introduction of innovative artistic developments and their application to interior environments and architecture. Many of the creative accomplishments of the 1910s did not appear in interior environments until the 1920s. As previously discussed, some Western European artists focused on rejecting traditional art and were inspired by native cultures in "exotic" places, such as Africa, South America, Asia, and islands in the South Pacific (an example is primitive art, evident in the Cubist movement, developed by Pablo Picasso and Georges Braque). Western

European ballet was transformed by the music, choreography, costumes, and décor (set designs) of the Ballets Russes, even though the war caused the closure of the 1915 and 1916 seasons in London and Paris.

Performing Arts: Ballets Russes (1909–1929)

The Ballets Russes had an enormous impact on the performing arts throughout the world and subsequently affected interior environments and architecture. Specifically, interior designers and architects were inspired by the Ballets Russes' avant-garde approach to costumes and décor. Exotic costumes in bright colors were complemented with exceptional music and extravagant scenery painted by master artists, including Pablo Picasso, Henri Matisse, and Russians Léon Bakst, Natalia Gontcharova, Mikhail Larionov, and Alexandre Benois (Figure 3.17).

In 1909 Russian Sergei Diaghilev (Diaghileff) founded the Ballets Russes in Paris. Diaghilev had the charisma to attract the world's most famous artists, composers, choreographers, and dancers to create ballet performances. His training in music and art was reflected in his approach to assembling a performance. To create a season's program, Diaghilev formed an "artistic committee," comprised of the artistic director, artists, choreographers, and composers. A critic during this period, Valerien Svetlov, explained the committee's unique collaborative approach, noting, "Diaghileff's new ballets are quite a different matter. Painters, composers, choreographers, writers, and people belonging to the artistic world in general, all meet and discuss their future plans. Somebody puts forward a subject. It is at once examined down to the smallest detail. Somebody makes a suggestion, others back it or reject it, in fact it is hard to say who is the real author of the libretto, which is thus created by common discussion" (Lifar, 1954, p. 226).

The results of the committee were astounding. Diaghilev's dance company created some of the most revered ballet performances in the world, including

Figure 3.17 For performances at the Ballets Russes in Paris, exotic costumes in bright colors were complimented with exceptional music and extravagant scenery painted by master artists. This sketch by Léon Bakst was a setting for Rimski-Korsakov's ballet *Shéhérezadé* (1910).

Source: Erich Lessing/Art Resource, NY.

Igor Stravinsky's *L'Oiseau de Feu (The Firebird)* (1910), *Petroushka* (1911), *Le Sacre du Printemps (The Rite of Spring)* (1913), and Claude Debussy's *L'Après-Midi d'un Faune (Afternoon of a Faun)* (1912). From an interior environment perspective, the most influential ballets were originally performed in Paris starting in 1909 until the outbreak of World War I. The overwhelming success of the performances prompted the company to perform on international stages, including Monte Carlo, Venice, Spain, Russia, London, the United States, and South America. As a fresh and modern approach to dance, the Ballets Russes had a profound effect on the public, artists, architects, interior designers, fashion designers, and graphic designers. Diaghilev's artistic approach to *designing* performances could help to explain his widespread influence. For example, Svetlov noted that Diaghilev's artistic committee's first step was to design the "background" for the choreography, explaining

> The painter most inspired by the subject undertakes the décor; he creates the setting, costumes, accessories, down to the smallest detail. That is why the ballet gives such an impression of unity in its idea and its production. The painters, who have devoted their whole lives to studying problems of style, period, modelling [sic], colour, and line, ought to be his ceaseless helpers on an equal footing. After learning from the painter what groups are likely to create the most powerful effect on stage and the most attractive design, the ballet master can use this as a background for his choreography. (Lifar, 1954, p. 226)

Diaghilev's reformist approach to ballet also reflects issues and concerns that were prevalent among architects, interior designers, and artists. He was concerned with respecting the past while creating new, modern performances. Diaghilev assembled seasons that included classical ballet and innovative costumes, music, décor, and choreography. At a time when classical dance in Western Europe had become mundane, the Ballets Russes exhilarated Western European audiences, including artists, interior designers, and architects. Diaghilev's Russian artists and the designs from "exotic" locations provided inspiration that would continue into the next two decades. Many of the performances resulted from a synthesis of Russian music, painting, and dancing. During this period, Russian art and decorative ornamentation were basically unknown to Western audiences. Most Western European art galleries open to the public did not display Russian paintings. Therefore, people were astounded and impressed with "new" creative uses of contrasting colors and patterns. The ballet *Schéhérazade* (1910) was known for its "riot of colors," which included scarlet, orange, purple, gold, and silver. Russian folk art was "fresh" and innovative in the ballet *Le Coq d'Or* (1914). *Cléopâtra* (1910) brought a rich, colorful, and vibrant Egypt to Western Europe, and exoticism was derived from the Orient and Northern Africa. Pablo Picasso designed the costumes and décor for the ballets *Le Tricorne, Parade,* and *Pulcinella*. The simultaneous Cubism Movement (1907–1914) in Western Europe reinforced the vibrant colors, patterns, and geometric abstraction featured in the performances of the Ballets Russes. The Ballets Russes and Cubism had a tremendous influence on interior environments and architecture in the interwar decades, most notably in the Art Deco style.

Visual Arts: Favrile Glass by Louis Comfort Tiffany

Louis Comfort Tiffany started creating fine art glass in the 19th century in New York, but the power of his genius becomes apparent by noting his continued success even though the Art Nouveau style was in decline. Tiffany had a dramatic impact on the decorative and applied arts in the 19th, 20th, and 21st centuries. In writing about the potential of "modern" glass architecture, the Berlin-based poet and essayist Scheerbart (see next section) contended that "The famous American Tiffany, who introduced the 'Tiffany glass,' has by this means greatly stimulated the glass industry; he put coloured [sic] clouds into glass" (Sharp, 1972, p. 47). As with Diaghilev, Tiffany was also attracted to and inspired by the colors, patterns, and motifs derived from "exotic" lands and non-Western styles. An influential colleague suggested to Tiffany early in the latter's

Figure 3.18 Tiffany's success as a decorator was evident by acquiring the remodeling project for the entrance hall of the White House.
Source: White House Museum.

career that he "acquire objects of interest and to study the values of non-European cultures" (Koch, 1982, p. 9). Tiffany took the advice and traveled the world to experience fresh and innovative approaches to design. These experiences were reflected in many of his paintings and interiors and influenced the variety of colors, shapes, and patterns in his art glass.

Tiffany is internationally known for his innovative **favrile** glass, but he also had a successful career as an interior designer. He initially had wanted to be an artist. The subject matters of his oil and watercolor paintings were landscapes, flowers, and urban environments. He was involved with many artistic societies, such as the Society of American Artists and the American Water Color Society. Tiffany's paintings were displayed at national and international exhibitions, including the 1876 Philadelphia Centennial, the 1878 Exposition Universelle in Paris, and the 1893 World's Columbian Exposition in Chicago. When Tiffany realized that his paintings were not at the caliber of renowned artists, he explored other artistic endeavors, including "decorating" (the term used in that era) and stained glass. Tiffany's success as a decorator was evident by his acquiring the remodeling project for the White House and for the Palace of the President of Cuba. Tiffany and the Associated Artists became known for colored glass; windows above fireplaces; ornamental **transoms**; Islamic carvings; and custom textiles, wallpaper, furniture, and glass mosaic sconces (Figure 3.18).

Tiffany became even more famous as a designer of stained glass windows and mosaics. However, after 1900, Tiffany's fame catapulted with his innovative vessels made from favrile glass. Favrile glass is created when numerous colored glasses are blended together while they are hot from the furnace. Extremely talented artisans, such as Arthur John Nash, worked for Tiffany and provided invaluable knowledge in the development of favrile's unique chemical formulas and the glassblowing techniques used to create the glass vessels. In a brochure written by Siegfried (Samuel) Bing, a German art dealer in Paris (see Chapter 1), he describes a Tiffany peacock-feather vase: "Just as in the natural feather itself, we find here a suggestion of the impalpable . . . this power which the author possesses of assigning in advance to each morsel of glass, whatever its color or chemical composition, the exact place which it is to occupy when the article leaves the glassblower's hands—this truly unique art is combined in these peacock's feathers with the charm of iridescence which bathes the subtle and velvety ornamentation with an almost supernatural light" (Koch, 1982, p. 121).

In addition to being inspired by exotic colors, Tiffany's innovation was derived from various sources, including silversmith artists from his father's jewelry store, Tiffany & Company, Japanese sword-guards, ancient textiles, embroidery, and East Indian carvings. An amazing example of his artistic expression and his ingenuity is the enormous mosaic glass curtain for the National Theatre in Mexico City (Figure 3.19). The fireproof curtain has over a million favrile glass tiles embedded in a steel frame with a weight of 21 tons. The glass is painted with a view of the countryside and mountains visible from the Palace of the President of Mexico. In 1911, thousands of people viewed the glass curtain in New York City prior to its installation in Mexico City. The success of favrile glass was the result of Tiffany's creative genius and the artisans who executed his vision by perfecting the materials, colors, glazes, and formulas. Tiffany had an enormous impact on the fine and applied arts through his mastery of glass, art pottery, enameling, glass vessels, lamps, bronzes, ceramics, and jewelry. Today, Tiffany's art is in museum collections throughout the world.

Figure 3.19 An amazing example of Tiffany's artistry and ingenuity is the enormous mosaic glass curtain for the National Theatre in Mexico City. The fireproof curtain has over one million favrile glass tiles embedded in a steel frame with a weight of 21 tons.

Source: http://media-cdn.tripadvisor.com/media.photo

GLOBAL BUSINESS AND ECONOMICS

Even though World War I affected the economic conditions of most countries, new industries and businesses were founded that were based on the technological developments of the late 19th and early 20th centuries. Specifically, new corporations and industries were established to profit from the "new age" materials: glass and steel. Increased international travel and improved communication networks continued to affect sources of inspiration. Designs of new products were influenced by locations such as Japan, North Africa, and Southeast Asia, which were seen as exotic. A different facet of business was the response to deadly fires—some manufacturers researched properties of fireproof materials to make products safer. In contrast to most of the world, the late entry of the United States into World War I resulted in an economic boom for the country. Established railroads, steel production, and escalating demands for oil created multimillionaires, such as John Pierpont Morgan, John D. Rockefeller, and Andrew Carnegie.

Industry: Glashaus (Glass House) (1914) by Bruno Taut

The possibility of constructing glass buildings became apparent during various exhibitions in the 19th century, including London's Crystal Palace in 1851 (see Chapter 1). The escalating demands for glass resulted in the formation of new glass businesses and industries. In the early 1910s, the German glass industry was interested in promoting its new products. The 1914 Deutscher Werkbund Exhibition in Cologne, Germany, was an ideal venue for demonstrating to international visitors Germany's progressive approach to "modern" glass. The German glass industry's promotional interests

occurred simultaneously with the visions and aspirations of a Berlin poet, Paul Scheerbart, and the German architect Bruno Taut. The result was Taut's transformational *Glashaus* (Glass House), sponsored by Germany's glass industry at the 1914 Exhibition. The pavilion had a profound impact on the use of glass for interior environments and architecture, and is an excellent example of the **Expressionist movement** in architecture. As in the fine and performing arts, the Expressionist movement is associated with challenging classical perspectives and distorting objects to create a response. New materials, such as glass, were often used to prompt emotions.

Scheerbart was consumed with promoting glass architecture. His fictitious architect, Klug, flew in an "airship" to supervise the design and construction of glass buildings all over the world, including Arabia, Ceylon, and Japan. Scheerbart was convinced that glass was the material to create a "new culture." Scheerbart met Taut through a mutual friend, and the two visionaries started to engage in various collaborative activities that were based on advancing the concept of glass architecture. Taut wrote articles regarding the potential of glass architecture and was actively involved with a group called the Glass Chain. To explore the possibilities of glass architecture, members of the Glass Chain shared sketches, concepts, and ideas. Taut also had a deep appreciation for the potential of glass and had the skills to implement Scheerbart's fantasies.

The two innovators collaborated on the design of the *Glashaus*. Almost the entire pavilion was made of transparent or translucent glass. Taut's intent was to design the "lightest possible concrete structure, destined to demonstrate the use of glass in all its varied aesthetic charm" (Whyte, 1982). The *Glashaus* was built on a concrete podium with glass balls surrounding its base. A glass dome with concrete ribs covered the two-story pavilion. The prismatic dome was mounted on a 14-sided drum that had 14 aphorisms written by Scheerbart inscribed in the narrow band of concrete. Over the entrance was that statement "Coloured glass Destroys hatred."

Figure 3.20 At the Glashaus by Bruno Taut, visitors experienced tactile and visual textures from the variety of glass used for walls, ceilings, floors, and the interior staircase.

Source: Wikimedia Commons.

In designing an emotional experience, Taut incorporated elements that responded to sound, touch, and sight. Soothing sounds came from music and the cascading water in the lower level. Visitors experienced tactile and visual textures from the variety of glass used for walls, ceilings, floors, and the interior staircase (Figure 3.20). The exterior application of each diamond-shaped element of the dome was plate glass, and their interior sides were lined with a layer of Luxfer prismatic glass tiles and colored glass. In use prior to electrical lighting, the Luxfer prism tiles were known for their ability to distribute daylight to dark interior corners. The light and color spectacle must have been stupendous when sunlight passed through the prismatic dome. The experience was enhanced by the inclusion of a mechanical kaleidoscope.

In the same year of the Exhibition, Scheerbart published *Glasarchitektur* (Glass Architecture), a thesis that widely explored glass architectural applications and identified solutions to any disadvantages associated with glass, such as heat gain. The book has 111 brief chapters that discuss various glass applications, including "double glass walls, light, heating and cooling," "the chair," "the door," "ghostly illumination," "the effects of Tiffany," and "floating architecture." Many of Scheerbart's concepts were derived from "exotic" locations, including

Japan, Arabia, Syria, and Egypt. For example, in the chapter titled "Ancient Greece without glass, the East with ampullae and majolica tiles," he explains, "In ancient Greece glass was almost unknown. But before the Hellenic civilisation [*sic*] there were already many colourful [*sic*] glass ampullae and lustrous majolica tiles in the countries bordering the Euphrates and Tigris, a thousand years before Christ. The Near East is thus the so-called cradle of glass culture" (Sharp, 1972, p. 47). Scheerbart used Japanese partition-screens as an example of how to have movable glass partitions in residences. He concluded by proclaiming that the "new glass environment will completely transform mankind, and it remains only to wish that the new glass culture will have ever fewer opponents" (Sharp, 1972, p. 74).

Industry and Management Principles: The Metal Furniture Company (Modern Steelcase)

In addition to glass manufacturers, the metal industry was pursuing new ventures by exploring possibilities with steel. The development of steel furniture, cabinets, and accessories has had an obvious impact on interior environments. For this to have occurred required visionary leaders that were willing to work with new materials, develop new processes, and transform traditional management philosophies. In the early 1910s, one of the world's most successful furniture manufacturing companies was founded at the same time as the development of one of the most influential management philosophies of the 20th century.

In 1911, Frederick W. Taylor wrote the *Principles of Scientific Management*, and the Metal Furniture Company (modern Steelcase) was founded in 1912 in Grand Rapids, Michigan (Figure 3.21). Over the years, Taylor's management principles have influenced the efficiency of tasks and processes in innumerable organizations, including hospitals, schools, universities, corporations, and manufacturing institutions. The Metal Furniture Company's first patent was for fireproof steel wastebaskets. The next product was a steel desk, followed by an amazing success story. Today Steelcase has more than 1,400 patents, more than $3 billion in annual revenue (2009), more than 500 product lines, and numerous worldwide manufacturing facilities and dealers (www.steelcase.com, 2009).

Time has revealed the impact that the Metal Furniture Company and Taylor's management principles have had on interior environments. Leaders at Steelcase had the vision to create steel furniture, but

to improve the mechanical production processes that were required to mass-produce furniture, at reasonable prices, required transformational management policies and procedures. Reviewing Steelcase's vision and Taylor's management philosophy reveals three commonalties that are still important to the work of today's designers:

1. A focus on efficiency and effectiveness,
2. Creating an environment that maximizes the potential of people in the workplace, and
3. Identifying solutions by engaging in research studies.

Based on President Roosevelt's call for "national efficiency" in an address to governors in 1908, Taylor engaged in several experiments and research studies to determine the most efficient and effective production processes. He also advocated for maximizing the potential of people, stating, "The principal object of management should be to secure the maximum prosperity for the employer, coupled with the maximum prosperity for each employé [*sic*]" (Taylor, 1911, p. 9).

Effectiveness and "prosperity" for people are also evident in the description of the "Steelcase Story" on the company's website: "Whatever you need to accomplish, Steelcase can provide you with the environment and the tools to do it better, faster and more effectively. That's because we're passionate about unlocking the potential of people at work. It's the fundamental principle on which our company was founded in 1912 and it remains our single-minded focus in the 21st century" (2007, p. 3).

Research, the third concept, was fundamental to Taylor's ability to suggest the most effective and efficient means to manufacture products. As also practiced by Steelcase, Taylor engaged in countless hours of observation to determine the most appropriate materials, tools, motions, and work sequence. Interior designers can benefit from Taylor by applying his philosophy to practice. Successful interior environments maximize the potential of people by applying research-based design solutions.

Figure 3.21 The Metal Furniture Company (modern Steelcase) in Grand Rapids, Michigan, was founded in 1912.

Source: Bettmann/Corbis.

SUMMARY

World War I was the dominant event of the decade of the 1910s and affected lifestyles, technological developments, architecture, interior environments, and the visual and performing arts, among other things. The Palais des Nations in Geneva, Switzerland, was conceived to help prevent future devastating international wars. Revolutions in China and Russia resulted in either the opening or closure of important architecture. Public access was granted at the Temple of Heaven in Beijing and the Winter Palace and the Hermitages in St. Petersburg. Discoveries and excavation activities, such as Machu Picchu and Stupa I, revealed ancient civilizations that had amazing engineering and artistic skills.

Technological advances concentrated on improving transportation and developing new "modern" materials. The war effort consumed great resources, which resulted in the bankruptcy of some of the countries that had fought in the war. Security concerns prompted the U.S. government to construct the Panama Canal. After the deaths of thousands of people during its construction, the canal opened, linking the Atlantic and Pacific oceans. By producing materials for the war, the Formica Corporation developed its corporate foundation and also altered the design of kitchens and bathrooms, an influence that would extend throughout the 20th century and into the 21st century. Life and work styles were also changed by the professional practice and writings of Elsie de Wolfe and Frank A. Parsons. Both interior designers were visionary leaders in the profession and helped to define the modern home.

The 1918 influenza pandemic killed more than 50 million people and infected more than two billion worldwide. Radical measures had to be taken to curtail the spread of the disease, including the use of makeshift hospital tents and the passage of laws forbidding coughing and sneezing in public.

The visual and performing arts in the 1910s were enriched by the innovative performances of the Ballets Russes and the continued excellence demonstrated by Tiffany's favrile glass. Even though Tiffany's art started in the 19th century, his creative genius in working with art glass provided inspiration for interior designers and architects who wanted to explore the beauty of "modern" glass architecture in the early decades of the 20th century.

Bruno Taut's Glashaus was a defining example of the reality of building glass architecture. Manufacturers continued to explore the many uses for steel, including the revolutionary designs created by Steelcase. In reviewing the events and developments of the period from 1910 to 1920, this chapter emphasized global perspectives by describing and explaining interior environments and architecture of cultures in China, Switzerland, Russia, South America, Mexico, India, the Panama Canal Zone, Paris, Germany, and the United States. The next chapter examines how the end of World War I affected interior environments and architecture during the 1920s.

KEY TERMS

architrave

Bakelite

bochka

conical dome

cupola

drum

egg-shaped dome

Expressionist movement

favrile

Formica

fretwork

harmika

ogive-shaped projections

onion dome

tent roof

toranas

transom

vedikás

EXERCISES

1. Philosophy and Design Project. To create a season's program, Diaghilev formed an "artistic committee" with a philosophy that focused on a unique collaborative approach. Identify a commercial or residential project and design the interior environment using a collaborative approach similar to Diaghilev's "artistic committee." Write a summary of the collaborative activities and submit sketches and drawings of the interior environment.

2. Human Factors Research Project. The Panama Canal project provides many examples of social injustice. Research examples of how housing and public buildings have been used to execute social injustices. In a written report, summarize your findings and provide suggestions for how interior designers can be involved with social justice.

3. Research Design Project. The first three chapters have identified examples of sustainable designs. To reinforce the concept of sustainability, review the chapters and develop a summary of the solutions. Select five examples that could be applied to contemporary interiors. Write a report that includes the summary, recommendations for contemporary interiors, and drawings, sketches, or photographs.

CHAPTER 4

EMPHASIS: THE 1920S

OBJECTIVES

After reading this chapter, you should be able to describe and analyze:

■ How selected global political events in the 1920s, such as colonization in India and revolutions in Beijing, China, affected interior environments and architecture.

■ How natural environmental conditions and earthquakes in the 1920s affected selected global interior environments and architecture as evident by the discovery of the preserved tomb of Pharaoh Tutankhamun and Frank Lloyd Wright's Imperial Hotel in Tokyo.

■ How selected global technologies and materials in the 1920s affected interior environments and architecture as evident by the Bauhaus and the development of tubular steel furniture.

■ How selected global work styles and lifestyles in the 1920s affected interior environments and architecture as evident by Le Corbusier's "Esprit-Nouveau" and Parisian Art Deco inspired by Parisian fashions.

■ How selected global visual arts in the 1920s affected interior environments and architecture as evident by Eileen Gray and Jean Dunand's lacquer pieces and De Stijl.

■ How selected global business developments and economics in the 1920s affected interior environments and architecture as evident by the Barcelona Exhibition, Constructivism, and workers' housing in Russia.

■ How to compare and contrast selected interior environments and architecture of the Americas, Asia/Oceania, Europe, and the Middle East/Africa in the 1920s.

The 1920s were dominated by the recovery from World War I. However, the extent of recovery efforts varied between countries. Germany in particular endured severe hardship due to the demands imposed by the Treaty of Versailles, including losing territories, limited armed forces, and payments of billions of dollars for war damages. Other European countries also suffered due to shortages of raw materials, such as iron ore and coal, and exorbitant taxes that were levied to pay for the war. In contrast, the United States experienced a significant economic boom until the stock market crash in October 1929. From a cultural perspective, archeologists continued to discover ancient civilizations, including the extremely influential items in the tomb of Pharaoh Tutankhamun near Luxor, Egypt. **Art Deco** became a popular style in both Western Europe and the United States; this design trend continued into the 1930s. The design, function, and materials used in machines and technologies influenced the Art Deco style and the new Modernist movement. The women's rights movement finally was successful in attaining women's right to vote when the 19th Amendment was passed in 1920. At the start of the decade, very few people owned radios and telephones, but by the end of the decade, many homes had electricity, wireless radios, and automobiles.

Corporations manufacturing automobiles, such as Chrysler, and General Motors, flourished in the 1920s and demonstrated their success with the construction of skyscrapers in New York City. The cause of air travel progressed with Charles Lindbergh's nonstop flight between New York City and Paris in 1927. Modernism was evident in the visual arts with Picasso's development of **Abstract Art** in the mid-1920s and the opening of The Museum of Modern Art (MOMA) in New York City in 1929. In addition, architect Walter Gropius founded the transformational Staatliches **Bauhaus School** in Dessau, Germany, whose program had international influence on numerous aspects of design, including architecture, furniture, textiles, photography, ceramics, film, graphics, and painting.

GLOBAL POLITICS AND GOVERNMENT

World War I had a significant effect on territorial boundaries and colonization. Former empires were dissolved, and new states were formed in Eastern Europe. Independent states included Finland, Poland, Hungary, Romania, Egypt, and Tibet. Australia was independent and possessed territories in the South Pacific. Prior to the war, Australians were British citizens and Great Britain controlled Australia's foreign policies. As prescribed in the Treaty of Versailles, Germany's colonial possessions in Africa were distributed among Western European nations. Japan's quest for dominance in the East was evident by its possessions, which included Korea, Formosa, and islands in the Pacific. In Russia, the Bolshevik victory in 1920 against the czarists ended the civil war, and the Union of Soviet Socialist Republics (USSR) was established in 1922. After the death of Vladimir Lenin in 1924, Josef Stalin became the leader of the USSR and formulated a "5-year plan" to industrialize the country. The rise in power of the prime minister of Italy, Benito Mussolini, resulted in the establishment of a fascist government. To gain independence from Britain, political unrest in India was stimulated by the initiatives of Mohandas Gandhi. China endured a civil war that began in 1925 and led to an eventual reunification of the country by Chiang Kai-shek, leader of the Nationalist Party.

Colonization: Viceroy's House (1912–1931) in New Delhi, India

Colonial unrest in India began with the unsuccessful revolution of 1857–1859. Consequently, Britain became an occupying colonial power and Queen Victoria was declared the Empress of India. In an attempt to maintain control during World War I, Britain restricted Indians' freedom of speech, press, and right to assemble. These restrictions continued after the war with the Rowlatt Act of 1919. At this time, reformist Mohandas Gandhi worked to achieve India's independence from British rule, which had existed for more than 300 years. To protest Britain's occupation, Gandhi (or Mahatma, "great soul") ordered a nonviolent strike of workers in 1919. His rules to the Indian strikers were simple: (1) never resort to violence, (2) never molest non-strikers, (3) never beg for food, and (4) never give in. Unfortunately, violence erupted in Amritsar, and due to an "unlawful" public assembly, the British army killed 379 people and wounded over a thousand Indians, including many women, children, and unarmed individuals.

To demonstrate opposition to Britain's tactics, Gandhi asked Indians to boycott British institutions, organizations, and products, including factory-produced textiles. To substitute for British textiles, Gandhi started to weave fabric for his clothing and encouraged Indians to revitalize their ancient craft by weaving textiles (see Chapter 1). He was often seen with his spinning wheel and dressed in a plain, white, cotton fabric draped over his body. The tool was a symbolic representation of his nonviolent approach to independence, and it also represented India's self-sufficiency prior to Britain's occupation. In March of 1922, Gandhi was arrested for encouraging people to disobey British laws and was imprisoned for 2 years. After his release, he continued his peaceful efforts to gain India's independence, eliminate racial prejudice, and establish peace between the Hindus and Muslims.

The political unrest that occurred in India during the early 20th century coincided with Britain's decision to move India's capital from Calcutta to Delhi. To establish the new capital and several government buildings, Britain formed the Delphi Planning Committee, which included the English architect Sir Edwin Lutyens. Sir Herbert Baker, the English architect responsible for the Union Building in Pretoria (see Chapter 2), was selected to collaborate with Lutyens. Work was suspended during World War I but resumed in the early 1920s. The project was extensive. The committee had to identify an appropriate site, develop a city plan for approximately 30,000 people, and oversee the design and construction of the governmental buildings. The committee selected a site approximately three miles southwest of Delhi and developed a plan for the city that resembled the network of monuments and radiating boulevards in Paris and Washington, D.C. (see Chapter 1). Lutyens was assigned to design the palace, including administrative facilities for the viceroy, the individual who governed India as the representative of the king (Figure 4.1). Baker was responsible for two buildings for the secretariat. There was a great deal of controversy regarding the architectural style. Lutyens

Figure 4.1 The Viceroy's House in New Delhi, India, designed by Sir Edwin Lutyens.

Source: © Tibor Bognar/Dinodia.

and Baker preferred the aesthetics of classical Western architecture, but many other influential individuals recommended that for political and cultural reasons, governmental buildings in the "heart" of India should have Indian motifs. Ultimately, the design solution was to employ "Western architecture with an Oriental motif" (Irving, 1981).

Lutyens' design for the Viceroy's Palace is predominantly classical, but the massive building has Indian motifs that are derived from Mughal architecture, a style influenced by designs during the Mughal Empire (1526–1858) (see Figure 4.1). The H-shaped plan has more than 300 rooms, and its square footage exceeds the Palace of Versailles in France. Located under the palace's central dome, the most magnificent room is Durbar Hall, the viceroy's throne.

Some of the features adapted from Mughal architecture were selected to counteract India's climate and intense sunlight. For example, the upper level of the palace is outlined with an 8-foot-deep (2.44-meter) **chujja,** a very thin ledge of stone. The chujja helps to absorb heat from the intense sun and provides shade to the upper-level windows. Its deep projection protects the stone façade by shielding the surface from rainwater, which is especially critical during a monsoon. Aesthetically, when sunlight strikes the edge of the chujja, the palace's plain façade is decorated with a ribbon of light and shadow. To help reduce the sun's intense heat and brightness, the palace has a limited number of small windows that are recessed or protected by deep overhangs. Local sandstone was selected to help the structures endure India's climate and intense sun. Nearly all of the interior and exterior stone was the regional Dholpur red, pink, and beige sandstone.

To contend with India's hot climate, Lutyens incorporated Mughal-inspired gardens, fountains, pools, terraces, courtyards, and verandas. Other Mughal architectural features are evident in the design of the palace's central dome and the numerous **chattris,** the small pavilions located on the rooftop. The cen-

Figure 4.2 Bells carved from stone are used as part of the decorative element of the Viceroy's House.

tral dome resembles the design of Stupa I in Sanchi (see Chapter 3). Similarly, the palace's dome is a solid, egg-shaped stone structure with a flattened top. In the middle of the dome, the broad band of beige sandstone resembles the ground-level vediká that surrounds Stupa I. The palace has other motifs that are important symbols of the cultural heritage of India. The lotus flower and bells, which are important for Indian religious ceremonies, are common ornamental motifs. Bells carved from stone are used as part of the decorative element of the Viceroy's House (Figure 4.2). When the people of India gained their independence from Britain in 1947, the Viceroy's Palace became the home of the President of the Republic of India.

Revolutions and Governments: Forbidden City (1406–1420) (Modern Palace Museum 1924) in Beijing, China

As reviewed in the previous chapter, China's revolution resulted in the overthrow of the Qing Dynasty in 1911 and the establishment of the Republic of China in 1912. These events had a significant impact on the world's knowledge and understanding of interior environments and architecture because the new Nationalist government declared that, beginning in 1924, the previously private Imperial Palace (Forbidden City) in Beijing would be open and available to the public as a museum (Palace Museum). The Imperial Palace was named the Forbidden City because only the Chinese Emperor and his court were allowed to live within its surrounding walls (Figure 4.3). For more than 500 years, this spectacular example of Chinese architecture, craftsmanship, and artistry was the home for the Ming (1368–1644) and Qing (Manchu) (1644–1911) dynasties.

In 1924, the Nationalist army invaded the palace and forced the abdicated emperor, Puyi (P'u-i or Henry P'u-i), to leave the Forbidden City. The Forbidden City was converted into the Palace Museum. Thus, not only did the 1920s mark the beginning of the world's ability to study, appreciate, and understand traditional Chinese architecture, historical furnishings, and artwork, but the removal of the imperial family revealed objects, in impeccable condition, that were used in the daily life during the Qing period. Some of the historical articles include the emperor's platform bed with embroidered silk quilts, a red lacquer bathtub, commodes made of pewter and silver, enamel hat stands, cupboards, and mats made from ivory strips, which was a cool material to sleep on during the summer.

Located close to the Ming-Qing Temple (Altar) of Heaven, Ming Emperor Yongle started the construction of the Forbidden City in 1406 by utilizing hundreds of thousands of workers every day. Completed in just 14 years, the Forbidden City is one of the world's greatest masterpieces. Located in the center of Beijing, the Imperial Palace was built on 180 acres (73 hectares) and is surrounded by a moat and a wall 35 feet (11 meters) tall. Odd numbers, especially nine—the most "perfect" number in Chinese philosophy—are auspicious numbers for the emperor, and so the palace has 9,999 rooms. In abiding by the principles of **feng shui** (wind water), for auspicious reasons a hill was built to the north of the palace to deflect the cold northerly winds and to deter invasions. Feng shui is an ancient Chinese philosophy that is premised on people being in

Figure 4.3 The palace was named the Forbidden City because only the Chinese Emperor and his court were allowed to live within its surrounding walls until 1924, the year the Forbidden City became the Palace Museum. The Hall of Supreme Harmony is the center of the photograph.
Source: Erich Lessing/Art Resource, NY.

harmony with nature and their physical environment. The primary buildings are along the north-south axis. Entrances face the south to take advantage of the positive southerly breezes and to shield the emperor from the inauspicious northerly winds.

Entry to the Imperial complex begins by crossing one of five bridges that arch over the Golden River. Upon passing through the Gate of Supreme Harmony and an enormous courtyard, one reaches the Outer Court complex that was used by the emperor for important public ceremonies, such as weddings and coronations. The structures include the magnificent Hall of Supreme Harmony, the Hall of Central Harmony, and the Hall of Preserving Harmony. Progressing in a northerly direction, one approaches the private living area for the emperor and his wives, concubines, and attendants. The Inner Court is comprised of the Palace of Heavenly Purity, Hall of Union, and Palace of Earthly Tranquility. The north-south axis ends with the Imperial Garden, the Hall of Imperial Tranquility, and the Gate of Martial Spirit.

Within the walls of the Forbidden City, the wooden buildings feature tiled roofs in yellow, a color that could only be used by the emperor. There are several roof styles, but the most elaborate designs were used for the ruler's most distinguished buildings, such as the Hall of Supreme Harmony (see Figure 4.3). This double-eave building has a hip roof with sloping ridges that terminate with several carved wooden figures. The yellow-tiled roofs sharply contrast with the intense royal red façades and columns and the white marble terraces and balustrades.

A variety of mythological animals, such as dragons, cranes, lions, serpents, phoenixes, and tortoises, are represented throughout the palace. A pair of bronze lions with tails and paws of a dragon "protect" the entrances of buildings. The powerful male lions grip a ball, representing the earth or a pearl, and the paws of a female lion hold a cub. As a symbol of the emperor, five-clawed dragons are carved in wood and stone and are embroidered in silk brocades. To extinguish fires,

vessels such as bronze cauldrons were filled with water and placed indoors and outdoors.

As illustrated in Figure 4.4, furniture and wooden surfaces were decorated with richly carved motifs and finished with gilding, lacquer, or paint. Painted surfaces in red, yellow, green, and blue resembled the deep hues of precious stones. The atmosphere of the interior was intensified by the smoke from numerous incense burners. The smoke gave the impression that the emperor, known as the son of heaven, was floating on clouds. Clouds surrounding dragons were often used as a royal motif, such as the Imperial Way, a magnificent stone relief ramp that extends from the back of the Hall of Preserving Harmony.

Throughout its 500 years and 24 emperors, the Imperial Palace endured war, revolutions, occupations, fires, looting, and earthquakes. The Chinese have faithfully restored and preserved its historical cultural heritage. Beginning with the dynasties Ming and Qing, the Chinese people have rebuilt the palace's wooden structures. On each occasion the restorations were executed by following the original 15th-century plans, colors, and construction techniques. An unknown number of priceless works of art and furniture were stolen, lost, or destroyed over the centuries; however, the collection was so vast that today the Palace Museum still has over a million pieces of art, including paintings, ceramics, bronzes, jade, restored sculptures, and objects made from gold and precious stones.

The Palace Museum is currently open to visitors from all over the world. To preserve China's heritage, the government maintains the museum and continuously restores its structures using ancient paint formulas and the original 15th-century construction technologies. The Imperial Palace was inscribed on UNESCO's World Heritage List in 1987 for meeting several criteria, including its representation of "masterpieces in the development of imperial palace architecture in China" and its "testimony to Chinese civilisation [sic] at the time of the Ming and Qing dynasties" (UNESCO, 1986, p. 1).

Figure 4.4 Throne, Palace of Heavenly Purity. Furniture and wooden surfaces at the Forbidden Palace are decorated with richly carved motifs and finished with gilding, lacquer, or paint.

Source: Vanni/Art Resource, NY.

EFFECTS AND CONDITIONS OF THE NATURAL ENVIRONMENT

China's Forbidden City was not the only historical site to be viewed by the public in the 1920s. Government actions enabled the public to experience one of the world's greatest museums. From another perspective, the world has been able to study and understand ancient civilizations because their remains were preserved by environmental conditions. In the 1920s, archeologists continued to search for the remains of lost civilizations and were enormously rewarded by the century's most important discovery, the tomb of Pharaoh Tutankhamun in Egypt in 1922. British archeologist Sir Arthur Evans was involved with excavating the Palace of Knossós in Crete throughout the decade, not ending until 1931.

Several major natural disasters occurred in the 1920s, such as the devastating 1923 earthquake, fires, and subsequent tsunami that killed more than 100,000 people and nearly destroyed Tokyo and Yokohama.

Four years later, an earthquake in China in the Qinghai region killed 200,000 people. The 1920s were also affected by the deaths of more than 200,000 people from an influenza epidemic beginning in 1918. When these disasters occur, interior environments and architecture are destroyed and modifications are made that enhance the safety and stability of future structures.

Environmental Conditions: Discovery of the Tomb of Pharaoh Tutankhamun (1922) in Egypt

For centuries, archeologists and grave robbers have been searching for the tremendous riches that were buried with Egyptian royalty. The Pyramids at Giza, which were constructed during Egypt's Old Kingdom (ca. 2650–2134 BCE) period, were easy to find; thus, often their contents were removed soon after entombment. Consequently, to avoid their tombs being disturbed, the Pharaohs in the New Kingdom (ca. 1550–1080 BCE) identified secret burial sites in what is currently called the Valley of the Kings, close to modern Luxor. Tombs were constructed in the mountains and in the floor of the valley. Throughout the years, many tombs were discovered, but the location of the boy king Tutankhamun's tomb remained a mystery for more than 3,000 years, until English archeologist

Howard Carter located the site in November 1922. The task was not easy and was only possible because of the financial support of another Englishman, Lord Carnarvon, and the cooperation of the Egyptian government. Carter and his crew searched the Valley of the Kings for more than 5 years before a member of the team accidentally found the opening of the tomb. The man had been poking a hole in the ground next to old huts, and his stick hit one of the stone steps that led to Tutankhamun's tomb.

Upon removing the huts, Carter was able to find the 16 steps and two covered doorways that protected the four rooms in the tomb. The floor plan of the tomb consisted of an antechamber, an annex, and the burial chamber that was connected to a Treasury. The first two doorways had been opened, and objects in the first room, the antechamber, were in disarray (Figure 4.5). Jewelry wrapped in linen was found on the ground, implying that the grave robbers were caught and ran without their treasures. At this time grave robbers could be executed without a trial. Another indication that the robbers had to immediately leave the site was the untouched condition of the doorways of the burial chamber and the annex. These two unopened doorways were critically important; their position meant that the contents in these rooms had not been touched since the king was buried more than 3,000 years ago. Carter and a large team of professionals, including representatives from the Egyptian government, started the extensive process of cataloguing, photographing, and preserving the thousands of artifacts that were discovered in the tomb. The entire process took more than 10 years to accomplish.

The discovery had a tremendous impact on interior environments; most notable was the influence that Egyptian forms, colors, patterns, and objects had on Art Deco (discussed later in this chapter). Technological advances in transportation, printing, and communication (specifically radio) let people throughout the world learn about the discovery and follow the excavation process. To Carter's dismay, tourists began to travel to the site and photographed the excavation, sometimes defacing objects. The quality and number of artifacts were astounding. The Egyptians believed that people should be buried with items they would need for the next life. For a king, the list was extensive and items had to be of the same quality the rulers were accustomed to when they were alive. Therefore, in addition to Tutankhamun's gilded coffins and shrines, the tomb contained furniture, jewelry, clothing, weapons, games, musical instruments, glass, guardian statues, wine jars, pottery, oil lamps, cosmetics, and food.

Colors, materials, motifs, patterns, and textures that were discovered had an influence on interior designers, architects, and fashion. These elements served as inspiration for designing textiles, wall coverings, furniture, and decorative arts. Inspirational colors included lapis blue, gold, turquoise blue, black, and sienna brown. Popular motifs, such as the falcon and cobra, were often derived from the frequently published photograph of Tutankhamun's gold death mask. One of the most striking designs was the striped nemes headdress made from bright gold and the dark blue lapis stone. Other attractive motifs were lotus flowers, beetles, ankhs, scarabs, solar disks, sunrays, and the two

Figure 4.5 The floor plan of Tutankhamun's tomb consisted of an antechamber, annex, and the burial chamber that was connected to a Treasury. The first two doorways had been opened and objects in the first room, the antechamber (shown above), were in disarray.

Source: © François Guenet/Art Resource, NY.

Figure 4.6 King's Golden Throne is made from wood with an overlay of sheet gold and silver. The inlays consist of faience, colored glass, and semiprecious stones.

Source: © François Guenet/Art Resource, NY.

implements held in the king's hands: a crook and flail. The crook represented the king's role as the shepherd of the flock, and the flail signified strength.

Figure 4.5 illustrates many of the furniture pieces found in the tomb, including three ritual couches, the king's childhood chair, chests, and stools. The gilded ritual couches had animal sides resting on a rectangular wooden stand. The curved beds had footboards between the tails of the animals, and separate gilded headrests were positioned between the animal's heads. Each couch featured a different animal. The couch on the left in Figure 4.5 is similar to the goddess Ammut (devourer of the dead), with the head of a hippopotamus, sides of a crocodile, and legs and paws of a lion. The gilded middle couch is Mehetweret, a cow goddess with a pattern made of **trefoils** of dark blue glass. The third couch is believed to be the lioness goddess, Sekhmet. Contrasting blue and black glass used for its eyes, "tears," and nose highlights the gilded finish.

Located under the lioness couch is the ebony wood child's chair made with inlaid ivory and gilded panels on each side of the armrest. The lion paw legs have ivory claws and rest on wooden drums. The ebony wood stool also has inlaid ivory in a faux leopard pattern (see Figure 4.5). The crossed legs terminate in carved heads

of ducks. Under the Ammut couch is the King's Golden Throne, which is made from wood with an overlay of sheet gold and silver (Figure 4.6). The inlays consist of **faience,** colored glass, and semi-precious stones. The scene on the back of the chair depicts Ankhesenamun, the king's wife, rubbing perfume on his left arm while the intense rays of sunlight shine on their union. The pierced armrest panels are filled with the open wings of cobras. Other objects to look for in Figure 4.5 are several alabaster perfume vases, a wooden box with a panel of faience inlay, chairs, chests, a bed, stools, and food baskets. Many of the attributes of these objects, such as inlaid ivory, lion paw legs, and colored glass, were reinterpreted in the 1920s interiors designed by Art Deco designers, including Jean Dunand, Paul Poiret, Armand-Albert Rateau, and Jacques-Émile Ruhlmann.

Natural Disasters and Mount Fujiyama (Fuji): The Imperial Hotel (1915–1922) in Tokyo, Japan, by Frank Lloyd Wright (Demolished 1968)

While the world was mesmerized by the unveiling of Tutankhamun's treasures, the Kantō (Kwanto) region of Japan was experiencing one of the worst earthquakes of the 20th century. On September 1, 1923, an earthquake erupted beneath the populous cities of Tokyo and Yokohama. Registering 7.9 on the Richter scale, the quake triggered a series of natural disasters that included countless simultaneous fires, firestorms, cyclones, tsunamis, and landslides. The widespread devastation resulted in the deaths of 142,800 people, and thousands more were injured. More than three million people were left homeless. The worst devastation occurred in Yokohama, where approximately 86 percent of homes suffered damage. Tokyo's losses were also significant, exceeding 70 percent. Similar to the situation in San Francisco's 1906 earthquake, fires caused most of the damage. However, many of the fires that erupted in Japan were started by small hibachis people were using at the time to prepare lunch (the earthquake occurred at noon). Hot coals flew from the open-fire stoves and quickly ignited the small wood kitchens. Spurting gas lines, highly dense urban areas, wooden structures, very few grassy areas, and industrial chemicals created the ideal formula for rapid firestorms. Broken water mains prevented firefighting success. Fire prevention and rescue activities were further curtailed by the destruction of roads, railroads, and streetcars and damage to and destruction of electric, telephone, and telegraph lines.

On September 1, 1923, the opening day of the Imperial Hotel, the building withstood damage from the Kanto earthquake and extensive fires. The chairperson of the Imperial Hotel sent a telegram to the architect and designer Frank Lloyd Wright on September 13, 1923: "FOLLOWING WIRELESS RECEIVED FROM TOKIO [sic] TODAY HOTEL STANDS UNDAMAGED AS MONUMENT OF YOUR GENIUS HUNDREDS OF HOMELESS PROVIDED BY PERFECTLY MAINTAINED SERVICE CONGRATULATIONS SIGNED OKURA IMPHEO" (James, 1968, p. 45).

Japan is located in a region of the world with significant geological movements. As a result of the shifting, Japan experiences numerous earthquakes every year and is highly susceptible to volcanic eruptions. Frank Lloyd Wright was very much aware of these conditions when he was commissioned to design the Imperial Hotel (Figure 4.7). In addition to knowing the volatile nature of Japan's earthquakes, Wright was also familiar with the horrific fires that accompany eruptions of the earth as well as intentional acts by humans. In 1914, an employee set fire to Wright's home, Taliesin, in Spring Green, Wisconsin. At the time of this fire, Wright was working on early sketches of the Imperial Hotel. After the fire, Wright revised the design and created a structure that was more resistant to being destroyed by fire. Perhaps remembering the tragedy at Taliesin, Wright describes nature's forces: "The dreaded force that made the great mountain takes it toll of life from this devoted people. . . . Whole villages disappear. New islands appear as others are lost and all on them. Shores are reversed as mountains are laid low and valleys lifted up. Always flames! The terror of it all faces configuration at the end" (James, 1968, p. 35).

The Imperial Hotel in Tokyo was originally constructed by German architects in 1890. In the quest to

Figure 4.7 Wright's presentation drawing of his design for the Imperial Hotel in Tokyo.
Source: © The Frank Lloyd Wright Foundation, AZ/Art Resource, NY.

modernize and Westernize Japan during and after the Meiji Dynasty (1868–1912), it was determined that the Imperial Hotel should be updated and enlarged. The hotel was located close to the Imperial Palace and used by Western government officials, business leaders, and important foreign visitors. The idea behind the renovation of the hotel was that a new, modern hotel would demonstrate to the world Japan's progressiveness and the viability of investing in Japanese industries. Wright, a long-time admirer of Japanese art and architecture, intended to design a hotel that was modern but also conveyed respect for Japan's culture heritage, including Mount Fujiyama (Fuji). He explained his thoughts: "Japanese fine-art traditions are among the noblest and purest in the world, giving Chinese origins due credit. It was my instinct not to insult them. The West has much to learn from the East—and Japan was the gateway to that great East of which I had been dreaming since I had seen my first Japanese prints—and read my first Laotze" (James, 1968, p. 36).

In addition to commemorating Japanese artistic traditions, Wright focused on the "sacred" mountain of "old Japan": Mount Fuji. "From infancy, a sort of subjective contemplation, minds and hearts of Japanese are fixed upon the great calm mountain God of their nation—sacred Fujiyama brooding in majesty and eternal calm over all" (James, 1968, p. 35). As the dominant backdrop for Tokyo and the Imperial Hotel, Mount Fuji's profile inspired the design of the hotel, and the volcano's eruptive forces provided the rationale for constructing a building that could withstand nature's most devastating attacks.

In considering Mount Fuji, earthquakes, and fires, Wright designed the Imperial Hotel with several engineering features that prevented its destruction during a mild earthquake that occurred during construction—as well as the deadly 1923 earthquake. Wright at first conceptualized the hotel as a modern "steamship," but after the Taliesin tragedy, the design became a "battleship." The idea of a boat floating on water was critical to designing a structure that would withstand the violent motion of an earthquake. Wright worked with engineers to design a shallow foundation that would float on the area's muddy soil. Thus, during an earthquake the building would fluctuate with the rise and fall of the earth rather than resist the forces. To enhance the building's flexibility, Wright divided the structure into parts and designed a cantilever balancing system that supported floors in a manner similar to the way "a waiter carries his tray" with his arm and fingers. Wright specified a light copper roof as a way to reduce the hazards associated with falling heavy roof tiles. Using oya, a local lightweight volcanic stone, Wright reduced the overall weight of the structure. Oya and bricks were also excellent fireproofing materials. Wright was adamant that late cost-cutting measures, due to the project's escalating expenses, would not eliminate the large pool of water in the front of the hotel, which was an excellent resource for fighting fires.

In addition to engineering a structure that could "battle" nature, Wright's design integrated Eastern and Western perspectives. For example, he substituted modern concrete crafted using local techniques for the wood that had been used in Japan's time-honored tradition of timber framing and bracketing (Figure 4.8). During construction, Wright worked with local craftsmen and attempted, unsuccessfully, to provide them with exact masonry methods. He therefore relinquished to the experts and proclaimed, "How skillful they were! What craftsmen! So instead of wasting them by vainly trying to make them come our way—we went with them their way" (James, 1968).

Guest and public rooms faced beautiful Japanese gardens, which were sunken, terraced, or located on the roof (see Figure 4.8). Similar to Japanese dwellings, the hotel's guest rooms were simple and compact and had low ceilings. Public areas, such as the lobby, main dining room, promenade, and parlor, featured tall ceilings resembling Mount Fuji's profile. Furniture such as dining chairs and tables was Western in design, but Japanese influences were evident in the light fixtures

Figure 4.8 At the Imperial Hotel in Tokyo, guest and public rooms faced beautiful Japanese gardens that were either sunken, terraced, or on the roof. As with Japanese dwellings, the hotel's guest rooms were simple, compact, and had low ceilings.

Source: © The Frank Lloyd Wright Foundation, AZ/ Art Resource, NY.

and textile patterns. Wright contended that a building's worst enemy was an earthquake. The Imperial Hotel won the battle in 1923; however, the building was torn down in 1968 to make room for a new hotel.

GLOBAL TECHNOLOGICAL DEVELOPMENTS

As mentioned previously, people and governments focused on recovering from World War I during the early part of the 1920s. The hard economic times, hyper-inflation, famine, material shortages, and destruction of homes, schools, factories, and communities primarily in Europe made it difficult to develop new technologies. However, many of these conditions provided the incentive to find solutions for constructing dwellings quickly, economically, and with minimum resources. Using the automobile as an example, many people were convinced that building millions of homes required industrial production techniques. The automobile industry in the United States had become enormously successful by using Henry Ford's mass-production

processes. Mechanizing the production of automobiles resulted in large quantities and low prices. World War I especially devastated Europe; thus, it was the location of intensely focused affordable-housing initiatives.

Technologies and Industrialization: The Bauhaus (1919–1933) in Weimar, Dessau, and Berlin, Germany

After its defeat, Germany was in severe need of materials, resources, and shelter for its people. Prior to the war, architects such as Bruno Taut, Walter Gropius, Ludwig Mies van der Rohe, and Gerrit Rietveld had already begun to conceptualize modern architecture for the new age. Throughout his career, the German architect Walter Gropius contended that prefabrication using industrial production was the solution for building large quantities of dwellings at reasonable prices. At the beginning of the 1920s, houses were constructed by hand, which was prohibitively expensive for most people. The solution had to be components that could be mass-produced at a factory and then assembled on the construction site. As an example of the feasibility of prefabrication, Gropius often noted houses that could be purchased in Sears catalogues. He contended that standardized components were aesthetically pleasing, and their inter-changeable attributes enabled people to choose from a variety of plans. To demonstrate these criteria and to meet societal needs, Gropius designed several housing developments, including the 60-unit Dammerstock housing project (1927–1928) near Törten (1926–1929) and the Am Weissenhof development in 1927 (Figure 4.9). In the later years of Gropius's career, he wrote a letter to the *New York Times* that defended prefabrication, stating

> *The true aim of prefabrication is certainly not the dull multiplication of a house type ad infinitum: men will always rebel against attempts at over-mechanization which is contrary to life. But industrialization will not stop at the threshold of building. We have no other choice but to accept the challenge of the machine in all fields of production until men finally adapt it fully to serve their biological needs. . . . Prefabrication, as a logical progressive process, aimed at raising the standards of building, will finally lead to higher quality for lower prices. . . . Prefabrication will thus become a vital instrument to solve the housing problem economically. (Gropius, 1947)*

Gropius's letter to the *Times* demonstrates many principles that he applied to his architectural practice and to the founding of the German design school the Bauhaus (House of Building) in 1919. As noted in previous chapters, interior designers and architects working at the end of the 19th and beginning of the 20th centuries grappled with understanding how to mechanize creative endeavors. Gropius believed there was "no other choice"; therefore designers had to identify the best ways to use mechanization within aesthetic ideals. This premise formed the foundation for the Bauhaus: "The Bauhaus believes the machine to be our modern medium of design and seeks to come to terms with it" (Bayer, Gropius, W., & Gropius, I., 1938, p. 27). To "come to terms" with machines, Gropius created a plan that involved the merger of two institutions located in Weimar, the Grand-Ducal Saxon Academy of Fine Art, and the Grand-Ducal Saxon School of Arts and Crafts. These two academies became the Bauhaus, Weimar, and its first manifesto proclaimed, "The complete building is the final aim of the visual arts" (Bayer, Gropius, W., & Gropius, I., 1938, p. 18).

Gropius's understanding of industrialization styles and processes resulted from his work as an assistant to Peter Behrens on the AEG Building in Berlin (1910) (see Chapter 2). In private practice, Gropius and Adolf Meyer designed the extremely influential Fagus Works (Faguswerk) Shoe Last factory (1911–1913) in Alfeld-an-der-Leine. Faguswerk demonstrated the potential for integrating contemporary design with industrialization. As the Bauhaus's first director, Gropius was responsible for hiring "masters" (faculty) and for developing the curriculum.

Figure 4.9 Gropius designed several housing developments, including the Am Weissenhof development in 1927.
Source: Getty Images.

The list of talented artists and architects was extraordinary and included Josef Albers, Marcel Breuer, Johannes Itten, Wassily Kandinsky, Paul Klee, László Moholy-Nagy, and Oskar Schlemmer. Curriculum started with *Vorkurs*, a preliminary 6-month course that emphasized creativity, natural materials, and understanding form. The course description read, "Elementary instruction in form together with exercises in materials, in the special workshop for the preliminary course. Result: admission as apprentice to a workshop" (Dearstyne, 1986, p. 85). The "apprentice to a workshop" phase of the program involved 3 years of learning a craft from two masters: an artist and a craftsman. Workshops included furniture, pottery, print, weaving, stained glass, wall painting, sculpture, theater, and metal. The purpose of the workshop was to understand how to design aesthetically pleasing functional objects and the mass-production processes necessary to produce the item. For example, in a similar manner demonstrated by Behrens's electric kettle (see Chapter 2), in the pottery workshop students designed a teapot for mass-production that had only six major parts. A minimal number of parts helped to facilitate mass-production processes and made it easy to manufacture different versions of the same teapot. The workshop also developed methods to mechanize traditional hand-woven textiles. Upon successful completion of the workshop courses and apprenticeship, students had to pass the journeyman's certificate. At this stage the students had merely *qualified* for training in architecture and the technologies of mass-production. To complete the degree, students had to be accepted into the final phase of the curriculum.

Continuous conflicts between the conservative Weimar community and the Bauhaus resulted in Gropius moving the school to Dessau in 1925. The Bauhaus was enthusiastically welcomed to Dessau, which was evident by the city's purchase of land for the school's facilities. Gropius designed the internationally recognized Bauhaus buildings (1925–1926) (Figure 4.10), including workshops, studios, classrooms, a technical school, an auditorium, and a dining hall (Figure 4.11).

He also designed residences for the director, masters, and students. Gropius designed the asymmetrical buildings in the modern industrial style using steel, concrete, large spans of glass, flat roofs, and sparse interiors. Many of the interior furnishings—such as the wall paintings, electrical fixtures, and furniture—were designed and made in the Bauhaus workshops. Gropius resigned as the director of the Bauhaus in 1928 to return to practice privately as an architect in Berlin, and Hannes Meyer

Figure 4.10 Model of the Bauhaus (1925–1926) in Dessau, Germany.
Source: Foto Marburg/Art Resource, NY.

Figure 4.11 The third floor lobby of the Technical School Wing (1926–1927) with Marcel Breuer's Wassily chair (1925). Gropius designed the internationally recognized Bauhaus buildings (1925–1926), including workshops, studios, classrooms, a technical school, an auditorium, and a dining hall.
Source: Vanni/Art Resource, NY.

resumed the role until 1930, when the mayor of Dessau dismissed Meyer from the position. Upon recommendation from Gropius, Ludwig Mies van der Rohe was appointed the last director of the Bauhaus. In 1932 the Nazi party had a majority in Dessau and cut off financial support for the Bauhaus, forcing Mies van der Rohe to close the school and move the school to Berlin to establish the new, private Bauhaus. In 1933, the Berlin police closed the school under orders from the new Nazi government. However, the short 14 years in existence had a profound impact on modern architecture and initiated the **International Style.**

Technologies and Industrialization: Marcel Lajos Breuer and Tubular Steel

Marcel Breuer, a Hungarian, was extensively involved with the Bauhaus. At the age of 18, Breuer was one of the first students of the school. Soon he became an instructor of the *Vorkurs* and ultimately he was a master in the furniture workshop. Breuer was an architect and furniture designer, but his fame is derived from his genius in inventing and developing tubular steel furniture. Tubular steel was invented during the late 19th century, but initially people believed that the cold, hard material was only appropriate for industrial or mechanical purposes.

In the mid-1920s, Breuer noticed the soft curves of tubular steel used for the handlebars on bicycles and was inspired to use the material for furniture. He found that it was perfect for modern interiors; the thin steel tubes could give the appearance that the furniture piece was floating on air, yet the material could provide the strength to allow people to sit on a chair without the traditional support of four legs. Substituting metal for wood was ideal for promoting an industrial appearance and shedding "old" furniture construction materials and joineries. The shiny finish invited viewers to trace the curves with their eyes. This sense of movement gave the impression that the tubular steel was one continuous piece, and it reinforced the overall form of the chair in a person's mind.

As a derivative of the industrial setting, tubular steel was also easy to manufacture in quantities using mass-production processes. Thonet had already formulated the principle of bending a material to create furniture in the 19th century (see Chapter 1). Therefore, in the furniture workshop of the Bauhaus, Breuer was able to develop the prototypes for mass-produced tubular steel furniture. To create the desirable shiny finish, many of the original furniture pieces were nickel-plated, but items were subsequently made with chrome plating. Based on earlier experiments with wood and stretched fabric, Breuer had already discovered that he could create comfortable seating without the bulk of springs or heavy fabric. As another modern statement, chairs had minimum amounts of fabric (black leather was the most popular) (see Figure 4.11). Tables and stools were designed with the same machine aesthetics. For example, Breuer's classical nesting stools were made from two pieces of tubular steel and a wooden seat painted black.

Other important modern characteristics of tubular steel furniture were its small scale, light weight, ease of assembly, and ability to fold into a compact size. As an aftermath of the war, interior designers and architects were advocating for smaller spaces; thus, lightweight tubular steel furniture enabled people to easily move furniture throughout a building, and when necessary the piece could be folded or nested. The tubular steel chairs Breuer designed for the Bauhaus Theatre were actually attached to the floor, but when the seat flipped up, the entire area in front of the chair was clear. He also was known for designing storage units that were either built-in or freestanding cabinets, other methods of conserving space. To facilitate mass-production processes for the cabinetry, Breuer created a standardization system that involved cabinet sizes in 13-inch (33-centimeter) increments.

Tubular steel was imperative to construct the cantilever chair. Using tubular steel to "float" a chair was a perfect reflection of how designers envisioned modern furniture. As illustrated in Figure 4.12, Breuer

Figure 4.12 Breuer merged the resilient properties of tubular steel with beechwood and cane to create the ubiquitous Cesca (B-33) chair (1928).

Source: Digital Image © The Museum of Modern Art/Licensed by SCALA/Art Resource, NY.

merged the resilient properties of tubular steel with beechwood and cane to create the ubiquitous Cesca chair. Named after his daughter, Francesca, the chair is a modern classic, but there is controversy regarding the first person to create the steel cantilevered chair. Several architects and furniture designers, including Mart Stam from the Netherlands, Breuer, and Mies van der Rohe, were developing the design concurrently and were seeking patents. The first displays of the cantilever chair in public were at the 1927 Am Weissenhof Housing Exhibition in Stuttgart (see Figure 4.9). The rightful owner of the patent had the potential for significant financial compensation because there was a demand for modern furniture in industrial and commercial interiors. Traditional wood furniture, which was associated with handicrafts, was not viewed as appropriate in modern interiors. Therefore, modern interiors were photographed with either no furniture or very few pieces. At this same time, furniture designers started to name their furniture after themselves, such as MR-10 (Mies), B-33 (Breuer), and S-33

(Stam). Eventually, Breuer and many other designers contracted with Thonet to manufacture their tubular steel furniture. Concerns regarding patent rights were accurate; many of the tubular steel chairs, including the cantilevered versions, have become modern classics with multimillion-dollar international sales over the years.

GLOBAL LIFE AND WORK STYLES

The destructive forces of World War I and the depletion of building materials and labor precipitated a considerable housing shortage in the warring countries, except for the United States and Japan. Before the war, socially conscious interior designers and architects were already concerned about how to design housing for those with low incomes. The dire situation following the war escalated housing programs, most notably with government-sponsored initiatives. In contrast to the housing shortage during this same period, people who had profited from the war and the new generation of industrial wealth were interested in luxurious living standards. These were many of the individuals who were attracted to the stylish glamour of Art Deco or the very modern International Style.

The "Esprit-Nouveau": Le Corbusier in the 1920s

The war obviously changed life and work styles in Western Europe. The destruction demanded new housing that was built quickly and inexpensively. The only way to accomplish this was to apply successful industrial production processes to housing. Mass housing was desperately needed near employment opportunities in urban settings. Architects and interior designers had to respond to the changes in life and work styles by identifying solutions for mass-produced housing. Throughout his long career, Le Corbusier, the Swiss-born architect (and eventual French citizen), focused on identifying societal solutions for housing large numbers of people (Figure 4.13). Born Charles-Édouard Jeanneret-Gris, who later changed his name to Le Corbusier, as noted below, was a strong advocate for mass-produced housing. He expressed many of his views in writing. Le Corbusier (also known as "Corbu") was a prolific writer and wrote numerous books and articles on architecture, interior environments, furniture, fine arts, and city planning. Several articles that he wrote for the journal *L'Esprit Nouveau* were reprinted in his famous and extremely influential 1923 book, *Vers une Architecture* (*Towards a New Architecture*). Corbu addressed mass-produced housing in his writings, stating, "A great epoch has begun. There exists a new spirit [Esprit-Nouveau]. . . . Mass-production is based on analysis and experiment. Industry on the grand scale must occupy itself with building and establish the elements of the house on a mass-production basis. We must create the mass-production spirit. The spirit of constructing mass-production houses. The spirit of living in mass-production houses. The spirit of conceiving mass-production houses" (Le Corbusier, 1923; translation 1927, p. 210).

Corbu designed numerous examples of mass-produced houses in a variety of styles, sizes, settings, and price ranges. Many of these buildings were designed with his cousin, Pierre Jeanneret. Critical features of the designs were standardization and the use of reinforced concrete. Corbu contended that doors, cupboards, and windows could be mass produced in modular units or standard sizes. Mass-produced units would reduce costs, and the modules would ensure that "good proportion is assured automatically."

To expedite construction, Corbu suggested that a house could be finished in 3 days by pouring concrete "from above as you would fill a bottle." The village of Pessac, near Bordeaux in France, provided Corbu and Jeanneret with one of the first opportunities to design standardized houses that could be built quickly (see Figure 4.13). Approximately 50 houses were built in less than 1 year (1925–1926) by employing standardized "cells," or cubes, and reinforced concrete. Standard cells were combined to create the multilevel units complete with terraces, gardens, and patios. Unfortunately, due to opposition from local authorities who did not appreciate Corbu's nontraditional designs, occupancy permits were not granted until 3 years after the buildings were completed.

The cube and designs for mass-production became familiar elements in Le Corbusier's architecture. The world was directly introduced to Corbu's theories at the 1925 Exposition Internationale des Arts Décoratifs

Figure 4.13 Le Corbusier was always focused on identifying societal solutions for housing large numbers of people. The Village of Pessac, near Bordeaux in France, provided Corbu and Jeanneret with one of the first opportunities to design standardized houses that could be built quickly.
Source: © FLC/ARS, 2009.

et Industriels Modernes in Paris. Corbu had difficulty getting his avant-garde project accepted for exhibition, and judges denounced his work as not being "architecture." In retrospect, Corbu and Jeanneret's exhibit, the Pavillon de L'Esprit Nouveau, influenced countless architects who attended the Exposition and, as described below, contributed to the development of the modern International Style (Figure 4.14).

The Pavillon was a prototype for standardized mass-produced housing that could be constructed with steel and reinforced concrete. Its single "cell-unit" and its roof-terrace could become "multiple villa-flats." The cell-unit was connected to an annex that was used to display two large dioramas of urban planning studies, the 1922 "Plan for a Modern City of 3,000,000 Inhabitants" and the "Voisin Plan," a conceptualization for a new business center in Paris. The cell-unit's living room with a two-story height and balcony became a common feature in the architect's private residences (Figure 4.15). To create a "modern interior," Corbu and Jeanneret eliminated traditional wood furniture and replaced the "fossilized" pieces with metal equipment that was built in, including wardrobes, cupboards, and shelves. Modern equipment would help to eliminate clutter and all of the unnecessary furniture that often fulfilled only a single purpose. The only pieces needed in a modern interior in addition to what was present in the Pavillon were artwork, tables, and chairs. Paintings in the Pavillon were by Corbu and Fernand Léger. The only chairs were the leather club chair and Thonet's bentwood no. 9 with wickerwork seats. Soon after the Exhibition, Corbu's interiors included tubular steel chairs and chaises.

Beginning in 1925, Corbu, Jeanneret, and Charlotte Perriand created several iconic modern furniture designs and displayed them in the 1929 Salon d'Automne in Paris. Their "Interior Equipment of the Dwelling" included the LC4 Chaise-longue (1925–1928); an armchair with a pivoting back, B301 Basculant (1928); and the cube-shaped club chair, LC2 Gran Confort (1928).

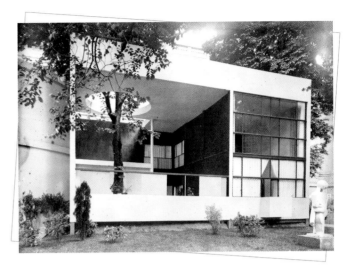

Figure 4.14 Corbu and Jeanneret's exhibit, the Pavillon de L'Esprit Nouveau, influenced countless architects and contributed to the development of the modern International Style.
Source: © FLC/ARS, 2009.

Figure 4.15 The Pavillon de L'Esprit Nouveau's cell-unit was connected to an annex that was used to display two large dioramas of urban planning studies. The cell-unit's living room with a two-story height and balcony became a common feature in Corbu's private residences.
Source: Photo Les Arts Décoratifs, Paris/Editions Albert Lévy.

These "equipments" of tubular steel and leather are still manufactured today. The Gran Confort style is available in a sofa version and the smaller chair, Petit Confort.

Corbu continued his manifesto in *Vers une Architecture* by suggesting, "If we eliminate from our hearts and minds all dead concepts in regard to houses and look at

Figure 4.16 In collaboration with Pierre Jeanneret, Le Corbusier demonstrated the "Five Points" in their masterpiece of modern architecture, Villa Savoye (1928–1931) in Poissy, northwest of Paris.

Source: Anthony Scibilia/Art Resource, NY.

the question from a critical and objective point of view, we shall arrive at the 'House-Machine,' the mass-production house, healthy (and morally so too) and beautiful in the same way that the working tools and instruments which accompany our existence are beautiful. Beautiful also with all the animation that the artist's sensibility can add to severe and pure functioning elements" (Le Corbusier, 1923; translation 1927, p. 210).

References to the "House-Machine" often have been abbreviated to Le Corbusier's famous quote, "The house is a machine for living in." Out of context, it can appear that Corbu was suggesting that houses should be like a machine, cold and unemotional. But considering Corbu's words and explanations, it is apparent that he marveled at the beauty of mass-produced technologies. For example, in *Vers une Architecture*, three chapters are dedicated to the designs of "Liners" (ocean liners), "Airplanes," and "Automobiles." His intent is for designers to analyze the beauty of their mechanized designs and to apply their minimalist principles to houses. Critical to his appreciation of these "machines" was their functionality and the elimination of superfluous ornamentation or space. For example, in the book, a caption for a photograph of an ocean liner's promenade reads, "Architecture pure, neat, clear, clean, and healthy. Contrast with this our carpets, cushions, canopies, wall-papers, carved and gilt furniture, faded

or 'arty' colours [*sic*]: the dismalness of our Western bazaar" (Le Corbusier, 1923; translation 1927, p. 94).

Le Corbusier's minimalist perspectives are reinforced in his renowned philosophy, reflected in his *Five Points of a New Architecture*: (1) placing the house on *les pilotis* (columns), (2) *les toites-jardins* (roof gardens), (3) *le plan libre* (the open or free plan), (4) *la fenêtre en longueur* (the long or strip window), and (5) *la façade libre* (the free or plain façade). In collaboration with Jeanneret, Le Corbusier demonstrated his genius and the "Five Points" in their masterpiece of modern architecture, Villa Savoye (1928–1931) in Poissy, northwest of Paris (Figure 4.16).

The architecture responds to the needs of its inhabitants by efficiently providing healthy sunlight, fresh air, views of the countryside, and immediate connections with nature via sliding glass walls and rooftop terraces. A tiled, deep bathtub adjoined with a reclining surface emphasizes hygiene and relaxation. To accommodate the needs of the modern lifestyle, Villa Savoye has a garage for three automobiles, the *new* form of transportation. In addition to the sculptural spiral staircase, Corbu included ramps that progress from the ground level all the way to the second-level roof terrace. Ramps tend to have a calming effect as one casually ascends the incline, and the gradual movement provides adequate time to appreciate and absorb the surrounding countryside. The architecture expresses a perfect "interplay of light and shade," and the principle of proportion is flawlessly applied to its elements.

Fashion: Parisian Art Deco

Le Corbusier's Pavillon de L'Esprit Nouveau did not receive positive reviews at the 1925 Exposition Internationale des Arts Décoratifs et Industriels Modernes, but Hôtel du Collectionneur, a residential design by Jacques-Émile Ruhlmann, was an enormous success (Figure 4.17). Ruhlmann's Hôtel du Collectionneur became one of the defining characteristics for Parisian Art Deco. Subsequently, part of the name of the exposition, Internationale des Arts Décoratifs (Art Deco), was used as the name for the style. Ruhlmann's Art Deco

Figure 4.17 Hôtel du Collectionneur designed by Jacques-Émile Ruhlmann became many of the defining characteristics for Parisian Art Deco.

Source: © Ministère de la Culture/Médiathèque du Patrimoine, Dist. RMN/Art Resource, NY.

interior had luxurious and exotic furniture, objects d'art, and rich materials, such as silk damask and ivory.

Parisians' enthusiasm for glamorous couture and interiors was cultivated prior to World War I, but the war had suspended its development. Paris's 1925 Exhibition was the perfect arena to internationally demonstrate that the city was once again the world's premier leader in design. Art Nouveau had been an influential style with origins in Paris, but interest in the style waned during and immediately following the war. Parisian couture was a source of inspiration for the city to once again be the world center for modern interiors. Paris's leadership in fashion began before the war, transcended through the battle years, and was reconfirmed in the 1920s. As discussed below, the career of a Parisian couturier, Paul Poiret, provides an outstanding example of the connectedness between couture and interior design and how prevailing fashions can influence interior environments and architecture.

Poiret is renowned for designing the "modern" dress and for creating the contemporary fashion industry. Known in the United States as the "king of fashion," Poiret became famous for eliminating corsets, petticoats, and bustles. In contrast to the antiquated, restricting styles, Poiret's dresses and gowns were draped over women's bodies. His momentous couture designs, "lampshade" tunics, and "harem" trousers were inspired by Léon Bakst's costumes for the Ballets Russes performance of *Schéhérazade* (see Chapter 3).

Poiret was brilliant at promoting his fashions by hiring artists to draw illustrations for advertisements in the leading Parisian magazines. To create stunning advertisements, Paul Iribe and Georges Lepape used the time-consuming stenciling and hand-coloring process *pochoir*. The illustrations were elegant, featured vibrant colors, and resembled the techniques used to create the popular Japanese woodblock prints (see Chapter 1). Some of the illustrations blended Poiret's couture with "modern" interiors with elegant Classical style furniture (Figure 4.18). To experiment with avant-garde couture,

Poiret designed costumes for the stage. This exposure and reactions from the audience provided Poiret with immediate feedback from the public at a minimal cost.

Poiret's interest in advocating designs for a "total lifestyle" was brought to fruition by the opening of his perfumery, Les Parfums de Rosine, and his interior design business, Martine, established in 1911. Both businesses were named after Poiret's daughters. Les Parfums de Rosine was the first time a couturier had formed the relationship between perfume and couture. Martine comprised three different but interrelated activities. École Martine was an art school for young students. Les Ateliers de Atelier Martine was a design studio that created a wide range of interior furnishings, such as furniture, lighting, wallpaper, and textiles. Furnishings from Atelier Martine were sold in La Maison Martine. La Maison Martine also offered interior design services. To promote Martine's products and services, Poiret had an exhibit at the 1925 Internationale des Arts Décoratifs Exposition. He decorated three river barges that were floating on the Seine River. The *Amour* barge featured the work of La Maison Martine, *Délice* promoted Rosine's perfumes, and *Orgue* was the boat featuring parties and entertainment.

Poiret's chic fashions and interiors helped fuel a fascination with luxurious modern Parisian residences because people wanted their interiors to harmonize with what they were wearing. Rhulmann responded to the demands by designing furniture and interiors that were exotic, were very expensive, and promoted a self-indulgent lifestyle. Couture influences become apparent when analyzing Poiret's dresses and gowns and Rhulmann's interior environments. Both designers were extremely influenced by the exoticism and daring, vivid colors displayed in Ballets Russes performances. For example, couture and interiors had heaps of pillows, draped fabrics, and dramatic colors, such as vibrant yellow, royal blue, and blood red.

Poiret and Rhulmann used similar motifs and decorative materials, such as pebbles, stylized roses, swirls, fur, and silk tassels. Poiret's use of expensive materials for fashion—such as handmade lace, sequins, lead-crystal rhinestones, and silk—translated into Rhulmann's interiors with the use of expensive exotic woods, marquetry, and silk damask wallcoverings. As with Poiret's Bataille evening dress, for emphasis Rhulmann contrasted colors with black (Figure 4.19). Rhulmann's dark color came from exotic woods, including American bur walnut, bur Amboina-wood, macassar ebony, amaranth, and rosewood. Decorative inlays of ivory contrasted with the dark wood. The ivory motifs were spirals, thin **fillets,** diamond-shapes, flowers, **dentils,** and "pearls." Rhulmann often used an inlay "strand" of small circular ivory "pearls" to decorate surfaces. Poiret designed evening dresses with embroidered pearls, and a frequent couture accessory was a long strand of pearls.

Rhulmann's fame was derived from his Art Deco designs for private residences. An extraordinary number of sketches and notes accompanied projects,

Figure 4.18 Some of Poiret's illustrations blended his couture with "modern" interiors and elegant Classical furniture.

Source: The Metropolitan Museum of Art, The Irene Lewisohn Costume Reference Library, Special Collections, Image © The Metropolitan Museum of Art.

Figure 4.19 Bataille evening dress (1925). Couture influences become apparent when analyzing Poiret's dresses and gowns, and Rhulmann's interior environments.

Source: Courtesy of Sandy Schreir; Image © The Metropolitan Museum of Art.

wrought-iron banisters. Fashionable motifs included stylized flowers, leaves, arabesques, sunbursts, and zigzags. Dark furniture, sometimes covered with fur, contrasted with light-colored damask silk wallcoverings. Materials for objects d'art were engraved frosted glass, enamels, lacquered boxes, silver-chrome frames, and cheval mirrors.

In addition to luxurious materials, Rhulmann dictated a self-indulgent lifestyle by including several superfluous rooms, each with a separate passageway. Bedrooms had a boudoir and a lounge, and other rooms had antechambers. Rhulmann designed impeccable handcrafted furniture for the entire residences of wealthy clients. The wide variety of furniture also revealed a focus on excess: make-up cabinets, **chiffoniers, divans** (day-bed, canapé), dressing tables, tripod tables, and "drinks" cabinets. Often furniture doors closed with octagonal lock plates with a silver-chrome finish. Rhulmann became well known for his fluted details, elephant armchairs, and tapered **fuseau** legs with ivory **sabots.** In contrast to typical streamlined, machine-like Art Deco materials, Rhulmann used **shagreen,** rough leather, and lacquer.

including his correspondence with clients. Rhulmann was a perfectionist and specified every detail in a furniture piece, inlay, light fixture, or textile. The Hôtel du Collectionneur is an excellent illustration of his design expertise (see Figure 4.17). Rhulmann designed the architecture, decoration, furniture, and objects d'art. The Hôtel had a round and an oval-shaped room, shedding the typical square or rectangular-shaped plan. Large rooms had a peristyle with **fluted** pillars and **coffered ceilings.** Lighting was derived from crystal chandeliers and "wall-lights" (fixtures mounted on the walls) and was concealed behind cornices. Frescoes of elongated naked women covered walls. Marble was used in bathrooms and steps. Stairways were ornamented with

GLOBAL VISUAL AND PERFORMING ARTS

The designs of Western interiors in the 1920s were derived from the boldness of the Ballets Russes, Cubism, and art from "exotic" locations, including Japan and Africa. As illustrated with Rhulmann's furniture, the use of contrasting colors and materials to emphasize ornamental motifs was considered an avant-garde statement. To create exquisitely handcrafted furniture, Rhulmann hired individuals with the skills of an 18th-century **ebéniste,** or master cabinetmaker. However, during this same period, the Asian art of **lacquer** was revitalized due to its shiny finish and its ability to contrast colors with black. Rhulmann designed some lacquer for his interiors, but other designers who specified lacquer pieces mastered the art themselves. Eileen Gray and Jean Dunand were renowned for their lacquer furniture and objects d'art. These two, and many other architects and interior designers, were influenced by the flatness and two-dimensional abstraction of Cubism. Cubism is believed to have started with Picasso's *Les Demoiselles d'Avignon* (1907). However, the public did not view Picasso's painting until 1916 when it was displayed at Paul Poiret's Galerie Barbazanges, a commercial gallery located on the premises of Poiret's couture house. As reflected in the De Stijl style, architects and interior designers were still inspired by the modern geometry and primary colors of Cubism.

Visual Arts: Lacquer—Eileen Gray and Jean Dunand

Lacquer is an Asian art with origins in China, but many countries, including Japan, Korea, Vietnam, India, and Iran, have mastered the craft. Lacquer is a specialized finish that is applied to a surface. Applying a very thin layer of lacquer numerous times creates a lacquered piece. After each application, the lacquer must dry and harden in a climate-controlled room with high humidity. One layer of lacquer takes approximately 3 days to dry, and each layer must be rubbed smooth prior to the next application. Depending on the decorative treatment, there could be 300 layers of lacquer, which would require about 900 days to create. The three types of lacquer are **true lacquer, resin lacquer (lac),** and **Japanning** or **Japan work.** True lacquer is the most traditional form and is made from the sap of the *rhus vernicifera* tree, which is indigenous to China. The sap is extracted from the tree by collecting the substance as it oozes from numerous horizontal cuts made in the bark. Resin lacquer is made from a substance excreted by female scale insects. A European version of Asian lacquer, Japanning is a shellac or varnish finish. Japanning became popular in the 17th and 18th centuries when there was a great demand for Japanese lacquered objects d'art.

The lacquering craft is one element of the art. To create an ornamental design, artists use several techniques. For example, inlaying a material, such as mother-of-pearl, precious stones, or ivory, could make a decoration. Broken or cracked eggshells create a fascinating pattern when inlaid on a black surface. Another beautiful and difficult technique, **maki-e,** involves sprinkling gold or silver particles over the wet lacquer. The most complicated carved decoration involves numerous multi-colored layers of lacquer. After all of the layers have been applied, an artist carves the design from the lacquer. The depth of a cut determines the color that is revealed. A frequently seen example is when the bottom layer is black and the top layer is red. Designs are often landscapes, figures, flowers, plants, trees, birds, or geometric patterns.

Common lacquered objects are screens, lidded boxes, religious figures, trays, chests, bowls, and **inrōs,** a small nested boxed unit that was used to hold small items, such as medications.

Eileen Gray was known for her lacquered screens, desks, benches, and tables (Figure 4.20). Gray, the Irish-born architect and interior designer, started as an art student in England. In Paris she became an expert artist in lacquer after training with the Japanese lacquer master Seizo Sugawara. Gray's lacquer technique was flawless, and she designed several screens that have become timeless and iconic, such as the screen made from numerous black lacquered brick-shaped panels that are hinged together. Another artist in Paris, Jean Dunand, also created exquisite lacquer objects d'art. Dunand, a sculptor, created lacquered screens, panels, small boxes, and vessels. Dunand's most popular designs were African-inspired geometric patterns in black, red, and touches of gold (see Chapter 1). Rhulmann

Figure 4.20 Jacques Doucet's studio with a dark green lacquer table with silk tassels (1913) designed by Eileen Gray.

Source: The image is reproduced with the kind permission of the National Museum of Ireland.

Figure 4.21 Eileen Gray's residence, E. 1027 (Roquebrune-Cap Martin, France 1926–1929) is an excellent example of her minimalist approach to architecture, interiors, and furnishings. Living room of E. 1027 with Bibendum armchair, Transat chair, and Centimetre carpet.

Source: The image is reproduced with the kind permission of the National Museum of Ireland.

commissioned Dunand to create lacquer furniture for his elite clientele.

Even though Gray was living and working in Paris during the 1925 Exposition Internationale des Arts Décoratifs et Industriels Modernes, she did not have a strict preference for either the fashionable Art Deco or

for Le Corbusier's avant-garde modern architecture. In a very unique manner, Gray combined the two styles together into a cohesive whole. Her lacquer furniture designs had popular Art Deco details, such as ivory handles, silk tassels, lotus shapes, silver inlays, Egyptian motifs, and figures. As illustrated in Figure 4.21, Gray's design for her residence, E. 1027 (Roquebrune-Cap Martin, France 1926–1929), is an excellent example of her minimalist approach to architecture, interiors, and furnishings. The architecture employs all of Le Corbusier's "Five Points of a New Architecture." The interior was designed to be as efficient as the compactness and sparseness of cabins of an ocean liner. Gray was familiar with ocean liner features because the *Transatlantique Oceanliner* inspired her design for the renowned Transat (1925–1926) reclining chair. Most of the furniture for E. 1027 was made from chrome-plated tubing, including another famous armchair designed by Gray, Bibendum (1925–1926). Gray's custom handcrafted carpets were inspired by her visits to North Africa. African artists taught Gray how to naturally dye fibers and weave carpets. From 1922 until its closing in 1931, Gray sold lacquered furniture, light fixtures, screens, and carpets at her Parisian shop, Jean Désert.

Visual Arts: De Stijl—Gerrit Rietveld

Interior environments and architecture in the 1920s were also influenced by the aesthetics and principles of **De Stijl** (The Style). The Netherlands had been neutral during the war, which allowed several Dutch professionals to collaborate to establish the group De Stijl in 1917. The group comprised artists, architects, sculptors, graphic designers, and even a poet, A. Kok. The avant-garde members included Theo van Doesburg, Jacobus Johannes Pieter Oud, Gerrit Rietveld, Bart van der Leck, and Piet Mondrian. The artists collaborated to share their perspectives of art and to demonstrate their opposition to old traditions. To publish their manifesto and their projects, van Doesburg created the journal *De Stijl* (1917–1932). De Stijl theories advocated for designs that were more abstract than Cubism. For example, objects in Cubist paintings were angular and distorted, but they were generally recognizable. Abstract Art, on the other hand, is not recognizable and lacks representation of the external world. De Stijl members contended that simple abstraction equated to a "universal" style that was constant. This philosophy was translated into two dimensions through paintings and into three dimensions via interior environments, architecture, furniture, and light fixtures. The best two-dimensional example of De Stijl is Dutch painter Piet Mondrian's work after 1920. The Schröder house, designed by Dutch architect Gerrit Rietveld in 1924, is the defining three-dimensional representation of De Stijl.

An understanding of Mondrian's *Composition* paintings is fundamental to appreciating how Rietveld translated the artist's tenets to three-dimensional forms and volume. Mondrian created numerous paintings of *Composition* that explored the relationships between square and rectangular forms, straight lines, right angles, and *only* the colors, white, black, gray, red, blue, and yellow. Mondrian's abstract painting *Composition with Great Blue Plane* (1921) is an example of his analysis of the relationship between shapes, colors, and divisions. Each painting in his *Composition* series illustrates a unique approach to asymmetrically balancing these basic elements. Black lines define shapes, and balance is created by manipulating the voids and the masses. White and light gray are the voids. The primary colors and black create mass. Overlapping lines connect the disparate parts. A remarkable attribute of Mondrian's *Composition* abstract paintings is that the elements retain their balance when viewed from each side of the painting.

De Stijl aesthetics, revealed in Mondrian's *Composition* paintings, are also apparent in the residence designed by Rietveld for the Schröder family in 1924. This structure illustrates the relationships between square and rectangular forms, straight lines, right angles, and *only* the colors, white, black, gray, red, blue, and yellow (Figure 4.22). Mrs. Schröder was an extraordinary client who was willing to allow Rietveld to "experiment" with her home, and, as acknowledged by Rietveld, she was actively involved with the design process. She had commissioned the project and had requested a program that included a countryside site, had openness, and was flexible. The result was one of the most important modern architecture designs and a design that exhibits important principles related to sustainability.

The two-story residence is filled with natural daylight via strip windows and a skylight above the

Figure 4.22 The Schröder house by Rietveld illustrates the relationships between square and rectangular forms, straight lines, right angles, and only the colors, white, black, gray, red, blue, and yellow.

Source: Rietveld Schröder House, Centraal Museum.

centrally located spiral staircase. When corner windows are open, the space is completely free of any structural member. Minimizing the quantity of furniture, incorporating built-in cabinets, and creating flexible spaces conserves resources. The ground level is the utilitarian area, which consists of a studio, reading room, kitchen with an adjoining small dining space, and maid's bedroom. Originally Rietveld had designed a one-car garage for the residence, but Mrs. Schröder converted the space into a studio.

The spiral staircase connects the ground floor with the upper floor. The upper level was for "living-dining" and "work-sleeping" (see Figure 4.22). The hyphenated words reflect how Rietveld and Mrs. Schröder created flexible spaces. Through the installation of sliding panels, the upper floor was designed to be totally open, partially closed, or completely closed. The entire floor, including the hallway and bathtub area, could convert into an open-plan for living, dining, and working. Closing the floor-to-ceiling sliding panels provided privacy for sleeping and bathing. At this time, an open plan was a novel and modern approach to interiors and to a lifestyle. After living in the residence for 58 years, Mrs. Schröder explained how the upper floor evolved into an open-plan with the option of closed areas:

> You see, I'd left my husband on three occasions because I disagreed with him so strongly about the children's upbringing. Each time, they were looked after by a housemaid, but still I thought it was horrible for them. And after my husband died and I had full custody of the children, I thought a lot about how we should live together. So when Rietveld had made a sketch of the rooms, I asked, 'Can those walls go too?' To which he answered, 'With pleasure, away with those walls!' I can still hear myself asking, can those walls go, and that's how we ended up with the one large space. But I was still looking for the possibility of dividing up that space. That could be done with sliding partitions.

Figure 4.23 Free-standing furniture designed by Rietveld have become icons for De Stiljl, including the *Rood Blauwe* (Red Blue) lacquered chair and the *Military* chair in the background.
Source: Rietveld Schröder House, Centraal Museum.

> I think that was an idea of Rietveld's though he found it a shame. He did it, but he thought it was a pity. Personally, I'm eternally thankful that it was done. (Overy, 1988, p. 56)

As illustrated in Figure 4.22, to accommodate storage needs, Rietveld designed built-in cupboards, cabinets, and shelves. These units and their surrounding surfaces created a harmonious composition with De Stijl colors, forms, and overlapping planes. Red was frequently used as a horizontal element, and blue was reserved for most vertical forms. Freestanding furniture pieces designed by Rietveld have become icons for De Stijl, including the Rood Blauwe (Red Blue) lacquered chair (original 1918, chair in Figure 4.23 is a 1923 version), the Military series (tables and chairs 1923–1925), Divantafeltje (end table 1923), and the Zigzagstoel (zigzag chair 1934). As reflected in their inclusion in art museums, Rietveld's light fixtures, the neon tube Hanglamp (Hanging lamp, 1920) and

Figure 4.24 Weissenhofsiedlung apartment building, Stuttgart, Germany. For an exhibition in Stuttgart, Mies designed a modern apartment complex with ribbon windows, a flat roof, balconies, and roof terraces.
Source: © Arcaid/Alamy.

the Tafellamp (Table lamp, 1925), have also become important modern designs (Figure 4.22). Rietveld and the aesthetics of the De Stijl had far-reaching effects on the development of modern design. Most notable was the impact that De Stijl had on the philosophy and designs of the Bauhaus. For example, chairs designed by Rietveld inspired Breuer, and in 1923 Gropius created a ceiling light fixture for an office in Bauhaus that resembled Hanglamp.

GLOBAL BUSINESS AND ECONOMICS

The large-scale destruction of homes during World War I resulted in significant stressors on many of the combatant countries, but rampant inflation necessitated low-cost housing. This condition was particularly relevant in Germany and Russia. The war and subsequent revolutions created dire situations that left millions of homeless people dying of starvation. To help address the desperate need for low-cost housing and urban planning,

several architects established the **CIAM (Congrès International d'Architecture Moderne)** in 1928. Le Corbusier was instrumental in creating CIAM and was involved with the organization for many decades. As previously discussed in this chapter, to build, furnish, and provide utilities for housing required a revitalization of several industries (see "Impact of Technologies and Industrialization," Corbu's "Esprit-Nouveau," and De Stijl). By the mid-1920s, countries had begun construction projects, manufacturers were provided housing for their workers, and industries were starting to focus on promoting their products at international exhibitions. All of these initiatives came to a halt, however, after the stock market crash of 1929. The investment losses and other consequences of the crash became a worldwide crisis in the following decade, creating the Great Depression.

Industry and Exhibitions: Barcelona Pavilion (1929) in Barcelona, Spain, by Ludwig Mies van der Rohe

As the son of a master mason, German architect Ludwig Mies van der Rohe's (also known as Mies) life began in the building industry. Mies did not have formal architectural training but learned about materials and building technologies by working on construction sites. As with Le Corbusier and Walter Gropius, Mies also learned about architecture by eventually working in the architectural office of Peter Behrens. After his military service in World War I, Mies designed five projects (never built) that had important characteristics of modern architecture. Two buildings conceptualized the potential of glass skyscrapers (1919–1921). A design for an office building (1922) was revolutionary for the alternating cantilevered concrete slabs and ribbon (continuous horizontal band) windows. The plans of the other two villa designs resemble a painting in the De Stijl style. Mies designed the earlier project (1923) with brick, a material he favored due to its inherent structural integrity. The 1924 villa was designed with modern reinforced concrete.

Mies's growing notoriety resulted in his selection as vice president of the Deutsche Werkbund in 1926. Postwar conditions in Germany warranted effective and progressive international exhibitions sponsored by the Werkbund. In an effort to improve the severe housing situation, the city of Stuttgart and various industries were willing to provide financial assistance with Werkbund's 1927 Am Weissenhof Housing Exhibition. The exhibition proved to be critical to the development of modern furniture and architecture.

As mentioned earlier in this chapter, the 1927 exhibit introduced cantilevered tubular steel chairs to the public, including a version designed by Mies that today is known as MR. As vice president of the Werkbund, Mies' responsibilities included serving as the director of the exhibition. Mies invited 16 avant-garde architects, including Behrens, Gropius, Le Corbusier, Jeanneret, and Oud, to design residences for the exhibition. More than 30 residences were designed and constructed in Stuttgart. All of the single-family dwellings and apartment buildings were examples of modern architecture. Mies designed a modern apartment complex with ribbon windows, a flat roof, balconies, and roof terraces (Figure 4.24). After the exhibition, the city used the structures for community housing, but only a few of the houses remain today.

In 1927 Mies also became involved with designing exhibition space for industry with colleague Lilly Reich.

Figure 4.25 Barcelona Pavilion designed by Mies is one of the most outstanding examples of modern architecture in the world.
Source: Erich Lessing/Art Resource, NY.

Most notable was an installation they designed for the Mode der Dame Exhibition in Berlin. The Velvet and Silk Café was exhibit space for a silk textile manufacturing company. In contrast to the usual format of using an assortment of cardboard displays, Mies and Reich designed an exhibit that was simple and elegant. The manufacturer's silk fabric was subtly featured by suspending long lengths of the material from the ceiling. The only other addition to the installation was Mies's MR chairs and tubular steel tables. This innovative approach to designing exhibit space seems to have influenced Mies throughout his long career. Most important, these installations affected how he designed the Barcelona Pavilion, one of the world's most outstanding examples of modern architecture (Figure 4.25).

After the successful Am Weissenhof exhibit, Mies was asked to design the 1929 Barcelona Pavilion (disassembled 1930) because German government officials and industrial leaders were aware that he had incredible talent and impeccable taste. The purpose of the pavilion was to promote Germany and demonstrate the progressiveness of German industry. In maintaining his elegant and subtle approach to advertising, Mies focused all of the attention on the exquisite proportions of the architecture, perfection in the level of detail, and use of the finest materials available. Rather than presenting German exhibits *in* the pavilion, the pavilion *was* the exhibit. As in a Mondrian painting, the plan of the pavilion was a series of overlapping rectangular forms (Figure 4.26). Walls and partitions were the black lines that separated and joined disparate parts. To inspire visitors to flow through the pavilion, areas were never completely enclosed and within each space one could always catch a glimpse of another space that was intriguing to explore (see Figure 4.26). The precise positioning of the partitions and the use of rich surface materials accomplished this channeling effect.

Differences between the interior and exterior were blurred by partitions that were topped by the flat roof and were open to the sky (see Figures 4.25 and 4.27). The two pools that were lined with black glass balanced the high gloss finish of the stone and glass partitions. The chrome-plated mullions supporting the glass and the eight cross-shaped support columns heightened the effects of shiny surfaces. In contrast to De Stijl color aesthetics, Mies relied on the natural hues from Roman travertine, green Tinian marble,

onyx, and coloring glass in gray and bottle green. To contrast smooth and shiny surfaces, the double panels in the center of the pavilion were etched glass and were illuminated by a hidden light source.

Mies perfected the pavilion by selecting a sculpture by the German sculptor Georg Kolbe that appeared to float in one of the two pools and by designing furniture that exemplified elegance (see Figures 4.26 and 4.27). Currently known as the "Barcelona Series," the chair, stool, and table designed by Mies for the pavilion have become modern classics. The exquisite design is synonymous with quality, grace, and flawlessness. Mies demanded the highest quality craftsmanship and materials. He designed *every* detail of the Barcelona Series, including the size of the upholstery buttons, welting, leather straps, depth of the cushions, and distances between the tufting. The tufting on the cushions is exactly spaced between the leather straps that support the cushion. The precisely calculated, gentle curves of the *X* legs are an elegant application of a design that has origins in ancient Egyptian stools. The flat, chrome-plated steel frame was welded and polished by hand. The ample width of the chair emphasized the horizontal

Figure 4.26 Rather than presenting German exhibits *in* the Barcelona Pavilion, the pavilion *was* the exhibit. As in a Mondrian painting, the plan of the pavilion was a series of overlapping rectangular forms.
Source: Digital Image © The Museum of Modern Art/Licensed by SCALA/Art Resource, NY.

Figure 4.27 Mies completed the pavilion's perfection by selecting a sculpture by Georg Kolbe that appears to float in one of the two pools.

Source: Digital Image © The Museum of Modern Art/Licensed by SCALA/Art Resource, NY.

line and was a comfortable size for most people. Mies was also very attentive to the position of a piece of furniture in a space and the distances between furniture in a grouping. The careful positions reflected his mastery of applying the principles of proportion and scale. The Barcelona furniture line is still produced today by Knoll, but contemporary stainless steel has been substituted for the 1920s chrome-plated material.

Industry: Constructivism and Workers' Housing in Russia

As Western Europe was exploring definitions of modern interior environments and architecture in the 1920s, the USSR was engaged in its own interpretations of the new spirit. After becoming leader of the country in 1924, Josef Stalin formulated plans for the government to industrialize the USSR and to control aspects of Soviet life, including agricultural production. The program began in 1928 and continued into the 1930s. The opposition of state control of their farms led to the death and imprisonment of millions of peasants.

The quest to industrialize manufacturing resulted in the construction of hundreds of new buildings, and the prevailing interest in modern architecture was applied to industrial buildings. Vladimir Tatlin was

leading the Modern movement in the country by creating **Constructivism.** The Constructivist aesthetic had been established in Tatlin's Monument to the Third International (1920) (Figure 4.28). The building was intended to be a facility for governmental functions but was never constructed because engineers feared the design was not feasible after evaluating a model of the building. However, Tatlin's concept was revolutionary and was influential in Western Europe when architects and designers were formulating the philosophies of De Stijl and the Bauhaus. Tatlin had presented his drawings at international exhibitions in several cities, including Berlin, Paris, Vienna, and New York. Designers were intrigued by the double spiral structure that surrounded the buildings, the total glass structures, and the planned rotation of each form. The cube form at the lowest

Figure 4.28 The Constructivist aesthetic was established in Tatlin's *Monument to the Third International.* The building was intended to be a facility for governmental functions, but was never built.

Source: Digital Image © The Museum of Modern Art/Licensed by SCALA/Art Resource, NY.

level was for legislative assemblies and was to rotate at a speed of one rotation per year. The pyramid form above the cube was designed for the government's executive bodies. This form's rotation was intended to take 1 month to complete. The cylinder form at the top was for communication services—with a full rotation to be executed in 1 day.

The Constructivist elements conceived in Tatlin's architecture were applied to numerous buildings constructed in the USSR during approximately 10 years beginning in the early 1920s. The diversity of structures is astounding, such as Modernist water towers, garages, "palaces of culture," bakeries, offices, radio towers, and numerous workers' clubs. Many of the buildings in the 1920s were commissioned by the Soviet government and reflected the new industrial ideals of integrating factories with workers' clubs and communal facilities.

The Zuev workers' club (1926) in Moscow is an outstanding example of how the architect Ilia Golosov interpreted Russian Constructivism (Figure 4.29). The glass cylinder suggested in Tatlin's Monument to the Third International exists in the corner of the structure. Tatlin's suggested rotation of the form is translated into a spiral staircase (Figure 4.30). The structure employs the Constructivists' preference for glass, steel, and concrete. These modern materials and technologies and the geometric forms provide the ornamentation for the structure. Golosov achieved asymmetrical balance by precisely positioning the plain concrete masses with voids created by rectangular forms of glass. As illustrated in Figure 4.30, Golosov created aesthetic spaces for the workers by incorporating imposing views of the city and flooding the interior with natural daylight. The modernity of steel is emphasized in the space by the graceful banister and the steel beams that form a star-shaped ceiling. The Zuev workers' club is just one of the countless examples of masterful applications of Modernist architectural aesthetics in the Soviet Union.

Figure 4.29 The Zuev workers' club (1926) in Moscow is an outstanding example of how the architect, Ilia Golosov, interpreted Russian Constructivism.
Source: Richard Pare.

Figure 4.30 The glass cylinder suggested in Tatlin's *Monument to the Third International* exists in the corner of the workers' club. Tatlin's suggested rotation of the form is translated into a spiral staircase.
Source: Richard Pare.

SUMMARY

In the 1920s, previously warring countries focused on recovering from World War I, which had resulted in a depletion of resources, higher taxes, and severe housing shortages. Newly independent states were formed, such as Austria and Czechoslovakia, and the USSR was established in 1922. Britain tried to maintain control of India by resuming construction of governmental buildings in the new capital, Delhi, and the Viceroy's House was completed. China's revolution resulted in the overthrow of the Qing Dynasty in 1911 and the establishment of the Republic of China in 1912. The last Chinese emperor lived at the Palace until 1924, the year the Forbidden City became the Palace Museum.

During the decade, archeologists continued to search for the remains of lost civilizations and discovered the tomb of Pharaoh Tutankhamun in Egypt. The decade also saw several natural disasters, including a devastating earthquake, fires, and a subsequent tsunami that nearly destroyed Tokyo and Yokohama, Japan. However, on September 1, 1923, the opening day of the Imperial Hotel designed by Frank Lloyd Wright, the building withstood damage from the Kanto earthquake and extensive fires.

The postwar economic difficulties, hyperinflation, famine, material shortages, and destruction of homes, schools, factories, and communities slowed development of new technologies. However, to address the needs for low-cost housing, architects examined ways to use industrial production methods for prefabricated dwellings. Walter Gropius founded the transformational Staatliches Bauhaus School in Dessau, Germany, whose program internationally influenced every aspect of design. Breuer, a student and instructor at the Bauhaus, became famous for inventing and developing tubular steel furniture. Le Corbusier's focus on low-cost housing and mass-production was on display at the extremely influential 1925 Exposition Internationale des Arts Décoratifs (Art Deco) et Industriels Modernes in Paris. Corbu and Jeanneret's exhibit, the Pavillon de L'Esprit Nouveau, influenced countless architects and contributed to the development of the modern International Style. The exposition also featured interiors created by Ruhlmann and the designs of Parisian couturier Paul Poiret. The latter's chic fashions and interiors inspired a fascination with luxurious modern Parisian residences. Rhulmann responded to the demands by designing furniture and interiors that were exotic, were very expensive, and promoted a self-indulgent lifestyle.

The visual and performing arts also influenced interior environments and architecture. The designs of Western textiles and decorative arts in the 1920s were derived from the boldness of the Ballets Russes, Cubism, and art from "exotic" locations, including Japan and Africa. Eileen Gray and Jean Dunand were renowned for their lacquer furniture and objects d'art. Many architects and interior designers were influenced by the flatness and two-dimensional abstraction of Cubism. In addition to Cubism, interior environments and architecture in the 1920s were influenced by the aesthetics and principles of De Stijl. The best two-dimensional example of De Stijl is Mondrian's work after 1920. The Schröder house, designed by Rietveld, is the defining three-dimensional representation of De Stijl.

To promote Germany and the progressiveness of German industry, Mies was asked to design the 1929 Barcelona Pavilion. Even though the pavilion was disassembled after the exhibition, the design has become one of the most important examples of modern architecture in the world. As Western Europe was exploring definitions of modern interior environments and architecture, Russia was engaged in its own interpretations of the new spirit. Vladimir Tatlin was leading the Modern movement in that region with his creation of Constructivism. The prevailing interest in modern architecture was applied to industrial buildings, as well as other types of structures. Many of the buildings in the 1920s were commissioned by the Soviet government and reflected the new industrial ideals of integrating factories with workers' clubs and communal facilities.

KEY TERMS

Abstract Art

Art Deco

Bauhaus School

chattri

chiffoniers

chujja

CIAM (Congrès International d'Architecture Moderne)

coffered ceiling

Constructivism

De Stijl

dentils

divans

ebéniste

faience

feng shui

fillets

fluted

fuseau

inrōs

International Style

Japan work

Japanning

lacquer

maki-e

resin lacquer

sabots

shagreen

trefoils

true lacquer

EXERCISES

1. Research Design Project. Gropius was responsible for developing the Bauhaus curriculum. The curriculum started with *Vorkurs*, a preliminary 6-month course that emphasized creativity, natural materials, and understanding form. Research, and then following the course structure developed by Swiss Bauhaus designer Johannes Itten, create a collage that is a "detailed study of nature especially: (a) representation of materials and (b) experiments with actual materials" (Bayer, H., Gropius, W., & Gropius, I., 1938, p. 32). Prepare a presentation of the collage that includes a research summary and an analysis of the design with respect to the elements and principles of design.

2. Philosophy and Design Project. Yongle started the construction of the Forbidden City in 1406 by utilizing hundreds of thousands of workers every day. The palace was designed by abiding to the principles of feng shui (wind water). Research the principles of feng shui and the development of the Forbidden City. Apply the results to a design project in a studio course. In a written report, summarize your understanding of feng shui and how the principles were applied to the Forbidden City. The report should include a summary of how feng shui was applied to your design project.

3. Human Factors Research Project. The Constructivist elements conceived in Tatlin's architecture were applied to numerous buildings constructed in Russia for approximately 10 years beginning in the early 1920s. Many of the buildings in the 1920s were commissioned by the Soviet government and reflected the new industrial ideals of integrating factories with workers' clubs and communal facilities. Identify a local not-for-profit organization that provides facilities for the disadvantaged. Identify an interdisciplinary team of professionals and students, such as the social science discipline, that would be appropriate for the project. Using interviews, surveys, and/or observations, determine the appropriateness of the facilities. In a written report, summarize your results and include recommendations for future practice. The report could include sketches, drawings, or photographs. Your interdisciplinary team should prepare a presentation to the directors of the not-for-profit organization.

CHAPTER 5

EMPHASIS: THE 1930S

OBJECTIVES

After reading this chapter, you should be able to describe and analyze:

■ How selected global political events in the 1930s, such as totalitarian leaders and a revolution in Rio Janeiro, affected interior environments and architecture.

■ How the natural environment affected selected global interior environments and architecture in the 1930s as evident by Frank Lloyd Wright's Fallingwater and sustainable buildings in Finland.

■ How selected global technologies and materials in the 1930s affected interior environments and architecture as evident by developments in silk textiles and fluorescent lamps.

■ How selected global work styles and lifestyles in the 1930s affected interior environments and architecture as evident by designs of ocean liners and Tugendhat Villa in Brno, Czech Republic.

■ How selected global visual arts and performing arts in the 1930s affected interior environments and architecture as evident by Rockefeller Center and the popularity of the Empire State Building.

■ How selected global business developments and economics in the 1930s affected interior environments and architecture as evident by buildings in Shanghai, China, and the Johnson Wax Building in Racine, Wisconsin.

■ How to compare and contrast selected interior environments and architecture of the Americas, Asia/Oceania, Europe, and the Middle East/Africa in the 1930s.

The 1930s began with the response to the U.S. stock market crash, which occurred during the last few months of 1929. The economic collapse in October 1929 signaled the beginning of the devastating Great Depression, an economic crisis that lasted until 1939. Because of the global nature of the economy, the collapse of European banks quickly followed the collapse of those in the United States. Subsequently, the entire world was affected by the economic crisis. Many businesses were forced to close, and industrial production was significantly reduced. This led to massive unemployment and shortages of food, equipment, supplies, clothing, and housing. Major industrial countries, including Britain, Germany, and the United States, exceeded an unemployment rate of 25 percent at the nadir of the Great Depression. In attempts to protect national industries, severe and ineffective tariffs were imposed on international products. To revive the economy, many governments sponsored public works projects, such as agricultural programs, and the construction of new roads and government buildings. The dire situation provided the stimulus for the rise in totalitarian leaders—economic hardships were tied to the rise of the Nazi party and Hitler in Germany, for example—and the start of World War II in 1939.

The streamlined designs of modes of transportation, most notably cars and trains, were transposed to architecture, interior environments, decorative arts, industrial arts, and graphic arts. Associated with the public's excitement for speed and technological advancements, Art Deco was still a popular style and inspired new skyscrapers in New York City, such as the Chrysler building (1928–1930) by William Van Alen, and increasingly popular movie theaters. The Modernist movement continued to inspire architects and interior designers, such as Lúcio Costa, Le Corbusier, and Mies, as evidenced by the construction of modern architecture in cities around the world, including Rio de Janeiro, Prague, and Budapest. Names of some cities and nations changed in the 1930s. Constantinople, Turkey, was renamed Istanbul, and Siam became Thailand.

Many more people owned radios, automobiles, and electric appliances by the end of the decade. Progress continued in the field of women's rights during the 1930s, as evidenced by the first appointments of women to government positions in the United States. Explorers and adventurers continued to capture the public imagination: Amelia Earhart became the first woman to fly solo across the Atlantic Ocean in 1932 and the first person to fly solo across the Pacific Ocean in 1935. Howard Hughes successfully flew around the world in 1938 in 3 days. Passenger air travel also progressed, but the explosion of the *Hindenburg* in 1937 soon arrested flight by passenger airships. The Museum of Modern Art (MoMA) in New York City mounted an important and controversial Surrealist (super-real) Art exhibition in 1936, with the catalogue preface written by one of the founders of the Surrealist movement, the French poet and essayist André Breton. Artists associated with the movement included Man Ray, Salvador Dali, Joan Miró, Yves Tanguy, and Giorgio de Chirrico.

GLOBAL POLITICS AND GOVERNMENT

The 1930s saw several leaders who were interested in power and wealth via aggressive expansionary plans. After an unsuccessful bid for the presidency, Getúlio Vargas, the governor of Rio Grande do Sul, led a revolution in Brazil in 1930, resulting in a new dictatorship. Japan, while undergoing a series of military machinations and assassinations by army officers to gain control of the government under the Emperor Shōwa (Hirohito), continued its assaults on China.

Japan conquered Manchuria in 1931, and after winning the Second Sino-Japanese War (1937–1945), controlled other regions in northern and eastern China. Italian dictator Benito Mussolini invaded and seized control of Abyssinia (now Ethiopia) in 1935 and Albania in 1939. An attempted *coup d'état* and subsequent maneuvering for power by competing political factions in Spain initiated a 3-year civil war that involved Italy, Germany, and Russia. Picasso captured the brutality of the war in his famous *Guernica* mural in 1937, which he painted in response to the atrocities committed in April 1937 in Guernica, a small village in the Basque province in northern Spain. The painting was displayed at the Spanish Pavilion at the 1937 World's Fair in Paris.

Stalin's strategies to turn the Union of Soviet Socialist Republics (USSR) into a powerful industrial state started in 1928 and continued into the 1930s, resulting in the deaths of tens of millions of people. Due to the Depression and the difficulties associated with maintaining control of various colonies, Britain granted independence to several countries, including Iraq, New Zealand, and South Africa. Germany, led by Hitler, first ignored the Treaty of Versailles by reoccupying the Rhineland (1936), which the treaty had made into a demilitarized zone, and then invaded Austria (1938), Czechoslovakia (1939), and finally Poland (1939). Germany's invasion of Poland in 1939 began World War II.

Totalitarian Leaders: Hitler, Mussolini, and Stalin

During the 1930s, Hitler, Mussolini, and Stalin ordered the construction of monumental structures for administrative functions and to give the impression that they were improving the lives of their citizens by sponsoring public work projects during a time of economic hardship. The buildings were planned adjacent to large squares, enabling masses of people to hear their speeches and other propaganda. Hitler had an immediate effect on the arts, literature, science, and philosophy when prominent

professionals in these fields were among the tens of thousands of people to flee Germany beginning in 1933. Many architects and interior designers, including the architect Ludwig Mies Van der Rohe, the founder of the Bauhaus Walter Gropius, and Bauhaus architect and furniture designer Marcel Breuer, eventually moved to the United States. Hitler's autocratic rule extinguished the Modernistic perspectives that had developed in Germany. The fascist policies of Hitler and Mussolini affected interior environments and architecture in dramatically different ways; each dictator had an impact on the buildings that were constructed during the 1930s, but their stylistic preferences were distinctly varied.

Hitler's focus on ancient Rome and Greece architecture is revealing of his obsession with establishing Germany as the greatest state that ever existed. His rise to power and authority began in 1930 when the Nazi party won a large number of seats in the legislature. At this time, Germany was suffering from the substantial debt imposed on it after World War I and from the economic turmoil resulting from the stock market crash. Hitler was able to attract supporters because he was willing to address the perceived injustices imposed on Germany by the Treaty of Versailles, such as the loss of territory and the imposition of reparation payments, and he promised to establish an economic recovery program that would provide employment opportunities and prosperity. After a series of political maneuvers, in 1933 Hitler was named the chancellor of Germany with absolute dictatorial powers, which enabled him to enact laws that affected every aspect of German life.

Hitler had always had an interest in the arts and architecture; these areas especially appealed to him and were used as propaganda tools. To demonstrate Germany's supremacy, Hitler and a select few of his favorite architects developed a grandiose program to rebuild the cities and construct new buildings in Berlin, Munich, and Nürenberg. World War II obviously stopped a good number of the intended construction projects, but several projects—such as a monumental

Figure 5.1 Hitler's *Hall of Mirrors* in his administrative building, Reich Chancellery, was purposely designed longer, wider, and taller than the *Hall of Mirrors* at Versailles.
Source: Courtesy of Prof. Randall Bytwerk.

building for his administrative offices, an Olympic stadium, and an entire complex of multiple buildings for Nazi rallies—were rapidly completed.

Hitler wanted his architecture to last thousands of years; therefore buildings had to be constructed with massive blocks of stone rather than modern materials and technologies. He preferred interior environments and architecture that were intimidating and massive, appeared to be impenetrable, and referenced classicism. To demonstrate to the world German supremacy, Hitler ordered his architects to design buildings that were superlative to the Western world's most important monumental interiors and architecture. For example, he demanded a design for a triumphal arch that would dwarf the Arc de Triomphe in Paris. The façade of the U-shaped section of Congress Hall (1936–1939, incomplete) in Nürenberg resembles the Roman Colosseum but is more austere. A concept for a meeting hall called for an enormous dome with a cupola more than 800 feet (243.84 meters) wide, dwarfing the size of the domes in St. Paul's Cathedral in London, and the Pantheon and St. Peter's Basilica in Rome. Berlin was to have boulevards wider and longer than the Champs Elysées in Paris. The Hall of Mirrors in the German administrative building, Reich Chancellery (1938–1939, destroyed), was designed

to be longer, wider, and taller than the Hall of Mirrors at Versailles (Figure 5.1). The architect Albert Speer used a variety of materials, including a tremendous amount of red marble, to decorate the interior and Hitler was said to be greatly impressed with the results. The Reich Chancellery eventually was demolished by the Soviets after the war and, legend has it, used to create a Soviet monument honoring Russians killed in World War II.

Benito Mussolini was similarly a fascist dictator, but his approach to architecture in Italy was different from Hitler's monumental edifices in Germany. Whereas Hitler attempted intimidation through architecture, Mussolini, or Il Duce ("The Leader"), wanted interiors and architecture to glorify the ancient Romans while reflecting Modernism. Mussolini approved of the use of modern materials and technologies, including glass, steel, and reinforced concrete. To improve and modernize Italy, Mussolini ordered the design and construction of several urban planning projects. In Rome, Città Universitaria (University City) (1933–1935) was built to consolidate educational facilities. Using thousands of manual laborers, the beautiful town of Sabaudia was created from marshland southwest of Rome. A new and modern railroad station, Santa Maria Novella (1932–1934) in Florence, is a superlative example of exploring the interplay of light and volume.

Perhaps the most important architecture ordered by Mussolini was the fascist headquarters, Casa del Fascio (1933–1936) in Como, by Giuseppi Terragni (Figure 5.2). The travertine façade is elegantly designed with a grid that becomes three-dimensional by the inclusion of balconies. Responding to the Mediterranean climate, the plan integrates indoor and outdoor spaces. Rooms and porticos surround a courtyard with a glass brick ceiling. The building's deeply recessed balconies provide shelter from the rain. Numerous large windows provide an abundant amount of daylight, while the deep overhangs prevent the ill effects of direct sunlight. As with Hitler's concept for totalitarian architecture, Il Duce had a large square in the front of the building for political rallies. However, in contrast to Hitler's formidable style, architecture commissioned by Il Duce suggested an open, modern approach to the fascist state.

As discussed in Chapter 4, Stalin's intention was to create the USSR as the world's most powerful industrial state. This mandate continued in the 1930s via Stalin's 5-Year Plan with the construction of more power plants, factories, and mines. Every aspect of Soviet life was supposed to reflect symbols of the new state power, including textiles and porcelain (Figure 5.3). To reinforce the power of the new communist state in 1931, Stalin initiated an international competition for a Palace of the Soviets. Numerous architects, including Le Corbusier, Gropius, and several Soviets, submitted drawings and proposals. As a reflection of totalitarian monumental architecture, the program required gargantuan-size rooms that could accommodate thousands of people. The rooms included a conference room for 6,000 people and a main hall for 15,000.

Ukrainian architect Boris Iofan's neoclassical design was selected for the palace (Figure 5.4). The multi-tiered structure resembled a wedding cake and was topped by a 100-meter (328-foot) statue of Lenin in a pose similar to the Statue of Liberty. Construction began with the destruction of a building associated with the czars, the Church of Christ the Savior (1832; 1839–1883; razed 1931). The start of World War II halted construction, but the huge hole in the ground that was excavated for the foundation became the largest open swimming pool in the world. In the 1990s, the Church of Christ the Savior was reconstructed according to its original design.

Figure 5.2 Perhaps the most important architecture ordered by Mussolini was the fascist headquarters, Casa del Fascio in Como by Giuseppi Terragni.
Source: © Matt Nardella, Architect/Artifice Images.

Figure 5.3 Stalin's *Five-Year Plan* included the construction of more power plants, factories, and mines. Textiles reflected the new state of power.

Source: Scala/Art Resource, NY.

Figure 5.4 Boris Iofan's neoclassical design was selected for the palace. The multi-tiered structure resembled a wedding cake and was topped by a 328-foot-high (100-meter) statue of Lenin, in a similar pose as the Statue of Liberty.

Source: Wikimedia Commons.

Revolution and Politics: Rio de Janeiro and Brazilian Modernismo

On the other side of the Atlantic Ocean, political unrest was occurring in Brazil. Exports and subsequent profits were already declining in the 1920s, but when the stock market crashed in 1929, the economic consequences devastated Brazil. The dire economic conditions in the United States and Europe resulted in significant reductions in luxury imports, such as Brazilian coffee and sugar. The urban middle class blamed the affluent exporters and landowners for the conditions. In 1930, a military revolution resulted in the authoritarian presidency of Getúlio Vargas and a "New State." Vargas had determined that Rio de Janeiro (at this time the capital of Brazil; Brasília did not become the nation's capital city until 1960) would benefit from his new social, educational, and industrial program for Brazil. Central to the initiative was the construction of new ministry and monumental buildings in the Modern style. Prior to the revolution, Brazilian architects and designers were aware of the Modern movement in Europe, but the Modern movement in Brazil did not begin until Vargas became the president.

One year after Vargas's presidency began, the enormous Art Deco statue that has become synonymous with Rio, Christ the Redeemer (1926–1931), was completed. Designed by Brazilian engineer Heitor da Silva Costa, the figure's outstretched arms appear to welcome visitors to the city. The statue's sculptor, Paul Landowski, a French sculptor of Polish descent, carved the statue from green-colored soapstone. The purpose of the statue was to commemorate the 100th anniversary of the country's independence from Portugal in 1822. Completing the statue reinforced Brazil's independence and demonstrated an incredible engineering accomplishment. The enormous 125-foot-high (38-meter) statue had to be reinforced with steel to withstand the tremendous winds that constantly whirl around the top of Mount Corcovado, the site of the statue.

New ministry buildings were also representative of the changes for the "New State." A new ministry building for education and health was an excellent way for Vargas to promote his new social and educational program. In 1936, an international competition was initiated for a new Ministry of Education and Health (MEH) building (1937–1943) (Figure 5.5). To further advance his agenda, Vargas wanted Modern architecture rather than the old neoclassical styles that were preferred by the overturned establishment. The traditional project that was selected by the conservative jury was not constructed. Instead, the French-born Brazilian Modernist architect Lúcio Costa was commissioned to design the new MEH. Brazilian architects revered Le Corbusier; thus Corbu was hired by Costa as a consultant for the MEH project and was very involved with the final design. Costa went on to hire a team of professionals for the project, including Oscar Niemeyer, Carlos Leão, Jorge Moreira, Affonso Eduardo Reidy, and Ernani Vasconcelos. Later, many of those who worked on the project, including Costa, Niemeyer, and Reidy, would become internationally known for extraordinary Brazilian architecture in the 1940s and 1950s.

Reflecting Corbu's "Five Points of a New Architecture" (see Chapter 4), the main building of the MEH had les pilotis, roof gardens, open plans, glass curtain walls, and predominantly plain façades. Costa blended Corbu's Modern elements with traditional Brazilian details. The MEH therefore evolved into a unique national architectural style that is now referred to as **Brazilian Modern,** or **Modernismo.** Brazilian Modernismo is a combination of local traditions and international avant-garde. As an expression of the native environment and culture, MEH was designed with the Brazilian environment and climate in mind; it also featured Brazilian fine and decorative arts. To protect the occupants from the harsh tropical sun, the exterior of the north façade has vertical and horizontal sun-breakers (see Figure 5.5). Vertical shielding is derived from the concrete walls, and the horizontal blue asbestos **brise-soleil** rotate to constantly control the light as the sun moves across the sky. The openings of the brise-soleil allow ventilation, even during tropical rainstorms. The importance of the beach and water in the Brazilian culture is revealed in the repeated use of the aforementioned blue, as well as in views of the Atlantic Ocean from the rooftop terrace gardens.

Brazilian landscape designer Roberto Burle Marx joined the team; his task was to reinforce the beauty of the local rainforest. Marx designed the lush tropical gardens on the ground level and the curvaceous rooftop gardens. The traditional Baroque-inspired curves were also used on floors, furniture forms, and various decorative arts. In reference to a historic Brazilian handicraft, mosaic tiles were used as a decorative element. The entrance plaza has a blue and white

Figure 5.5 In 1936, an international competition was initiated for a new Ministry of Education and Health (MEH) building in Rio de Janeiro. Lúcio Costa was commissioned to design the MEH and hired a team of professionals for the project.
Source: Wikimedia Commons.

mosaic tile mural designed by Candido Portinari. On the rooftop, the protruding elevator tower and water tank are covered with blue tiles. The MEH also features many sculptures, including *Prometheus Chained* by Swiss sculptor Jacques Lipchitz, which is mounted on the exterior wall of the amphitheater. Costa and the team's approach to MEH, including the new Brazilian modern forms, soon became internationally admired when Niemeyer designed the Brazilian Pavilion for the 1939 New York World's Fair.

EFFECTS AND CONDITIONS OF THE NATURAL ENVIRONMENT

The power of water had a significant impact on the 1930s. Flooding of the Yellow River in China contributed to the deaths of approximately two million people in 1931. To harness the Colorado River for hydroelectric power, Boulder Dam (now known as Hoover Dam) was completed in 1936, about 30 miles (49 kilometers) southeast of Las Vegas, Nevada. A deadly hurricane drenched the New England coast in the early fall of 1938, killing nearly 700 people. In dramatic contrast to the destructive force of water, Frank Lloyd Wright integrated rushing waters with Fallingwater (1936–1938), a house built over a waterfall, which has become a modern icon of organic architecture.

A lack of water was also a problem in the 1930s. A severe and long-lasting drought in what is known as the Dust Bowl region (Colorado, Kansas, New Mexico, Oklahoma, and Texas) of the United States led to the destruction of millions of acres of farmland. In Europe, weather conditions and Stalin's farm policies in the

Soviet Union contributed to the starvation of more than five million people.

Oil was discovered in Saudi Arabia in 1938, and subsequently land became very expensive. From a design perspective, nature proved to be an inspiration to Jorge Ferrari-Hardoy, Antonia Bonet, and Juan Kurchan, the designers who created the famous "butterfly chair" in 1938. Originally called "Horde," the chair is currently manufactured by Knoll. Finnish architect Alvar Aalto also was inspired by nature and climatic conditions when he designed the Paimio Sanatorium and the Library at Viipuri in Finland.

Geographical Features: Fallingwater (1935–1937) by Frank Lloyd Wright

Thousands of miles away from Brazil's Ministry of Education and Health and *Prometheus Chained,* another architect selected a sculpture created by Lipchitz. *Mother and Child* was placed at the edge of Fallingwater's plunge pool. Fallingwater, Wright's masterpiece located in the Appalachian Mountains in southwest Pennsylvania, exemplifies how nature can inspire interior environments and architecture (Figure 5.6). Edgar Kaufmann, the owner of Kaufmann's department stores in Pittsburgh, commissioned Wright to design a family weekend "cabin" in the mountains. When Wright visited the site, he was drawn to the sounds and dynamics of Bear Run stream. The stream rapidly cascades down Laurel Hill, creating waterfalls and meandering brooks. From the beginning, Wright was committed to designing a residence that enabled people to connect with the stream. Rather than employing the typical solution by designing a building that faced the water, Wright created a residence that was integrated with the waterfalls and streams. Blending the architecture with cliffs, boulders, trees, and native plants expanded the connection with nature.

The task was formidable from an engineering perspective. Engineering reports warned Kaufmann that it was not advisable to construct a house over a waterfall. Fortunately, Kaufmann had the vision, patience, and resources required to construct enormous cantilevered structures over rushing water. As a result, the horizontal cantilevered planes appear to be extensions of the natural cliffs. Natural integration was also accomplished by constructing the residence with the same sandstone that created Laurel Hill. A quarry was built on the site, and as construction progressed, masons cut the stones according to what was needed at a particular time. Wright specified that the smoothest stones were to be used for the floors. Stones used for the walls were carefully selected to form a harmonious pattern. Highlights and shadows created by different thicknesses emphasized the texture of the sandstone.

Fallingwater has several attributes to which the senses respond (Figure 5.7). Rough walls of stone and the smooth wood furniture stimulate the sense of touch. To ensure that people would hear the water rushing over the boulders, there are numerous casement windows and doors over the waterfalls. The living room has an open stairway that leads to the water. Corner casement windows and glass double-door openings allow the sounds and scents of nature to flow through the interior. Window openings were so essential to the experience of Fallingwater that Wright designed a semicircular cutout in a desk in order to provide space for the swing of a casement window. Visual connections with nature are achieved by separating the interior and exterior with sheets of glass. Even corners of the structure become invisible by eliminating vertical members and using a series of short casement windows that open to the outdoors. The abundance of windows, skylights, and glass doors enables natural daylight to fill the spaces. To simulate natural daylight, Wright used **cove lighting** above wardrobes and stepped ceilings that were covered with white muslin and wood grilles (see Figure 5.7).

Figure 5.6 Fallingwater, Wright's masterpiece located in the Appalachian Mountains in southwest Pennsylvania, exemplifies how nature can inspire interior environments and architecture. *Mother and Child* was placed at the edge of Fallingwater's plunge pool.

Source: © The Frank Lloyd Wright Foundation, AZ/Art Resource, NY.

Figure 5.7 To create a residence that inspired people to connect with nature, Fallingwater has several attributes that respond to the senses.

Source: © Ezra Stoller/Esto.

People could interact physically with the extensive areas dedicated to the outdoors. Fallingwater has numerous terraces that adjoin all of the living and sleeping areas, and many of the terraces are actually larger than their adjoining interior space. To retain as many trees as possible and provide another source of interaction with nature, some terraces and trellises were constructed with openings for the tree trunks. "Plunges" into the stream were easily accessible from the living room steps, covered with a hatch. An in-place boulder used as a hearth in the living room can be touched and climbed on. Wright's custom-designed furniture made from black walnut, including desks, tables, pedestal ottomans, wardrobes, bookshelves, radiator casings, and built-in seating, appeal to the sense of touch. To help prevent mildew in the wardrobes, air circulates through the open weave of the cane shelves. Wood grain was vertically aligned on units that opened, such as doors, and horizontal on fixed cabinetry. These directional differences are also evident with many of the windows and doors. Vertical apertures open, and horizontal units often are fixed. Mrs. Kaufmann, not Wright, was responsible for selecting the lounge chairs, the inverted tree-trunk side tables, and the Alpine dining chairs with backs edged with Baroque curves (see Figure 5.7).

References to nature are also evident in the choice and application of colors and patterns. Natural stone is used for the colors of walls and floors. Natural cork is used in the bathrooms. Fabrics have a rough texture and are void of pattern. Animal-skin throws provide another tactile experience. The beige color of the upholstery fabric blends well with the sandstone. As in nature, bright colors are used sparingly. Red and yellow are used for pillows, seat cushions, wall hangings, throws, and rugs. The earth color red is an important accent element throughout Fallingwater. Earth red outlines the windows, doors, outdoor metal furniture, and streamlined metal shelves. Earth red is also the dominant color of folk craft rugs and the large cast iron kettle that dominates the fireplace in the living room. Wright designed a crane that enables the kettle to swing from the fireplace into a carved niche in the wall of stone. The residence also had all of the modern conveniences of the 1930s, including hot water heating, Kohler bathroom fixtures, St. Charles metal kitchen cabinets, an Aga stove, and latex foam cushions.

Nature and Climate: Alvar Aalto—Paimio Sanatorium (1929–1933) and the Library (1930–1935) at Viipuri (Modern Vyborg)

Frank Lloyd Wright and Alvar Aalto both had a deep appreciation for the beauty of the natural environment, and they designed interiors and architecture to stimulate and enhance the relationship between people and nature. Aalto's designs were inspired and determined by the natural environment of his native Finland. Valuing handcrafts and designing for the physiological and psychological needs of people, Aalto's Scandinavian cultural heritage also affected his designs. The origins of **ergonomics,** applying science to equipment design to blend smoothly with a person's body or actions, started with the work of Kaare Klint at the Royal Danish Academy of Fine Arts. In the 1930s, Aalto designed in the International Style the Paimio Sanatorium and the Library at Viipuri, two buildings with vastly different functions that exemplify his approach to the natural environment, handcrafts, and designing for people. These structures, as well as other projects designed by Aalto, provide numerous examples of how to apply the principles of sustainability to interior environments. Most notable are Aalto's solutions for integrating daylight, controlling for sunlight, improving the indoor air quality, planning maintainable interiors, and using local materials and resources.

The original purpose of the Paimio Sanatorium was as a medical facility to treat people who were suffering from tuberculosis. At this time, the medical profession believed that the only way to cure the disease was for the patient to exercise and be exposed to fresh air and sunlight. Therefore, the natural environment of Finland had to be integrated with the design of the sanatorium. A site was selected that was far from any urban pollution and was surrounded by a dense forest of healthy "ozone-producing" pine trees. Hiking in the woods was encouraged; therefore, Aalto incorporated into his design storage facilities for hiking boots. To maximize exposure to sunlight, the building was constructed on a hill that overlooked the forests. Aalto positioned the six-story patients' wing along a southwest axis to take full advantage of sunlight. Every room for patients faced the southeast and had three large casement windows. This orientation allowed the morning sun to fill the rooms, while eliminating the harsh west sunlight later in the day. Communal areas, such as the dining room, were filled with natural daylight from entire walls of glass, corner windows, and skylights (Figure 5.8). On the inside of the dining room glass walls were flowerboxes filled with plants that emitted healthy oxygen. Aalto designed an ingenious method for distributing fresh air in the patients' rooms even in the cold winter. Air would enter an opened out-swinging casement and flow to an area between two sheets of glass. The fresh air was gently warmed and then flowed into the room via an opened in-swinging casement window. Additional opportunities to breathe fresh air, absorb the sun's radiant heat, and enjoy views of the forests were provided by roof decks, balconies, and cantilevered terraces.

As a functionalist designer, Aalto was concerned about ambient temperatures, comfortable furniture, acoustics, and maintainable interiors. Warmth was especially critical for a building in a region with long, harsh winters. Patients' rooms were heated with hot water pipes in the ceiling, and the units were positioned above the end of the beds to keep feet warm. In keeping with Scandinavian preference for the warm touch of wood, Aalto designed furniture using native birch for the facilities. Aalto was very successful experimenting with bent laminated woods and painted molded plywood. Addressing the needs of people in the sanatorium created one of Aalto's most famous furniture designs. The curved sides of "armchair 41" are made from laminated birch, and the seat and back is one continuous sheet of painted, molded plywood. The warm, tactile qualities of wood are used on surfaces that will be touched. Ergonomic comfort is derived from the curved seat, slightly reclined back, and chair's springiness. The slots

Figure 5.8 Designed by Alvar, Aalto communal areas at the Paimio Sanatorium were filled with natural daylight from entire walls of glass, corner windows, and skylights. On the inside of the dining room, glass walls were flowerboxes filled with plants that emitted healthy oxygen.

Source: Martti Kapanen, Alvar Aalto Museum.

cut in the back of the chair allow for air circulation. The sled base makes it easy to move the chair for conversation, catching the sun, and cleaning the floor. All of the chair's surfaces are easy to maintain. This sustainable feature helps extend the life of the furniture and improves the long-term costs of interiors. Aalto was also able to reduce the cost of furniture by creating designs that appeared to be handcrafted but could be mass-produced. Other maintainable features are curved corners, a warm gray-colored paint on wall surfaces prone to be touched, and durable linoleum, which is also an excellent sustainable flooring material.

In addition to the Paimio Sanatorium, Aalto designed another important building in the International Style. The architecture of the Library at Viipuri (now called Viborg and part of Russia) illustrates the elements of the new Modern style and demonstrates outstanding approaches for enabling people to effectively see and hear in large spaces. During the day, a tremendous amount of daylight fills the library's reading room and stacks from numerous 6-foot (1.83-meter) circular skylights. The unique conical-shaped skylights provide indirect illumination on desk surfaces and library bookshelves. The indirect lighting from above eliminates shadows. In the evening, excellent lighting is achieved using ceiling-mounted fixtures, which are aimed at the perimeter walls. The reflected light from opposite directions illuminates surfaces while eliminating shadows.

The ceiling of the library's lecture hall has an elegant wooden sculpture; the undulating curves were designed to deflect sound at every location in the room (Figure 5.9). This acoustical format is quite different from a traditional room that has been designed to project a speaker's voice from the front podium. The uniform distribution of sound is ideal for discussions: regardless of where a person is standing, everyone in the room can hear the person speak. To enhance the multidirectional discussion format, Aalto designed stools for the room, rather than the traditional chair with a back, which suggests seating in one direction. The legs on chairs and stools were made with Aalto's famous bent corner, or L-leg. Aalto's designs were in such high demand that he founded the furniture company Artek in 1935 with Maire and Harry Gullichsen. Artek is still producing modern furniture and light fixtures (www.artek.fi). In addition to initiating a successful business with Aalto, the Gullichsens commissioned him to design their country residence, Villa Mairea (1938–1939), which has become a very important architectural structure. It is an excellent example of blending the modernity of whitewashed brick with natural timber, Finland's organic architectural element.

Figure 5.9 The ceiling of the Library at Viipuri's lecture hall has an elegant wooden sculpture and the undulating curves were designed to deflect sounds at every location in the room.

Source: Gustaf Welin, Alvar Aalto Museum.

GLOBAL TECHNOLOGICAL DEVELOPMENTS

The introduction of new industries, technology, and international developments to the world continued with the 1933–1934 Century of Progress in Chicago, the 1937 Exposition Internationale des Arts et Techniques dans la Vie Moderne in Paris, the 1939 New York World's Fair, as well as other world's fairs and expositions in Antwerp, Stockholm, Brussels, and Johannesburg. By the mid-1930s, General Electric was selling the first fluorescent lamps. Commercial television made its debut in 1939, but radio was still the most important medium for news and entertainment. The invention of the helicopter and jet engine, and the development of radar during the 1930s helped expand the possibilities of flight. The construction of the Golden Gate Bridge in California (1937) gave people the impression that they could *fly* over the San Francisco Bay. The first electron microscope (1933) would impact the design of modern textile prints in the future. The DuPont Company's discovery of nylon (1935) had multiple effects on many products, including carpets and upholstery fabric. In contrast to claims about it as an "artificial silk," nylon could not substitute for the beauty of genuine silk, as demonstrated by the Scalamandré Silks, Incorporated manufacturing company.

Technologies and Materials: Scalamandré Silks, Incorporated

"Technology" is a very broad term that includes devices that are operated by hand and by mechanical means. Today some interior furnishings are still made by hand, with or without a handloom. Fortunately, there are artisans who have retained the knowledge and skills to create furnishings that would be impossible to make with machines. Technology and skills require raw materials, and fortunately for manufacturers working in the 1930s, the price per pound for raw silk plummeted during this decade. An economist explains the conditions and the prices: "when the Great Depression set in and worldwide commodity markets collapsed in the late 1920s and the early 1930s, silk prices dove to their historical low (the 1935 price was only one-fifth of the level of predepression years, say 1926 or 1927). Between 1930 and 1937, nominal prices of silk slide downward at 4 percent on average per annum" (Ma, 1996, p. 343). Scalamandré Silks, Inc. is a textile manufacturer that had the technology, skills, and reasonably priced silk to successfully launch their company in the 1930s.

Scalamandré is a high-end design and manufacturing company that specializes in the restoration of historic textiles, manufacturer's designer fabrics, **passementerie,** and wallpaper. The company's founders, Franco and Flora Scalamandré, created a successful business by understanding the art of weaving, design, and quality materials. Franco Scalamandré was an Italian engineer who immigrated to the United States after an uncomfortable encounter with Mussolini in 1923. Franco, with his new wife, Flora, an artist, started Scalamandré in 1929 with one loom, one weaver, and imported silk from Italy. The Scalamandré Company became better known after opening one of the first showrooms in the new wholesale building, Chicago's Merchandise Mart, in 1930. Scalamandré developed and flourished in the 1930s after successful restorations of historic textiles for the White House, Hearst Castle in the California coastal town of San Simeon, and Colonial Williamsburg in Virginia.

To reproduce the historic textiles, Franco had to build special looms and eventually filled a large red-brick textile mill in Long Island City, New York. The mill's wooden floors were critical for flexing with the vibrations of the looms. To ensure quality textiles, Franco developed a design and manufacturing company that performed every part of the process—starting with dyeing imported yarns and ending with detailed inspections. For example, in the 1930s Franco reproduced just 7 yards of an old brocatelle fabric for William Randolph Hearst's West Coast mansion in San Simeon. However, the defining attribute that contributed to its authentic reproduction occurred by accident (Coleman, 2004). To age the textile, Franco washed the fabric and placed it on the mill's roof to dry. An unusual March snowstorm buried the textile, but rather than ruining the fabric, Franco discovered that the weather condition had created "an exact match for the original!" (Coleman, 2004, p. 5).

Scalamandré had, and continues to have, the ability to create flawless passementerie, or decorative trimmings. Passementerie includes **gimp, cords, ropes, fringes** (loop, cut, **bullion, tassel**), **tiebacks,** and **rosettes** (Koe, 2007). Gimp is a narrow flat trim that can be a decorative band on fabric, or gimp is used on furniture between a hard surface and upholstery fabric. To make cords, plied yarns are twisted together. A cord becomes a rope when the thickness exceeds 1 inch (2.5 centimeters). Fringes have a heading with an attached decorative treatment, such as silk loops or tassels. Bullion fringe has looped cords or ropes in a variety of lengths. Tiebacks are trimmings used to hold a drapery treatment, and rosettes are decorative trims sewn to look like a rose. Passementerie can be made by hand, using a handloom, or using a mechanical loom. Trimmings handmade at Scalamandré include tiebacks, tassels, fringes, and rosettes. As illustrated in Figure 5.10, generations of artisans have been making passementerie by hand. Tassels are hand sewn to the silk heading. Tassels can be a wooden mold that has been wrapped with silk yarns. The end of the tassel is finished by hand trimming the numerous fine silk yarns. Scalamandré has a special ruffing machine that only makes **ruffs,** a pleated trim that can be used at the top of fringes and bullions.

Scalamandré is still a family-owned business, still using antique looms from the 1930s. Many of the company's looms and equipment are tagged for eventual inclusion in the Smithsonian collection. Frank Koe, author of the textbook *Fabric for the Designed Interior*, included as a supplement to his book an excellent DVD featuring Scalamandré's original textile mill that demonstrates the entire design and manufacturing process. Interesting features of the DVD are the interviews

Figure 5.10 At Scalamandré, generations of artisans have been making passementerie by hand.

Source: Dan Mayers.

and explanations from those responsible for specific processes. The company is able to reproduce a textile from an illustration, period photographs, written descriptions, or fragments of the original.

Technologies: Fluorescent Lamps

The research and development of **fluorescent lamps** started in the 19th century, but a practical lamp was not available until 1938. General Electric and Westinghouse introduced fluorescent lamps to the public at the 1939 New York World's Fair and followed that with the Golden Gate International Exposition (1939–1940) in San Francisco. A fluorescent lamp is an electrical discharge light source that most often uses a glass tube, electrodes, phosphors, low-pressure mercury, and other gases (Figure 5.11). **Discharge lamps** do not have filaments and produce optical radiation by operating with low or high pressure. Discharge lamps use gases for illumination, and must have a **ballast** to maintain an even flow of electrical current. Numerous patents were awarded to specific individuals and corporations; however, there are a number of scientists and engineers from many countries who are responsible for researching and developing fluorescent

lamps. *Every* attribute of a fluorescent lamp required significant research and experimentation. The ideal solution had to be discovered for the size of tubes; coating techniques; circuitry; ballasts; production methods; and properties of its glass, gases, and phosphors.

Prior to the 20th century, scientists experimented with mercury vacuum pumps and tried to identify the most effective luminescence substance that could be stimulated by electricity. At the turn of the century, scientists focused on creating a lamp with a longer life by maintaining gas pressures. Two lamps were developed that led directly to the practical fluorescent, the mercury vapor lamp by Peter Cooper Hewitt in 1901 and the neon light by Georges Claude in 1909. Both electrical light sources had limitations related to color and the use of toxic gases. The mercury vapor lamp emitted a bluish-green color, and neon lights were either red when the electrical current was passed through the neon gas or blue when argon gas was inserted into the glass tube. Significant progress occurred in Germany when Friedrich Meyer, Hans Spanner, and Edmund Germer patented the first fluorescent lamp in 1927.

In the 1930s, several corporations were involved with developing a practical fluorescent lamp, including a British company called General Electric Company, Ltd.; Philips in the Netherlands; Osram in Germany; and General Electric and Westinghouse in the United States. In 1934, the General Electric Company in Britain produced a fluorescent lamp that was three times more efficient than the enormously popular incandescent lamp. This significant advance prompted immediate fluorescent development by a team of eight engineers working at General Electric's industrial research site, National Electric Lamp Company Park in Cleveland, Ohio. George Inman and Richard Thayer were responsible for directing the team; thus their names have been associated with developing the world's first commercial fluorescent lamp.

Initially, fluorescent lamps were produced in four standardized sizes, but soon engineers realized that

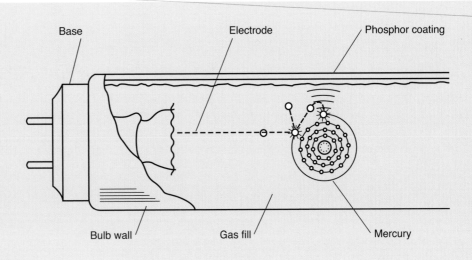

Figure 5.11 A fluorescent lamp is an electrical discharge light source that most often uses a glass tube, electrodes, phosphors, low-pressure mercury, and other gases.

Source: Winchip, S. M. (2005). *Designing a quality lighting environment.* New York: Fairchild. Figure 3.5.

Labels: Base, Electrode, Phosphor coating, Bulb wall, Gas fill, Mercury

the 48-inch (121.92-centimeter) length using 40 watts was the most effective configuration. This standardized length and wattage became a common application for fluorescent lighting systems. Early fluorescent lamps were energy efficient, emitted a good level of illumination, had a long life, radiated little heat, and had a low operating cost. However, these lamps were made with a phosphate substance that produced an unappealing bluish color. The lamp was ideal for commercial and industrial applications (for example, warehouses) that did not require quality color. The research and development of the fluorescent lamp had a staggering impact on fields such as architecture, interior environments, sustainability, and economics. Its ubiquity in commercial, industrial, and eventually residential interiors has had physiological and psychological effects on people, such as triggering seizures, changes in heart rate, and depression.

From a design perspective, the appearance of interiors was changed by the multiple rows of fluorescent fixtures installed on ceilings. New fixtures had to be designed to conform to the shape and sizes of the fluorescent tubes. The drawback of the lamps' energy effectiveness was that it encouraged windowless spaces in the 1930s most notably in offices for typists and people working on tabulating machines. Today people are still experiencing the effects of the development of the fluorescent lamp and its pervasive use in the 1930s

but the lamp's energy efficiency is important for sustainable designs.

GLOBAL LIFE AND WORK STYLES

The effects of the Great Depression from 1929–1939 were pernicious; it had a significant impact on the lives of people throughout the world. Millions of people were unemployed and starving, unable to find work because of the collapse of many businesses. In the United States, unemployment reached its peak in 1933, when more than 25 percent of all workers and 37 percent of nonfarm workers were jobless. Construction was stifled, and new buildings were generally intended to either glorify dictators or fulfill the wants of the few wealthy. Popular books in the 1930s included *Gone with the Wind* by Margaret Mitchell (1936), *The Hobbit* by J.R.R. Tolkien (1937), and John Steinbeck's *Of Mice and Men* (1937). Other forms of entertainment during the decade included going to the local movie theater to watch films such as the Busby Berkeley musical *Gold Diggers* (1933), *Mr. Deeds Goes to Town* (1936), and *The Wizard of Oz* (1939); watching Babe Ruth hit home runs for the New York Yankees; playing the new board game Monopoly (1935); and watching the launch of the British Broadcasting Corporation (BBC) in 1936.

Travel: Ocean Liners

Transportation improvements of the late 19th and early 20th centuries provided people with the ability to travel around the world in a much more convenient manner than had been previously available. Travel was for pleasure as well as for people who were seeking employment during the Depression. Enormous interest in international travel and immigration prompted companies in many countries to build ocean liners. The goal was to constantly stay ahead of the competition by building liners that were faster, larger, and more luxurious. The *Blue Ribband* was an award given to the liner that made the fastest crossing—eastward and westward—of the North Atlantic between Bishop Rock lighthouse off the Scilly Isles in the UK and the Ambrose lightship off New York harbor. Generally, countries in contention were Britain, France, Germany, Poland, Italy, the Netherlands, and the United States. Some of the most notable ocean liners during the 1930s were the *Europa* (1930), *Empress of Britain* (1931), *Orion* (1935), *Normandie* (1935), and *Queen Mary* (1936).

The four categories of passengers on ocean liners prior to the 1920s were first class, second class, third class, and steerage. As can be imagined, first class offered the largest lounges, dining rooms, and cabins. Each reduction in class resulted in smaller and fewer rooms and less service. Generally, on westbound trips, immigrants to the "New World" occupied the horribly crowded steerage areas, which often had no windows. Steerage was located at the bow (front) of the ship, which experienced every pitch and roll of the liner. Dining was at rows of collapsible tables, and sleeping arrangements lacked any privacy. Steerage was the cheapest ticket, but the profits from these passengers were significant to the companies because of the minimum service. The number of steerage passengers often exceeded the combined number of the other three classes. Fortunately,

steerage tickets were outlawed after the passage of the U.S. Immigration Act of 1924.

The positive economic climate of the roaring 1920s encouraged the building of larger and more glamorous liners, which were then used in the 1930s despite the Great Depression. Larger liners meant larger profits, but spacious, highly decorated interiors of the ships were needed to entice people to make the long and dangerous journey. In the initial years of the early 20th century, some transatlantic passenger service ships sank crossing the North Atlantic due to the speed of the new steam turbines, high winds, high waves, potential for icebergs, and ever-present fog. The passage took between 8 and 12 days. The "bon voyage" celebration began because people feared they would never see loved ones again. Thus, in the 1930s, to promote sales, companies like White Star Line and Cunard still had to persuade passengers that long voyages across the Atlantic or Pacific were going to be safe, comfortable, and healthy experiences. This was accomplished by designing spaces that were familiar to the passengers. First-class lounges, dining rooms, and cabins were designed to resemble the finest hotels in period styles, such as Louis XVI, Adam, French Renaissance, Louis XIV, and even hunting lodges. An advertisement for an Italian liner showed a photograph of a woman being served breakfast in bed in a spacious cabin in the Louis XVI style. Because the ocean cannot be seen in the photo, it appears that the woman's guest room is in a luxury hotel. Early liners always had "men-only" first-class smoking rooms in a clubby style. Daylight from large stained-glass skylights filled rooms that were two or three decks high (Figure 5.12). Avoiding windows helped to distract passengers from thinking about the risky journey and helped to eliminate seasickness from watching the movement of the horizon.

To promote the therapeutic value of spending several days in sunshine and fresh air, the ocean liners were designed to have winter gardens filled with potted palms, outdoor promenades, and swimming pools. In the 1930s, liners added gymnasiums, massage salons, and exercise equipment. Chairs with openings in the back and seat, such as rattan furniture or designs with slats, were chosen to help passengers benefit from the fresh ocean breezes. Deck chairs with wooden slats became synonymous with liners and were often photographed with a comforting blanket. Other ocean liner traditions were serving high tea on the promenade deck, writing letters, and reading novels. To accommodate these activities, liners had luxurious, daylight-illuminated libraries and writing rooms. The numerous desks were filled with complimentary postcards and stationery engraved with the liner's insignia.

Other traditions were serving bouillon in the morning and chefs preparing gourmet food from some of the finest hotels in the world, including the Ritz-Carlton. Gourmet menus themselves became a form of entertainment that blended with the formality of dressing for dinner. Women in evening gowns and extravagant jewelry paraded down an elaborate staircase in view of all the guests in the dining room. Orchestras from balconies and choruses provided entertainment during dinner. Bars adjoining the dining rooms were used before and after dinner. After dining, guests could dance in nearby ballrooms. Eventually, theaters were added for motion pictures, and live musical and stage performances.

All travel between the continents for the general public (as well as designers and architects) had to be done by ocean liners. Passengers were therefore exposed to the design of interiors for a concentrated period. Chapter 4 introduced the influence that ocean liners and other forms of transportation had on the designs of interior designers and architects, including Le Corbusier and Eileen Gray. In addition to a liner's architecture, which Corbu contended was "pure, neat, clear, clean, and healthy," ocean liners had an effect on the popularity of Art Deco. Liners designed in period interiors generally did not influence passengers, but this changed in the 1930s when companies started to design their new liners in the Art Deco style.

Art Deco was an ideal style to promote their modern form of transportation. The cabins, lounges, smoking rooms, and other first-class areas of the *Normandie* (1935), for example, had outstanding Art Deco interiors, furnishings, murals, sculptures, and paintings (Figure 5.13). The first-class dining room became famous for bas-relief landscapes of peasant life in Normandy carved in gilded stone and mounted on

Figure 5.12 Early ocean liners had two- or three-deck high rooms filled with daylight from large skylights.
Source: Popperfoto/Getty Images.

Figure 5.13 *Normandie*'s first-class dining room. The *Normandie*'s cabins, lounges, smoking rooms, and other first class areas had outstanding Art Deco interiors, furnishings, murals, sculptures, and paintings.

Source: Popperfoto/Getty Images.

red marble. The cascading glass chandeliers by Lalique became a defining Art Deco motif. The old stained-glass skylights were replaced with modern indirect lighting. The "floating" modern Art Deco style had a lasting impression on wealthy passengers throughout the world, as evidenced by their interest in designing their own residences in the new modern style.

When World War II began, ocean liners were used to transport troops or supplies. Many liners were destroyed either by enemy fire or from striking underwater mines. After the war, ocean liners had a successful return, until the late 1950s, when jet travel reduced the transatlantic voyage time to just 7 hours. Cruise ships are common now, but they are not able to replace the aura, glamour, or service provided by the luxurious ocean liners.

Perceptions of Living Space: Tugendhat Villa (1929–1930), Brno, Czech Republic, by Mies Van der Rohe

The early 20th century saw the introduction of new concepts in the design of residential living space. In contrast to traditional residences with rooms that were partitioned with doors and walls, designers were creating multifunctional spaces that flowed together. Rooms were no longer prescribed for a specific purpose but could be adapted to

meet the needs of individuals at various times. Prairie Houses designed by Frank Lloyd Wright initiated the concept of open plans for living areas by removing partitions and combining social rooms together (see Chapter 2). Wright's designs featured plain surfaces, minimal furniture, and selective decorative arts. Subsequently, Gerrit Rietveld's Schröder house (see Chapter 4) was designed with an upper level for living-dining and work-sleeping. Sliding panels enabled the multifunctional spaces to be totally open, partially closed, or completely closed. Wright and Rietveld incorporated large windows in their designs to maximize daylight and to enhance the relationship between the indoor and the natural environment. Not only did the openness alter perceptions of the space by creating a connection with nature, but the continuous views also gave the impression that the rooms were larger than their actual square footage. However, spaces were not fully exposed to the environment. Mies first challenged this concept when he designed the Barcelona Pavilion (1929). Walls of glass and seamless floor transitions blurred the divisions between interior spaces and the natural environment. The stark openness was intriguing but not alarming because the Pavilion was for exhibition purposes. To actually live in a glass house *and* an open living space required people who were willing to transform their lifestyle. Fortunately, Mies was able to connect with a client who was willing to live in what became the first "glass house." The generous wedding gift from the bride's father enabled Fritz and Grete Tugendhat to commission what has become a "masterpiece of the Modern Movement in architecture" (UNESCO, 2000).

The three-story Tugendhat Villa was built into the elevation of a sloping site (Figure 5.14). Therefore, at street level, the entrance adjoins the top level of the residence. This level has bedrooms, private study areas, bathrooms, and a milky glass–enclosed staircase that connects to the second story. The second story has an open plan for the living spaces that resembles the design of the Barcelona Pavilion (Figure 5.15). Freestanding partitions and built-in furniture provide only hints of separate spaces for living and dining, as well as a library. A pale gold-and-white African onyx partition separates the living area from the study. A semicircular wall of dark striped Macassar ebony wood subtly isolates the dining room. Glass curtain walls surround the living space and provide dramatic views of the gardens. In replicating the design of the Barcelona Pavilion, chrome-plated, cross-shaped columns support the roof, and double glass panels in the center of the plan are illuminated by a hidden light source.

As in other interiors in the Modern movement, Mies designed a small kitchen that was separate from the living space. The lowest level was for utility rooms, but the walls fulfilled an important function for concealing the panels of glass in the living space. To enhance the connection with the natural environment, some of the glass panels in the living space electrically opened by sliding down into the walls of the lowest level. Connecting with nature was also possible with the winter garden and the numerous terraces that surrounded the residence (see Figure 5.15).

Nature dominated the color scheme for the villa. Color was derived from the gardens, onyx, travertine marble, metal, and wood. Textiles were made from

Figure 5.14 The three-story Tugendhat Villa was built into the elevation of a sloping site. This level has bedrooms, private study areas, bathrooms, and a milky-glass enclosed staircase that connects to the second story.
Source: Digital Image © The Museum of Modern Art/Licensed by SCALA/Art Resource, NY.

Figure 5.15 The second story of Tugendhat Villa has an open plan for the living spaces that resembles the design of the Barcelona Pavilion (see Chapter 4). Tugendhat chairs and coffee table are on the right. The library is on the left.
Source: Digital Image © The Museum of Modern Art/Licensed by SCALA/Art Resource, NY.

natural wool, silk, and leather. Interior furnishings were subtle shades of white, gray, and tan. These muted colors and plain textiles provided the optimum background to enhance the forms of the classic furniture that Mies designed for the villa. Mies' furniture plan included his new Barcelona chairs and stools, and he designed two pieces specifically for the villa, the Tugendhat Chair (1929–1930) and the Tugendhat Coffee Table (1930).

The cantilevered Tugendhat Chair was made from chrome-plated flat steel bars (modern stainless steel) that flexed with movement (see Figure 5.15). The original cushions were leather or a light gray–colored textile. Wide bands with belt buckles were used to support the cushions. The Tugendhat Coffee Table had an X-frame made from chrome-plated flat steel bars (modern stainless steel) and a beveled clear glass that was three-quarters of an inch thick (1.91 centimeters).

Mies used the villa as an opportunity to introduce his Brno chair (1929–1930) in the dining area and bedrooms. The Brno chair was designed with either chrome-plated steel tubes or chrome-plated flat steel bars. The upholstered chair cover was leather or a textile. Mies's Side Chair with Arms (1927) (Modern MR) with a black-lacquered cane seat was used in the library (see Figure 5.15). The furniture, as well as every other element in the villa, illustrates Mies's phenomenal ability to precisely design every detail. He lived by his philosophy: "God is in the details." As previously noted, Mies was a perfectionist who demanded the highest quality craftsmanship and materials. Precision required impeccable placement and proportions. This is evident in the asymmetrical furniture layout in the living space. Mies precisely placed every chair, table, and the pedestal under a bust sculpted by Wilhelm Lehmbruck. Vertically, the sculpture and the floor-to-ceiling draperies harmonize with the shiny cross-shaped columns. The precisely scaled wool area rug defines the arrangement. Three small Tugendhat chairs are perfectly spaced to balance two wide Barcelona chairs. To balance the long rectangular table in front of the onyx wall, Mies placed the glass Tugendhat coffee table with a Barcelona stool. Now known as the Barcelona Series, the chair, stool, and table that Mies designed for the pavilion have become modern classics and are synonymous with quality, grace, and flawlessness.

The Tugendhat family was forced to leave their villa when Hitler invaded Czechoslovakia in 1939. The villa survived World War II, but restoration work included having to replace all of the original furniture. In 2001, Tugendhat Villa was inscribed on the UNESCO World Heritage List for many reasons, including its important contribution to the International Style of the Modern movement in residential architecture.

GLOBAL VISUAL AND PERFORMING ARTS

Advances in film technologies contributed to a growing number of movies being produced and a growing number of Hollywood stars, including many fictitious creatures. The 1933 "moving picture" *King Kong* had a significant impact on the adventure film genre and attracted worldwide attention to New York City's new Empire State Building. Animated characters became popular due to Disney's first full-length film, *Snow White and the Seven Dwarfs*. Other stars in the 1930s were Shirley Temple, Joan Crawford, Clark Gable, Charlie Chaplin, John Wayne, and Bette Davis. People were enamored with the remarkable dancing of Fred Astaire and Ginger Rogers. Louis Armstrong, Cole Porter, Bing Crosby, and Benny Goodman were some of the stars providing musical entertainment during the decade. To support the performing and the visual arts, Rockefeller Center in New York City was completed in 1939.

Performing and Visual Arts: The Metropolitan Opera and Rockefeller Center (1928–1939) in New York City

Rockefeller Center is a large, multibuilding complex located in midtown Manhattan between Fifth and Sixth Avenues from 48th to 51st Streets. Known as the "City Within the City," the 22-acre complex comprises commercial offices, restaurants, shops, theaters, television studios, gardens, a plaza, and promenades (Figure 5.16). In the 1920s, the Metropolitan Opera (Met) wanted to construct a new opera house with an "Opera Plaza" and move out of its existing opera house on Broadway and 39th Street with its adequate stage facilities, where the Met had been since 1883. Met board members looked to philanthropist John D. Rockefeller, Jr., the son of Standard Oil Company founder John D. Rockefeller, to assist in the project as a "highly important civic improvement." To develop initial plans for the new location, the Met commissioned architect Benjamin W. Morris. Original plans for the project included additional revenue sources, such as commercial space, hotels, apartments, department stores, an underground garage, and perhaps other theaters for the performing arts. After reviewing and rejecting several sites, a realtor suggested a large, rundown area in midtown that was owned by Columbia University. Rockefeller negotiated a lease for the property from the university in 1928; however, the Met was forced to withdraw from the plan after the stock market crash in 1929.

Rockefeller became personally involved with every aspect of the comprehensive project, which eventually employed over 40,000 people. He hired John R. Todd to manage the project, and Raymond Hood, known for his American Radiator Building in New York, became the principal architect. By 1930, three architectural firms were involved with the development of the center: Reinhard & Hofmeister; Corbett, Harrison, & MacMurray; and Goodley & Fouilhoux. The primary architects responsible for the project were Hood, Harrison, Reinhard, and Hofmeister.

Without the involvement of the Met, Rockefeller had to focus attention on a revised plan that included tenants. The solution came from the rapidly emerging Radio Corporation of America (RCA). RCA needed space for offices, theaters, broadcasting, and radio operations. The location for the opera house became the site for the 70-story RCA Building (now the GE Building; see Figure 5.16). The shift from opera to mass entertainment affected the development of the project, and the center's

theme was applied to every decision. The involvement of RCA precipitated a series of changes, including the addition of a "moving picture" studio, RKO (Radio-Keith-Orpheum Company), and a producer of entertainment shows, S. L. "Roxy" Rothafel. In 1934, the previously planned "loft or apartment buildings" became Radio City Music Hall (6,000 seating) and an RKO building (31 stories). Apartment buildings planned for 49th Street were changed to an RKO Roxy Theater (3,500 seating) and a "proposed" opera house (4,300 seating). The original plans for department stores, shops, and an apartment hotel became office buildings and two buildings separated by an arcade, La Maison Française, and the British Empire Building. The proposed sunken outdoor plaza remained with the new plans and, with its gilded statue *Prometheus* by Paul Manship, is an icon

Figure 5.16 Known as the "City within the City," Rockefeller Center's comprehensive planning project has commercial offices, restaurants, shops, theaters, television studios, gardens, a plaza, and promenades. The RCA building is in the center.

Source: Smithsonian Museum of American Art, Washington D.C./Art Resource, NY.

of New York City and Rockefeller Center. The flag-lined outdoor plaza is also renowned for its spectacular annual Christmas tree, a tradition that began in 1931 while the center was still under construction.

The flags bordering the plaza are an excellent example of a detail that supported the theme of the center. To develop a theme, Rockefeller hired a philosophy professor from Southern California. After reviewing numerous concepts and revisions, Rockefeller decided that to communicate a message to the world, the center's theme would be "New Frontiers and the March of Civilization." The theme was the source of inspiration for the interior environments, architecture, promenades, gardens, and an extensive art collection. "New frontiers" of entertainment included the expansion of radio, moving pictures with sound, phonographs, and television. The center housed corporations, such as RCA, The Associated Press, and Eastern Airlines, which were creating these "new frontiers" in the field of entertainment and news. Architecture was designed with the "new frontiers" associated with building technologies, including air conditioning, high-speed elevators, and offices that were filled with natural daylight and fresh air. Every office space was within 27 feet (8.33 meters) of a window.

Interior furnishings and architecture were designed using the progressive Art Deco style. "New frontiers" of interiors were highlighted in Radio City Music Hall. The interior designer Donald Deskey was commissioned to primarily design the Music Hall's lounges, smoking rooms, and powder rooms. The interiors have become synonymous with many of the defining characteristics of Art Deco (Figure 5.17). "New frontier" materials for furniture included bronze, chrome metal, lacquer, and black glass. Deskey's "Nicotine" wallpaper for the second mezzanine men's smoking room was printed on aluminum foil. Deskey designed furniture, light fixtures, wallpaper, and commissioned the art, including textiles by Ruth Reeves and Marguerite Mergentine. Deskey's selections of artists obviously had a significant impact on the design of the interiors and the center's art collection.

Painters included Stuart Davis, Louis Bouché, Witold Gordon, Henry Billings, and Yasuo Kuniyoshi; the sculptors were Robert Laurent and Gwen Lux. A mural for a men's lounge painted by Davis, *Men without Women*, was moved to the Museum of Modern Art in 1975.

The mural painted for the first mezzanine men's lounge, Gordon's *Decorative Map of the World*, is an excellent example of Rockefeller's theme of "new frontiers" of international relations (see Figure 5.17). In addition, the center originally included La Maison Française and the British Empire Building. As a reference to the English Channel (which separates France

Figure 5.17 Men's lounge, first mezzanine. Wall mural is by Witold Gordon and the furniture was designed by Donald Deskey. Deskey designed the Music Hall's lounges, smoking rooms, and powder rooms. The interiors have become synonymous with many of the defining characteristics of Art Deco.
Source: James Kirkikis.

and Britain), the two buildings were separated by the Channel Gardens. Although Rockefeller failed to get Mussolini's support for an Italian building, the center nevertheless included a Plazzo d'Italia. The "new frontiers" of international relations and the "march of civilization" are evident in the center's indoor and outdoor paintings, carvings, mosaics, relief panels, and sculptures. In these works, the artists captured the importance of wisdom, happiness, health, and freedom while celebrating dance, drama, song, labor, and technologies. The art collection illustrates new technologies, such as radios, moving pictures, still pictures, phonographs, airplanes, trains, and ocean liners, which enabled people to connect globally. A carved limestone screen at the entrance to the International Building by architectural sculptor Lee Lawrie celebrates the "march of civilization" by illustrating past accomplishments, such as old symbols of imperialism and trade ships, with future advances associated with industrialization and factories.

Despite the Depression, Rockefeller Center became tremendously successful: 7 more buildings were eventually added to the original 14, and the project influenced urban planning strategies throughout the world. Urbanists were inspired by Rockefeller Center's integration of public and private spaces, its access to the subway system, and its plan for efficient street patterns within a large complex.

"Moving Pictures": Skyscrapers, the Empire State Office Building (1930–1931), and *King Kong* (1933)

The Empire State Building is a unique example of how world occurrences from a variety of sources affect interior environments and architecture. The movie *King Kong* did not affect the appearance or design of the Empire State Building, but from a different perspective *King Kong* influenced the popularity of the Empire State Building as well as perceptions of skyscrapers. The "moving picture" *King Kong* (1933) brought badly needed national attention

to the Empire State Building, or as it was known, the "Empty State Building." History has demonstrated that this attention was essential to boost the building's occupancy rates during the Great Depression, and to help people accept and become familiar with skyscrapers, the tallest structures in the world. Currently, most people have become accustomed to seeing, visiting, working, or living in skyscrapers; however, in the 1930s, experiencing a view from the top of these tall structures was equivalent to flying in an airplane, which most people had not done at this time. People were—and some still are—concerned about the sway and movement of skyscrapers, and some individuals had fears of heights and fires. *King Kong*, a movie seen by millions, familiarized the public with tall structures, created curiosity in going to the top of the building, and helped to overcome some of the negative reactions to tall buildings.

In 1929, John Jakob Raskob and Pierre S. du Pont joined Coleman du Pont, Louis G. Kaufman, and Ellis P. Earle to form Empire State, Inc., to build a premier office building on the former site of the Waldorf-Astoria hotel. John Jakob Raskob was a businessman and financier who had held directorships and other executive positions in the DuPont Company. Raskob had been a major factor in the transformation of General Motors, and its stock into one of the historic giants of American industry. Pierre S. du Pont, the great-grandson of the founder of the DuPont Company, Eleuthère Irénée du Pont, led the company in its transition from a family firm to a multinational chemical company, and was also chairman of General Motors from 1915 to 1929. Part of their vision for the Empire State Office Building stemmed from a competition between Walter Chrysler, head of the Chrysler Corporation (a General Motors rival) and John Jacob Raskob to see who could build the world's tallest building. Ground was broken for the Empire State Office Building in January 1930, just a few months after the U.S. stock market crash, and construction of the building began on March 17, 1930. William Lamb of the New York firm Shreve, Lamb, and

Harmon was commissioned to design the architecture. Speed in construction was imperative. The quicker the building could be finished and occupied, the sooner the investors would receive revenue from office rent. Speed became even more critical as the country slid further into the Great Depression. To quickly construct the building, more than 3,400 people were employed during peak periods and mass-produced parts were delivered to the site exactly when they were ready to be installed, referred to as just-in-time management practices. **Fast-tracking** the project allowed construction to actually begin before the completion of all of the working drawings. To reduce eating time, lunch stands were located on different floors of the construction site. Full medical services were also available on the site.

Some of the construction techniques that were identified to reduce time and costs affected the design of the architecture. For example, the building's subdued Art Deco architecture has minimal decoration on the exterior. To help reduce time-consuming masonry work, the joints between windows and the limestone cladding were covered with chrome and nickel mullions. Covering the stone's edges meant that the stone could be rough-cut at the quarry and then placed without final cutting or fitting, thus saving a great amount of time. Areas above and below the windows were covered with aluminum spandrels embossed with a chevron-like pattern. The results produced a shiny metal that glistens in sunlight, and the vertical aluminum members reinforce the building's soaring architectural style. The telescoping shape is derived from the setbacks, a requirement of city zoning ordinances to allow sunlight and fresh air to penetrate the street level.

The most decorative area was the three-story main lobby, which was lined with a gray-red colored marble. The lobby's focal point was the stainless steel relief image of the Empire State Building superimposed on the map of New York, the Empire State (Figure 5.18). The top of the mooring mast radiates rays of sunshine.

A phenomenal coordinated effort enabled the workers to construct more than four and a half floors per week. The 102-story building (1,250 feet [381 meters]; 1,472 feet [443 meters] to the top of the antennae), including the glass and metal mooring mast, was completed in 1 year and 45 days, finishing in May 1931. Because of the Great Depression, the skyscraper was several million dollars under the original budget of $50 million and was 200 feet (61 meters) taller than the Chrysler Building. In 1931, the Empire State Building was the tallest structure in the world, and it retained that status until the completion of the twin World Trade Center buildings in 1973.

As could be expected, the grip of the Great Depression had a serious effect on the Empire Building's occupancy rates. The two million square feet (185,806 square meters) of office space was not fully occupied

Figure 5.18 The focal point in the Empire State Building's lobby was the stainless steel relief image of the building superimposed on the map of the *Empire State*, New York. *Source:* Bettmann/Corbis.

Figure 5.19 Upon reaching the top of the Empire State Building, King Kong gently places Ann on a ledge while he combats fighter planes that are firing bullets.
Source: Getty Images.

until the 1950s. During low occupancy years, a major source of income was derived from fees charged to visit the observation platform. This became especially popular after the New York City premiere of *King Kong* in 1933, which featured the Empire State Building (Figure 5.19). The RKO film became a huge box office success and was seen by thousands of people, including audiences at Radio City Music Hall. It was the highest grossing film in 1933. This was the first time most people were able to see panoramic views from the tallest building in the world. Some shots included Central Park and a seemingly "short" Chrysler Building.

The Empire State Building dominated the film's finale. The action centered on the giant gorilla, King Kong, scaling the side of the Empire State Building while he was holding Ann (Fay Wray), the woman he loved. Kong is soon killed by fighter planes and falls to his death. Romance continues at the top of the building when Ann's true love rescues her from the ledge. Their embrace is framed by a spectacular view of the Manhattan skyline.

Beginning with *King Kong*, the Empire State Building has become an icon for New York City and is one of the most recognized buildings in the world. More than 120 million people have visited the top of the building, which has become synonymous with romance. Nearly 100 films have featured the Empire State Building, many of them romantic movies, such as *An Affair to Remember* and *Sleepless in Seattle*. Today, couples enter a contest to have the opportunity to be married on Valentine's Day at the Empire State Building.

GLOBAL BUSINESS AND ECONOMICS

Many businesses were forced to close due to the economic circumstances initiated by the 1929 stock market crash, which led to massive unemployment in many nations. The automobile industry was affected by the crisis. The opening of the Empire State Building in 1931 was a promotional opportunity for General Motors to help the company stand out against fierce rival Chrysler

Corporation (whose namesake building had been constructed in 1928–1930). To stimulate sales, Ford Motor Company introduced the new Model B in 1932, essentially an updated version of its iconic Model A, as well as a similar vehicle with a Flathead V8 engine marketed as the Model 18. Due to the effects from the Great Depression, manufacturers at this time started to offer long-term payment plans to encourage sales. Companies in other countries—for example, Toyota in Japan and Volkswagen in Germany—also created new automobiles.

In the East, many industrial and commercial buildings were developed during this period along the Bund, the waterfront road along the Huangpu River, regarded as the symbol of Shanghai, China, for hundreds of years. Other business initiatives and inventions in the 1930s included the development of the frozen food industry by Clarence Birdseye Corporation (1930) and the legalization of gambling in Las Vegas (1931). The invention of photocopiers (1937) and ballpoint pens (1938) facilitated clerical work at businesses, such as the Johnson Wax Company in Racine, Wisconsin.

Industry and Economic Modernization: Shanghai, China

Thousands of years ago, Shanghai was a small fishing village, but its location in eastern China would eventually have a significant impact on the city's development. Shanghai (meaning "on the sea") is located on the East China Sea at the end of the important Yangtze River. Shanghai's unique port location was ideal for trade with the remote areas of the country, as well as regional and international maritime trade. In recognizing the strategic importance of this location, Britain declared Shanghai as the first treaty port after the British won the first Opium War in 1842. This proclamation forced foreign trade, and the British were able to seize and control areas within Shanghai. To oversee commerce and shipping activities, Britain created its foreign concession close to the Huangpu River, a branch of the lower reaches of the Yangtze River. During this colonial

period, other nations (including France, Germany, Japan, Australia, and the United States) also established foreign concessions in the region. Several of the countries (France was an exception) merged their concessions to develop the Shanghai International Settlement. This resulted in a commercial, political, and administrative division of Shanghai that included the walled area of ancient China (removed in 1912), the International Settlement, and the French concession.

To develop industry and commerce in this area, many buildings were constructed along the Huangpu River. These developments helped to provide employment opportunities for the local people. During what is known in Shanghai as the "Golden Age" of the 1920s and 1930s, traditional Chinese architecture was replaced by an eclectic assortment of Western-inspired architecture, including Art Deco, Gothic, Modern, Neoclassical, and Renaissance. A significant number of Western-inspired styles were built as banks, insurance companies, post offices, theatres, utility companies, national organizations, custom officials, and municipal administration. Many of the Western-inspired buildings built by foreign merchants lined the Bund, a street in Shanghai that faces the harbor. An example of the replication of Western architecture is the resemblance between Manhattan's Flatiron Building (1902) by Daniel Burnham and Shanghai's International Savings Society Apartments (later called the Normandie Apartments) (1934) by Hungarian architect Ladislaus (László) E. Hudec (Figure 5.20). Both buildings took the form of their triangular site and used a heavy projected cornice. Each building also has three major horizontal divisions, but the materials and colors used for their façades differ. The façade of the Flatiron Building is limestone and glazed terra-cotta.

Art Deco and Modern were two styles that reflected Shanghai's quest to transform its image in order to expand international economic opportunities. The decision to design buildings in the Art Deco style is reflective of how the business executives and Shanghai administrators were trying to promote the city's import-export trade by using a style that was associated with modernism and advancements in technologies. The Art Deco style reflected a new look for Shanghai that helped erase the city's ties to colonialism and traditional Chinese architecture.

By the 1930s, Shanghai had become the "premier port of the Far East and the fifth port of the world" (*Encyclopedia Britannica*, 1937, p. 456). Shanghai has become well known for its collection of buildings in the Art Deco style, such as the Sassoon House/Cathay Hotel (1929) (modern Peace Hotel North Building); Picardie Apartments (1935) (modern Hengshan Hotel); and the Park Hotel (modern Jin Jiang Park Hotel) (1934). The 22-story Park Hotel was designed in the classic Art Deco style with a pyramidal, set-back tower that resembles cascading water. This creation by Hudec was the tallest building in Asia and Shanghai until 1952 and 1983, respectively. The Park Hotel is located on Nanjing Road (modern Nanjing Dong Lu), the main shopping road in Shanghai.

Economic modernization in commerce was also evident in Shanghai's developments in retail stores.

After the 1911 revolution, in an effort to promote retail commerce, Nanjing Road became the site for several large department stores, including the "Big Four Companies"—Sincere Department Store (1917) (modern Shanghai Fashion Company); Wing On (1918) (modern Hualian Commercial Building; Sun-Sun (1926) (modern Shanghai No. 1 Provisions Store); and The Sun (1936) (modern The No. 1 Department Store) by Kwan, Chu, and Yang. These were some of the first large department stores in China. The interior plan of Wing On was important because the design established a consumer demand format that other large department stores subsequently emulated (www.shme.com, 2008). For example, a strategic element of the plan involved giving shoppers immediate access to inexpensive merchandise that they would need to purchase repeatedly, while locating the expensive products (which required more time to buy) much farther away. The ground level featured products for everyday use, such as food and cigarettes. The displays on the ground floor were elaborate to encourage impulse purchases. Textiles and clothing were offered on the first floor. The third

Figure 5.20 Replicating Western architecture is the resemblance between Shanghai's La Normandie Apartments and Manhattan's Flatiron Building by Daniel Burnham. Both buildings took the form of their triangular site and used a heavy projected cornice.

Source: Wikimedia Commons.

and fourth floors were dedicated to items that could be considered *intentional* purchases, such as furniture, porcelain, musical instruments, and clocks.

The products sold in the large department stores reflected Shanghai's commercial and political climate in the 1920s and 1930s. In the early 20th century, when the International Settlement controlled the city, the stores sold goods from Britain, France, and other countries. The Chinese eventually started to protest imperialism and foreign interference, and their efforts for a semblance of local control of their commerce began to succeed during World War I—when the Western powers were battling. Foreign countries eventually started releasing commercial concessions back to the Chinese.

By the mid-1930s, Shanghai had over three million people. As the societal sentiment began shifting toward nationalism and economic expansion, retailers started selling products made by Chinese workshops and factories, including textiles and yarn spinning. This progress was halted when the Japanese invaded and controlled Shanghai at the start of the Second Sino-Japanese War (1937–1945) but continued after the war and well into the 21st century.

Advertising and Office Productivity: The Johnson Wax Building (1936–1939) in Racine, Wisconsin, by Frank Lloyd Wright

The leaders of many corporations in the early 20th century believed that constructing new, modern buildings could be a means of promoting their business through associating the corporation's name with a building, such as the Bata Building (1937–1938) in Zlin, Czechoslovakia (modern Czech Republic), and the McGraw-Hill (1930–1931) and Chrysler (1928–1930) buildings in Manhattan. The Chrysler Building not only took its name from the company, but its Art Deco style incorporated motifs that were associated with the streamlined design of automobiles. For example, the gargoyles resembled ornaments on the hoods of cars

and the sunburst at the top of the building was similar to an automobile's front grill.

Herbert F. Johnson, the president of S.C. Johnson & Son Company (and grandson of its founder), also believed that an innovative corporate building would be an excellent way to raise the company's profile, promote the company's wax and paint products, and improve its sales. In the short term, the company would benefit from the extensive publicity that accompanies groundbreaking architecture, and in the long-term, perceptions of the corporation as a progressive company would influence consumers' acceptance of new products. After rejecting a traditional design from a local architect, Johnson determined that the innovative and internationally known Frank Lloyd Wright would be the perfect architect to design a modern, new administration building for the company.

To promote the company's image, Wright wanted to design a building that incorporated the most progressive concepts associated with modern architecture. This involved using modern styles, materials, technologies, space planning, and pioneering concepts regarding efficient office productivity. In the 1930s, streamlined designs were popular due to their associations with the escalating speeds and other technological advances of automobiles, ocean liners, trains, and airplanes. To present a fast image, transportation vehicles were designed with multiple horizontal lines in a silver-colored metal along the sides. For example, fast passenger trains, such as the *Pioneer Zephyr* (1934), were made of stainless steel. A series of shiny horizontal lines became a design feature associated with modern and was applied to any product that was supposed to be futuristic, such as refrigerators or plastic radios.

Wright transferred this streamlined image to the design of the Johnson Wax Building. Alternating Pyrex® glass tubes and different sizes and shapes of brick to form the angles and curves, Wright created a series of horizontal lines along the exterior elevations. Horizontal lines appeared to be continuous by substituting curves

Figure 5.21 Wright designed the Johnson Building with a modern open plan in the center of the building. Wright opened the *Great Workroom* by creating a space that resembles being "among pine trees breathing fresh air and sunlight."

Source: Courtesy of S. C. Johnson & Son, Inc.

Great Workroom

for corners wherever possible. Rooms had curved walls made from bricks or glass tubes. Glass tubes were used to emphasize the curve of the barrel-vault ceiling of a bridge between the main building and the rooftop squash court. Office desks designed by Wright also had a streamlined appearance through his use of curved corners and a series of horizontal planes. A futuristic impression was derived from cantilevered elements, such as the "pads" on the top of interior columns and planning for the modern automobile by connecting the building to a carport.

Wright used modern space-planning techniques to eliminate "the box." In a 1956 interview, he explained his disdain for "the box," stating, "the box has had a long and credible history in architecture because there was no way of building a building except, practically, to make it a box or columns that form a box. But when we, in modern times, got steel we had an element, and glass, we had two elemental materials that abolish a box" (Meehan, 1984, p. 89).

Wright used steel and glass in many ways to avoid and eliminate boxes in the Johnson Wax Building. Following his earlier success of the Larkin Building (1904), Wright designed the Johnson Building with a modern open plan in the center of the building (Figure 5.21). Wright opened the "Great Workroom" by creating a space that resembled being "among pine trees breathing fresh air and sunlight" (Lipman, 1986, p. 41). This was accomplished by placing sleek "dendriform" columns resembling tree trunks in a tall, two-story space that reach toward the sky. The glass tubes allowed sunlight to penetrate the space, and the "pads" resembled canopies created by leaves and branches. Wright also attempted to eliminate "the box" by using rows of glass tubes for clerestories, a horizontal row of windows located on a wall, close to the ceiling. Bending the glass in corners and over curved surfaces intensified the effect.

The Great Workroom's open plan was a modern approach to office space planning and reflected Wright's application of informal research findings to the design process. Johnson wanted a building that would be efficient and a pleasant work environment, explaining his motivation in the following statement: "Let's not try to build only a bigger business—let's not let mere size be the goal of our ambitions—let's build a finer, more perfect corporation, so as to make our chosen life's work fine, and more enjoyable" (Lipman, 1986, p. 1). To identify an environment that would create a "more perfect corporation," Wright interviewed employees and observed work in the factories. He applied the results to the space plans and the design of the furniture (see Figure 5.21). People who frequently worked together were placed close to each other. Any functions that were used by many people were centralized. Shared files for each department were located in the center of the building under the mezzanine. File cabinets on casters were designed to transport the files. Using the same shapes, materials, and colors unified the designs for the furniture, but Wright included several variations to accommodate the tasks of the employee (Figure 5.22). For example, all desktops had rounded corners, wooden tops, and earth red–colored tubular steel supports. To meet the specific needs of an employee, some desks had recessed areas for rows of files and others had clear surfaces for writing. To provide the ideal height for typing, desks had a lowered surface for typewriters. The three-legged office chair was designed to force people to sit straight while working; improper posture resulted in people falling out of these chairs. However, Wright also designed a four-legged version of the chair that is still produced today by Steelcase.

Employees' physiological and psychological needs were designed for by incorporating features that would improve the **indoor environmental quality (IEQ).** For example, Wright reduced noise levels in open areas by insulating the walls with cork and using rubber tiles for the floors. Loud office equipment, such as a duplicating machine, was placed in separate rooms. Wright specified modern mechanical systems to be used, including air-conditioning and radiant floor heat. Air-conditioning vents were concealed in the calyx, and fresh air vents were located on the roof rather than

the traditional location along exterior walls, which was adjacent to polluted streets. To provide quality illumination, rooms had daylight and indirect lighting, and desks were designed so that each individual had control of his or her task lighting. Installing wooden blinds reduced glare from the clerestory windows. Other amenities for employees included a recreation deck over the carport, a squash court, and a theater.

A great deal of publicity accompanied the completion of the Johnson Wax Building, and the entire Racine community was invited to the official opening on April 22, 1939. Some of the publicity focused on the 15 to 25 percent increases in employee productivity efficiency due to the improvements in the IEQ. From a different perspective, in an article published in the Milwaukee Journal, the financial editor described the design of the Great Workroom: "A silly urge comes over you to lie flat upon the bottom of this pool of liquid light and stare up at the lily pads—of concrete—that float upon its glassy surface" (Lipman, 1986, p. 93).

Figure 5.22 Using the same shapes, materials, and colors unified the designs for the furniture in the Johnson Building, but there were several variations to accommodate the tasks of the employee.
Source: Courtesy of S. C. Johnson & Son, Inc.

SUMMARY

For millions of people throughout the world, dealing with the Great Depression and its consequences was the focus of the 1930s. Approximately 25 percent of the world's working population was unemployed during at least part of the 1930s. The destabilizing economic situation created circumstances that contributed to the rise of totalitarian leaders, including Hitler, Mussolini, and Stalin, who each ordered the construction of monumental structures for administrative functions. Large squares were included in the front of these buildings, making it possible for masses of people to hear the leaders' speeches. In Brazil, Getúlio Vargas initiated the construction of a new ministry building and other monumental buildings in the Modern style. New concepts regarding how to design residential living space were introduced; the world's first "glass house" was designed by Mies for a family in Brno, Czech Republic.

Water played a role in design and construction in the 1930s: Boulder Dam (modern Hoover Dam) was constructed to both control and benefit from the power of the Colorado River, and Frank Lloyd Wright harnessed a stream in Pennsylvania to create the Fallingwater house. Geography and climate inspired Alvar Aalto when he designed the Paimio Sanatorium and the Library at Viipuri in Finland during this decade.

New industries, technologies, and international developments continued to be introduced. Scalamandré Silks, Inc., a textile manufacturer, had the technology, skills, and silk to successfully launch their company in the 1930s. By the mid-1930s, General Electric was selling the first fluorescent lamps. Possibilities related to the area of flight expanded with the invention of the helicopter and jet engine and the development of radar. The DuPont Company's invention of nylon affected many products, including carpets and upholstery fabric. Improvements to modes of transportation provided people with the ability to travel around the world faster and easier. Despite the ravages of the Great Depression, interest in international travel and immigration continued in the 1930s and sustained the ocean liner industry that had expanded in the 1920s. The early 20th century saw the introduction of new concepts in the design of residential living space. To actually live in an open living space and a glass house required people who were willing to transform their lifestyle. Mies's Tugendhat Villa was the first "glass house" and its design became a "masterpiece of the Modern Movement in architecture" (UNESCO, 2000).

The 1930s also saw the completion of Rockefeller Center in New York City, a project that had been conceived before the stock market crash of 1929; today it features commercial offices, restaurants, shops, theaters, television studios, gardens, a plaza, and promenades. Advances in film technologies made possible the 1933 movie *King Kong*, which attracted worldwide attention to New York City's new Art Deco Empire State Building. The Art Deco style and business initiatives were also evident in Shanghai, China, during this period. To promote commercial business, the city developed many industrial and commercial buildings along its Huangpu River. Nanjing Road, the city's major shopping thoroughfare, became the site for several new, large department stores, such as The Sun. The leaders of many corporations believed that the designs and architecture used in their buildings could be a means of promoting their business. The Johnson Wax Building, a new and modern administration building for S.C. Johnson & Son Company in Racine, Wisconsin, designed by Frank Lloyd Wright, featured the most progressive concepts associated with modern architecture, including a modern approach to the open office plan.

KEY TERMS

ballast

Brazilian Modern

brise-soleil

bullion fringe

cords

cove lighting

discharge lamps

ergonomics

fast-tracking

fluorescent lamp

fringe

gimp

indoor environmental quality (IEQ)

Modernismo

passementerie

ropes

rosette

ruffs

tassel

tiebacks

EXERCISES

1. Human Factors Research Project. Brazilian Modernismo is a blending of local traditions and international avant-garde. Research Brazilian Modernismo and the architects involved with the style. Your research should include an examination of the contextual factors that affected Brazilian Modernismo, including politics, economics, cultural heritage, and environmental factors. Select a project in a studio course and design the interior in the Brazilian Modernismo style. Write a report that has the research findings and could include drawings, sketches, and photographs.

2. Research Design Project. To conserve space and resources, many architects and designers have designed multipurpose built-in cabinetry for residential interiors. In a team of designers, research custom cabinetry and appropriate sustainable materials. Design cabinetry for contemporary residential interiors that is multifunctional and reflects the principles of sustainability. Present the design solutions using sustainable materials and methodologies.

3. Philosophy and Design Project. Rockefeller hired a philosophy professor from Southern California to develop the theme for the center bearing his family name in New York. Rockefeller decided that to communicate a message to the world, the center's theme would be "New Frontiers and the March of Civilization." Conduct a visual field trip of an interior on the Internet. Examine the interior and identify the theme for each project. Select a project and create a collage that reflects its theme. Include a written report that summarizes your thoughts and observations.

CHAPTER 6

EMPHASIS: THE 1940S

OBJECTIVES

After reading this chapter, you should be able to describe and analyze:

■ How selected global political events in the 1940s affected interior environments and architecture as evident by buildings in the Warsaw ghetto and furniture designed by Charles and Ray Eames.

■ How the natural environment affected selected global interior environments and architecture in the 1940s as evident by organic furnishings, the Farnsworth House, and the Glass House.

■ How selected global technologies and materials in the 1940s affected interior environments and architecture as evident by the designs of Raymond Loewy and R. Buckminster Fuller.

■ How selected global work and lifestyles affected interior environments and architecture as evident by the *For Modern Living* exhibition and the L'Unité d'Habitation in Marseille, France.

■ How selected global visual arts and performing arts in the 1940s affected interior environments and architecture as evident by the designs of Isamu Noguchi, Gunta Stölzl, and Anni Albers.

■ How selected global business developments and economics in the 1940s affected interior environments and architecture as evident by the Herman Miller Furniture Company and hotels on the Las Vegas strip.

■ How to compare and contrast selected interior environments and architecture of the Americas, Asia/Oceania, Europe, and the Middle East/Africa in the 1940s.

Germany's invasion of Poland in 1939 helped trigger the conditions that millions of people lived with for most of the 1940s. World War II battles consumed the first half of the decade; the remaining years focused on recovering from its devastating consequences. World War II ended in Europe on May 8, 1945. The U.S. decision to use the atomic bomb and the subsequent obliteration of Hiroshima and Nagasaki brought the war to an end in the Pacific on September 2, 1945. During the war, the world witnessed the inhumane, depraved conditions that resulted from the German persecution of Jews in the Holocaust. To help prevent and resolve future world conflicts, the United Nations was founded in 1945. The end of World War II saw the beginning of the Cold War between the Soviet Union and the United States. The tensions between these two countries contributed to the establishment of the North American Treaty Organization (NATO) in 1949.

The concluding years of the decade saw a civil war in China (1945–1949) and, after an evacuation by the British, the creation of the state of Israel in 1948. Britain also granted independence to India and Pakistan in 1947. A year after India gained independence, Mohandas Gandhi, who, along with his followers, had been instrumental in achieving that success, was killed by a Hindu radical as he walked to a community prayer session. The Philippines, Sri Lanka, Burma, and Indonesia also achieved their independence from colonial rule by the end of the decade.

As had been the case during the First World War, most of the resources in the early 1940s were dedicated to the war effort. This huge demand stimulated the economy of many countries, such as Canada and the United States, which ended the Great Depression but also contributed to rationing policies due to severe shortages of food and materials. Technologies developed for the war led to new products that eventually could be used by general consumers. Jet engines and radar invented in the 1930s were further developed and subsequently used to advance commercial passenger air travel. Charles Eames and his wife Ray Eames, an artist, applied war technologies, including plywood parts for aircraft and synthetic glues, to the development of molded plywood furniture.

The war had destroyed innumerable cities and towns all over the world, leaving millions of people homeless. As a result, significant attention was focused on addressing massive housing shortages, which involved developing mass-produced prefabrication technologies. Optimism during the postwar years fueled new technologies and businesses, including the microwave oven (1947), mobile phone (1947), Velcro (1948), and the first computer able to store programs (1949) (developed by British engineers).

GLOBAL POLITICS AND GOVERNMENT

World War II began on September 1, 1939, when Germany invaded Poland. The battles lasted for 6 years, spanning three continents. A key turning point in the war was the Allies' landing at Normandy, France in 1944. Germany's inability to successfully defend against the Normandy campaign begun on D-Day, as it became known, loosened Germany's grip on Europe. Most of the world—including Germany, France, England, Italy, Soviet Union, Japan, and the United States—was involved in some aspect of combat until 1945. During the war, millions were killed and hundreds of thousands lived in horrendous conditions, like those in the Warsaw ghetto, where a large population of Jews was forced to live. Technologies developed and used for the war effort resulted in new materials for architecture, buildings, and interior environments. To build a massive structure that would house the entire

U.S. war department, the government broke ground to construct the Pentagon Building in Washington, D.C. on September 11, 1941 and completed the military structure (more than 3 million square feet or 278,709 square meters) in mid-February of 1943. Charles and Ray Eames developed and designed new products that revolutionized the furniture industry. Jens Risom was another designer who applied wartime technologies to interior furnishings. Risom used parachute straps to create a basket-weave pattern for the backs and seats of lounge chairs. His **Scandinavian Modernism** chair with woven cotton or cotton/nylon webbing is one piece in a series for the Knoll furniture manufacturer.

World War II: Worldwide Destruction and the Warsaw Ghetto

It has been estimated that more than 80 million people died or were injured as a result of World War II. Combat also led to the destruction of major cities and countless small towns. As discussed in this section, the ways that World War II affected people, interior environments, and architecture are countless and include topics that are not normally explored when one examines the built environment. This includes a discussion of the thousands of residences, commercial buildings, and historic sites that were damaged or destroyed during the war. Examples also include buildings and interiors that were converted into warring facilities and the construction of new buildings, such as the Pentagon, that were constructed to manage the war effort.

Dissemination of design concepts and movements was facilitated when architects, artists, and interior designers fled the battlefields and immigrated to countries such as the United States. Sadly, the war also affected the built environment when the Nazis created buildings in concentration camps for the purpose of killing millions of people. Moreover, to hide from the Nazis, people living in the wartime ghettos created new approaches to the design of interior environments and identified unconventional uses for furniture.

The widespread devastation in World War II was due in part to the decisions of leaders and to advances in technologies that had been discovered and developed in the 19th century, including U-boats (underground boats or submarines), tanks, radio communications, planes, and the atomic bomb. Significant loss of life and property had occurred in World War I, but a defining feature of that conflict, trench warfare, helped to reduce widespread destruction.

In World War II, entire villages, towns, farmland, and large areas of major cities were destroyed due to "modern" warfare, which was much more mobile and on a significantly larger scale than 30 years previous. Consequently, thousands of homes, churches, schools, and businesses representing centuries of civilizations were lost in just 6 years. Probably the most significant damage occurred in Hiroshima and Nagasaki as a result of the atomic bombs. However, significant damage also occurred in London, Berlin, Poland, Rotterdam, Russia, Tokyo, and major port cities. This devastation was primarily due to *Blitzkrieg* (lightning war). Initially, Germany was very successful employing Blitzkrieg, which resulted in a rapid occupation of Poland, Denmark, Norway, Holland, Belgium, France, Rumania, and Greece in a little over 2 years.

The first phase of the Blitzkrieg was executed by dive-bombers, airplanes that were used to terrify citizens and destroy a city's important infrastructure such as railroads, highways, bridges, and governmental buildings. The great domes of cathedrals were easy targets from the air; numerous churches were therefore either destroyed or heavily damaged. After a city was immobilized, Hitler ordered the next phase: rapid deployment of a motorcycle infantry, armored cars, and tanks. To complete the occupation, the last phase was the deployment of foot soldiers. Key to Germany's success was striking fast with a powerful air force and army.

After declaring war on Germany in 1939, London endured numerous air raids and rocket bombs and more than 1,500 fires from a variety of sources.

St. Paul's Cathedral in London was attacked by German airplanes (December 1940), but the local firewatchers saved the burning structure; this act became a symbol of British resistance and helped to inspire the country's resolution to win the war. The widespread bombing on Coventry, England, demolished that city's cathedral. The fragments of the church have been preserved as a reminder of the perils of war (Figure 6.1). Other historic sites, many of them cathedrals, that were damaged during the War include the Houses of Parliament, London; the Berlin Cathedral; the Zwinger Palace, Dresden, Germany; St. Stephen's Cathedral, Vienna; Church of St. Mary, Gdańsk, Poland; St. John's Cathedral, Warsaw; Mátyás Church, Budapest; and St. Isaac's Cathedral in St. Petersburg.

A fragmented structure also remains in Hiroshima, Japan, which had been at war with the United States since its attack on Pearl Harbor on December 7, 1941. Horrendous devastation occurred on August 6, 1945, when the United States attacked Hiroshima with an atomic bomb. More than a hundred thousand civilians were instantly killed or injured. Sixty percent of the city was destroyed. The intense heat of the explosion was felt 10 miles (16 kilometers) away from the city, and radiation burns caused victims to suffer lifelong disfigurement, scars, and sickness. No buildings were left intact, but a structure that appeared to demonstrate resistance was the Industrial Exhibition Hall. The dome's skeletal frame withstood the atomic bomb and still stands as one more reminder of the horrific consequences of war.

Three days later, the city of Nagasaki, Japan was destroyed in the same manner when the United States dropped another atomic bomb on this city of 250,000 people. Japan surrendered on August 14, 1945. Three months later, the first session of the General Assembly of the United Nations established the United Nations Atomic Energy Commission to develop "effective co-operation in the field of atomic energy" (United Nations, 1945).

Buildings in various parts of the world were converted to support wartime activities, including the Akershus Castle in Oslo, Norway, which was converted into a Nazi prison. As mentioned in the previous chapter, many of the luxurious ocean liners that sailed the oceans

Figure 6.1 The widespread bombing on Coventry, England, demolished its cathedral. The fragments of the church have been preserved as a reminder of the perils of war.
Source: INTERFOTO/Alamy.

in the 1930s with wealthy passengers were converted into troop transport vessels, their elegant furnishings stripped, their rooms turned into mess halls, and sleeping quarters filled with military bunks. Indoor swimming pools were covered to provide additional sleeping space. Some of the liners were scrapped for metal, which was melted and then used to produce materials for the war.

The war prompted many architects, designers, artists, scientists, writers, and musicians—including Einstein, Stravinsky, Gropius, and Mies—to emigrate to the Americas. In fact, Einstein was the scientist who signed a letter to President Franklin Roosevelt written by physicist Leo Szilard in 1939 urging that the atomic bomb be built. Interior design and architecture were significantly impacted in the late 1930s when Gropius became the chairman of the Harvard Design School and Mies was named the director of the Armour Institute School of Architecture (modern Illinois Institute of Technology, or IIT) in Chicago. Gropius and Mies were able to directly share their philosophies with architects and designers in the United States. Moreover, their positions at higher education institutions created the opportunity to disseminate their modern perspectives with faculty and students. If Mies had not immigrated to Chicago, perhaps the renowned buildings on the IIT campus might never have been conceived or built (see Chapter 7). However, millions of people were unable to flee from the persecution of the Nazi party. To accommodate the Nazis' Final Solution, a policy of annihilating the Jewish people, new, horrific buildings were constructed in concentration camps for the sole purpose of gassing and incinerating hundreds of thousands of people.

The Nazis also turned existing structures and areas into ghettos for Jewish people. The most notorious ghetto was in Warsaw, Poland. Soon after Germany occupied that country in 1939, Warsaw's extensive Jewish community, almost a third of the city's population, was forced to live in a small area of the city behind walls and barbed wire. Existing buildings became apartments that were shared with strangers. The overcrowded apartments had approximately 15-people-per-livable rooms and lacked adequate sanitation, heat, and water (Figure 6.2). Furniture and anything else made of wood in an apartment were burned for heat. People starved, and easily contracted and died from typhoid fever caused by the poor sanitary conditions.

Figure 6.2 In the Warsaw ghetto, overcrowded apartments also had hiding places that were complete with food supplies for months.

Source: U.S. Holocaust Museum.

To record the horrific conditions, Józef Kaliszan, a Polish artist who survived the war, later painted 40 drawings of the Warsaw ghetto in 1966. The collection has ten drawings in each of the following categories: "Exodus," "Ghetto," "Ghetto Fighting," and "Massacre." In 1942, the Nazis sent hundreds of thousands of people from the Warsaw ghetto to the gas chambers in the Treblinka concentration camp. The remaining Jews in the ghetto were outraged, and in 1943 there was an uprising that significantly challenged the German army. The German response was to quickly send many people to concentration camps. Anyone remaining was brutally killed, and the ghetto was burned and destroyed.

After the war, a historical recording of life in the Warsaw ghetto, written by Emmanuel Ringelblum, was found buried in two secret locations. Ringelblum was a prisoner of the ghetto and his journal describes the horrendous conditions, but he also explains how people redesigned buildings to save their lives. (Anne Frank's diaries are perhaps the best-known example of information about how interiors were adapted in order for people to hide from the Nazis.) Titled "Hiding Places," Ringelblum's journal entry on December 14, 1942, provides the following details about "popular" and ingenious secretive rooms:

> Everywhere, in all the shops and elsewhere in the Ghetto, hiding places are being built. Their construction has actually become a flourishing specialized craft. Skilled workers, engineers, etc. are making a living out of it (Ringelblum, 1958, p. 338). Successful "hiding places" required trap doors, hidden corners, sound control, food supplies for months, access to water, and concealed entries and windows. Apartment buildings with identical layouts were a special problem, which he discussed in the following manner: "As everyone knows, modern apartment houses are so constructed that all the apartments in the same line have the same layout. Walling up an alcove in one apartment does not provide an adequate hiding place, because it is quite easy to find the same alcove on a higher or lower floor in the same line of apartments. The way out of this dilemma was for all the persons living in the same line to wall up their alcoves. In one house, the residents all walled up one corner of a room built an entry through a bakery oven, and put in a passageway from one floor to the next through a chain of ladders pushed through the holes cut into the floors. An impressive hideout like that accommodates up to sixty persons. (Ringelblum, 1958, p. 343)

"Professional informers" revealed many hideouts, which resulted in immediate executions. After the ghetto uprising, the Germans found the hiding place of Ringelblum, his wife, and their 12-year-old son. The family and 35 other people who were hiding together were executed on March 7, 1944.

World War II Warfare Technologies: Charles and Ray Eames

World War II was a total effort involving people of every age group, both genders, and all levels of physical and mental ability. Everyone sacrificed, and to maximize the number of troops available for the war those at home began to do the work previously done by men who were fighting on the battlefields. The degree of sacrifice made by people in many countries resulted in starvation, disease, and death. Women and children worked in factories to produce warfare supplies and equipment, including planes, rifles, ships, tanks, and ammunition. The home fronts of every warring nation were impacted by rationing or eliminating any commodity that was important for the war effort, including food, clothing, soap, nylon, paper, gasoline, coal, metal products, batteries, rubber, tin, and nickel. Even wallpaper became part of the war effort; glued to helmets and jackets, it was used for camouflage, which worked well when a soldier was hiding in an abandoned house. Children also contributed to the war relief by selling war stamps and scouring streets and homes for any metal product, such as tin cans, lead foil, and aluminum pots and pans. These were needed to build warring technologies such as tanks, guns, bullets, and planes.

In occupied countries civilians formed resistance groups that sabotaged the operations of the enemy. For example, in France the members of "The Committee of Public Safety" sabotaged German transportation networks, set fire to oil supplies, smuggled communications, and were espionage agents. When caught by the Germans, the members of the resistance were immediately executed, but the possibility of this fate did not deter them. Another country deeply involved on the home front during the war was the Union of Soviet Socialist Republics (USSR). Due to severe food shortages and that country's harsh climate, the Soviets endured some of the worst conditions of all the warring nations. However, the remarkable strength and resilience of Soviet civilians contributed to the country's victory over the German army in the fierce and deadly battles at Stalingrad (modern Volgograd) in 1942.

The sacrifices, living conditions, destruction, and focus on warfare technologies during the first half of the decade had a significant impact on people, interior environments, and architecture in the postwar years. First and foremost people were committed to practical lifestyles, economizing, and living with less, which they had become accustomed to during the Great Depression.

The comprehensive destruction of cities and towns resulted in a severe housing shortage in most of the warring nations. As soon as possible after the end of hostilities, government officials enacted city planning committees and initiated commissions for mass-produced housing developments. In anticipating housing shortages, the July 1944 issue of *Arts and Architecture* magazine was dedicated to industrial housing, including prefabrication, employing wartime technologies, and mass-production techniques. In the 1940s, articles in the *Arts and Architecture* magazine focused on not only architecture and the visual and performing arts, but also cultural, political, and social

issues. The versatile American architect and designer Charles Eames and John Entenza, the editor and publisher of *Arts and Architecture,* wrote an article, "What Is a House?" in the July 1944 issue that reflects the principles of sustainability by describing the relationships between people, economics, and the environment. Their exploration of "materials and techniques" recommended that solutions to the housing shortage involve "all our experience as a nation organized for war production and from all related scientific development" (Eames and Entenza, 1944, pp. 22–49).

One year later, to stimulate concepts for "good housing" in southern California, the magazine sponsored a multi-year project that resulted in the construction of several prototypes. Charles and Ray Eames and the Finnish architect and furniture designer Eero Saarinen collaborated on the design for a house and studio for the Eameses, Case Study #8 (modern Eames House) (Figure 6.3). In following the spirit of the project, Case Study #8 had minimal square footage (approximately 2,000 square feet or 185.81 square meters), prefabricated elements, and "off-the-shelf" materials, such as windows, doors, trusses, decking, and columns. The modular system of the steel framing required less than 2 days to complete. The combination of industrial materials was harmonized by designing asymmetrically balanced elevations that resemble a Piet Mondrian *Composition* painting (see Chapter 4). The influence of Mondrian's paintings is further evidenced by the use of red, blue, white, black, and gray for the exterior colors.

The Eameses and Entenza were in an ideal position to participate in the *Arts and Architecture* project. During the war they were extensively involved with the design, experimentation, and production of objects made using technologies developed during wartime, including molded plywood splints, litters, aircraft parts, and gliders. The Eameses and Saarinen began experimenting with molding wood into compound curves in 1940. The living room seating units and **case goods,** or furniture for storage, such as dressers, that

Figure 6.3 The house and studio for the Eameses, Case Study #8 (modern Eames House). In following the spirit of the project, Case Study #8 had minimal square footage, prefabricated elements, and "off-the-shelf" materials such as windows, doors, and trusses.

Source: © Tim Street-Porter/Esto.

they created won first place in the Museum of Modern Art's (MoMA) competitive exhibition in 1941, "Organic Design in Home Furnishings." For the purpose of the competition, MoMA's definition of **organic design** was as follows: "A design may be called organic when there is an harmonious organization of the parts within the whole, according to structure, material, and purpose. Within this definition there can be no vain ornamentation or superfluity, but the part of beauty is none the less great—in ideal choice of material, in visual refinement, and in the rational elegance of things intended for use" (Noyes, 1969 reprint edition, p. 1). The purpose of the competition "was to discover good designers and engage them in the task of creating a better environment for today's living" (Noyes, 1969 reprint edition, p. 4). The contest also intended to encourage a collaborative relationship between designers, manufacturers, and retailers. Thus, designers of the winning entries were supposed to work with manufacturers through the production process and then collaborate with sponsoring retailers to develop the most effective displays. Prototypes were built and displayed at the MoMA; however, World War II precluded fruition of the project.

The Eameses' and Saarinen's furniture was not put into production due to the war, but the initiative served as the foundation for the development of molded plywood chair seats, sculptures, and other experiments. The Eameses became involved with splint and litter products when a physician familiar with the Eameses' experiments suggested that the molded technologies might lessen problems associated with metal splints. On the battlefields, metal splints were used to help protect a soldier's leg or arm during transport. Due to slippage and shapes that did not conform to the shape of legs, metal splints often failed to secure a leg, which resulted in further injury and medical complications. This prompted the Eameses to develop prototypes of molded-plywood leg splints, which they demonstrated to the U.S. Navy. After an order from the U.S. Navy, the Eameses collaborated with publisher and financier John Entenza to found the Plyformed Wood Company. This arrangement provided the Eameses with the resources, equipment, and time for extensive experimentation and for the development of prototypes. Contracts with the military provided the Eameses privileged access to rationed materials and large quantities of electricity, which was needed to mold the plywood. To expand its mass-production capabilities, the company merged with the industrial manufacturer Evans Products Company in Detroit. For approximately 3 years, more than 150,000 leg splints were produced for the war effort.

The Eameses' considerable experimentation with war-related products, such as very large gliders, provided the ideal background for designing and manufacturing molded plywood interior furnishings in the postwar years. Developing splints that conformed to the human shape was excellent training for designing comfortable seating. Accommodating the military's demands for products that were durable, flawless, and cost-effective and could be quickly manufactured in mass quantities gave Charles and Ray Eames the ideal experience and know-how to design and produce practical and reasonably priced furnishings. The Eameses transferred this knowledge to design furniture that was inexpensive, was lightweight, used minimal materials, was easily stored, and could be mass-produced.

To facilitate mass production processes, the earliest plywood chairs were designed in separate components. The Eameses experimented with three- and four-legged chairs and legs made of both metal and wood. They identified material differences with the name of the chair,

thus the DCW (dining chair wood) (1946) had wooden legs and the DCM (dining chair metal) (1946) featured metal legs (Figure 6.4). The 1945 molded plywood tables had a tray top and were made with metal and wooden legs. The Eameses experimented with rosewood plywood lounge chairs, but their ubiquitous leather lounge chair and ottoman were not perfected until 1956.

To expand the availability of practical furniture, the Eameses designed a system for storage units, Case Goods, that was based on their award-winning designs in the MoMA's 1946 exhibition (see Figure 6.4). Other than a small unit for storing records, each wooden unit in the Case Goods system was 18 inches (45.72 centimeters) wide, 16 inches (40.64 centimeters) deep, and approximately 15 inches (38.1 centimeters) high. Units could be combined to form a sliding door case and could be arranged in numerous configurations. The low-profile units rested on benches, and a unit could have drawers, doors, sliding doors with an embossed "dimple" pattern, open shelves, or wiring for radios (see Figure 6.4). The Eameses also experimented with radio enclosures, plywood folding screens, children's furniture, and toy animals that were large enough for children to ride. In 1947, the Eameses contracted with the Herman Miller Furniture Company to manufacture

Figure 6.4 "New Furniture designed by Charles Eames" exhibition at The Museum of Modern Art in 1946. The exhibit includes the Eameses' Case Goods and their molded plywood chairs.

Source: Digital Image © The Museum of Modern Art/Licensed by SCALA/Art Resource, NY.

and distribute their plywood furniture. The company is still producing their furniture today.

As a means to explore various approaches to determining what is "good design" (MoMA, 2009, p. 1), MoMA sponsored a competitive exhibition called "The International Competition for Low-Cost Furniture Design" in 1948. The competition was held in collaboration with furniture retailers like Herman Miller, who agreed to produce the winning designs. For the contest, the Eameses developed a metal-stamped chair that became the first molded plastic chair. The chair won second place, and Herman Miller is still manufacturing Eameses' chair today in five different "colorful shells," including a stackable side chair. The base of the chair can be made from metal tubes, metal wire with wood runners to enable rocking, or metal wire styles that resemble a cat's cradle and the Eiffel Tower. The original molded plastic chair was supposed to be made by metal-stamping laminates, with a production cost of $27.00. In 1948, the Eameses also designed La Chaise, an innovative organic form inspired by French-American sculptor Gaston Lachaise's 1927 sculpture "Reclining Nude" that allowed the user(s) to determine seating or lounging arrangements. La Chaise proved to be too expensive to manufacture at the time; it did not go into production until 1990.

EFFECTS AND CONDITIONS OF THE NATURAL ENVIRONMENT

MoMA's "Organic Design in Home Furnishings" competition in 1941 also included a division that encouraged Latin American participants to use local materials and methods of construction. The winning entries from Mexico, Uruguay, Argentina, and Brazil demonstrated unique designs with regional materials and processes. The natural environment also had an effect on architects who designed residences that appeared to seamlessly blend interiors with the landscape, as evidenced by the work of Ludwig Mies van der Rohe and Philip Johnson, each of whom designed iconic glass residences in the United States. The beauty of wood was exemplified by the Danish designer Hans Wegner when he created three wooden chairs that have become classics: the elegant Chinese chair (1943), the Windsor-inspired Peacock (1947), and the Round or what was simply known as The Chair (1949).

In contrast to the built environment, two mountain ranges separated by the Atlantic Ocean were in the headlines for activities that occurred thousands of years apart. In the southwest region of France, Paleolithic cave paintings were discovered by four teenagers in Lascaux in 1940, and in South Dakota the granite sculpture Mount Rushmore National Memorial was completed in 1941. The Pacific Ocean was also in the headlines in 1947 after the successful voyage of *Kon-Tiki,* a raft made from the trunk of a balsa tree, that was sailed by a crew of six more than 4,000 miles (6,437 kilometers) to determine the feasibility of prehistoric civilizations making the journey from South America to the Polynesian Islands.

The destructive force of earthquakes during the decade resulted in the deaths of more than 130,000 people in San Juan, Argentina (1944); Turkmen SSR of the USSR (now Turkmenistan) (1948); and Ecuador (1948). In addition, millions of Chinese people died of starvation in 1946 due to a civil war and drought conditions.

Natural Environment: MoMA's "Organic Design in Home Furnishings"—Mexico, Uruguay, Argentina, and Brazil

Saarinen's and the Eameses' winning designs for the MoMA's 1941 competitive exhibition "Organic Design in Home Furnishings" was in the United States category. The exhibition had another category whose

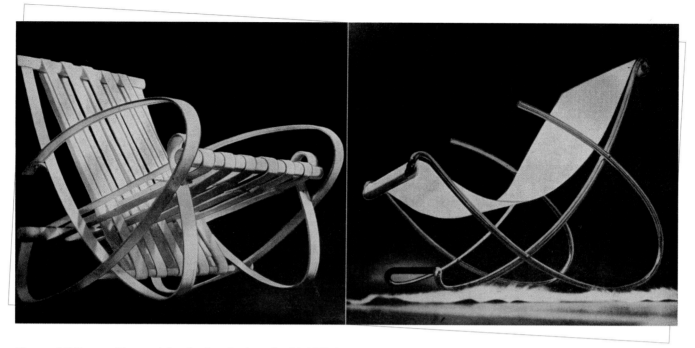

Figure 6.5 Roman Fresnedo's winning designs for MoMA's Latin American competition included rattan pieces, and chairs made with steel frames and skins and leather straps.

Source: Digital Image © The Museum of Modern Art/Licensed by SCALA/Art Resource, NY.

entries were also juried as winners. The second category was for Latin America entries, which included Mexico, Central America, and South America.

The competition's program was distributed to 20 Latin American "republics" and delineated that "The purpose of the Latin American contest was not primarily to procure designs for production in this country, but to discover designers of imagination and ability and bring them to New York to observe and study the work being done here" (Noyes, 1969 reprint edition, p. 39). The program encouraged designers to "submit suggestions as to the manner in which their own local materials and methods of construction might be applied to the making of furniture for contemporary American requirements" (Noyes, 1969 reprint edition, p. 39). In encouraging the Latin American designers to use local materials and technologies, the organizers were hoping to expand the "range of materials available for furniture." From the sustainability viewpoint, encouraging the use of local materials is important because resources and pollutants associated with transportation are reduced, which conserves energy, the natural environment, and costs.

The five winning entries used local materials; many of these were indigenous to South America. The winning Latin American designers were Roman Fresnedo, Montevideo, Uruguay; Julio Villalobos, Buenos Aires, Argentina; Bernardo Rudofsky, São Paulo, Brazil; and Xavier Guerrero and the team of Michael van Beuren, Klaus Grabe, and Morley Webb, Mexico City, Mexico. Looking at the winning furniture provides insight into the geography, climate, and industry of these countries. For example, Fresnedo's winning designs included **rattan** pieces and chairs made with steel frames, animal skins, and leather straps (Figure 6.5). Uruguay is a small country on the Atlantic Ocean between Brazil and Argentina. The climate is moderate, and the land is predominantly grasslands, rivers, and lakes. The environment is ideal for grazing cattle and sheep. This gave Fresnedo access to local skins and leather for his furniture designs. The region also grows the quebracho tree, which produces tannin, a substance used for tanning leather.

Villalobos was from Argentina, which has diverse climates and geographical features due to its extensive north-south land area that exceeds 1 million square miles

(~2.6 million square kilometers). Argentina's geographical features include the Andes Mountains, which adjoin Chili; glaciers in the country's southwest region; and 2,900 miles (4,700 kilometers) of coastline. Other regions include deserts, tropical rainforests, and grasslands. Argentina has a temperate climate that is warmer in the north and cooler in the south. The Andes Mountains create desert conditions along Argentina's west-central border, and the steep mountain range blocks most of the moisture from the Pacific Ocean. These conditions are ideal for growing giant cacti and other arid plants. The inner section of a cactus species found in South America has a woody composition that can be used for structural support and furniture. Villalobos used cactus wood for the slats of the chaise's seat and back (Figure 6.6). Junco reed was another indigenous material that Villalobos specified for the chaise's awning. Because junco has insulating properties, the straw-like reed was perfect for the chaise's awning.

Rudofsky also designed a chair with an awning, but his winning entries were made with fabric from Brazilian fibers, including **jute,** caroã, cánhamo, and others. The dominant element of Rudofsky's outdoor seating was a plain textile made from a variety of Brazilian fibers, including jute and caroã, which was attached to a wood or metal frame. Most of his seating pieces had one continuous piece of fabric that served as the back and the seat. An emphasis on fabrics was appropriate for a Brazilian entry because textiles are a major industrial product of São Paulo and the rest of the country. The southeast region of Brazil has an environment that is ideal for growing fibers for textiles and other crops: The region's rich soil receives ample rainfall, and temperatures are moderate.

Both of the winning Mexican furniture entries used a local fiber for woven webbing. Guerrero's "peasant furniture" used woven **ixtle** webbing for a cot and a chair seat. The fibers from the leaves of the ixtle plant can be woven into a coarse textile. Native to Mexico, the plant requires dry, sunny, and hot conditions. Guerrero's wall cabinet was uniquely designed by using local jute for the sliding door. Van Beuren, Grabe, and Webb's chaise was made of woven **mecate** webbing and **primavera wood.** Mecate is a sisal-like fiber, and primavera is a blond-colored wood with graining that resembles mahogany. (From a sustainability perspective, primavera should be used sparingly because the tree's large canopy provides important shade in the rainforest and the species has a very slow growing period.)

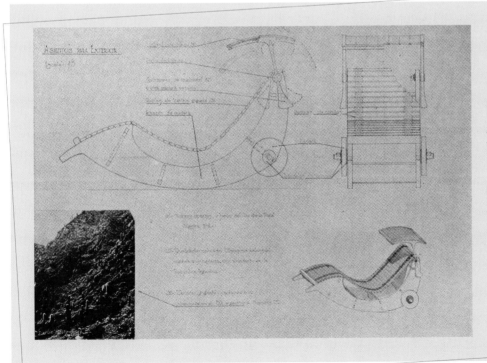

Figure 6.6 For MoMA's Latin American competition, Julius Villalobos used cactus wood for the slats of the chaise's seat and back. Junco reed was another indigenous material that Villalobos specified for the chaise's awning.

Source: © The Museum of Modern Art/Licensed by SCALA/Art Resource, NY.

Natural Environment: Farnsworth House (1946–1951) by Ludwig Mies Van der Rohe and Glass House (1949) by Philip Johnson

German architect Ludwig Mies Van der Rohe appreciated the beauty of primavera wood when he designed the cabinets for the Farnsworth House in Plano, Illinois, his first completed domestic project in America. In the 1940s, Mies and Philip Johnson each designed a residence that enabled its users to feel at one with the natural environment. Mies first conceived the all-glass residence as a country retreat for Dr. Edith Farnsworth in 1945 (Figure 6.7). He had already experimented with the concept of eliminating opaque walls when he designed the Barcelona Pavilion and the Tugendhat residence, discussed in the previous chapter. However, an all-glass residence introduces an entirely novel approach to experiencing nature.

Johnson's early career as a critic and historian provided him with an understanding of the universal qualities of architecture. Specifically, Johnson and architectural historian Henry-Russell Hitchcock were responsible for naming the International Style exhibit for the MoMA in 1932 and became associated with creating the name for the style. Johnson's all-glass structure (modern Glass House) was his personal residence in New Canaan, Connecticut (Figure 6.8). Designed in 1948 and completed in 1949, the Glass House was a radical departure from traditional design, with exterior walls of glass and no interior walls.

While the Farnsworth House and the Glass House are both all-glass structures, each design has a unique response to the natural environment and provides different experiences. The Farnsworth House, built on a meadow close to the Fox River, is set 5 feet, 7 inches (170 centimeters) above the ground with eight steel columns. This interior level is essential when the river overflows its banks. The house can be seen as a modern Mont Saint-Michel (see Chapter 1) when the river completely surrounds the structure. An intimate connection with nature is also present in the way that Mies determined the location of the residence with respect to the site's enormous trees. In several areas, the residence touches trees, shrubs, and prairie grasses. A large sugar maple shades the house and the entry terrace. Other large trees are just inches away from the structure; at times low branches scrape the walls of glass. From the interior, tree trunks, branches, and leaves are so close to the glass that they become the exterior walls. When it rains, the reflections of trees appear on the surface of the **terrazzo**-tiled patio.

Johnson's Glass House was built on the summit of rolling hills and responds to its natural environment by being close to the ground. A secure anchoring to the earth appears necessary in order to prevent strong winds from blowing away the glass structure. Large trees, which could fall during a storm, are not located close to the glass walls; a manicured lawn adjoins the structure instead. The dominant brick tower containing a fireplace and bathroom further emphasizes a secure attachment to the earth. A low concrete railing that runs along the edge of a cliff in the backyard separates people and the residence from a perilous condition created by nature (see Figure 6.8).

Each residence has a unique entry that provides a different approach to interacting with nature. To reach the *hidden* front door of the Farnsworth residence requires a person to climb steps and walk across two large **travertine**-tiled surfaces. To arrive at the exposed front door of the Glass House, one gradually ascends a grassy knoll. Mies blurred the separation between nature and structure by the elimination of columns at the corners and by extending the residence's roof over the patio. When glare from the glass is eliminated, the interior and patio appear to be outdoor space that is protected by one roof. The separation between nature and the Glass House is more defined by the use of corner columns and a roof that conforms to the exact size of the residence.

Different approaches to interacting with nature are also evident in the way that people transition between the interior and the outdoors of each structure. There

Figure 6.7 Designed by Mies, the Farnsworth House in Plano, Illinois, enabled its users to feel one with the natural environment.

Source: The Museum of Modern Art/Licensed by Scala/Art Resource, NY.

Figure 6.8 Philip Johnson's all-glass structure (modern Glass House) was his personal residence in New Canaan, Connecticut.

Source: Time Magazine, March 13, 2008.
Photographer: Eirik Johnson.

is only one set of double doors to enter and exit the Farnsworth residence. To provide immediate access to the outdoors, Johnson's residence has four doors (a single door is located in the center of each elevation).

Mies's and Johnson's designs provide different visual and physical experiences when users transition between the interior and the outdoors. Both residences have floor-to-ceiling glass doors, but the progression between the interior and outdoors appear to be seamless in the Farnsworth house. Mies merged the floors together by continuing the travertine tile flooring from the patio into the residence. The Glass House has a step that separates the lawn from the interior, and the separation is further emphasized by the use of a herringbone-patterned wood floor. The two residences also differ in the ways that people interact with nature. Mies planned stone decks for outdoor seating; Johnson anticipated that people would sit on chairs in the grass. Both architects designed small galley kitchens, but Mies's design requires people to look at cabinets instead of the opposite view of a meadow. By eliminating upper cabinets, people working in Johnson's kitchen are able to enjoy the views of the outdoors.

When seen from the outdoors as the glass reflects nature, the walls appear to be a photograph of the trees and sky. To emphasize the murals of nature, both architects used a minimal number of furniture pieces and natural-fiber textiles in earthen colors. Today, both residences are classics of design and architecture and are National Trust Historic Sites.

GLOBAL TECHNOLOGICAL DEVELOPMENTS

As previously discussed, technological developments in the 1940s primarily focused on equipment and machinery for the war, and the careers of many designers, including Raymond Loewy and R. Buckminster Fuller, were suspended while they assisted the war effort. The most notable technological development during the war was the Manhattan Project in the United States, which resulted in the experimental explosion of the atomic bomb in 1942 and the subsequent bombing of Japan in 1945. Automobile manufacturers used their mass-production processes to produce military vehicles and equipment, and wartime development of communication technologies facilitated the invention of the transistor radio in 1948.

Materials developed during the 1940s included nylon, artificial rubber, and new plastics. Plastic became important for the invention of long-playing records (LPs) in the late 1940s. Earl Tupper's Tupperware Company capitalized on the development of new plastics by creating revolutionary food-storage containers beginning in 1946. The postwar years witnessed a renewed interest in the automobile and the introduction of television.

Technology and Industry: Raymond Loewy, Industrial Designer

The internationally renowned industrial designer Raymond Loewy was born in France at the end of the 19th century, when the focus of technological developments was on the fields of transportation, electricity, mechanization, and mass-production (see Chapter 1). The simultaneous births of Loewy and the machine age eventually contributed to the establishment of the American industrial design profession. Ultimately, Loewy International (with offices and major clients in many cities throughout the world) was responsible for designing automobiles, steamships, railroad locomotives, motor coaches, aircraft, consumer products, commercial equipment, interiors, "specialized architecture," packaging, graphic design, and eventually space stations. His designs, such as the Coca-Cola bottle, the Shell gasoline logo, and the Lucky Strike cigarette package, became iconic. Loewy's guidelines for design were to "Simplify products, make them more economical, easier to maintain and fail-safe so as not to burden further the consumer's already hectic life; avoid unnecessary costly annoyances and irritations; do not indulge in 'yearly model' changes unless they are justified by sound functional, technological, and/or cost advantages" (Renwick Gallery, 1975, p. 9).

The principles of sustainability designers use today are evident in Loewy's recommendations to design products that are cost-effective, easy to maintain, and effortless to use and have enduring styles. Furthermore, Loewy hinted at the creation of designs that reflect the principles of universal design when he said, "Industrial design means a concern for the broadest spectrum of humanity, not only for ideal forms" (Loewy, 1979, p. 122). Loewy demonstrated this philosophy when he improved the design of seats mounted on tractors. He found that a lower seat accommodated farmers who were "old, paunchy, or arthritic" (Loewy, 1979, p. 122).

Loewy moved to the United States in 1919 after serving in World War I. He started his career in the 1920s, drawing fashion sketches for prominent New York department stores; his work as an industrial designer began as a consequence of the Depression. In the 1930s Loewy tried to convince manufacturers to produce attractive products to stimulate purchases. Several decades later, he explained his motivation when he wrote that "good appearance was a salable commodity, that it often cuts costs, enhanced a product's prestige, raised corporate profits, benefited the customer, and increased employment" (Loewy, 1979, p. 52). World War II caused Loewy to shift his attention from business ventures to the war effort. He was given a unique commission by government officials in Washington, D.C. To "help maintain the morale of American woman," the government hired Loewy to design a lipstick container that did not require the essential metals that were needed for warfare. Loewy's solution was a "swivel cardboard" lipstick container. The product was very successful and was purchased by millions of women.

After the war, that creativity was applied to commerce and industry. Enthusiasm for technologies and mass-produced products enabled Loewy to actualize his business philosophy that "good appearance was a salable commodity." Several major corporations—including the Frigidaire Division of General Motors, the Greyhound Bus System, Pennsylvania Railroad, and United Airlines—hired Loewy to design their products. He also became involved with prototypes for futuristic automobiles. Aesthetics were mandatory; however, Loewy's designs also accommodated mass-production technologies and the physical and psychological attributes

of users. For example, to help reduce anxieties of people who were afraid to fly, which was very common in the early years of air travel, the interior of the 1945 Lockheed Constellation was "cheerful and colorful" (Figure 6.9). Understanding how to design interiors to accommodate physical and psychological attributes was critical when Loewy, as a "habitability consultant," later designed the interior of NASA's Skylab in the 1960s.

Loewy applied his experience with designing transportation to a range of products that impacted the design of interior environments, including furniture, appliances, televisions, vacuum cleaners, radios, tableware, and textiles. For example, streamlined styles used in the design of automobiles and railroad locomotives were applied to the fronts of refrigerators, radios, and desks. To create simple designs that had smooth, curved lines, in addition to the visual appraisal, Loewy used his sense of touch. Prototypes of transportation and consumer products were made by sculpting clay. Streamlined designs were perfected when Loewy moved his hands along the profile of a product.

In designing automobiles, Loewy created substantial door handles and aluminum radiator grilles that resisted rust. He adapted these concepts to consumer products by specifying solid handles for refrigerators and desks. To solve the problem of rusty metal wire

Figure 6.9 To reduce anxieties of people who were afraid to fly, which were very common in the early years of flight, Raymond Loewy designed a "cheerful and colorful" interior for the 1945 Lockheed Constellation.
Source: Raymond Loewy™/® by CMG Worldwide, Inc./www.RaymondLoewy.com.

shelves in refrigerators, he designed new units from aluminum radiator grilles. After Loewy's new design was implemented, annual refrigerator sales for the Sears *Coldspot* jumped from 65,000 to 275,000 in the 1930s and 1940s. Desks were designed with drawers that opened smoothly, had solid handles, and included a finish that prevented stains and scratches. To help conceal stains on the seats of Greyhound buses, Loewy designed a patterned fabric that had the same colors as the most common stains found on bus seats.

Loewy's "design cross-pollination" was also applied to department stores. He contended that a department store was a "sales machine" and an "implement for merchandising." To design a "machine," Loewy created plans that were streamlined and functional for shoppers and employees (Figure 6.10). He was concerned about illumination, traffic flow, and convenient stock storage areas. In addition to artificial illumination, Loewy integrated daylight into the environment via large fixed windows, an outdoor terrace, and a special "daylight selling area."

Creating wide aisles and clustering display cabinets streamlined traffic flow. Smooth movement through the store was further emphasized by the use of curved display cases. Loewy designed nine separate stock storage areas throughout the store to provide easy access to reserve merchandise (Figure 6.10). Immediate access to merchandise helped employees and was a tremendous time saver for shoppers. Loewy became very successful in designing and planning department stores and soon established a Store Planning and Design Division in his company. His international success was recognized in 1949 when *Time* magazine featured Loewy on the cover with the caption "He Streamlines the Sales Curve."

Technologies and Furnishings: Dymaxion Machines and Geodesic Domes by R. Buckminster Fuller

Richard Buckminster Fuller ("Bucky") became famous for inventing **geodesic domes** in 1949, but his visionary

abilities were developed well before the world acknowledged his genius. In an autobiographical monologue, he explained, "I'm not trying to imitate nature, I'm trying to find the principles she uses" (Snyder, 1980, p. 196). Fuller was born in the United States in 1895, just 2 years after Loewy. Both pioneers shared the same vision of maximizing the industrial machine but pursued its development in very different ways.

Fuller's lifelong pursuit was "what he called 'Comprehensive Anticipatory Design Science'—the attempt to anticipate and solve humanity's major problems through the highest technology by providing 'more and more life support for everybody, with less and less resources'" (Buckminster Fuller Institute, 2008, p. 1). Specifically, Fuller was concerned about solving the problem of adequate and affordable shelter. Universal shelter was so important to his life's work that *Shelter* became the name of the magazine

Figure 6.10 Ground floor of the Lord & Taylor store, Manhasset, New York. To design a retail "machine," Raymond Loewy created plans that were streamlined and functional for the shoppers and the employees.

Source: Raymond Loewy™/® by CMG Worldwide, Inc./www.RaymondLoewy.com.

he founded in 1930. Fuller's search for the optimum design for shelter was always predicated on following the principles of sustainable development and design. For example, in the 1940s when Fuller was designing the **Dymaxion Deployment Unit (DDU),** a shelter based upon a grain bin, the product was accompanied by a list of the "design responsibilities of the DDU." Fuller believed that a product had a responsibility that exceeded its physical contribution. His "comprehensive design responsibility" or **"cradle-to-grave"** philosophy for a housing program included nine areas:

1. **Mass Production**

2. **Package Distribution**

3. **Quick Erection**

4. **Low Cost**

5. **Flexible Orientation**

6. **Fire Resistance**

7. **Concussion Resistance**

8. **Air Protection**

9. **Demountability (Marks, 1960, p. 113).**

Fuller's "comprehensive design responsibility" was applied to every project, beginning with his earliest experiments. In the late 1920s, he started his historic exploration of universal shelter as a result of being frustrated with "old" architectural concepts and the building industry. Aware of the rapid advances in flight and communications, he expected the building industry technologies to develop at the same pace. In contending that a building should be "flexible" and "demountable," he often asked architects to identify the "weight" of their structures. Of course architects did not have an answer and failed to understand its importance. Buildings were supposed to stay in one place. However, from Fuller's perspective, weight was critical. Heavy structures consumed a great deal of resources, required hundreds (if not hundreds of thousands) of hours of labor to construct, resisted force from winds, and could not be transported.

In trying to technologically advance the building industry in the late 1920s, Fuller began experiments with shelters that could *fly*. He developed his 4-D (fourth-dimension) house by adapting dirigibles, or blimps. By standing a dirigible on its end, Fuller created a house with ten decks. The mast at the top of the house had a hook that could be attached to a dirigible and then flown anywhere in the world. The 4-D house became known as Dymaxion by combining the words "dynamic," "maximum," and "ion." Dymaxion became the name of the design when a model was on display with other "modern" furniture at the Marshall Fields department store in Chicago in 1928. A marketing professional had suggested this modern-sounding name to Fuller after listening to his description of the 4-D house.

In addition to conceptualizing a visionary, transportable house, Fuller's design for the Dymaxion's interior was remarkable. He envisioned a house that had extremely advanced technology, and his design reflected the principles of sustainability and universal design (Figure 6.11). Fuller conceptualized the design in the 1920s, but at this time the materials needed to construct the house were costly and some were still in the development stage. Finally, in the early 1940s he was able to persuade a manufacturer to build a prototype.

Using the methods of the auto industry as a model, the Dymaxion house was designed so that the parts could be mass-produced using an assembly line in a factory. The total price of the house including installation was $6,500. To reduce transportation costs and packaging, Fuller designed the parts to be assembled on the building site. Prefabricated and interlocking parts enabled construction in *1 day*. The Dymaxion house was a series of decks, which were supported by tension cables and a central hollow mast. The building's footprint was minimal, approximately 300 square feet (27.87 square meters), and it even included a garage under the first deck. The exterior walls were a double layer of glass, and partitions and floors were soundproof. The central mast contained an elevator, solar reflectors, wiring for electricity, and the tubing for ventilation, heat, and air conditioning. Fuller designed the mechanical system to create an optimum indoor environmental quality (IEQ) with the ideal temperature, humidity, ventilation, and sound control. As a self-contained unit, the base had a septic system and fuel storage.

The flexible floor plans could be easily reconfigured, and decks could be added or deleted. The efficient floor plans economized on space by eliminating hallways, and partitions served a functional purpose, such as shelving or a laundry unit. In addition to the living room, kitchen, bedrooms, and bathrooms, the house had a library, gymnasium, and swimming pool at the lowest level. The library, or "go-ahead-with-life-room," encouraged "self-education" by including areas for drawing, reading, and the newest technologies, radio and television. Storage for books and clothes was accommodated by "ovolving" or revolving units. An ovolving unit had a series of shelves that rotated in a vertical loop. Only one shelf was visible to a user at a time.

To mechanize cleaning and maintenance, Fuller conceptually designed "catch-up-with-your-life," or laundry units, where clothing could be cleaned, dried, and pressed. Dishwashers washed, dried, and placed dishes on shelves. Compressed air removed dust. To enable people to select an optimum setting, the house had built-in pneumatic beds and sofas. Doors opened and closed by moving a hand across photoelectric cells.

All mechanical and electrical systems were also integrated in the Dymaxion prefabricated bathroom. The efficiency and compactness of the Dymaxion bathroom became a prototype for restrooms on aircraft and trains. The 5- by 5-foot (1.52- by 1.52-meter) room was shipped in four parts. Each section was lightweight and small enough to fit through narrow doorways and stairways. One half contained the shower/bathtub, and the other side had a wash basin (lavatory), toilet, and illuminated medicine cabinet. Curved corners and plastic surfaces helped to facilitate maintenance.

From a sustainability perspective, minimal water was consumed, and technologies were included to filter, clean, and recycle water from the basin and shower/bathtub. The waterless toilet packaged waste for compost material. Fuller's "fog gun" for the shower required just a quart (0.95 liter) of water. While serving in World War I, he had noticed that the combination of wind and fog removed the dirt and grime from the faces of men as they stood on the decks of ships. He applied this same phenomenon to his "fog gun" showers. Other unique features in the Dymaxion bathroom were the red (hot) and blue (cold) plastic control handles, a knee-activated toilet control, grab bars, and a hammered finish applied to the tub to prevent bathers from slipping.

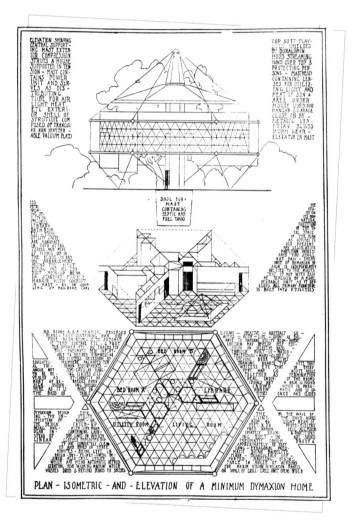

PLAN - ISOMETRIC - AND - ELEVATION OF A MINIMUM DYMAXION HOME

Figure 6.11 In addition to conceptualizing a visionary transportable house, Buckminster Fuller's design for the *Dymaxion*'s interior was remarkable. Fuller envisioned a house that had extremely advanced technology, and his design reflected the principles of sustainability and universal design.

Source: Courtesy Estate of R. Buckminster Fuller.

Figure 6.12 Buckminster Fuller's patent description for the geodesic dome was that it "relates to a framework for enclosing space."

Source: Courtesy Estate of R. Buckminster Fuller.

Fuller then designed the infamous Dymaxion map, which depicts Earth on a flat surface. As an important sustainability symbol, the map illustrates the world as a "one-world island" in a "one-world ocean." The map also depicts a series of triangles, which are the structural foundation for Fuller's geodesic dome. His patent description for the geodesic dome was that it "relates to a framework for enclosing space" (Figure 6.12). Fuller started the geometric development of the structure in the 1940s by experimenting with balls. By placing balls next to each other and on top of one another, he was able to identify the optimum spherical arrangement. He discovered that by compressing balls together, triangular shapes were formed on their surface. The dome became stronger as the size increased.

Based on these experiments, in 1949, Fuller and students at Black Mountain College in North Carolina developed the first prototype of a geodesic dome. The geodesic dome is exceptional for a variety of reasons. The dome is lightweight, consumes minimal resources, is easily transportable, is cost-effective, can be installed in any climatic conditions, and is wind resistant even in Arctic conditions. Furthermore, when inside the dome,

people perceive a space that is larger than reality. By the 1950s, the invention's success and its adaptability to various regions in the world were evident by its installation at international trade fairs:

> *There, on the grounds of the 1956 International Trade Fair [Kabul, Afghanistan], a great domed structure was rising. . . . The men knew nothing about the techniques of building construction and spoke only their native language. The single engineer who directed them had issued simple instructions: "Bolt blue ends to blue ends and red ends to red ends." That was all. Two days later, the workmen found to their amazement that they had built a great dome fashioned of aluminum triangles and covered with a skin of nylon cloth. (Rosen, 1969, p. iv)*

GLOBAL LIFE AND WORK STYLES

For the warring countries, there was a dramatic difference between life and work styles during the war and in the postwar years. In the early 1940s, commodities such as gasoline, oil, canned foods, and sugar were rationed. Many women were employed, and their efforts were championed through the iconic "Rosie the Riveter." Despite severe housing shortages, high unemployment, and economic conservatism, people were searching for optimistic approaches to living after enduring the Great Depression and the war. Exhibitions featured designs for modern living and architects such as Le Corbusier designed modern residential units. To help support returning veterans, the U.S. government passed the GI Bill of Rights, which covered the service person's educational expenses, among other things. The postwar years also saw a spike in the birth rate that is now referred to as the baby boomer generation. Progress in the world of medicine resulted in the invention of the kidney dialysis machine and the discovery of antibiotic streptomycin. The United Nations established the World Health Organization (WHO) in 1948.

Modern Living: *For Modern Living* Exhibition (1949) in Detroit, Michigan

The end of World War II prompted people to embrace *living*. The deadliest war in the history of civilization was finally over, and those who survived had witnessed awful devastation. Mechanization and scientific advances were in the forefront during the war, which changed the way people viewed these developments. Mass production was inevitable. The challenge was to design products that maximized the advantages of mechanization, served the needs of modern living, and were aesthetically pleasing. All of these conditions were explored in an exhibition at the Detroit Institute of Arts in the fall of 1949. As the center of the modern U.S. automobile industry, Detroit was an ideal location for exploring technological possibilities.

The purpose of the *For Modern Living* Exhibition was to ask prominent designers to respond to the following questions: "What does the best modern design have to offer? Can you, using modern technology, modern materials, give us a new and better setting for our daily lives? Have you, or have you not, discovered a new style—a new ideal of beauty—which will be the expression of our age as other ages of the past created their styles?" (Girard & Laurie, 1949, p. 7). The exhibition demonstrated the answers to these questions by creating four display areas: "Background of Modern Design," "Steinberg Mural," "Hall of Objects," and interior modern vignettes designed by leading architects and interior designers.

To provide context for the exhibition, the first display visitors saw was the "Background of Modern Design," beginning in the 19th century. This display included examples of objects that had been designed out of necessity, such as farm tools. The space also had examples of furniture that illustrated the development of new technologies, including tubular steel and bent plywood.

The next space in the exhibit was a semi-circular mural drawn by cartoonist Saul Steinberg (Figure 6.13). The multi-panel mural comically illustrated how Steinberg perceived people were living in the 1940s. Each apartment illustrated the eclectic way people tried to personalize their living space and sometimes even blend with their surroundings. The drawings provide insight regarding how people were adapting to technology, smaller spaces, and the number of products that lacked integrity. For example, as shown in the apartment in Figure 6.13, in attempting to accommodate "new" electricity, a variety of existing objects were used for light fixtures, such as a bust of a man and musical instruments. In a "modern" apartment, there were multiple light fixtures aimed in pointless directions. In another illustration, a woman instructed a deliveryman where to place her new fireplace, which was attached to a long electrical cord. The rooftop of an apartment building had countless television antennas aimed in various directions. An obsession with new televisions, which first went on sale in 1939 and resumed production in 1946 following the war, was also illustrated in a living room with all of the people and furniture positioned in front of the television to watch a boxing match. In a different apartment, a woman was cleaning the head of an animal-skin rug with a vacuum cleaner that had an electric cord that appeared to be thousands of feet long.

To contrast many of the poor design solutions that were illustrated in Steinberg's drawings, the next exhibit area was the "Hall of Objects." The everyday items in this space were selected for their excellent response to technology and their design integrity. As in museums throughout the world that display ancient bowls and utensils, everyday objects were selected to demonstrate the "living art of our own life and times." Objects in the exhibition included pruning shears, toys, tableware, casserole dishes, Tupperware containers, cookie jars, glasses, textiles, clocks, irons, sewing machines, typewriters, and a communications receiver designed by Raymond Loewy. At this time, small "household-size mechanisms" were considered "symbols of modern living" (The Detroit Institute of Arts, 1949, p. 62). Objects had to be aesthetically pleasing and solve everyday living problems, such as eating, drinking, ironing, sewing, playing games, telling time, typing, pruning trees, and preparing and storing food. In reflecting the exhibition's purpose to illustrate designs for modern living, the objects were readily available, mass-produced, and ergonomically designed to fulfill a specific purpose.

This same utilitarian perspective was on display in the rooms for living. The exhibition concluded in a large area that had modern living rooms designed by leading designers. Rooms for modern living included furniture and materials that were readily available, mass-produced, and ergonomically designed to fulfill a specific purpose. The rooms had to be aesthetically pleasing and solve everyday modern living problems. Interestingly, the rooms selected for the exhibition did not include kitchens or bathrooms. All of the vignettes were living/dining areas, except for one bedroom.

Alvar Aalto, Bruno Mathsson, Jens Risom, Charles Eames, and George Nelson each designed a room. A collaborative design for a bedroom and living/dining area was created by Richard Stein, Florence Knoll, Eero Saarinen, Franco Albini, Pierre Jeanneret, Abel Sorensen, Isamu Noguchi, André Duprés, and Hans Bellmann. To illustrate outdoors for modern living, Van Keppel-Green designed a garden patio. Amazingly, the entire list of designers for the 2-week exhibition included 200 prominent individuals, primarily from the United States, but also including designers from Denmark, Finland, Italy, and Austria.

An analysis of the designs and the written descriptions of rooms provides insight into the designers' solutions "for modern living" (Figure 6.14). For example, Knoll contended that designs for modern living had to be "practical, durable, and inexpensive" (The Detroit Institute of Arts, 1949, p. 78). From this

same perspective, Eames envisioned modern design as "objects that will serve their purposes better than ever before and at a lower cost" (The Detroit Institute of Arts, 1949, p. 80). The rooms demonstrated practicality and had cost-effective interior furnishings as a result of being mass-produced. Rooms were small, were multipurpose, and had a minimal number of furniture pieces. The only bedroom had a small "retreat" area for when the living/dining room became too congested.

The multifunctional style of chairs and small tables enabled pieces to be used for a variety of purposes.

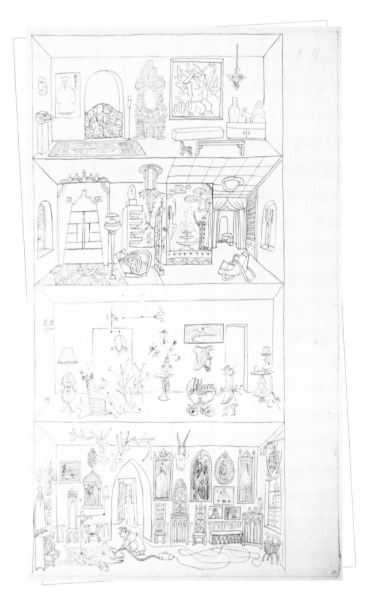

Figure 6.13 In the *For Modern Living* exhibition there was a semicircular mural drawn by the cartoonist, Saul Steinberg. The multi-panel mural comically illustrated how Steinberg perceived people were living in the 1940s.

Source: Detroit Institute of Arts.

Figure 6.14 The *For Modern Living* exhibition included George Nelson's solutions for modern living.
Source: Detroit Institute of Arts.

Built-in cabinets and open shelving were used in every room. The rooms had very few accessories and walls lacked artwork. Practical living objects for the period included ashtrays, magazine racks, desks, radios, liquor decanters, and record players. Durability was demonstrated by easy-to-clean surfaces, such as plastic, glass, and wood. Floors were usually hard surfaces with area rugs. Walls were made from inexpensive and durable materials, such as plywood. Many chairs had woven cotton webbing for the seats and backs. Few lighting fixtures were used in the rooms, which reduced costs and eased maintenance. Some spaces relied on display lighting for illumination. The apparent modern living approach to illumination was the use of fixtures made from steel tubing or concealed in a built-in cabinet. The considerable number of floor fixtures provided a flexible approach to illuminating rooms. Wall-mounted fixtures next to a table or desk were also common solutions to modern lighting and living.

Modern Life: L'Unité d'Habitation (1945–1952) in Marseille, France, by Le Corbusier

As they did in the United States, in the postwar years people in many countries searched for optimum dwellings that were well designed, were functional, and accommodated modern lifestyles. As previously noted, countries that had been bombed and served as the battlefields were undergoing severe housing shortages. Even before the war ended, policymakers were starting to create plans for rebuilding cities and towns. The French government established the Department of Reconstruction for this purpose.

The Minister of Reconstruction, M. Raoul Dautry, commissioned Le Corbusier to design a large residential unit in Marseille to house primarily government employees. Le Corbusier created the Unité d'Habitation, Marseille, as "the first manifestation of an environment suited for modern life" (Figure 6.15). A "modern life" required harmony between the "individual and collectivity." Unité d'Habitation was designed to enable the individual to have solitude, as well as interact with other family members and people in the Unité's community. Conceptually, Le Corbusier had been sensitized to resolving potential conflicts between the individual and the group by his visit to the Ema monastery in Italy in 1907. He marveled at the tranquil coexistence of the monks in seclusion and the monastery's community. As with the monastery, the Unité d'Habitation provided corbu with the opportunity to create a large residential unit that supported both the individual and the group (or collectivity).

The Unité d'Habitation was also influenced by Le Corbusier's long-term interest in urban planning. As noted in Chapter 4, for the 1925 Exposition in Paris, Corbu and Jeanneret displayed the 1922 "Plan for a Modern City of 3 Million Inhabitants" and the "Voisin Plan," a conceptualization for a new business center in Paris. Corbu's dedication to improving urban planning continued in the 1930s when he proposed La Ville Radieuse (The Radiant City). Le Corbusier contended that La Ville Radieuse, "inspired by the laws of the universe and by human law, is an attempt to guarantee the men of a machine civilization all this world's *basic pleasures. For all men, in cities and farms: sun in the house, sky through the widowpanes, [sic] trees to look at as soon as they*

Figure 6.15 Le Corbusier created the Unité d'Habitation, Marseille, as "the first manifestation of an environment suited for modern life."

Source: Banque d'Images, ADAGP/Art Resource, NY.

step outside, I say: the basic materials of city planning are: sun, sky, trees, steel, cement, in that strict order of importance" (Le Corbusier, 1933, pp. 85–86). Corbu's concept for his proposed large residential units for La Ville Radieuse was realized when he designed the Unité d'Habitation. His goal for the Unité d'Habitation was to "provide with silence and solitude before the sun, space, and greenery a dwelling which will be the perfect receptacle for the family" (Le Corbusier, 1933, pp. 85–86). Le Corbusier's goal for Unité encapsulates his views toward planning for the individual, collectivity, and interacting with nature.

Designed to accommodate 1,600 people, the Unité d'Habitation was an 18-story structure with 337 apartments in 23 different arrangements. The smallest unit was for hotel rooms and for singles. The largest apartments were for families with as many as eight children. Le Corbusier designed Unité d'Habitation for the individual and collectivity by planning solitude areas for individuals, and shared spaces for families and community interactions. Whenever possible, he included a private space within an apartment that an individual could use for alone time (Figure 6.16). Some spaces were designed for children to play together that were separate from their parents' living area. To encourage drawing, the sliding walls that separated children's rooms were made from blackboards. Individual privacy between apartments was accomplished by soundproofing walls and floors, and all views were restricted to the countryside. Family collectivity was planned for via the living/dining/kitchen area.

Interactions within the community of the Unité occurred in several locations. The Unité d'Habitation was built in a park—this was an area of interaction. Corbu planned collectivity opportunities in several locations within the building. Each corridor had "youth centers," and the rooftop had many facilities available for everyone. Inspired by the designs of ocean liners, Unité's rooftop "deck" had a gymnasium, playground, restaurant, outdoor theater, gardens, solariums, running track, and shallow swimming pool. Unité's ventilation chimneys even resembled a ship's smokestacks. Residents could also interact while shopping along the two-story-high "internal street." Located on the seventh floor, businesses included a hotel, grocery stores, medical facilities, pharmacies, clothing shops, laundry facilities, and beauty salons.

One of the most interesting collectivity designs in the Unité d'Habitation is the nursery school (ages 2–6), located on the 17th floor with a ramp to the rooftop garden and playground. To illustrate the success and uniqueness of the design, Corbu wrote the book *The Nursery Schools* (1968). The book demonstrates collectivity through numerous photographs of children playing together in the wading pool, drawing on blackboards, painting, gardening, dancing, sculpting with clay, and exercising. A photograph of a residential corridor reveals three children walking home from school without adults. Corbu explained that living in a vertical city eliminates dangers associated with traffic and crossing streets. In addition, immediate access between home and school provides more time with family or being alone. All of the children appear happy, and they shared correspondences with Le Corbusier via their teacher. Corbu was also very involved with designing an environment that encouraged the visual and performing arts.

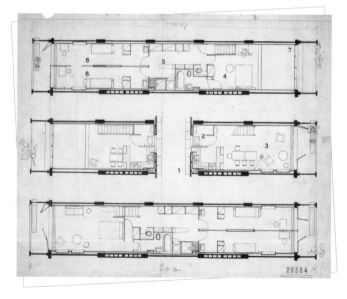

Figure 6.16 The Unité d'Habitation, Marseille. Plans for two interlocking apartments on three levels. 1, corridor; 2, entrance; 3, living room and kitchen; 4, main bedroom and bathroom; 5, storage, boiler; 6, children's bedrooms; and 7, open area to living room below.

Source: Archives of the Foundation of Le Corbusier, Paris/ARS 2009.

The **parapet** surrounding the rooftop garden became a canvas for children to paint. The concrete tables were added for molding clay. A series of short walls in various shapes could become imaginary "play" rooms. Unité fairs were held on the rooftop and included theatrical performances, donkey rides, and picnics.

Essential to the healthy development of the children was the continuous interaction with the "sun, space, and greenery." From a child's perspective, the importance of the sun was evident in their artwork. Corbu noted that every painting and drawing created by the children had a bright sun. Therefore, in addition to planning for the individual and collectivity, Unité was designed to enhance the relationship between people and the natural environment. This is evident in the structure's park setting and the communal rooftop garden. From the rooftop, people could see only the sky, sun, hills, treetops, Mediterranean Sea, and its islands. The parapet prevented views of the surrounding deteriorated neighborhood.

To ensure that people could always see trees from their apartments Le Corbusier set a maximum height for the structure. Apartments were designed to maximize daylight penetration and views (see Figure 6.16). The main elevations of the building faced east and west. To protect people from cold winds, the north elevation was solid and devoid of windows. The interlocked two-story floor plans either passed over or under a centralized corridor. This reduced typically wasteful corridor space and enabled apartments to extend along the east/west axis. Therefore, as illustrated in Figure 6.16, nearly every apartment had rooms with morning and afternoon sun exposure.

To control sunlight, balconies were deeply inset, and some walls had brise-soleils, as in the façade of the Ministry of Education and Health in Rio de Janeiro (see Chapter 5). Brightly colored awnings and draperies were also used to control sunlight. Living rooms had Corbu's customary layout of a two-story height with a balcony. Natural daylight was maximized by the use of light shelves below the upper wall of glass.

The success of the Unité d'Habitation later translated into the development and construction of four similar Unité d'Habitation complexes in the cities of Rezé-les-Nantes (1952), Briey en Forêt (1956), Berlin (1957), and Firminy-Vert (1960).

GLOBAL VISUAL AND PERFORMING ARTS

As it had affected all other aspects of life during the decade, World War II also had a significant impact on the visual and performing arts. Commissions essentially disappeared, and performances were limited until the postwar years. Many artists, musicians, and actors immigrated to the Americas to avoid the Nazi regime. Surrealism inspired sculptural architectural and furniture forms, such as Eero Saarinen's Grasshopper chair (1946) and Womb chair (1948). Isamu Noguchi applied his sculptural talents to the creation of interior environments and furnishings. **Abstract Expressionist** artists, including Jackson Pollock, created a novel approach to patterns, colors, and textures. Martha Graham exemplified performing arts' interpretation of modern dance in the ballet *Appalachian Spring* in 1944. People were listening to B.B. King, Frank Sinatra, and music written by Rodgers and Hammerstein. Bing Crosby sang the timeless song *White Christmas* in the war-related movie *Holiday Inn* (1942). The war also inspired the successful Broadway musical production *South Pacific* in 1949.

Sculpture and Performing Arts: Isamu Noguchi in the Early Years

As Le Corbusier and designers involved with the 1949 *For Modern Living* Exhibition were identifying the essential elements of a dwelling for modern living, Isamu

Noguchi was creating sculpture for the "lived environment." Throughout his long career, Noguchi's main purpose was "art as it related to life," and was manifested in sculpture, interiors, furniture, light fixtures, gardens, parks, theater sets, earthworks, fountains, and memorials. How Noguchi's oeuvre affected interior environments and architecture is demonstrated by his perspectives regarding the work of artists: "It is my opinion that sculptors as well as painters should not forever be concerned with pure art or meaningful art, but should inject their knowledge of form and matter into the everyday, usable designs of industry and commerce. This necessitates their learning why things are the way they are, why the bend of a road, why the streamline of airplanes" (Apostolot-Cappandona & Altshuler, 1994, p. 19).

To learn "why things are the way they are," Noguchi engaged in extensive international travel, and collaborated with artists, artisans, interior designers, architects, and choreographers. His international experiences began at an early age when Isamu and his American mother, Leonie Gilmour, moved with his father, Yonejiro (Yone) Noguchi, from Los Angeles (where Isamu was born) to Japan, the home of his father, in 1906. Noguchi's childhood in Japan exposed him to ancient Japanese traditions, including wood joinery, pottery, spatial compositions, and Japanese gardens. Exposure to Western concepts and designs began during his adolescent years when his mother sent him back to the United States for an education in Indiana.

Upon graduation in 1923, Noguchi moved to New York City to begin premed studies at Columbia University, and in 1925 he enrolled at the Leonardo da Vinci Art School to study sculpting. Subsequently, Manhattan became his home while traveling and living in Europe, China, India, Mexico, and Japan. These countries and the people who mentored Noguchi affected his oeuvre. For example, in Paris while apprenticing with the Rumanian abstract sculptor Constantin Brancusi, Noguchi learned how to carve stone, including intricate details. Brancusi also reconfirmed the value of working in wood, which Noguchi had already experienced when he helped to construct buildings as a child living in Japan. Kitaoji Rosanjin, a master potter and "cook," taught Noguchi how to create pottery with integrity. Noguchi explained Rosanjin's philosophy: "With cooking, as with pottery, the ingredients count above all else for Rosanjin."

Living in Manhattan exposed Noguchi to other artists, and he became close friends with both Buckminster Fuller and dancer/choreographer Martha Graham. He received a prominent Manhattan commission for a sculpture above the entrance of the Associated Press Building at Rockefeller Center. *News* (1938–1940) is a monumental stainless steel relief depicting the work of journalists with their technologies, such as a teletype, camera, and pad and pencil. In his Manhattan studio, Noguchi often sculpted portrait heads of his close friends, including Fuller, Graham, and Mexican painter José Clemente Orozco (see Chapter 1). Each portrait was sculpted to reveal the subject's personality. For example, to illustrate Fuller's visionary qualities, Noguchi sculpted his friend's head from shiny, chrome-plated bronze.

These friendships influenced Noguchi's values and his oeuvre. He noted that Fuller influenced his use of aluminum for sculptures, the synergetic placement of rocks, and a building with a geodesic dome. Noguchi designed the geodesic dome for the unrealized Martha Graham experimental theater and museum. Graham's influence on Noguchi revolved around "sculpture as space." Noguchi's vision was "that the frontiers of sculpture might open up by relating to the land and to the walkable space. From this would come a new consciousness free of the constraints set on art by the art market" (Noguchi, 1987, p. 143). Graham gave Noguchi the opportunity to experiment with "walkable space" by commissioning him to design more than 20 dance sets.

Noguchi's experiences with Eastern and Western cultures are reflected in his "pure art" and his designs for "everyday, usable designs." In the 1940s, Noguchi's designs for everyday objects and spaces included playgrounds, walls, ceilings, furniture, and lighting.

Noguchi sculpted the earth to create *Contoured Playground* (1941), a proposal for a free-form playground in Central Park. Sculptural forms were applied to the ceilings and walls of his Lunar interiors (Figure 6.17). A Lunar interior was designed for the lobby ceiling of the American Stove Company Building (1947) in St. Louis, Missouri. Noguchi's sculptural forms had a magical effect on structural elements. For example, in the American Stove Company Building's lobby, the massive column appears to dissolve as it flows into the curvaceous forms of the ceiling. Unexpected openings in the ceiling provide intrigue and create alluring light and dark contrasts. A similar undulating surface, *Lunar Voyage* (1948), was created for a stairway wall on the ocean liner *Argentina* (scrapped 1959) (see Figure 6.17). *Lunar Voyage*'s curved forms and openings resemble the eyes and tentacles of sea creatures. Concealed

Figure 6.17 *Lunar Voyage* on a stairway wall on the ocean liner *Argentina*.
Source: Jacob Burckhardt.

illumination plays an important role in directing the eye to the sculptural shapes, textures, and forms. Noguchi had already experimented with integrating light with a sculpture when he created a suspended light fixture, Lunar Infant (1944). The light source was concealed behind the curves of its form, but the effects from illumination grazed its rough **magnesite** surfaces. Noguchi's experiments with Lunar Infant provided the inspiration for the development of his world-renowned Japanese Akari Lamps in the 1950s.

Noguchi also achieved notoriety in 1948 when he sculpted the functional forms of an organic coffee table (modern Noguchi Table) for the Herman Miller Furniture Company (Figure 6.18). He created the **biomorphic** design when Herman Miller's design director, George Nelson, contacted him to create a table for an article Nelson was writing, "How to Make a Table." The tripod wood base is made from two identical sculptural forms that are reversed. A rod connects the two pieces and enables the forms to pivot. The perfectly balanced surface can support the glass without any attachments. Noguchi explained that the table was designed from an idea to use "a continuous loop of wood and cut it in two so that, swiveled in the middle, it would still serve to support a glass top—thus to make a table" (Noguchi, 1987, p. 242). In the 1940s, he designed other sculptural functional designs for Herman Miller, including a biomorphic sofa, an ottoman, three-legged tables, stools, and a chess table. The chess table was made from plywood and cast aluminum. On the table's top, white plastic insets mark the chessboard and the surface rotates to expose pockets for storing chess pieces. Noguchi continued to explore sculptural space, illuminated interiors, and the dichotomies of Eastern and Western cultures in subsequent decades.

Visual Arts: Functional and Aesthetic Textiles—Gunta Stölzl and Anni Albers

To demonstrate textiles for modern interiors, MoMA's 1941 *Organic Design in Home Furnishings* Exhibition and the 1949 *For Modern Living* displayed several

Figure 6.18 Noguchi attained enormous success when he sculpted the functional forms of an organic coffee table (modern Noguchi Table) for the Herman Miller Furniture Company.

Source: Herman Miller, Inc.

examples created by designers, including Ray Eames, Benjamin Baldwin, Stanislaus V'Soske, and Alexander Girard (Figure 6.19). The textiles were either plain fabrics with subdued tones, or had an open weave that allowed air and light to pass through. Generally, patterned textiles were geometric shapes or stylized forms of nature. There were many sources of inspiration for the weaves, fibers, colors, and patterns of the modern textiles. Many of the patterns and colors reflect the artistic styles that had been prevalent in Western art since the turn of the century. Simple geometric shapes used by De Stijl artists (see Chapter 4) are evident in the textile patterns in MoMA's 1941 exhibition. For example, prints by Antonin Raymond have black grids contrasted with white circles. Weaves by Marli Ehrman were repetitive horizontal lines in alternating white and black.

Figure 6.19 Displays in the "Hall of Objects" exhibition area. To demonstrate textiles for modern interiors, MoMA's 1941 *Organic Design in Home Furnishings* exhibition and the 1949 *For Modern Living* displayed several examples created by designers, including Ray Eames, Benjamin Baldwin, Stanislaus V'Soske, and Alexander Girard.

Source: Detroit Institute of Arts.

Designers of textiles displayed at the later 1949 exhibition appeared to be influenced by Abstract Expressionist artists, part of a movement that started in the 1940s in New York City. Jackson Pollock's paintings are an excellent example of Abstract Expressionism. Pollock used **gestural abstraction** to splatter, splash, pour, and drip paint on canvases. In a similar manner, Alexander Girard's printed cotton textiles had free-flowing narrow curvaceous lines that could have been made by dripping paint from a container. The spontaneity of open weaves and nubs found in the woven fabrics resembled paint splatter.

The textiles displayed at the exhibitions also reflected the work of weavers at the Bauhaus (see Chapter 4) and other modern weaving businesses in locations such as Holland, Switzerland, and Czechoslovakia. A weaving workshop was included in the Bauhaus curriculum when the school was established in 1919 and continued when the program moved to Dessau. Using the dobby or jacquard loom, students created tapestries, knotted carpets, woven rugs, wall hangings, wall coverings, blankets, and eventually yard goods. Initially, the emphasis was to explore the potential of materials and forms for artistic purposes. These "one-off" woven pieces were made on hand looms and were time-consuming and expensive. This changed in 1925 when German textile artist Gunta Stölzl became the "young master" of the weaving workshop, the only female to receive a formal title at the Bauhaus.

In following the principles of the Bauhaus, Stölzl restructured the weaving curriculum by connecting art with industry. Students were able to pursue artistic woven pieces or develop prototype textiles for mass production. Experimentation with designs for mass production focused on textiles that were inexpensive and durable, and utilized new synthetic fibers. To meet the needs of everyday life, weavers experimented with textures and fibers that could reflect light, absorb sound, repel moisture, and deter dust. In a novel approach, in the 1940s designers created new textiles for a specific purpose, such as curtains, draperies, or "furniture covers." Under Stölzl's artistic abilities and leadership, textile prototypes created at the Bauhaus weaving workshop were purchased by industry. The weaving workshop became one of the most profitable programs of the Bauhaus.

The inspiration for many of the Bauhaus designs was derived from the visual arts. Weavers were exposed to the paintings of the Bauhaus masters, including Paul Klee, Josef Albers, and Wassily Kandinsky. One of the students was Anni Albers, the wife of Josef Albers. She began her studies in 1922 and received her diploma in

1930. Anni was also an instructor and acting director of the weaving workshop. Many of her initial textiles were wall hangings made of silk, cotton, and artificial fibers (Figure 6.20). A resemblance to De Stijl is evident in the timeless nonobjective shapes. Repetition and intersecting vertical and horizontal directions organized the restrictive colors and shapes. Anni received her Bauhaus degree for an innovative textile that reflected light and absorbed sound. The textile, made from cotton, **cellophane,** and **chenille,** was created for a stage curtain in a new auditorium in Bernau, Germany.

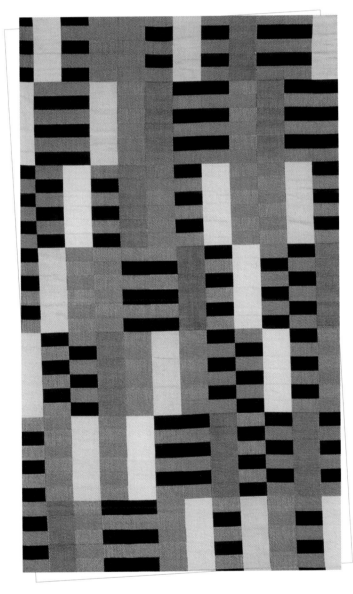

Figure 6.20 Many of Anni Alber's initial textiles were wall hangings made of silk, cotton, and artificial fibers. A resemblance to De Stijl is evident by the timeless nonobjective shapes.

Source: Victoria and Albert Museum, London/Art Resource, NY.

After the Bauhaus closed in 1933, Anni and Josef emigrated to North Carolina to teach at Black Mountain College. In the United States, she continued to experiment with different materials and created numerous textiles for draperies, partitions, wall hangings, and "pictorial weavings." Desert colors and the primitive shapes and symbols of ancient Peruvian textiles inspired her to create drapery textiles using the **leno weave**; twisting warp yarns results in an open weave that allows the passage of light and air. In 1949, MoMA recognized Anni's art by sponsoring its first one-person weaving exhibition. The exhibition included her innovative approach to "free-hanging room dividers." The dividers were approximately 3 feet (0.9 meter) wide and were made from jute, cellophane, walnut lath, dowels, and "waxed-cotton harnessmaker's [*sic*] thread."

Subsequently, to provide visual and tactile interest, Anni's cotton and linen textiles were knotted and intertwined with metallic threads, metal foil, **fiberglass,** and cellophane. Her extraordinary career continued until her death in 1994. Fuller offered a succinct analysis of her artistic achievements: "Anni Albers, more than any other weaver, has succeeded in exciting mass realization of the complex structure of fabrics. She has brought the artist's intuitive sculpturing faculties and the agelong [*sic*] weaver's arts into historical successful marriage" (Weber & Asbaghi, 1999, p. 9).

GLOBAL BUSINESS AND ECONOMICS

As was the case with all the other areas discussed in this chapter, global business and economic activities in the 1940s centered on supporting and then recovering from World War II. Factories were converted into manufacturing facilities for production of war-related materials and equipment. People were employed in jobs that supported the war effort. In the postwar years, the demand for housing and consumer goods stimulated the growth of businesses throughout the world. After the War, the Herman Miller Furniture Company experienced enormous growth and worldwide recognition for modern furniture due to the considerable contributions of D. J. De Pree, Gilbert Rohde, and George Nelson. From a vastly different business perspective, numerous individuals and corporations experienced financial success from gambling and entertainment when the first Las Vegas hotels were constructed on the Strip during the postwar years.

Business Philosophies: Herman Miller Furniture Company—D. J. De Pree, Gilbert Rohde, and George Nelson

Noguchi's commission to design sculptural furniture for Herman Miller is just one example of how the architect, designer, and writer George Nelson affected the success, philosophy, and development of the furniture company. The Herman Miller Company began as the Michigan Star Furniture Company in Zeeland, Michigan, in 1905. Four people, including Herman Miller, owned the company. Michigan Star manufactured reproductions of residential period furniture and sold most of its furniture to Sears.

In 1923, Miller purchased the company from the other owners and changed its name to Herman Miller. Dirk Jan (D. J.) De Pree started as a clerk with Michigan Star but studied manufacturing efficiency research, including the work of Frederick Taylor (see Chapter 3). De Pree was the president of Michigan Star and subsequently became the president of Herman Miller in 1923. Initially the company continued to manufacture period furniture, but during the late 1920s, competition with other manufacturers significantly affected revenues; then the Great Depression had an even greater negative impact. De Pree contended that the "four major

evils" associated with the furniture industry were: (1) the buyer's market, (2) four seasonal markets, (3) "ear-to-the-ground attitude," and (4) individual contractors controlling sales. He was able to begin addressing the "four major evils" when he met Gilbert Rohde in 1930. Rohde was an illustrator who designed modern furniture and tried to convince De Pree that his designs were those for the future. In seeking to differentiate Herman Miller from other furniture manufacturers, and to avoid bankruptcy, De Pree hired Rohde to design new *modern* furniture for the company.

Rohde contended that *modern living* was changing the design of houses. The new mobile society translated into smaller houses and rooms. This required new furniture that was smaller, functional, and flexible. In demonstrating a tremendous amount of respect for Rohde's design abilities and his forecasting skills, De Pree agreed to eventually stop production of period furniture, and Herman Miller began manufacturing furniture that was simple and versatile (Figure 6.21).

De Pree also had a great appreciation for Rohde's designs because of their honesty and integrity. Rohde's simple designs were original, and required expert craftsmanship and quality materials. This was in contrast to many reproductions of period furniture, and the practice of using ornamentation to conceal defects and flaws. Rohde's designs also responded to the needs of users in a modern world. Designing furniture that solved modern living problems helped to eliminate the "evils" associated with the "buyer's market," "seasonal markets," and "ear-to-the-ground attitude."

Rohde did not have his "ear to the ground" to hear what buyers thought they wanted in a particular season; in contrast, he studied modern living patterns, and applied the results to the designs of furniture and interiors. An understanding of how to select and plan for new modern designs, which were modular and versatile required education. Therefore, De Pree and Rohde determined that the traditional sales format prevalent in the furniture industry would not provide the education that was needed. Individual contractors, the fourth "evil," represented numerous manufacturers; thus they had little interest in investing their time to learn a complex product line. To provide important production information and service, De Pree initiated a policy that required buyers to purchase through a Herman Miller dealer. In 1939, De Pree opened a showroom at Chicago's Merchandise Mart that is still operating today.

De Pree had to search for a replacement for Rohde after his death in 1944 and a January 22, 1945 article written by George Nelson for *Life* magazine intrigued him. Nelson had described his Storagewall furniture, which was designed to resolve modern living problems. In Nelson and Henry Wright's book, *Tomorrow's House: A Complete Guide for the Home-Builder*, they described what became systems furniture. The book explains in great detail how to create "Tomorrow's House," including how to plan every room in a house, "sound conditioning," "manufacturing climate," "solar heating," and "organized storage." Nelson and Wright's argument for "organized storage" was based on their theory that houses were "shrinking" because of the elimination of basements and attics. Nelson's focus on saving space,

designing for the users, and functional furniture designs reflected Rohde's legacy.

De Pree hired Nelson in 1945 as the company's design director and empowered him to determine the future design direction for the company. To assist with the development of futuristic designs, Nelson hired Fuller as a consultant. Within 3 years, De Pree's faith in Nelson's talents was confirmed by new furniture designs by Nelson, Charles Eames, Isamu Noguchi, and Paul Laszlo. By 1948, Nelson created for *purchase* a bound, hardcover product catalogue that featured furniture designed by the four designers. In the Foreword, Nelson articulated aspects of what he perceived to be Herman Miller's philosophy: "What you make is important." "Design is an integral part of the business." "The product must be honest." "You decide what you will make." And "There is a market for good design" (Nelson, 1948, p. 4).

Nelson also explained the "program" for the furniture. The first assumption was that furniture could be made from a variety of materials besides plywood and lumber. Nelson contended that the program was strengthened by the "participation of a group of designers who share Herman Miller's particular attitudes." Lastly, the program was to have a "*permanent*

Figure 6.21 Furniture designed by Gilbert Rohde for Herman Miller, Inc.
Source: Herman Miller, Inc.

collection designed to meet fully the requirements for modern living." The furniture in the residential catalogue reflects the philosophy and program that Nelson described in the Foreword. The catalogue included modern living storage units designed by Nelson and what have since become classic pieces by Eames, Noguchi, and Laszlo. Most of the catalogue included descriptions and photographs of Nelson's standardized, multi-purpose storage system (Figure 6.22). The system was designed for every room in a house, and could appear to be a "custom-designed built-in" unit or serve as a wall divider. For example, Nelson's famous platform bench was made in four different lengths and could be used for seating, as a coffee table, or as a base for cabinets (Figure 6.23). Units were available with cabinets, chests, open shelves, and sliding glass doors.

To accommodate modern living requirements, special cabinets were designed for radios, record players, album storage, and typewriters. Vanities were complete with mirrors, illumination, and compartments for cosmetics. Coffee tables had built-in trays for serving food and inset copper pans for plants. Furniture with extensions supported by **gatelegs** helped to resolve problems associated with "shrinking" rooms. Nelson continued to have an impact on modern design by solving problems for users during the next several decades.

Figure 6.22 Herman Miller's catalogue included descriptions and photographs of George Nelson's standardized, multipurpose storage system.

Source: Herman Miller, Inc.

Figure 6.23 George Nelson's famous platform bench was made in four different lengths and could be used for seating, a coffee table, or a base for cabinets.

Source: Herman Miller, Inc.

The Gambling Business: Origin of Las Vegas Hotels on the Strip

As the furniture industry was identifying attributes of a modern living environment, businessmen in Las Vegas, Nevada, were creating a modern entertainment destination. It was a challenge for entrepreneurs to create an intriguing destination—prior to 1940. Las Vegas was basically a railroad depot in the Mojave Desert with a population of just 8,400. At the turn of the century, Las Vegas, meaning "The Meadows" in Spanish, was only a railroad station linking Salt Lake City with Southern California. Subsequently, several events stimulated growth. In 1931, Nevada legalized gambling and President Franklin Roosevelt released the funds to build Boulder Dam (modern Hoover Dam). The effects of legalized gambling took many years to materialize; however, the infusion of substantial governmental funds to build the dam during the Great Depression had an immediate impact. Thousands of people moved to Las Vegas to work on the massive construction project.

In addition to offering critical employment opportunities, controlling the Colorado River reduced flooding and supplied Las Vegas with very inexpensive electricity. When the dam was completed in 1935, tourists started to visit Las Vegas to see the stupendous engineering feat.

The start of World War II also impacted the development of the city. To establish a training site for pilots, the government built Nellis Air Force Base close to Las Vegas. The base brought military personnel to the area and provided employment opportunities for the many people who were unemployed after the completion of Boulder Dam.

To continue creating the Las Vegas destination, California hotel entrepreneur Tommy Hull built the first hotel-casino on Highway 91, or the Strip (modern Las Vegas Boulevard). Hotel El Rancho Vegas was finished in 1941, and the Hotel Last Frontier soon followed in 1942. The hotel-casinos had to attract large numbers of people who were willing to gamble for extended

Figure 6.24 The "Pioneer Lobby" of the Last Frontier hotel. In early Las Vegas, the hotel-casinos El Rancho Vegas and Last Frontier developed enticements by using a western theme.

Source: Pomona Public Library.

periods. Las Vegas and its remote location were basically unknown at the time. Moreover, the city lacked typical vacation services, such as restaurants, shops, recreation, and entertainment. To entice people to vacation in Las Vegas required spectacular complexes that included all of the amenities. The original hotel-casinos had the customary guest rooms, "fine foods," and several casinos, outdoor swimming pools, cocktail lounges, bars, marriage chapels, and ample free parking. In addition to gambling, the facilities included dancing, floorshows, and entertainment from the "stars of radio, stage, and screen." El Rancho Vegas and the Last Frontier developed a further enticement by adapting a Western theme (Figure 6.24). According to the Last Frontier's slogan, guests could experience "The Early West in Modern Splendor." The slogan of the competing El Rancho Vegas boasted "Western America's Finest."

The Western theme was evident in every detail, such as employees wearing cowboy outfits, lighting made from wagon wheels, animals used for wall decorations, and hewn logs used for columns and ceilings. The "Pioneer Lobby" at the Last Frontier featured a painting of Will Rogers, "A Tribute to America's Most

Beloved Cowboy," and a miniature covered wagon was suspended from the ceiling. The lobby also had an *open* display of "Guns used by Geronimo's Warriors in His Last Battle." Guests could have a stagecoach party, sit on saddles, and visit "Frontier Village." All of these adventures were photographed and printed on free postcards. The financial success of the first two hotel-casinos prompted the involvement of organized crime.

The glamorous Hollywood atmosphere of the Flamingo Hotel (1946) stood in dramatic contrast to Las Vegas's original Western-themed hotel-casinos. Elected to create a glamorous Hollywood atmosphere, the Flamingo's developer, Billy Wilkerson, started construction on the Flamingo, but by January 1945, he was deeply in debt. Benjamin (Bugsy) Siegel stepped in to fund the project using money from organized crime. He spared no expense in the design of the modern hotel-casino, and conceptually the project transformed how people perceived gambling.

Construction of the Flamingo coincided with the end of World War II and the war-imposed gas rationing. This was beneficial to the city's growth, as people were able to use significant quantities of gasoline to drive the long distance to Las Vegas—it was 270 miles (435 kilometers) just to Los Angeles. The design of the Flamingo capitalized on this by aligning its entrance with the highway, building large parking lots, and creating tall neon signs that could easily be seen from a distance. The hotel entrance featured slot machines, a game table area, and a long bar (Figure 6.25). There were 77 modern guest rooms, a swimming pool, a golf course, a gymnasium, a shooting range, restaurants, and shops. Bugsy invited Hollywood stars to the Flamingo, and many of them performed in the lounges of the hotels, including Jimmy Durante, Danny Thomas, and Lena Horne.

As previously noted, building a casino with all of these modern amenities changed perceptions associated with "saloon" gambling. In addition, affordable gaming tables in a glamorous setting enticed people from every income level to visit Vegas to gamble. Inexpensive electricity, due to the construction of Boulder Dam, enabled a limitless use of neon signage, and the facilities were air-conditioned, which was critical to assuring that people would continue to visit the city in the hot summers. The mob continued to operate the Flamingo (after a dispute with Siegel, which ended in his death). The Flamingo set the standard for the quality and design of the many hotel-casinos that followed. Its tremendous success prompted the construction of several new hotels along the Strip in the 1950s, including the Desert Inn (1950), Sahara (1952), Sands (1952), and the Riviera (1955), all designed to make Las Vegas an international destination.

Figure 6.25 To emphasize gambling, the Flamingo Hotel's entrance had slot machines, a game table area, and a long bar.
Source: Pomona Public Library.

SUMMARY

Tens of millions of people were killed and injured during World War II, and major cities and countless towns throughout the world were destroyed or damaged. The widespread devastation was due in part to the decisions of world leaders and the technological advances that had begun in the 19th century. World War II was a total effort involving people of every age group, both genders, and the spectrum of physical and mental abilities. Everyone sacrificed, and to maximize the number of troops available for the war effort, people at home assumed the work previously done by men who left to fight in the war. Sacrifices in many countries led to starvation, disease, and death. Thousands of residences, commercial buildings, and historic sites were damaged or destroyed during the war. The war also affected the built environment when the Nazis created buildings in concentration camps for the purpose of killing millions of people. Moreover, to hide from the Nazis, people living in wartime ghettos created new approaches to the design of interior environments and identified unconventional uses for furniture.

Charles and Ray Eames and Eero Saarinen began experimenting with molding wood into compound curves in 1940, and their living room seating units and case goods won first place in the MoMA's 1941 *Organic Design in Home Furnishings* competition. Two distinct divisions in MoMA's *Inter-American* competition were the United States and Latin America, which included Mexico, Central America, and South America. Mies van der Rohe and Philip Johnson designed residences that enabled their users to feel at one with the natural environment. Mies designed the Farnsworth house as an all-glass residence as a country retreat for Dr. Edith Farnsworth, and Johnson's all-glass structure (modern Glass House) was his personal residence in New Canaan, Connecticut.

The machine age resulted in the establishment of the American industrial design profession. The Raymond Loewy Company, with offices throughout the world, had been responsible for designing automobiles, ships, railroad locomotives, aircraft, and consumer products. R. Buckminster Fuller, concerned about solving the problem of adequate and affordable shelter, became famous for inventing geodesic domes in 1949.

The end of World War II prompted people to embrace *living*. The people who had survived had witnessed devastation and horrific conditions. The challenge was to design products that maximized the advantages of mechanization, served the needs of modern living, and were aesthetically pleasing. All of these conditions were explored in a 1949 exhibition at the Detroit Institute of Arts called *For Modern Living*. In the postwar years, people the world over searched for optimum dwellings. Countries that were bombed and had been the battlefields of the war had severe housing shortages. Le Corbusier created the Unité d'Habitation in Marseille, France, as "the first manifestation of an environment suited for modern life."

As Le Corbusier and designers involved with the 1949 *For Modern Living* Exhibition were identifying the essential elements of a dwelling for modern living, Isamu Noguchi was creating sculpture for the "lived environment." Throughout his career, Noguchi's main purpose was "art as it related to life," which was manifested through sculpture, interiors, furniture, and light fixtures. To meet the needs of everyday life, weavers such as Gunta Stölzl and Anni Albers experimented with textures and fibers that could reflect light and absorb sound and resembled the creativity of Abstract Expressionist artists.

The Herman Miller Company, which began as the Michigan Star Furniture Company in Zeeland, Michigan, in 1905, hired designers to create new, modern furniture. George Nelson was hired as the design director and was empowered to determine the company's future design direction. In keeping with the philosophy of the previous director, Gilbert Rohde, Nelson focused on saving space, designing for the users, and functional furniture designs. To create a destination, Tommy Hull built the first hotel-casino on the Las Vegas Strip. Hotel El Rancho Vegas was finished in 1941, and the Hotel Last Frontier soon followed in 1942. In dramatic contrast to the original Western-themed hotel-casinos, mobster Bugsy Siegel opened the Flamingo Hotel (1946), which featured a glamorous Hollywood style.

KEY TERMS

Abstract Expressionist

biomorphic

case goods

cellophane

chenille

cradle-to-grave

Dymaxion Deployment Unit (DDU)

fiberglass

gateleg table

geodesic dome

gestural abstraction

jute

leno weave

magnesite

mecate

organic design

parapet

primavera wood

rattan

Scandinavian Modernism

terrazzo

travertine

EXERCISES

1. Philosophy and Design Project. The home fronts of every warring nation were impacted by rationing or eliminating from the general marketplace any commodity that was important for the war effort. The combination of two events that were close together, World War II and the Great Depression, prompted designers and architects to develop designs that were cost-effective and functional and economized materials. In 1948, MoMA sponsored another competition, "The International Competition for Low-Cost Furniture Design." In an interdisciplinary design team, create designs for contemporary residential and commercial interiors that reflect the philosophy of designers working in the immediate postwar years. Use a sustainable format to prepare the presentation of your design.

2. Research Design Project. MoMA's 1941 competition "Organic Design in Home Furnishings" included a division for Latin American entries. The program encouraged designers to "submit suggestions as to the manner in which their own local materials and methods of construction might be applied to the making of furniture for contemporary American requirements" (Noyes, 1969 reprint edition, p. 39). Research the geographical, climatic, and economic conditions of two non-Western countries. Based on your findings, develop prototypes of furniture that use local materials and methods of construction. Display the prototypes in a public space and include a pamphlet that profiles the project and how the design reflects the principles of sustainability.

3. Human Factors Research Project. Ultimately, Loewy International had offices in many cities and was responsible for designing automobiles, ships, railroad locomotives, motor coaches (e.g., tour buses), aircraft, consumer products, commercial equipment, interiors, "specialized architecture," packaging, graphic design, and eventually space stations. Some of Loewy's guidelines for design reflect the principles of universal design. In an interdisciplinary team, research the work of Loewy and determine which designs best exemplify the principles of universal design. Write a report that summarizes your observations and include recommendations for applying concepts to assignments in other courses. The report could include sketches, drawings, or photographs.

CHAPTER 7

EMPHASIS:
THE 1950S

OBJECTIVES

After reading this chapter, you should be able to describe and analyze:

■ How selected global political events in the 1950s, such as the Korean War and the policies of Stalin and Khrushchev, affected interior environments and architecture.

■ How nature and environmental conditions affected selected global interior environments and architecture in the 1950s as evident by the Guggenheim Museum in New York City and the excavation of Wat Mahathat in Sukhothai, Thailand.

■ How selected global technologies and materials in the 1950s, such as fiberglass and the large-scale introduction of television, affected interior environments and architecture.

■ How selected global work styles and lifestyles in the 1950s affected interior environments and architecture as evident by three special homes in Calcutta established by Mother Teresa as well as educational facilities at the Cranbrook Academy of Art, Illinois Institute of Technology, and the Universidad Nacional Autónoma de México (UNAM).

■ How selected global visual arts in the 1950s affected interior environments and architecture as evident by the Chapel at Ronchamp, and the designs of Arne Jacobsen and Harry Bertoia.

■ How selected global business developments and economics in the 1950s affected interior environments and architecture as evident by mass-produced furnishings and McDonald's restaurants.

■ How to compare and contrast selected interior environments and architecture in the Americas, Asia/Oceania, Europe, and the Middle East/Africa in the 1950s.

The 1950s began with the consequences of World War II still being felt, including the Cold War, the continuing state of conflict and competition between the Soviet Union and the United States. Due to the extreme devastation caused by the war, Japan and most of the countries in Europe were still rebuilding during the 1950s. However, by the end of the decade, Germany and Japan demonstrated the beginnings of strong economic growth. In Asia, the Korean conflict began in 1950 and lasted 3 years. After the death of Josef Stalin in 1953, Nikita Khrushchev became the First Secretary of the Soviet Union's Communist Party—the new leader of the Union of Soviet Socialist Republics (USSR). During this time, many countries throughout the world gained independence after years of colonial rule (see following section).

Individuals demonstrated that some aspects of nature could be conquered when beekeeper and mountain climber Edmund Hillary and Sherpa Tenzing Norgay reached the summit of Mount Everest, the world's tallest mountain, in 1953. Frank Lloyd Wright was inspired by nature when he designed the renowned Guggenheim Museum in New York City. The peeling away of nature, the excavation of Wat Mahathat in Sukhothai, Thailand, enabled the world to study and appreciate architecture and sculpture that was created in the 13th to the 15th centuries.

In dramatic contrast, the governments of the United States and Soviet Union focused on creating nuclear weapons and developing technologies for space exploration. Finnish-American architect and furniture designer Eero Saarinen explored how fiberglass could be used for furniture and as a reflection of modern "permanence." Saarinen designed the stainless steel arch in St. Louis, Missouri. Technological advances in television, including color programming, had a significant impact on lifestyles and interior environments.

Mother Teresa affected interior environments and the lives of thousands of people as she created homes for the "unwanted" throughout the world (although a significant portion of her work was in India). The Cranbrook Academy of Art in Michigan, the Illinois Institute of Technology in Chicago, and the Universidad Nacional Autónoma de México (UNAM) in Mexico City advanced the study and practice of interior design, architecture, and the visual arts. Sculpture played an important role in inspiring Le Corbusier's design for a new Chapel at Ronchamp in France, as well as the furniture created by Arne Jacobsen and Harry Bertoia. Eventually, furniture designed by all three was mass-produced and became classics. Furniture manufacturer Knoll Associates became instrumental in promoting work created by celebrated designers. McDonald's restaurants are not known for their designer interiors; nevertheless, the hugely successful corporation has had a pervasive influence on the design of food-service facilities throughout the world (currently, there are more than 31,000 McDonald's restaurants on six continents).

GLOBAL POLITICS AND GOVERNMENT

The treaties signed to end World War II had long-lasting ramifications. Many countries were divided and had new borders, including Poland, Germany, and the USSR, and some gained independence from colonial rulers. Countries acquiring independence included Libya (1951), Cambodia (1953), Sudan (1956), Ghana (1957), Malaya (1957), and Cyprus (1959). Ideological differences between the United States and the USSR during World War II negotiation processes resulted in what has became known as the Cold War. In supporting capitalism, the United States feared the spread of communism, especially after mainland China became a Communist country in 1949. Although the

United States and the Soviet Union were concerned about the devastating consequences of a nuclear war, the two countries began to develop nuclear technology for weapons arsenals.

Philosophical differences between the two powers became apparent during the Korean War. Communist states supported North Korea, and democratic states assisted South Korea. Today, the people of Korea remain divided by the 38th parallel north, a line of latitude across the middle of the country. Other conflicts occurred in Israel, Egypt, Tibet, Algeria, and Kenya; a political assassination occurred early in the decade when King Abdullah of Jordan was murdered in 1951. Following a revolution, Colonel Gamal Abdel Nasser attained power in Egypt in 1954.

The first Geneva Summit—a meeting of the leaders of the United States, France, Britain, and the Soviet Union, the first meeting between the leaders of the United States and the USSR since the Potsdam conference following World War II—was held in 1955. Charles de Gaulle became the Prime Minister of France in 1958, and in 1959, through the course of revolution, Fidel Castro became the leader of Cuba.

A Divided Country and the Korean War (1950–1953): North and South Korea

The location of Korea played a significant role in the country's history and culture, as well as its involvement in World War II. Located in northeast Asia, Korea is a peninsula with the Sea of Japan (East Sea) on its eastern coast and the Yellow Sea (West Sea) to the west. The southern coast is separated from Japan by the Korea Strait (Tsuchima Strait). The country's northern border is shared with China and Russia. This close proximity to China, Russia, and Japan resulted in numerous invasions and eventually the division of the country at the 38th parallel by the Soviet Union and the United States (which divided the country into roughly two equal parts) at the end of World War II. Korea had been a colony of Japan since 1910, after that country's victory

over Russia in the Russo-Japanese War (1904–1905). Japanese rule continued until Japan's defeat in World War II. The armistice included specific details regarding the dispersion of Japanese possessions, including Korea. To oversee Japanese activities, both the USSR and the United States stationed troops in what became North and South Korea, respectively. In the late 1940s, the Soviet Union supported the establishment of a communist government in North Korea and the United States advocated for a democratic republic in South Korea.

By 1948, North Korea had become known as the Democratic People's Republic of Korea and South Korea was the Republic of Korea. In the first months of 1950, Soviet and U.S. troops left Korea and the country remained a divided nation. The effects of this division on Koreans and interior environments and architecture become evident when the nations had to rebuild their cities and towns after the widespread destruction caused by the Korean War (1950–1953).

The Korean War began on June 25, 1950, when North Korea attacked South Korea. The United Nations sent troops to defend South Korea, and China sent troops to assist North Korea. The fighting continued for 3 years. Four million soldiers were either killed or injured; civilian casualties numbered a million. Both countries suffered extensive destruction of cities, homes, and forests. In 1953 there was a ceasefire, but the two countries are still working on a peace treaty in the 21st century. The 38th parallel became the Demilitarized Zone (DMZ), which continues to separate Korean families and friends. Interestingly, the 2-mile-wide (3.22-kilometer) DMZ has become an undisturbed natural habitat for wildlife, trees, and plants.

The Korean War and the DMZ affected people, interiors, architecture, and the natural environment in various ways. Both countries had to reconstruct their built environments and rehabilitate their various natural resources (e.g., forests) that had been damaged by the extensive fighting, which included artillery, tanks, and relentless bombings. Both North and South Korea had to establish viable agricultural and manufacturing sectors. Prior to the Korean War, most industry was in North Korea, which had more mineral resources. South Korea had the rich soil for agriculture. Therefore, North Koreans had access to materials required to rebuild their cities, towns, and buildings, but they had the challenge to develop farmland. South Korea had the natural resources to grow food, but to rebuild their country required international trade.

The source of materials and political ideologies affected the design of new buildings, interiors, cities, and towns on each side of the DMZ. North Korea rebuilt their country using local materials, and to demonstrate self-reliance the government limited imports from a few countries, such as China and Russia. South Korea rebuilt their country with diverse materials and products that were derived from international trade.

Political differences also affected housing and interior environments. North Korea's housing was controlled by the government, and thus authorities determined architectural styles and maintenance policies, including the operation of utilities. Urban housing designed by the government consisted of monotonous high-rises with limited heating, and unreliable electricity and water. As a democratic republic, South Korea's international trade policies resulted in the development of a strong industrial base with most people living in privatized high-rises in urban areas. South Koreans had the opportunity to select where they wanted to live as well as the type of dwelling. Therefore, high-rises were designed in a variety of styles, sizes, and amenities. Furthermore, employment opportunities derived from the country's strong industrial base enabled people to buy modern furnishings and to pay the costs for reliable utilities, including heating, air conditioning, electricity, and water.

Even though the political situation in Korea led to the development of two forms of government and approaches to housing, there are many ways the Korean people on both sides of the DMZ have sustained their commitment to their cultural heritage, reflecting their desire to reunify their country. For example, North and South Koreans are ethnically homogenous and speak the same language; many also value education and respect nature. Korea developed conservation laws in the 6th century. Both countries established reforestation programs after the war. The desire to reestablish their heritage is also evident in the building of traditional architecture and reviving of cultural arts. Thus, to study the interior environments and architecture in North and South Korea in the 1950s requires an exploration of Korea's historical traditions.

Korean history begins 5,000 years ago and was significantly influenced by its neighbor, China. The Chinese introduced Koreans to Buddhism, Confucianism, the written language, and many fine arts, including painting, handicrafts, and architecture. Handicrafts involved ceramics, pottery, porcelain, papercrafts, lacquer, and working with bamboo, stone, and wood. Koreans developed their own unique style and were responsible for creating woodblock printing and **celadon porcelain** (Figure 7.1). The most extraordinary example of Korean

Figure 7.1 Koreans developed their own unique style, and were responsible for creating celadon porcelain.
Source: TongRo Image Stock/Alamy.

Figure 7.2 To respect their cultural heritage, in the 20th century Koreans built traditional Korean houses, or hanok.
Source: © Atlantide Phototravel/Corbis.

wood carving is the *Tripitaka Koreana,* a collection of wooden printing blocks of Buddhist scriptures. Carved during the Koryŏ Dynasty (918–1392), the *Tripitaka Koreana* includes more than 80,000 woodblocks and is displayed in the Buddhist temple, Haein, located in South Kyŏngsang (Gyeongsang) province, South Korea. The Koryŏ Dynasty is well known for the construction of numerous Buddhist temples and celadon porcelain.

Koryŏ celadon porcelain is internationally famous for its semitransparent bluish-green glaze. Artistic and functional pieces were made in a range of greenish colors, but the turquoise blue color, or "kingfisher blue," is considered the most valuable. Common decorations on celadon porcelain considered auspicious in Korean culture include lotus flowers, clouds, cranes, butterflies, and chrysanthemums. Decorations on the porcelain are applied by painting with liquid clay (**slip decoration**) or by inlaying clay into its surface (**slip inlay decoration**). Interest in Koryŏ celadon was renewed in the early 20th century, when during the construction of railways, many pieces were found in tombs near the capital of Koryŏ. In another effort to sustain their cultural heritage despite the imposed DMZ, Korean artists have restored and are using ancient kilns that were used to fire Koryŏ celadon.

Another example of Koreans' respect for their cultural heritage is evident in the 20th-century practice of building traditional Korean houses, or **hanok** (Figure 7.2). The military conflict and political situation did not deter Koreans from constructing these houses, which have traditional thatched roofs, wood beams, and the ancient **ondol** (**warm stone**) method of heating. The ondol heating system dates back to the Koguryŏ (Three Kingdoms) (37 BCE–668). Ondol was an underfloor heating system that used ducts beneath the clay or stone floor to heat the rooms of a house. Originally, heat from the cooking stove was the energy source. Warm floors encouraged people to remove their shoes and to sit on the floor. Small rooms and low ceilings helped to retain the heat. A tradition used in the houses of the wealthier members of society was the "one room—one building" concept, which included enclosing several buildings within stone walls. These complexes had buildings for specific purposes, such as sleeping rooms, and separate areas for males and females. People with lower incomes had one building with a kitchen, storage area, and two or more multifunctional spaces.

Korea is sometimes called Chosŏn (Chosŏn Dynasty 1392–1910), or "Land of the Morning Calm," which is reflected in the simple design of interior environments and the diffused lighting created in rooms as daylight passes through paper in the sliding doors. Traditional Korean houses were one-story dwellings with sliding doors made with wooden grilles and paper. Traditional Korean paper, or hanji, is made from the bark of mulberry trees. The multistage process results in a beautiful translucent material that enhances the quality of illumination. Fragments and strands of the mulberry bark create an interesting texture and provide color variation to the cream-colored paper.

Interiors of traditional Korean houses were simple with minimal furniture. People sat on mats, on cushions, or on the floor. When dining, people sat on mats next to a low table. Padded mats were used to sleep. Chests in a variety of forms were important storage pieces and typically were placed along the walls. Traditional Korean chests were made from wood and were decorated with iron and brass metalwork. Some chests were veneered with strips of bamboo. Chests made from the locally grown persimmon wood had additional decoration. The graining pattern of persimmon wood has large areas of extremely dark and light colors. Consequently, persimmon wood graining can have a strip pattern or can appear to be an abstract painting. Chests were made in a variety of sizes in a box form or with multiple units stacked on top of each other. Preserving traditional chests as well as other cultural traditions is important to Koreans living in the south and the north.

World War II: Stalin's High-Rise Buildings (1949–1953) and Khrushchev's Palace of Congresses (1959–1961) in Moscow, USSR

An interesting outcome of war is the apparent need for people to re-establish their heritage by rebuilding traditional architecture and reviving their cultural arts. This occurred in Korea as well as in the Soviet Union. Even though the Soviet Union was one of the victors in World War II, the people and country suffered substantial damage and destruction. The Soviet Union lost approximately 10 percent of its prewar population, 11 million soldiers and 7 million civilians were killed or wounded, and more than 1,700 cities and towns were destroyed. Over 25 million people were homeless, and 32,000 industrial enterprises were destroyed. The war's financial costs ruined approximately one-third of the USSR's entire national wealth. What might be called the country's national pride was especially offended by the purposeful defacement of national architecture by enemy forces and the theft or vandalism of museum art collections. Subsequently, the Soviet government started creating plans to rebuild its cities and towns. The "Stalinist" construction plans included

Figure 7.3 Stalin initiated a grand plan for transforming Moscow's skyline by building eight high-rise buildings in a similar architectural style. Only seven buildings were ultimately built, and these were constructed between 1949 and 1953. Compare details of this architecture to the buildings in Figure 7.4.

Source: © Ivan Vdovin/JAI/Corbis.

comprehensive urban planning, monuments, and several new buildings for the homeless, public services, government offices, worship, and education. Designs were inspired by traditional Russian architecture. This was important for national pride, and also for demonstrating opposition to Western norms and customs. After World War II, distrust between the USSR and United States (the new "superpowers"), which stemmed in part from their opposing political and economic philosophies, escalated into a situation that became known as the Cold War. Tensions between the two nations—which in part led to the development of huge arsenals of nuclear weapons—did not ease until the 1990s.

Modern architecture, including designs during the Constructivist Movement in the 1920s and 1930s, was abandoned by authorities because of its connection to the West, and what was perceived as inferior construction materials and methods. For inspiration, architects and designers referenced traditional Russian architecture with an emphasis on 18th-century Neoclassicism and 19th-century Eclecticism. Many of the decorative motifs were traditional Russian symbols, such as the five-pointed red star, sheaves of Siberian wheat, and the hammer and sickle. Symbols were carved on medallions, panels, and bas-reliefs. Most buildings had numerous statues that were associated with Soviet and Russian history, such as depictions of Josef Stalin, farmers, factory workers, and the venerated St. George of the Eastern Orthodox religion slaying a dragon.

After the war, Stalin initiated a plan for transforming Moscow's skyline by building eight high-rises in a similar architectural style (Figure 7.3). Only seven buildings were ultimately built, and these were constructed between 1949 and 1953. The high-rises consisted of two apartment buildings, two hotels, a government office building, Moscow State University, and the Ministry of Foreign Affairs and Foreign Trade. The location of each building was strategically designed to balance the skyline and to emphasize topographical features of the city, predominantly the Moskva River and the surrounding hills. Crowning the arrangement was Moscow State University, built on the top of the Lenin Hills.

The university's high-rise buildings have a similar architectural style that is easily recognizable in

Figure 7.4 Stalin's high-rise buildings have tall central towers surmounted with spires and have a resemblance to the multiple towers of Moscow's Kremlin. Some of the high-rise towers repeat the Kremlin's use of clocks, bells, and the five-point stars at the top of spires. Compare these historical buildings to the architecture in Figure 7.3.

Source: © José Fuste Raga/Corbis.

the Moscow skyline. All of the Gothic Revival buildings have a central tower, spires, golden-yellow stone façades, **finials,** figurative carving, **pinnacles,** and a vertical emphasis. Each high-rise has a pyramid shape formed by multiple tiers. The tall, central towers are surmounted with spires and resemble the multiple towers of Moscow's Kremlin (Figure 7.4). Some of the high-rise towers repeat the Kremlin's use of clocks, bells, and the five-pointed stars at the top of spires. Generally, the lobby interiors were highly decorative. For example, the Leningrad Hotel was decorated in a Russian Byzantine style with elaborately carved stucco, floral paintings, and patterned carpets. Rooms were spacious, and the dominant colors were red and gold.

Nikita Khrushchev was another Soviet leader who affected Moscow's architectural heritage in the 1950s. After the death of Stalin in 1953, Khrushchev became the Premier of the Soviet Union (1953–1964). Khrushchev opposed Stalin's excessive use of valuable land, labor, and resources and ordered statues and paintings of Stalin removed from public buildings. To demonstrate a new stewardship ethos, Khrushchev commissioned the rational design of the Palace of Congresses inside the walls of the Kremlin (Figure 7.5). The palace's unadorned design illustrates how architecture in the Khrushchev era was dramatically different from the traditional towers, which inspired Stalin's high-rise buildings. In addition to projecting a statement, the Palace of Congresses was built to accommodate activities of the state, including meetings, conferences, concerts, and ballet and theater performances. The palace had an auditorium that could accommodate more than 6,000 patrons, and hundreds of rooms for offices and state functions. Khrushchev's modern design also emphasized his interest in new technologies. One of the technological areas the USSR was dedicating significant national resources to was space exploration. In 1957, the Soviet Union launched Sputnik I, the world's first satellite.

Figure 7.5 To demonstrate a new stewardship ethos, Khrushchev commissioned the rational design of the Palace of Congresses (on the left) inside the walls of the Kremlin. The palace illustrates how Khrushchev's architecture was dramatically different than traditional towers, which inspired Stalin's high-rise buildings.
Source: Peter Titmuss/Alamy.

EFFECTS AND CONDITIONS OF THE NATURAL ENVIRONMENT

A series of floods in China, Holland, India, and the United States killed millions of people during the 1950s. In 1950, China suffered a flood when the Hwai and Yangtze Rivers overflowed its banks. As a result, 10 million people were made homeless. In 1953, a storm in the North Sea caused dikes in Holland to breach, causing the drowning of over 1,800 people and the destruction of 3,000 houses. Floods and an earthquake left more than 5 million people homeless in Assam, India in 1950. The Great Smog of 1952, which lasted only 5 days, killed more than 4,000 people in London, mostly due to pneumonia, bronchitis, and tuberculosis. The deadly smog was created by a combination of unusually cold weather, high humidity, a heavy fog, and air pollution from an endless burning of coal to heat buildings. Two years later, the British scientists Sir Richard Doll and Sir Austin Bradford-Hill confirmed a link between smoking and cancer.

Another disaster, the Great Chinese Famine (1958–1961), resulted in the deaths of millions of people, primarily due to starvation. The famine was primarily caused by the policies of the Chinese government in its quest to industrialize the country, a process that continues into the 21st century. Excavations in the 1950s enabled the world to experience and appreciate the splendor of Wat Mahathat in Sukhothai, Thailand. The territory of the United States grew when Alaska and Hawaii joined the nation in 1959.

Organic Forms: Solomon R. Guggenheim Museum (1956–1959) in New York City by Frank Lloyd Wright

Using nature for inspiration, Frank Lloyd Wright's Solomon R. Guggenheim Museum in New York City opened in 1959; revolutionizing the museum experience. The Solomon R. Guggenheim Museum was Frank Lloyd Wright's last major project and essentially his only project in New York City. Unfortunately, two of the people most responsible for the museum's revolutionary design, Wright and Solomon Guggenheim, died before the museum opened. Wright, Guggenheim, and the eventual director of the museum, Baroness Hilla Rebay, began conceptualizing the museum in 1943. However, for numerous reasons, including World War II, the death of Guggenheim in 1949, and problems related to building codes, the project took 16 years to complete.

The project's conceptualization can be traced back to Rebay's extraordinary commitment to "Non-Objective" Art. Her artistic background and life in Europe exposed her to some of the most famous 20th-century Abstract artists (see Chapter 4), including

Wassily Kandinsky, Paul Klee, and Rudolf Bauer. In the late 1920s, Rebay moved to New York City and eventually met the Guggenheims. Rebay inspired Guggenheim, a wealthy businessman and art collector, to invest in Non-Objective Art, a type of abstract art that is not representational, containing no recognizable figures or objects. Ten years later, Guggenheim had amassed a collection that exceeded 800 paintings. As Guggenheim approached the age of 80, he established the Guggenheim Foundation in 1937 "for the promotion and encouragement of art and education in art and the enlightenment of the public, especially in the field of art" (Guggenheim Museum, 1960, pp. 8–9). After displaying his collection of Non-Objective paintings in temporary museums, Guggenheim asked Rebay to begin the process of building a permanent museum in New York City to be funded by his Foundation.

Guggenheim's decision to give Rebay considerable responsibility for the project had a significant impact on the museum's conceptualization. The "memorial" museum was to be designed for Guggenheim's collection of Non-Objective Art. According to Guggenheim and Rebay, this required a transformational approach to museum architecture. After considering several architects, Rebay and Guggenheim determined that Frank Lloyd Wright had the vision, fortitude, and talent to design a museum that would reflect the spirit of Non-Objective Art.

To ensure a comprehensive understanding of what was envisioned for the presentation of this type of art, Wright, Guggenheim, and Rebay engaged in correspondence with each other over several years. Rebay explained in great detail her philosophical perspectives regarding Non-Objective Art and expected Wright to translate these concepts into the museum's organic architecture. Rebay contended that Non-Objective Art was "order creating order and [is] sensitive (and corrective even) to space. As you feel the ground, the sky and the 'in-between' you will perhaps feel them too; and find the way . . . I have never seen a building you made but photos, and I feel them-while I never felt others' work as much, [theirs being] lacking in organic perfection and adapting to the task's originality. I want a temple of spirit, a monument!" (Pfeiffer [Ed.], 1986, p. 4). The "temple" museum was to be an "elevating sanctuary" that was contemplative, peaceful, and quiet (Lukach, 1983, pp. 62–63). Rebay proclaimed that "Functionalism does not agree with non-objectivity," but there was a strong connection between Non-Objective Art and the universal qualities found in nature. Rebay explained that Non-Objective Art had "a spiritual rhythm" and was "organic with the cosmic order."

Wright was already a longstanding advocate of organic architecture (see Chapter 5). Thus, he was able to respond to Rebay's philosophical tenets of Non-Objective Art and design the Guggenheim Museum, or what Wright referred to as "The Modern Gallery." In a letter to Guggenheim in 1946, Wright proclaimed that the museum would be "the first advance in the direction of organic architecture which the great city of New York has to show" (Guggenheim Museum, 1960, p. 16). Wright incorporated many organic elements and forms in the design of the museum, including water, plants, natural light, the spiraling forms of seashells, seedpods, and the shapes of the moon and the sun.

The transformational organic "Modern Gallery" was designed so that viewers would visually, physically, and "spiritually" connect with Non-Objective Art. Wright's concept for "The Modern Gallery" was not "to subjugate the paintings to the building. . . . On the contrary, it was to make the building and the painting an uninterrupted, beautiful symphony such as never existed in the World of Art before" (Guggenheim Museum, 1960, p. 48). To "make the building and the painting an uninterrupted, beautiful symphony" he created a revolutionary architecture that "never existed in the World of Art before." As has been noted previously, art museums were initially located in private residences and palaces (see Chapter 1). Generally, the interiors had a series of square- or rectangular-shaped

rooms with very tall ceilings and excessive ornamentation. Paintings were hung on straight walls without consideration for the museum experience. Many of the rooms had numerous paintings mounted on all four walls. "Museum fatigue" easily occurred when people were overwhelmed by the quantity of paintings within a room and the subsequent confusion resulting from the ability to see even more paintings in the adjacent rooms. The continuous progression of rooms can intensify fatigue when a person is in an area far from the entrance and is unable to easily determine how to leave the museum or find a place to relax.

Wright's design for the organic "Modern Gallery" completely transformed traditional museum experiences. Rooms with corners were replaced by "clean beautiful surfaces throughout the building, all beautifully proportioned to human scale" (Guggenheim Museum, 1960, p. 15). To create an intimate experience with the Non-Objective Art, Wright created small alcoves with comfortable 9-foot-high (2.74-meter) ceilings.

Paintings were to be mounted without the traditional frames or glass. Within each alcove, paintings were "set in a wall" rather than "mounted on a wall." Most paintings were "set in" one wall, which was angled for ease in viewing. Wright's description of the walls demonstrates his focus on organic unity: "Walls slant gently outward forming a giant spiral for a well defined purpose: a new unity between beholder, painting, and architecture. . . . The flat-plane of the picture thus detached by the curve of the wall is presented to view much as a jewel set as a signet in a ring. Precious—as itself" (Guggenheim Museum, 1960, p. 19).

To avoid viewer confusion when moving from gallery to gallery, Wright designed one continuous spiraling "Grand Ramp" (Figure 7.6). His cantilevered design of the ramp, "like that of a seashell, is clear of interior supports of any kind, the fibrous floors being carried throughout from the outer walls." The ramp represented organic progress in the "chambered nautilus." Entrance to the ramp was located on the ground

Figure 7.6 Wright designed one continuous spiraling "Grand Ramp" for the Guggenheim Museum in New York City. Wright's intent with the cantilevered design of the "Grand Ramp" was "like that of a seashell, is clear of interior supports of any kind, the fibrous floors being carried throughout from the outer walls."

Source: Ambient Images, Inc./Alamy.

level next to the "oval seed-pod"–shaped pool filled with water. Wright also envisioned that people would take an elevator to the top level and then slowly follow the Grand Ramp down to the ground level. To reduce "museum fatigue," he planned an elevator stop on every level so that people could easily leave the museum or relax by visiting the cafeteria. The "oval seed-pod" pool with a fountain was also a "peaceful" spot to rest.

Wright considered the "seed-pod" symbolic of sprouting life and used the oval shape in details throughout the museum, such as the structural columns,

benches, and a staircase. As had Non-Objective artists, Wright used geometric shapes, such as circles and semicircular shapes, symbolically. He viewed the circle as representing infinity and associated it with the sun and moon. Wright used the circle for the plans of the main gallery, the gallery's dome, the auditorium below ground level, and the administration building. Circular and semicircular shapes are evident in the vestibule, terrazzo flooring, restrooms, elevators, window grills, front entrance doors, and information desk.

The new museum experience had to involve nature and natural light. Natural light emitted from the enormous glass dome could be experienced at any gallery level along the "Grand Ramp." Wright explained his concept for illuminating art in "The Modern Gallery" in the following way: "But the charm of any work of art, either of painting, sculpture or architecture is to be seen in normal, naturally-changing light. . . . Instead of light fixed and maintained in two-dimensions, this more natural lighting for the nature of a painting is a designed feature of the new Solomon R. Guggenheim Museum" (Guggenheim Museum, 1960, p. 23). Natural light provided a three-dimensional light source for the art and helped reduce museum fatigue. The low parapet walls along the spiraling ramp enabled a viewer to contemplate the "temple" by absorbing sunlight and listening to the soft sound of water generated by the fountain. Another source of rest was the view of the Fifth Avenue garden, which could be seen through an enormous glass wall in the main gallery.

Unfortunately, Wright died 6 months before the opening of the museum and was never able to learn how his "Modern Gallery" "would add up to a reposeful place in which the paintings would be seen to better advantage than they have ever been seen" (Guggenheim Museum 1960, p. 16). In the first 9 months after it opened, more than 750,000 people visited the Guggenheim Museum and were able to have a new museum experience. In 2009 the Guggenheim celebrated its 50th anniversary.

Environmental Conditions: Wat Mahathat (13th–15th Centuries; Excavation 1956), in Sukhothai, Thailand

As with previous sites discussed in this textbook, Wat Sukhothai is an example of a place where environmental conditions preserved a cultural heritage until excavation. In 1956, Thailand's Fine Arts Department's excavation of Wat Mahathat provided the world with the opportunity to examine and learn about the interiors, architecture, sculpture, and art of a civilization that existed hundreds of years ago. The city of Sukhothai (meaning "Dawn of Happiness") was critically important to the development of Siam (modern Thailand). Sukhothai was the first independent kingdom in Siam and became the kingdom's capital city when its boundaries expanded. The magnificent Buddhist architecture of Wat Mahathat, "Temple of the Great Relic," was built between the 13th and 15th centuries.

The architectural style of Wat Mahathat reflects an assimilation of cultures that border Sukhothai / Siam and is synonymous with today's defining characteristics of Thai architecture. Thailand shares a northwest border with Burma (modern Myanmar), and Laos is to the northeast. Cambodia is to the southeast, and the two countries border the Gulf of Thailand. To the south, Thailand shares the Malay Peninsula with Malaysia. The country's interior environments and architecture have been and still are influenced by these countries, and because Thailand, "Land of the Free," was never a European colony, styles were not affected by Western designs during the 19th and early 20th centuries.

Pho Khun Sri Indraditya (1257–1277) founded the Kingdom of Sukhothai when he defeated the Khmer Empire (800s–1200s) of Angkor. The son of Pho Khun Sri Indraditya, Pho Khun Ramkhamhaeng (1279–1298), continued the expansion and development of the kingdom, and was responsible for establishing political relationships with China. Interactions with China were very important to the development of many of Thailand's cultural traditions and techniques, such as the art of ceramics, architecture, and producing silk. The reign of Pho Khun Ramkhamhaeng was referred to as the "Golden Years."

During the Sukhothai era (1235–1438), one of the most important architectural sites built in the center of Sukhothai was the Buddhist temple complex, Wat Mahathat (Figure 7.7). Buddhism, the national religion of Thailand (currently practiced by 95 percent of the population) began more than 2,500 years ago in India

Figure 7.7 Aerial view of Wat Mahathat, Sukhothai.

Source: Yann Arthus-Bertrand/Corbis.

Figure 7.8 Wat Mahathat is a style that reflects an assimilation of cultures that geographically border Thailand.

Source: International Photobank/Alamy.

and spread to Thailand in the 3rd century BCE. The construction of Wat Mahathat occurred during the 13th and 15th centuries, and Phra Maha Dharmarãja Li Thãi (1298–1346) commissioned a restoration during the 14th century due to a collapse of the original structure. During the Sukhothai era, nearly all paintings, sculpture, woodcarvings, and architecture were created for religious purposes.

Wat Mahathat is a complex of several religious buildings that were constructed with local materials. Original structures, some of which are no longer in existence, were made from wood. Later buildings were made with stone, Khmer sandstone, bricks, and **laterite,** a clay-like substance that hardens when exposed to air. Generally, bricks were covered with white stucco and carvings were gilded. Chinese influence is evident in ceramic roof tiles; intense blue and orange colors are reflective of Thailand's architecture. Perceived as auspicious, repetition is evident in multiple roofs, repeated motifs, and recurring arches above windows, niches, and doors. Structures had multiple steep roofs with

flared points and highly decorated gables (Figure 7.8). Ornamentation included glass mosaic pieces, lacquer, gilt, mother-of-pearl, and porcelain fragments. The end points of the roofs were finished with **chofa** (sky tassels), a finial in the shape of a horn. Common forms of decoration along the edges of eave boards were **hang hongse** (swan's tail) or **nagas,** a mythical serpent-like creature that symbolizes water. Nagas were also used on balustrades. Other mythical creatures used for ornamentation and for auspicious purposes were **singha,** a guardian lion; **kinnara,** a creature that was half human and half bird; **makara,** a reptile that spews objects; and **kala,** a head of a demon with pointed ears, sharp teeth, and claws for fingers (Figure 7.9). Other examples of uniquely Thai details are towers with lotus-bud spires and the flickering leaf decoration (Figure 7.10).

As with other Buddhist **wats,** or temples, the Wat Mahathat complex served as the center of community activities, including religious ceremonies, prayer, meditation, education, and the monks' residence. To acquire merits in the Buddhist religion, community members assisted in the construction of the wat's religious structures, and donated paintings and sculptures. Monks were given food, clothing, and educational materials. Numerous buildings, courtyards, ornamental ponds, and trees were enclosed within stone walls.

Religious structures of Wat Mahathat were the **bot** or **ubosot** (ordination hall), **wihan** or **vihãra** (assembly hall), a central **chedi** (stupa), and approximately 200 minor chedis. The bot is the most sacred building in the wat. The bot is used by the monks for prayer and mediation and is the site for ordination ceremonies. The ground must be consecrated and is designated by boundary and marker stones that surround the structure. The wihan is a religious building constructed on ground that is not consecrated. The wihan is used for ceremonies, prayer, and meditation and can be used by worshippers as well as monks. Chedis can contain ashes and relics of Buddha, monks, and royalty.

Figure 7.9 Mythical creatures used for ornamentation and for auspicious purposes at the Wat Mahathat complex were singha, kinnara, makara, and kala.

Source: Ben Pipe – Details/Alamy.

Figure 7.10 Examples of uniquely Thai details are towers with lotus-bud spires (background) and the flickering flame finial on top of Buddha's head.

Source: Jon Arnold Images Ltd./Alamy.

The religious buildings in a wat played an important role in educating people about the teachings and life of Buddha. Most people during this time were illiterate; therefore, learning was derived from depictions in paintings, murals, statuary, and wood and stone carvings. Wat Mahathat is well-known for a stucco bas-relief of walking monks along the base of the central chedi (Figure 7.11). The seated statue of Buddha and a walking Buddha in a niche are also masterpieces at the complex. Sukhothai artists had a very elegant and refined approach to creating Buddha images. To create a Buddha image, an artist must adhere to precise criteria. Buddhists believe that the spirit of Buddha will be sustained when images adhere to specific guidelines. For example, human attributes, such as bones, veins, and muscles, were not revealed on surfaces. The fluidity

of bronze enabled the Sukhothai artists to craft images that emphasized Buddha's elongated arms, fingers, and legs. Buddha's image had the customary distended earlobes and the ushnisha, or cranial proturbence on top of his head, and his locks of hair were curled in a clockwise direction. However, a unique adaptation created by the Sukhothai artists was an egg-shaped head and the flame finial protruding from the top of the head (see Figure 7.10). The four postures of Buddha images are standing, walking, sitting with the right leg resting on the left leg, and reclining, which is associated with nirvana. Seated and standing Buddha images are common, but Sukhothai's sculptures of Buddha walking are considered to be rare. The seemingly sheer fabric draped over the Buddha image's left shoulder cascades to the ground and appears to move as he walks.

Figure 7.11 Wat Mahathat is well-known for a stucco bas-relief of walking monks along the base of the central chedi.
Source: Corbis RF/Alamy.

Sukhothai was added to UNESCO's World Heritage List in 1991 because it "represents a masterpiece of the first Siamese architectural style" and the historic towns characterize "the first period of Siamese art and the creation of the first Thai state" (UNESCO, 1991, p. 54). Today the ancient monuments of Sukhothai and other nearby sites are managed by the Department of Fine Arts, Thailand, and are open to visitors. In the National Park, the department still celebrates Loy (float) Krathong (small boat), a late-autumn festival associated with a bountiful rice harvest. To thank the gods for the rain that was needed to grow crops, during a full moon candles are placed on lotus leaves that float on Sukhothai's ornamental ponds.

GLOBAL TECHNOLOGICAL DEVELOPMENTS

Technologies that advanced in the 1950s included nuclear energy and weapons, space exploration, and television. The first nuclear bomb test occurred in Nevada at the beginning of the decade, and the Soviets launched Sputnik I toward the end of the 1950s. To promote the space program in 1958, the U.S. government established the National Aeronautics and Space Administration (NASA). The RCA Corporation broadcast the first color television programs from the top of the Empire State Building in 1954. To support the growing automobile industry, Eero Saarinen and his father Eliel Saarinen designed a modern-day technical complex for the General Motors Corporation in Warren, Michigan. The U.S. government responded to the ascendance of the private automobile by initiating the construction of the interstate highway system in 1956.

The 1950s also witnessed the invention of robots, solar cells, and video recorders. Computer technology was advanced by the development of the modem, microchips, and IBM's 1401 mainframe. The Xerox Corporation launched the first commercial copy machine in 1959. Synthetic fiber advances included the invention of acrylic and polyester in 1950 and 1953, respectively, by E. I. du Pont de Nemours & Company, Inc. New materials contributed to George Nelson's ability to design the Coconut (1955) chair and the Marshmallow (1956) sofa. Charles and Ray Eames's infamous molded plywood lounge chair and ottoman in leather were produced in 1956.

Technologies and Materials: Eero Saarinen

During the 1950s, advances in organic chemistry, physics, and machinery enabled designers to experiment with new approaches to the design of furniture and architecture. Fiberglass had been developed to the extent that designers were able to apply the technology to industrial designs. Melting glass marbles and extruding the liquid through very tiny holes produces fiberglass. The fine fibers, resembling silk, are resistant to fading and burning, and are very strong. Fiberglass reinforced with plastic creates a product that is strong and lightweight, and can be molded into a variety of forms. The availability of fiberglass inspired Eero Saarinen, the son of renowned Finnish architect Eliel Saarinen, to design furniture made from the innovative material.

The ability to mold fiberglass into shapes that would be strong enough to support the weight of people resulted in Saarinen's revolutionary Pedestal Collection, including the modern Tulip chair (1955–1957) (Figure 7.12). The Pedestal Collection of chairs and tables is still manufactured by Knoll and has become a modern classic. To understand how to work with the new material, Saarinen consulted with industrial designers, including people who were experimenting with using lightweight fiberglass for the construction of boats. Due to its infancy in development, Saarinen was only able to use molded fiberglass for the chair's shell. The base was made from cast aluminum. To give the appearance that the base and chair were one unified form, the aluminum had a white plastic finish. In reflecting on his designs in 1958, Saarinen explained the rationale of the Collection:

> The undercarriage of chairs and tables in a typical interior makes an ugly, confusing, unrestful [sic] world. I wanted to clear up the slum of legs. I wanted to make the chair all one thing again. All the great furniture of the past from Tutankhamun's chair to Thomas Chippendale's have always been a structural total. With our

Figure 7.12 Fiberglass's ability to be molded into shapes that would be strong enough to support the weight of people resulted in Eero Saarinen's revolutionary Pedestal Collection.

Source: Knoll, Inc.

> excitement over plastic and plywood shells, we grew away from this structural total. As now manufactured, the pedestal furniture is half-plastic, half-metal. I look forward to the day when the plastic industry has advanced to the point where the chair will be one material, as designed. (Saarinen [Ed.], 1968, p. 66)

Saarinen's innovative designs for his Pedestal Collection are a result of considerable experience working with new technologies and materials. As discussed in Chapter 6, he collaborated with Charles Eames in the design and development of two furniture designs that won first prizes in the Museum of Modern Art's (MoMA) 1941 "Organic Design in Home Furnishings" competition. Saarinen continued to experiment with innovative technologies and materials when he focused on designing affordable housing. In the early 1940s, he applied mass-production techniques, prefabrication processes, and modular construction methods to two new conceptual projects. A Community House (1941) was a conceptual project that was based on Fuller's 4-D, or Dymaxion, house (see Chapter 6). Similar to Fuller's design, the Community House had a central mast that supported its roof and the structure had prefabricated mechanical systems. The building could be expanded or reduced in size depending on the needs of the community. The Unfolding House (1945) project was a modular trailer that had an expandable metal roof. The roof could unroll when the modular unit was enlarged.

A definitive example of how modern materials affected the design of Saarinen's interior environments and architecture is the Technical Center (1948–1956) for the General Motors Corporation in Warren, Michigan (Figure 7.13). The Saarinens, father and son, started the development of the Technical Center in 1945, but General Motors delayed the project until 1948. Although Eliel died in 1950, aspects of the design of the Technical Center still reflect his style, such as using water as a dominant element and the incorporation of strong vertical structures as a means to balance horizontal forms.

In discussing the project, the younger Saarinen noted that "General Motors is a metal-working industry; it is a precision industry; it is a mass-production industry. All these things should, in a sense, be expressed in the architecture of its Technical Center" (Saarinen [Ed.], 1968, p. 30). To express the "metal-working industry," Eero used steel and buildings made from "mass-produced units" on an "assembly line" (Saarinen [Ed.], 1968, p. 30). To provide "maximum flexibility," the "mass-produced units" were 5-foot (1.52-meter) modules. The standardized modules were used for steel construction, mechanical systems, wall partitions, storage units, and furniture. Another strategy to reinforce the "metal-working industry" was Eero's designs for the furniture and interior staircases, or "technological sculptures." As illustrated in Figure 7.14, the industrial interior reflects influences from the Bauhaus (see Chapter 4). Eero's cube-shaped furniture made with tubular steel and leather resembles Le Corbusier's LC2 Gran Confort (1928) (see Chapter 4).

The precision and strength of metal is dramatically illustrated in the apparently floating staircase. Thin metal wires support the broad and sweeping "technological sculpture."

In addition to an "appropriate architectural expression," Saarinen sought to "provide the best possible facilities for industrial research" and "to create a unified, beautiful, and human environment" (Saarinen [Ed.], 1968, p. 30). According to Eero, the unifying elements were the large centralized pool, the forest of trees, the modules, color, and the repeated use of glass and metal walls. Water and trees were unifying elements because they carefully balanced the complex of buildings with the natural environment. The dynamic qualities of water were emphasized by additional elements that were installed in the pool. A shiny spherical-shaped water tower contrasted with the horizontal form of the buildings and the pool (see Figure 7.13). Additional, contrasting vertical elements in the pool were the 50-foot (15.24-meter) fountain and Alexander Calder's *Water Ballet* sculpture that used jets to create the illusion that water was dancing in the air. All of the buildings were unified in the use of materials, but variety was achieved by different colors on the ends of the buildings. All of the long elevations of the buildings had glass and metal walls. The ends of the buildings were brick painted in a variety of colors, including orange, blue, black, red, and yellow (see Figure 7.13).

Saarinen's mastery of new materials was exemplified in his award-winning design for the Jefferson National Expansion Memorial (1948–1964) in St. Louis, Missouri. In direct competition with his father, Eliel, Eero's design for a dramatic stainless steel arch with an interior that was large enough for people to walk through has become an icon for that Midwestern city. Saarinen explained that the arch shape had "permanence" and "its dynamic quality seemed to link it to our own time" (Saarinen [Ed.], 1968, p. 22). To reflect "permanence" and "to belong to our time," Saarinen specified stainless steel.

Figure 7.13 A definitive example of how modern materials affected the design of Saarinen's interior environments and architecture is the Technical Center (1948–1956) for the General Motors Corporation in Warren, Michigan.

Source: General Motors Corp. Used with permission, GM Media Archives.

Figure 7.14 Eero Saarinen's cube-shaped furniture made with tubular steel and leather resembles Le Corbusier's LC2 Gran Confort. The precision and strength of metal is dramatically illustrated in the apparently floating staircase.

Source: © Ezra Stoller/Esto.

Eero Saarinen had many other commissions in the 1950s, including several college campuses, research centers, and a U.S. Chancellery building in Oslo, Norway, and London. Saarinen's airport terminal buildings were the Trans World Flight Center (modern John

F. Kennedy Airport) (1956–1962) in New York; Dulles International Airport Terminal Building (1958–1962) in Chantilly, Virginia; and the International Airport (1960–1964) in Athens, Greece. Saarinen died in 1961 at the age of 51. Many projects, including the St. Louis Arch, were not completed until after his death.

Impact of Television on the Built Environment

The founding of General Motor's Technical Center is an example of how corporations in the postwar years focused on researching and developing new technologies for modern living. Television was another technology that advanced significantly after World War II. By the end of the 1950s, ownership of television sets had increased to more than 85 percent of U.S. households. Several inventors in the United States and Europe experimented with television broadcasting in the 1920s and 1930s, but the start of World War II stopped their work.

Initial research related to television was based on the technologies that were developed for the radio. Dr. Vladimir K. Zworykin, a physicist at the Radio Corporation of America (RCA), is credited with inventing the first electrical television in 1929. During the 1930s, the British Broadcasting Corporation (BBC) in Britain developed broadcasting technologies in the interest of public service, and in the United States, RCA's National Broadcasting Company (NBC) created commercial programs. After World War II, television technology progressed rapidly in the United States, but the pace was much slower in Europe due to the widespread rebuilding that had to occur in most major European cities, as well as the economic hardships of the war. David Sarnoff, a producer and founder of NBC, provided a definition for television and anticipated its success: "I believe that television, which is the technical name for seeing as well as hearing by radio, will come to pass in the future" (Winship, 1988, p. 6). As the successful forerunner of home entertainment, radio was an excellent example to follow, and television executives were very familiar with the medium. Three of the four initial networks, NBC, Columbia Broadcasting System (CBS), and American Broadcasting Corporation (ABC), had origins in the radio industry. The other original network was the short-lived Du Mont Television Network.

In addition to improving television's technology, corporations had to identify funding sources, and create programs and schedules. Television executives once again used radio as the source of inspiration. Like radio, television was home entertainment for the entire family. Executives approached the same sponsors that funded radio programs, such as General Electric, Texaco Gasoline Dealers, and manufacturers of soap and tobacco products. Initial schedules were similar to radio's format of repeating the same morning, afternoon, and evening programs every week. Television programs also featured radio's genres, which included dramas, situation comedies (sitcoms), game shows, soap operas, variety shows, musicals, sports events, and news. Many successful radio stars and programs became even more famous on television, such as Lucille Ball, Bob Hope, *The Jack Benny Program, The Adventures of Ozzie and Harriet, The Red Skelton Show,* and *The Burns and Allen Show.*

Similarities between radio and television also occurred with the design of the product. In the earliest years, people had only one radio per household. To enable everyone in the family to hear the radio, the ideal placement was in the living room. To look attractive in the living room, radios were designed to resemble quality wood furniture. Subsequent designs were streamlined and made from modern **Bakelite,** a resin material developed in the early 20th century. Executives applied this same strategy to the design of early television sets. Television equipment was installed in attractive cabinets (Figure 7.15). However, in contrast to radio, television sets had to be placed in a location that let everyone see the screen. Interior environments were affected by not only the inclusion of a large unit

in living rooms, but furniture arrangements were altered to accommodate viewing angles. Consequently, focal points in many living rooms, such as a fireplace or views to the outdoors, shifted to television sets.

In addition to the physical characteristics of television sets, the design of interior environments was also affected by corporate sponsors and programs. In the early years of television, a corporation sponsored an entire program, such as *Texaco Star Theater* or *Kraft Television Theatre.* Associating their product with a program prompted corporations to align themselves with shows that would be watched by their consumers. Because many of the sponsors were manufacturers of food products and household equipment, television programs were set in pristine domestic situations, such as *Leave it to Beaver* (CBS: 1957–1958; ABC: 1958–1963) or *Father Knows Best* (CBS: 1954–1955; NBC: 1955–1960).

These middle-class homes were in the suburbs and had the newest household equipment as well as a garage for their automobile. Characters and neighborhoods lacked ethnic, racial, religious, and socio-economic diversity. Typically, families with children lived in comfortable single-family dwellings in the suburbs,

Figure 7.15 To look appropriate in the living room, television equipment was installed in attractive cabinets.
Source: Corbis.

Figure 7.16 There was a social distinction between the suburban home used in *Leave it to Beaver* and the Brooklyn apartments of the Kramdens and the Nortons on *The Honeymooners*.

Source: Jackie Gleason Enterprises/Photofest.

and couples without children lived in crowded apartments in New York City. The distinction is especially apparent when comparing the suburban home of *Leave it to Beaver* and the Brooklyn apartments of the Kramdens and the Nortons on *The Honeymooners* (CBS: 1955–1956) (Figure 7.16).

Beaver's spotless suburban home became associated with an idyllic family lifestyle, which included his mother, June Cleaver, routinely wearing dresses, aprons, high heels, and a pearl necklace. In dramatic contrast, Alice and Ralph Kramden's dingy, crowded urban apartment was the scene of fighting, yelling, and scheming (even though the plots always had a happy ending). Ralph's two-room unit had few furnishings and antiquated appliances, and the single window, which lacked a window treatment, faced the fire escape of another apartment building (see Figure 7.16). Unsurprisingly, the networks created more programs that depicted happy suburban lifestyles, and *The Honeymooners* had a very brief run from 1955 until 1956.

When network executives first supported *The Honeymooners,* they might have assumed an urban apartment setting could be successful because *I Love Lucy* (CBS: 1951–1960) was the top television program in the country, and that show's setting was a New York apartment building. However, even though the main characters Lucy and Ricky Ricardo were initially childless, their apartment was dramatically different from the Kramden's unit.

The Ricardos' apartment was spacious and well furnished, and the living room had a piano, artwork, a writing desk, and a "fireplace." The living room was remodeled in subsequent seasons, which exposed millions of viewers to modern furniture and textiles. (One remodeling erroneously changed the living room's solid wall behind the piano to a large window with an elaborate window treatment.) The kitchen had modern appliances, and the bedroom windows had frilly curtains, star decals on the walls, and a vanity table for applying makeup. A single upholstered headboard gave the impression that the Ricardos were sharing the same bed, but the division between the two twin beds was apparent. At this time, filming scenes of a television program in the couple's bedroom was an exception. The sponsors and network executives only allowed this to occur with *I Love Lucy* because Lucy and Ricky were actually married in real life.

Controlling access to specific rooms and activities was very common in early television. Generally, the only rooms that were filmed were the front entries, living rooms, dining rooms, children's bedrooms, and kitchens. On occasion an episode might be filmed outdoors or in a garage, but viewers rarely saw a bathroom or the parents' bedroom. Eventually, programs filmed parents in their bedroom, but the room had two separate twin beds. After years of living in New York City, the Ricardo family (by this time, with a child) moved to a traditional single-family home in suburban Connecticut. Interestingly, this was 1 year after the short-lived urban *Honeymooners* had left the air.

GLOBAL LIFE AND WORK STYLES

The destructive forces of World War II caused the need to construct many schools, and the growing demand for higher education resulted in the expansion of many institutions worldwide. For example, the Soviet Union's launch of Sputnik in 1957 stimulated education in the fields of science and mathematics. The importance of global education was exemplified by the United Nations' establishment of UNESCO immediately after the War. UNESCO's vision is "that education is key to social and economic development. We work for a sustainable world with just societies that value knowledge, promote a culture of peace, celebrate diversity and defend human rights, achieved by providing Education for All (EFA)" (UNESCO, 2009, p. 1). Mother Teresa included education with her charitable activities in India as well as providing a home for the dying and the "unwanted."

The sheer numbers of those in the baby-boomer generation—approximately 79 million people born between 1946 and 1964—spurred the construction of schools and low-cost housing. In the legal case *Brown v. Board of Education of Topeka* (1954), the U.S. Supreme Court decided that public school segregation was unconstitutional. The case was named for Oliver Brown, whose daughter, a black third-grader named Linda Brown, had to attend a black elementary school a mile away even though a white elementary school was only seven blocks away. In 1955, Rosa Parks was arrested in Montgomery, Alabama, for refusing to relinquish her seat on a bus to a white passenger. These conditions contributed to the rise of the Civil Rights Movement during this decade as well.

As a result of advances in nuclear science and weaponry, many people in the 1950s constructed bomb shelters filled with food supplies in their backyards. More people moved to the suburbs during the decade. Francis Crick and James Watson discovered the DNA structure in 1953. Medical researcher Jonas Salk announced his discovery of a vaccine for the disease of polio in 1954. Subsequently, millions of people were vaccinated, preventing the deaths and paralysis that had been associated with polio. Readers in the West were exposed to the 1917 Russian Revolution with the publication of the successful novel *Doctor Zhivago* (1957) by Boris Pasternak.

Charity: Mother Teresa—Nirmal Hriday (1952), Shishu Bhavan (1955), and Shanti Nagar (1957) in Calcutta (modern Kolkata), India

In stark contrast to the advertising and related consumerism that was promoted on television, in Calcutta (modern Kolkata) Catholic nun Mother Teresa was tirelessly committed to helping "the poorest of the poor." During the 1950s, she established three special homes in Calcutta. The first, Nirmal Hriday (Home for the Pure Heart) (1952), was for people who were dying. In 1955, Mother Teresa founded Shishu Bhavan, a home for orphaned and abandoned children, and then two years later Shanti Nagar (Town of Peace) was created for people with leprosy. These initiatives resulted in the eventual development of hundreds of centers in more than 100 countries, including the United States and Britain.

The homes she established were extraordinary for this time period because they were constructed in a city that "was a vast sea of suffering and despair. The streets, where people were born and died hourly, were crowded with beggars and lepers, together with a host of refugees from the countryside who had never known a home. Unwanted infants were regularly abandoned and left to die in clinics, on the streets, or in garbage bins. There were thousands of pavement dwellers within the city itself; 44 percent of the city did not have sewers" (Greene, 2004, p. 39). Mother Teresa had to establish homes in a city where people "lived in small hovels with dirt floors" (Greene, 2004, p. 40). Mother Teresa's perspective regarding the plight of abandoned people was "Being unwanted is the worst disease that any human being can ever experience."

In 1910, Mother Teresa was born Agnes Gonxha Bojaxhiu in Skopje (modern capital of the Republic of Macedonia). As early as 12, she was interested in becoming a Catholic nun. Specifically, Mother Teresa was attracted to the order of the Sisters of Loreto because of their missionary work in India. Because India was still a colony of Britain (see Chapter 1), to prepare for work in India, Mother Teresa studied English at the Loreto Abbey in Ireland. Upon taking her vows, Agnes chose "Teresa" as her adopted name in honor of St. Thérèse of Lisieux, a patron saint known for helping people by engaging in simple tasks.

Mother Teresa traveled to India when she was 18 to begin teaching geography and history primarily to children of wealthy British families. In 1931, she was transferred to St. Mary's High School in Calcutta. On the other side of the high walls that surrounded the school was one of the worst bustees (slums) in India. Eventually, helping to alleviate the horrific conditions that Mother Teresa saw on a daily basis became her mission in life. The "call within a call" came when she was on a train returning to Calcutta from a religious retreat. She explained that on September 10, 1946, the "Day of Inspiration," she received a message: "I was to leave the convent and help the poor while living among them. It was an order. I knew where I belonged, but I did not know how to get there" (Egan, 1985, p. 25).

Mother Teresa understood that her "calling" was to help serve the poor, but the task had to be done by living with the poorest people in Calcutta. After finally receiving permission from the Pope, Mother Teresa left the convent in 1948 and in 1950 created a new order of Catholic nuns, the Missionaries of Charity. To begin her life living with the poor, Mother Teresa only had five rupees (less than $1), one pair of sandals, and clothing worn by poor Indian women, a white cotton sari. The white sari trimmed in blue became the clothing for all of the sisters who eventually became nuns in the order of Missionaries of Charity.

Mother Teresa began her work in the streets of Calcutta during an extremely tumultuous era in Indian history, shortly after the country had achieved its independence from Britain. Indians were elated by this, but the terms of the negotiations resulted in riots, bloodshed, and mass confusion. The terms included an attempt to resolve differences between Muslims and Hindus by partitioning the country. Consequently, the independent nation of Pakistan was created with regions east (East Pakistan, modern Bangladesh) and west (West Pakistan, modern Pakistan) of India. The intent was to establish Pakistan as the nation for Muslims, and India would be the home for Hindus. The immediate consequence was deadly mayhem because there were Muslims and Hindus living in Pakistan and India. Approximately eight million people emigrated from Pakistan to India.

Calcutta is located very close to East Pakistan; therefore, the city, which was already overcrowded, became inundated with thousands of Hindu refugees in a very short period. Calcutta was not able to handle the situation; consequently, thousands of people lived in the streets or tried to create shelter from garbage found in heaps throughout the city. People were forced to live without sanitation, clean water, and adequate food or clothing. Therefore, when Mother Teresa started to walk the streets of Calcutta, conditions were even worse than what she had witnessed while teaching in the convent's schools.

She started her work with the poor by establishing a kind of open-air school, teaching abandoned children the alphabet outdoors. Classrooms were created without walls, desks, equipment, or supplies. The ground became a blackboard, and sticks served as chalk. Mother Teresa was able to attract more pupils every week. Her service to the poor expanded when she saw a dying woman on the ground outside a hospital. Mother Teresa carried the woman into the hospital for medical help. The hospital initially refused to care for the woman because she did not have any money and she had a contagious disease. The woman's situation prompted Mother Teresa to establish Nirmal Hriday, a home for people who were dying alone.

Mother Teresa established Nirmal Hriday by acquiring an abandoned building from city officials (Figure 7.17). Located adjacent to a Hindu temple, the building had been used as a dormitory for pilgrims. The purpose of Nirmal Hriday was to care for people who were dying alone in the streets. The numbers were staggering due to the crisis in Calcutta and the caste system associated with the Hindu religion. Traditionally, the caste system divided people into five main categories according to occupation and subsequent social status:

1. **Brahmins—priests and teachers**
2. **Kshatriyas—warriors and rulers**
3. **Vaishyas—farmers, merchants, artisans, minor officials**
4. **Sudras—laborers, unskilled workers**
5. **Harijans—untouchables, polluted laborers**

People were supposed to engage only with other individuals in their caste. Therefore, able-bodied people with economic means generally did not help poor

Figure 7.17 Men's ward at Nirmal Hriday. Mother Teresa established Nirmal Hriday by acquiring an abandoned building from city officials. Located adjacent to a Hindu temple, the building had been used as a dormitory for pilgrims.

Source: Wikimedia Commons.

people they saw dying on the streets. Mother Teresa and subsequent volunteers helped the dying by making them feel wanted and providing them with food, minor medical attention, baths, and a place to sleep. The design of the Nirmal Hriday building helped to facilitate the needs of the hospice. The rooms were filled with natural light streaming through the wide windows and reflecting off white surfaces. The tall ceilings and rotating fans helped dissipate India's intense heat. The large space was divided into separate sleeping quarters for men and women. To accommodate as many people as possible, rows of cots were placed close together. This arrangement also helped the nuns and volunteers observe the condition of many people at one time. Patients close to death were placed toward the front of the room for immediate care. The home had facilities for cooking and laundry, and the back of the building had a morgue.

After establishing a home where people could die with dignity, Mother Teresa established two other homes in Calcutta for people who were unwanted. In 1955 she opened Shishu Bhavan, a home for children who had been orphaned or abandoned. Many of these children had disabilities, and some of the babies had been found lying on the street or on a pile of garbage. Shanti Nagar was established to provide a community for "untouchable" people with leprosy, a disease that has caused its victims to be ostracized for centuries. Leprosy is not fatal, but it causes severe skin rashes and its bacteria attack the body's nervous system. Left untreated, the disease can cause severe deformities, most often affecting extremities, such as fingers and toes. Leprosy was considered a highly contagious disease, and therefore lepers were forced to live in isolation, often without adequate living conditions or medical assistance. Shanti Nagar provided the unwanted lepers with a home and care from people who wanted to serve the poorest of the poor. In addition to having their physical needs met, lepers were provided with the materials and training to create crafts.

Currently, scientists understand that leprosy is mildly contagious, and treatment medications have been developed. A vaccine does not yet exist to prevent the disease, and the World Health Organization estimates that more than five million people are currently living with leprosy in primarily warm climate regions of the world.

Mother Teresa's work spread to hundreds of other communities throughout the world. In 1969, Mother Teresa's services and homes for unwanted people gained international attention when a British journalist, Malcolm Muggeridge, created a BBC documentary of her accomplishments in Calcutta. She received numerous honors and awards, including the Nobel Peace Prize in 1979. The focus of her homes expanded to include HIV/AIDS victims, drug addicts, and battered women. Mother Teresa's perseverance and vision inspired the development of hundreds of interior environments that have contributed to the quality of life of tens of thousands of people.

Education: Cranbrook Academy of Art in Bloomfield Hills, Michigan; Illinois Institute of Technology (IIT) in Chicago; and Universidad Nacional Autónoma de México (UNAM) in Mexico City

As Mother Teresa was teaching children how to read in classrooms without walls, several educational facilities were being constructed around the world with massive walls. In the 1950s, some of these endeavors expanded existing campuses, such as the Cranbrook Academy of Art and Illinois Institute of Technology, as well as created brand new campuses, such as the Universidad Nacional Autónoma de México.

The Cranbrook Academy of Art in Bloomfield Hills, Michigan, a suburb north of Detroit, was formally established in 1932, but the Academy originated in 1924 when George G. Booth hired architect Eliel Saarinen to develop the Cranbrook Educational Community. Booth asked Eliel Saarinen to develop a master plan and to create a community where "artists . . . live at Cranbrook and execute their work there. Those artists form a more or less permanent staff of the Art Council" (Clark, 1983, p. 29). Saarinen was responsible for designing buildings on the campus and worked with Booth and faculty in developing an experiential program that integrated the academy with a traditional arts and crafts school. An important element of the program was involving students with successful working artists, designers, and architects through the artists-in-residence initiative. The program included architecture, urban design, interior design, furniture, metalwork, bookbinding, textiles, ceramics, sculpture, and painting. When the Academy was formally established in 1932, Booth named Saarinen its first president. Saarinen's international reputation helped attract talented students, instructors, and lecturers, such as Frank Lloyd Wright and Le Corbusier.

The Academy during the 1940s and 1950s had a significant impact on interior environments and architecture. During these decades, innovative designers were students, instructors, or both at Cranbrook. For example, Charles Eames began his work with Eero Saarinen, an Instructor of Design, while at Cranbrook. The sculptor Harry Bertoia was a student and an instructor in the metalwork department. A special exhibition of Bertoia's work in the 1950s was displayed in the Academy's museum in 1957. From the late 1930s through the 1950s, other designers associated with Cranbrook included Benjamin Baldwin, Niels Diffrient, Jack Lenor Larsen, Ralph Rapson, Harry Weese, and Florence and Hans Knoll. During the 1940s and 1950s, classes at the Academy included sculpture, survey of modern art, ceramics, weaving, painting, metalsmithing, architecture, woodworking, design, graphic arts, art history, and aesthetics. After the death of Eliel Saarinen in 1950, the Academy discontinued its studies in urban design.

Mies van der Rohe was another internationally renowned architect and designer hired to create a campus master plan and an architectural curriculum for a Midwest institution. The Illinois Institute of Technology (IIT) was created when the Lewis Institute and the Armour Institute of Technology, two Chicago institutions with origins in the 19th century, merged in 1940. The purpose of the new institution was "empowering young people to lead independent, meaningful lives" (Collens, 2005, p. 4). Mies's Bauhaus-inspired curriculum developed skills sequentially, beginning with drawing, followed by materials courses and construction principles, and concluding with architecture. The site for the newly formed institution was Armour Institute's campus, which had three buildings in the Romanesque Revival style. Mies had the extraordinary opportunity to create a symbiotic relationship between the plan of the campus, its architecture, and its curriculum.

Between 1940 and Mies's retirement in 1958, the Modernist campus expanded over several acres and included 22 buildings designed by Mies. Many of these were built after the war, including the Commons (1953), IIT Electrical Engineering and Physics Building (1954–1955), and S. R. Crown Hall (1956). The highly celebrated Crown Hall, the Architecture and Institute of Design Building, is often cited as one of Mies's greatest architectural creations (Figure 7.18).

Figure 7.18 The highly celebrated Crown Hall, or the Architecture and Institute of Design Building, is often cited as one of Mies's best architectural creations. Crown Hall is extraordinary for its flawless proportions and its completely column-free interior.

Source: Edward Parker/Alamy.

Crown Hall is extraordinary for its flawless proportions and column-free interior. Continuing to create floor-to-ceiling walls of glass, Mies used four steel-frame structures to support the one-story plan with a basement. Each unit had two columns and a plate girder running the short span of the floor plan. The walls of glass and steel mullions were divided horizontally. The upper section was clear glass, and the lower section had sandblasted glass.

The walls of glass and the column-free interior provided an ideal environment for teaching and learning design and architecture. The walls of glass allowed natural daylight to fill the drafting area, including the center section of the plan. Daylight was ideal for tasks requiring **visual acuity,** such as seeing drawing details. A larger floor plan would have prevented daylight from reaching the center of the building. To ensure the spread of daylight through the building, cabinetry was designed at the same height as the sandblasted glass. Sunlight was controlled by blinds and the sandblasted glass. Using sandblasted glass for the lower walls provided daylight, diffused glare, and eliminated shadows on the drafting tables. Louvers below the sandblasted glass provided fresh air. In addition to maximizing the benefits of daylight and the dispersion of fresh air, the column-free interior supported Mies's curriculum. The open space helped instructors and students at various levels in the program to collaborate and interact with each other easily.

As Crown Hall was being constructed in Chicago, an enormous educational project, including a department of architecture and design, was being constructed in Mexico City. The entirely new facilities and open areas were the physical component of the Central University City Campus of the Universidad Nacional Autónoma de México (UNAM). The University of Mexico was founded in 1551 and added buildings as needed. Consequently, the university lacked a unified location, and its academic buildings were scattered throughout the city. The resultant campus, constructed in just 3 years (1949–1952), is a "testimony to the modernization

Figure 7.19 Fresco by Diego Rivera, *Ancient Mexico*, National Palace, Mexico City, 1929–1935.

Source: Schalkwijk/Art Resource, NY.

of post-revolutionary Mexico in the framework of universal ideals and values related to access to education, improvement of quality of life, integral intellectual and physical education and integration between urbanism, architecture, and fine arts" (UNESCO, 2007, p. 1).

In the 1940s, to construct the new campus, officials identified a location on the then-outskirts of Mexico City. Extraordinarily, the 3-year construction timeline involved more than 6,000 workers and more than 60 architects, engineers, designers, and artists. The campus master plan had four major areas, which were separated by green open spaces. The areas were the teaching/research facilities; sports/recreation; an Olympic stadium; and residence halls for faculty, staff, and students.

In addition to consolidating the campus, an important goal for the university was demonstrating the government's commitment to educating the people of Mexico. This was imperative in helping to overcome the divisiveness that occurred during the Mexican Revolution (1910–1920). More than one million people had died during the revolution. An outcome of the revolution was a rejection of life associated with Spanish

colonialism (1521–1821) and a strong allegiance to Mexico's indigenous cultural heritage. These sentiments were portrayed in much Mexican art, including the art for new buildings at the University by David Alfaro Siqueiros and Diego Rivera. Rivera and José Clemente Orozco (see Chapter 1) have become internationally known for their large murals painted in public buildings (Figure 7.19). Some of the murals illustrated the history of Mexico and included scenes of Mexicans being attacked by Spaniards.

In the 1940s and 1950s, the pride that Mexicans had for their indigenous history and culture was translated into the design of the buildings for the University City campus. The overall design for the campus was Modernist but also followed traditions that were thousands of years old. An outstanding example is the stone mosaic façades of the university's main library (Figure 7.20). Dating back to paintings on the walls of lava pyramids, murals have been an important aspect of Mexico's cultural history and heritage. As exterior and interior decoration, murals of glass and ceramic tiles depicted important historical events and included many of Mexico's indigenous symbols, motifs, crafts,

Figure 7.20 Dating back to the lava pyramids, murals have been an important aspect of Mexico's cultural history and heritage. An outstanding example is the stone mosaic façades of the University City's main library.

Source: © Rainer Kiedrowski/Arcaid/Corbis.

and colors, such as the Quetzalcoatl god (feathered serpent), jaguar, and skeleton masks. One of the most important illustrations was an eagle perched on a cactus while devouring a snake. According to the Tenochtitlan legend, the Aztecs knew the location of their settlement when they saw an eagle eating a snake while perched on a cactus. The emblem was associated with the founding of Mexico City and is centered on Mexico's national flag.

GLOBAL VISUAL AND PERFORMING ARTS

The rapid increases in **globalization,** as evidenced by the worldwide interchange of ideas, goods, services, and capital, had an effect on the visual and performing arts. In the world of popular music, the sounds of the big bands were fading away as rock and roll became popular; the Western world was listening to Elvis Presley sing on the Ed Sullivan television show and in his first movie,

Love Me Tender (1956). The stage play *The Mousetrap* by Agatha Christie premiered in London in 1952. The play is the longest continuously running performance in the world and is still being performed in London today. In New York City, the Broadway musicals *My Fair Lady* and *West Side Story* were very successful commercial hits, winning Tony awards in 1957 and 1958, respectively.

Abstract art and sculpture had a significant impact on Le Corbusier when he designed the celebrated Chapel at Ronchamp in France. In Le Corbusier's book on the Chapel at Ronchamp, he explained the role of fine arts in the following way: "Abstract art which, rightly, nourishes so many passions in these days is the raison d'être of Ronchamp, the language of architecture" (Le Corbusier, 1957, p. 123). Corbusier also explained the sculptural aspects of the Chapel, noting, "The interior is also sculpture in the round (hollow). The four walls, the ceiling, the floor, everything is pressed into service in a disarming simplicity" (Le Corbusier, 1957, p. 120). Biomorphic sculptors, such as Henry Moore and Constantin Brancusi, also had an impact on the furniture designs of Arne Jacobsen and Harry Bertoia. Biomorphic sculpture reflects the forms of living organisms. The dichotomy between the East and West was evident in the philosophy and lifestyle of sculptor Isamu Noguchi. Noguchi's parentage (one parent was American; one was Japanese) resulted in his considerable international travel and feelings that he was at "home everywhere."

Sculpture and Abstract Art: The Chapel at Ronchamp (1950–1955) in Ronchamp, France, by Le Corbusier

In 1944, German artillery destroyed a small pilgrimage chapel on the summit of a hill overlooking the village of Ronchamp and the Vosges Mountains. When Le Corbusier first visited the site in 1950, stones and rubble from the ruined chapel were still scattered over the hilltop. Destruction of the chapel was an occurrence that the people of Ronchamp had been accustomed to for centuries—because the Vosges Mountain range is located along France's eastern border, opposing armies constantly fought for control of the strategic site. The entire countryside can be viewed from the chapel's site (Figure 7.21). In describing his initial experience on the hilltop, Le Corbusier explained that he "spent three hours getting to know the ground and the horizons, so as to become permeated with them" (Le Corbusier, 1957, p. 88). Corbu translated the site's mountains, plains, valleys, and a village into "four horizons." As Le Corbusier sketched the "four horizons," he noted a "phenomenon of visual acoustics." These inspired Le Corbusier to sculpt a new chapel for the village of Ronchamp, which became a masterpiece of Modernist architecture.

Le Corbusier integrated sculpture, abstract art, nature, and human dimensions to create a chapel that was to be "a place of silence, of prayer, of peace, of spiritual joy." The isolated hilltop surrounded by beautiful mountains and streams provided the ideal setting for Corbu's serene environment. He adapted the tranquility of the natural environment to the design of the chapel. The smooth, undulating forms of the hills are present in the sculptural shapes of the walls, towers, choir galleries, and roof. The shell of a crab provided the

inspiration for the chapel's organic roof. Abstract drawings of the sun, moon, stars, clouds, water, flowers, and birds are painted on the windows. Clear glass windows enabled worshippers to view the sky and grassy knolls. The randomly placed windows echo the positioning of forms in abstract paintings. Rainwater became an element of the organic architecture by flowing through a double-barrel gargoyle into a tub that contained three pyramidal forms and a cylinder. Conserving rainwater was especially important to the parishioners because the hilltop lacked an adequate water supply.

As with sculpture, light played a critical role in the chapel's architecture and in the emotional effects on people. Corbu described the importance of light in the book that he wrote about the chapel, stating, "The key is light and light illuminates shapes and shapes have an emotional power" (Le Corbusier, 1957, p. 27). Daylight and candlelight were the only sources of illumination for the interior. Natural light was especially important for emphasizing the architecture's

Figure 7.21 To design the Chapel at Ronchamp, France Le Corbusier translated the site's mountains, plains, valleys, and a village into "four horizons."

Source: FLC/ARS 2009.

sculptural forms and for evoking emotional responses. On the exterior, sunlight emphasized the shapes of the chapel by contrasting illuminated surfaces and textures with shade and shadows. For example, the sculptural form of the roof can be observed by its shadow on the main tower and the wall behind the outdoor altar (Figure 7.22). The chapel's tallest peak was emphasized when sunlight illuminated the vertical form and the adjoining surfaces were in shade. Corbu carefully orchestrated the combined effects of forms, light, and shadow, noting, "Observe the play of shadows, learn the game. . . . Precise shadows, clear cut or dissolving. Projected shadows, sharp. Projected shadows, precisely delineated, but what enchanting arabesques and frets. Counterpoint and fugue. Great music. Try to look at the picture upside-down or sideways. You will discover the game" (Le Corbusier, 1957, p. 47).

From the interior, each façade had a unique method for the penetration of light. The vivid south elevation had a scattering of deeply recessed openings (Figure 7.23). Light passing through the glass had a different quality depending on the size and shape of the opening, and the treatment of the glass. In contrast to traditional religious stained-glass windows, the *vitrages* in the chapel were clear, colored, or painted with images and religious words. The south and west elevations shared a narrow band of light that separated the walls from the roof. Le Corbusier intended to "amaze" people with this lighting effect. The wall behind the main altar was pierced with a few small, square-shaped openings that appeared to twinkle when sunlight entered the chapel. In echoing how light enhances a sculpture, a dramatic illumination effect was created in the three side chapels as "light flows down" from the apertures of the towers. As daylight grazed the walls of the side chapels, the textural qualities of the stucco walls were enhanced and the backlighting created an emotive silhouette of the altar.

As with sculpture, to achieve interesting textural effects on surfaces and objects required tactile materials. During Le Corbusier's initial visit to the chapel,

Figure 7.22 At the Chapel at Ronchamp, France, the exterior sunlight emphasizes the shapes of the Chapel by contrasting illuminated surfaces and textures with shade and shadows. The unique form of the roof can be observed by its shadow on the main tower and the wall behind the outdoor altar.

Source: Marion Kaplan/Alamy.

he noted that the road to the hilltop was not suitable for transporting many building materials. Corbu's solution significantly affected the design of the chapel. The building was constructed at the original site using the existing stones and rubble from the ruined chapel, and new materials, such as sand and cement, were selected for their ease of transport. The deteriorating stones and rubble could be used only for fill. To achieve different effects with the same material, Le Corbusier specified two different techniques for working with reinforced concrete. The roof was made of **béton brut** (unfinished concrete), and the sprayed concrete walls were finished with a contrasting white paint. Béton brut was also used for the frames of wooden benches. As with the Unité d'Habitation in Marseille (see Chapter 6), Corbusier intentionally did not finish the concrete. He contended that some of the beauty of concrete was derived from its natural color and the interesting textural imprints that remained from the framing boards' joints and wood grain.

Figure 7.23 From the interior of the Chapel at Ronchamp, France, each façade has a unique technique for the penetration of light. The vivid south elevation has a scattering of deeply recessed openings.

Source: Jon Arnold Images Ltd./Alamy.

Le Corbusier used human dimensions as the guide for the sizes of the benches and other objects as well as the architecture. Dimensions were proportionally based on Corbu's **modulor system**, a mathematical formula derived from **anthropometric** data. Human dimensions served as the basis for creating the intimate nave and the outdoor altar. As explained by Le Corbusier, "Inside, alone with yourself. Outside, 10,000 pilgrims in front of the altar" (Le Corbusier, 1957, p. 103). His interest in people and his respect for "masters of their craft" are evident in his comments and selection of a concluding image in his book, *The Chapel at Ronchamp*. The "Concerning Men" section honors those who were responsible for the project; the only image is a construction-site photograph of the eight men who built the chapel.

Biomorphic Sculpture:
Arne Jacobsen and Harry Bertoia

Arne Jacobsen and Harry Bertoia were also having an impact on Modernism by creating furniture that reflects biomorphic sculpture created by artists, such as Henry Moore and Constantin Brancusi. The Danish architect Arne Jacobsen had an extremely long and successful career designing numerous residential and commercial

buildings, including private houses, housing developments, banks, restaurants, theaters, a hotel, schools, town halls, factories, and sports facilities. Jacobsen's oeuvre also included nearly every object and detail in interior environments, such as furniture, light fixtures, textiles, glassware, flatware, tabletop pieces, door hardware, and bathroom fittings. Most of Jacobsen's projects were in the Scandinavian countries, and many of his designs are classics and are still in production. Reflecting Scandinavian ethos, Jacobsen had a reputation for expecting quality workmanship, emphasizing functionalism, and selecting excellent natural materials.

Jacobsen began his career designing private houses in the late 1920s and continued working until his death in 1971. In 1952, his architectural career expanded into furniture designs when he was involved with a new factory for the Novo Pharmaceutical Company in Copenhagen. Jacobsen wanted chairs for the factory's cafeteria that were lightweight, stackable, durable, comfortable, inexpensive, and easy to maintain. The chairs did not exist, but Jacobsen was intrigued with the work of his friend, Alvar Aalto, and the experimental molded plywood chair seats that had been developed by Eames and Saarinen in 1940 (see Chapter 6). Using

Figure 7.24 Arne Jacobsen adapted the design of The Ant chair for the classrooms in his new architecture for the Munkegårds Elementary School in Vangedevej Søborg, Copenhagen. Jacobsen maximized daylight in the classrooms by having two vertical surfaces with windows.

Source: Strüwing.

their work as a source of inspiration, Jacobsen created the iconic hourglass-shaped chair, The Ant, or FH3100 (1952). Creating the biomorphic back and the seat with one continuous piece required a layer of fabric between the layers of molded plywood. To provide more space for the user's feet, Jacobsen initially designed the chair with just three steel legs, but for stability subsequent chairs were made with four legs. Jacobsen contacted Fritz Hansens, a local furniture manufacturer, to produce the first 300 chairs. Jacobsen adapted the design of The Ant chair for the classrooms in his new architecture for the Munkegårds Elementary School in Vangedevej Søborg, Copenhagen (1951–1958) (Figure 7.24).

As illustrated in Figure 7.24, Jacobsen maximized daylight in the classrooms by having two vertical surfaces with windows. The lower wall provided daylight to approximately half of the room. The clerestory windows mounted in the upper wall, and the reflected light from the light-colored angled ceiling, illuminated the remaining areas of the classroom. To further maximize the integration of the built environment with nature, each classroom adjoined a courtyard. Jacobsen created

a unique landscape design for each courtyard that included custom water fountains, stone sculptures, and sculptural shrubs that resembled animals.

Jacobsen's designs continued to be inspired by biomorphic forms, as evidenced by his Series 7 chair (1955), and the furniture for the SAS (Scandinavian Airline System) Royal Hotel and the SAS Terminal Building (1956–1961) in Copenhagen. The low horizontal structure served SAS's air terminal functions, and the 22-story high-rise was designed for the hotel's purpose of housing guests. The SAS project is an outstanding example of *Gesamtkunstwerk,* or total artwork. Jacobsen designed every object and detail, including the furniture, carpets, light fixtures, textiles, door handles, glassware, tableware, graphics, packaging materials, and even the elevator control panels. In contrast to the geometric lines of the architecture, Jacobsen designed biomorphic-inspired furniture that was meant to comfort people (Figure 7.25).

By using styropore, a new plastic material that hardened after being heated, Jacobsen was able to sculpt shell chairs in various biomorphic shapes. To create the prototypes, Jacobsen sculpted the forms (1:1 scale) from clay. The four shell chairs (1958) Jacobsen designed for the SAS Building were The Egg, The Swan, The Pot, and The Giraffe. As illustrated in Figure 7.25, The Egg's biomorphic form tends to warmly embrace its occupant and shelters the user from strangers, cold drafts, and unwanted noise. The Pot and The Giraffe have been discontinued, but The Swan and The Egg have become modern classics.

Harry Bertoia was born in Italy, but as child he moved to the United States with his family in 1930, and he became a U.S. citizen in 1946. Bertoia was a student and then an instructor of metal crafts at Cranbrook from 1937 to 1943. Bertoia created jewelry, graphics, and pieces made from metal, including screens, sculptures, fountains, and furniture (Figure 7.26). In 1953, Eero Saarinen commissioned one of Bertoia's metal screens for the General Motors Technical Center. Bertoia

Figure 7.25 The SAS Royal Hotel project is an outstanding example of *Gesamtkunstwerk*. Arne Jacobsen designed every object and detail. In contrast to the geometric lines of the architecture, Jacobsen designed organic furniture that was meant to comfort people, including The Egg.
Source: Strüwing.

became involved with furniture while he was working with Charles Eames in California. The two stopped working together in 1946, and by 1950 Bertoia and his family had moved to Pennsylvania to design furniture for Knoll Associates. Florence Shust Knoll (Basset) was a fellow student at Cranbrook and was very familiar with Bertoia's work and his potential.

By 1951 he had developed a prototype for what became The Diamond chair (see Figure 7.26). An analysis of Bertoia's previous work illustrates how he developed this metal chair. Initial grids were drawn on paper, and then drawings became metal roof grids, which were twisted into planar curves. The metal grid was positioned at an angle and created a concaved area in the center, which formed the seat. Based on The Diamond chair, Bertoia created several chairs for Knoll, including The Bird (1952), a child's chair (1955), and the Asymmetric Chaise (1952), just recently in production due to its structurally complicated design. In 1952, Bertoia explained his metal furniture: "In the sculptures,

Figure 7.26 Knoll's Chicago showroom with Bertoia's Bird Lounge Chair and Ottoman (left side), Diamond chair (center), and Bertoia side chair (front).
Source: Florence Knoll Bassett papers, 1932–2000, Archives of American Art, Smithsonian Institution.

I am concerned primarily with space, form and the characteristics of metal. In the chairs many functional problems have to be satisfied first . . . but when you get right down to It [sic], the chairs are studies in space, form, and metal, too" (Schiffer & Bertoia, 2003, p. 41).

GLOBAL BUSINESS AND ECONOMICS

The 1950s initiated an economy in the West that was fueled by consumerism and credit cards. People were demanding new technologies, including the automobile, telephones, and televisions. Automobile manufacturers responded by offering long-term payment plans. The Diners Club was the first consumer credit card. The rationing of items and materials imposed during World War II had been lifted, which increased the demand for many products that had been previously deemed luxuries. Demand and supply economics also provided the foundation for the strengthening of labor unions.

Increase in travel prompted the construction of the first Holiday Inn hotel in 1952. Fast-food restaurants began to grow in popularity during the decade. The Swanson Company maximized a combination of fast food and television by creating TV dinners in 1954. Significant technological and economic advances were occurring in Japan, West Germany, and Australia, including Sony Corporation's first transistor radio and magnetic tape recorder. Sony Corporation in Japan exported its first product, the transistor radio, to Canada. The European Common Market (Common Market), also known as the European Economic Community (EEC), was established in 1957. The Common Market's founding organization was the European Coal and Steel Community (ECSC) in 1951. Original members were Belgium (modern headquarters location), France, Italy, Luxembourg, the Netherlands, and West Germany (modern Germany). The purpose of the organization was to advance political and economical initiatives by fostering partnerships between European nations. In 1993, the Common Market became the European Union (EU).

Furniture-manufacturing companies were established in Australia that featured designs by Australian designers, including Gordon Andrews, Grant and Mary Featherston, and woven webbing chairs with wooden frames by Douglas B. Snelling. In the United States, Knoll Associates was involved with new mass-produced furniture systems, textiles, and the innovative Knoll's Planning Unit.

Corporations: Mass-Produced Furnishings

Harry Bertoia's collection for Knoll Associates originated in 1952 and is an example of the discovery by corporations that "good design is good business" (Knoll, 2008, p. 1). Hans G. Knoll founded Knoll Associates in 1938 and started to hire "world-class" architects and designers, such as Charles Eames and Jens Risom, by the early 1940s. Hans hired the most influential designer, Florence Schust, in 1943. Schust had impeccable credentials, having studied architecture and design at the Cranbrook Academy of Art and with Mies at IIT. She was responsible for establishing an interior space-planning department, *Knoll's Planning Unit*, and for designing Knoll's first showroom, located in New York City.

In 1946, Schust married Hans Knoll. The couple remained "business and design partners" until his death in 1955 and in that time had significant impact on the business of interior design and modern designs for workplace furnishings. During Hans's leadership (1938–1955), Knoll Associates began manufacturing furniture by Eero Saarinen, Ralph Rapson, Pierre Jeanneret, Don Knorr, Don Petitt, Isamu Noguchi, and Florence Knoll. Knoll Associates also received the legal rights to manufacture Mies's Barcelona Collection, and Knoll Textiles was established in 1947. Today Knoll has more than 140 designers responsible for designing its products; approximately 40 of the company's pieces are in the permanent collection of the MoMA.

From the collection
of fabrics and wallpapers
designed by Alexander Girard
for Herman Miller.

Figure 7.27 Herman Miller started a textile collection when they hired Alexander Girard, a colorist and textile designer, in 1952.

Source: Herman Miller, Inc.

To become successful, in addition to commissioning "good design," Knoll had to establish factories that were able to mass-produce the new pieces. Knoll Associates' first factory was in East Greenville, Pennsylvania, and was followed by three other main sites (two in Michigan and Toronto) and two factories in Italy. To sell modern furniture in the mid-century, Knoll Associates, as well as other corporations, had to establish modern textile collections. For example, Herman Miller started a textile collection when the company hired Alexander Girard (see Chapter 6), a colorist and textile designer, in 1952 (Figure 7.27). Textile divisions were a smart business initiative and were necessary from a design perspective because most of the contemporary textiles were not appropriate for modern furniture, which required textiles with abstract designs and contemporary fibers, dyes, and weaves.

Initially some manufacturers commissioned internationally known artists, such as Alexander Calder, Henri Matisse, Joan Miró, and Salvador Dalí. Pablo Picasso's last textile design, created for the 1951 Festival de la Jeunesse et des Étudiants pour la Paix (Festival for Youth and Students for Peace) in Berlin, had a "dove of peace" uniting "the four parts of the world," which was a frequent image used by Picasso in the 1950s. The designs of printed textiles were also inspired by developments in science, mathematics, space exploration, automobiles, and television. These influences translated into textile designs using stylized cell structures, amoebic forms, atoms, steel rods, small geometric patterns, and abstract versions of microscopic views of plant materials. For residential interiors, many of the motifs were printed on **barkcloth,** a crepe-weave fabric with a slightly nubby appearance.

To meet the demands for high yardage quantities and to be cost-effective, textiles had to be mass-produced. Printing became more cost-effective because of technological advances in silkscreening. Automated silkscreen printing was more economical than conventional block or roller printing. Printing was also more cost-effective than creating a design through the weaving process. However, contemporary weaving techniques that used innovative fibers and dyes were also important to the development of modern textiles in the 1940s and 1950s.

A source of inspiration for modern textiles was the weaving department at the Cranbrook Academy. Eliel Saarinen's wife, Loja Saarinen, founded the weaving department with a staff of Swedish designers and weavers. Initially, the department focused on "hand woven art fabrics, rugs, and window hangings" (Detroit Institute of Arts, 1983, p. 176), but eventually the curriculum included powerloom weaving. Swedish designs and weaving techniques created beautiful modern textiles (Figure 7.28). The textiles had geometric forms, abstract designs, and muted colors made from natural dyes and fibers. The combined weaving of linen, silk, and wool created subtle variations in colors and textures. In addition to weaving many of the textiles for Cranbrook's interiors, Loja's weaving studio received numerous commissions, including for textiles designed by Frank Lloyd Wright and Charles Eames.

Upon Loja Saarinen's retirement in 1942, Marianne Strengell became the new director of Cranbrook's weaving department. As the Head of the Department of Weaving and Textile Design until 1961, Strengell also had a tremendous influence on modern textiles and acknowledged the importance of learning the business of interior design. In 1944, Strengell wrote the following statement, which subsequently affected the program's curriculum: "I feel, and Mr. [Eliel] Saarinen agrees with me fully, that it is of utmost importance for the student of weaving and textile design to be able to execute work for orders of sale. Learning how to handle the client, analyze the problem as to environment, personality, etc., learning to present

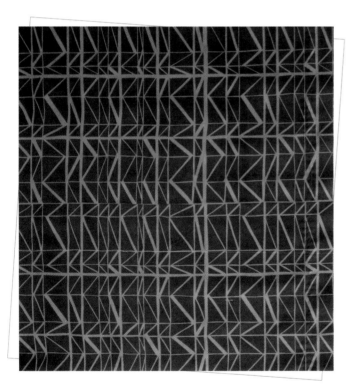

Figure 7.28 Swedish designs and weaving techniques created beautiful modern textiles. The textiles had geometric forms, abstract designs, and muted colors made from natural dyes and fibers.

Source: Curtain material, © 1954 (screen-printed cotton) by Marianne Strengell (1909–1998). The Detroit Institute of Arts, USA/The Bridgeman Art Library.

a sketch that will give a layman an exact picture of the goods he will receive and carrying out the order is of great educational value to the student" (Detroit Institute of Arts, 1983, pp. 196–197).

Upholstery, curtain, and wall-covering materials designed by Strengell and woven by Gerda Nyberg were made of natural and synthetic fibers, including nylon, rayon, and metal threads. Looped mohair in a contrasting color created a very modern texture. Strengell's fabrics were displayed at the Academy's museum in 1950, and she was a volunteer for UNESCO's Technical Assistance Administration, New York in 1951. In this role, Strengell was a consultant for textile designs and the cottage industry. As the number of students increased in the program in the 1950s, the weaving department had a greater influence on modern textiles.

Strengell's influence is evident with the designs and career of Jack Lenor Larsen. Larsen's innovative textiles are an example of Cranbrook's impressive alumni register. Larsen received his MFA from the academy in 1951 and founded his eponymous textile corporation in 1952, adding the Larsen Design Studio in 1958. Larsen is internationally known for his inventive weaving techniques and resist-dyeing technologies. The "Larsen Look" is synonymous with modern 20th-century design. Larsen designed curtains for Lever House as well as fabrics for Braniff and Pan Am jets. His clients included Louis Kahn, Frank Lloyd Wright, and Marcel Breuer. His work can be found in the Metropolitan Museum of Art, Philadelphia Museum of Art, and the Art Institute of Chicago. Jack Lenor Larsen textiles merged with Cowtan & Tout in 1998.

The Fast-Food Industry: McDonald's Restaurant (1955) in Des Plaines, Illinois

Another entrepreneurial venture that affected interior environments and architecture (as well as the American culture and diet) was the launch of fast-food restaurants in the 1950s. McDonald's "Golden Arches," one of the most recognized symbols in the world, began as an architectural decoration on the sides of the building (Figure 7.29). The original design of the restaurant was created by two brothers, Dick and Mac McDonald. They started working in the food industry while living in Los Angeles in the late 1930s. The McDonalds opened their car-hop, barbecue restaurant in San Bernardino, California in 1940. The small, octagonal-shaped building basically held the kitchen. The front of the building featured glass from the counter to the ceiling. Below the counter, the exterior façade was covered with stainless steel. There were a few stools for the outdoor counter. The carhops placed and picked up their orders through two front windows. The large spans of glass gave customers a complete view of the food-preparation process. An enormous rooftop sign advertised "McDonald's Famous Hamburgers—Buy 'Em By The Bag" for 15 cents. Many of the attributes of the first San Bernardino restaurant became trademarks for the McDonald's Corporation, including the open view of the kitchen, the use of stainless steel, and the large "HAMBURGERS" signage.

This McDonald brothers' restaurant was successful, but by 1948, to improve their business and reflect postwar concerns with value, the brothers implemented numerous developments that ultimately changed the food industry—and created a revolutionary design for restaurants. The McDonald brothers created a design for *family* restaurants that emphasized the combination of self-service and fast, inexpensive food. The focus was speed and sales volume. To be "Speedee," they eliminated the carhops, dishwashers, and many food items that had been on the menu. These changes required renovated facilities, such as windows for self-service, trash receptacles for paper products, and new kitchen equipment and layouts.

To create efficient kitchens, the McDonald brothers conducted extensive time and motion studies of their crew preparing a limited menu of hamburgers, cheeseburgers, french fries, soft drinks, milkshakes, and coffee. The exact size and shape of each preparation

Figure 7.29 McDonald's "golden arches," one of the most recognized symbols in the world, began as an architectural decoration on the sides of the building. *Source:* Used with permission from McDonald's Corporation.

area, and the design of the equipment were determined to prepare food quickly and efficiently. Until this period, traditional restaurant equipment was not designed to accommodate the quantities of food that the McDonald brothers wanted to sell on a daily basis. For example, a new grill was designed that was twice as large as traditional styles; this allowed the cooks to prepare twice as many burgers at one time. A "lazy Susan" was designed to accommodate 24 hamburger buns. To ensure a speedy application of the correct amount of ketchup, a special dispenser for condiments was created. The equipment needs were so specialized that a local metal shop was commissioned to fabricate the custom items.

The McDonald brothers wanted their restaurants to appeal to the family market. They had learned from their San Bernardino store that traditional drive-ins appealed to teenagers and bikers. This was a problem because the business from that demographic was inconsistent and discouraged families. Therefore, to appeal to families, their new operation focused on children. The brothers noticed that children enjoyed watching food preparation, and thus the new restaurant kept its "fishbowl" design. To use the "fishbowl" as a form of entertainment required a very clean kitchen and equipment, and white uniforms. The company initiated strict cleaning policies and specified materials that were easy to maintain, such as stainless steel. Other tactics they used to attract families included giving free items to children and charging low prices (which was possible due to high sales volume). During the 1950s, the cost of taking a family to a restaurant made the occasion a special event. McDonald's low prices allowed a family to eat out on a regular basis, with the added bonus of entertainment.

The restaurant's new exterior was also designed to appeal to children and present a clean appearance. The exterior façade featured the iconic red and white tiles and the large "Golden Arches," which projected through the roof. The original sign was altered to include a large golden arch and a mini chef, "Speedee," with a hamburger for a face. To advertise their success, the artist's rendering of the sign included "Self Service System" and "We Have Sold Over 200 Million." Customers walked up to the windows for service, which especially appealed to children, who enjoyed buying their own food.

The McDonald's success attracted national attention, and the brothers sold their first franchise to an operator in Phoenix. The brothers met food-service equipment salesman Ray Kroc in 1954 when he traveled to California to learn about the success of a product he was selling at the time, the Multimixer, a multi-spindled milkshake maker. Making 24 milkshakes at one time required eight machines at McDonald's. A traditional drugstore fountain only had *one* Multimixer. Kroc was very impressed with their automated approach to food preparation and their incredible success. He believed that having multiple McDonald's restaurants would be an outstanding way to sell many Multimixers.

In 1954, Kroc proposed a contract with the McDonald brothers for the rights to open and operate McDonald's restaurants throughout the country. The first restaurant Kroc opened was located in Des Plaines, Illinois, a suburb of Chicago in 1955. Kroc intended it to be the experimental prototype for all future restaurants. The Des Plaines building is now a McDonald's museum.

The contract with the McDonald brothers included the rights to the building plans, the "McDonald's" name, signage, and operating procedures and policies. The first problem Kroc had to resolve was adapting a building that had been designed for a warm climate to Midwestern winters. For example, the California slab foundation was replaced with a basement. To accommodate a furnace, the engineers designed a rooftop mechanical system. Steel used for the counters had to be thicker in order to retain adherence to its wood surface during weather fluctuations. The McDonald brothers stored the potatoes for french fries in wired bins outdoors. Kroc kept the potatoes in the basement but soon realized that the damp storage affected the taste of the french fries. To replicate an outdoor environment, Kroc installed large fans that circulated air around the potatoes. He also had to resolve problems with balancing the exhaust and HVAC systems. Initially, the kitchen exhaust system extracted too much air, which made the restaurant either cold in the winter or hot in the summer.

The McDonald brothers' original building design purchased by Kroc was successful for the McDonald's Corporation and was not changed until 1968. In a very risky and expensive initiative, the corporation developed a new building design that included a brick exterior, mansard roof, and, for the first time, indoor seating. In addition to the cost of construction, risks associated with a new building design centered on the possibility that the public would not like the new appearance and consequently would stop patronizing the franchise. The venture has proven successful, but people are still eating in their cars. Newer fast-food restaurant designs have changed the traditional drive-in to the drive-thru.

SUMMARY

Following the Korean War, both North and South Korea had to form their own governments and reconstruct their cities, which affected people, architecture, and interior environments in various ways. North Korea became a communist country, and South Korea established a democratic republic. In defiance of Germany's aggression toward the USSR, during the initial years of the war the Soviet government started the process of creating plans to rebuild cities and towns. The Stalinist construction plans included comprehensive urban planning, monuments, and several new buildings.

A museum was planned for Solomon Guggenheim's collection of Non-Objective Art. According to Guggenheim and Rebay, this required a transformational approach to museum architecture. After considering several architects, Baroness Hilla Rebay and Guggenheim determined that Frank Lloyd Wright had the vision, fortitude, and talent to design a museum that would reflect the spirit of Non-Objective Art.

The city of Sukhothai ("Dawn of Happiness") was critically important to the development of Siam (modern Thailand). Ancient Sukhothai was the first Kingdom of Siam, its capital city, and its remarkable Buddhist temple complex was built in an era that is referred to as the "Golden Years." The magnificent Buddhist architecture was built between the 13th and 15th centuries, but due to centuries of neglect, modern civilizations were not able to see the complexes until excavations in 1956.

Advances in organic chemistry, physics, and machinery allowed designers to experiment with new materials and approaches to the design of furniture and architecture. Fiberglass was a material that had developed to the extent that designers were able to apply the technology to industrial designs. Eero Saarinen used fiberglass to create his Pedestal Collection. Many corporations in the 1950s focused their attention and resources on the research and development of new technologies for modern living. Television was one such technology. In 1950, approximately 9 percent of U.S. households had a television, but by 1960 this had increased to 87 percent. In addition to the physical characteristics of television sets, television programs and their corporate sponsors had a significant impact on the design of interior environments.

In stark contrast to the consumerism that was promoted on television, in Calcutta (modern Kolkata) Mother Teresa was tirelessly committed to helping "the poorest of the poor." During the 1950s, she established three special homes in Calcutta. As Mother Teresa was teaching children how to read in classrooms without walls, several towns and cities throughout the world were constructing educational buildings. In the 1950s, some of these endeavors expanded existing campuses, such as the Cranbrook Academy of Art and IIT, and built new campuses, such as the Universidad Nacional Autónoma de México (UNAM) in Mexico City.

Le Corbusier integrated sculpture, abstract art, nature, and human dimensions to create the Chapel at Ronchamp, "a place of silence, of prayer, of peace, of spiritual joy." As with all of Le Corbusier's projects, light played a critical role in the chapel's architecture and in the emotional effects on people. Two other designers, Arne Jacobsen and Harry Bertoia, also had an impact on Modernism by creating furniture that was inspired by biomorphic sculpture. Bertoia's Collection for Knoll Associates is one example of the discovery by corporations that "good design is good business." Hans G. Knoll had founded Knoll Associates in 1938 and started to hire "world-class" architects and designers, such as Charles Eames and Jens Risom, by the early 1940s.

Another entrepreneurial venture that affected the interior environments and architecture of fast-food restaurants was established in the 1950s: Taking over from the McDonald brothers, Ray Kroc started the McDonald's Corporation with the opening of his first McDonald's restaurant in Des Plaines, Illinois, in 1955. McDonald's "Golden Arches," one of the most recognized symbols in the world, began as an architectural decoration on the sides of the building.

KEY TERMS

anthropometric

Bakelite

barkcloth

béton brut

bot

celadon porcelain

chedi

chofa

finials

globalization

hang hongse (swan's tail)

hanok

kala

kinnara

laterite

makara

modulor system

nagas

ondol (warm stone)

pinnacles

singha

slip decoration

slip inlay decoration

ubosot

vihāra

visual acuity

wats

wihan

EXERCISES

1. Research Design Project. The magnificent Buddhist architecture at Sukhothai in Thailand was built between the 13th and 15th centuries, but due to centuries of neglect, modern civilizations could not see the complexes until Thailand's Fine Arts Department initiated excavations in 1956. The excavations enabled Sukhothai and other historic towns to be included on UNESCO's World Heritage List in 1991. Research other examples of Buddhist architecture. Compare and contrast attributes of their architecture, interiors, and artwork. Write a reflective paper on your results. The report should include sketches, drawings, or photographs.

2. Human Factors Research Project. Eero Saarinen noted that "General Motors is a metal-working industry; it is a precision industry; it is a mass-production industry. All these things should, in a sense, be expressed in the architecture of its Technical Center." Conduct a virtual field trip of several corporate headquarters on the Internet. Identify how the architects and designers expressed a corporation's industry in its architecture, and how the design accommodated human factors. Create a digital learning tool that demonstrates the results and can be used for future projects.

3. Philosophy and Design Project. Since Ray Kroc opened his first McDonald's restaurant in Des Plaines, Illinois, in 1955 and started the McDonald's Corporation, McDonald's has sold billions of hamburgers in thousands of worldwide restaurants. Visit the McDonald's Corporation Web site and review the descriptions of the McDonald's restaurants that are located outside of the United States. Analyze three restaurants located on three different continents and determine similarities and differences between the locations. Be sure to examine and discuss how McDonald's implements its philosophical approach to social responsibilities. In a written report, summarize your findings and provide suggestions for an oral presentation. In a team with other students, prepare a presentation that is supported with visual materials.

CHAPTER 8

EMPHASIS: THE 1960S

OBJECTIVES

After reading this chapter, you should be able to describe and analyze:

■ How selected global political events in the 1960s, such as colonization and independence in Chandigarh, India, Brasília, and Algeria, affected interior environments and architecture.

■ How the natural environment affected selected global interior environments and architecture in the 1960s as evident by designs in Mexico by Luis Barragán and the Sydney Opera House in Australia by Jørn Utzon.

■ How selected global technologies and materials in the 1960s affected interior environments and architecture as evident by designs by Raymond Loewy and Joe Colombo.

■ How selected global work styles and lifestyles in the 1960s affected interior environments and architecture as evident by the John Deere Headquarters by Eero Saarinen and Kenzo Tange's designs for the National Gymnasiums for the Tokyo Olympics.

■ How selected global visual arts and performing arts in the 1960s, such as the music of the Woodstock generation and Pop Art, affected interior environments and architecture.

■ How selected global business developments and economics in the 1960s affected interior environments and architecture as evident by the Italian Industrial and Furniture Design Industry and the need for modern office buildings, furniture, and space planning.

■ How to compare and contrast selected interior environments and architecture of the Americas, Asia/Oceania, Europe, and the Middle East/Africa in the 1960s.

The Cold War between the Soviet Union and the United States had a significant effect on the 1960s. Most notable were the competitions and wars between communist and capitalist states. The decade witnessed hostile actions that included the Cuban missile crisis, the beginning of the Vietnam War, and the construction of the Berlin Wall. Fighting continued between India and Pakistan, and the Six-Day War between Israel and Egypt, Jordan, and Syria occurred in the Middle East in 1967. Also during the decade, 15 African nations gained their independence. As was the case during every other decade of the 20th century, numerous natural disasters occurred in the 1960s that resulted in the deaths of thousands of people, including an earthquake followed by a massive tidal wave in Agadir, Morocco, on February 29, 1960, and a cyclone that devastated the entire Orissa district in India on October 12, 1967. Informal international efforts by European countries focused on sustaining the natural environment. For example, government funding for military purposes prompted the development of improved techniques for measuring gas levels in the atmosphere, which enabled scientists to better determine the extent of climatic changes.

As the Soviet Union and the United States continued the "space race," interior designers and architects applied the newly developed technologies and materials to the built environment. "Space Age" interiors used lightweight plastic, compact furniture systems, and featured objects that had gravity-defying appearances, such as clear "bubble" chairs that were suspended from the ceiling. While space exploration expanded the horizons of the planet, discriminatory practices in the United States and South Africa had limited the horizons of a large portion of their citizens. But the decade also featured the tireless work of activists who protested social injustices, war, and discrimination. These views were often showcased at the outdoor concerts during the decade and were captured and expressed by the music of the time. The baby-boom generation inspired new designs and materials that were reflected in textiles,

objects, and Pop Art. Despite inflationary conditions, several entrepreneurs founded businesses that manufactured furniture at the forefront of contemporary designs, such as Artemide, Cassina & Buselli (C & B) Italia, and Centro Cassina. Successful businesses created a need for more office buildings, as well as new furniture and layouts that accommodated new management philosophies, practices, and policies.

GLOBAL POLITICS AND GOVERNMENT

The decade witnessed the beginning of the Vietnam War, and in response to English control of Ireland, the Irish Republican Army (IRA) began a concerted paramilitary campaign against the British. The Berlin Wall was erected in 1961, effectively dividing communist East from capitalist West. The continuing Cold War between the United States and the Soviet Union, between communist and capitalist societies, fueled the Cuban missile crisis—a nuclear arms confrontation between the United States, the Soviet Union, and Cuba, in 1962. The situation amplified the specter of nuclear war, and people continued to build bomb shelters in their backyards that contained food, water, and medical supplies.

Fighting over the territory of Kashmir continued between India and Pakistan until the signing of a peace treaty in 1966. In the Middle East, the Six-Day War in 1967 resulted in Israel gaining more territory. The 1960s was an important decade for many African countries: Fifteen nations gained their independence from France, Britain, Spain, and Belgium. The effects of colonization and the rebuilding process can be seen in Le Corbusier's designs for Chandigarh, India, and in the work of Oscar Niemeyer in Brasília and Algeria.

Colonization and Independence: Chandigarh, India (1950–1969), by Le Corbusier, Pierre Jeanneret, Jane Drew, and Maxwell Fry

Mohandas Gandhi and his philosophy of peaceful civil disobedience were key elements in the success of India's independence movement. India gained its independence from Britain on August 15, 1947. As discussed in the previous chapter, the terms of the negotiation between India and Britain resulted in a partitioning of territory, which created India, East Pakistan (modern Bangladesh), and West Pakistan (modern Pakistan). India's first president was sworn in and its constitution ratified on January 26, 1950, which then became known as the country's Republic Day. A portion of the Indian state of Punjab became part of the newly created West Pakistan, including Punjab's capital city of Lahore. Indian officials, including Prime Minister Pandit Jawaharlal Nehru, determined that Chandigarh would become the new capital city of Punjab as well as the capital of Haryana; Chandigarh was formed in 1966 and administered separately as a Union Territory.

Chandigarh is a Hindu word derived from the name of the goddess Chandi. Nehru's vision was to create a modern city: "Let this be a new town, symbolic of the freedom of India, unfettered by the traditions of the past, an expression of the nation's faith in the future" (Boesiger [Ed.], 1970, p. 52). Located at the foothills of the Himalayan Mountains, Chandigarh is close to Pakistan and Tibet. The area is in India's northern plains and includes two major rivers, the Patiali and the Mani Majra. For approximately 10 months each year, the plain's extremely hot weather causes the rivers to become dry, rocky beds. Nehru initially commissioned Americans Albert Mayer and Matthew Novicki to design the new city. Novicki's death in a plane crash precipitated Nehru contacting Le Corbusier to resume the project.

Corbu's collaborative team included several Indian architects and engineers, and fellow members of the Congrès International d'Architecture Moderne (CIAM) (or International Congress of Modern Architecture): Pierre Jeanneret, Jane Drew, and Maxwell Fry. At this time, Chandigarh was basically an undeveloped site. Therefore, Le Corbusier had the opportunity to design the entire urban site, including the size of sectors, a road classification system, commercial districts, government buildings, industrial areas, and recreational areas. Corbu's road system, or "7V" ("V" represented *voie* or road), consisted of seven categories of roads and was designed to contain the fastest traffic on the V1 highways. As the number increased, the traffic and size of the roads decreased. The highest numbers prohibited vehicular traffic and were intended only for pedestrians. The initial plan for Chandigarh was created for 150,000 inhabitants with the intent that by expanding to an area south of the city, the urban population could be 500,000 in the future.

Le Corbusier's design for Chandigarh did not represent the first planned city in India. The country's history of city planning dates back to Emperor Akbar's (1555–1605) development of Fatehpur-Sikri (City of Victory), the capital city of the Mogul Empire in the 16th century. Fatehpur-Sikri's group of monuments was inscribed on UNESCO's World Heritage List in 1986 for influencing town planning and as an "exceptional testimony to the Mogul civilization at the end of the 16th century" (UNESCO, 1982, p. 3). In the 18th century, King Jai Singh was responsible for planning and developing the former capital city of Jaipur.

In addition to the "7V" road system, Le Corbusier's plan for Chandigarh included open spaces, parks, schools, health centers, community centers, swimming pools, promenades, industrial areas, business/commercial districts, and Lake Sukhna, an artificial body of water. Buildings (1952–1965) included the Capitol complex, the City Centre, the Club House, the Museum and Art Gallery, the College of Art, the College of Architecture, and housing units. The Capitol complex was created to accommodate governmental functions and administration. Le Corbusier designed the

Assembly (Parliament) (1955–1962), the High Court (1952–1955), and the Secretariat (1953–1958) (Figure 8.1).

Historically, Indian architecture is unique for sculpting a structure directly from stone. The Ellora Caves, sculpted in the 7th century, are extraordinary for the incredible feat of carving 34 interiors out of the cliff's rock. Inscribed on UNESCO's World Heritage List in 1982, the caves were noted as "one of the most invaluable properties of the World Heritage." In addition, because the caves include temples for Buddhism, Brahmanism, and Jainism, the site was commended for illustrating "the spirit of tolerance, characteristic of ancient India, which permitted these three religions to establish their sanctuaries and their communities in a single place, which thus served to reinforce its universal value" (UNESCO, 1983, p. 2).

It appears that Corbu made a conscious effort to make the Capitol's massive structures appear hand carved,

Figure 8.1 The Assembly (Parliament) in Chandigarh designed by Le Corbusier.

Source: Chris Hellier/Corbis.

in keeping with India's architectural traditions and to reflect the sculpting of the Ellora Caves. Modern reinforced concrete was used in lieu of a hillside, but Le Corbusier's extensive use of béton brut (unfinished concrete) had the qualities of rough stone. During the construction period, hundreds of Indians were employed to carry baskets filled with wet concrete, which they did on their heads. The absence of advanced industrialization at this period also affected the height of buildings. For example, the lack of elevators resulted in shorter buildings, but in lieu of traditional staircases, Corbu specified ramps, a common element in his oeuvre.

The design for Chandigarh reflects a synthesis of Corbu's most important architectural theories, many which had been developed over the course of his long, productive career. Many aspects of Le Corbusier's "Five Points of a New Architecture" (see Chapter 4) were evident in the buildings designed for the Capitol, with modifications to help control India's harsh sun and climate. For example, the long strips of windows (la fenêtre en longueur) had to be protected with brise-soleil. As with the Ministry of Education and Health building in Rio de Janeiro (see Chapter 5) and L'Unité d'Habitation in Marseille (see Chapter 6), Le Corbusier designed horizontal and vertical brise-soleil depending on the orientation of a building's façade and the path of the sun.

To provide shade, Corbu's traditional les pilotis (columns) were used to support the enormous sculpted roof of the Parliament building (see Figure 8.1). To help absorb the heat from the sun, buildings were constructed with two roofs. The second roof was the **"parasol."** The Secretariat had a roof garden (*les toites-jardins*), and its façades had plain surfaces (*la façade libre*) with deep balconies. The recessed balconies helped control sunlight and created an interesting pattern of alternating light and dark forms. Le Corbusier also applied his modulor system (see Chapter 7) to the design of the structures and incorporated its human form as a decorative motif.

As with all of Corbu's projects, to gain an understanding of the site, the people, and their customs, he spent time traveling in India and sketching impressions of the country (see Chapter 7). Many of the images Corbu captured inspired architectural forms, colors, and symbols used for decorative purposes. He sketched numerous drawings of villages, the Himalayan Mountains, rivers, plains, trees, flora, weather conditions, sunbeams, farm animals, fauna, and birds. Initial sketches of the Capitol skyline illustrate that Le Corbusier designed each of the buildings in the complex to follow the profile of the Himalayan Mountains. The horns of Indian cattle are apparent in the profile of the Parliament's roof.

Some of the most outstanding examples of the incorporation of Corbu's impressions of the Indian landscape can be seen in his designs for tapestries (Figure 8.2) and the enamel plates for the enormous pivoting gate of the Parliament building. The large tapestries that covered entire walls in the Palace of Justice and the Parliament were hand-woven in Kashmir, located near Chandigarh. In the Palace of Justice, nine tapestries were woven in just 5 months. Eight of the tapestries were 210 square feet (20 square meters), and one tapestry was 472 square feet (44 square meters). The magnificent tapestries pay homage to India's long history of traditional crafts, including textiles, basket weaving, and metalworking. From a technical perspective, the tapestries were not only visually beautiful, but they also improved the acoustics in the Council's Chamber. As illustrated in Figure 8.2, the composition includes many of Corbu's drawings of local impressions, which included the grassy plains, trees, rivers, birds, cattle, turtles, snakes, wheels, lightning strikes, a representation of the seasonal path of the sun, and the modulor symbol of a man. Another example of an acoustical device that reflected nature was the cloud-like insulation mats mounted on the dome of the Assembly Chamber.

To symbolize the philosophy that formed the basis for the Capitol, Le Corbusier designed the sculpture

Figure 8.2 Corbu's impressions of the Indian landscape were incorporated in his designs for tapestries. The large tapestries were hand-woven by the weavers of Kashmir.
Source: Getty Images.

Open Hand. Using another traditional Indian craft, metalwork, the sculpture resembled a bird and freely rotated with the wind. In *Volume 5* of Corbusier's oeuvre, he explained the design, noting, "This *Open Hand* will turn on ball bearings like a weather-cock, not to show the incertitude of ideas, but to indicate symbolically the direction of the wind (that is, the state of affairs). A movement of the spirit in 1948 has taken in 1951 an eminent part in the composition of a capital in India" (Boesiger [Ed.], 1953, p. 151). Due to a lack of funds, the *Open Hand* and buildings in Chandigarh were not constructed until after Corbu's death in 1965. Decades later, in reflecting on the design of Chandigarh, there have been critical assessments, some of which focus on inadequate control of India's brutal heat, low-density structures for a highly populated country, and unsatisfactory plans for the users of the space. Mumbai-based Indian architect Charles Correa identified these problems in a 1987 essay but concluded his analysis by noting, "A hundred years from now, perhaps Chandigarh will also fit seamlessly into the Punjab ethos; perhaps it will be perceived as a famous old Indian town, and Le Corbusier will be acknowledged . . . as the greatest Indian architect of them all?" (Brooks [Ed.], 1987, p. 202).

Independence: Oscar Niemeyer in Brasília and the University of Constantine (1969–1977) in Algeria

As Le Corbusier was planning the new capital city of Chandigarh in India, architects Lúcio Costa and Oscar Niemeyer were in Brazil creating Brasília, the nation's new capital city. Brazil had gained its independence from Portugal in 1822. Rio de Janeiro had served as the capital of Brazil since 1808, but its location on the shores of the Atlantic Ocean was far removed from most of the country. For decades, Brazilians had discussed the importance of creating the capital city in the center of the country. In 1956, the newly elected president of Brazil, Juscelino Kubitschek, resolved to move forward with the creation of a capital city on the Central Plateau. The approval by the Congress to move the capital from Rio de Janeiro to Brasília, making the name formal, was granted later that year. Shortly thereafter, Oscar Niemeyer, who had worked with Costa and Le Corbusier on the Ministry of Health and Education building (see Chapter 5), was appointed as the architectural advisor to the organization implementing the plans for Brazil's new capital; in 1959 he was named director of the Department of Architecture and Urban Affairs. Kubitschek then sponsored a national design competition for a master plan for the new capital, and Lúcio Costa's entry was the winning project. Thus, Niemeyer was responsible for designing the architecture, Costa executed the city's master plan, and Roberto Burle Marx was the landscape architect.

Costa's urban plan for Brasília was designed in the shape of a cross, or what appears to be a bird flying southeast. The Plaza of Three Powers was located at the "head" of the bird and included the primary governmental buildings designed by Niemeyer, including Alvorada Palace and Chapel (1957), National Congress (1958), Planalto Palace (1960), and the Federal Supreme Court (1960). The buildings located along the "body" of the bird, or the east-west Monumental Axis, were the Esplanade of the Ministry and the National Theatre (1958), the National Cathedral (1970), and the JK Memorial (1980) for Juscelino Kubitschek. As with Le Corbusier's plan for Chandigarh, Costa planned for a population of 500,000 and separated the government buildings from the residential sectors. The "wings" of the bird featured a residential area, and the outskirts included additional residential neighborhoods, an airport, foreign embassies, and a cemetery. The "tail" of the bird included a bus and train station. Brasília was inaugurated as the capital city in 1960.

The Plaza of Three Powers and the Monumental Axis included Niemeyer's most renowned architecture of the city. He explained how he conceptualized the architecture for Brasília, saying, "As an architect my concern in Brasília was to find a structural solution that would characterize the city's architecture. So I did my very best in the structures, trying to make them different with their columns narrow, so narrow that the palaces would seem to barely touch the ground. And I set them apart from the façades, creating an empty space through which, as I bent over my work table, I could see myself walking, imagining their forms and the different resulting points of view they would provoke" (www.pritzkerprize.com).

Excellent examples of Niemeyer's "structural solution that would characterize the city's architecture" are the National Cathedral, Planalto Palace, and the Federal Supreme Court (Figure 8.3). Remarkably, the buildings are supported by the elegantly thin columns in a free-form shape. The cathedral's boomerang-shaped white columns create a crown form that delicately supports the building and the waves of free-flowing blue, green, and transparent stained glass. The elongated triangular white columns of the Planalto Palace and the Federal Supreme Court appear to be weightless, as one narrow point seems to "barely touch the ground." The floating appearance is further emphasized by the deeply inset glass façades that are separated from the columns.

The City of Brasilia was inscribed on UNESCO's World Heritage List in 1987, with the administrative evaluation noting, "Because of the enormity of the challenge, the extravagant scale of the project, and the massive resources poured into it, the creation of Brasilia is unquestionably a major feat in the history of urbanism" (UNESCO, 1986, p. 2).

The construction of the new capital city in Brazil was affected by a military coup in 1964. Construction was brought nearly to a standstill, and there was even some pressure to transfer the capital back to Rio. The takeover established a dictatorship that controlled the country until 1985. The architects involved with the Brasília projects were removed, as were the

Figure 8.3 Excellent examples of Niemeyer's "structural solution that would characterize Brasília's architecture" include the Federal Supreme Court.

Source: Pedro Luz Cunha/Alamy.

standards and codes they had developed to sustain the beauty and functional requirements of the program.

The new regime was especially problematic for Niemeyer due to his political activism and his membership in the Brazilian Communist Party. Niemeyer explained his perspectives, noting, "I believed as I still do, that unless there is a just distribution of wealth reaching all sectors of the populace, the basic objective of architecture, that is its social base, would be sacrificed, and our role as architects only relegated to satisfying the whims of the wealthy" (Underwood, 1984, p. 89). Niemeyer's involvement with politics during the upheavals in 1964 caused him to go into exile in France, which proved to be an extraordinary opportunity for countries that were seeking innovative architecture and what Niemeyer cited as the "advancements of Brazilian engineering." His remarkable free-form modern Brazilian architecture was adapted to many cities in the United States, Europe, and Africa. In reflecting upon his oeuvre, Niemeyer explained, "I must design what pleases me in a way that is naturally linked to my roots and the country of my origin" (www.pritzkerprize.com). Niemeyer received commissions in Italy and France, including the Mondadori Publishing House Headquarters (1975) in Milan, Italy, the French Communist Party Headquarters (1965–1980) in Paris, and the Maison de la Culture (1972–1982) in Le Havre, France.

By the time Niemeyer was exiled from Brazil, Algeria achieved its independence from France after a long and hard fight. Algeria's central location along North Africa's Mediterranean coast had a significant impact on its history, including the many battles Algerians fought to retain control of their country. Algeria's location made it very easy for rulers from Europe and the Arabian Peninsula to travel to its rocky coastline and overcome the Algerians. The country has been ruled by the Carthaginians, Romans, Vandals, Arabs, several Muslim dynasties, Ottoman Turks, and French. The French took control of Algeria in 1848, and

Figure 8.4 Niemeyer's Brazilian free-form modern architecture and "advancements of Brazilian engineering" were featured in the design of the auditorium at the University of Constantine in Algeria.
Source: Fabio Pili/Alamy.

even though many African countries, such as Morocco, Tunisia, and Guinea, gained their independence peacefully after World War II, France did not want to relinquish control of this particular country. Algeria's agricultural products, such as wine that was exported to France, strengthened the French economy. Algeria's war for independence resulted in years of deadly battles (1954–1962). Finally, amid student antiwar protests in France, President Charles de Gaulle acquiesced and granted Algeria the opportunity to vote for its independence in 1962.

To improve economic conditions and establish a modern country, President Houari Boumediene (president, 1965–1978) created several new initiatives, including a new university in the city of Constantine in eastern Algeria. Constantine the Great, a Roman emperor, built the city in AD 313. Boumediene commissioned Oscar Niemeyer to design the new campus in 1968. In an interview for a book about his oeuvre, published in 2002, Niemeyer was asked, "And of all the buildings you have designed, is there any special one? One which has marked your life?" Niemeyer's response: "In Brazil, the National Congress and the Niteroi Museum of Contemporary Art. Abroad, the Mondadori headquarters and the University of Constantine in Algeria.

They are different and surprising, and that's important in architecture" (Salvaing, 2002, p. 11).

Niemeyer's "different and surprising" architecture for the university (modern Université Mentouri Constantine) was a compact campus design that consolidated educational facilities. The University of Constantine's "Campus Central" (1969–1977) had a central esplanade with reflecting pools and academic buildings. Classrooms were in the long block building that ran the length of the esplanade, and the central library was housed in the round structure. The block building for science laboratories was located away from the central core. Niemeyer's Brazilian free-form, modern architectural style and "advancements of Brazilian engineering" were featured in the design of the auditorium (Figure 8.4). The walls of glass beautifully reflect the Algerian landscape and the adjoining reflecting pool. The ultra-thin roof appears to be a piece of paper that gently fell on top of the structure. The roof's large size provides a wide area of shade that is needed to control Algeria's hot sun. Psychologically, the combination of the large, shady area and the rippling water has a cooling effect. Niemeyer also designed Constantine's Zoological Gardens and the Foreign Office.

EFFECTS AND CONDITIONS OF THE NATURAL ENVIRONMENT

The founding of the World Wide Fund for Nature (WWF) in 1961 helped bring attention to the value of sustaining the natural environment. Likewise, scientist and ecologist Rachel Carson's 1962 book *Silent Spring* attracted attention to problems associated with pesticides and environmental pollution. Scientist and environmentalist James Lovelock's discovery of chlorofluorocarbons (CFCs) in the 1960s was the first step to understanding their negative effects on the ozone layer. Natural disasters during this period also killed thousands of people and destroyed many communities. Deadly earthquakes occurred in Chile (1960), Libya (1963), Venezuela (1967), and Sicily (1968). On February 29, 1960, an earthquake followed by a massive tidal wave killed 12,000 people in Agadir, Morocco, more than one-third of the city's population. In 1966, a horrendous flood in Florence, Italy, killed people and caused destruction or damage to historical buildings, such as Basilica di Santa Croce, and innumerable priceless artworks, including the gilt bronze doors (Gates of Paradise) of the baptistery of the Florence Cathedral by artist Lorenzo Ghiberti. As they have done throughout history, however, humans were also harnessing the forces of nature in the middle of the 20th century. For example, the Aswan Dam in Egypt was completed in 1958, and the energy generated by Niagara Falls started to produce hydroelectric power in 1961. Interior designers and architects were inspired by water and nature in the 1960s, this time resulting in magnificent architecture created by Luis Barragán in Mexico and Jørn Utzon in Australia.

Landscape and Climate: Luis Barragán in Mexico

Another designer was connected to the beauty of North Africa and the Mediterranean Sea during the middle of the century. While traveling in Africa in the 1920s, the Mexican-born architect Luis Barragán was inspired by Morocco's Moorish architecture, gardens, and fountains. He was also influenced by Le Corbusier's lectures and the architecture and gardens of Spain, Italy, and France. Barragán (1902–1988) blended these international influences with his childhood memories of living on a ranch near Guadalajara, Mexico. In a book about his architecture, Barragán reminisced:

> My earliest childhood memories are related to a ranch my family owned near the village of Mazamitla. It was a pueblo with hills, formed by houses with tile roofs and immense eaves to shield passersby from the heavy rains which fall in that area. Even the earth's color was interesting because it was red earth. In this village, the water distribution system consisted of great gutted logs, in the form of troughs, which ran on a support structure of tree forks, 5 meters high, above the roofs. This aqueduct crossed over the town, reaching the patios, where there were great stone fountains to receive the water. The patios housed the stables, with cows and chickens, all together. Outside, in the street, there were iron rings to tie the horses. The channeled logs, covered with moss, dripped water all over the town, of course. It gave this village the ambience of a fairy tale. (Ambasz, 1976, p. 9)

Many elements of Barragán's childhood memories are reflected in his designs, including attributes of pueblos in the hills, with their tile roofs and deep eaves. Explosive colors, including "red earth," are hallmarks of his minimalist architecture. Memories of his village are revived through his use of color, enormous troughs, aqueducts, and water drips. The village patios, cobblestones, fountains, stables, animals, and "iron rings to tie the horses" all reappear in Barragán's designs for subdivisions, landscapes, residences, and gardens (Figure 8.5).

He was also inspired by his Catholic religion and the quiet serenity found in churches and convents. Beauty found in solitude was a critical element in his oeuvre. "To my dismay, I have found that an alarming proportion of publications devoted to architecture have banished from their pages the words beauty, inspiration, magic, spellbound, enchantment, as well as the concepts of serenity, silence, intimacy and amazement. All these have nestled in my soul, and though I am fully aware that I have not done them complete justice in my work, they have never ceased to be my guiding lights" (Burr, 2000, p. 3). An exceptional illustration of Barragán's "serenity, silence, intimacy and amazement" is the Chapel for the Capuchinas Sacramentarias del Purísimo Corazón de Maria (1952–1955), Tlalpan, in Mexico. Barragán used natural sunlight to evoke serenity. Diffused rays pierce through grid walls and screens. Indirect lighting that penetrates gold glass and strikes a gold-leaf sculpture creates a warm glow on the altar. The glass and sculpture were created by German sculptor Mathias Goeritz, an artist who collaborated with Barragán on various projects.

Essential to Barragán's designs was a serene connection between nature, architecture, and people. He created an intimate bond with nature when he designed the El Pedregal (1945–1950 original; 1960) San Angel, a garden residential subdivision near Mexico City (Figure 8.6). The subdivision was built in an abandoned volcanic rock area. Barragán designed the paths, roads, gates, and buildings to conform to the natural shapes of the site's volcanic rocks and plant life. The perimeter walls of the subdivision were made of volcanic rocks, which resembled the construction techniques used by the ancient Aztec Empire. Fundamentally, Barragán's overall design made a clear distinction between nature and modern elements. For example, he specified the *unnatural* straight line for the residential architecture, gates, and concrete pools. Residences in the subdivision were required to use a Modern architectural style, and most of the property had to be reserved for natural vegetation. Following the Mexican village tradition of private patios, most residences had multiple interior courtyards and inner gardens.

Figure 8.5 Luis Barragán's stable residential subdivision. Memories of Luis Barragán's village are revived through his use of color, enormous troughs, aqueducts, and water drips. The village patios, cobblestones, fountains, stables, and animals reappear in Barragán's designs for subdivisions, landscapes, residences, and gardens.

Source: Armando Salas Portugal © Barragán Foundation, Switzerland/ProLitteris, Zürich, Switzerland.

Other noted Mexican architects involved with designing residences for the subdivision included Max Cetto and Francisco Artigas. Residences designed by Cetto and Artigas had flat roofs and glass walls, and some structures were raised on pilotis. The interior and exterior walls for Cetto's personal residence were made from lava rocks. The wide spans of unprotected glass walls were a problem in an area with intense sunlight. During the day, to reduce the glare and heat from the sun, residents had to close the draperies, which prevented magnificent views of the countryside. Unfortunately, many of the residences were not designed according to Barragán's specifications, and by 1960 there were hundreds of houses sprawled over thousands of acres.

A comprehensive interplay between Barragán's memories of his childhood, international travels, and serenity culminated in his extensive designs for Las Arboledas (1958–1961), Los Clubes (1963–1964), and San Cristobal (1967–1968), all in Mexico City (see Figure 8.5). Las Arboledas and Los Clubes were residential subdivisions designed for people who owned horses, and San Cristobal was a private residence within Los Clubes. Over the years, innumerable publications have printed photographs taken at San Cristobal. Serene photographs illustrate the beauty of a single person walking his horse across the open plaza with brightly colored walls and pools of water.

The scene encapsulates many of Barragán's philosophies and influences. For example, his renowned use of bright and unexpected colors can be attributed to the Mexican culture and its landscape. Mexicans have traditionally used vibrant colors in their hand-painted pottery, textiles, costumes, murals, and paintings. Barragán's hometown of Guadalajara is well known for pottery, glass, textiles, and the brightly colored murals of José Clemente Orozco (see Chapter 1). However, Orozco's brightly painted figures were politically motivated and sought to evoke anger over the injustices to workers and underprivileged people. In dramatic contrast, Barragán covered planes with bright colors in a

Figure 8.6 Luis Barragán created an intimate connection with nature when he designed the El Pedregal San Angel, a garden residential subdivision near Mexico City. The subdivision was built in an abandoned volcanic rock area.

Source: Armando Salas Portugal © Barragán Foundation, Switzerland/ ProLitteris, Zürich, Switzerland.

noncontroversial manner. Depending on the color and its context, Barragán's plain walls invoke feelings of tranquility, surprise, or delight. In echoing Mexico's natural landscape, walls painted in bright red, purple, and orange mimic the colorful flowers of the bougainvillea. The pink walls also reflect the colors of the thousands of flamingos that live in Mexico's Yucatán Peninsula. It is easy to assume that Barragán also would have been influenced by the bright colors of the village plazas, especially during the lively Mexican fiestas and in the outdoor marketplaces filled with vegetables and fruits. A contemporary of Barragán, Mexican artist Rufino Tamayo, was very inspired by the colorful markets. Many of Tamayo's paintings are of bright fruits and vegetables.

White is surprising when used with Barragán's intense colors. However, the neutral surface was ideal for revealing shadows and emphasizing the ripples of water. In a forest of eucalyptus trees, Barragán used an extremely tall white wall next to a large rectangular trough. The single wall, approximately half the height of the trees, catches the shadows of the trunks, branches, and leaves while providing a reflected white image on the surface of the water. Barragán created many other innovative techniques for integrating water with the landscape, horses, and architecture. In reflecting his childhood memories of aqueducts and "great gutted logs," many of the plaza areas have walls that are topped with a beam that pours water into a shallow, cobblestone-lined pool. Some partitions have water spouting between two walls (see Figure 8.5). When one looks directly at the side of the wall, it appears that the surface itself is expelling the water. As with Barragán's childhood village, the source of the water is unknown.

Barragán's use of contrasting natural textures is as varied as Mexico's geography and climate. Mexico's abundant natural diversity includes two majestic mountain ranges, stark deserts, rich soils of the Plateau of Mexico, colorful tropical rainforests, and the blue waters of the Pacific Ocean, the Gulf of Mexico, and the Caribbean Sea. Stucco walls are blended with bare wood, smooth pebbles, coarse cobblestones, rushing waters, jagged vegetation, and calm reflecting pools.

In addition to phenomenal commissioned projects, Barragán has been internationally recognized for the design of his house and studio. UNESCO's description of the property reads "The concrete building, totalling 1,161 m², consists of a ground floor and two upper storeys, as well as a small private garden. Barragán's work integrated modern and traditional artistic and vernacular currents and elements into a new synthesis, which has been greatly influential, especially in the contemporary design of gardens, plazas and landscapes" (2004, p. 142). With contrasting textures, innovative colors, and intimate connections with nature, Barragán's sparsely furnished house/studio demonstrates how sustainable architecture can be extraordinary and "serene." Barragán's oeuvre has been internationally recognized in many venues and was inscribed on UNESCO's World Heritage List in 2004. In commending Barragán's house/studio, UNESCO's evaluation committee concluded, "The House and Studio of Luis Barragán represents a masterpiece of the new developments in the Modern Movement, integrating traditional, philosophical and artistic currents into a new synthesis" (UNESCO, 2004, p. 145).

Water and Nature: Sydney Opera House (1957–1973) in Sydney, Australia, by Jørn Utzon

Danish architect Jørn Utzon was also inspired by Moroccan architecture as well as the pre-Columbian pyramids in Mexico. The Mayans' approach to integrating nature with "platforms" had a significant impact on Utzon's design for the Sydney Opera House, one of the most recognized structures in the world and a modern masterpiece. In 2003, Utzon described his impressions of Mayan architecture, noting:

> As an architectonic element, the platform is fascinating. I lost my heart to it on a trip to Mexico in 1949, where I found a rich variety of both size and idea, and where many platforms stand alone, surrounded by nothing but untouched nature. All the platforms in Mexico are placed very sensitively in the landscape, always the creations of a brilliant idea. They radiate a huge force. You feel the firm ground beneath you, as when standing on a great cliff. Let me give you an example of the power in this idea. Yucatan is a flat lowland area covered by an impenetrable jungle which everywhere attains a certain height. The Maya people used to live in this jungle in villages surrounded by small cultivated clearings. On all sides, and also above, there was the hot, humid, green jungle. No great views, no vertical movements. But by building up the platform on a level with the roof of the jungle, these people had suddenly conquered a new dimension that was a worthy place for the worship of their gods. They built their temples on these high platforms, which can be as much as a hundred metres [sic] long. From here, they

had the sky, the clouds and the breeze, and suddenly the roof of the jungle was transformed into a great, open plain. By means of this architectonic device they had completely transformed the landscape and presented their eyes with a grandeur that corresponded to the grandeur of their gods. (www.pritzkerprize.com)

Becoming familiar with Utzon's impressions of Mayan architecture helps one to understand how he developed the design for the Sydney Opera House and how the natural environment can affect interior environments and architecture. Utzon's design for the building had a substantial platform, or **podium** (Figure 8.7). However, in lieu of being surrounded by a jungle, the rocky site of the proposed structure had water on three sides and the Royal Botanical Gardens to the south. As with the Mayan pyramids, by using a platform the facility was "surrounded by nothing but untouched nature" and provided stability "as when standing on a great cliff." By building the opera house's platform above the "roof" of Sydney's landscape, Utzon "conquered a new dimension" and created "views" with "vertical movement." People visiting the opera house had "the sky, the clouds and the breeze," and the "roof" of the harbor was "transformed into a great, open plain." Utzon described the relationship between the roof and the landscape the following way: "in the schemes for the Sydney Opera House . . . you can see the roofs, curved forms, hanging higher or lower over the plateau" (Futagawa, 1972).

To catch the "breeze," Utzon designed the top of the platform with *billowy*, interlocking white *sails* or shells. The iconic ceramic shells were the perfect free-form shape over Sydney Harbor, but unlike traditional sail-making, the opera house's roof was extraordinarily complex and required years of development. When Utzon won the international competition for the Sydney Opera House in 1957, he had submitted visionary sketches of the design, but the architecture

was conceived without adequate consultation with engineers or acoustical experts. To suppress concerns regarding a delayed project, the construction of the platform began in 1959, which was prior to the full development of the project. Even though the project had the strong endorsement of architect Eero Saarinen (see Chapter 7), a member of the jury, the lack of specifications was one of many factors that contributed to extensive delays. The actual construction timeline was 16 years, and numerous overruns resulted in a final project cost that exceeded 10 times the original estimates. After several years of working on the project, Utzon was replaced with the architectural firm Hall, Todd, and Livermore, but he remained in communication with the firm during the remaining years of construction.

Although any major (or for that matter, minor) project can be complicated and plagued by technical difficulties, political issues, and poor communication, the problems associated with the construction of the Sydney Opera House were so significant that many books and articles have been written to chronicle the events. One of the initial accounts was written after Utzon claimed he was "forced to resign" from the project prior to the completion of the building. The book, *The Sydney Opera House Affair*, written by Michael Baume in 1967, provides a valuable lesson in problems to avoid while working on a project and demonstrates how inadequate planning can have a negative impact on sustainable practices. Upon analyzing correspondence and documents related to the construction of the opera house, Baume described a "framework for disaster" that centered on (1) a lack of planning; (2) misunderstandings regarding roles and responsibilities; and (3) miscommunication between the architect, engineers, consultants, and multiple clients.

The clients for the project included the Australian Broadcasting Corporation (A.B.C.), the Elizabethan Theatre Trust, the Opera Theatre Committee, and Sydney's Public Works Department. At various times throughout the construction, each organization had

Figure 8.7 Construction of the Sydney Opera House. The Mayans' approach to integrating nature with "platforms" had a significant impact on Jørn Utzon's design for the Sydney Opera House, one of the world's most recognized structures and what has become a modern masterpiece.

Source: © Eric Sierins/Corbis.

a different influence, new participants, and changing requirements. These confluences resulted in dramatic changes from the original plan for a dual-purpose major hall for A.B.C. concert symphonies and opera performances. After Utzon's departure from the project and 9 years of construction, the dual-purpose hall became two structures. Designed to seat 2,679, the Concert Hall was the largest structure, and on the east side of the platform was the Opera Theatre with seating for 1,507. A third major structure was added, the Bennelong Restaurant, located at the southwest corner of the Foyer Concourse.

These changes and many other subsequent developments significantly affected the already-constructed platform. Utzon intended the platform to "separate primary and secondary functions completely. On top of the platform the spectators receive the completed work of art and beneath the platform every preparation for it takes place" (www.pritzkerprize.com). Consequently, to accommodate the revised plans, rooms that had been built below the platform had to be reconfigured at considerable time, expense, and waste of materials. For example, the original stage lifts required for opera

performances were renovated to become the Recording Hall. A small experimental theater became a larger Drama Theatre. Important and complex requirements for these renovations focused on redesigning acoustics, creating soundproofing systems, and new lighting plans. Furthermore, to dissipate heat from the additional patrons, the structures needed a revised cooling and ventilation system.

Another problem and expense with the project was a lack of understanding of how Utzon's free-form design could be built, including the *sails* or shells, and its multiple glass walls. Viewed from all angles, the shells would be seen from the harbor, the Sydney Harbour Bridge, and the city of Sydney. A significant amount of research and experimentation were involved with identifying the ideal shape and material to cover the buildings. Originally, the shells were designed using the geometry of the parabolic form, but after 6 years of development and numerous models, Utzon discovered that the best design for structural integrity was the shape formed at the intersections of overlapping spheres. These shapes became the *sails* and were formed using precast concrete ribbed arches (see Figure 8.7). To cover the surface of the roof, Utzon's remarkable solution was a series of ceramic tile panels in a chevron shape. The centers of each panel are glazed white tiles that glisten in the sunlight and subtly contrast with a border of buff-colored tiles in a matte finish. Computers, fundamentally unsophisticated at the time, had to be used to calculate the complex size, and placement of every tile and panel. Without computers, these calculations would not have been possible, nor would many of the other geometrical solutions that had to be calculated for Utzon's free-form design, which was applied to the interior spaces of the auditoriums, and the watertight and soundproofed glass walls (Figure 8.8).

Utzon's solution for the "top of the platform" included an incredible approach to entering the auditoriums. Patrons begin their experience by ascending the platform's pink granite Monumental Steps to the Foyer Concourse. Each auditorium has a southern foyer and side foyers encased in glass. People walk through these

Figure 8.8 To solve the complex geometrical computations for Jørn Utzon's Sydney Opera House required computers. Calculations had to be performed for the free-form designs of the concert hall.

Source: © Marcus Vetter/Corbis.

spectacular spaces to reach the entrance of the auditorium, which adjoins the northern foyer. The glass walls of the northern foyers expose impressive views of the harbor and the Sydney Harbour Bridge.

Upon entering the Concert Hall, the white birch–paneled ceiling and walls resemble the waves of an ocean (see Figure 8.8). The "completed work of art" includes an acoustically perfect interior in each auditorium. The Concert Hall was planned to create a longer reverberation time needed for instruments. The Opera Theatre has a design for the shorter time required for voice. This required specific materials for each auditorium and an ideal shape, size, and placement of the walls and the ceilings. The Sydney Opera House had a tumultuous beginning, but Utzon's masterpiece has become an undisputable international icon. According to UNESCO, "The Sydney Opera House is a great architectural work of the 20th century. It represents multiple strands of creativity, both in architectural form and structural design, a great urban sculpture carefully set in a remarkable waterscape and a world famous iconic building" (2006, p. 96). In 2007, Utzon's design was inscribed on UNESCO's World Heritage List.

GLOBAL TECHNOLOGICAL DEVELOPMENTS

As discussed earlier, the Cold War affected many aspects of life in the 1960s. Technological advances focused on the competition between the two superpowers, the USSR and the United States. Some of the developments included communication and weather satellites, moon landings, human space travel, space docking, and space walks. The futuristic images associated with and made available by these technological developments were reflected in the designs of interior environments and architecture. Industrial designer Raymond Loewy became the world's first cosmic designer when he consulted for NASA on the design of the Skylab project (1967–1973), the United States' first experimental space station. New technologies included fiber optics, laser lights, and **LEDs (light-emitting diodes)**, and new discoveries were made in the field of artificial or electrical lighting. Designers started to experiment in their designs using newly developed "space-age materials." The U.S. Department of Defense launched the precursor to the Internet, ARPANET, a computer network developed to facilitate communication between military operations. What became the first compact disk (CD) was invented by James Russell in 1965, and by the end of the decade 95 percent of households in America had a television. World travel was improved by the Hovercraft, an air-cushion vehicle first put into scheduled commercial service across the English Channel in 1962. The world's first high-speed rail network, the Shinkansen (bullet train) in Japan, began operating in 1964, and the first flight by the Concorde, the supersonic airliner, took place in 1969. The emergence and importance of plastic was reinforced in the 1967 film *The Graduate*. In the movie, actor Dustin Hoffman portrays a recent college graduate trying to determine his career. Another character in the movie provides one word that summarized his recommendation: "Plastics." Raymond Loewy and Joe Colombo were two designers who understood this recommendation and developed innovative materials, products, and interiors made from plastics.

Space Exploration: NASA's Skylab Project and Raymond Loewy

As previously mentioned, computers were essential for executing the engineering plans for the Sydney Opera House. Computers were critical for space exploration. What quickly became known as the "Space Race," between the Soviet Union and the United States, required the development of faster and more powerful computers. For centuries, civilizations have been intrigued with exploring the universe and people have dreamed about flying to another planet. Successful journeys to the moon were sensationalized through the popular writings of Jules Verne (*From the Earth to the Moon*) and H. G. Wells (*The First Men in the Moon*). The feasibility of space flight originated in the early 1900s with Konstantin Tsiolkovsky, a Russian. Known as the "Father of Space Travel," Tsiolkovsky developed theories associated with using rockets for space exploration. The development of liquid-fuel rockets by a German scientist, Wernher von Braun, in the early 1940s led to the creation of Vengeance weapon (V-2) rockets, which Germany used to bomb England during World War II.

Another space-related outcome of the war was competition. When the Soviet Union launched Sputnik I in 1957, the United States feared that this "first" would lead to deadly missiles that could reach North America. In the United States, numerous atomic bomb test explosions were conducted in New Mexico and Nevada. Subsequently, the United States and the Soviet Union invested heavily in the research and development of space exploration.

Successful satellite launches precipitated the determination to initiate human space flight and numerous other firsts in space exploration during the 1960s. Soviet cosmonaut Yuri Gagarin was the first human in space: he orbited Earth one time for 90 minutes on April 12, 1961. The U.S. response to the Soviet Union was the flight of Alan B. Shepard, Jr. on May 5, 1961. Soon after this flight, President John F. Kennedy proclaimed in a speech to Congress on May 25, 1961, "I believe that this nation should commit itself to achieving the goal, before this decade is out, of landing a man on the Moon and returning him safely to the Earth. No single project in this period will be more impressive to mankind or more important for the long-range exploration of space" (JFK Library, 2009, p. 4). John H. Glenn, Jr. was the first American to orbit around Earth on February 20, 1962, less than 1 year after Gagarin's journey. The enormous global investment (the Apollo program alone was $25 billion in 1967) in space exploration in the 1960s resulted in many other firsts, including the first woman in space (1963), Valentina Tereshkova, and the first spacewalk (for 10 minutes) by Alexei A. Leonov in 1965. Finally, on July 20, 1969, Neil Armstrong, Buzz Aldrin, and Michael Collins landed on the moon with the spacecraft Apollo 11. Armstrong was the first human to walk on the moon. While the world watched on live television, Armstrong took his initial steps and said his famous line, "That's one small step for man, one giant leap for mankind." The successful landing on the moon was followed by several manned and unmanned missions.

During this period of space exploration, scientists worked to develop technologies that would enable people to live in space for several months. The Soviets started to experiment with creating space stations in the late 1960s and had a successful orbit of Salyut I in 1971. The U.S. version of a space station was Skylab. To provide a fairly comfortable living and working environment for three people for an extended period required major revisions to the cramped conditions that astronauts endured while traveling to the moon.

Early spacecrafts were extremely small, were filled with exposed wires, and lacked attention to reducing the physiological effects of weightlessness. Larger spacecrafts had to be very carefully designed to minimize weight. Extra weight from people and equipment, or payload, translated into additional fuel that added weight and required that the craft have more space. To help resolve interior design concerns, NASA officials contacted Raymond Loewy (see Chapter 6) in 1967. NASA hired the Loewy Company as "habitability" consultants "to help insure the psycho-physiological safety and comfort of the astronauts" (Loewy, 1979, p. 205). As a consultant on the development of the Skylab, Loewy can be considered one of the first "cosmic" interior designers. His work on the Skylab provides insight for current practice, such as the importance of applying research findings to design solutions and designing for

human factors. For example, first and foremost was the extensive research he used to enhance solutions. Loewy reported that during a 6-year period his organization completed "Eight habitability studies comprising over eight hundred pages and over a thousand illustrations, statistical analyses, diagrams, and scale models" (Loewy, 1979, p. 205). Research involved not only gaining an understanding of space travel and its complicated equipment; Loewy also researched anthropometric data and the potential psychological and physiological effects of living in space. These factors had to be designed for within a compact configuration. As with Utzon's engineering studies, to determine an ideal shape, Loewy experimented with various geometrical forms, such as the polyhedron and concentric spheres.

He applied research findings to his recommendations for the design of the Skylab interior. For the Earth Orbital Workshop (EOW) project, Loewy's suggestions focused on (1) a mandatory porthole, (2) 8 hours of solitude for each astronaut every day, (3) dining arrangements that required the astronauts to face each other, and (4) surfaces that were "smooth and flush to make it easy to keep them clean in the event of uncontrollable space sickness" (Loewy, 1979, p. 205).

Loewy's reports, *Habitability Study: Earth Orbital Space Stations*, included many drawings, sketches, photographs of mock-ups, and detailed specifications. For the "Shuttle Orbiter Crew Compartment / X-Axis Docking" specifications, the parameters read: "1. Consider operation in 3 modes of operation—launch, Zero-G [zero gravity], re-entry. 2. 6-man crew—maximum of 4 crewmen occupy crew compartment at launch. 3. Crew compartment consisting of a 94"H × 108"W × 196"L module. 4. Immediate access necessary to emergency escape hatch and head during launch. 5. A 39" passage through the crew compartment extending from the airlock to the rear bulkhead" (Loewy, 1979, p. 209). The document continued by identifying problems, such as difficulties in maneuvering through entrances, the lack of visual contact between the astronauts, and the

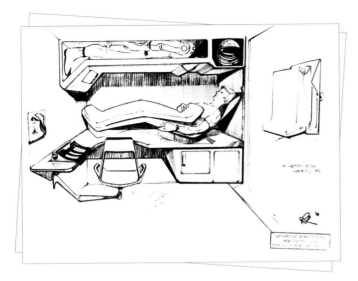

Figure 8.9 Many of Raymond Loewy's published works included drawings of improvements to personal hygiene facilities, and living/working configurations. As an integrated and multipurpose design, an astronaut had sleeping, work, and storage facilities.

Source: Raymond Loewy™/® by CMG Worldwide, Inc./www.RaymondLoewy.com.

Figure 8.10 Another work/sleeping arrangement designed by Raymond Loewy. The hinged-desk top flipped down after sleeping and demonstrates how Loewy planned for zero gravity.

Source: Raymond Loewy™/® by CMG Worldwide, Inc./www.RaymondLoewy.com.

need for an "integrated plan." Many of Loewy's published works included drawings of improvements to personal hygiene facilities and living/working configurations (Figure 8.9). The illustration in Figure 8.9 is an excellent example of Loewy's "integrated" and multipurpose designs. In a very compact area, an astronaut had sleeping, work, and storage facilities. The desk and credenza could become a bed and the attached seat swiveled into different positions. A "hinged hammock stows against the wall," and the astronaut's pressure suit was stored in the upper cabinets.

Another work/sleeping arrangement is illustrated in Figure 8.10. The hinged-desk top flipped down after sleeping and demonstrates how Loewy planned for zero gravity. For example, shoulders were positioned under a bar, arms were strapped to the chair, and feet were wedged between upper and lower poles. Loewy also suggested a sliding seat arrangement with foot restraints that would be useful for monitoring space control panels. Eventually, there was a collaborative Soviet Union–United States program, the 1975 Apollo-Soyuz [Test] Project (ASTP). ASTP, or "Handshake in Orbit," was a space flight that linked Soviet and American spacecrafts while in operation. The astronauts appeared to benefit from Loewy's design recommendations. In Loewy's book, he included a space photograph, autographed by five astronauts, with a message to Loewy and his wife: "With admiration and appreciation for enriching the life style of our world through your imaginative designs. The ASTP Crews" (Loewy, 1979, p. 217).

Space Exploration and Plastic Technologies: Joe Colombo

To meet NASA's criteria, Loewy's designs for the Skylab would not have been possible without using plastics. The origins of plastic date to American inventor John Wesley Hyatt's discovery of celluloid in 1870. Composed of cellulite from plant materials, celluloid also made it possible to develop film. The first synthetic resin was Bakelite, created by Leo H. Baekeland in the early 1900s (see Chapter 7). Bakelite, the phenol-formaldehyde resin, was used for many products, including the new black rotary-dial telephones, radios, jewelry, and electrical insulators. Raw materials for synthetic resins

Figure 8.11 The injection molding machine used to produce Joe Colombo's Universale chair (1965).

Source: Kartell Photographic Archive.

include coal and petroleum (crude oil). Chemists found that plastic was lightweight, tough, a good insulator, and resistant to moisture and corrosion. At this time, the positive attributes of plastics overcame any current concerns about depleting petroleum and coal supplies.

Plastic products are basically made by using heat to melt plastic chips or pellets. The **molten plastic** is then poured into a mold, which becomes hard during the cooling process. The two major classifications of plastic materials are **thermoplastic** and **thermosetting.** Thermoplastic materials will become soft if they are reheated. Thermosetting materials will not become soft if they are reheated. Fundamentally, this is due to another step in the production process. Thermoset materials are reheated while they are in the mold. The additional heat causes a chemical reaction that "sets" the material.

Each classification is used for different types of plastic and uses. For example, some of the thermo-plastics are **cellulose acetate, polycarbonate, ABS (acrylonitrile-butadiene-styrene), acrylic, polypro-pylene,** and **polyvinyl chloride (PVC).** Cellulose acetate's flexibility and toughness is ideal for decorative

objects, packaging, and photographic film. Due to its high impact resistance, polycarbonate is used for light diffusers, office equipment, and windows. ABS (acrylonitrile-butadiene-styrene) is long lasting and strong, and thus the material is used for pipes, furniture, and small appliances. Acrylic's transparency is used in light fixtures, textiles, and paint. Polypropylene's ability to be easily extruded (defined below), as well as its resis-tance to heat and chemicals, enables it to be used for carpeting. A combination of strength and a resistance to sunlight and abrasion has resulted in many uses for polyvinyl chloride (PVC), including flooring, imitation leather, textiles, electrical insulation, and pipes.

Thermoset plastics include **epoxy, melamine,** and **polyurethane.** Epoxy's resistance to chemicals and weather make it good for adhesives, flooring, and protective coatings. Melamine is used for tableware, lampshades, and laminates due to its resistance to heat and most chemicals. Polyurethane's foaming ability makes it suitable for padding, seat cushions, insulation, and stretch fabrics.

The basic processing methods used to shape plastic materials are **molding, casting, extrusion, calendaring, laminating, foaming,** and **thermoforming.** All of these methods are used to produce furniture, furnishings, and equipment. Products made by molding, such as Colombo's Universale chair, require intense heat and pressure (Figure 8.11). The casting method does not require pressure. A synthetic resin is poured into a mold, and a solid object is formed when the material hardens. For the extrusion method, resins are forced through a heated form. The method is ideal for fabricating tubes and pipes. Calendaring is a method to adhere a plastic sheet to a material, such as fabric or paper. Heated rollers are used to melt plastic to a surface. The rollers might inc-lude a design that is then embossed on the surface. This method is used to create imitations of natural textiles.

Laminating is used extensively for plywood, furni-ture, **luminaires** (light fixtures), and numerous other products for the building industry. The laminating process involves layering sheets of a material, such as paper or wood, with thermosetting resins. Foaming methods blend gas-producing chemicals with resins to create polystyrene or polyurethane. **Polystyrene** (Styrofoam) is lightweight, and is used for packaging and flotation equipment. Additional chemicals are added to resins to stiffen polyurethane. The thermoforming method uses heat to adhere plastic sheets over a form. A vacuum pump removes air from the surfaces. Thermoforming (vacuum forming) is a common method to fabricate shower stalls, boats, and parts of aircraft (Figure 8.12).

While plastic materials and processing methods were being developed, Italian designer and artist Joe Colombo was working in Italy. The death of Colombo's father in 1959 precipitated his becoming responsible with his brother Gianni for his family's factory, which manufactured electrical equipment, and his involvement with the development of plastics. Because plastic is an ideal material for electrical parts, insulation, and appliances, Colombo became involved with experimenting with various resins and production processes. Colombo soon applied this experience to futuristic designs of luminaires, furniture, containers, exhibition stands, cabinetry, and "multi-function units." As aerospace engineers were using plastics for space exploration, Colombo used the material to create environments that appeared to exist in space. He explained his interest in the new materials, stating, "It is clear that the appearance of new materials presents new possibilities for the solution of problems and it is equally clear that the designer cannot ignore this" (Favata, 1988, p. 22). To be able to use new materials, Colombo had to help solve the complexities of producing products using new manufacturing processes. Building equipment to manufacture plastic products is extremely complicated and expensive. After a manufacturing process is successful, a product can be mass-produced in enormous quantities. Due to the uncertainty of the public's acceptance of a new material, Colombo and other designers were challenged to find manufacturers willing to invest in what was considered a risky business.

Fortunately, Italian companies such as Kartell, Comfort, Bieffeplast, and Bellato/Elco developed the technologies to manufacture Colombo's designs, many of which are in the collections of museums throughout

Figure 8.12 Thermoforming was used to produce some of the pieces in Joe Colombo's *Visiona*, a "habitat for the future, 1969."
Source: Studio Joe Columbo.

the world. Plastics were the dominant material used by Colombo. Because the new plastics were heat-resistant, Colombo was able to create many new designs for luminaires using a variety of lamps. Some of his early designs for portable and surface-mounted luminaires used clear acrylic. The transparent material appeared futuristic and had superior optical qualities. Colombo designed a scattering of pyramid-shaped ceiling-mounted fixtures made of Plexiglas (acrylic) for the entrance of the Pontinental Hotel, Golfo dell'Asinara, Sardinia (1962–1964). In collaboration with his brother Gianni, Colombo designed the iconic Acrilica light fixture using a fluorescent lamp in its metal base (1962). The Colombos have received awards for the way light seems to float through Acrilica fixture's elegant "C"-shaped Plexiglas form.

Revolutionary furniture designs included Colombo's Elda armchair (1963), Universale chair (1965) (see Figure 8.11), Additional System armchair (1967), and Tube-Chair (1969). Named after Colombo's wife, the Elda chair rotated and was the first armchair made entirely from fiberglass. The leather-covered tubes of foam required developments in polyurethane. The tubes tend to resemble the bulky arms and legs of astronauts dressed in spacesuits. The Universale chair was inspired by the child's chair 4999 designed by Marco Zanuso and Richard Sapper. Colombo's stackable chair with flat sides was originally made entirely of ABS plastic. The novelty of the new material and production processes resulted in two years of experimentation. Subsequently, the chair was made of polypropylene and was available in various heights (achieved by unscrewing its legs).

Polyurethane foam and plastic were also used to design the Tube-Chair. The PVC circular rollers can be made into a variety of shapes and sizes. Metal joints with rubber ends were attached to the tubes, which were covered in a polyurethane-coated textile. The modular Additional System armchair was also made of various units that could create seating in a variety of sizes and shapes. Each cushion was made of polyurethane and covered in a stretch fabric.

Similar to Loewy's concepts for Skylab, Colombo's most outstanding examples of inspiration from space exploration are his "multi-function units," including Visiona (1969), "a habitat for the future"; Roto-living (1969); and Cabriolet-Bed (1969). In describing future interiors, Colombo introduced another dimension: "In the past space was static; this has been the classic notion for our millennia. Our century is characterized by dynamism instead . . . there is a fourth dimension: time. It is necessary to introduce this fourth dimension into space" (Favata, 1988, p. 12). Even today, Visiona appears to be a residence for living on the moon (see Figure 8.12). The experimental project featured bright colors and "furniture-blocks" made of plastic, and the spaces had a "dynamism" that could be reconfigured to accommodate any requirements in the "fourth dimension." The three primary "blocks" included the "Central-Living," the "Night-Cell," and the "Kitchen-Box." The other designers who collaborated with Colombo to fantasize Visiona were T. Bonaretti, I. Favata, A. Grieco, and M. P. Valota. Colombo died of heart failure in 1971; he was 41 years old.

The extraordinarily large quantities of plastic products have become a very significant environmental problem in the 21st century. According to the Environmental Literacy Council, "in 2002 about 107 billion pounds of plastic were produced in North America" (2009, p. 1). Consuming nonrenewable resources was not perceived as a problem 50 years ago because commodities such as gasoline and electricity were not in nearly as high demand and, initially, manufacturers did not consume a great deal of petroleum to make plastic products. But in this century, depletion of nonrenewable resources has escalated to the extent that today's prolific use of plastic products is a major sustainability issue. In addition to consuming petroleum, other sustainability issues related to plastics focus on the substantial energy required to heat and form plastic products, the toxic emissions resulting from their creation, and the detrimental consequences of disposing of huge quantities of nonbiodegradable substances in landfills, oceans, and other waterways.

GLOBAL LIFE AND WORK STYLES

Discriminatory practices based on race in the United States and South Africa resulted in violence and bloodshed in the 1960s. The Civil Rights Movement was on the rise, led by Rev. Martin Luther King, Jr., who delivered his "I Have a Dream" speech on the steps of the Lincoln Memorial in Washington, D.C., in 1963. Nelson Mandela was sentenced to life in prison in South Africa in 1964, and the U.N. General Assembly condemned the South African practice of apartheid, its nationwide official policy of racial segregation. To outlaw discrimination, Congress passed the Civil Rights Act of 1964, the Voting Rights Act of 1965, and an expanded Civil Rights Act in 1968. In an era of violence marked by assassinations and unrest in major U.S. cities, "hippies" demonstrated for peace and reflected their views through anti-establishment clothing, hairstyles, and lifestyles. In dramatic contrast, Eero Saarinen was involved with designing new headquarters for the conservative John Deere Corporation in Illinois, and Japanese architect Kenzo Tange was commissioned to design the National Gymnasiums for the 1964 Summer Olympics in Tokyo, Japan.

Human Research Studies: John Deere in Moline, Illinois, by Eero Saarinen

Architect Eero Saarinen's life and career also ended prematurely; he died after brain surgery at the age of 51. Saarinen's death in 1961 preceded the completion of many of his most important projects, including the Trans World Airlines terminal (1956–1962) at New York's then Idlewild Airport (now John F. Kennedy International Airport); IBM Research Center (1957–1961) in Yorktown, New York; Bell Telephone Corporation (1957–1962) in Holmdel, New Jersey; John Deere & Company Headquarters (1957–1963) in Moline, Illinois; Colleges at Yale University (1958–1962);

the terminal building at Dulles International Airport (1958–1962) in Chantilly, Virginia; North Christian Church in Columbus, Indiana (1959–1963); Columbia Broadcasting System (CBS) Headquarters (1960–1964) in New York City; and the St. Louis Arch (1947–1948 competition; 1959–1964) in St. Louis, Missouri.

Eero Saarinen's untimely death did not preclude his recognition as the Project Designer for projects completed after 1961. Fortunately, Saarinen's interdisciplinary and collaborative work ethic, which was relatively uncommon in the 1950s, allowed for the projects to be successfully completed. Interviews with people who worked in Saarinen's firm have indicated that he encouraged design input from architects, designers, engineers, landscape designers, users of the space, and clients. Saarinen's collaborative approach unexpectedly ensured that the designers who remained with the firm after his death understood the projects and his designs for the completed buildings. Many of the architects who worked for Saarinen became internationally known and received numerous awards for their work with Saarinen as well as their later architecture, including Kevin Roche, Cesar Pelli, and Robert Venturi. Saarinen also gathered research data that was applied to the design of the interior environments and architecture. He utilized the data to create hundreds of sketches, models, and mock-ups, intently studying every prototype and identifying better solutions.

Many critics contend that Saarinen's last projects featured his best solutions, most notably the soaring free-form architecture of the Dulles International Airport, and the bold and elegant design for the John Deere & Company Headquarters. These two projects are excellent examples of how Saarinen conducted extensive human behavior research and applied the results to innovative design solutions. Data were used to create efficient and functional spaces that reflected the physiological and psychological needs of users.

For the terminal building at Dulles Airport, Saarinen was extensively involved with researching the most ideal conditions for a commercial airport for jet airplanes, an entirely new concept when the project began in the 1950s (Figure 8.13). Saarinen explained the research process, noting, "We sent out teams with counters and stop-watches to see what people really do at airports, how far they walk, their interchange problems. We analyzed special problems of jets, examined schedules, peak loads, effect of weather. We studied baggage handling, economics, methods of operations, and so on. We reduced this vast data to a series of about forty charts" (Saarinen, A., 1968, p. 102).

From this research, he concluded that the three critical areas to address were: (1) "the time and inconvenience of getting passengers to and from planes," (2) "heavy cost of taxiing jet planes," and (3) "the increasing need for greater flexibility in operations and servicing of aircraft" (Saarinen, A., 1968, p. 102). A major solution was to bring "the passenger to the plane rather than the plane to the passenger" via the "mobile lounge: a departure lounge on stilts and wheels." In addition to resolving functional aspects of the airport, Saarinen's design for the terminal's roof and columns was elegantly spectacular (see Figure 8.13). He was even enthralled with its beauty. A few months before he died, Saarinen commented, "I think this airport is the best thing I have done. I think it is going to be really good. Maybe it will even explain what I believe about architecture" (Saarinen, A., 1968, p. 102).

Saarinen's design for the Deere & Company Headquarters reflects a thorough understanding of the needs of his client and the company's employees. For several years he collaborated with the chairman and chief executive of the company, William A. Hewitt. Hewitt's vision for the new headquarters was to: (1) "pull the company together and improve employee working conditions," (2) "help the company attract and hold superior personnel," and (3) "be outstanding aesthetically" (Hall & Hall 1975, p. 11). Hewitt explained that an aesthetic building was important "to improve the company's image in the world at large and raise the architectural standards of the local community." Hewitt's goal to have an "aesthetic" building was unique for a conservative Midwest company that manufactured farm machinery. However, time has proven that Saarinen's "aesthetic" design has been enormously beneficial to the Deere Company. The headquarters have received international attention, thousands of visitors have toured the facilities over the years, and the "aesthetic" design has been important for employee recruitment and sales.

As noted by Hewitt, employee interest and retention was a priority because of the company's relatively

Figure 8.13 For the terminal building at Dulles airport, Saarinen was extensively involved with researching the most ideal conditions for a commercial airport for jet airplanes, an entirely new concept in the 1950s.

Source: Visions of America, LLC/Alamy.

remote location. Prior to the construction of the new headquarters, the company was located in several old buildings in downtown Moline. To attract excellent employees and to consolidate operations, Saarinen collaborated with Hewitt to identify a large, "aesthetic" site for the new headquarters. They identified a beautiful area in the country close to Moline. The site's 600 acres (242.812 hectare) had rolling hills, streams, extensive forests, and wildlife.

Saarinen's earliest designs were based on an inverted pyramid, but designers who were working with him have explained that his design changed radically after a trip to Japan. The pyramid form was eliminated, and Saarinen created the Japanese-inspired design that exists today. Designers, including Cesar Pelli, have noted similarities between Deere and the Japanese "tea house tradition, Katsura Palace" (discussed in the next section). Saarinen was intensively involved with blending the architecture with the landscape design, a feature of many Japanese designs. In echoing the design for the General Motors Technical Center project (see Chapter 7), Saarinen added an artificial lake with fountains next to the administrative building. He carefully positioned the buildings, roads, and parking lots to maximize the views and to conserve thousands of trees.

Responding to Hewitt's vision, Saarinen's preliminary designs for the headquarters sought to: (1) "provide functional, efficient space which would take care of future expansion in flexible ways," (2) "create the kind of pleasant and appropriate environment for employees which is part of Twentieth Century thinking," and (3) "express in architecture the special character of Deere & Company" (Hall & Hall, 1975, p. 12). To create "functional" spaces, the three buildings Saarinen designed for Deere's headquarters were the eight-story administration building, an exhibition building with an auditorium, and a laboratory building (Figure 8.14). The three buildings were linked with glazed "flying bridges." To allow for future expansion, the plans for the administration building had movable

Figure 8.14 To create functional space for the John Deere Headquarters in Moline, Illinois, Saarinen designed an administration building that was linked with glazed "flying bridges."
Source: © Ezra Stoller/Esto.

partitions and the large site could accommodate additional buildings.

Saarinen created a "pleasant and appropriate environment for employees" in numerous ways. The walls of glass enabled employees, customers, and visitors to enjoy views of the beautiful countryside. On all of the plans, except for the executive floor, a corridor was placed in the windowless center area and offices were positioned adjacent to the glass walls. To reduce glare and solar heat, some of the glass was tinted and all of the buildings had steel brise-soleil.

The steel louvers and the projecting eaves that protect the buildings became critical elements in the design of the façades (see Figure 8.14). An abundant use of bold steel was Saarinen's approach to "express in architecture the special character of Deere." Saarinen explained his rationale for using a type of steel that did not have to be treated with a finish, noting, "Farm machinery is not slick, shiny metal but forged iron and steel in big, forceful, functional shapes. The proper character for its headquarters' architecture should likewise not be a slick, precise, glittering glass and spindly metal building, but a building which is bold and direct, using metal in a strong, basic way" (Saarinen, A., 1968, p. 82). The unfinished steel Saarinen specified for the architecture, Cor-Ten, is maintenance free, and the natural weatherizing process results in a warm reddish-brown patina. Saarinen repeated the exposed steel in the interiors, including the desks he designed for the offices—an H-shaped steel beam supported the desks' surfaces.

To analyze the success of the Deere project from a human behaviorist perspective, anthropologist Edward Hall and his wife author Mildred Hall initiated a research study with many of Deere's executives and employees. In the Deere project, the Halls identified "the impact of building on man's behavior as the fourth dimension in architecture." During the 5-year study, the Halls conducted several interviews with randomly selected Deere employees. Initially 47 people took part in the study, but at its conclusion only 33 of them were available for interviews. The interviews were conducted prior to occupancy and via two post-occupancy studies. One set of post-occupancy interviews took place 4 months after move-in, and the final interviews were conducted approximately 5 years after occupancy. The researchers also conducted numerous observations to gather additional information.

The results of the study help assess how well Saarinen addressed the needs of the client and provide insights for improving future practice. Overall, the Halls reported that most people had a "strong positive reaction" to the building and employees became accustomed to the constant attention from working in a place that was "world famous." People worked hard in their new environment, the Halls also noted, stating, "Many people originally commented on how efficiency had increased since the company moved into the building. Five years later we had this same strong feeling that an atmosphere of hard work prevails everywhere" (Hall & Hall, 1975, p. 45). To gain meaningful results regarding the impact of a building on behavior, the Halls emphasized the importance of examining a group of individuals over a long period of time (longitudinal study), and employing multiple methodologies that could involve a variety of sources of information, such as surveys, observations, and documents.

The 1964 Summer Olympics and the Katsura Temple: National Gymnasiums for the Olympics (1961–1964) in Tokyo, Japan, by Kenzo Tange

The ancient Greek tradition of the Olympic Games began in 776 BCE at the religious site in Olympia, Greece. The games were held in midsummer to honor Zeus and to promote peace among the city-states. The popular event occurred every 4 years for 1,170 years, until it was abolished in 393 CE by the Christian Byzantine Emperor Theodosius I. It was not until centuries later, in the late 19th century, that French Baron Pierre de Coubertin began a campaign to revive the Olympics. de Coubertin wanted fitness and athleticism to be part of everyday life and wanted the return of the Olympics both for the athletic contests and to bring the nations of the world together at a peaceful event. In 1894 he founded the International Olympic Committee, and the first modern Summer Olympic Games was held in 1896 in Athens, Greece. Winter Games were added in 1924.

World War I and World War II forced cancellation of the Olympics in 1916, 1940, and 1944, but they resumed in 1948. Winter and Summer Olympics were held in either Western Europe or the United States until Melbourne, Australia, hosted the 1956 Summer Olympics. The first time the games were held in Asia was at the 1964 Summer Olympics in Tokyo. This international event gave Japan the opportunity to demonstrate its technological and economic advances, and recovery since the devastation of World War II.

The career of Japanese architect Kenzo Tange was significantly affected by both the U.S. bombing of Hiroshima and the Olympic Games 19 years later. Tange, Takashi Asada, and Sachio Otani designed Hiroshima's Centre of Peace (1949–1955), a complex on the site where the atomic bomb hit the city on August 6, 1945. In addition to a library and conference facilities, a highlight of the center is the Museum of Remembrance, which houses documents related to the bombing.

Along with engineers Yoshikatsu Tsuboi and Uichi Inove, Tange was commissioned to design the National Gymnasiums for the Tokyo Olympics (1961–1964) (Figure 8.15). The gymnasium complex included two stadiums, gardens, a promenade, a parking lot, and two subway stations. The larger stadium—which had capacity for 16,246 spectators—had an Olympic swimming pool, concrete diving boards, and an interior garden. The smaller stadium was for boxing events and had a maximum seating capacity of 5,351. Tange's design for the gymnasiums received international acclaim and was often cited for its technological accomplishments, such as the suspended roof-span and its innovative approach to space. Fortunately, a few

Figure 8.15 Kenzo Tange, with the engineers, Yoshikatsu Tsuboi and Uichi Inove, were commissioned to design the National Gymnasiums for the 1964 Tokyo Olympics. The gymnasium complex included two stadiums, gardens, a promenade, a parking lot, and two subway stations.
Source: Angelo Hornak/Alamy.

designers, including architects Matthew Nowicki and Eero Saarinen, had already used technology that was required to create the dramatic roof of the larger stadium. These projects provided Tange with practical information, such as efficient installation methods, that he could apply to the design of the gymnasiums. Similarities exist between Tange's gymnasiums and Saarinen's design for the David S. Ingalls Hockey Rink at Yale University (1956–1959). The two architects conversed during Saarinen's visit to Japan. Saarinen used the soaring roof design to "motivate the hockey players to excel."

Undoubtedly, Tange also intended to create a design that would motivate the Olympic athletes, but a close examination of the National Gymnasium Complex, as well as of a book that Tange wrote during the same period, tends to suggest other parallels. By analyzing the gymnasia in light of Tange's book *Katsura* (1960), one can gain a greater appreciation for Tange's contemporary design, as well as an overview of one type of traditional Japanese architecture.

The Katsura Palace described in Tange's book was built in multiple phases during the 17th century. The present country villa, located close to the previous capital city, Kyoto, was initiated by Hachijo no Miya Toshihito and then was completed by Prince Toshitada (Figure 8.16). Tange was extremely fond of the palace and noted that Katsura was "an ultimate integration of function and expression," an important element for the Olympic Games (Tange, 1972; redesigned edition of the original 1960, p. 2). He also contended that "the structural relationship between tradition and creation in Japanese history is visible in the typical form at Katsura."

These perspectives provide insight into Tange's design for the National Gymnasium Complex. For example, in Tange's book *Katsura*, he declares, "The dialectical synthesis of tradition and anti-tradition is the structure of true creativeness" (Tange, 1972, p. 44). Thus, the "true creativeness" of his design for the gymnasium complex can be derived from Tange's synthesizing the architectural "traditions" reflected in the

Katsura Palace and the "anti-tradition" use of modern materials and technologies. A comparative analysis of Tange's "traditional" book and his "anti-tradition" design for the gymnasium complex is feasible due to the unique approach Tange and photographer Yasuhiro Ishimoto used to create their book on Japanese architecture. Tange explains that their intent was not to create a historical book about the Katsura Palace. The book "is a visual record of the living Katsura as it exists in the minds of an architect and a photographer" (Tange, 1972, p. 1). Rather than capturing photographs of the Katsura complex, Tange and Ishimoto "trained" their attention to "details." Thus, the two collaborated to photograph details of the palace that reflected what they felt were "inspired by a personal experience or emotion." For example, many of the illustrations are close-up photographs of details in the gardens, such as moss growing between stones, rock arrangements, a pond, the lawn, rain gutters, or stepping stones leading to a building.

Exterior and interior photographs capture joinery details, a door handle, a cabinet, a grille wall, or a pantry. Generally, as with traditional Japanese architecture, photographs taken from the interior illustrate the magnificent views of nature. Tange explains, "The spaces create vistas and perspectives flowing gently along in time. The interpenetration of interior and exterior at Katsura reveals a world of perfect time-space relationships" (Tange, 1972, p. 122).

These "visual records" captured in *Katsura* seem to reappear in Tange's "anti-traditional" design for the National Gymnasiums for the Olympics. To showcase Japan's technological achievements, Tange designed soaring "anti-traditional" vertical structures that seem to float around the complex's "traditional" gardens. The vertical emphasis was in dramatic contrast to horizontal spaces found in "traditional" Japanese architecture. Tall, vertical spaces required the use of "anti-traditional" materials and technologies, such as steel, aluminum, and reinforced concrete. However, the "anti-traditional" structures and materials have

subtle details found in "traditional" Japanese architecture. For example, the roofs for the gymnasium were made of "anti-traditional" steel and aluminum panels with ridges, and are supported with cables that are attached to two reinforced-concrete pillars (see Figure 8.15). The pattern created with these "anti-traditional" materials resembles "traditional" patterns that were illustrated in *Katsura*, such as bamboo fencing, wooden grille windows, bamboo ceilings, and tatami mats. The thick cables with rings resemble bamboo (see Figure 8.15), a common Asian woody treelike plant that was frequently photographed for *Katsura*. The apexes of the roofs use "anti-traditional" materials but follow the "traditional" forms of the gable details of the Ise Shrine illustrated in *Katsura*.

The "anti-traditional" plans of the gymnasiums could be traced to the "traditional" shape of the moon, which Tange often referred to in *Katsura*, such as the palace's "Moon-viewing Platform," the "Singing of the Moon" plaque, or a "door handle shaped like the Chinese ideograph for 'moon' in the New Palace." The smaller arena could represent the full moon, and the larger stadium appears to be two half-moons that are slightly shifted.

The palace and the National Gymnasiums are both complexes that include several buildings, gardens, and

Figure 8.16 Garden and Shoin, Katsura Rikyu Imperial Villa, Kyoto.
Source: Arcaid/Alamy.

entrance gates. The larger gymnasium has an interior courtyard that is made with "anti-traditional" materials; however, the design is very similar to Ishimoto's photograph of a "traditional" Zen-style garden at the Ryoanji Temple. The temple's enclosed stone garden has the "traditional" raked stones and large-rock arrangements. At the gymnasium complex, rather than the difficult-to-maintain raked stones, Tange used "anti-traditional" concrete. The "traditional" large-rock arrangements were replaced with "anti-traditional" light wells, which provide illumination for the arena's gallery at the gymnasium. The "anti-traditional" addition of seating had references to "visual records" of the palace; the seats of the benches are the identical C-shape of the palace's "traditional" sinks and hearths. As with the temple, the interior courtyard and the other gardens at the gymnasium complex became "vistas and perspectives." This connection between the built environment and nature pays homage to Japan's important architectural "tradition" of "interpenetration of interior and exterior" (Tange, 1972, p. 122).

GLOBAL VISUAL AND PERFORMING ARTS

In the world of pop culture, the 1960s was the decade of the Beatles and rock music. The band's first album, *Please Please Me*, became a hit in 1963, but their most successful year was 1964. The Beatles had 13 singles on Billboard's Hot 100 list at the same time, including "I Want to Hold Your Hand" and "All My Loving." They also appeared on *The Ed Sullivan Show* in 1964, and in 1965 they became even more famous with their movie and album *Help!* Other popular musicians that defined this decade were the Rolling Stones,

Bob Dylan, the Animals, the Supremes, the Grateful Dead, Led Zeppelin, and Janis Joplin. Many of these artists performed at the plethora of outdoor concerts that occurred in the 1960s, including the Woodstock Festival in 1969. The Woodstock generation and their music inspired new designs and materials, which were reflected in products created by Marimekko, a Finnish fashion and furnishings company. Innovative and bold patterns and colors similar to those used in Marimekko's textiles also were reflected in the Pop Art of Andy Warhol. With a focus on the impact of the media, Warhol became famous for his iconic images of everyday objects (e.g., soup cans) and celebrities (e.g., movie stars).

The Woodstock Generation: Marimekko

There were many cultural events in the 1960s that affected Western music, theater, and film, which subsequently impacted the design of interior environments. Dominant social issues included the Vietnam War, the civil rights movement, and the emergence of counterculture philosophy that rejected the "establishment." Musicians had a significant role in promoting things like political activism, "free love," psychedelic experiences, the so-called "hippie lifestyle," and experimental drugs, including LSD. Musicians with long hair and "sloppy-looking" clothing performed at seemingly chaotic outdoor concerts. The sounds, lyrics, and volume of rock music were perceived as a source of trouble by the establishment because they seemed to encourage unruly behavior. During this time, however, folk singers, such as Joan Baez, Bob Dylan, Pete Seeger, and Peter, Paul, and Mary were gently singing poems with themes such as civil rights, opposition to the Vietnam War, and the possibility of nuclear apocalypse.

The most popular ways for musicians to share their message included recorded versions of their songs on singles and albums, as well as performing the music live at open-air concerts, and shows in theaters and smaller venues. A trend that continues to this day, outdoor rock concerts "came of age" in the late 1960s (many of the shows at that time were free). The Monterey International Pop Music Festival occurred during the 1967 "Summer of Love." This seminal concert—which featured the Who, Jimi Hendrix, the Mammas & the Papas, and Janis Joplin—was held in Monterey, California, about 100 miles (161 kilometers) south of San Francisco. The concert helped to reinforce the hippie culture that had been developing and gaining media attention in that city's Haight-Ashbury district. But the event that came to define the new generation was the Woodstock Music Festival in upstate New York, held August 15–17, 1969. Many of the musicians and young people in the audience wore flowers in their long hair, headbands, love beads, blue jeans, and loose floral shirts. As described below, the unconventional lifestyles of both the performers and the fans at the festivals translated into new fashions and interior environments.

The peace sign and bright, often psychedelic colors became symbols for the counterculture generation. Psychedelic colors were created by contrasting bright hues, such as hot pink, orange, and purple. These impressions and values also became part of interior environments. Communal living arrangements, another nontraditional choice of some during this time, featured simple interiors with few material possessions due to their association with the "establishment." The back-to-nature lifestyle included nudity, growing one's own food, and creating handicrafts. Living spaces often had a collection of pillows on the floor, which served as the smoking area for pot parties. Colorful beads in doorways separated spaces, and mats were used in lieu of beds. It is interesting to note that hippies chose to use mats at the same time George Harrison of the Beatles traveled to India to study Eastern religions.

Tie-dyed fabrics, **Pop Art,** and the flowing bubbles in **lava lamps** seemed to be perfect for staring at when stoned. The Volkswagen Bus became a home for hippies and was filled with the same decorative furnishings used in other dwellings. It was a vehicle of choice for the hippies for various ideological reasons, such as being built in Germany rather than by a U.S. company that was owned by the "establishment." The Bus accommodated a communal lifestyle by allowing people to travel and live in the Bus in groups. The Bus was also easy to repair, which enabled hippies to be self-reliant.

Many of the colors, forms, objects, and nonconventional attitudes and music of the hippies were reflected in furnishing fabrics designed by Maiji Isola for Marimekko (Finnish translation: Mary's dress) (Figure 8.17). The Finnish company Marimekko was started by textile artist Armi Ratia in 1951. Ratia's approach to

Figure 8.17 Many of the colors, forms, objects, and nonconventional attitudes of the hippies were reflected in furnishing fabrics designed by Maiji Isola for Marimekko. This fabric is Isola's *Unikko* pattern (1964).

Source: Marimekko Corporation.

creating decorative arts and fashion for everyday life was to empower textile artists. Printed fabrics were designed by full-time and freelance artists. Ratia provided the artists with the freedom to use their creativity and discretion in creating designs that were innovative while reflecting Finnish traditions. To create "beautiful things for everyday life" within a "complete environment," Ratia concentrated on fabrics, fashion, and architecture. Maiji Isola was one of Marimekko's most successful and prolific textile artists. During her 38-year career, Isola created more than 500 designs for Marimekko.

Isola's printed fabric designs in the 1960s reflect many of the cultural perspectives of the Woodstock generation. In the early 1960s, Isola had an interest in Slovakian folk art and historical European textiles. Folk art inspired the Ornamentii (Ornament) series; the Barokki (Baroque) series reflected historical textiles. Patterns included in the Ornamentii series were the lacy designs of Pidot (Feast) (1960) and Tantsu (Country Dance) (1960). The intricate patterns used in both series tended to resemble the small floral designs in the loose shirts worn by the hippies and the posters for psychedelic rock musicians such as Jimi Hendrix.

Isola's Joonas (Jonah) series initiated designs in large-scale, simple patterns with few but bright colors, often with a white ground. Original patterns in red, brown, or black were 98 feet (30 meters) long. The Lokki (Seagull) pattern (1961) repeated large, alternating red and white "waves." Each large-scale circle with "tentacles" of the Joonas pattern (1961) nearly filled the size of a seat cushion placed on Marimekko's Kameleontti sofa.

Large-scale patterns became **supergraphics** in Isola's Arkkitehti (Architect) series in the mid- to late 1960s. The large, stylized, bright pink and red flowers used in the Unikko (Poppy) and Kaivo (Well) patterns (1964) seem to foreshadow the flower children, and Isola's Lovelovelove pattern (1969) echoes the famous Beatles song (Figure 8.18). The pattern's repeated waves of perhaps roads or rivers were filled with apples and flowers. The design appears to symbolize the peaceful

Figure 8.18 Isola's *Lovelovelove* pattern (1969) for Marimekko echoes the famous Beatles' song.

Source: Marimekko Corporation.

and loving existence musicians were singing about. Isola repeated the dreamy, fantasizing theme and another Beatles song in the Mansikkavuoret (Strawberry Hills) pattern (1969). Billowy clouds separating supersize strawberries capture the idyllic concept of being in "strawberry fields forever."

Visual Arts: Pop Art and Andy Warhol

Billowy clouds, everyday objects, and large-scale images were also critical elements in Pop Art, a style popular in the 1960s. Pop Art began in Britain by the Independent Group at the Institute of Contemporary Art in London in the 1950s, but the style attained international fame from Pop artists in the United States, including Jasper Johns, Robert Rauschenberg, Roy Lichtenstein, and Andy Warhol (Figure 8.19). The concept of "mass" within the context of popular culture was a primary source of inspiration for Pop artists. Mass media was a subject matter and drew on material from newspapers, magazines, and television. Artistic content focused on mass obsessions related to movie stars, political leaders, sex symbols, death, dying, violence, food, drinks, shoes, comics, and money. Mass production of consumer products that were promoted with mass advertisements translated to mass-produced art. References to mass production were made by the famous Pop artist Andy Warhol with the statement "I want to be a machine."

The amazing mass quantity of paintings and film created by Warhol in a relatively short period demonstrates that he indeed worked like a machine. Warhol was well acquainted with mass consumerism and processes when he began his career in 1949 as a commercial artist in New York City. Working like a machine, he achieved success drawing advertisements for mass media. As described by Warhol, "The process of doing work in commercial art was machine-like, but the attitude had feeling to it" (McShine, 1989, p. 459). From 1949 until approximately 1957, Warhol's many drawings of shoes were advertised in newspapers and magazines, such as *Vogue*, *Glamour*, *Life*, *Seventeen*, *The New Yorker*, and *Harper's Bazaar*. He worked for companies that were selling merchandise in large cities, including Bergdorf Goodman, Bonwit Teller, I. Miller, and Tiffany & Co. However, Warhol's strongest desire was to be a serious artist.

Fundamentally, Warhol's success as an artist began with a $50 check. In the early 1960s he met an art consultant, Muriel Latow, at a party in New York City. To obtain ideas for subject matter, Warhol frequently asked people, "What should I paint?" Warhol reportedly wrote a check

for $50 after Latow told him, "What do you like most in the world? You like money. You should paint that. And you should paint something that everybody sees every day . . . like cans of soup" (Greenberg & Jordan, 2004, p. 42). Latow's $50 suggestion initiated Warhol's paintings of Campbell's soup cans and drawings of $1 and $2 bills. In following the popular style of the Abstract Expressionist artists (see Chapter 6), some of the paintings had "drips," but Warhol soon developed his own style. He became famous for 32 works of *Campbell's Soup Cans* (1962). Each of the synthetic polymer paint on canvas works was 20 by 16 inches (50.8 by 40.6 centimeters). The installation was a perfectly spaced grid consisting of four rows and eight columns. One message from Pop artists was that people could be fooled by ordinary objects. At first glance the repetitive soup can images look alike, but a closer inspection reveals that each can's label lists a different type of soup.

Repetitive paintings of everyday images and symbols became synonymous with Pop Art. Warhol created many other paintings of soup cans, including cans with big, torn labels; cans with small, torn labels; cans being opened; cans with dollar bills; crushed cans; soup boxes; and tomato soup cans redesigned in psychedelic colors. The Campbell's soup can series attained a unique emphasis when mass quantities were presented in large scale. Warhol's *Two Hundred Campbell's Soup Cans* (1962) and *One Hundred Cans* (1962) featured large-scale proportions. The overall size of the 200 images of different types of Campbell's soup was 72 by 100 inches (182.9 by 254 centimeters). One hundred cans of "Beef Noodle" soup measured 72 by 52 inches (182.9 by 132.1 centimeters).

Warhol continued painting mass images on large canvases. However, the subject matter expanded to other images that people see every day. Movie stars, sex symbols, and disasters became material for numerous of his paintings. In echoing mass media's obsession with the death of famous people, Warhol created many paintings of Marilyn Monroe after her suicide, and images of Jackie Kennedy and the assassination of

Figure 8.19 Philip Johnson collected Pop Art and exhibited the pieces in a gallery built next to his *Glass House* in Connecticut. From left to right, the paintings are *Portrait of Philip Johnson* (1982) by Andy Warhol, Roy Lichtenstein's *Girl with Ball* (1961) and *Studio Wall* (1973), and Frank Stella's *Abra Variation I* (1969).

Source: Richard Payne; *Portrait of Philip Johnson* © 2009 The Andy Warhol Foundation for the Visual Arts/ARS, New York; *Girl with Ball* and *Studio Wall* © Estate of Roy Lichtenstein; *Abra Variation I* © 2009 Frank Stella/ARS, New York.

President John F. Kennedy in 1963. Warhol's multiple paintings of Marilyn Monroe focused on her head and lips. *Gold Marilyn Monroe* (1962) had garish colors that were somewhat smeared over her eyelids, lips, and hair. Many paintings of her had multiple images of the same photograph, but half of the work was in color and the other side was black and white. Warhol's *Sixteen Jackies* (1964) had four photographs of the former First Lady repeated four times. The images included two photographs of Jackie prior to the assassination and two photographs after Kennedy's death.

Warhol's *Death and Disaster* series (1962–1968) continued a focus on death and dying. Paintings had repetitive images of people dying by violent means, including falling from a high-rise, car crashes, a fatal ambulance crash, and a photograph of an electric chair. After the *Death and Disaster* series, Warhol had his own experience with violence when Valerie Solanis, an acquaintance, shot him in his New York studio, The Factory, in 1968. The near-fatal wound required life-saving surgery and months of recovery.

Warhol's shocking photographs and gaudy colors had an even greater impact when the images were repeated on large canvases. Perfecting the commercial-silkscreen printing process enabled Warhol to create large-scale paintings in mass quantities. These large-scale paintings had an impact on interior environments. Traditional room sizes were not appropriate for the enormous canvases. For example, as an art collector, architect Philip Johnson had to solve the problem of displaying his extensive collection of contemporary art, which included paintings by Warhol, Roy Lichtenstein, and Frank Stella (Figure 8.19). Johnson purchased *Gold Marilyn Monroe* (1962) for $800 at Warhol's first show in New York City. To house his collection of large-scale paintings, Johnson designed a gallery at his Glass House (1949). To avoid competing with the iconic residence, Johnson designed an underground painting gallery (see Figure 8.19).

In addition to design with large-scale canvases in mind, architects and interior designers were influenced by Pop Art in other ways. For example, furniture was designed using everyday images and objects. The beanbag lounge chair, Sacco (Sack) (1968), was designed by Piero Gatti, Cesare Paolini, and Franco Teodoro. In 1970, Paolo Lomazzi, Donato D'Urbino, and Jonathan De Pas created Joe Sofa, the oversized baseball-glove chair made of polyurethane covered in leather. The chair/sofa was named for Joe DiMaggio, the baseball player who had been married to Marilyn Monroe in 1954. A large-scale ribbon became a chair designed by Pierre Paulin in 1966. Studio 65 designed a sofa in the shape of Marilyn Monroe's red lips. Light fixtures were made of large-scale pills, vacuum cleaner hoses, automobile headlights, and parts from fishing poles.

Warhol directly became involved with interior furnishings when he designed Cow Wallpaper (1966) for the Galerie Ileana Sonnabend in Paris (Figure 8.20). Expanded interest in the Cow Wallpaper was evident in the gallery installation at Leo Castelli, New York, in 1966, and Warhol's new colors (brown and yellow) of

Figure 8.20 Andy Warhol's *Cow Wallpaper*.

Source: Digital Image © The Museum of Modern Art/Licensed by SCALA/Art Resource, NY.

the cow and its background (blue and purple) in 1971 and 1976.

GLOBAL BUSINESS AND ECONOMICS

Inflation, or the level of consumer prices against the purchasing power of money, rose during the 1960s from below 2 percent in the early part of the decade to 7 percent in 1969. Despite the inflationary circumstances, several entrepreneurs founded businesses during the decade that became extremely successful. Sam Walton opened the first Wal-Mart discount store in Bentonville, Arkansas, in 1962. As described in this section, in Italy there were several innovative businesses that were willing to invest in plastic technologies as well as other contemporary materials. The Italian industrial- and furniture-design industries were eventually honored for those accomplishments and contributions at a special exhibition at the Museum of Modern Art (MoMA) in New York City. Business developments also stimulated the need for more office space and buildings. The furniture industry

responded by designing and manufacturing new office systems that accommodated contemporary open office layouts. The need for more office space was evidenced by the groundbreaking of the World Trade Center office building complex in New York City in 1966.

Italian Manufacturers: Collection of Modern Designs

In 1972, the MoMA in New York produced the exhibition "Italy: The New Domestic Landscape." The director of the exhibition, Emilio Ambasz, provided the following explanation for the show:

> *. . . to recognize the cultural achievements of modern Italian design, to honor the accomplishments of Italy's gifted designers, and, by presenting a selection of the most outstanding examples of their works during the last decade, to illustrate the diversity of their approach to design. We have also wanted to stress that Italian design is important not solely because of its remarkable formal production, but also because of the high level of critical consciousness. (Ambasz, 1972, p. 419)*

"The last decade" refers to an amazing collection of designs that were primarily created in the 1960s. To create "the cultural achievements of modern Italian design" required gifted designers and visionary leaders in the Italian Industrial and Furniture Design Industry. Ambasz referenced this fact by acknowledging Italy's "remarkable formal production." The world has since become accustomed to the Italian designs created in the 1960s; however, in the immediate postwar years, modern designs required the development of new industrial production processes. Without the commitment, financial investment, and risk-taking initiatives of several Italian manufacturers, MoMA would not have been able to "recognize the cultural achievements of modern Italian design."

Italian manufacturers created "workshop" laboratories that allowed designers to collaborate with factory engineers. To produce the new, modern designs, companies worked with their suppliers as well as other manufacturers. Designers were inspired by new plastics, Pop Art, and space exploration. The creation of innovative products required capital investments, research, experimentation, and a willingness to make unforeseen and expensive adaptations to manufacturing equipment. The Italian manufacturers that accepted the risks and were willing to invest in new production processes were featured in the MoMA exhibition. The "Collaborators in the Exhibition" included Artemide, Cassina & Buselli (C & B) Italia, Centro Cassina, Citroën, Kartell, Pirelli, Saporiti, and Sleeping International System Italia (SISI).

The accomplishments of the Italian manufacturing industries were presented in the exhibition's "Objects" division. The products were selected for their "formal and technical means." Nearly all of the objects were produced in the 1960s, and, in following the requirements of the exhibition, the products were designed to be mass produced (Figure 8.21). Demonstrating

Figure 8.21 *Jarama* chair and table (1969) by Alberto Rosselli.

Source: Digital Image © The Museum of Modern Art/Licensed by SCALA/Art Resource, NY.

technological advances, almost all of the objects were made of some type of plastic, including ABS plastic, PVC plastic, reinforced polyester, fiberglass, polyurethane, and melamine. Furniture included puffy lounge chairs, plastic armchairs, an inflatable armchair, various folding chairs, stackable chairs, desks, folding tables, stacking storage units, and stacking shelves.

Light fixtures were made from lacquered metals, aluminum, or ABS plastic (Figure 8.22). The collection included the iconic Arco (Arc) (1962) floor lamp designed by Achille and Pier Castiglioni. Arco is well known for its rectangular-shaped marble base, stainless-steel shade, and a hole in its base the size of a broomstick. The purpose of the hole was to make it easier to move the heavy fixture. Other objects in this category were televisions, record players, portable radios, clocks, dishes, ashtrays, a red Olivetti typewriter, utensils, desk accessories, and vases.

In addition to the Italian manufacturers that were "collaborators" in the exhibition, other companies were engaged in progressive production processes with Italian designers. For example, Italian industrialist Dino Gavina had a profound impact on modern Italian design by founding successful manufacturing companies. In 1960 he started Gavina SpA and appointed designer Carlo Scarpa as the president of the company. Gavina entered into a contract with Marcel Breuer to manufacture Breuer's 1920s tubular furniture (see Chapter 4), including his Cesca (1928) chair and the Wassily (1925) chair, a name suggested by Gavina. The company also manufactured and exported other furniture designed by Breuer and many other designers who became internationally renowned, including Kazuhide Takahama, Vico Magistretti, Marco Zanuso, Richard Sapper, Tobia Scarpa (son of Carlo Scarpa), and Achille and Pier Giacomo Castiglioni. In 1968, Gavina sold Gavina SpA to the Knoll Company.

To create quality lighting fixtures in 1962, Gavina and Cesare Cassina formed the company Flos. The Flos Company has been enormously successful by

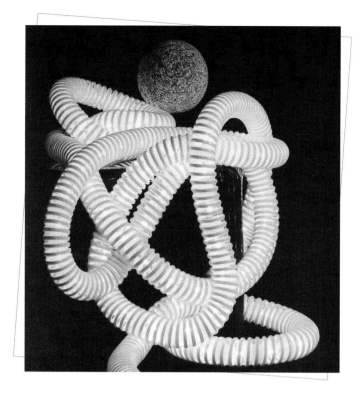

Figure 8.22 A futuristic flexible luminaire, *Boalum* (1969), designed by Gianfranco Frattini and Livio Castiglioni. Displayed at the Museum of Modern Art's exhibition, "Italy: The New Domestic Landscape."

Source: Digital Image © The Museum of Modern Art/Licensed by SCALA/Art Resource, NY.

manufacturing numerous luminaires designed by accomplished designers. Many of the Flos luminaires have become contemporary classics. Celebrated light fixtures produced by Flos include several designs by Achille and Pier Giacomo Castiglioni, such as Viscontea (1960), Toio (1962), Taraxacum (1960), Splügen Bräu (1961), Taccia (1962), and Arco (1962). After selling Gavina SpA, Gavina founded Simon International, a manufacturing company that started producing Ultrarazionale (Ultra-rationale), furniture designed to move beyond the rationalist perspective. Other projects continuing into the 1970s were Ultramobile (Ultra-furniture), Metamobile (Meta-furniture), and Paradisoterrestre (Heaven-on-Earth).

The Service Sector and Corporations: The Office Building and Space Planning

The 1960s witnessed the creation and expansion of many international companies that required additional office buildings. Examples of these companies are Thorn Electrical Industries, London; Chase Manhattan Bank, New York City; Pirelli, Milan; and C. F. Boehringer & Söhne in Germany. Demands for office buildings and qualified employees were precipitated by industrialization and advances in the service industries (see Chapters 1, 2, and 5). Companies that were expanding during this time and required large office buildings included banks, investment corporations, marketing firms, insurance companies, and large manufacturers. During the late 1950s and early 1960s, numerous office buildings were built in New York City, London, Chicago, Germany, Japan, Italy, and the Scandinavian countries (Figure 8.23). Corporations' need for office buildings and well-designed environments had an enormous impact on interior environments, architecture, and the interior design profession. Generally, office buildings were built for one major occupant, such as an administration building for the Chase Manhattan Bank or the headquarters building for CBS. As a reflection of the high number of construction projects, by the early 1960s books and magazines were published that featured the designs of new office buildings throughout the world.

By the 1960s, office furniture and equipment had changed radically from the rigidity that had been the norm since the turn of the century. A brief review of historical office design helps provide an understanding of the dramatic changes between offices in the 1920s and the 1960s. In the 1920s, mechanical engineer and writer Frederick Taylor's (see Chapter 3) *The Principles of Scientific Management* (1911), which had been used to improve productivity in factories, was adapted to the office environment. For example, Leffingwell's 1925 book *Office Management Principles and Practices* proposed efficient practices for office management that were based on Taylor's principles. W. H. Leffingwell was an engineer, a member of *The Taylor Society*, and a consultant to office managers. Leffingwell's 1925 book included "efficient practices," such as stenographers' desks that were adjustable by placing the desk and chair on

Figure 8.23 An "open layout" office in the Lever House Building designed by SOM. During the 1950s and early 1960s, numerous office buildings were built in major cities.

Source: © Ezra Stoller/Esto.

pedestals. To change from a sitting to a standing position, the occupant rolled the chair off the pedestal. Roll-top desks were eventually phased out of the office environment because the desks' pigeonholes were a convenient place to lose, hide, or forget papers. Furthermore, the tall back on roll-top desks obstructed the views of supervisors. A "modern efficiency desk" had a flat surface with three small drawers. Office training manuals included descriptions of the mandatory contents of each drawer. To avoid "gossip and chatter," W. H. Leffingwell suggested an 8-foot-high (2.44-meter) partition between typists. The very small space within the cubicle could only accommodate a desk and the typist's chair. Eventually, an adjustable typist chair was made with padded support for the small of the back.

In 1950, to compete with the opportunities offered by higher-paying industrial work, Leffingwell coauthored with Edwin Robinson another edition of office management, which included chapters on "Working Conditions," "The Office Worker and His Job," "Providing Office Space," and "The Office Manual" (1950, p. xiii). The 1950 edition included black-and-white photographs of the new modern office. For example, to create a better work environment, Leffingwell and Robinson suggested eliminating any "distracting

influences" by having plain walls, a clean desk, and minimal furniture and equipment (1950, p. 17). They suggested that an office manager should provide a "desk that fits the worker" by having "interchangeable units" (1950, p. 266). This arrangement would allow the office manager to "fit the desk to the clerk, instead of fitting the clerk to the desk, and at the same time secure a desirable appearance" (1950, p. 266). A photograph in the book illustrates an L-shaped secretarial unit that was designed to accommodate a proper arrangement for typing by having the typewriter at a lower level than the desk surface. Leffinwell and Robinson also suggested that to "visualize the flow of work and show how suggested changes might affect" the space an office manager could position scaled wooden blocks (furniture and equipment) on a sheet of plywood (modern space planning).

In 1962, to help building owners and architects understand how to design new office interiors, German architectural theorist and writer Jürgen Joedicke wrote *Office Buildings*. The book included examples of new office buildings and covered topics for office planning, such as "The Structure," "External Wall Construction," and "Heating, Air-Conditioning and Lighting." Joedicke's book discussed the details of designing and constructing modern offices that met the needs of corporations.

In the first chapter the author provided numerous line drawings that illustrated planning suggestions for low, medium, and high multi-story structures. He included layouts and arrangements for the offices, corridors, and utility cores. Examples included minimum spacing of office desks, depths of rooms, orientation exposures, and module arrangements. Joedicke divided the "room units in office buildings" into two categories: "individual-room system" and "open layout."

Photographs of an "individual-room system" illustrate an office environment with minimal furniture: a modest-size desk, a credenza, and a small stand for the telephone. The space had an additional area that was designated for an assistant or conferences. The large windows in the office provided significant levels of natural daylight, and artificial illumination was supplied from suspended light fixtures. Joedicke provided the following explanation for the open layout: "This system permits better utilization of the available space, cuts out the considerable cost of installing and rearranging movable partitions, facilitates supervision of employees, and permits much more economical lighting installations. Noise is a disadvantage of the open layout; it can, of course, be mitigated by suitable design of the ceilings and walls, but it cannot be eliminated entirely" (Joedicke, 1962, p. 17). Joedicke's examples of the open layout included offices in New York City's Lever House Building and the Connecticut General Life Insurance Company Building in Bloomfield, Connecticut. Both office buildings were designed by Skidmore, Owings, & Merrill (SOM).

As discussed in the office books, managers decided to create pleasant work environments to help attract and keep qualified employees. The industrial appearance of offices was therefore eliminated over time; the modern office interiors featured a comfortable, residential appearance. Dramatic improvements occurred in the design of furniture and office equipment. **Contract** became the term for commercial interior design, and the concept was reinforced by the first *Contract* magazine publication in 1960. Office buildings illustrated in magazines included bright colors, artwork, and supergraphics. To reduce the glare from the glass walls of buildings, casement, or sheer fabrics for window treatments, became very popular.

In 1968 the Herman Miller Company introduced Action Office, the first open-plan **furniture system,** a transformational system of panels and components designed by Robert Propst (Figure 8.24) that allowed the physical office environment to be changed easily. The **open office layout** created large, open spaces for groups of office workers. The open office layout became a "landscaped office" by eliminating traditional grid patterns and adding other amenities associated with residential interiors, such as carpeting throughout the building. German company Quickborner Team played a significant role in developing office landscaping by planning an office to facilitate communication, paper flow, and tasks. The company started in the late 1950s, and by the late 1960s its esteemed reputation in Europe enabled it to open a subsidiary in Milburn, New Jersey. The Quickborner Team continues to be responsible for projects throughout the world today.

Figure 8.24 In 1968, Herman Miller introduced Action Office, the first open-plan furniture system originally designed by Robert Propst. The transformational system of panels and components enabled management to easily change the office environment.

Source: Herman Miller, Inc.

SUMMARY

The 1960s were a decade filled with numerous advances in interior environments and architecture and reflected the results of the long building process required after the destruction during World War II. India attained its independence from British rule, and as a consequence Indian officials determined that the city of Chandigarh would become the new capital of the state of Punjab. Le Corbusier was commissioned to design the entire urban site, including the size of sectors, a road classification system, commercial districts, government buildings, industrial areas, and recreational areas. As Le Corbusier and colleagues Pierre Jeanneret, Jane Drew, and Maxwell Fry were planning Chandigarh, architects Lúcio Costa and Oscar Niemeyer were in Brazil creating Brasília, the new capital city. Niemeyer's subsequent exile from Brazil coincided with Algeria's independence from France. Niemeyer traveled to Africa and was invited to design a new university in the city of Constantine in Algeria.

Luis Barragán's designs also reflected the beauty of North Africa and the Mediterranean Sea. Essential to Barragán's work was a serene connection between nature, architecture, and people, as demonstrated in his designs for subdivisions and developments in Mexico. The Danish architect Jørn Utzon was also inspired by Moroccan architecture and the pre-Columbian pyramids in Mexico. These images, as well as references to white *sails* and *shells*, were reflected in Utzon's masterpiece, the Sydney Opera House in Australia.

For centuries, civilizations have been intrigued with exploring the universe. The 1960s saw the development and escalation of the Cold War between the United States and the Soviet Union, as well as a competition between the two nations for the lead in space travel and exploration. One element of these programs was considering the possibility of creating colonies in space. The U.S. version of a space station was Skylab. To help resolve interior design concerns, officials hired Loewy Company as "habitability" consultants. Ray Loewy's designs for Skylab would not have been able to meet NASA's criteria without using plastics, which were gaining prominence in the world of manufacturing at the time and were made by using heat to melt plastic chips or pellets. As plastic materials and processing methods were being developed, Italian artist and designer Joe Colombo experimented with various resins and applied the processes to numerous futuristic designs.

In the United States, Eero Saarinen was involved with human behavior research that he applied to the design of the John Deere & Company Headquarters, demonstrating a thorough understanding of the needs of his client and the company's employees. In 1964, the Summer Olympics were held in Tokyo, Japan. Architect Kenzo Tange and engineers Yoshikatsu Tsuboi and Uichi Inove were commissioned to design the National Gymnasiums for the Olympics (1961–1964). The gymnasium complex included two stadiums, gardens, a promenade, parking lot, and two subway stations. A close examination of the National Gymnasium complex and Tange's book, *Katsura* (1960), written roughly during the same period, illustrates many parallels between the complex he designed and the Palace of Katsura, which had been constructed centuries earlier in Japan.

Many events in the 1960s affected Western performing arts, which subsequently impacted the design of interior environments. Some of the colors, forms, objects, and nonconventional attitudes of the members of the baby boom generation (who were going through adolescence then) were reflected in furnishing fabrics designed by Maiji Isola for Marimekko. Pop Art, with mass media as a subject matter, used material from newspapers, magazines, and television as launching points for some creations. Artistic content focused on mass obsessions related to movie stars, political leaders, food, and many other products and interests. In contrast, Italian designers and manufacturers made more long-lasting, significant contributions to the world of interior design during the 1960s; these achievements were celebrated at a MoMA exhibit in 1972.

The postwar years also featured the creation and rapid growth of international companies, which led to a demand for more office buildings and employees. By the 1960s, office furniture and equipment had changed radically from the rigidity that had been the norm at the turn of the century. Commercial interior design was given the term "contract." In 1968, the Herman Miller Company introduced Action Office, the first open-plan furniture system.

KEY TERMS

ABS (acrylonitrile-butadiene-styrene)

acrylic

calendaring

casting

cellulose acetate

contract

epoxy

extrusion

foaming

furniture system

laminating

lava lamps

LEDs (light-emitting diodes)

luminaires

melamine

molding

molten plastic

open office layout

parasol

podium

polycarbonate

polypropylene

polystyrene

polyurethane

polyvinyl chloride (PVC)

Pop Art

supergraphics

thermoforming

thermoplastic

thermosetting plastics

EXERCISES

1. Philosophy and Design Project. To develop a project, Le Corbusier spent considerable time understanding the site, the people, and their customs and philosophies. Corbu traveled in India and sketched impressions of the country. Select a local site and research the community, the people, and their customs and philosophies. Sketch multiple impressions of the site and images of the community. Develop designs that are inspired by the site, the community, and the people. Write a report that includes drawings, sketches, and a synopsis of the community.

2. Research Design Project. Research several international space programs. Identify materials and products that could be applied to the built environment. In addition, identify solutions for living in a compact environment for an extended period. As a "habitability" consultant, provide recommendations and sketches of the proposed built environment. Summarize your findings in a written report and provide suggestions for an oral presentation. The report and sketches should include solutions based on international space programs. In a team with other students, prepare a presentation that is supported with visual materials.

3. Human Factors Research Project. When Eero Saarinen worked on a project, he was known for gathering research data and then applying the information to create hundreds of sketches, models, and mock-ups. Saarinen intently studied every prototype and identified better solutions. This was the process he used for the John Deere & Company Headquarters. Identify a project in a studio class, and in a team of designers create numerous sketches, models, and mock-ups of the building and record reactions to the changes in a journal. The entries should identify positive as well as negative reactions. Record your team's activities and reactions, and develop an evaluation of how your designs changed as the number of drawings and sketches increased over time. Write a report that summarizes your observations and include recommendations for future practice. The report must include sketches, models, and mock-ups.

CHAPTER 9

EMPHASIS: THE 1970S

OBJECTIVES

After reading this chapter, you should be able to describe and analyze:

■ How selected global political events in the 1970s affected interior environments and architecture as evident by Vietnamese housing conditions and the extensive project, Sher-E-Banglanagar in Dacca, Bangladesh.

■ How natural environmental conditions affected selected global interior environments and architecture in the 1970s as evident by energy-conservation initiatives in response to the 1973 oil crisis and excavations in Mexico City and China.

■ How selected global technologies and materials in the 1970s affected interior environments and architecture as evident by computer-aided drafting/computer-aided manufacturing (CAD/CAM) programs and the exposure of mechanical systems at the Centre Georges Pompidou (Beaubourg) in Paris.

■ How selected global work styles and lifestyles in the 1970s affected interior environments and architecture, as evident by public housing policies in the United States, Australia, and South Africa.

■ How selected global visual arts and performing arts in the 1970s affected interior environments and architecture as evident by disco clubs, the Institute for Music/Acoustic Research and Coordination (IRCAM) in Paris, and temporary vast-scale wrapped buildings.

■ How selected global business developments and economics in the 1970s affected interior environments and architecture as evident by commissions sponsored by the Cummins Engine Company, the Sears Tower (modern Willis Tower) in Chicago, and the CN Tower in Toronto.

■ How to compare and contrast selected interior environments and architecture of the Americas, Asia/Oceania, Europe, and the Middle East/Africa in the 1970s.

The Cold War continued through the 1970s; however, beginning in 1972, the Soviet Union and the United States began negotiations to limit their military arsenals. The Vietnam War ended in 1975, when North Vietnamese troops took control of South Vietnam as U.S. troops withdrew from the country. This resulted in thousands of South Vietnamese refugees who became "boat people" for several years after the war. Thousands of people died at sea, and the newly formed communist government sent thousands of people who supported the South Vietnamese to refugee camps. Several nations won their independence from colonial rule during the decade. In 1975, Portugal relinquished control of Mozambique, Cape Verde, São Tomé and Príncipe, and Angola. In 1979, St. Lucia, Vincent, and the Grenadines gained independence from Great Britain.

The 1970s also saw numerous human-caused events that had severe negative impacts on the natural environment. Most notable was the nuclear disaster after a fire in a reactor at Three Mile Island, Pennsylvania (1979), and oil tankers that spilled hundreds of thousands of gallons of petroleum into waterways, such as the groundings of the *Urquiola* at La Coruña, Spain, in 1976 and the *Amoco Cadiz* at Portsall, Brittany, France, in 1978. Natural disasters made their mark on the decade as well. A cyclone in East Pakistan (modern Bangladesh) killed 500,000 people in 1970, and in 1976 an earthquake centered northeast of Beijing, registering 8.3 on the Richter scale, killed 655,000 in China. The natural environment benefited from the consciousness-raising event known as Earth Day, first celebrated in 1970. By the end of the decade, the world population reached 4.4 billion.

The 1970s can be seen as the era when the modern world began to step into the digital and electronic age. Transistors and integrated circuits provided the technologies for many new consumer electronics, such as the Texas instrument pocket calculator in 1971 and the first desktop computer, MITS *Altair*, in 1975. Other inventions included the floppy disk in 1971, ink-jet printers in 1976, and the first cellular mobile phone system,

developed by AT&T and Bell Labs in 1978. The development of the microprocessor stimulated the progress of home computers and helped launch Microsoft Corporation and Apple Computer. Computer-aided design/computer-aided manufacturing (CAD/CAM) was introduced to industry in the 1970s. Technology was featured in the bold design for the Centre Georges Pompidou cultural and artistic complex in Paris.

The decade also saw an increase in terrorism, the use or threatened use of force or violence, often as part of a policy or ideology of violence, by a person or an organized group. Terrorist acts usually are committed for political or ideological reasons with the intent to intimidate or cause terror in order to coerce other groups or governments. During the 1970s, there were bombings (Irish Republican Army [IRA] terrorists bombed the Tower of London and the British House of Parliament in 1974), hijackings, and numerous people held hostage in various parts of the world. In 1976, Palestinian and West German terrorists hijacked an Air France aircraft traveling to Paris from Athens. The terrorists demanded a diversion to an airport in Uganda and held over 100 hostages. Three hostages were killed when the Israel Defense Forces raided the plane.

These terrorist acts have forced officials, interior designers, and architects to reanalyze their roles and responsibilities in the design of the built environment. Conventional approaches used in the design process had to be supplemented with solutions that would deter terrorists and reduce injuries in the event of an attack. On the economic front, the 1970s saw global inflation, recessions, high interest rates, and unemployment. These conditions affected the housing industry and contributed to severe problems in **public housing projects** in the United States. In South Africa, the segregation system known as apartheid continued to cause hardship and violence for the country's people.

Rock festivals like Woodstock faded in the early 1970s and were replaced by the short-lived disco craze, which drove demand for the creation of disco dance clubs throughout the United States as well as in many other countries. At the other end of the spectrum, scientific research into music and ideal acoustic conditions was advanced by the construction of a building for the Institute for Music/Acoustic Research and Coordination (IRCAM) in Paris. As has been the case throughout history, in the 1970s artists of all types looked to the outdoors for their inspiration. Site-specific art installations were created in valleys, waterways, and grassy fields. Outdoor sculptural artists Christo and Jeanne-Claude became internationally known for their temporary vast-scale natural and urban environment projects, which included wrapped or covered monuments (Wrapped Monuments, Milan, 1970), objects (The Wall, Rome, 1972), and landscape (Valley Curtain, Rifle, Colorado, 1972).

In the fields of business, technology, and industry, Japan continued strong economic growth through the sales of fuel-efficient automobiles and innovative consumer electronics. In a continuation of tradition begun earlier in the century, many corporations commissioned internationally renowned architects and designers to create their corporate headquarters. One competitive aspect was the perception that the taller the structure, the more successful the corporation. Thus, some of the tallest structures in the world were completed in the 1970s, including the World Trade Center's twin towers in New York City (1973), Chicago's Sears Tower (modern Willis Tower) (1973), and the CN Tower in Toronto (1976).

GLOBAL POLITICS AND GOVERNMENT

Many political and military struggles of the 1960s continued into the next decade. The Cold War struggle between capitalist and Communist countries still existed in the 1970s, and fighting continued in the Middle East and Vietnam. After decades of Cold War anxiety, the Soviet Union and the United States initiated discussions for nuclear arms limitations in 1972. The United States withdrew its last troops from Vietnam in 1975, and communists took control of Saigon (which had been the capital of the Republic of South Vietnam) and renamed it Ho Chi Minh City in honor of the North Vietnamese ruler. The country was reunited under communism. During this period, genocide occurred in the neighboring country of Cambodia. The Khmer Rouge guerrilla movement under leader Pol Pot seized power of the nation and killed over two million civilians. After Pol Pot was overthrown by the Vietnamese in 1979, mounds of skeletal remains were found throughout the countryside.

One highlight of the decade was that colonial rule essentially ended after several nations, including Guinea-Bissau, Angola, Mozambique, Qatar, Sierra Leone, Bangladesh, Suriname, and Seychelles, won their independence. The decade ended with the Camp David Accords, brokered by President Jimmy Carter, signed by Israeli Prime Minister Menachem Begin and Egyptian president Anwar el-Sādāt, which led to the 1979 Israel-Egypt Peace Treaty. In 1979, Ayatollah Ruhollah Khomeini returned to Tehran, Iran, and became imam (successor to Muhammad).

The Vietnam War: Boat People and Refugee Camps

Vietnam, an S-shaped country in Southeast Asia, is bordered by the South China Sea along its east coast. China lies to the north, and Laos and Cambodia share Vietnam's western border. The combined countries of Vietnam, Laos, and Cambodia are sometimes referred to as Indochina. The French took control of the country as a colony in the 1800s (1859–1940). Germany's takeover of France during World War II made it possible for Japan to take control of Vietnam. After the war, Japan withdrew, but France was not able to adequately assert itself to retake control. France fought with the Vietnamese to regain control of Vietnam but was defeated by the Vietnamese in the First Indochina War (1946–1954). The conflict was resolved with an agreement, created at an international conference in Geneva 1954, which "temporarily" divided the country into north and south. Reunification elections were scheduled for 1956 but were never held. Fears about the domino effect of communism that were pervasive during the Cold War prompted President Dwight D. Eisenhower to send U.S. military advisors to South Vietnam in the 1950s.

Eisenhower's successor, President John F. Kennedy, sent more advisors, financial assistance, and significant military equipment. Following the assassination of President Kennedy in 1963, President Lyndon Johnson became involved with Vietnam. Over 500,000 U.S. combat troops were in Vietnam by 1969. Sending combat troops to Vietnam prompted immediate antiwar demonstrations in Washington, D.C., followed by protests in New York, San Francisco, and Chicago. Opposition to the war escalated, and eventually, political pressure forced President Nixon to initiate a peace treaty with North Vietnam. The Paris Peace Accords were signed on January 27, 1973, which stipulated a cease-fire and the withdrawal of U.S. combat troops from Vietnam.

Estimates vary of the number of soldiers and civilians killed, wounded, captured, and orphaned during the Vietnam War. The U.S. military has reported that more than 57,000 U.S. soldiers were killed, and approximately 300,000 were estimated wounded. The combined estimated losses for North and South Vietnamese were 1.2 million soldiers killed, over 1.6 million wounded, and 26,000 captured. The number of Vietnamese civilian dead was nearly 2.5 million, and hundreds of thousands of children became orphans.

The war destroyed most of Vietnam's cities, villages, homes, industrial factories, and croplands (Figure 9.1). The natural environment was significantly affected by the poison dioxin (or Agent Orange, the U.S. military's code name for the chemical). The destruction of croplands was especially devastating because Vietnamese were in desperate need of food, and the country was reliant upon an agricultural economy. Residential rebuilding initiatives after the war were confined to areas perceived as safe, stable, and able to support vegetation. Agent Orange had a devastating effect on the people's ability to rebuild homes in rural areas because of the fear of building on toxic sites as well as the difficulty of finding safe vegetation, a primary material used to construct buildings. As in present day, most rural houses

Figure 9.1 Destruction from the Vietnam War.
Source: Topham/The Image Works.

in Vietnam were simple structures made with bamboo walls, wood beams, and heavily thatched grass roofs (see Figure 9.1). Wood was especially important because the Vietnamese use lumber to elevate their homes high from the ground to deter snakes, and help reduce damage from flooding and insects. As an indication of the continuing economic challenges, most rural houses are still small one- or two-room dwellings, and a frequent arrangement is for extended families to live together in multiple dwellings. These crowded arrangements are intensified by the lack of modern conveniences. Before the Vietnam War, electricity and plumbing were not common in rural Vietnamese houses, but after the war, the situation became worse because the country's infrastructure was so badly damaged and destroyed.

Prior to the Vietnam War, architecture in the cities was influenced by the countries that had colonized Vietnam. For example, for decades buildings were constructed that reflected Chinese architecture. In the 19th century, French colonizers designed Vietnamese cities with wide avenues and French Colonial architecture was the prevailing style. During the war, these buildings and others were converted to military headquarters. In Saigon (modern Ho Chi Minh City), the U.S. military used Independent Palace (modern Unification or Reunification Palace) until the city and the U.S. headquarters were attacked and taken over by the North Vietnamese in spring of 1975.

Conquering Independent Palace demonstrated the strength of the communist forces and signaled the end of the Vietnam War. The conquest was symbolic because it had been the site for Vietnamese national leaders since French government constructed the original palace (1868) during the colonial years. French governors used the palace for their home until Japan took control of Vietnam during World War II. The Japanese government occupied the palace as a military post until the French regained control of some Vietnamese cities, including Saigon. In opposition to France's interest in recapturing Vietnam, Independent

Palace was badly damaged by bombs and fighting in 1962. That same year, Prime Minister Ngo Dinh Diem ordered the demolition of the building and commissioned Ngo Viet Thu to design a new palace.

To reflect the culture of the Vietnamese people, Ngo Viet Thu incorporated Chinese symbols into the design of the new modern palace. For example, the plan view of the palace is in the shape of the Chinese character for good (ji), meaning good fortune. Architectural elements of the palace's front façade, such as the placement of columns and openings, resemble the Chinese characters for prosperity (xing) and fidelity (zhong). In 1975, after the Vietnam War, the communist government restored the palace and renamed the building Unification Palace (1962–1966), a name that represents the reunification of North and South Vietnam.

As mentioned previously, the war affected where in Vietnam the Vietnamese would be able to rebuild their homes and communities. The flood of refugees caused by the fall of Saigon created unthinkable accommodations for several years. Overcrowded and filthy boats became homes to "boat people" as they waited in the South China Sea for approval from a host country, such as Thailand, Malaysia, or the Philippines, to grant them citizenship (Figure 9.2). Their new homes on the water were basically hulls with flimsy roofs. Some boats did not have walls, and thus in their crowded conditions people were forced to stand or sit close to the edge of the boat. Generally, when walls existed, they were mounted on the sides of a boat, and ventilation and daylight were restricted to one small opening in the wall.

Roofs and walls of the new floating homes leaked, and they lacked privacy, sanitation, electricity, furniture, and adequate facilities to prepare food. Most boats were so crowded that people had to take turns standing, and it was impossible to walk around the craft. Thousands died at sea, and many had to combat pirates who assaulted the unarmed refugees. Refugee camps in Indonesia, the Philippines, Hong Kong, and Thailand also became crowded as they accepted the

Figure 9.2 When North Vietnamese captured Saigon, millions of South Vietnamese fled for their lives. Overcrowded and filthy boats became homes to "boat people."

Source: Bettmann/Corbis.

Vietnamese who had fled the country. The refugee camps often lacked adequate water, food, clothing, and health care, so, like the boat people, the refugees in camps continued to suffer for long periods.

Because the Vietnam War was divisive in the United States and the country had not been victorious, many Americans wanted to forget the war and sought to recover from the national wound. Others, however, thought it was important for the country to remember the war. At the end of the 1970s, Jan Scruggs, a Vietnam veteran, convinced Congress to approve a memorial to Vietnam veterans. Artist and architect Maya Ying Lin won the design competition for the memorial in 1981 while she was an undergraduate student at Yale University. The Vietnam Veterans Memorial ("The Wall") was built on the Mall in Washington, D.C., and dedicated in 1982. The elegant sculpture is made of polished black granite and bears the etched name of each American service person who died in the war.

War and Independence: Sher-E-Banglanagar in Dacca, Bangladesh (1962–1983), by Louis I. Kahn

Bangladesh (previously East Pakistan) in southern Asia also was affected by war in the 1970s, as well as in many previous decades and centuries. Bangladesh is a small developing country that is surrounded by India on the north, west, and east. To the south are the Bay of Bengal and a small section of Myanmar (modern Burma). As discussed in Chapter 7, one of the consequences of World War II was Britain's decision to divide Pakistan into east and west. The independent nation of Pakistan was created with regions east (East Pakistan, modern Bangladesh) and west (West Pakistan, modern Pakistan) of India. The intent was to establish Pakistan as the nation for Muslims, and India would be the home for Hindus. Pakistan's two regions were separated by India, with a land area of more than 1,000 miles (1,609.34 kilometers). Most of the financial resources, government officials, and military were already established in what became West Pakistan, but most of the people lived in East Pakistan, one of the poorest countries in the world. The new locations resulted in many cultural differences, such as different languages, customs, and ethnic backgrounds.

Tensions between East and West Pakistan escalated until war erupted in 1971. The Civil War, or the War of Independence, was fought between March and December of that year. More than one million people were killed during the battles, and millions of refugees fled to India. In addition to support from India, East Pakistan also received funds from a "nontraditional source": a former Beatle. A charitable rock concert was held at New York City's Madison Square Garden on August 1, 1971. Ravi Shankar, the world-renown Indian sitar master, organized the concert. Many rock stars performed, including George Harrison (who had been a devotee of Shankar's for several years at that point). Former Beatle Ringo Starr, Bob Dylan, and Eric Clapton also performed, and millions of dollars were raised from concert tickets, albums, and movie receipts. The funds helped East Pakistan in its fight for independence, as well as assisted the people who were trying to recover from a deadly cyclone, with subsequent tidal waves and flooding, that occurred in 1970 and killed more than 300,000 people. With military support from India, East Pakistan was able to defeat West Pakistan, and East Pakistan declared its independence at the end of 1971 and renamed itself Bangladesh.

Prior to Bangladesh's declaration of independence, the prime minister was involved in establishing the second capital of Pakistan at Dacca (modern Dhaka), East Pakistan. To explore concepts and costs for the project, government officials contacted the extremely successful American architect Louis I. Kahn in 1962. At this time, Kahn already had years of experience working as a consultant architect for the Philadelphia Housing Authority and the Philadelphia City Planning Commission. Kahn also designed renowned buildings such as the Salk Institute in the United States, but the extensive project Sher-E-Banglanagar or Sher-e-Bangla Nagar (The City of the Bengal Tiger) in Dacca, Bangladesh, and the Indian Institute of Management (1962–1974), in Ahmedabad, India, attracted international attention to Kahn's architecture.

Kahn was commissioned by the Pakistani government to design several buildings for the new governmental center in Dacca, Bangladesh. Sher-E-Banglanagar was to include several governmental buildings, including a national assembly, prayer hall, hospital, and residences for government officials. According to Kahn, initially the project in Dacca was "a Supreme Court and the program amounted to *Allow so many square feet*. There was also a prayer room asked for, with a closet for prayer rugs" (Wurman, 1986, p. 24). Kahn explained that he suggested that the original 3,000-square-foot (278.71-square-meter) prayer room should become a 30,000-square-foot (2,787.1-square-meter) mosque because he believed "A house of legislation is a religious place . . . when you enter the assembly, there is something transcendent about your view" (Wurman, 1986, p. 24).

Kahn's concept for the Dacca project was embraced by the officials. One aspect of Kahn's concept focused on the interaction between light and forms:

In the assembly I have introduced a light giving element to the interior of the plan. If you see a series of columns you can say that the choice of columns is a choice in light. Now think of it just in reverse and think that the columns are hollow and much bigger and that their walls can themselves give light, then the voids are rooms, and the column is the maker of light and can take on complex shapes and be the supporter of spaces and give light to spaces. (Tyng, 1984, p. 167)

Kahn's integration of columns, voids, and light for Sher-E-Banglanagar included the Assembly with a Prayer Hall that was accessed through the Ambulatory (Figure 9.3). Kahn also contended that the Assembly was "really the maker of the institutions" that were important for people. He explained that the Assembly "gave the right for the school to exist, for the place of health to exist, and even for the house of legislation to exist—all the institutions of man" (Wurman, 1986, p. 25).

From this perspective, Kahn divided the numerous required structures into two main areas. One group of buildings would serve the "institutions of man," and the other cluster would be "associated with the sense of legislation." Buildings in the "institutions of man" (Citadel of the Institutions) complex were schools, libraries, and cultural institutions. The "sense of legislation" (Citadel of the Assembly) structures were the Assembly, Prayer Hall, dining halls, and hostels for ministers, secretaries, and members of the Assembly. As illustrated in Figure 9.3, the architecture has a medieval fortress appearance and shares a similar sense of strength and grandeur as the Shait Gumbad Mosque (1459) in Bagerhat (ancient Khalifatabad), Bangladesh (Figure 9.4). The historic Mosque City of Bagerhat was inscribed on UNESCO's World Heritage Site in 1985. As shown in Figure 9.3, the site plan also had a lake, and Kahn wanted "nothing but grass as a setting, a great carpet in front of a strong geometry." He developed sketches, drawings, and models of Sher-E-Banglanagar

Figure 9.3 Kahn's unique design for Sher-E-Banglanagar included the Assembly Hall on the right and hostels on the left.

Source: © Le-Dung Ly/Science Faction/Corbis.

Figure 9.4 Kahn's architecture of the Assembly Hall has a medieval fortress appearance and shares a similar sense of strength and grandeur as the Shait Gumbad Mosque (1459) in Bagerhat (ancient Khalifatabad), Bangladesh.

Source: MARKA/Alamy.

in the 1960s, and in the 1970s work was halted during the Pakistani Civil War in 1971.

Bangladesh's hard-fought independence had an impact on Kahn's final design for Sher-E-Banglanagar. "I toured the land and saw what happened during time of war. They are very different people. They hold the state first, religion second. What held the East and West together was supposedly the religious agreement [shared Muslim faith], but when the East was freed from the West, they considered the country first" (Wurman, 1986, p. 235). Consequently, in the early 1970s, Kahn's preliminary drawings developed in the 1960s were modified, which included additional executive office space. The Prayer Hall remained an important element, along with the National Assembly Hall Building. In addition to reconsidering the facilities, Kahn's attention focused on Bangladesh's rainy monsoon season, which occurs annually from June until October: "I visited the land again in the height of the monsoon, and I realized how thorough the hardship is during those times when almost half the land is inundated" (Wurman, 1986, p. 234). To help resolve the problems caused by intense flooding during the monsoon, Kahn conceived that roads could be designed as bridges. "These bridges were brick bridges with arched areas. During the dry season, you can walk under them, or grow under them if you like" (Wurman, 1986, p. 235).

As with any developing country, Bangladesh lacked adequate resources for constructing buildings with modern materials, including concrete. Kahn therefore had to develop strategies that enabled buildings to be constructed using his favored material, reinforced concrete. He minimized the use of concrete to the construction of the National Assembly Hall Building. Other structures, such as the dining halls and hostels, were made with red brick, a common local material (see Figure 9.3). In addition to recognizing that the quality of the concrete work would be unsatisfactory due to the lack of skilled concrete finishers and adequate concrete forms, Kahn added marble to the design of the façades, later explaining, "But still, my choice of the marble in unison with cement is inspired technology. I wanted to recognize the fact that the concrete would not turn out well" (Wurman, 1986, p. 232) (see Figure 9.3).

A modern concrete project in Bangladesh also was intended to be an educational experience. An engineer who worked with Kahn for 18 years, August Komendant, explained, "First, we will use local architects and engineers and teach and train them from the design phase to the finished structures. Second, we will use construc-

tion methods and equipment which could be used after our work is finished" (Komendant, p. 79). The structures made of concrete with bands of marble were especially challenging given Kahn's design for double façades (see Figure 9.3). The thick outside walls were incised with slits and openings in the shapes of triangles, circles, and rectangles. The double façades are an excellent means to reduce the heat and glare from Bangladesh's intense sunlight and created interesting lighting effects. The glow from the indirect sunlight created an aura of "transcendence" within the interiors. The metal grids in the openings of the Prayer Hall's corner light wells created interesting light and shadow patterns on the plain concrete walls (Figure 9.5). The Sher-E-Banglanagar was not completed until 1983, 9 years after Kahn's death.

EFFECTS AND CONDITIONS OF THE NATURAL ENVIRONMENT

Humans and nature both affected the environment in the 1970s, but compared to the previous decade, humans had a significant impact on destroying the environment. For example, in 1979 a fire occurred in a nuclear reactor at Three Mile Island, Pennsylvania, which caused the release of radioactive gases. This disaster coincides with how the natural environment was affected by the world's growing dependence on oil. Shipments of oil resulted in two major oil tanker–related ecological disasters. The tanker *Pacific Glory* spilled 100,000 gallons of crude oil into the English Channel (1970), and *Amoco Cadiz* ran aground in Brittany (1978). The 18-mile (29 kilometers) oil slick in Brittany spread to an area 80 by 200 miles (129 by 322 kilometers) and affected 200 miles

Figure 9.5 The interior of Kahn's Prayer Hall, Sher-E-Banglanagar. The metal grids in the openings of the corner light wells created interesting light and shadow patterns on the plain concrete walls.

Source: © Shahidul Alam/Drik/Majority World/The Image Works.

(322 kilometers) of coastline. Western nations' dependency on oil became apparent during the 1973 oil crisis when the Organization of the Petroleum Exporting Countries (OPEC) stopped exporting oil to the United States and other countries.

During this decade, scientists reported in academic journals the results of their research on the continuing destruction of tropical rain forests and the increases in greenhouse gas emissions. Researchers discovered the detrimental effects of the chlorofluorocarbons (CFCs) in aerosol cans, and Sweden quickly banned aerosol cans. On the positive side, the first Earth Day was celebrated in 1970.

By the end of the decade, the world population reached 4.4 billion, and in an attempt to control its population growth, China enacted a law that restricted each family to one child. Population densities were dramatically different across the globe. For example, in 1970 the United States and Japan had 85 and 1,083 people per square mile (2.6 square kilometers), respectively.

As previously mentioned, a cyclone (a storm with very strong winds moving around a center of low pressure) in East Pakistan (modern Bangladesh) killed more than 300,000 people in 1970. In 1974, Cyclone Tracy destroyed Darwin in Northern Territory, Australia. In 1977, a cyclone in India's Bay of Bengal resulted in the deaths of 20,000 and left more than two million people homeless. In 1970, an earthquake with a magnitude of 7.9 in Peru killed 67,000. There were earthquakes in eastern Turkey in 1975 with a 6.7 magnitude and earthquakes in Ghir, in southern Iraq, in 1972. A 7.5-magnitude earthquake in Tangshan, China, killed more than 240,000 people (although some estimates put it as high as 655,000) in 1976. In the same year, there was a 7.5 earthquake in Guatemala that killed 22,000 people. But in dramatic contrast to destroying cities and buildings, archeological discoveries in the 1970s revealed that the earth had preserved the Templo Mayor in Tenochtitlán, Mexico City, and the Qin Shi Huang Mausoleum in Shaanxi Province, China.

Environmental Conditions: The Templo Mayor (Discovery 1978) in Tenochtitlán, Mexico City, Mexico, and Qin Shi Huang Mausoleum (Terracotta Warriors) (Discovery 1974–1978) in Shaanxi Province, China

Two very important archeological discoveries occurred in the 1970s. In Mexico City, the Templo Mayor (Great Temple), which had been built in the 14th century, was rediscovered, and an enormous subterranean complex including thousands of terracotta warriors was found in the Xi'an area of China. Both of these sites provide newly discovered knowledge and understanding of ancient cultures, architecture, artistic skills, building techniques, and the use of materials and colors. In addition to providing a better understanding of global cultures, placing the discoveries within the context of an era provides the background for analyzing how the rediscovered interiors, architecture, and decorative arts influenced contemporary designs. It was not until the rediscoveries in the 1970s that interior designers and architects were able to apply the designs to their practice, such as restorations and inspiration for new colors, furniture designs, and architectural elements.

Located in the heart of Mexico City, the Templo Mayor of Tenochtitlán (1324–1521) was rediscovered in 1978 by workers employed by the Electric Light Company. Tenochtitlán was on one of the many islands in Lake Texcoco. The Aztecs built a very advanced city with 500,000 inhabitants, including a ceremonial center, various temples, schools, palaces, steam baths, recreational facilities, and residential areas. As mentioned in Chapter 7, the Aztecs selected this site because they believed they were supposed to build their capital city where they witnessed an eagle devouring a snake while perched on a cactus.

In 1521, the Spanish Conquistadors, led by Hernán Cortés, destroyed Tenochtitlán and built the current Mexico City over the ruins. The rediscovery has revealed the use of stone and lava rocks for the construction of the Templo Mayor, and as with the statue at Chichén-Itzá (see Chapter 2), the city had a stone chacmool in a reclined position holding a tray. Fragments remaining on the Tenochtitlán chacmool reveal that the statue had been painted in blue and red earth colors. Other statuary included a polychrome stone Quetzalcoatl (mythical feathered serpent), standing bearers, incense burners, and a stone that was sculpted to resemble a skull rack. Aztecs used skull racks to display the heads of victims who were sacrificed during rituals. In 1987, UNESCO inscribed Mexico City's Historic Centre, which included the ruins of Tenochtitlán, on the World Heritage List. The evaluation committee noted, "from the 14th to the 19th century, Tenochtitlán, and subsequently, Mexico City, exerted decisive influence on the development of architecture, the monumental arts and the use of space first in the Aztec kingdom and later in New Spain" (UNESCO, 1986, p. 2).

China's Qin Shi Huang (221–210 BCE) Mausoleum, known also as the Terracotta Warriors, was also inscribed on UNESCO's World Heritage List in 1987 (Figure 9.6). "Because of their exceptional technical and artistic qualities, the terracotta warriors and horses, and the funerary carts in bronze are major works in the history of Chinese sculpture prior to the reign of the Han dynasty" (UNESCO, 1986, p. 2). The amazing discovery of the Terracotta Warriors occurred when a Chinese farmer found fragments while digging a well in 1974. An archeologist was sent to the site, and subsequent excavations found a total of four pits approximately 1 mile (1.5 kilometers) from the tomb of the first emperor of China, Qin Shi Huang. The four pits contained more than 8,000 life-size warriors, horses, chariots, and weapons. To protect him in the afterlife, Qin Shi Huang ordered the construction of the subterranean complex more than 2,000 years ago. Qin Shi Huang was a ruthless totalitarian, but he was responsible for many important developments in the country. Qin Shi Huang unified China in 221 BCE, and established a code of law and the Chinese coinage system, weights, measurements, and script. Qin Shi Huang also ordered the construction of a wall that subsequently became the Great Wall of China.

Figure 9.6 China's Qin Shi Huang (221–210 BCE) Mausoleum, also known as the Terracotta Warriors, was inscribed on UNESCO's World Heritage List in 1987. The amazing discovery of the Terracotta Warriors occurred when a Chinese farmer found fragments while digging a well in 1974.

Source: Tom Till/Auscape/The Image Works.

Historical records indicate that Qin Shi Huang forced 700,000 slaves to construct the funerary complex. The time required to complete the project was approximately 40 years, and in addition to the slaves, there were 85 master sculptors. Warriors were posed for battle and held weapons made with wood handles and bronze blades. There were armored and unarmored warriors, and chariots were pulled by horses (see Figure 9.6).

The entire subterranean complex was approximately 15 feet (4.7 meters) below the soil level. The floors of the pits were brick, and the wooden ceilings were covered with a grassy mat, clay plaster, and soil. Pit number one was the largest area, with 11 corridors and 6,000 warriors. Each corridor was filled with infantrymen that, depending on their military role, were either kneeling or standing. Pit number two was smaller and contained approximately 1,400 soldiers, saddle horses, and four-horse war chariots. The "command" center with the officers resided in pit number three, the smallest of the three chambers. Pit number four, totally empty, was found in the 1990s. The reasons for the empty chamber are not completely understood, but explanations center on the idea that the last pit was intended to be a sacrificial site for the soldiers who helped to construct the complex. However, historians believe the killings never occurred because the men were needed for battle.

The life-size warriors were made using mass-production processes, but each sculpture had unique facial features and expressions. The warrior's legs, arms, torso, and head were made from separate molds, fired, and then assembled at the site. Master sculptors completed details on each head, including unique hairstyles, mustaches, eyebrows, cheekbones, noses, scars, and lips. Hairstyles involved elaborate braiding and the traditional Chinese topknots. Originally, all of the items were painted, but only fragments of color exist today. Archeologists have reported that the primary colors used were green, lavender, blue, and red. Rivets on amours were painted white, red, and light green. Cords were purple and orange, and some shoes were black with red ties.

In addition to the magnificent terracotta figures, the funerary complex included two large bronze chariots (Figure 9.7). The chariots exemplify Chinese mastery of metalwork more than 2,000 years ago and provide insights regarding their sense of proportion and scale, as seen in the dimensions and divisions of the chariot in Figure 9.7. The broad parasol appears to gently hover over the body of the chariot. Remaining color fragments reveal that the chariots were gilded and the

Figure 9.7 The Terracotta Warriors funerary complex included bronze chariots. The chariots exemplify Chinese mastery of metalwork over 2,000 years ago.
Source: © Aldo Pavan/Grand Tour/Corbis.

horses were highly ornamented. The public is able to view the chariots displayed at the Shaanxi Provincial Museum. Pit number one has been enclosed and is also open to the public, but to protect the contents until archeologists can conduct proper excavations, the government re-covered pit numbers two and three.

Nonrenewable Natural Resources: The 1973 Oil Crisis and Energy-Conservation Initiatives

The finite quantity of *natural resources*, such as oil and natural gas, has forced nations and individuals to develop conservation practices and policies. To sustain natural resources, engineers, scientists, architects, and interior designers have been applying new and old technologies to the designs of the built environment. As discussed in this section, developments include architectural and interior designs that incorporate renewable forms of energy, including solar, wind, water, and geothermal. Conservation technologies also include energy-efficient windows, earth-sheltered housing, and passive solar interiors.

It can be argued that the adverse environmental consequences of the Industrial Revolution began to appear during the economic boom in the 1970s. Increases in demands for transportation, heating, electric energy, and consumer products caused significant rises in the consumption of **fossil fuels.** Oil, coal, and natural gas are fossil fuels made from decomposing plant and animal material over a period of millions of years. Fossil fuels are **nonrenewable,** that is, there are finite amounts of them and they cannot be replaced after they have been used; therefore, without conservation practices, these energy sources can be depleted. Furthermore, there are environmental problems associated with the use of fossil fuels. Gases and particles emitted from burning petroleum cause pollution. One of the gases, carbon dioxide, is associated with global warming. Carbon dioxide and methane are two gases that contribute to the **greenhouse effect** by trapping the sun's heat in the atmosphere. Oil leaks and spills cause the destruction of wildlife (both plant and animal) and pollute water, land, and the air.

In 1960, OPEC was formed by countries involved in exporting petroleum. By the 1970s, many people in industrialized nations were reliant on fossil fuels. People had automobiles, single-unit dwellings, and many products that required electricity, including televisions and appliances. More people were traveling by air, which increased the consumption of aviation fuel. The industrialized nations' escalating dependency upon petroleum coincided with political unrest in the Middle East, a major source of oil in the world. Problems in the Middle East following World War II centered on Britain's withdrawal from Palestine and the subsequent dividing of the region into two states, Israel and Jordan. In 1948, Israel gained its independence, but Arab nations, including Egypt, Syria, Lebanon, Jordan, and Iraq, opposed this and declared war on Israel. An armistice was signed in 1949, but fighting resumed by the mid-1950s.

In 1967, Israel's victory in the Six-Day War against Egypt, Jordan, and Syria resulted in the expansion of Israel's territory, including the previously Syrian Golan Heights and the Egyptian area Sinai. Consequently, in opposition to the land acquisitions, terrorists launched a series of attacks, including the killings of Israeli athletes at the 1972 Olympic Games in Munich, West Germany. In 1973, the Yom Kippur War (Arab-Israeli War) began when Egypt and Syria attacked Israel on the Jewish holy day. During the war, the Arab countries decided to retaliate against nations that supported Israel by using oil as a weapon. The established OPEC organization helped to facilitate and coordinate decisions, initiatives, and actions involving the Arab nations. Therefore, in a very short period of time, the Arab countries were able to reduce the production of oil, raise prices, and establish an embargo of oil shipments to the United States and the Netherlands, a nation that also supported Israel. The Yom Kippur War lasted less than a month but resulted in the deaths of nearly 2,700 soldiers, and the total wounded was over 7,000. Israel won the war;

thus territorial possessions were essentially unchanged. The "oil war" had a dramatic and immediate impact on the industrialized world. A limited supply of a natural resource in high demand created a global crisis in industrialized nations as well as developing countries. Oil prices quadrupled, gasoline supplies were reduced, and the price for a gallon of gasoline nearly doubled in 1 year. By early 1974, people were paying high prices for gasoline while waiting in long lines at gas stations. Gas rationing was instituted by the government, thieves siphoned gas from automobiles, and it was common to see a sign in front of gas stations that read, "Sorry No Gasoline." Four hundred-percent increases in the price of crude oil soon impacted other uses for petroleum, including energy required for heat and electricity.

To conserve what became very expensive energy, people in most industrialized nations started to focus on ways to reduce dependency on nonrenewable resources and to explore using **renewable** forms of energy. To conserve energy and use renewable forms of power required transformational approaches to the design, orientation, and construction of buildings. Renewable energy sources include solar, wind, water, and geothermal. They are critical to a sustainable planet, and all these forms of energy have been used by civilizations for centuries. Many modern developments in these technologies started in the 19th century but were accelerated as a result of the 1973 oil crisis.

Solar energy is a means to use sunlight for the production of electricity and heat. Fundamentally, technologies and equipment are used to collect and store the energy of the sun. A simple approach is to mount light-collecting panels on a roof of a building. The panels contain solar or photovoltaic cells made from silicon, which convert the sun's energy into electricity. The power is then stored in batteries. To create heat for buildings, solar collectors can be mounted on a roof or located on the ground. To absorb the sun's energy, glass-covered collectors are lined with a black material and contain rows of metal tubes filled with a liquid. The heated liquid, usually water or oil, is transferred to an insulated storage tank.

Wind power creates electricity by using the kinetic energy from wind to operate generators. Windmills have long been used to create energy, and since the 1973 energy crisis, engineers have continued to develop wind turbine technologies. **Water power,** or hydroelectric power, utilizes the energy in falling or running water to generate electricity. The Hoover Dam, discussed in Chapter 6, is an example of hydroelectric power. **Geothermal energy** is the natural heat in the earth. The heat generated from geothermal energy can be used to heat buildings, and the energy of steam can be used to produce electricity.

To help overcome the problems caused by the energy crisis, scientists and engineers also explored **nuclear energy** (energy released by a nuclear reaction) as an alternative energy source. Advocates of nuclear energy explain that it can produce electricity without emitting carbon dioxide or other pollutants. Nuclear energy requires uranium for fuel, which is a nonrenewable resource that is also radioactive. Nuclear power creates radioactive waste, which is deadly and has the potential to be lethal for thousands of years. Moreover, any problem with a nuclear power station can be disastrous. Two prominent examples of this type of technological catastrophe occurred when a nuclear reactor overheated at Three Mile Island, Pennsylvania, in 1979 and the total devastation that was caused by the failure at the Chernobyl Nuclear Power Station in 1986 (discussed in Chapter 10).

In addition to exploring natural energy sources, people also concentrated on identifying technologies that would conserve energy as a result of the 1973 energy crisis. Individuals and organizations invested in energy-efficient double-glazed windows, insulated doors, and insulation with high **R-values.** The R-value designates a material's resistance to the flow of heat. In an attempt to nearly eliminate all costs for heating and cooling a residence, some people explored various

Figure 9.8 Earth-sheltered housing can be a bermed dwelling or a structure underground. In cold climates, a bermed house is entirely covered by the earth except for the south-facing elevation, which provides passive solar opportunities.

Source: John Angerson/Alamy.

approaches to **earth-sheltered housing.** Basically, earth-sheltered housing can be a bermed dwelling or a structure underground (Figure 9.8). In cold climates, a bermed house is entirely covered by the earth except for the south-facing elevation. The south-facing elevation provides **passive solar** opportunities, which also became very popular for many traditional dwellings. For example, to maximize the heat from the sun, numerous windows were installed on the south-facing elevation. Heat-absorbing materials, such as ceramic tile or bricks, were used on floors. Heat absorbed during the day was distributed through the room during the evening. To move warm air to the living space, ceiling fans were installed in rooms with high ceilings. Control of sunlight during the summer was achieved with awnings, overhangs, window treatments, and deciduous trees. Manufacturers designed energy-efficient window treatments that were insulated and had sealable tracks along the edges. The focus on the environment even translated to preferences for certain colors used in interiors. "Earth" colors, mainly brown, green, and gold, were used for carpeting, appliances, paints, and fabrics. The names of colors even referenced nature, such as "avocado green" and "harvest gold."

GLOBAL TECHNOLOGICAL DEVELOPMENTS

As mentioned in the introduction, the 1970s can be seen as the decade that launched the digital and electronic era. Transistors and integrated circuits provided the technologies for calculators and improved televisions. Home computers were developed and brought to the marketplace by Microsoft Corporation and Apple Computer, and the invention of the microprocessor had a dramatic effect on the fields of interior design and architecture. Technology for computer-aided design/computer-aided manufacturing (CAD/CAM) had its origins in the 1970s. Technological developments included video games, electronic card access, improved microwave ovens, barcodes, floppy disks, ink-jet printers, laser printers, commercial video cassette players, cellular mobile phones, global positioning system (GPS), and the Sony Walkman.

The 1973 oil crisis created significant demands for fuel-efficient vehicles. Air travel continued to improve and expand. One landmark achievement in this field was the first commercial supersonic flight in 1970. It took just 3½ hours for the Concorde to fly from New York to Paris. In the same year, the first Boeing 747 flight took to the skies, carrying 500 passengers. By the end of the decade, people worldwide were flying 700 billion total miles per year, approximately ten times the number in the 1960s. Attention also focused on Paris with the opening of The Centre Georges Pompidou.

The cultural institution focused on modern and contemporary creative arts in 1977, and its bold exposure of mechanical and electrical systems.

Computers: Computer-Aided Design/Drafting and Computer-Aided Manufacturing (CAD/CAM)

Mechanical devices that perform calculations, such as an abacus, were invented in ancient times. In the 1600s, several inventions occurred that were important to the development of computers. Three mathematicians, the Scotsman John Napier, Frenchman Blaise Pascal, and the German Gottfried Wilhelm von Leibniz, were all involved in creating systems that performed calculations. Napier designed a system to calculate logarithms, and Pascal's "Pascaline" device performed addition and subtraction. Subsequently, Leibniz designed a calculator with the added functions of multiplication and division. In the 1800s, the Jacquard Loom played an important role in the concept of using punched cards to program a system (see Chapter 1). In 1833, the first modern computer, the Analytical Engine, was invented by Charles Babbage (Figure 9.9). The device

Figure 9.9 In 1833 the first modern computer, the Analytical Engine, was invented by Charles Babbage. The device used Jacquard punched cards.

Source: TopFoto/The Image Works.

used Jacquard punched cards. Improvements in using punched cards occurred in the late 1800s. To help reduce the considerable amount of time required to perform census calculations, Herman Hollerith, a statistician for the U.S. Bureau of the Census, invented the Tabulating Machine, which used keypunched cards. In the 1930s, Howard Aiken studied Babbage's Analytical Engine and then worked with engineers at the IBM Corporation to design the Harvard Mark I, an electromechanical machine that could perform all types of mathematical equations in seconds, including addition, subtraction, multiplication, and division. Long computations, such as logarithms, were also possible but required more time. With funding from the U.S. Army, the ENIAC (Electronic Numerical Integrator and Computer) machine became important for various artillery calculations that had to be performed during World War II. Designed by J. Presper Eckert and John Mauchly, engineers from the University of Pennsylvania, ENIAC is considered the first large-scale electronic digital computer. ENIAC's size required an entire room and many technicians to operate the system.

Military investments and other inventions accelerated the technological developments of computers in the postwar years. To make computers lighter, smaller, and cheaper required the invention of the transistor (a small electronic device containing a semiconductor, the basic device used in miniaturized electronic systems) by Bell Laboratories in 1947. To program computers, FORTRAN language was developed by computer scientist John W. Backus. Several inventions in the late 1950s and 1960s also improved computers. The development of integrated circuits (ICs), or chips, by Jack Kilby and Robert Noyce enabled a semiconductor chip to contain all of the necessary electronic components. Integrated circuits translated into smaller, faster, and cheaper computers.

Today's Internet began in the 1960s by the Advanced Research Projects Agency (ARPA). Computer scientist Larry Roberts directed the development of a system that was created to connect military and university computers in several different locations throughout the country. The first personal computers were invented in the 1970s. This required the development of the first microprocessor, the 4004, invented by an Intel engineer, Ted Hoff. In 1975, the Altair 8800 was featured as the "World's First Minicomputer Kit to Rival Commercial Models." Steve Wozniak and Steve Jobs invented the Apple I microcomputer in 1976, followed by the Apple II in 1977. By 1978, the floppy disk was invented as a storage device.

Technology that combined two technologies together, **computer-aided design and computer-aided manufacturing (CAD/CAM),** also has origins in the 1970s but was primarily used at that time by large manufacturing industries using computer graphics to design and manufacture products. Some of the manufacturing industries were Ford Motor Company, Chrysler, General Motors, and Boeing. CAD/CAM systems were too expensive for most businesses, including those in the fields of interior design and architecture, before the invention of the microprocessor. Therefore, for several years, many professionals and firms had to be convinced that computer-aided technologies were a good investment. Arguments for using CAD/CAM systems focused on a more efficient operation, enhanced working drawings, fewer errors, and reduced time for execution.

Large architectural and engineering firms started to use CAD/CAM systems in the late 1970s, but the numbers increased dramatically in the subsequent decades. Located in Indianapolis, Everett I. Brown was an architectural, engineering, and construction firm with experience utilizing CAD/CAM systems beginning in the 1970s. In a 1982 article in *Computer Graphics World*, Patrick Brown, president of the company, described the company's perceptions and uses of a CAD/CAM system, noting, "Foreseeing total computerization of building design in the next five to ten years, the Everett I. Brown Company has developed one of the first computer graphic networks for computer-aided building design (CABD). This system speeds the execution of all architectural and engineering drawings, resulting in reduced construction and life-cycle costs, eliminating redundant drawings, simplifying and expediting design and drafting work, and giving facilities managers the data and drawings they need" (Teicholz [Ed.], 1985, p. 2.19). Brown reported that his company's system in 1978 was manufactured by Intergraph (originally M&S). For graphics, the company used a "DEC [Digital Equipment Company] PDP 11/34, an 80 megabyte hard disk, three workstations and a Calcomp 960 plotter."

Brown's brief description provides insight regarding the original designs of CAD/CAM systems (Figure 9.10). Most interesting was the type of user input devices and display devices. In addition to keyboards, the earliest user input devices were light pens, joysticks, and trackballs. Originally the most common graphics display was the cathode ray tube (CRT), a television picture tube.

Figure 9.10 One of the original designs of CAD/CAM systems.

Source: © Ed Kashi/Corbis.

Based on his experiences beginning in the 1970s, in 1983 Brown concluded, "There is little doubt within five to ten years computer graphics will be the accepted way to do nearly all architectural and engineering designs and drafting" (Teicholz, Ed., 1985, p. 2.20).

Brown's prediction was certainly accurate; "computer graphics" has had a significant impact on the design of interior environments and architecture and will continue to have a dramatic effect on design in the future. How computers have transformed the professions of interior design and architecture was reinforced in a 2009 special collection at the Chicago Art Institute's new Modern Wing (2009) by Pritzker Prize–winning architect Renzo Piano (discussed in Chapter 11). In three galleries of The Modern Wing, a special collection was arranged with selections from the Museum's Architecture and Design department. The collection displayed includes architectural drawings and models from 1910 through contemporary works of design (essentially the era covered in this book), including chairs, lighting, textiles, and graphic arts. The chronological layout of the collection is an excellent overview of primarily Western architecture and design in the 20th and 21st centuries as well as the changes that occurred in how professionals draw and present their concepts. For example, architectural drawings on display from the early-to-mid 20th century were hand drawn with pencil or ink on paper, such as four elevations of a private office (1930s/1940s) drawn in pencil by Josef Hoffmann. The collection included ink drawings by Le Corbusier and Mies. Erasing, inconsistent line qualities, and unreadable details were found on some drawings. Drawing with pen or ink was always a challenge because one mistake or a leaky pen could require someone to start a new drawing. Faint lines drawn with ink or pencil would not reproduce well, thus causing the loss of potentially important details.

As the collection progressed through the 20th century, examples included architectural drawings that were executed using computer-aided design, a process that enabled a designer to easily make changes on a drawing and create various views. The concluding works in the collection included examples of how **computer graphics** have expanded beyond a drafting medium and have transformed the way that interior designers and architects are able to design as well as present their concepts to their clients. Beyond a drafting tool, designers have been able to use computer graphics to create and change realistic three-dimensional images. These virtual-reality techniques enable a client to see different images while walking through a space.

Mechanical Technologies: Centre Georges Pompidou (Beaubourg) (1971–1977) in Paris, France, by Renzo Piano and Richard Rogers

As computers were beginning to impact the field of design, the Italian-born Renzo Piano and British architect Richard Rogers were developing a project that revolutionized the way people viewed and interacted with technology. The Centre Georges Pompidou, also referred to as "Beaubourg," is located in the center of Paris' historic district in the Marais Quarter (Figure 9.11). Named in honor of a former French president, Georges Pompidou, the mission of the interdisciplinary cultural center was "to spread knowledge about all creative works from the 20th century and those heralding the new millennium" (www.centrepompidou.fr). Hence, according to the rules of the competition for the building, "the architectural project had to meet the criteria of interdisciplinarity [*sic*], freedom of movement and flow, and an open approach to exhibition areas." Piano and Rogers' winning entry was the best of 600 proposals.

Their revolutionary design exposed the service functions of the building on the exterior and provided "freedom of movement and flow, and an open approach to exhibition areas." The resultant "X-ray" appearance of the building also emphasized modern mechanical systems from a "craftsmanship" perspective. In writing about Beaubourg, Piano explained this concept, stating, "I believe that it is also quite a mistake to consider this

Figure 9.11 The Centre Georges Pompidou, also referred to as "Beaubourg," is located in the center of Paris's historic district in the Marais Quarter.

Source: imagebroker/Alamy.

building a triumph of technology. Attention: it is not! This is a building of profound craftsmanship, practically made piece by piece. Its craftsmanship is that of every prototype. However, the techniques and processes obviously belong to today's culture. Nothing in Beaubourg is casual: everything was designed with a meticulous approach" (Donin, 1982, p. 23). The "techniques and processes" Piano referred to reflect the culture in the 1970s, including its emphasis on machines, mechanical systems, and space exploration. "Techniques and processes" are uniquely emphasized by Piano and Rogers's use of color. The mechanical systems handling air were painted blue. Electrical cables were painted yellow, and fluid ducts were green. Red was used for "elements of movement," including elevators, escalators, catwalks, and fire extinguishers. References to space exploration included the emphasis on mechanical systems and designs that promoted the illusion of zero gravity, such as the 360-degree glass tubular compartments that housed the escalators (see Figure 9.11). To accommodate the cultural needs of the 1970s, the program required space for a modern and contemporary art gallery, a library, a cinema, performance halls, a music research institute, interdisciplinary spaces for temporary exhibitions, a bookshop, and food service (Figure 9.12).

For Piano, an important element of employing the techniques and processes of "today's culture" was from a historical perspective, which he explained in the following manner: "I believe that the new has very deep roots in the old and that very often the way of conceiving architecture today and even the construction process has a lot to do with knowledge of history" (Donin, 1982, p. 26). Historically, Beaubourg has been associated with the boldness that British architect Joseph Paxton revealed in his revolutionary 19th-century design, the Crystal Palace in London (see Chapter 1). The design for the Eiffel Tower is another example of an innovative structure that employed the "techniques and processes" of the prevailing culture. In trying to understand and describe Beaubourg's revolutionary design, people used several names for the building, such as the "urban machine" or the "inside-out building." Piano explained that he appreciated a connection between Beaubourg and industry, stating, "I have to say that this notion of the Beaubourg as a machine or factory has always filled me with joy: I was always interested in the idea that a building can not only 'consume' but also 'produce' information" (Donin, 1982, p. 24).

Beaubourg has been able to "produce" information by meeting the needs of its users and the community (see Figure 9.12). Piano explained the importance of researching the needs of people, noting, "Another thing in which I strongly believe is the demands of the people. There are many projects in which the word 'participation' can be used. I believe in the discipline that is derived in planning from the systematic search for the needs of the people" (Donin, 1982, p. 29). The glass and steel structure is well-known for revealing its mechanical systems, but a closer examination of the architects' intent reveals an intriguing approach to creating a design that encourages people to interact with each other, the interior environment, and the building's immediate surroundings.

Piano and Rogers concentrated on creating interactive spaces both outside and inside Beaubourg. Outdoor space for the visual and performing arts reflected the center's interdisciplinary mission and provided a large, open public area in a very crowded section of Paris. Nearly half of the original site was dedicated to the piazza. The piazza was designed to encourage performances and exhibitions and for planned and impromptu concerts. From an interior perspective, placing the aforementioned color-coded mechanical systems, elevators, and escalators on the façades of the building resulted in large, open interior spaces that encouraged people to

Figure 9.12 Beaubourg's spaces are crowded with people. The popularity of the project illustrates its success in meeting the needs of its users and the community.

Source: George Kasotakis.

converse and exchange interdisciplinary perspectives. Even though Centre Pompidou has large, unrestricted areas, the popularity and success of the building has created challenging space problems (see Figure 9.12). Photographs of the interiors frequently include crowds. The center's open spaces also have allowed designers to create arrangements that support the specific needs of an exhibit, performance, or lecture. The avant-garde Beaubourg has been an enormous success—every year the center plays host to at least six million visitors.

GLOBAL LIFE AND WORK STYLES

Advances in air travel and increases in the number of passengers contributed to a growing number of international terrorist acts. On May 30, 1972, three gunmen killed 26 people by opening fire near a ticket counter at Lod International Airport (modern Ben Gurion Airport) in Tel Aviv, Israel. On October 13, 1977, Palestinian extremists hijacked a Lufthansa jet flying to the airport in Frankfurt, Germany. After refueling in Rome, the plane landed at several airports on the Arabian Peninsula. The crisis finally ended on October 18, 1977, when Somali forces stormed the plane and killed the four terrorists while the plane was on the ground at the Somalia airport. All of the passengers were safe, but the hijackers killed the captain of the plane. Palestinian extremists also hijacked an Air France plane en route from Greece to Paris on June 27, 1976. The plane was diverted to Entebbe, Uganda, where seven passengers and the four hijackers were killed during the rescue raid. Terrorism extended beyond aircraft and airports. There was a bus hijacking in Tel Aviv on March 11, 1978, that left 35 people dead and 100 injured. On November 4, 1979, 52 hostages were taken when Iranian militants stormed the American Embassy in Tehran, Iran. These hostages were not released until January 20, 1981—444 days after being captured by the militants.

On the economic front, during the decade, countries the world over experienced inflation, recessions, high interest rates, and unemployment. For example, in 1975, the United Kingdom had to deal with 24.2 percent inflation, and the price of petrol underwent a 70 percent increase in just 1 year. These economic conditions, as well as practices such as discrimination that had existed for decades in many places, obviously affected lifestyles and housing. As described in the next section, the effects of housing legislation that evolved after World War II began surfacing in the 1970s. Problems with public housing were documented, and people examined global solutions. Discriminatory policies and practices were especially horrendous in South Africa during the apartheid (separateness) years (1948–1994).

Global Social Issues: Public Housing in the United States and Australia

Providing safe, clean, and affordable housing for all people has always been a challenge across the world. As discussed in the early chapters of this textbook, the issue came to the forefront in the 19th century when the Industrial Revolution caused a population shift from rural to urban settings. The high demand for housing often resulted in the creation of overcrowded tenements that sometimes degenerated into slums. The problem escalated in the early 20th century. Cities had millions of homeless people, overcrowded, unsanitary conditions, and poorly constructed dwellings. Consequently, due to the deplorable conditions and public outcry, many industrial nations determined that the only way to address the issue was to enact new laws and to create public housing programs.

The United States was one of many industrialized nations that strove to develop adequate housing for those with low and moderate incomes. A number of U.S. legislative actions related to housing occurred between 1930 and 1980. For example, Congress passed the Housing Act of 1934, which created the Federal Housing Administration (FHA) and the Federal Savings and Loan Insurance Corporation (FSLIC). The two departments were formed to enable people to acquire home mortgages at reasonable interest rates. Soon after this legislation, in order to provide housing subsidies for low-income people, Congress approved the Housing Act of 1937. After World War II, the Housing Act of 1949 authorized federal dollars for slum clearance and the construction of 810,000 public housing units in 6 years. To coordinate housing programs in 1965, Congress created the Department of Housing and Urban Development (HUD).

Although well-intended, some of the provisions in the legislation resulted in grievous consequences. Hundreds of thousands of low-rent units were built throughout the United States without considering all of the factors, conditions, and services that are required to have a safe, secure, sanitary, sociable, and thriving living environment. Fundamentally, the prevailing perspective presumed that people simply needed shelter. During the 1950s and 1960s, thousands of "modern concrete slab" structures were constructed in the inner cities for low-income families (Figure 9.13). A quick solution was to build mass-produced, high-density structures in slum areas that were recently cleared through urban renewal programs. Many of these buildings resembled Le Corbusier's Unité d'Habitation, Marseille (see Chapter 6). For example, the Pruitt-Igoe (1951–1956; demolished 1972) housing project in St. Louis, Missouri, consisted of 33 apartment buildings (see Figure 9.13) for 10,000 people. Designed by the architect Minoru Yamasaki, each structure was 11 stories, and the total number of units was nearly 3,000.

The demolition of the Pruitt-Igoe complex just 21 years after its opening is indicative of a failed project. On the surface, Pruitt-Igoe's tall, densely populated, rectangular-shaped apartment buildings tended to resemble Unité d'Habitation; however, many of the elements that Corbu designed to support the individual and the collectivity were absent in the St. Louis project, as well as in most other large city public housing

Figure 9.13 During the 1950s and 1960s, thousands of "modern concrete slab" structures were constructed in the inner cities for low-income families. Designed by Minoru Yamasaki, the Pruitt-Igoe housing project in St. Louis, Missouri, consisted of 33 apartment buildings for 10,000 people. The demolition of the Pruitt-Igoe complex just 21 years after its opening is indicative of a failed project. Notice the St. Louis Arch (see Chapter 7) in the background.
Source: Bettmann/Corbis.

buildings constructed during the 1950s and 1960s. Le Corbusier described his perspective of what humans needed in their housing when he said, "For all men, in cities and farms: *sun in the house, sky through the widow-panes, [sic] trees to look at as soon as they step outside*, I say: the basic materials of city planning are: sun, sky, trees, steel, cement, in that strict order of importance" (Le Corbusier, 1933, pp. 85–86).

But public housing projects were designed in reverse of Corbu's concept. Cement and steel were most important. Unfortunately, trees, sky, and the sun were not considered an integral component of the residential units. In addition to the lack of opportunities to interact with the natural environment, such as Corbu's rooftop and park setting, public housing projects lacked many important amenities within the confines of a building that Le Corbusier designed for Unité d'Habitation. The projects lacked recreational facilities, restaurants, outdoor theater, gardens, grocery stores, medical facilities, pharmacies, clothing shops, laundry facilities, and beauty salons. They also lacked areas for privacy within an apartment for alone time. Corbu planned solitude areas for individuals and shared spaces for families and the community, focusing on designing for the needs of people. But the ill-conceived public housing projects were created and constructed to quickly provide a building to meet the demands.

As a result of the quick and cheap construction, the buildings soon had structural problems.

The U.S. Census Bureau's annual housing surveys reveal several deficiencies in structural characteristics of public housing buildings. For example, in 1973 and 1976, the results of the surveys found that structural deficiencies included "loose steps or railings on common stairways," "some or all electrical lighting exposed," "roof with signs of water leakage," and "broken plaster in ceilings and walls," and the most frequent problem was "basements with signs of water leakage" (Pynoos, Schafer, & Hartman [Eds.], 1980, p. 4). In addition to structural problems, the projects were located in areas that often lacked adequate transportation, medical facilities, flourishing schools, commercial businesses, and social services.

A number of problems developed for those living in the public housing projects, including high crime rates, vandalism, drug addiction, arson, unsanitary living conditions, vacancies, abandonment, and eventually occupation of the rooms by squatters. The projects were available only to low- and moderate-income families, and during this period the average income of non-whites in the United States was less than that of whites. Thus, the projects were primarily occupied by minorities and became associated with discriminatory housing practices. Political activism in the 1960s helped to create the Civil Rights Act of 1964. However, it was not until after the assassination of Martin Luther King, Jr. in 1968 that Congress finally acted on housing discrimination.

The Civil Rights Act of 1968 prohibited housing discrimination on the basis of race, color, creed, or national origin. Unfortunately, discriminatory practices remained a problem and there were social stigmas associated with public housing projects. To determine the human effects of public housing, hundreds of social science research studies were conducted by university professors in the 1960s and 1970s, such as Daniel R. Mandelker, Roger Montgomery, and William Michelson. The studies revealed conflicting and often inconclusive results about the effects of the physical environment on human behavior. Generally, social scientists examined variables associated with high-rise apartments, single-family homes, suburbs, downtowns, crime rates, life-cycle considerations, interpersonal relationships, finances, and social and community services.

In an attempt to identify effective public housing policies for Australia in the 1970s, social psychologist Paul Wilson analyzed subsidized housing programs in the United States and studied the prevailing social science research literature. Based on his research, Wilson's book *Public Housing for Australia* provided suggestions that focused on alternatives to public housing, management performance, the social environment, and the physical environment. In discussing his analysis of the research studies and various housing programs, Wilson noted, "the critical issue is concerned with isolating those particular aspects of successful housing programmes [*sic*] which allow one to propose a series of policies that can meet the objectives of any particular housing programme" (Wilson, 1976, p. x).

Wilson emphasized an examination of management performance, which he noted was often forgotten in public housing analyses. Wilson advocated for effective management practices at every organizational level, starting with the federal authorities and trickling down to the residential managers. At each level the focus

should extend beyond merely providing a building. Managers must concentrate on continuously maintaining and improving housing. Constant improvements must occur with the social and physical environments. Wilson suggested that each project should have specific social policies and procedures that are developed with input from a tenant advisory group. Items in a "master plan" listed by Wilson were a tenant newspaper, accessible transportation, child care provisions, recreational activities, youth organizations, rehabilitation programs, and projects designed to reduce maintenance costs and crime.

From the physical environment perspective, Wilson focused on the importance of the site, social stigmas associated with public housing high-rises, and crime-prevention strategies. Frequently, to fulfill the obligations prescribed in urban renewal programs, many public housing projects were built in deteriorating neighborhoods that had high crime rates and lacked essential services. But Wilson contended successful public housing projects required a location in a thriving neighborhood with convenient transportation, schools, commercial businesses, recreational facilities, health care, and social services. As previously mentioned, high-rises that were built in deteriorating neighborhoods were stigmatized and associated with crime, drugs, and violence. Many social scientists therefore contended that the physical characteristics associated with high-rise buildings, such as Pruitt-Igoe, negatively affected human behavior. Clearly, the large number of successful high-rise residential buildings in cities throughout the world reveals a lack of a direct relationship between high-density living and criminal behavior. Wilson also indicated that high-rise buildings were more appropriate for families with older children because of supervision issues. Institutional appearances should be replaced with aesthetic amenities, such as quality lighting, and attractive colors and materials. Improving the physical environment included crime-prevention strategies (Figure 9.14). Wilson suggested that to help prevent crime, strategies

Figure 9.14 Crime-prevention strategies included neighborhood participation and clustering residential units.

Source: Provided by Housing NSW. Illustration by Steven Stankiewicz.

should include neighborhood participation, citizen interdependence, individual expression, clustering residential units, and effective lighting at the entries and shared outdoor spaces.

Wilson's proposals for public housing were created for the unique conditions in Australia, specifically New South Wales, but his strategy to conduct a global analysis to find effective solutions is commendable. Every country contends with housing problems. The combined wisdom gained from global research studies, policies, procedures, and practices is critical to the successful designs of local and regional public housing projects.

Apartheid: South African Housing Policies

The practice of apartheid (separateness) in South Africa, especially during the apartheid years (1948–1994), was even worse than the wide range of discriminatory practices in the United States, which the Civil Rights Act was passed in 1964 to address. The origins of apartheid were derived from racial segregation instituted by early European settlers. The first European settlement was in 1652 when Jan van Riebeeck arrived as a representative of the Dutch East India Company. Settlers from the Netherlands were joined by people from France and Germany. The three nationalities became known as the Boers (farmers). The descendants of marriages

between the Boers and indigenous people of South Africa, such as the San peoples, were referred to as "Coloured" people. Fundamentally, white Europeans were classified as "white" and all other races were considered "non-white." Britain took control of South Africa in the 19th century.

The discovery of diamonds and then gold at the end of the 19th century had a profound impact on the previously agrarian lifestyle of the country's residents, and initiated various separate and unequal practices. Work shifted to mining operations, and economic pursuits attracted corporations and laborers. "Non-white" and "white" people migrated to South Africa to work in the mines, but the two groups were treated very differently. The white-owned mining corporations gave white employees the best jobs, the highest pay, and comfortable living conditions. To retain political and economic advantages, the minority white leaders established policies and regulations that separated the laborers by "white" and "black."

In 1910 the Union of South Africa, a dominion of the British Empire, was created; Louis Botha was appointed the country's first prime minister. The new government established the first of many laws that were used to control what "blacks" could possess and where they could live, work, learn, shop, eat, travel, worship, and receive health care. In opposition to the new laws and practices, the African National Congress (ANC) was established by the black Africans in 1912. The ANC organization was founded to promote civil rights for black Africans through peaceful means. Nelson Mandela was one of its members. But numerous laws (beginning with the Natives Land Act of 1913) delineated where "blacks" could go for entertainment and recreation. After a narrowly won election in 1948, the conservative National Party, a new South African government, concentrated on developing apartheid, most notably for economic exploitation.

By creating apartheid, the minority European population would be assured economic advantages because the laws specified who received what type of employment and education. In the 1950s, to ensure racial segregation, the "white" National Party revised previous legislation and created several new laws. Collectively, laws and enforcement policies controlled every level of life in South Africa. Maps were used to designate the location of "black" and "white" regions, cities, towns, business districts, housing, schools, churches, recreational facilities, parks, and beaches.

Apartheid policies not only had a dramatic impact on the people and geography of the country, but the laws also affected the layout of buildings. Geographic boundaries were used to separate "non-white" and "white" buildings. Public buildings had to be enlarged to create separate entrances and rooms. A. J. Christopher, a geologist professor, discovered a floor plan for a post office near Port Elizabeth, a city along South Africa's eastern coast (Figure 9.15). The floor plan reflects compliance with the apartheid laws that were established with the 1949 Prohibition of Mixed Marriages Act and the 1950 Immorality Act Amendment Act. Even though most of the population in Port Elizabeth was "non-white," the space allocated for the "whites" was the largest. The "white" residents also had special amenities, such as telephone booths and a fireplace. Christopher's book also had an illustration of a floor plan for a "white" residence that had an adjoining small, one-room structure with an outdoor W.C. for the "non-white" servant. Eventually, living conditions for many "non-whites" became deplorable and health care was basically nonexistent (Figure 9.16).

Descriptions of living arrangements of patients in Groote Schuur Hospital in Cape Town in the 1970s provide an understanding of the living conditions. One document read, "George, an assistant maintenance mechanic hospitalized for lymphoma was living with 16 other people in a dwelling with two bedrooms, living room and kitchen . . . the mother-in-law sleeps in the room with the family" (Dewar & Ellis, 1979,

p. 239). The description of another patient who lived in two rooms was:

> Sheets of corrugated iron make up the walls and roof, with occasional spaces left for windows. One room is used for sleeping and the other for everything else, i.e.: cooking, eating, bathing, relaxing, etc. The inside walls have been laid out with cardboard. There is no electricity. Uses a tiny gas stove for cooking and paraffin lamps for lighting. Water is obtained from a single tap on a pole. The toilet is outside and another family shares it with them. The house is rather low-set and the family are frequently flooded out of the house, and have to go and stay with relations. This means splitting up the family. The overcrowding and outbreak of infectious disease could be a problem, especially in the rainy winter months. (Dewar & Ellis, 1979, p. 240)

Another example of overcrowding in the 1970s was reported by the Social Investigator of the City Health Department: "Family A live in a house in Bridgetown, with 2 bedrooms, a kitchen, a living room, and a bathroom. Altogether, 23 people share the house; they consist of 2 people aged 66, 1 aged 41 and 1 aged 39, 4 between 20 and 30 years old, 3 teenagers, and 12 children under 11. Of these people 7 either have, or have had, TB" (Dewar & Ellis, 1979, p. 241). A case study from child welfare noted that "The Mother has lived in a shanty for about 15 years. This shanty is situated on the premises of her reputed husband's mother's house. There are also several other shanties on these premises—all occupied by her reputed husband's relatives. . . . It is felt that the mother's lack of suitable alternate accommodations is one of the major problems in the family" (Dewar & Ellis, 1979, pp. 242–243).

To combat the atrocities of apartheid, there were a number of demonstrations in the 1960s. An anti-apartheid demonstration by thousands in Sharpeville

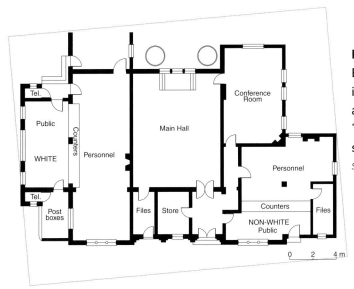

Figure 9.15 A floor plan of a post office in Port Elizabeth. Even though most of the population in Port Elizabeth was "non-white," the space allocated for the "whites" was the largest. The "white" residents also had special amenities, such as telephone booths and a fireplace.

Source: Illustration by Steven Stankiewicz.

Figure 9.16 Living conditions in South Africa for many "non-whites" became deplorable and health care was basically nonexistent.

Source: © Hervé Collart/Sygma/Corbis.

resulted in the massacre of 69 black protestors in 1960. In 1964, Mandela was tried, convicted of plotting to overthrow the government, and sentenced to life in prison. In 1973, the United Nations condemned apartheid and stated the racist rule was a "crime against humanity."

Opposition to apartheid reached a fevered pitch after the uprisings in the city of Soweto in 1976 and the killing of Steve Biko, a Black Consciousness movement leader while being detained by police in 1977. Thousands of protestors started the riot to demonstrate opposition to a new apartheid law that required nonwhites to learn Afrikaans, a perceived oppressive language, rather than English. Nearly 600 student protestors were killed by police. Eventually, "white" leaders became concerned about the continuing protests and demonstrations, and were financially affected by the recession and high inflation in South Africa. In 1984, Bishop Desmond Tutu received the Nobel Peace Prize for his peaceful approach to opposing apartheid. Many Western nations, including the European Economic Community (EEC) and the United States, levied economic sanctions against South Africa as a means of protest; the South African nation was shunned. In 1990 Nelson Mandela was released from prison, and finally in 1994 South Africa held its first democratic elections and Mandela became president. Apartheid was dissolved, but the country is still working to overcome the decades of discrimination, segregation, oppression, and deprivation that it caused.

GLOBAL VISUAL AND PERFORMING ARTS

Rock festivals continued to be popular in the 1970s, but the decade witnessed the disbanding of the Beatles. The first *Saturday Night Live* show was broadcast in 1977, and the impact of space exploration could be seen in the enormously successful films *Star Wars* (1977) and *Close Encounters of the Third Kind* (1977). The power of film was made apparent by the disco craze that swept the world after the showing of *Saturday Night Fever* (1977) starring John Travolta. Music and music research gained international attention with the Institute for Music/Acoustic Research and Coordination (IRCAM) in Paris, designed by Renzo Piano and Richard Rogers. Artists brought attention to architecture and the natural environment by site-specific art installations. Works that became part of the landscape altered traditional perspectives regarding where one could appreciate art. Some of the artists who extended art museums to the outdoors were Robert Smithson, Richard Serra, and Christo and Jeanne-Claude.

Figure 9.17 The 1977 block-buster film, *Saturday Night Fever* starring John Travolta, fueled disco clubs throughout the United States.

Source: © Sunset Boulevard/Sygma/Corbis.

Music: Disco Clubs and the Institute for Music/Acoustic Research and Coordination (IRCAM) (1973–1977) in Paris, France, by Renzo Piano and Richard Rogers

The 1970s saw a marked shift in the styles of popular music, dancing, and fashion from the rock concerts, folk music, and casual dress of the 1960s. Instead of listening to music performed on an outdoor stage by a band wearing secondhand clothing, people wanted to wear flashy clothes to dance on a stage in a club with music played by a disc jockey (DJ). In the early 1970s, a number of clubs in New York City created an interest in disco by playing music with a pulsating beat. Two successful disco artists who helped advance the trend in both music and fashion were the Bee Gees (the Gibb brothers from Australia) and American Donna Summer. By the mid-1970s, disco music and discothèques were popular in urban settings, but the 1977 blockbuster film *Saturday Night Fever*, starring John Travolta, fueled the trend throughout the United States (Figure 9.17). In the film, Travolta aspired to be a Brooklyn disco star and frequently danced in a local discothèque and practiced to win the ultimate competition. The popular film and soundtrack by the Bee Gees provided a generic formula for disco dancing, dress, music, and clubs. Disco dancers dressed in glittery "stage" fashion such as tight polyester pants, gold chains, and platform shoes. Women wore revealing dresses, halter tops, sparkly jewelry, and high heels.

By the end of the decade, more than 20,000 disco clubs were thriving; they could be found in every major city in the United States, and some type of disco format was created in many rural communities. There were disco weddings and proms, and most hotels opened a disco in one of their existing spaces. The disco experience was a synthesis of music, fashion, dance, and the design that was created exclusively for the clubs. All of the elements combined together for the total experience. Disco music's nonstop thumping beat inspired people to dance, and for many people, dancing required a "stage" and a "costume." A dance performance needed an audience and theatrical lighting. Thus, clubs were designed to support and reinforce the important elements of a disco experience. In order to constantly play music, a disco had to have at least two turntables, but some clubs featured very sophisticated sound systems. The dance "stage" was the focal point of the disco and had to be in a location that was in clear view of the "audience." As illustrated in Figure 9.17, to create a 360-degree lighting experience and to attract attention to the dancers, some clubs had dance floors made of **Plexiglas.** The most spectacular lighting and special effects were reserved for the dance "stage." Some of the lighting and special effects included

flashing strobes, pulsating colored lights, laser-beam systems, mirrored balls, fog machines, and computer-controlled projections. The trend, which had been seen by some as self-indulgent and escapist, gradually faded as the decade came to a close.

Meanwhile, in Paris, Renzo Piano and Richard Rogers were designing the Institute for Music/Acoustic Research and Coordination (IRCAM) (1973–1977). The IRCAM project coincided with the construction of the Centre Pompidou. In addition to wanting a new and innovative cultural center in Paris, French President Georges Pompidou established an institute to research and produce contemporary music. In 1970, President Pompidou commissioned the composer and conductor Pierre Boulez to establish and direct IRCAM. The purpose of IRCAM "was to bring science and art together in order to widen instrumentarium [*sic*] and rejuvenate musical language" (www.ircam.fr). The interdisciplinary mission of the cultural centre was reinforced by connecting Beaubourg with IRCAM. The site selected for IRCAM was adjacent to Saint Merri Church, but the building is not visible at street level (Figure 9.18). To create optimum acoustic conditions, IRCAM was designed as a subterranean building, and its roof is Place Igor-Stravinsky, with a playful water sculpture by Niki de Saint-Phalle and Jean Tinguely.

The design of the building involved a comprehensive interdisciplinary team of professionals that

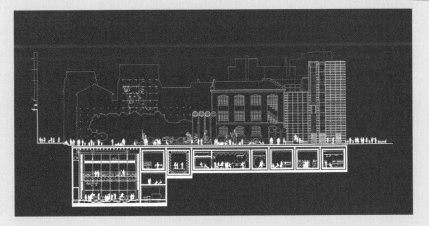

Figure 9.18 Renzo Piano and Richard Rogers designed the facilities for the Institute for Music/Acoustic Research and Coordination (IRCAM). IRCAM was established to research and produce contemporary music.
Source: G. Berengo Gardin/RPBW.

included architects, acoustical engineers, musicians, mathematicians, and mechanical engineers. IRCAM was designed as a "cluster of means and techniques necessary for musical exploration." Musical exploration required several unique designs for the interior environment. The interdisciplinary team designed an acoustic projection chamber, a recording chamber, research offices, and a public area. The acoustic projection chamber or the experimental concert hall was designed as an ultimate flexible space (see Figure 9.19). Because it was going to serve as a research facility, the chamber's acoustics had to accommodate a wide range of musical works, instruments, and vocals. The IRCAM website explains that the hall's "variable acoustic characteristics" allow a "reverberation time from 0.4 to 4 seconds." Factors that contributed to the flexibility are prismatic units mounted on the walls that absorbed, reflected, and diffused sounds. In addition, adjustments were derived from the movable ceiling (Figure 9.19). Currently, IRCAM sponsors numerous activities including music research, music software, concerts, conferences, films, training, school programs, colloquiums, seminars, and various publications. According to their website, IRCAM has over 150 people, including

composers, researchers, performers, and engineers who contribute to the institute's activities (www.ircam.fr, 2009). These individuals have contributed to IRCAM becoming "the world's leading center for computer-music training" and "the major site for contemporary music creation" (www.ircam.fr, 2009).

Visual Arts: *Running Fence* (1972–1976) and *Wrapped Reichstag* (1971–1995) by Christo and Jeanne-Claude

Interdisciplinary teams of professionals, politicians, and the members of the general public were essential to the creation of the public art projects designed by the husband-and-wife artists Christo and Jeanne-Claude. Bulgarian-born Christo and French-born Jeanne-Claude are internationally famous for their vast-scale natural and urban environment projects (Figure 9.20). They purposely select sites that are "already prepared and used by people, managed by human beings for human beings" (www.christojeanneclaude.net). Although some contend that their large-scale projects are best viewed from the air, Christo and Jeanne-Claude explain that their projects were scaled to "be enjoyed by human beings who are on the ground." The beauty and serenity of their natural environment projects focus attention on the importance of taking responsibility for sustaining the planet.

Christo and Jeanne-Claude's urban projects that involved wrapping a structure present the design profession with an innovative approach to studying forms, proportions, objects, color, light, and the draping qualities of fabrics (Figure 9.21). In addition, all of their large-scale projects, especially in the public domain, demonstrate to professionals the importance of involving all stakeholders, respecting diverse views, empowering people, collaborating with multiple disciplines, and recycling. Their first project, *Packages and Wrapped Objects* (1958), initiated several efforts that involved wrapping or covering an object, building, monuments, walls, walkways, or an element in the

Figure 9.19 The design of the IRCAM building involved a comprehensive interdisciplinary team of professionals. Musical research required several unique acoustical designs for the interior environment.
Source: G. Berengo Gardin/RPBW.

Figure 9.20 The temporary *Running Fence* (1972–1976) project in Sonoma and Marin counties, California, designed by Christo and Jeanne-Claude. The 24¼-mile (40-kilometer) fence was an 18-foot high (5.5-meter) shirred curtain that was suspended from a steel cable and attached to the ground by another cable.

Source: CNAC/MNAM/Dist. Réunion des Musées Nationaux/ Art Resource, NY.

natural environment. A woven fabric was used to wrap an element, and the materials for tying the objects were cords, twine, or ropes. Their first temporary vast-scale natural environment project was *Wrapped Coast, One Million Square Feet* (1968–1969) along the coastline of Little Bay, Australia. One million square feet (92,903.04 square meters) of a white-colored synthetic woven fabric and 35 miles (56.3 kilometers) of polypropylene rope were used to attach the fabric to the rocky cliffs of the coast.

Christo's drawings, collages, and scale models "reflect the years of research involving the location of the site, the accumulated knowledge of the site and the people using that area, and the technical aspects of the structure slowly evolving towards the final engineering and the construction blue prints" (www.christojeanneclaude. net). Two temporary natural environment projects in the 1970s were spectacular and amazing feats. An enormous orange-colored curtain was draped between two mountains in the temporary *Valley Curtain* (1970–1972) in Rifle, Colorado. The span was 1,250 feet (381 meters), with a height of 185–365 feet (56–111 meters). A curtain was made of nylon polyamide fabric and suspended from steel cables. The second environmental project was the temporary *Running Fence* (1972–1976)

in California's Sonoma and Marin counties in the San Francisco Bay Area (see Figure 9.20). The 24¼-mile (40-kilometer) fence was an 18-foot-high (5.5-meter) shirred curtain suspended from a steel cable and attached to the ground by another cable. The beautiful colors of the sunset were displayed on the white fibers while the wind caused the fabric and metal components to create soft fluttering sounds. The fence extended over the hills and valleys of the California countryside until it meandered into the Pacific Ocean. The long distance involved the private property of 59 ranchers in two counties.

Christo captured both of these projects in a documentary video, which provides great insight regarding the complexity of the process. The films documented the overall steps involved with creating a vast-scale public arts project. In addition to the years of research and the complicated task of engineering vast projects, Christo's projects entailed thousands of hours dedicated to meetings, hearings, discussions, lectures, presentations, and exhibits. These activities were necessary to obtain permits from city and county officials, and to receive approvals from private property owners. Upon approvals, Christo and Jeanne-Claude become involved with the engineers and technicians responsible

Figure 9.21 An extremely complicated political project was the temporary *Wrapped Reichstag* (1971–1995) in Berlin, designed by Christo and Jeanne-Claude.

Source: © Régis Bossu/Sygma/Corbis.

for executing the structural details of the project. The creative process continues until "the work is completed." Their public projects are temporary, with a typical exhibition period of 2 weeks. Precautions are taken to prevent damage to a site, and after the project "the sites are restored to their original condition and most materials are recycled." On their website, Christo and Jeanne-Claude provide an example of how they recycled materials used in *The Umbrellas, Japan-USA* (1984–1991):

> The Umbrellas *were removed from the land. They were taken apart and most of the materials were recycled. The paint was scraped off the aluminum parts, (poles, ribs and struts) which was melted down and used again as aluminum. Like soda cans or whatever aluminum is used for. The steel bases became scrap metal or were used as bases for satellite dishes. The fabric used in the projects is always industrial man made fabrics, which are manufactured for ecological purposes (air and water filters, or sand bags against floods), or agricultural purposes, such as "erosion control mesh" which was used for the Wrapped Coast in Australia in 1969, and for construction purposes. (www.christojeanneclaude.net)*

Two other temporary projects in the 1960s were art museums: The Wrapped Kunsthalle (1968) in Berne, Switzerland, and Wrapped Museum of Contemporary Art (1969) in Chicago. An extremely complicated political project was their third temporary wrapped public building, *Wrapped Reichstag* (1971–1995) in Berlin (Figure 9.21). In describing *Wrapped Reichstag*, Christo and Jeanne-Claude noted, "the very essence is about architecture." In an interview with Masahiko Yanagi in 1986, Christo explained his interest in doing the Reichstag public project, saying:

> *The idea to go to Berlin and to work on the* **Reichstag** *project was so much more inspirational because of my links with Eastern Europe, and I was in some way expecting that finally I would do a project that could be visible from both East and West Berlin. This is why we were so keen right away on the* **Wrapped Reichstag**, *because that building is the only structure which is under the jurisdiction of the four Allied forces: the British, Soviet, American, and French military forces, plus the two Germanys, East and West. The building is paramount importance to the German nation and to European history, and it is dramatically related to what Germany is today. (Baal-Teshuva, 1993, p. 23)*

The Reichstag had been designed in 1894 to house the German Parliament. In 1933 it was badly damaged by a fire, and during World War II it was heavily attacked and nearly destroyed during the bombing of Berlin in 1945. The skeleton building was ignored until restoration efforts in the 1960s; however, restorative work did not include replacing its original glass and steel dome (see Figure 9.21). This was not accomplished until after Christo's wrapped exhibition. The architectural/design firm Foster and Partners' restoration project of the Reichstag (1992–1999) included a spectacular new glass dome.

International tensions surrounding Berlin and the Reichstag building created a complicated and arduous situation for Christo and Jeanne-Claude. A significant problem was that the east façade of the Reichstag building shared air space with the Communist-controlled East Berlin. There were countless conversations, meetings, presentations, and explanations to mayors, governors, and legislators. Politically, Christo had to negotiate with officials from Berlin, Bonn, West Germany, East Germany, Britain, France, and the United States. The project was denied in 1977 and 1978, but Christo continued his campaign with international exhibitions and by creating a Board for Christo's *Reichstag* Project. The Board, comprised of prominent West German professionals, was instrumental in communicating Christo's project to authorizing bodies in Bonn and the Soviet bloc. After 24 years, and the reunification of Germany in 1990, Christo finally received approval from officials in Bonn to install *Wrapped Reichstag* (see Figure 9.21).

His plan for the building was to wrap the structure in a "thick woven polypropylene fabric with an aluminum surface and 15,600 meters (51,181 feet) of blue polypropylene rope." There were three phases planned for the project. Initial work was conducted off-site and involved preparing the fabric, and constructing units that were designed to protect the building and its statues. The next two phases were at the site. Phase two entailed installing the protective structures, including cages around statues, and removable columns used to attach the fabric. Fabric panels were hoisted to the roof, and during the third phase the fabric was released and descended to the ground. Christo had a clear vision for how the folds of the fabric covered the building and how to retain the shapes with ropes. Christo explained that how a building was wrapped "is everything." A close analysis of *Wrapped Reichstag* reveals Christo's vigilant attention to the even spacing between folds of the fabric, the careful positioning of ropes, and an emphasis on the divisions of the architecture (see Figure 9.21). Viewing the *Reichstag* building as a wrapped package reveals architectural forms and proportions that tend to

be obscured by the competing shapes and ornamentation that cover the façades of the unwrapped structure. The temporary public art project was completed in 1995 and remained for 2 weeks, and the materials used in the project were recycled after the teardown.

In addition to starting *Wrapped Reichstag* in the 1970s, Christo and Jeanne-Claude were involved with several other temporary public art projects that were completed in the 1970s and into the 21st century, including *Wrapped Monument to Vittorio Emanuele, Piazza Duomo* (1970) and *Wrapped Monument to Leonardo da Vinci, Piazza Scala* (1970), both in Milano, Italy; *The Wall, Wrapped Roman Wall* (1974), Rome, Italy; *The Mastaba of Abu Dhabi: Project for the United Arab Emirates* using 390,500 oil barrels (1977–in progress); *Wrapped Walk Ways, Loose Park* (1977–1978), Kansas City, Missouri; *The Gates Project for Central Park* (1979–2005), New York City; and *The Pont Neuf Wrapped* (1975–1985), Paris.

GLOBAL BUSINESS AND ECONOMICS

As previously discussed, in the 1970s many nations experienced excessive inflation, recessions, and high unemployment. However, the economic recovery in Japan was strong, as evidenced by the tremendous increases in automobile production and innovative consumer electronics. Japan's automobile industry, including Toyota, Nissan, and Honda, experienced newfound success in the 1970s largely due to their economical price, fuel efficiency, and compliance with the government's pollution standards, established in 1970 with the Clean Air Act. Fuel efficiency was especially desirable in the 1970s after the 1973 oil crisis. At the end of the 1970s, approximately one out of every four cars sold in the

United States was manufactured by a Japanese company. New businesses were launched with far-reaching implications that would continue in the 21st century. Fred Smith started Federal Express in 1971, and two major computer corporations were founded by the end of the decade. Bill Gates and Paul Allen founded Microsoft Corporation with the BASIC program for the Altair 8800 in 1975. Two years later, Steve Wozniak and Steve Jobs founded Apple Computer Corporation in California. The Cummins Engine Company, an already established company, had a significant impact on architecture by establishing a program for the community (see below). Architecture as a symbol of commercial power remained a significant force with the completion of Chicago's Sears Tower (modern Willis Tower) and the CN Tower in Toronto.

Cummins Engine Company: The Community of Columbus, Indiana

In 1970, the National Society of Interior Design (modern American Society of Interior Design) presented the small city of Columbus, Indiana, with an award for exemplifying "environmental rebirth." Located in southern Indiana between Indianapolis and Louisville, in the 1970s Columbus had a population of 27,000. The award was the result of design initiatives that fundamentally began in the 1950s. Amazingly, in less than 20 years, Columbus had established an international reputation for modern architecture. Columbus was coined "The Athens in the Prairie" due to the visionary leaders at the Cummins Engine Company, a manufacturer of diesel engines and other related products. In 1919, mechanic and inventor Clessie Lyle Cummins founded the company with the financial backing of a local banker and investor, W. G. Irwin. Irwin, and most notably his great-nephew J. Irwin Miller, had significant roles in developing the town's modern architecture. Irwin believed in the importance of community service, social responsibility, and providing support to local entrepreneurial initiatives. In 1937, W. G. Irwin and his sister, Linnie I. Sweeney, donated land for the construction of a new building for the First Christian Church in Columbus. Eliel Saarinen was commissioned to design the First Christian Church, which was the beginning of Columbus's modern architecture and public art collection. In coordination with Saarinen, furniture for the church was designed by Charles Eames (see Chapter 6). Completed in 1942, the brick and limestone building was known for its campanile (bell tower), which stood 166 feet (50.60 meters) high and was "one of the first contemporary churches in the United States."

As the leader of the Cummins Company, Irwin Miller was able to advance his influence on the development of modern architecture and philanthropic activities. In the early 1950s, the city suffered from a housing shortage and needed new elementary schools. Cummins agreed to provide funding for new housing units and to help build new elementary schools. Charitable contributions continued in 1953 with funds for city enhancements. In 1954, the Cummins Engine Foundation was established to support "religious, educational, and charitable purposes" (www.cummins.com).

To encourage a serious architectural program for the city, the foundation presented a proposal to the school board. The foundation proposed to "pay architectural fees for new schools, with the stipulation that distinguished national architects be selected as designers. Criteria indicated the School Board would have independent control of the project, design and budget, including selection of the architect from a list of at least six proposed by a panel of leading architects" (Columbus Area Chamber of Commerce, 1984, p. 5). The school board approved the proposition, which initiated the construction of buildings designed by numerous renowned architects. At a dedication ceremony in the 1960s, J. Irwin Miller explained the company's vision for Columbus, including views regarding social injustices, noting:

> We would like to see [Columbus] become the city in which the smartest, the ablest, the best young families anywhere would like to live . . . a community that is open in every single respect

Figure 9.22 One of the many architectural "gems" in Columbus, Indiana, "The Athens in the Prairie." The Irwin Union Bank & Trust Company addition by Kevin Roche, John Dinkeloo, & Associates.

Source: Balthazar Korab.

to persons of every race, color and opinion; that makes them feel welcome and at home here . . . a community which will offer their children the best education available anywhere . . . a community of strong, outspoken churches, of genuine cultural interests, exciting opportunities for recreation . . . a community whose citizens are themselves well paid and who will not tolerate poverty for others, or slums in their midst. (Columbus Area Chamber of Commerce, 1984, p. 118)

As the foundation was being established, Eero Saarinen (see Chapters 7 and 8) was commissioned to design the Irwin Union Bank & Trust Company (1954) in Columbus. The one-story building surrounded by a "landscaped park" designed by landscape architect Dan Kiley from Charlotte, Vermont, was to "provide an efficiently functional structure for present-day banking, which would have dignity and yet reflect the friendly atmosphere of an old-fashioned country store" (Columbus Area Chamber of Commerce, 1984, p. 26). The Irwin Union Bank continued to commission renowned architects to design several new branches and a 1973 addition to the original bank designed by Kevin Roche John Dinkeloo & Associates (Figure 9.22).

The first building, completed in 1957 with architectural fees paid by the Cummins Engine Foundation, was the Lillian C. Schmitt Elementary School designed by Harry Weese. This project was followed by several schools and other public buildings, including the Quinco Consulting Center, a collaborative mental health project serving and involving the resources of five counties (modern Columbus Regional Hospital Mental Health Center) (1972) (Figure 9.23). Designed by James Stewart Polshek, the Center is built over Hawcreek and has facilities for training, research, and outpatient services. The Fodrea Community School, the "people-centered" school (1973) by Paul Kennon of Caudill Rowlette Scott, was unique for its use as both a community center and an elementary school.

The architectural program established by the Cummins Engine Foundation had an amazing domino effect in the community. Public and private entities contributed to the city's architectural prestige by investing in architecture and public art. Renovation of historic structures became a priority, including the downtown 19th-century buildings. In 1964, the downtown merchants acquired a master plan for storefronts and signage created by Alexander Girard (see Chapters 6 and 7). Currently, in a town of only 39,000 people, Columbus has more than 70 buildings and pieces of public art designed by internationally renowned creators, including Eliel Saarinen, Eero Saarinen, Dan Kiley, John Warnecke, Harry Weese, I. M. Pei, Cesar Pelli, James Polshek, Richard Meier, Robert Venturi, Kevin Roche, Romaldo Giurgola, Alexander Girard, Dale Chihuly, Henry Moore, Cork Marcheschi, and Jean Tinguely.

It is a phenomenal experience to stand on a corner in downtown Columbus and see in every *immediate* direction multiple buildings and pieces of public art designed by internationally noted architects, designers, and artists. The wide assortment of buildings includes churches, a fire station, schools, a library, health-care centers, recreation centers, factories, courthouse, a retirement center, a newspaper facility, banks, offices, apartments, clubhouses, a post office, and a prison. The American Institute of Architects ranked Columbus as one of the top U.S. cities for "architectural innovation and design," and *Smithsonian* magazine cited Columbus as a "veritable museum of modern architecture."

Figure 9.23 The Quinco Consulting Center, a collaborative mental health project involving five counties (modern Columbus Regional Hospital Mental Health Center). Designed by James Stewart Polshek, the center is built over Hawcreek and has facilities for training, research, and outpatients.

Source: Balthazar Korab.

Businesses: Sears Tower (Modern Willis Tower) (1970–1974) in Chicago, Illinois, by SOM and CN Tower (1973–1976) in Toronto, Ontario, by John Andrews

Columbus has amazing architecture and public art, but the city does not have a skyscraper. The closest structure to a skyscraper is the campanile Eliel Saarinen designed for the First Christian Church. Columbus's situation is to be expected in a community with only 39,000 people and comparatively reasonable land values. Since the 19th century, escalating costs for land in large cities has prompted property owners to build skyscrapers. By the end of the 1960s, several skyscrapers existed in the world, including the Economist Building (1959–1964) in London by Alison & Peter Smithson; Australia Square Tower (1965–1967) in Sydney by Harry Seidler & Associates; in Chicago the John Hancock Center (1965–1969) by SOM (Skidmore, Owings, and Merrill) and Lake Point Tower (1965–1968) by Schipporeit & Heinrich Associates. As discussed in previous chapters, many businesses were prospering, and executives anticipated needing more office space. This was the situation experienced by Sears, Roebuck and Company. In the 1960s, Sears was the largest retailer in the world, with stores throughout the United States and in Cuba, Mexico, Canada, Europe, and Central and South America. Employees of the Chicago-based company were housed in buildings in Chicago and a suburb on the north side of the city. Based on expected increases in sales, executives had determined that Sears's headquarters would need considerably more office space in the immediate future. To accommodate operational needs and to consolidate departments located in different buildings, executives decided to build a new building in downtown Chicago, the Sears Tower (modern Willis Tower) (1970–1974) (Figure 9.24).

Sears commissioned the architectural firm Skidmore, Owings, and Merrill (SOM) to design the new building. The firm had been founded by Louis Skidmore and Nathaniel Owings in 1936. Three years later, John Ogden Merrill became the third partner. In the 1960s, SOM had considerable experience designing skyscrapers in Chicago and New York City. Most recently was the mixed-use 100-story John Hancock Center (1970) in Chicago designed by two SOM partners, Bruce Graham and structural engineer Fazlur Khan. Colombian-born Graham and Khan, who was born in Dacca, Bangladesh, were assigned to design the Sears Tower. The tallest building in the world in 1974, the 110-story Sears Tower is 1,454 feet (443.18 meters) high, with 4.5 million square feet (418,064 square meters) of office space. The Sears Tower was clad with black anodized aluminum panels and bronze-tinted windows. To accommodate easy access to public transportation for its employees, Sears selected a 3-acre (1.21 hectare) site on the west side that was very close to train stations and several bus routes. As a showcase piece for the lobby, the company commissioned Alexander Calder to create *Universe* (1974), a large metal kinetic art sculpture. The metal elements were painted red, yellow, blue, black, and brown, and each component moved at a different speed.

Collaboratively, Graham and Khan developed new structurally efficient systems that enabled buildings to be built taller while using fewer materials and reducing costs. They designed the "**bundled tube**" structural system for the Sears Tower. Fundamentally, the bundled tube structural system employs open space units, or tubes that are supported by massive columns and girders around its perimeter. One free-standing tube would not be structurally viable, but a collection of tubes was very strong. Similar to a Rubik's cube, the Sears Tower had nine 75- by 75-foot (22.86- by 22.86-meter) tubes at the base of the building. Seven of the square-shaped tubes became setbacks at various heights, and the remaining two tubes became the tall rectangular unit at the top of the building. The setbacks were created at the 50th, 66th, 90th, and 109th floors (see Figure 9.24).

The structural system not only enabled the Sears Tower to become the tallest building in the world in 1974, but the "bundled tube" structure was an ideal solution for addressing the space needs of the client. Originally,

Figure 9.24 The Sears Tower (modern Willis Tower) in Chicago designed by SOM. The exterior reveals the bundled tube structural system.
Source: Stephen Lockett/Alamy.

Sears intended to use approximately half of the space in the building and lease the remaining areas. As the business expanded in the future, executives were planning to use the entire building for the corporate headquarters. The "bundled tube" structural system was ideal for their strategic business plan because the first 50 floors had the square footage (square meters) Sears required for its operations. In addition, the 75- by 75-foot (22.86- by 22.86-meter) column-free spaces around the perimeter of the building provided Sears with the flexibility to accommodate future departmental changes. Due to the setbacks, the floors above the 50th had less square footage (square meters), which was ideal for the rental market.

In writing about the Sears Tower, Graham discussed the tubes as well as the concept of a tower:

Tall buildings are man-made. Towers have historically been not only the pride of their temporary owners, but of their cities as well. So, the Sears Tower, one more mountain, was created for this city on the plains. Sears is very direct in its structural solution, a new concept of cluster tubes, originally fifteen, reduced to nine when the hotel was eliminated from the plan. The Sears Tower itself is much like the idea behind San Gimignano, but unlike most tall buildings in New York, it is a tower of people, not the palace of a bank. (Graham, 1989, p. 56)

Using the word "Tower" in the name of the Sears building demonstrates the corporation's pride in being the world's largest retailer (at the time).

The word also reinforces the height of the building by using a term that is typically reserved for communication towers, the tallest structures in the world. Technological advancements in the communication industry created the need for tall towers that supported antennas. Extremely tall towers are needed to transmit signals for long distances. Toronto was experiencing trouble with transmissions due to the construction of many skyscrapers in that city. To alleviate the problem, the Canadian National (CN) Railway built the world's tallest self-supporting structure, the CN Tower (1976) (Figure 9.25).

Interestingly, railroads were necessary for Sears to develop into a successful mail-order business, and that traditional transportation mode provided the financial means to build the contemporary CN Tower (see Figure 9.25). Prosperous times for the Canadian National (CN) Railway enabled the company to diversify and invest in modern technologies, including communications. Designed by John Andrews, the structure is a triangular-shaped concrete tower that is 1,815 feet (553 meters) tall. Once it was determined that the tower could be built to be the tallest structure in the world, CN decided to generate additional revenue by including facilities for the public. At the tower's observation level, on a clear day visibility is 100 miles (160 kilometers). The CN Tower was designed with a revolving restaurant, *360*, which originally included a disco. The highest observation level was the *Sky Pod*, and a lower level was outdoors and had a glass floor.

The CN Tower is still a popular tourist destination in Toronto today, but due to unexpected declining retail sales, Sears sold the Sears Tower in 1994 and moved its corporate headquarters to smaller facilities in the Chicago suburb of Rolling Meadows.

In the summer of 2009 Willis Group Holdings, a London-based insurance broker, became a tenant in the Sears Tower and legally was able to rename the building, Willis Tower. That same summer the Sears Tower received national attention for the exhilarating experience of being able to look directly to the ground 1,353 feet below (412.39 meters). Visitors experience new views of the city by standing in "The Ledge," glass bays that extend out 4 feet (1.2 meters) from the sides of the building on the 103rd floor.

Figure 9.25 To alleviate transmission problems, the Canadian National (CN) Railway built the world's tallest self-supporting structure, the CN Tower.
Source: Robert Harding Picture Library Ltd./Alamy.

SUMMARY

The Vietnam War was a major focus for more than half of the 1970s. Sending U.S. combat troops to Vietnam prompted immediate antiwar demonstrations in the United States, which began in the 1960s and gained momentum as time went on. In addition to the killings, the war destroyed most of Vietnam's cities, villages, homes, industrial factories, and croplands. The natural environment was significantly affected by the poison dioxin, or Agent Orange, a defoliant sprayed on the jungles. When North Vietnamese troops captured Saigon in 1975, thousands of South Vietnamese fled the country. Overcrowded and filthy boats became homes to "boat people" as they awaited approval from some country to grant them citizenship. New homes for hundreds of thousands of Vietnamese became crowded refugee camps in locations that included Indonesia, the Philippines, Hong Kong, and Thailand. Some of the camps lacked adequate water, food, clothing, and health care.

Bangladesh was another country in southern Asia that was affected by war in the 1970s. The prime minister established the second capital of Pakistan at Dacca (modern Dhaka). Government officials contacted Louis I. Kahn to design Sher-E-Banglanagar in Bangladesh and the Indian Institute of Management in Ahmadabad, India. Stretching from the present into the past, two very important archeological discoveries occurred in the 1970s. In Mexico City, the Templo Mayor, built by the Aztecs in the 14th century, was rediscovered. And an enormous subterranean complex including thousands of terracotta warriors from more than 2,000 years ago was found in the Xi'an area of China.

Collective oil policies of Arab nations had a dramatic and immediate impact on the industrialized world. A limited supply of a natural resource in high demand created a global crisis in industrialized nations as well as developing countries. Oil prices quadrupled, gasoline supplies were reduced, and the price of a gallon of gasoline nearly doubled in 1 year. To conserve what became very expensive energy, people in most industrialized nations focused on ways to reduce dependency on nonrenewable resources and to explore the possibilities of using renewable forms of energy.

Technology for computer-aided design/computer-aided manufacturing (CAD/CAM) had origins in the 1970s but was primarily used by large manufacturing industries. Prior to the invention of the microprocessor, CAD/CAM systems were too expensive for most businesses. Initially professionals and organizations had to be convinced that computer-aided technologies were a good investment. As computers were impacting design, Renzo Piano and Richard Rogers were involved with a project that revolutionized the way people viewed and interacted with technology. The exposure of the service functions of the Centre Georges Pompidou provided freedom of movement and emphasized modern mechanical systems.

Providing safe, clean, and affordable housing for all people has always been a global problem. Due to deplorable housing conditions and public outcry, many industrial nations developed new laws and created public housing programs during the 1970s. Horrendous practices were even worse in South Africa, especially during the apartheid years (1948–1994). The origins of apartheid were derived from racial segregation instituted by early European settlers. Collectively, laws and enforcement policies controlled every level of life in South Africa. Maps were used to designate the location of "black" and "white" regions, cities, towns, business districts, housing, schools, churches, recreational facilities, parks, and beaches. Apartheid policies not only had a dramatic impact on the geography of the country, but the laws affected the layout of buildings.

Popular music, dancing, and fashion in the new decade changed from the rock concerts and hippie subculture of the 1960s. Instead of listening to music performed by a band on an outdoor stage, people danced on a stage in disco clubs with music played by a disc jockey. By the end of the 1970s, more than 20,000 discos were thriving in every major U.S. city, and some type of disco-style entertainment was available in many rural communities. In Paris, architects Renzo Piano and Richard Rogers were involved with designing the Institute for Music/Acoustic Research and Coordination (IRCAM). Christo and Jeanne-Claude are artists who are internationally famous for their vast-scale natural and urban environment projects, several of which have involved wrapping or covering objects, including entire buildings. An extremely complicated political project of theirs was the temporary *Wrapped Reichstag* (1971–1995) in Berlin.

In less than 20 years, the small city of Columbus, Indiana, developed an international reputation for modern architecture due to the visionary leaders at the Cummins Engine Company. The American Institute of Architects ranked Columbus as one of the top U.S. cities for "architectural innovation and design," and *Smithsonian* magazine cited it as a "veritable museum of modern architecture." As mentioned in the previous chapter, many businesses prospered in the 1960s, which led executives to anticipate the need for more office space. Sears, based in Chicago, commissioned SOM to design its new headquarters, the Sears Tower. The structural system enabled the Sears Tower to become the tallest building in the world in 1974. Then, in Toronto, Canada, to alleviate transmission problems, the Canadian National (CN) Railway built the world's tallest self-supporting structure, the CN Tower (1976).

KEY TERMS

bundled tube

computer-aided design/computer-aided manufacturing (CAD/CAM)

computer graphics

earth-sheltered housing

fossil fuels

geothermal energy

greenhouse effect resources

nonrenewable resources

nuclear energy

passive solar energy

Plexiglas

public housing projects

R-values resource

renewable resource

solar energy

water power (hydroelectric power)

wind power

EXERCISES

1. Human Factors Research Project. Perform an analysis of the social science research studies conducted in the 1960s and 1970s related to public housing and urban renewal. Identify international policies and practices. Contact not-for-profit organizations that provide housing for disadvantaged people. Compare and contrast the social science research with the practices at the not-for-profit organizations. In a written report, summarize your results and include recommendations for future practice. The report could include drawings, sketches, and photographs. If possible, present the recommendations to one of the not-for-profit organizations.

2. Philosophy and Design Project. Research the effects of segregation on the people, philosophical perspectives, and living conditions in South Africa. Analyze current conditions and the years during apartheid. In a written report, summarize your findings and provide suggestions for an oral presentation. In a team with other students, prepare a presentation that is supported with visual materials.

3. Research Design Project. Viewing Christo's *Reichstag* building as a wrapped package reveals architectural forms and proportions that tend to be obscured by the competing shapes and ornamentation that cover the façades of the unwrapped structure. In a team of designers, research and build a model of a building in Asia. Using three different approaches, wrap the structure with textiles and ties. Record your team's observations. Write a report that summarizes your observations and include comments regarding how the architectural forms and proportions were altered depending upon how the structure was draped and tied. The report could include sketches, drawings, or photographs.

CHAPTER 10

EMPHASIS: THE 1980S

OBJECTIVES

After reading this chapter, you should be able to describe and analyze:

■ How selected global political events in the 1980s affected interior environments and architecture, such as the influence of communism on the built environments of Hungary and Berlin.

■ How the natural environment and disasters affected selected global interior environments and architecture in the 1980s as evident by high-rises in Hong Kong and the MGM Grand Hotel fire, respectively.

■ How selected global technologies in the 1980s affected global interior environments and architecture as evident by the nuclear disaster at the Chernobyl nuclear power station and an abandoned railroad station, the Orsay Station and Hotel in Paris.

■ How selected global work styles and lifestyles in the 1980s, such as air terrorism and religious beliefs, affected interior environments and architecture.

■ How selected global visual arts and performing arts in the 1980s affected global interior environments and architecture as evident by the new Globe Theatre and the Memphis movement.

■ How selected global business and economic developments in the 1980s, such as Japanese commerce and the international banking industry, affected interior environments and architecture.

■ How to compare and contrast selected interior environments and architecture of the Americas, Asia/Oceania, Europe, and the Middle East/Africa in the 1980s.

The collapse of communism and the end of the Cold War had dramatic effects on people, communities, and the built environment. Former communist states were involved with creating new constitutions, laws, and building programs. Hungary is an interesting example of how a nation transitioned from communist control to an independent country that was proud of its cultural heritage. A highly visible symbol of the end of communism was the dismantling of the Berlin Wall at the end of the decade and the reunification of Germany.

By 1980, the world population escalated to more than four billion; China alone had one billion people. Scientists were continuing their research regarding the impact humans have on the natural environment. Rapidly escalating populations were especially troubling in island nations with already extremely high-density living arrangements. Hong Kong was forced to build skyscrapers in its confined and populous city. As has been described throughout this text, the depletion of nonrenewable resources has consequences on the built environment. The design profession has an important role in safeguarding people, as well as the natural and built environment, by promoting and engaging in sustainability practices. Fortunately, the importance of sustainable development and design has come to the forefront in the 21st century (see Chapter 11).

The consequences of breakdowns in technology can be disastrous. The Chernobyl nuclear power station in Ukraine is an example of what can occur when technology fails, and how these occurrences as well as acts of terrorism redefine the roles and responsibilities of the design profession. Unexpected uses of technology can also be destructive, as when terrorists employ aircraft, automobiles, and trucks as weapons. Air terrorism has completely revolutionized the design of airports and the way that people travel. In the 1980s, air travel had an effect on previously popular modes of transportation. Considered obsolete, magnificent 19th- and 20th-century railroad stations were abandoned; some were saved, but some classical buildings were demolished in the name of progress by some individuals. Religion still played a major role throughout the world. But many of the new religious buildings incorporated modern technologies and featured immense structures.

Historically significant structures, which can be perceived as critical to sustaining cultural heritages, were reconstructed during the 1980s. The reconstruction of the Globe Theatre in London is an example of a project that will have long-lasting contributions for future generations. Memphis and Postmodern architecture did not last a long time, but their innovative motifs, colors, and forms had a role in attracting attention to the work of designers as well as posing debates regarding the purposes of ornamentation.

The effects of globalization—the efforts of businesses to expand operations into foreign markets as well as the connectivity between various countries and their economies—came to the forefront in the 1980s as Japanese corporations became world leaders in the production of automobiles and consumer electronics. Technological developments revolutionized the way people live, work, and play. Japanese inventions were surpassed only by the amazing advances in computers. Cited by *Time* magazine as the "Man of the Year" for 1982, computers and their progress in the 1980s enabled the machines' use on a daily basis and globally connected people and places. Many service industries, including banking, international finance, and trade, were dramatically affected by computers.

GLOBAL POLITICS AND GOVERNMENT

Numerous political events in the 1980s affected people living in Europe and the rest of the world. In Eastern Europe, opposition to communism reached a peak by 1989, when Communist parties began to lose control over governments in Czechoslovakia, East Germany, Hungary, and Poland. This was the decade when Polish workers formed a free labor-union organization, Solidarity, in 1981. In 1984, Prime Minister Margaret Thatcher signed the Joint Sino-British Declaration, agreeing to return Hong Kong to China in 1997 after 155 years of British rule. In the Soviet Union, Mikhail Gorbachev replaced Konstantin Chernenko as the Soviet leader in 1985 and initiated a reform program in Russia. Policies of perestroika (economic and political restructuring) and glasnost (openness) were at the base of the reforms. Glasnost contributed to the dismantling of the Berlin Wall in 1989 and the reunification of Germany in 1990.

In 1989, pro-democracy protestors in China were halted by government security forces when more than 100,000 people gathered in Tiananmen Square to demonstrate for democracy. Hundreds of civilians were killed and injured while the violence was broadcast on television and captured in photographs. An 8-year war (1980–1988) between Iraq and Iran over control of the Shatt al-Arab River concluded without resolution, but both countries suffered severe economic hardship and widespread devastation. Previous colonial states won their independence in the 1980s, including Zimbabwe (formerly Rhodesia) (1980), Antigua and Barbuda (1981), Brunei (1984), and Micronesia (1986).

Terrorists continued to strike, attacking embassies and taking hostages. Americans taken hostage in 1979 and held captive in Iran for 444 days were released on January 20, 1981. In Beirut, Lebanon, a bombing of the U.S. embassy killed 63 in 1983. The Irish Republican Army continued bombing Britain with specific targets in London; the high-profile London department store Harrods was bombed during the peak of the Christmas season in 1983, killing six people.

Communism: Hungary and Imre Makovecz

Hungary is located in Central Europe and is bordered by Romania, Serbia/Montenegro, Croatia, Slovenia,

Austria, Slovakia, and Ukraine. The country is enclosed by the Alps to the west and the Carpathian Mountains to the southeast, and is connected to the continent by the Danube and Tisza rivers. Hungary's centralized location and geographical features have significantly affected its history, culture, government, and the arts. Known as the "Crossroads of Europe," Hungary's vulnerable location precipitated attacks from several invaders, including the Mongols in the 13th century. Buda became the capital of Hungary in 1361 and was fortified by Matthias I Corvinus in the 15th century. In the 16th century, Hungary was taken and held by the Ottoman Turks (1541–1686).

From the 16th century until the present, Turkish rule influenced Hungary's interior environments and architecture. The Turks constructed hundreds of spas in Hungary, especially in the area that is now Budapest, the capital city of Hungary. Many of the spas had impressive architecture and were known for their domes, large pillars, and elegant stone interiors (Figure 10.1). Turkish spas have been renovated and continue to be very popular tourist destinations. Another continuing Turkish influence is coffee houses. The Turks introduced coffee to the Hungarians, which prompted the development of hundreds of coffee houses, many of which are still being used for coffee houses today. Since the 16th century, Hungary was producing earthenware and **majolica ceramics,** a highly decorated soft earthenware with tin and lead glazes with origins in Italy. The tradition of ceramics continued in Hungary during the Habsburg Empire with the establishment of Herend, a porcelain-manufacturing company, in 1826. Herend porcelains are known for their pure white color and the simple 24-karat gold edging and accents. Today, Herend is the largest porcelain manufacturer in Europe.

The Habsburg Empire, based in Vienna, Austria, ruled Hungary from 1699 until a compromise was established giving Hungary independence except in specific areas, such as foreign affairs, in 1867. The dual monarchy union between the two countries created the Austro-Hungarian Empire (1867–1918). The assassination of the heir to the Austro-Hungarian Empire, Archduke Francis Ferdinand, in 1914 precipitated the beginning of World War I (see Chapter 3). Hungary's monarchy ties with Austria forced that country to fight with Germany during the war.

Defeated, Hungary was dramatically impacted by the Treaty of Trianon, which was signed between Hungary and the Allied nations in 1920. Approximately 70 percent of Hungary's land area was distributed to several surrounding countries. This significant amount of territory reduced Hungary's population by more than 60 percent, and the country lost many natural

Figure 10.1 The Turks constructed hundreds of spas in Budapest, especially in Budapest, the capital city of Hungary. Turkish spas have been renovated and continue to be very popular tourist destinations.

Source: Robert Harding Picture Library Ltd./Alamy.

resources, factories, and some of its architectural heritage. Native Hungarians living in the newly established regions automatically became immigrants.

Hungary joined with German forces again during World War II. At the conclusion of that war, Soviet troops controlled Hungary, and it eventually became a satellite state of the Soviet Union with a communist government and constitution. To create a police state between 1949 and 1956, the communist leader of Hungary, Mátyás Rákosi, created unbearable living conditions that included torturing prisoners and incarcerations in concentration camps. In opposition to communist control, Hungarian students initiated a revolution in 1956. In less than 1 month of fighting, more than 2,500 Hungarians were killed during the revolt and the Soviet Union regained control of the country. In 1956, *Time* magazine named the "Hungarian Freedom Fighter" the "Man of the Year." Eventually their bravery had an impact on Hungary.

János Kádár became leader of Hungary, and the Soviet government gave him the task to clean up the political mess of 1956. Under the leadership of Kádár, the Soviet Union reduced some of its control. In the 1980s, Hungary opened its borders to allow people to travel from East Germany to West Germany. Allowing people to circumvent the barbed wire fences by traveling through Hungary essentially started to dissolve the "Iron Curtain"; the military, political, and ideological barrier created between Western Europe and the Soviet Union and its satellite states. Kádár's economic reforms started to take hold in the early 1980s, making Hungary more prepared for free commerce than many other countries in Eastern Europe as the Cold War ended and Eastern Europe was opened to the west. Antigovernment unrest in Hungary in the 1980s led to the declaration of the Hungarian republic and the end of communist control in 1989. The first free elections since 1945 were held in 1990, and the last Soviet troops left the country in 1991.

Hungary's architectural history from the postwar years until the end of communist control is an interesting analysis of how communism initially impacted the design of buildings as well as the changes that occurred as the Soviet Union withdrew from the country. As a communist satellite state, Hungary's government, farmlands, educational system, industry, businesses, foreign affairs, defense, and all public projects were controlled by the Union of Soviet Socialist Republics (USSR). Materials for housing were scarce, and thus private residences were small and state-owned apartment units were very crowded. Essentially, the state controlled Hungarian architectural initiatives. Most of Hungary was destroyed during World War II, and thus substantial rebuilding had to occur throughout the country.

The massive reconstruction program provided considerable work for Hungarian architects and designers, but initially their designs had to follow the ideals of Stalinist architecture (see Chapter 7). Public architectural drawings and artwork underwent a stringent review and proposal process. A means of communist propaganda, public statues and ornamentation on buildings depicted Soviet leaders and laborers as hardworking heroes. Noncompliance with communist ideals and themes resulted in censorship. These imposed restrictions occurred during a time when several talented Hungarian architects, such as Farkas Molnár, József Fischer, L. Kozma, L. Lauber, and I. Nyíri, had designed outstanding modern architecture prior to World War II.

Stalinist architecture continued until after the Hungarian Revolution in 1956. During the government's attempt to gain support from Hungarians in the 1960s, architects and designers had more liberty with their designs. In the 1970s, the design profession developed innovative theories for Hungarian architecture. By the 1980s, devastating economic conditions in the Soviet Union and its satellite nations nearly eliminated state-sponsored projects, but created opportunities for new private projects, including banks, offices, restaurants, and hotels. An excellent example is the Grand Hotel Corvinus Kempinski in Budapest, designed by the well-known Hungarian architects József Finta and

Antal Puhl. The relaxed restrictions and censorship of design prompted professionals to create architecture that reflected Hungarian values and vernacular traditions. Organic architecture (see Chapter 6), which included the use of natural materials and connections to the local natural environment, was an outgrowth of this movement.

The work of renowned Hungarian architect Imre Makovecz is an excellent example of organic architecture in the 1980s. Makovecz began his career working in state-sponsored design studios (1959–1977), but due to Soviet design restrictions, he accepted a position with the Pilis Forestry in 1977. Makovecz designed facilities for the Forestry Department, such as observation towers and camping units. Away from Soviet officials, the low-key position provided Makovecz with creative freedom. He became involved with the evolving theories of organic architecture, such as the concepts of Frank Lloyd Wright, and founded Makona Associated Architects in Budapest in 1981 (modern MAKONA Architectural Studio). An interesting example of Makovecz's organic architecture is Bak, Village Community Centre (1985). As illustrated in Figure 10.2, Makovecz used natural materials for the building, such as plank siding, and his design subtly references an eagle, the historical symbol of Hungary with origins in the Austro-Hungarian Empire. Makovecz's following explanation of the center includes Hungarian history: "This small multi-functional cultural institute planned for a small village in Western Hungary, contains a lecture hall, a library and club rooms. Its ground plan has a birdlike form, a feeling enhanced by the plank siding covering the building in a way that resembles bird wings. This was done in imitation of the mythical turul bird, an ancient, animalistic symbol representing the embodiment of the Hungarians. A turul monument erected in memory of those fallen in World War I—destroyed in the 1950s—stood in front of the new house" (www.makovecz.hu). Conceptually, a community center for lectures, group discussions, and fellowship was very important for people who were

Figure 10.2 Makovecz became involved with the evolving theories of organic architecture and founded Makona Associated Architects in 1981. A very interesting example of Makovecz's organic architecture is Bak, Village Community Centre.

Source: Adam Balog.

forced to live under communist control. The facility gave Hungarians the opportunity to connect with each other in public, a right that had been restricted controlled while living in a communist satellite state.

World War II: The Berlin Wall (1961–1989)

An outcome of World War II, determined at the Potsdam conference, was the "temporary" division of Germany into four military occupation zones, administered by France, the United Kingdom, the United States, and the Soviet Union. Each country had military oversight for its zone, and people could walk freely between each of the four sectors. Berlin, which was in the Soviet controlled (eastern) sector, also was divided into four

zones. The plan for these four nations to cooperatively administer Germany as a single unit broke down with the beginning of the Cold War. Political and military rifts, including issues such as currency reform and industrial disarmament, appeared between the western nations and the Soviet Union in the late 1940s.

In May 1949, the Federal Republic of Germany (West Germany) was established on the territory of the Western occupied zones, and in October 1949 the German Democratic Republic (East Germany) was established in the Soviet zone. West Germany was a democracy, and East Germany became a communist satellite of the Soviet Union. A barbed wire fence was constructed between the two countries, and the border was monitored by guards in watchtowers. Berlin, Germany's former capital, was in East Germany. East Berlin was controlled by the Soviet Union and became the capital of East Germany; West Berlin remained controlled by the other three Allies, its resident citizens of West Germany. France had the northwest section of West Berlin, the United Kingdom controlled the center area of the city, and most of the southern sector was controlled by the United States. Disparities in living conditions, wages, and food shortages between citizens living in East and West Germany prompted many people to emigrate to the west.

By the beginning of 1961, East Germany had lost millions of emigrants, including highly skilled workers, scientists, physicians, and other professionals. In just the early months of 1961, more than 200,000 people left East Germany. Communist leaders feared the consequences of the drain on the population. Soviet officials were intent on preventing further losses. Speculation focused on the need for barricades, but Walter Ulbricht, leader of the East Germany Communist party, suppressed the idea of constructing a dividing wall in 1961 when he proclaimed at a press conference in East Berlin and through posted signage in Berlin that "The construction workers of our capital are for the most part busy building apartment houses, and their working capacities are fully employed to that end. Nobody intends to put up a wall."

Ulbricht's June 16, 1961, statement was followed less than 2 months later with the secretive construction of what became known as the Berlin Wall. In the middle of the night on August 13, 1961, East German military and police forces quickly installed a fence made of concrete posts and barbed wire. Without resistance from the Western forces stationed in West Berlin, the 96-mile (155-kilometer) fence was completed in 4 days. The Berlin Wall was built between what became East and West Berlin and the entire perimeter area that separated West Berlin from East Germany. Eventually, in most locations, the barbed wire was replaced with a concrete slab wall that was approximately 13 feet (4 meters) high and was monitored by armed guards in more than 300 watchtowers.

The rapid and secretive construction of the fence resulted in the separation of thousands of families. Photos taken on the western side of the wall reveal people using binoculars to wave to their family members on the eastern side. To visit family living in West Berlin, a family member was required to remain in East Berlin. Communist officials believed that by retaining family members, it was more likely that the people who visited West Berlin would return to East Berlin.

Prior to the construction of the Berlin Wall, people living in East and West Germany had already experienced dramatically different living conditions, reflected in the quality of their housing, availability of technology, and employment opportunities. Interior environments and architecture had been affected by the differences in living in capitalist and communist societies. West Germany had contemporary skyscrapers and modern transportation, household appliances, and conveniences. East German architecture was state-sponsored; the interiors lacked modern amenities. As discussed in previous chapters many of the reasons for the contrasting living conditions are based on the philosophical divergences between capitalism and communism. Capitalism's free market system is based on private ownership and the principles of supply and demand. Thus, people working for successful businesses and manufacturing corporations are able to increase their income and have the opportunity to purchase quality goods and services. In a communist state, the national government controls the means for economic productivity, such as factories, the building industry, and farming. By controlling productivity, the government determines wages, prices, products, and housing. People are not able to select their housing, type of employment, or where they can live.

Construction of the Berlin Wall reinforced the differences between the two living conditions and illustrated how the callous attitudes of East Berlin officials affected people, interior environments, architecture, and the city. The East German army constructed the Berlin Wall without regard to families, ownership of businesses, church membership, place of employment, location of buildings, transportation networks, bridges, or street patterns. People lost their jobs because they had been located on the other side of the division. Buildings, roads, and railways were leveled to create the wall. With total disregard for functional aspects of the city, the wall was constructed directly in front of the doorways of buildings (Figure 10.3).

In one photograph, a woman can be seen hanging on the edge of a window on the third story of a building. The building was in East Berlin, but the ground next to the façade was in West Berlin. Freedom was waiting for her on the ground, and several West Berliners were waiting to catch her if she jumped. However, the woman was detained by East Berlin police, who had hold of her hands and arms. A West Berliner climbed the wall and rescued the woman. The façade of this building, and many other structures, became part of the Berlin Wall when East German officials boarded the windows and doors.

In another situation, fabric was used to attain freedom. Two families living in East Germany wanted to reunite with their families in West Germany. The families purchased yards of nylon fabric and stitched

Figure 10.3 A total disregard for functional aspects of the city resulted in the Berlin Wall being constructed directly in front of the doorways of buildings.

Source: Heiko Burkhardt.

the lengths into a giant hot-air balloon. On one evening with an easterly blowing wind, four adults and four children climbed into the balloon and safely crossed the border. Subsequently, East German officials imposed limits on the purchase of nylon fabric.

A look at Potsdamer Platz (Place), a very important and thriving commercial area of Berlin, reveals how the Berlin Wall affected people, the city, architecture, and interior environments. Figure 10.4 illustrates Potsdamer Platz as it appeared in 1932. The square was crowded with automobiles, trains, and people, and many prominent businesses faced the square. The 10-story building with alternating bands of opaque surfaces and strip windows was the Columbushaus (1931) building. Designed by German architect Erich Mendelsohn, the

streamlined design is an excellent example of how architects were reflecting the speed and movement of new forms of transportation. Columbushaus was unique for being a multi-functional building. The street level had shops, and other floors were dedicated to offices and restaurants. Berlin and Potsdamer Platz were badly damaged during World War II, but photographs reveal the skeletal existence of remaining structures, including Columbushaus. Figure 10.5 reveals how Potsdamer Platz was changed by the Berlin Wall. The previously thriving area with modern buildings and transportation systems was replaced by barren ground, barbed wire, concrete walls, and military police.

For nearly 30 years, people lived in the divided city and community. During this period on the west side only, the wall became a canvas for the public and artists. As a reflection of two distinctly different living conditions, the vivid expressions on the west side of the wall were in stark contrast to the east side's blank wall. Painted words, symbols, and figures covered the concrete walls on the west side—this graffiti art has been recorded for posterity in numerous media.

Ironically, to try to keep East Germans from fleeing, eventually the Soviet Union decided to remove the wall. Officials believed that by allowing people to travel between the two countries, the East Berliners were more likely to stay in their home. On November 9, 1989, the Berlin Wall was opened, and cranes started the long process of removing the concrete and barbed wire fences. Tearing down the Berlin Wall not only reunited Berlin, but symbolically its dismantling communicated to people an end of an era. As if political ideologies were the mortar between the concrete blocks, when the wall came down, so did communism, the Cold War, and the iron curtain. The people of Germany celebrated, and fragments of the wall were collected for sale and posterity. Today, the location of the wall is marked with rows of cobblestones, and the memories of the division are forever documented in countless "before and after" photographs.

Figure 10.4 Photograph of Potsdamer Platz as it appeared in 1932. The 10-story building on the right was the Columbushaus (1931) building designed by the German architect, Erich Mendelsohn. Compare this photograph with Figure 10.5.

Source: BPK/Art Resource, NY.

Figure 10.5 Potsdamer Platz after the construction of the Berlin Wall. Compare this photograph with Figure 10.4.

Source: akg-images.

EFFECTS AND CONDITIONS OF THE NATURAL ENVIRONMENT

Scientists continued to research the negative impact of humans on the planet. Studies focused on the effects of global warming, population growth, deforestation, and increases in the consumption of fossil fuels. In 1985, British Antarctic Survey scientists discovered a hole in the ozone layer, the protective layer that separates us from harmful ultraviolet radiation from the sun. In 1987, the European Community subsequently signed an agreement, the Montreal Protocol on Substances that Deplete the Ozone Layer, to halt the production of all chlorofluorocarbons (CFCs), a chemical that contributes to ozone depletion.

Also during this decade, more than a million people died from famine in Ethiopia, a crisis that prompted dozens of well-known musical artists to collaborate to help the country via the Live Aid benefit concert in 1985. The 1980s also saw disasters caused by technological developments. In 1984, more than 4,000 people were killed by a lethal gas leak at a Union Carbide Pesticide plant in Bhopal, India. Two years later, an explosion at a nuclear power plant in Chernobyl, Ukraine, released radioactive isotopes across Europe and the rest of the world.

The specific concept of sustainable development was identified in the 1987 United Nations (UN) report of the World Commission on Environment and Development

(WCED) entitled *Our Common Future*, also known as the Brundtland Report.

From a vastly different perspective death and destruction occurred when one of the worst hotel fires in U.S. history happened at the MGM Grand Hotel in Las Vegas. In Mexico, a volcanic eruption in 1982 killed more than 2,000 people, and an earthquake just 3 years later killed more than 10,000 people. Also in 1985, a volcanic eruption in Colombia killed more than 25,000 people. In 1987, a ferry accident in Manila, Philippines, killed more than 4,000 people after the ferry collided with an oil tanker. In Prince William Sound, Alaska, the *Exxon Valdez* ran aground and spilled 11 million gallons (42 million liters) of oil along the state's coastline in 1989. Disasters that destroy the natural environment focus attention on the precious value of the planet's natural resources, such as land, something that is well understood in high-density communities such as Hong Kong.

Nonrenewable Natural Resources: Hongkong and Shanghai Bank Corporation Headquarters (1979–1986) in Hong Kong by Norman Foster

From a sustainability perspective, complexities associated with balancing the needs of people, the natural environment, and the economy were revealed in the 1980s. The world's quickly escalating population hit new heights in the 1980s, reaching five billion by 1987. Highly dense living conditions were intensified in Hong Kong, which includes Hong Kong Island, the Kowloon Peninsula, New Territories, and several small islands. In the 1980s, Hong Kong had over five million people living in 426 square miles (1,103 square kilometers), or approximately 13,000 individuals per square mile (5,000 per square kilometer). These were the conditions when executives of the Hongkong Bank, known as 1QRC (One Queen's Road Central), branch (founded in 1866) requested a proposal from British architect Norman Foster for the redevelopment of its headquarters, located in the heart of Hong Kong's

political and financial district. At this time, Hong Kong was a colony of Britain (1898–1997). The request came after Norman Foster's innovative design for the large headquarters of an insurance company, Willis Faber & Dumas (1971–1975) in Ipswich, United Kingdom. Compared to conventional offices in the 1970s, unique concepts for the insurance company included a swimming pool, restaurant, and rooftop garden.

In the 1970s, the Hongkong Bank was still using a massive neoclassical building designed by Palmer & Turner in 1935. The building itself became a symbol of the banking industry and was printed on the red Chinese paper currency. In a country and city with millions of people who believed in the principles of feng shui, the bank building and its auspicious site and interior were associated with the city's strong financial health. Feng shui is the Chinese art or practice of positioning objects to create harmony and balance within an environment (see Chapter 4). Due to the bank's continued success, by the end of the 1970s, bank officials concluded that the building's 300,000 square feet (27,871 square meters) were no longer adequate for their operations and would not be able to accommodate the anticipated future growth. Executives determined they would need approximately 800,000 square feet (74,322 square meters) of space.

The bank's favorable site was imperative to their future plans. Land was at a premium in Hong Kong, one of the world's most densely populated cities. Since World War II, the city's population had increased annually by 125,000 people, many of whom were refugees from surrounding countries. To help resolve the massive housing shortages, thousands of high-rises were erected quickly and cheaply. In Hong Kong, the price for land can exceed construction costs—land could be 70 percent of the costs for a project.

Space within high-rises was also at a premium. Many units had only one or two rooms, and often these spaces were subdivided and leased. To double the area in an apartment, some occupants built another floor between the unit's original floor and its ceiling. By the 1980s, high-rises were essentially the only means to house and employ people. Hence, high-rises also were built for commercial and industrial purposes.

The practical solution for the Hongkong Bank was to build a tall skyscraper on the same site of the 1935 building. Foster's design for the bank had to maximize usable space and be constructed quickly (Figure 10.6). To develop the design for the 47-story structure, Foster and his associates researched the bank's auspicious site and studied the movements of people outside the building. The 1935 building faced Statue Square and Victoria

Figure 10.6 Foster's design for the Hongkong and Shanghai Bank in Hong Kong had to maximize usable space and had to be constructed quickly. Foster based some of the design on the movement of people.
Source: Peter Scholey/Alamy.

Harbour. The square was one of the few green areas in the city; therefore, the park had an important relationship to the bank. Mount Victoria (or "the Peak") was behind the building. According to feng shui, the location of these natural elements was very auspicious for the success and prosperity of the bank. A commercial building that faces water provides the basis for economic development and wealth. Mountains or "dragons" behind a structure protect the occupants from harsh winds and evil influences. The bank also had two bronze lions symbolically guarding its entrance. Over the years, the lions became associated with the good fortunes of the bank. Therefore, the lions would remain at the entrance of the new building. Feng shui masters also determined the most auspicious days for moving the lions during the construction phase and the date for reinstalling them upon completion of the new building.

In observing the flow of people, Foster noted that every day thousands of people came from the ferries and walked by the bank to other areas of the city. To create synergy between the bank and the public, Foster created an open plaza under the building (see Figures 10.6 and 10.7). Foster explained spaces that inspired his concept, saying:

> The spaces that the building makes at the ground are also important. We could not find a twentieth century building to explain to the bank what we were trying to achieve so we used one of our favourite [sic] buildings from the past, which is the Galleria [Vittorio Emanuele] in Milan by Giuseppe Mengoni. Apart from being a symbolic gateway it is also a very enjoyable short-cut with much interest, restaurants and bookshops, all related to the main offices above. Another favourite [sic] building in the same spirit is Paxton's Crystal Palace, a building which has not, in our view, been equalled [sic] since. (Lasdun, 1984, p. 125)

Thus, the plaza enabled people to interact with the bank by passing *through* the structure rather than walking around it. Foster also explored unique approaches to what people experienced as they moved through the interior of the bank (Figure 10.7). The architect was very much opposed to what had become the traditional means to move people in skyscrapers. Rather than totally relying on "sealed metal boxes" (elevators), he minimized the time in elevators by using high-speed one-stop systems to specific floors and then people used open escalators to take them to their destinations.

Foster also was concerned with people's perception of their work environment, stating, "Architecture is still about making appropriate space. It is about spaces for people, because the quality of the space influences the quality of life" (Lasdun, 1984, p. 119). As with public housing projects, the enormous size of skyscrapers can be dehumanizing, and the sense of alienation can be intensified by the lack of contact with the natural environment. Foster explained his views regarding the design of most skyscrapers, noting, "We tried to learn some lessons from the past in protest against the banality, the repetition, the institutionalized wastage, the poor performance, the miserable appearance of office towers the world over" (Lasdun, 1984, p. 125).

Foster's solution was to create human-scaled environments that included sunlight, gardens, and open areas. The interior consisted of "clusters" of office floors that were suspended from horizontal trusses. These "village-like units" were between large reception areas with outdoor gardens, or sky gardens (see Figure 10.7). As illustrated in Figure 10.7, to further enhance a connection to the natural environment, Foster designed a technology that reflected daylight into the center of the building. Sunlight strikes a large "sunscoop" mounted on the building's south façade, and then the light reflects to mirrors installed on the ceiling of the bank hall. Natural light reflects from the mirrors into the centrally located atrium, through the glass floor, and finally illuminates the plaza. Hong Kong's subtropical climate features an abundance of sunlight; this allows the bank's atrium and plaza to be filled with natural daylight.

Figure 10.7 The interior of Foster's Hongkong and Shanghai Bank building consisted of "clusters" of office floors that were suspended from horizontal trusses. "Village-like units" were between large reception areas with outdoor gardens, or sky gardens.
Source: Dennis Cox/Alamy.

To control the intense heat, Foster used sun shades on the façades and developed a new technology based on a traditional Eastern design. While engaged in research for the design of the bank, Foster and his associates traveled to Japan. In Kyoto, they lived in traditional Japanese houses and were especially fond of the diffused yet abundant level of illumination that passed through shoji screens. Subsequently, the firm researched the properties of the materials and developed "shoji windows" by inserting a layer of insulation between two panels of glass. Other references to traditional materials were the design of the floor coverings and scaffolding. The silver-gray carpet was divided into panels to resemble tatami mats. Foster noted that if scaffolding was needed for the project, workers would use bamboo, which he contended was more efficient than contemporary metal scaffolding systems. In addition, to follow a traditional Hong Kong building method, Foster explained that after machines removed the soil, "the caissons which go down to bedrock are hand dug by small family teams."

After occupancy, a feng shui master analyzed and made adjustments to the interior. For example, to avoid evil spirits and to enhance positive energy, plants, flowers, and mirrors were placed in specific locations. To further enhance positive energy, other changes included the removal of black metal file cabinets, which some people believed resembled coffins. Similarly, desks were placed in the most auspicious positions. To continue the bank's prosperity, on the outside of the building the two bronze lions were reinstalled in their former prominent position with the supervision of feng shui masters.

In 2009 with a population of 7 million, the density in Hong Kong reached 15,750 people per square mile (6,080 per square kilometer), and there are still more than 700,000 squatters living in shacks and tenements in the city of Kowloon.

Natural Disasters: MGM Grand Hotel Fire (1980) in Las Vegas, Nevada

The dramatic and rapid development of Las Vegas since the opening of its first hotel in the 1940s was astounding (see Chapter 6). By the 1970s, Las Vegas was attracting more than 12 million visitors per year. In contrast to high-density populated cities like Hong Kong, there was ample land in the vicinity of Las Vegas. However, land in the heart of the Las Vegas Strip was limited, which prompted hotel owners to build high-rise structures. High-rise mega-structures became synonymous with the Las Vegas experience. To attract tourists to their casinos and hotels, owners were constantly trying to outdo their competitors by building the biggest,

most complex, and, at times, most outlandish structure in the city. This was the situation when self-made billionaire Kirk Kerkorian, who had purchased the MGM movie studio, built the 26-story MGM Grand Hotel during 1972 and 1973. At this time, the MGM Grand Hotel was the largest hotel-casino in the world.

At the time of its deadly fire, on November 21, 1980, the hotel was extraordinarily profitable and had regular occupancy rates close to 100 percent. The MGM Grand Hotel fire killed 85 people, making it the second deadliest hotel fire in the United States (Figure 10.8). The most deadly hotel fire in the United States killed 119 at the Winecoff Hotel in Atlanta, Georgia, on December 7, 1946. The deadliest hotel fire in the world killed 163 people on December 25, 1971, at the Taeyokale Hotel in Seoul, South Korea. Deadly fires prompt architects, interior designers, city officials, and the National Fire Protection Association (NFPA) to reexamine fire factors in buildings, including combustible interior finishes, evacuation systems, and locations of fatalities.

The MGM Grand Hotel fire started in The Deli, a casual restaurant located on the main floor of the T-shaped hotel, in an *unsprinklered* area. An investigation of the fire by the NFPA revealed that the fire was caused by heat generated by an "electrical short-circuiting (a ground-fault) of an ungrounded electrical circuit conductor to a flexible metal conduit" (NFPA, 1982, p. 36). The investigation found that uninsulated wires belonging to a refrigeration unit for a pie display were being stretched and rubbed by the vibration of the unit. Heat from the electrical circuit caused a fire on a wall in The Deli, which soon spread along the ceiling through the restaurant and into the hallway adjacent to the casino. Within 10 minutes of the start of the fire, the entire casino was filled with smoke and flames. Fueled by multiple combustible materials, including the ceiling panels and wall coverings, the flame front continued to the main entrance of the hotel-casino, and soon the porte-cochère (coach door) was afire. Heavy smoke was billowing up the sides of the building. Authorities

Figure 10.8 The interior of the casino in the MGM Grand Hotel, Las Vegas, after the deadly fire in 1980. The Grand Hotel was the second deadliest hotel fire in the United States.

Source: AP Photo/Saxon.

estimated that the fire started at approximately 7:10 a.m., and by 8:00 a.m. the entire 67,500-square-foot (62,710 square-meter) casino was in flames and smaller fires had started on the fifth floor (see Figure 10.8).

The fire department was called at 7:15 a.m., and the first fire trucks arrived at 7:19 a.m. The fire in the casino was controlled by 8:30 a.m., but another fire erupted on a roof west of the casino at 9:24 a.m. The entire fire was extinguished by 3:00 p.m. The casino and the offices above the gaming area suffered the most destruction from the fire, but the entire building had smoke damage (see Figure 10.8). Rescue efforts included the help of several ironworkers who were on the construction site of the hotel's adjoining addition, and U.S. Nellis Air Force helicopters from the nearby air base. Helicopters were used to rescue approximately 300 people from the roof of the MGM Grand high-rise towers.

Even though several fire departments immediately responded to the fire alarm and the fire was soon contained, 84 hotel guests and employees were killed at the hotel, one guest died later in a hospital, and more than 600 people required medical attention. Sixty-one people had died in the high-rise tower, and 18 victims were found in the casino. The comparatively small number of people who died in the casino can be attributed to the fact that the fire happened early in the morning, a time period when few people gambled. The NFPA reported that "all of the fatalities in the high-rise tower died of asphyxiation secondary to carbon monoxide inhalation. Of the 18 victims located on the casino level, 14 died of smoke and carbon monoxide inhalation. Three victims died of burns and smoke and carbon monoxide inhalation, and one victim located outside on the roof of new construction died of a massive skull fracture" (NFPA, 1982, p. 26).

The tragic loss of life at the MGM Grand required the NFPA to conduct a close examination of how the hotel was designed, constructed, furnished, operated, and maintained. In addition, officials reviewed applicable building, fire, and life safety codes. The NFPA published the results of its investigation, and a subsequent study in which the NFPA examined human behavior during the fire. The design profession can learn a great deal about the causes and problems of fires by reading official reports and then applying the recommendations to improve practice. Frequently, disasters prompt the revisions of mandatory codes, but design solutions, such as interior finishes, furniture, and decorative materials, can be specified that are safer than the national or local requirements.

The NFPA report included important information regarding the nature of the fire and how the design of the building and its materials affected the spread of flames, smoke, and poisonous gases. Topics associated with the building were the "Main Casino and The Deli," construction, enclosure of vertical openings, **means of egress,** fire-alarm system, fire-suppression systems, mechanical systems, and elevator systems. The report concluded that the major factors that contributed to the loss of life were: (1) "Rapid fire and smoke development on the Casino level due to the available fuels, building arrangement, and the lack of adequate fire barriers," (2) "Lack of fire extinguishment in the incipient stage of fire," (3) "Unprotected vertical openings contributed to smoke spread to the high-rise towers," and (4) "Substandard enclosure of interior stairs, smoke-proof [sic] towers and exit passageways contributed to heat and smoke spread and impaired the means of egress from the high-rise tower" (NFPA, 1982, p. vi).

"Available fuels" included combustible interior finishes, furnishings, and fixtures. A substantial amount of the interior materials were made of plastics, which can emit lethal gases and, as was seen on the outside of the hotel, tremendous amounts of black smoke. Vinyl wall-covering and laminated plastic paneling were found on the walls of The Deli. The ceiling had plastic laminate glued to gypsum wallboard. The casino's interior finishes included plastic decorative trim that was used to simulate marble and wood. Mirrors in the ceiling were made of methacrylate. The plastic mirror panels extended to the porte-cochère, which had over three hundred panels. "Fuel load" was also provided in The Deli by the chairs, which had been padded in polyurethane foam, and wrap-around booths that were also padded in the foam and covered with a vinyl material. In the casino, the NFPA found plastic interior finishes made of polyvinyl chloride, polyurethane, polystyrene, and methyl methacrylate. Furnishings included gambling tables made with foam plastic padding and plastic covering along their edges. Plastic padding was also present in the casino's seating. Above the casino's ceiling was plastic insulation on electrical and communications wiring.

The large open space in the casino is an example of the building's "lack of adequate fire barriers." The "lack of fire extinguishment" included the building's sparse sprinkler system (Figure 10.9). When the building was constructed in the early 1970s, the sprinkling and fire-safety systems were in compliance with local codes. Most of the building did not have a sprinkling system, but the NFPA noted that the fire did not spread to the rooms

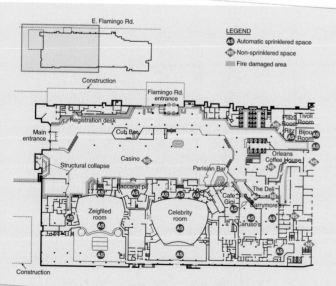

Figure 10.9 Floor plan of the MGM Grand Hotel in Las Vegas indicating automatic sprinklered space, nonsprinklered space, and fire damaged areas.

Source: Illustration by Steven Stankiewicz.

that had automatic sprinklers, including the theaters, the "Baccarat Pit," and three other restaurants. The casino, Deli, entrances, and lobby did not have sprinklers (the locations where most people were found dead). The MGM Grand had several "unprotected vertical openings," including openings in the interior partitions above ceilings, elevators, stairways, and **seismic joints,** which minimize damage to a building during an earthquake.

The primary objective of the NFPA's 1983 human behavior study of the MGM Grand Hotel fire was to determine when the guests became aware of the fire and how "their previous education, training, or experience relative to their selection of alternative responses" affected their actions (NFPA, 1983, p. 2). A few weeks after the fire, researchers mailed a questionnaire to hotel guests registered for the night of November 20–21, 1980. Of the 1,960 questionnaires sent to guests, 554 (28 percent) of the surveys were completed and returned to the researchers.

The results reveal that many of the guests learned about the fire by seeing fire equipment, smelling smoke, hearing yelling and knocking on doors, being "told by their roommate," and seeing the smoke outdoors. None of the guests who completed the survey indicated hearing an alarm or any type of internal signaling system, except for an announcement made in the casino area: "May I have your attention. Please evacuate the casino immediately and carefully. Thank you." Most of the guests used the stairs to leave the building, but there were some fatalities discovered in elevators.

Approximately 60 percent of the guests reported visibility of less than 5 feet (1.5 meters) as they moved through the building. Over 40 percent of the guests indicated that the fire department was an aid in their evacuation. They also reported that remaining calm and having a "will to survive" were aids in leaving the building. Clearly, the investigations revealed the importance of automatic sprinkler systems in the suppression of fires, fire evacuation alarm signals, and manual fire alarm pull stations along paths of egress. For political

reasons as well as to avoid expensive renovation costs, the Las Vegas 1970 building codes did not require retrofitted sprinkler systems in existing buildings. Retrofitting construction expenses are costly, and revenue losses during the process would also be very high. Just 3 months after the MGM Grand fire, the Las Vegas Hilton experienced an arson fire that killed eight people. In 1981, Nevada passed a law requiring sprinkler systems in hotels and other buildings taller than 55 feet (16.8 meters).

New laws were necessary in Nevada; however, investigative authorities have discovered that many factors or conditions that cause or intensify a fire could have been avoided if the owners had complied with *existing* national life safety codes. This situation becomes apparent by studying another publication compiled by the NFPA, 3 years after the MGM fire. NFPA's *Hotel Fires: Behind the Headlines* (1983) includes a summary of the MGM fire as well as other articles that described international hotel fires with fatalities between 1977 and 1982. The articles were published in fire-related journals, such as *Fire Journal* and *Fire Technology*, and the content was based on investigations and analyses by federal agencies.

The findings provide valuable information for architects, interior designers, clients, and city officials. For example, the articles describe effective ways to alert people of a fire (detection systems, evacuation alarms, hotel emergency training) and safe means of egress (adequate number and size of properly enclosed exits). How smoke and fire spread during a fire is explained, as well as construction features that contributed to many of the hotel fires, such as combustible interior finishes, a lack of fire/smoke barriers, and unprotected vertical openings (elevator shafts, pipe chases, etc.). The importance of the design profession knowing this information is evident by a deadly fire that occurred on November 28, 1942, at a nightclub in Boston. The Cocoanut Grove nightclub resulted in indictments against ten people, including the interior designer, because the interior finishes and decorative material were determined to have a significant role in the fire and the subsequent deaths of 492 people.

One of two main causes for the fire spread and the fatalities at the Las Vegas Hilton fire on February 10, 1981, was the combustible carpet on the walls and ceilings of the elevator lobbies. The National Bureau of Standards' Center for Fire Research tested undamaged carpet samples from the hotel, and found that its contents did not comply with the prevailing 1981 Life Safety Codes for interior finish on walls and ceilings. Carpet is tested in a horizontal position on the floor; thus to safely install carpeting on the walls and ceilings requires tests that are performed for interior finishes on walls and ceilings. Installing carpet that was classified for floor applications on the walls and ceilings of the Hilton's elevator lobbies contributed to the fire spread and the subsequent deaths, injuries, and substantial damage to the hotel.

Available fuel load from furnishings and combustible interior finishes were also contributing factors to the loss of life and damages that occurred during hotel fires at the Stouffer's Inn of Westchester (Harrison, New York) on December 4, 1980; Holiday Inn (Cambridge, Ohio) on July 31, 1979; the Ripplecove Inn (Ayer's Cliff, Quebec, Canada) on October 1, 1978; the Filipinas Hotel (Manila, Philippines) on November 14, 1978; and a Holiday Inn in Greece, New York, on November 26, 1978. Fuels for the hotel fires included mattresses, box springs, carpets, upholstery fabric, and vinyl wallcoverings. Other problems with the hotels reported by the NFPA were noncompliance with life safety codes, the lack of inspections by local officials, and inconsistencies in complying with the codes due to exemption clauses.

GLOBAL TECHNOLOGICAL DEVELOPMENTS

Advances in technology have inherent risks as well as benefits. In 1986, the world witnessed the death of seven crew members as the space shuttle *Challenger* disintegrated after takeoff. The technological malfunction at the Chernobyl nuclear power station resulted in widespread radiation exposure, with consequences that are still being studied today. From an interior environment and architectural perspective, the Chernobyl catastrophe had an immediate impact on at least 180 towns and villages in close proximity to the power station. The explosion of radioactive material at Chernobyl illustrates multiple problems associated with nuclear power, including the ever-present dilemma of how to dispose of the radioactive waste that is a by-product of the process of creating nuclear energy. As described in the next section, the Chernobyl disaster caused architects and interior designers to reanalyze their ethical and social responsibilities to people and the natural environment.

In contrast to disasters, several technological advances in the 1980s helped improve the lives of people. Engineers developed electronics that were increasingly smaller and cheaper. The 1980s saw the full-scale launch of the computer age as the components became faster, and innovative hardware and software programs lowered the cost of systems. In 1982, *Time* magazine named the computer "The Man of the Year." At the beginning of the decade, the World Wide Web was developed and video games were filling arcades. Japan became the world's largest automobile-manufacturing nation, and Motorola produced the first mobile phones. Outmoded transportation systems (which, according to some people, would include the railroad) precipitated discussions regarding appropriate uses for abandoned buildings, such as the Orsay Station and Hotel in Paris.

Nuclear Disaster: Chernobyl Nuclear Power Station 1986 in Ukraine

The energy crisis of the 1970s, high energy costs, and environmental consequences of burning fossil fuels all created a political climate that contributed to the acceleration of the construction of nuclear power plants. In 1986, the world's largest and most serious energy-related disaster occurred when a reactor at the Chernobyl Nuclear Power Station in Ukraine exploded and sent radioactive isotopes into the atmosphere (Figure 10.10). Millions of people were exposed to radiation and at least 180 towns and villages were impacted by the explosion. More than 20 years after the disaster, scientists and engineers are still studying the long-term global effects on people, plants, and animals. The final death toll attributed to radiation could reach the thousands or tens of thousands.

Chernobyl is located close to the north-central border of Ukraine, near Belarus. The Black Sea forms Ukraine's southern border. Similar to Hungary, Ukraine's central location in Europe has contributed to numerous wars, invasions, and control by foreign rulers over its long history. After existing as a state within the USSR since 1922, Ukraine gained independence in 1991. The country is currently bordered by several nations, including Russia, Belarus, Poland, Slovakia, Hungary, Romania, and Moldova.

In the 1970s and 1980s, the Soviet Union built the Chernobyl nuclear power plant as well as other nuclear facilities in Ignalina, Leningrad, Smolensk, and Kursk. During these decades, insufficient energy for the USSR's manufacturing industries had a significant impact on its sagging economy. The five nuclear power stations were constructed to provide approximately 50 percent of the electricity to the USSR.

The Chernobyl disaster occurred on the evening of April 26, 1986. Dr. Vladimir Chernousenko, a scientist invited by the Ukrainian Academy of Sciences to direct the task force in Chernobyl, described the events:

A sudden explosion at Block 4 [reactor 4] shattered the walls, lifted the roof, tilted it, and crashed it down into the reactor hall. This would have been a dreadful event even on a conventional scale—with fire, steam explosions, hot water, and falling steel and cement. But in the case of a nuclear reactor this constitutes a global disaster. Radiation kills people in the immediate vicinity; unchecked and leaked into the atmosphere or into aquifers, it can poison people and environment over huge territories. Because of high radiation levels, airplanes and helicopters were the best means to obtain an overall picture of the shattered reactor. (Chernousenko, 1991, p. 276)

The immediate response was to extinguish the fires and avoid igniting the other three reactors. Firefighters arrived at the site, but the radioactive flames, scalding

Figure 10.10 From an architectural and interior environment perspective as illustrated by this building, the Chernobyl catastrophe had an immediate impact on 180 towns and villages in close proximity to the power station.
Source: vladphotos/Alamy.

steam, and incredible heat (4,800°F/2,700°C) were insurmountable for typical fire trucks and equipment. Numerous helicopters flew over the reactors and delivered tons of sand and other firefighting substances. The materials buried the flames and the fires were put out within hours. The first casualties of the Chernobyl disaster were the firefighters, some dying within just a few months of being exposed to the extremely high levels of radiation.

As firefighters were combating the fires, radioactive isotopes were suspended in the atmosphere and drifting primarily in a northwesterly direction. Sweden was the first country to detect high levels of radiation at one of its nuclear power plant sites. In just a few hours, radiation levels were 25 times that of normal levels. Other Scandinavian countries, including Denmark and Norway, began reporting dangerous levels of radiation. Countries closer to Chernobyl, including Belarus, Germany, and Russia, experienced radiation levels that greatly exceeded the levels in the Scandinavian nations.

Within 5 days, due to variable weather conditions, nuclear fallout had spread throughout the continent of Europe and was drifting to the rest of the world. Rainfall was especially dangerous because radioactive materials cling to water and fall to the earth in concentrated forms. Immediate warnings were distributed to nearby communities that prohibited the consumption of fresh fruits, vegetables, fish, and, most importantly, milk. When cows eat contaminated grass, their milk immediately becomes radioactive. This was particularly problematic due to the fact that milk is consumed by infants and children. Children and the elderly are especially vulnerable to radiation poisoning. Initially, most of the world was unaware of the source of the radioactive contamination. In the mid-1980s, Soviet communication policies were very restrictive. Thus, officials were able to delay international public announcements of the disaster for 3 days.

The Chernobyl catastrophe was barely publicized in the Ukraine or in the Soviet Union as a whole. The lack of communication was especially serious for towns, villages, and cities close to the power plant. Built for the workers at the facility, the town of Pripyat with 40,000 inhabitants was less than 2 miles (3 kilometers) from Chernobyl. In the days after the explosion, the Soviet Union evacuated the entire town and everyone within a 6-mile (approximately 10-kilometer) radius, and then expanded the evacuation to everyone within a 19-mile (approximately 30-kilometer) radius, more than 150,000 people total. People had to leave all of their highly contaminated belongings in what became a ghost town (Figure 10.11). White substances in photographs were the result of a chemical reaction between the film and high radiation.

Figures 10.10 and 10.11 illustrate the devastating impact of a nuclear disaster on interior environments and architecture. The abandoned and decaying structures present a terrifying image of a nuclear catastrophe. A new "iron curtain" had to be constructed in the area surrounding Chernobyl. A barbed-wire fence was constructed to keep people away from the lethal levels of radioactive materials. Officials created a "10-kilometer Zone" (6 miles) and a "30-kilometer Zone" (19 miles) Recovery and clean-up efforts required more than 600,000 workers to enter these two radioactive zones, many of whom did not have appropriate safety gear, such as respirators and protective clothing. Any trucks, vehicles, equipment, or people leaving the contaminated zones had to be repeatedly washed to remove radioactive substances. After too much exposure to the radiation, equipment and vehicles were abandoned in one of many restricted radioactive fields. All of the firefighting trucks, equipment, and helicopters used to combat the fire were left to decay in these open fields.

In an attempt to contain the radioactive isotopes, the reactor was encased in a concrete "Sarcophagus." Thousands of tons of concrete piled 197 feet (60 meters) high covered the structure by the end of September 1986. Dr. Chernousenko, directing the task force, indicated that the structure had only a "30-year

Figure 10.11 An abandoned room in the town of Pripyat. The community was only a few miles from Chernobyl and immediately became a ghost town after the nuclear disaster.

Source: Viktor Chornobay.

lifespan." Leaks in the structure could cause another nuclear disaster. Another major concern was seepage into the local rivers and reservoirs. The nearby Dnipro River runs to the Kyiv Reservoir, which provided water to Kyiv, the capital of Ukraine, with a population of more than two million. To help avoid radioactive material from leaking into the ground, engineers dug a tunnel under the reactor and built a concrete platform. This dangerous task—as well as every other activity conducted in response to the disaster—has had serious health consequences.

Although reports indicate that only two people died at the scene of the explosion, numerous firefighters who worked at the site were airlifted to regional hospitals because of radiation sickness and burns. Many died within 4 months of exposure to the lethal doses of radiation. Although various reports have put the number of deaths that can be linked directly to the Chernobyl disaster at approximately 50, the long-term effects of the accident are still unknown. The final death toll attributed to radiation could reach the thousands or tens of thousands. Hundreds of thousands of people were exposed to high levels of radiation, which could take years to manifest into various forms of cancer.

Mutations occurred in infants, animals, trees, and plants that had been exposed. Numerous reports, books, and articles have been written about the Chernobyl catastrophe, and several myths have evolved over the years. Persistent myths and a lack of accurate information, along with the anxiety caused by fear of death or illness from radiation poisoning, have contributed to mental health issues manifesting in the affected population. Some reports indicate that mental health has become the largest public health problem stemming from the disaster.

In his book *Chernobyl: Insight From the Inside,* Chernousenko concluded that the primary causes of the explosion were: (1) "dangerous physical characteristics of the core," (2) "the defect inherent in the reactor's emergency protection system," (3) "the extremely slow operation of the emergency protection systems," and (4) "the poor quality of the design documentation and, hence also of the operating documents" (Chernousenko, 1991, p. 97). Eventually, Soviet officials reactivated the remaining three reactors to continue electricity production.

To better understand how to contend with the Chernobyl disaster, in 1986, the UN and other organizations initiated over 200 research studies and projects, including several related to the built environment, such as the development of radioactive waste management technologies, radiation protection, and decontamination policies and procedures. The entire Chernobyl nuclear power plant complex was shut down in December 2000.

In 2004, the UN reported that over eight million people in Belarus, Ukraine, and Russia were exposed to radiation, and millions of people continued to live in homes and work in buildings that had residual effects from contamination. The UN noted that after the Chernobyl explosion, professionals were not available to provide answers to simple questions related to the immediate or long-term safety of their homes, schools, stores, churches, or the contents of buildings. The consequences of a nuclear disaster focus attention on the design professions' social and ethical responsibility to assist people in need and to specify components of the built environment that reflect the principles of sustainability.

To concentrate on the changing and expanding roles of interior designers and architects in light of global events, interdisciplinary organizations have been established that focus on postdisaster and postconflict initiatives. For example, the International Crisis Group was formally established in 1995 by a group of international citizens and policymakers, and the Architects Without Frontiers (AWF) was founded in 1999 by Melbourne architects and planners Esther Charlesworth, Garry Ormston, and Beau Beza.

Air and Rail Transportation: Musée d'Orsay (Adaptive Reuse Project 1980–1986) in Paris, France, by ACT Group and Gae Aulenti

By the 1970s, air travel was making an even more significant impact on other modes of transportation, including railroads. Ornate railroad stations built in the 19th century were growing obsolete, except as homes for pigeons, rats, and the homeless. Often these terminus stations were located in the heart of a city and were visitors' first impressions of the city. To promote a city's image, railroad stations featured spectacular architecture and modern conveniences and amenities. This was the situation in Paris. The Orsay Station and Hotel (1900) was built in the heart of the city along the left bank of the Seine River and across from the Louvre Museum and the Tuileries Gardens (Figure 10.12). As with the Palais Garnier (see Chapter 1), the Orsay Station was built in the prevailing Beaux-Arts architectural style. Completed in 1900 for the International Exposition Universelle, Victor Laloux's station had a hotel, restaurant, elevators, lobby, reception area, great hall, and 16 underground rail tracks. Eventually, Orsay's platforms were not sufficient for electrified railroads. After 1939, the station fell into decline and was used for a variety of functions, including as a mail center during World War II.

By the early 1970s, Orsay Station was abandoned and scheduled for demolition. Public sentiment turned against this plan, however, following the destruction of Les Halles, the first Parisian marketplace, in 1971. The original Les Halles open-air market was established in the 12th century in an area close to the modern-day site of the Pompidou Centre (see Chapter 9). Parisian outrage over the destruction of Les Halles to build a shopping mall helped save the Orsay Station, and the building was listed as a Historical Monument in 1978.

When François Mitterrand became the president of France in 1981, he created a new plan for Paris: "Presidential Building Projects." The plan continued four projects that were initiated under the previous administration, including the Orsay Station. In preparation for the year 2000, Mitterrand's concept for the urban development project was to create a "city center" that "communicates with the suburbs and with marginal neighborhoods." In addition, Mitterrand wanted the projects to "provide meeting places for different kinds of people, for different forms of knowledge and for art. A new form of public facility must address a larger public—and our youth in particular—the cultural richness left us by generations of architects, artists, craftsmen, and scientists" (Fachard, 1987, p. 9).

The projects included the Orsay Museum, as well as the Great Arch of La Défense, the Grand Louvre, the Arab World Institute, the Ministry of Finances, the Bastille Opera, and La Villette. The concept for the Orsay Museum was initiated in 1974–1975. The architectural firm ACT Group, with Pierre Colboc, Renaud Bardon, and Jean-Paul Philippon, won the architectural competition to convert the station into a museum, and Italian architect and interior designer Gae Aulenti was responsible for the interior design.

In addition to the challenges of adapting a railroad station into an art museum, to have space for the collection, designers had to create an additional 215,278 square feet (20,000 square meters) within the existing structure. This formidable **adaptive reuse** project demonstrates the extraordinary results that can occur when historically significant architecture is modified for new purposes. Aulenti explained how she determined the interior design for the new museum: "The 'territory' of the new construction was largely determined by Laloux's building: the iron structure (pillars, beams, frames, joints, hinges), the stone walls which either reveal or hide the iron structure, the stucco-work and the decoration, even the conditions of its very existence" (Fachard, 1987, p. 65).

Natural light emitted through Laloux's enormous vault was also critical to Aulenti's lighting plan: "The various possibilities of Laloux's building for natural light were taken into account. The decision was made to combine natural and artificial lighting (overhead lighting in the galleries under the roofs, light from the central nave and from the windows along the rue de Lille, light for the oval rooms from the occuli). And, finally, these elements were classified, combined, or adapted to give clear sequences. As a result, each space is lit in a different manner, but the quality of light is consistent everywhere" (Fachard, 1987, p. 69).

The **museography,** the Orsay Museum's collection program, illustrates Mitterrand's desire for new projects that were designed "for different forms of knowledge and for art." Orsay's collection, confined between 1848 and 1914, includes a variety of Western-world forms, such as paintings, sculpture, decorative arts, photography, graphic arts, and architecture. The collection was derived from new acquisitions and artwork previously housed in the Louvre Museum, the Musée du Jeu de Paume, and the National Museum of Modern Art. Orsay has an outstanding Art Nouveau (see Chapter 1) collection, including works by Hector Guimard, Victor Horta, Louis Majorelle, Émile Gallé, Adolf Loos, Charles R. Mackintosh, Frank L. Wright, Otto Wagner, Josef Hoffmann, and Henry Van de Velde.

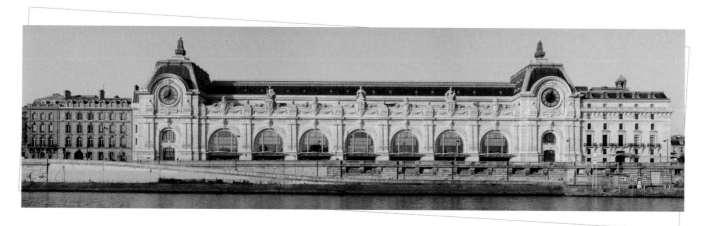

Figure 10.12 The Orsay Station and Hotel was built in the heart of Paris, along the Seine River and across from the Tuileries Gardens. Completed for the 1900 International Exposition Universelle, Victor Laloux's station had a hotel, restaurant, elevators, lobby, reception area, and a great hall.
Source: Wikimedia Commons.

Figure 10.13 Original architectural elements of the former station were retained for the Musée d'Orsay. To create an interior for the art collection, Aulenti collaborated with Orsay's curator, Michel Laclotte.

Source: Wikimedia Commons.

A significant portion of the original Orsay Station was restored, including the curved train shed made of glass and iron, mansard roofs, large gilded clock, giant busts of Mercury (the god of travel), glass awnings, stone façade, hotel ballroom, hotel dining room, and stone rose casings in the ceiling of the nave (Figure 10.13).

To create an interior for the art collection Aulenti collaborated with Orsay's curator, Michel Laclotte. Aulenti described the connection between the artwork and the interior design in the following way: "The museological program, the detailed analysis of the works, their groupings, and logical rhythms resulted in a set of rules that meant that the reconstruction of the museum itinerary as a whole was the sum of the typologies specific to the tradition of the various museums: rooms, galleries, and passageways, transfigured by the different formations imposed by their setting in Laloux's building" (Petranzan, 2003, pp. 27–28).

To facilitate Laclotte's museological program, Aulenti divided Laloux's building into three floors. The ground floor had the "Allée Centrale" (Central Avenue), several galleries, and an area for temporary exhibitions. In the architectural wing of this level, Richard Peduzzi designed an exhibit that included a polychrome model of the cross section of Garnier's Paris Opera House (1861–1875) and a 1/100-scale model of its district as it existed in 1914. The median level had terraces, galleries, a restaurant, and the Salle des Fêtes. Orsay's top floor had galleries along the north side and above the entrance. Aulenti added two towers, "buildings within a building," in the east end of the nave.

Orsay's lighting plan was complex, and Italian architect Piero Castiglioni, an expert in lighting, was commissioned as a consultant for the project. Beginning in the 1970s, Castiglioni had considerable experience designing fixtures and lighting for art galleries and trade exhibitions for OSRAM, a German lighting manufacturer. Aulenti described her principle for the project's lighting, noting: "The awareness that the study of lighting and the control of natural light define the architecture of a museum led to an analysis of the various spaces that the museological itinerary would create, isolating them and articulating the different possibilities for lighting engineering, defined by the common denominator of 'indirect light'" (Petranzan, 2003, p. 29).

An excellent example of connecting natural light with the "museological itinerary" was the illumination for the nave. Natural light penetrating the glass ceiling was an ideal source for the museum's sculptural collection. Paintings, drawings, furniture, and other fragile works were illuminated with indirect lighting from natural and artificial sources. To conserve the art collection and utilize natural light, sun screens and motorized awnings were incorporated into Laloux's iron and stone structure.

The result is a magnificent environment to view paintings, especially the Impressionist works on the top floor.

GLOBAL LIFE AND WORK STYLES

Technology that could be used to improve people's lives and work styles could also be used as a weapon. Commonplace modes of transportation like airplanes, buses, trucks, and automobiles were used to kill people and destroy communities. The 1980s witnessed hijackings, kidnappings, hostages, bombings, and air piracy. These acts of sabotage have also forced the design profession to expand their roles and responsibilities. To have safe and secure buildings, architects, interior designers, and city planners must understand acts of terrorism and strategies that can mitigate the effects of attacks.

An excellent source of information is the airline industry, because acts of terrorism forced them to either create safe travel conditions or fail. Consequently, government officials identified strategies to improve safety and security measures at airports throughout the world. Security systems designed to deter terrorists in airports were then installed for the same purpose in buildings perceived to be security threats, such as the Houses of Parliament in London, the Louvre Museum in Paris, Smithsonian museums in Washington, D.C., the Empire State Building, and the Eiffel Tower. Sadly, on June 10, 2009, passenger x-ray security machines installed at the entrance of the Holocaust Museum in Washington, D.C., were not effective because the gunman who killed one of the museum's security guards fired his rifle before reaching the x-ray machines.

Political disagreements resulted in some nations boycotting the Olympic Games in 1980 and 1984. At the same time, the human immunodeficiency virus (HIV), the virus that causes acquired immune deficiency syndrome (AIDS), was identified, followed by the development of the anti-AIDS drug AZT at the end of the decade. The highly addictive cocaine offshoot known as crack became a popular drug during this period, with devastating consequences.

Between 1984 and 1985, over one million people in Ethiopia died from famine due to weather-inflicted crop failures. From a positive perspective, Dr. Robert Jarvik, a medical scientist, successfully implanted the world's first permanent artificial heart in 1982, and as evidenced by new buildings with inspirational designs, Muslim religious beliefs prevailed in Morocco and Saudi Arabia.

Air Terrorism: Airport Security and Changi Airport, Singapore

While safety is always an important consideration in design, hijackings and terrorist attacks around the world led to serious analyses of security systems, most notably in airports, international landmarks, museums, and government buildings. The number and scope of international air terrorist events continued to escalate in the 1980s, especially the latter half of the decade. During this period, air terrorism resulted in the deaths of more than 1,200 people, while hundreds more were injured and held hostage.

Numerous aircraft were hijacked or seized, and jets were destroyed by bombs while in flight or parked at an airport. One tragedy involving a bomb was the destruction of the Pan American Boeing 747 aircraft while flying over Lockerbie, Scotland, on December 21, 1988. Two hundred fifty-nine passengers and crew were killed along with 11 people on the ground when fragments of the plane crashed on their homes. Prior to the Lockerbie tragedy on August 18, 1986, Sudanese rebels shot down a Sudanese aircraft in mid-flight by missiles from the ground. In 1985, there were at least five major incidents, including two in one month. In June, TWA Flight 847 was hijacked en route from Athens to Rome and its passengers held hostage in Beirut, Lebanon. One of the passengers was tortured and murdered by the terrorists. Also in June, Air India Flight 182 plunged into the Atlantic Ocean after a bomb exploded on the plane, resulting in the deaths of more than 300 people. Earlier that same day, a bomb in a bag intended for another Air India flight (flight 301) to Bangkok had exploded in the New Tokyo International Airport (now Narita International Airport), killing two people and injuring four. Several more major terrorist incidents took place the following year.

In 1986, a group from the Middle East claimed to have planted a bomb that exploded on a TWA jet as it flew over Greece. The jet landed safely, but the hole in the aircraft caused four passengers, including a small child, to be sucked out of the plane. Pan Am Flight 73 was hijacked at Karachi International Airport in India with 358 people on board; four armed men killed 20 people and injured more than 100 passengers. The years between 1987 and 1990 saw fewer major incidents per year, but the attacks still resulted in the deaths of significant numbers of individuals, including people living in their homes. In 1987, an explosive device carried onboard by members of the North Korean Workers Party caused the explosion of a Korean aircraft in flight, killing 115 people.

Although perpetrated by relatively few individuals, air terrorism significantly affected the lives of millions of people around the world, as well as the design of airports and other buildings accessible to the public. A critical look at international air transport security began with an agency of the United Nations, the International Civil Aviation Organization (ICAO). At the 1944 Convention on International Civil Aviation (Chicago Convention), 52 states signed an agreement that established the purpose of the ICAO: "the under-signed governments having agreed on certain principles and arrangements in order that international civil aviation may be developed in a safe and orderly manner and that international air transport services may be established on the basis of equality of opportunity and operated soundly and economically" (www.icao.int).

The ICAO has functioned to develop standards to address "unlawful acts of interference in international civil aviation" and to "limit its spread." In the wake of escalating international air terrorism, ICAO representatives developed standards at the Tokyo Convention (1963), the Hague Convention (1970), and Montreal Conventions of 1971, 1988, and 1991. The overarching goal of the conventions was to establish standards that would help ensure safe international travel. This was accomplished by identifying ways to suppress aircraft and airport terrorism as well as determining the punishments that would be inflicted in the event of an attack.

As terrorists identified new ways to hijack or destroy aircraft, the ICAO had to revise the standards at subsequent conventions. At the 1963 Tokyo Convention, the standards primarily focused on problems associated with offenses occurring on board an aircraft. Seven years later, the Hague Convention broadened the standards established at the Tokyo Convention by identifying ways to suppress aircraft hijackings and determine consequences for the hijackers. The 1971 Montreal Convention dealt with bombings of aircraft in flight or on the ground, and these standards were expanded by including airports in 1988. At the 1991 Montreal Convention, participants developed standards to deal with plastic explosives.

The early ICAO standards were very important to the proposal for a new airport in Singapore. In 1975, officials determined that the Paya Lebar Airport was no longer able to efficiently serve four million passengers annually. The Singapore government was in a position to build a new airport that was specifically designed to address terrorism by incorporating ICAO standards as well as other strategies. Cabinet Minister Howe Yoon Chong played an important role in developing the Singapore Changi Airport in 1975.

Changi Airport opened in 1981 and has received awards for its security, efficiency, service, air cargo facilities, amenities, eco-friendliness, and aesthetics (Figure 10.14). According to the Changi Airport Web site, from

1981 until 2009, the airport received over 230 awards; 29 of these awards were presented in 2008. Every year since its opening, Changi Airport received an award for its "deficiency-free" rating by the International Federation of Airline Pilots' Association (IFALPA). Rodney Wallis, a former director of security for the International Air Transport Association, provided a testimonial regarding Changi's airport security, saying, "At or near the top of any roster of major international locations whose performance earns top marks would be Singapore, which sets a standard against which others can be judged" (Wallis, 1993, p. 55). Ten years later, in another book written by Wallis, he claimed that Changi Airport had maintained its international reputation, writing, "Security at Changi is second to none. Opened 20 years ago, the airport made implementation of its security plan top priority" (Wallis, 2003, p. 92).

There are multiple and complex reasons that Changi Airport has acquired a reputation for excellent security, many of which are not published, for understandable reasons. However, airport and airline security experts have outlined critical components that should be included in policies and procedures. The design profession can apply these recommendations and guidelines to airports as well as other buildings, such as museums, court houses, government buildings, schools, theaters, historic landmarks, and ground-transportation terminals.

According to security experts, first and foremost is the collaboration and cooperation between international states, management, operators, and the airlines. There must be agreement and effective implementation of security standards, procedures, and policies. Safe civil aviation requires effective equipment, trained personnel, and quality performance. Professor and author Peter St. John, another specialist in intelligence, espionage, and terrorism, developed a plan for good security, and at the top of the list was "the physical layout and design [of the facilities]." Other items on St. John's list that must be coordinated with the design of the airport were "x-ray and sniffer technologies; security personnel; the airport's human communities; emergency response teams and policing; shared jurisdictions—airlines, airports, and government; and the role of the airport manager" (St. John, 1991, p. 78). As previously noted, Changi Airport has been cited for exemplifying these practices.

To explain important physical layout and design features for security purposes, St. John described what a passenger should encounter from the moment they arrive at the airport until they board the aircraft. The primary objective was to "keep the terrorist or his bombs off commercial airplanes." Preventing air terrorism begins on the ground with the design of the facilities and equipment. The perimeter and parking areas must be fenced,

Figure 10.14 Changi Airport was designed to address terrorism by incorporating ICAO standards as well as other strategies. Changi Airport opened in 1981 and has been lauded for its security, efficiency, and aesthetics.
Source: Andrew Woodley/Alamy.

guarded, well lighted, and may include watchtowers. The ramp, a previously frequent location for smuggling bombs on a plane, must be guarded, and personnel should be monitored on a continuous basis. Several security experts noted that the assortment of people and equipment that are required to prepare an aircraft for flight provided terrorists an ideal opportunity to plant bombs, guns, and other weapons. Airport personnel involved with preflight operations can include pilots, engineers, caterers, maintenance workers, mechanics, fuel attendants, baggage handlers, ticket agents, and flight attendants. In the chaos that occurred during preflight procedures, terrorists were able to easily acquire access to an aircraft or were disguised as airport personnel.

Security experts noted the importance of repeated surveillance and screening of passengers and any other individuals in the public areas. Security personnel observations were reported to be easier when spaces were small, and there were physical barriers between the public and items intended for the aircraft, such as baggage and packages. Airline and security personnel are trained to observe potential passengers. Therefore, to help in the detection of suspicious behavior, quality lighting should be installed at the ticket counters, passenger screening operations, lounges, corridors, and departure gates.

Airport layouts must be designed to create "sterile areas," which are rooms for passengers who have already passed through the screening operation. Sterile areas must be sealed from public access. Interiors must also be designed to accommodate x-ray machines, security cameras, and devices that track the movement of airport personnel. As a reflection of the efficacy of St. John's recommendations, security measures enacted in Changi Airport proved to be effective when a potential hijacking of an airbus was foiled by Singapore guards in 1991. Passengers and the crew were safe, but the four hijackers were killed by military troops.

In addition to specific recommendations for airport security, Government agencies such as the Federal Emergency Management Agency (FEMA) and the National Research Council in Washington, D.C., have developed guidelines that describe how to mitigate the effects of accidental occurrences or terrorism on new buildings. Beginning in the 1990s, the National Research Council has sponsored research on blast-effects and provided suggestions for applying the results to buildings, including impact-resistant glazing, seismic retrofits, and securing movable objects, such as furniture, light fixtures, and equipment. Some of the recommendations for new commercial buildings outlined by FEMA (2003) included using lightweight nonstructural elements on the exterior and interior; placing air intakes far above the ground; isolating entries and delivery areas from spaces with large numbers of people; and securing mechanical and electrical control systems.

Religion: Hassan II Mosque (مسجد الحسن الثاني) (1986–1993) in Casablanca, Morocco, by Michel Pinseau and the Hajj Terminal (1981) in Jeddah, Saudi Arabia, by SOM—Gordon Bunshaft

Morocco is located in northwest Africa along the coasts of both the Mediterranean Sea and the Atlantic Ocean; separated from Spain by the Strait of Gibraltar, only 8 miles (13 kilometers) wide. The land Morocco comprises has been settled for thousands of years by many different cultures. Berbers, descendants of ancient Numidians, a nomadic as well as sedentary culture, inhabited the area in the 2nd millennium BCE. Then Romans controlled the region beginning in the 2nd century BCE, followed by Muslims in the 7th century CE. In the 1500s, Portugal and Spain maintained territories in northern Africa, but by the middle of the 1600s, the Moroccan Dynasty Alawites (Alaouites) was established and still exists today.

The French fought with Morocco over the boundaries of Algeria in the 19th century; France's control soon spread to the west when Morocco became a protectorate of France in 1912. World War II weakened

Figure 10.15 Hassan II Mosque in Morocco is a magnificent religious house that overlooks the Atlantic Ocean.
Source: Wikimedia Commons.

France's ability to control Morocco, which enabled the country to gain its independence in 1956. Sultan Mohammed Ben Youssef was the third son of Sultan Moulay Youssef (1912–1927), chosen by religious scholars in Morocco (and approved by French authorities) to succeed his father as Sultan in 1927. When Morocco became independent in 1956, Sultan Mohammed Ben Youssef gave himself the title King Mohammad V.

In 1961, after the sudden death of his father, Hassan II became the second king of Morocco. During his reign (1961–1999), Hassan II decided to reinforce the country's dedication to Islam and declared on his birthday in 1980 his wish to build a new mosque in Casablanca. Construction of the Hassan II Mosque began in 1986. Created by French architect Michel Pinseau, Hassan II Mosque is a magnificent religious house that overlooks the Atlantic Ocean (Figure 10.15). It is the largest mosque in the world outside Mecca and Medina, and its style reflects Moorish influences, as evident by the horseshoe arches, stylized florals, and Arabic calligraphy (see Chapter 1). The mosque's square marble minaret is more than 50 stories high, the tallest minaret in the world, and contains a laser light that beams toward Mecca, Saudi Arabia, the holiest city in the Islam religion. More than 6,000 workers, including thousands of craftspeople and artisans, built the mosque and

decorated surfaces with elaborately carved and pierced materials—most of them from Morocco, including cedar, marble, onyx, granite, stucco, brass, bronze, and titanium (Figure 10.16). The interior of the mosque's magnificent dome is hand-carved cedar with painted decoration.

Knowledge about the Islam faith can provide a better understanding of the design of mosques. Islam is a monotheistic religion, founded in Arabia in the 7th century CE and practiced by more than a billion people (Muslims) worldwide. Islam is the dominant religion in the Middle East, North Africa, some regions in Eastern Europe, parts of western China, and a large portion of Indonesia. The Arab invasion in the 7th century introduced Islam to Morocco. Today, Morocco's population is nearly 99 percent Muslim.

Islam, an Arabic word meaning "submission," was founded by the Prophet Mohammad. Mohammad's teachings were based on revelations believed to be sent from God (Allah) by a messenger, Angel Gabriel (Jibril). The revelations focused on how to worship, how to treat others, and how to live the life of a good person. The revelations were written in Arabic script in the sacred book the Qur'an. As the revelations are believed to be Allah's words, every copy of the Qur'an is a precise duplication of the original except for its decorative details. Variations of the original Arabic script are derived from an artist's style of calligraphy and decorative motifs. To embellish the words of Allah, the borders on each page are beautifully illustrated with colorful geometric and floral patterns. Depictions of humans and animals are forbidden in the Qur'an due to the belief that only Allah can create life and that these images could contribute to the worship of false idols. To create the beautiful interiors in mosques, Muslim artists perfected exquisitely carved and painted designs that avoided the use of figures. Their designs consisted of unique and complex geometric patterns, flowers, vines, and verses from the Qur'an. Walls, pottery, and textiles were decorated with beautiful handwriting of verses from the Qur'an.

Duties of Muslims are described in the Five Pillars of Islam: (1) profess faith in Allah and Mohammad as his prophet, (2) pray five times each day, (3) provide alms to the poor, (4) fast during the holy days of Ramadan, and (5) if possible, make a pilgrimage to the holy city of Mecca once in a lifetime. From the top of the minaret, the crier, called a muezzin, calls the worshippers to prayer using a loud speaker or a horn. Prayer at a mosque can occur in the outdoor courtyard (**sahn**), covered arcades (**riwaqs**), and the musalla or zulla (prayer hall).

The musalla at the Hassan II Mosque can accommodate 25,000 worshippers, and the courtyard can hold 80,000 people. Some of the mosque's musalla was built over the Atlantic Ocean (see Figure 10.15). The musalla's glass floor enables the worshippers to see the ocean when they face the floor while praying on their knees. The room has a retractable roof that provides a view of the sky and stars. The design and decorative details of a mosque can vary, but all of them have a musalla and a **mihrab,** or niche. The mihrab indicates the direction of prayer, which is always toward the holy city of Mecca.

Believed to be a means to remove sins, before prayer Muslims wash their face, hands, arms, and feet and wipe their hair. At the Hassan II Mosque, water is

Figure 10.16 Hassan II Mosque. To create the beautiful interiors in mosques, Muslim artists perfected exquisitely carved and painted designs that avoided figures.
Source: Wikimedia Commons.

provided with several fountains (**fauwara**) covered with beautiful **zellij (zellige) tilework,** a specialized ceramic tile made from intricate mosaic pieces that are set into plaster. In addition to fountains, to wash before prayer, mosques may have rooms with rows of low-mounted sinks and benches. The musalla has separate entrances and prayer areas for men and women. One wall (**qibla**) in mosques has a mihrab that might have a stepped pulpit (**minbar**) next to the opening. The minbar is used by the cleric (imam) for noon sermons on Friday, Muslims' holy day. The floor of the musalla may be covered with small prayer rugs.

To create a quiet environment for prayer, the interior of a musalla does not have statues or paintings. Decorations on the walls and ceilings are painted or carved geometric patterns and quotations from the Qur'an. The eight-pointed star is a frequent motif. As illustrated in Figure 10.16, decorative materials include tile, wood, glass, stone, and sculpted plaster moldings. The women's gallery in the Hassan II Mosque has a beautiful pierced hand-carved wooden railing. Ornate entrances and doorways often have double horseshoe arches. The Hassan II Mosque utilized all local materials, except for the imported white marble and the crystal chandeliers from Venice.

Because a mosque is a center of community activities as well as a house of worship, the Hassan II Mosque includes a religious school, library, conference center, communal bath, and beautiful gardens. In following the Qur'an's description of paradise, gardens in mosques have scented flowers, shady trees, fountains, and birds. Although the Hassan Mosque II has become one of the most spectacular religious structures in the world, critics have noted that the hundreds of millions of dollars required to construct the mosque could have helped many of the needy people living in Morocco.

To accommodate Muslims able to fulfill the fifth pillar, the trip to Mecca, American architect Gordon Bunshaft of Skidmore, Owings, and Merrill (SOM) was commissioned by the Kingdom of Saudi Arabia's International Aviation Projects to design the Hajj Terminal (1981) north of Jeddah, the gateway to Mecca. Located at the King Abdul Aziz International Airport, the additional terminal was needed to accommodate the pilgrimage of millions of Muslims. The airport is located in Saudi Arabia on the coast of the Red Sea, and is approximately 45 miles (72.42 kilometers) from Mecca.

The pilgrimage occurs during Dhu-al-Hijja, the 12th month in the Islamic calendar. Millions of Muslims from around the world fly into the airport and wait to be transported by bus to Mecca. To provide accommodations for travelers, who needed to prepare for their pilgrimage and could wait many hours, Bunshaft designed a space with tent-like modular areas (100 acres, or 40.5 hectares), replicating traditional forms of shelter. Historically, to combat sweltering temperatures in the desert, inhabitants typically erected tents to shield them from the intense sunlight while allowing cool breezes to pass through the space. The Teflon-coated fiberglass white fabric roofs of the modular spaces at the Hajj Terminal were designed to provide similar protection and ventilation. The translucent fiberglass fabric reflects the heat from the sun while creating a soft illumination level in the terminal spaces. The combined effects of the heat-absorbing fiberglass fabric and the breezes flowing through the open terminal create a comfortable temperature of around 80°F (27°C). Fabrics, supported by radial steel cables, were attached to white steel pylons. The steel pylons also were roof drains and served as a surface for reflecting light emitted from indirect luminaires that were mounted on the pylons.

The open areas under the fabric roof provide the space to accommodate various activities. People waiting at the terminal pray, meditate, sleep on the floor, prepare their food, and buy or sell items, such as textiles and clothing. The terminal also has an information desk, post office, restrooms, a bus boarding area, and banking facilities. In receiving the 1983 Aga Khan Award, the jury noted, "The brilliant and imaginative design of the roofing system met the awesome challenge of covering this vast space with incomparable elegance and beauty" (Aga Khan Award, 1983, p. 1).

GLOBAL VISUAL AND PERFORMING ARTS

In each decade, the visual and performing arts are affected by both people and technology, and in turn the arts affect interior environments and architecture. Music was visually brought to the masses on a daily basis by the first broadcasts of Music Television (MTV) in 1981. The Live Aid concerts in 1985 were held to provide assistance to those starving in Ethiopia. Film director and actor Sam Wanamaker had the financial means and the desire to begin reconstruction of the Globe Theatre in 1987, on its original site in London, where Shakespeare's plays had been performed in Elizabethan England. A blending of contemporary and traditional styles achieved international attention with Ieoh Ming (I. M.) Pei's glass and steel entrance for the

Louvre Museum in Paris in 1989 (the Grand Louvre project mentioned earlier in this chapter). The dramatic pyramid was placed in one of the Louvre's courtyards and has become another icon for the city of Paris. References to theater and stage appeared in products and interiors designed by architects and designers who created **Memphis,** a contemporary design movement. In 1981, architect Ettore Sottsass and a group of Italian architects and designers (Memphis Group) originated the Memphis movement, which featured bright, colorful, and unexpected characteristics. Michael Graves included many characteristics of the group's design philosophy in the exaggerated elements of his design for the Postmodern Portland Building in Oregon.

Performing Arts: Globe Theatre (1987–1997) in London, United Kingdom, by Theo Crosby

"All the world's a stage, And all the men and women merely players. They have their exits and their entrances. And one man in his time plays many parts." These words from Shakespeare's *As You Like It* (Act II, Scene 7) can be seen as a metaphor for the relationship between the Globe Theatre and William Shakespeare (1564–1616) (Figure 10.17). The playwright, actor, poet, and shareholder in London's Globe Theatre worked during an era that grappled with conflicting perspectives regarding the value of players and their performances. Audiences were frequently loud and boisterous, and threw food and drink at the players. Traveling players, who performed in any location that attracted crowds, were often viewed as beggars of the streets.

After years of working as a traveling player, Elizabethan entrepreneur James Burbage decided that for players and theatrical drama to achieve creditability, their performances must be in permanent structures. In the 16th century, however, London's laws prohibited theaters within the city limits. Burbage built England's first public theater (1576) on land he leased in Shoreditch, an area beyond the medieval walls surrounding London, on the north side of the city. Known simply as "The

Theater," it was very popular. When the lease for the land was not renewed, the theater closed (1597). James Burbage died in 1597, and his sons Cuthbert and Richard, as owners of the theater, dismantled it and transported the wooden framework to Bankside, a section south of the Thames River. The first Globe Theatre was then constructed in Bankside in 1599, reusing the timbers from Burbage's Shoreditch Theatre and accommodating 3,000 people. Shakespeare referred to the Globe as the "wooden O," a shape derived from the circle that was formed when actors performed in town squares.

Located outside London's city limits, Bankside became notorious for "inappropriate" entertainment and behavior, including gambling, brothels, animal-baiting arenas, and theaters. When the Globe Theatre was built, the other large structures in Bankside were the Rose amphitheater, the Swan amphitheater, and the Animal-Baiting Arena. Design characteristics of the Baiting Arena were used in the design of the Globe Theatre. For example, the Globe was built with a "yard" that served as an area for animal battles. Other features of the Baiting Arena used in the theater included the perimeter galleries for the audience and the design of the arena's entrances. The number of entrances and their sizes were based on trying to prevent people from entering the theater without paying fees, a very common practice at the time. Thus, entertainment facilities had few entrances, and they were very small.

The Globe Theatre was a business; it had investors and hired employees. Shakespeare was a shareholder of the theater as well as the playwright and one of the players. Under these arrangements, most of Shakespeare's plays had to be written for the specific characteristics and dimensions of the Globe Theatre. For example, when writing scenes, Shakespeare had to consider how many people could be on the Globe's stage at the same time. He also had to plan for the Globe's limited backstage space, lack of sets, few props, and small *tiring house* (player's dressing rooms). The Globe's open stage could accommodate the lively action in Shakespeare's plays. This attribute was important

Figure 10.17 The first Globe Theatre in London was constructed in Bankside and accommodated 3,000 people. Shakespeare referred to the Globe as the "wooden O." Sam Wanamaker is responsible for reconstructing the theater as close to the original designs as possible.

Source: © terry harris just greece photo library/ Alamy.

because action helped to communicate a story to an audience in an era without modern sound systems and stage lighting. However, positioning the stage close to the audience made interactions between the players and the audience possible, which at times resulted in food fights. Due to the limits of lighting at the time, rehearsals were held in the morning and performances were in the afternoon. As an outdoor theater, performances ran during the summer months and moved to the Blackfriars Theater during the winter. However, summer was not a safe time of the year to use the theater due to the crowds. People believed that the plague could be spread in crowds during warm weather. At this period, London had significant problems with a series of plagues, and authorities closed the Globe as well as other public buildings during the Bubonic plague in 1593, 1603, and 1608.

The Globe's stage projected into the yard but was protected with a canopy, known as "heaven" (Figure 10.18). The stage and the costumes were very elaborate in order to create a memorable experience for audience members. The wooden pillars supporting the canopy were painted to resemble marble, and the capitals were finished with gold leaf. The ceiling was painted to look like the heavens and had an opening in its center for the occasional fairy or god that might appear in a play. The stage floor had a hatch that opened to allow a demon to appear at the appropriate time. The wide doors at the back of the Globe's stage allowed the players to make an entrance, and the rear curtains opened to expose surprises to the audience. The ground was covered with crushed hazelnut shells, sand, and ash. The yard had no seating; the audience had to stand during the entire performance. The galleries had wooden benches.

Shakespeare's writings, the players, and the theater were enormously successful until a fire destroyed the structure. In 1613, a canon shot during a performance of *Henry VIII* ignited the theater's thatch roof and destroyed the structure within a few hours. The theater was reconstructed on the same site in 1614. This structure existed until 1644 when the Puritans, then in power, declared that playhouses were illegal due to their association with inappropriate behavior.

For centuries a plaque marked the location of the original Globe Theatre, but it was not until the 20th century, in 1970, that Sam Wanamaker, a film director and actor, became interested in reconstructing the theater as close to the original design as possible (see Figure 10.17). Wanamaker commissioned South African–born British architect Theo Crosby to work on the reconstruction of the theater, in addition to numerous historians, archeologists, artists, and craftspeople. For many years several disciplines were involved in researching and determining how the Globe Theatre was constructed, was designed, and functioned. Their procedures provide insightful information regarding the variety of historical documents that can be used to identify a building's original condition, such as the type of materials, colors, and structural details.

The research process for the Globe Theatre involved archeological digs and the review of numerous illustrations and written documents. Most useful were construction contracts, diaries from individuals who attended performances, and a general knowledge of Elizabethan building techniques and preferred decorations. Construction contracts for the Fortune Theater, a theater operating during the same time as the Globe, were helpful to the reconstruction of the Globe Theatre. Researchers used these contracts because they were unable to locate the Globe's contracts, and they discovered in the Fortune Theater's documents that the owners wanted their builders to replicate many features of the successful Globe Theatre. The Fortune Theater's construction contracts read, "And the saide Stadge to be in all other proporcions Countryved and fashioned like vnto the Stadge of the saide Plaiehowse Called the Globe, Wth convenient windowes and lights glazes to the saide Tyreinge howse. And the saide fframe Stadge and Stearecases to be covered with Tyle" (Mulryne & Shewring, 1997, p. 181).

A journal entry from one of the first audience members at a performance at the old Globe, Thomas Platter, described the interior of the theater in the following way: "The [playing] places are so constructed that [the actors] play on a raised scaffold, and everyone can see everything. However there are different areas and galleries where one can sit more comfortably and better, and where one accordingly pays more" (Mulryne & Shewring, 1997, p. 191). Platter's reference to comfortable seating reflected the addition of a cushion that could be used on wooden benches. The Globe's three price levels were one penny for the "groundlings" who stood in the yard, two pennies for benches in the galleries, and an additional penny for a cushion.

Ground was broken for the new Globe in 1987; the reconstructed Globe Theatre adhered as much as possible to the original design, materials, colors, motifs, and construction methods (see Figures 10.17 and 10.18). When physical or recorded evidence was not available, historians referred to common Elizabethan construction and decorative practices: the stage design for the Globe Theatre was based on popular Elizabethan excesses, such as the gold leaf and imitation marble. The timber-framework for the reconstructed Globe used typical Elizabethan techniques, such as the use of slotted joints, wooden pegs, and thatched roofs. A carpenter used an authentic pole lathe to make the galleries' oak balusters.

In 1989, the foundations of the original building were discovered buried beneath a historic 19th-century

Figure 10.18 The Globe's stage projected into the yard, but was protected with a canopy, known as "heaven."
Source: ImageState/Alamy.

building. This discovery helped to establish an approximate size and shape of the original Globe. In reality, Shakespeare's "wooden O" was not a circle; the shape of the theater was instead made from 20 bays. The new Globe was built offsite. Each timber was numbered and was then reassembled at the site of the old theater. The theater was built with new green oak from 1,000 donated forest oaks, handmade Tudor bricks, plaster walls, and thatch from Norfolk.

Modern additions were a sprinkler system embedded in the thatched roof and 500 tapestries donated by the government of New Zealand. The Globe's entrance has an iron gate with 116 small objects (see Figure 10.17). Each flower, insect, or animal was created by a different artist and represents a phrase from a Shakespeare play. The theater also has a plaque commemorating Sam Wanamaker's vision. The first performance in the reconstructed Globe was on June 12, 1997, but Wanamaker and architect Crosby were not in the audience. The two individuals who invested years in the project died before they could enjoy the revival of Shakespeare's "wooden O."

Performing and Visual Arts: Memphis— Ettore Sottsass and Michael Graves

Theater and references to the stage, scenes, acts, and players became elements in the philosophy of the group of Italian architects and designers (Memphis Group) who created the Memphis movement, including Ettore Sottsass. While listening to Bob Dylan's song *Stuck Inside of Mobile With the Memphis Blues Again*, several designers discussed and developed the Memphis Group in 1980. Jan Burney, a former editor of *Designer* magazine, explained the connections between theater and Italian designers: "The main reason, [Ettore] Sottsass thinks, for the fervent compulsion Italians, particularly Italian designers, have to discuss as well as to produce and publish is that they see life as a stage play. Centuries of triumphs, invasions, destruction and rebuilding have left them devoid of any certainty about life as a possible,

real, trustworthy system. Thus everyone feels themselves to be simply a character in a play and in order to keep up with the script they must develop their own roles. Facts and reality do not exist, only the play—it must go on" (Burney, 1991, pp. 19, 22).

Burney's identification of "invasions," and other historical occurrences, was in reference to Italy's experiences with Mussolini's fascism and the massive destruction during World War II. Living through these years had a significant impact on people, including Italian architect and designer Ettore Sottsass and some of his colleagues. As "characters in a play," architects and designers worked on a "script" that identified "their own roles." Their script followed Pop art's drama by using popular culture and consumerism for inspiration (see Chapter 8). Their *roles* were to create designs that connected to a broader culture and elicited responses from expressive interpretations of everyday objects. The words and melody in Dylan's song reflected their design intent, and thus *Memphis* became the title of their *play*.

The first *performance* of the Memphis Group was at Milan's Design Gallery in September 1981. The *stage* designed by members of the group included furniture, light fixtures, ceramics, textiles, and accessories. Remarkably, more than 2,000 people were in the *audience*, including several members of the media. Some of the architects and designers who were involved in the *performance* were Michele de Lucchi, Michael Graves, Hans Hollein, Shiro Kuramata, Alessandro Mendini, Marco Zanini, and Ettore Sottsass. As with Pop Art, to provoke responses from the *audience*, the Memphis Group's designs had unexpected combinations of forms, colors, and materials (Figure 10.19). For example, furniture pieces were designed combining expensive and inexpensive materials. Marble was contrasted with inexpensive plastic laminates. Mother-of-pearl was combined with aluminum. As illustrated in Figure 10.19, Sottsass designed a traditional sideboard, Beverly (1981), with an unexpected

Figure 10.19 To provoke responses, Memphis designs had unexpected combinations of forms, colors, and materials. Ettore Sottsass designed a traditional sideboard, Beverly (1981) with an unexpected angled "tortoiseshell" table, metal bar, exposed red lamp, and a single handle on double doors.

Source: CNAC/MNAM/Dist. Réunion des Musées Nationaux/Art Resource, NY.

angled "tortoiseshell" table, metal bar, exposed red lamp, and single handle on double doors. The bright red and green and the unanticipated printed laminate used on the "snakeskin" doors of Beverly were other typical characteristics of Memphis. Printed plastic laminates often had patterns with diamond shapes, zigzags, and faux stones. Frequently, the designs were contrary to traditional fine arts and often exaggerated conventional elements, such as pediments, cornices, and arms of chairs. In challenging "functionalism," Sottsass explained, "When Charles Eames designs his chair, he does not design just a chair, he said. He designs a way of sitting down. In other words, he designs a function, not for a function" (Burney, 1991, p. 155). Sottsass indicated

that Memphis furniture is designed to be structure and decoration. Memphis designs are noted for how they create unconventional functions for furniture, light fixtures, and accessories. For example, the slanted, multicolor shelves in Carlton (1981), a "bookcase" designed by Sottsass, is an excellent example of how its angled surfaces present new challenges regarding the type of objects that can be placed on the shelves and where they should be placed.

Michael Graves also challenged traditional expectations in his designs of buildings, interiors, furniture, light fixtures, and accessories. The Portland Building in Portland, Oregon (1980–1982), exemplified many of the characteristics of **Postmodern architecture** as well as Memphis by exaggerating classical elements, including the podium, columns, "fluting," capitals, and repetitive application of small square windows (Figure 10.20). Unconventional colors on the building's façades were emphasized by Graves's symbolic use of hues, which he explained in the following manner: "As with form in a figurative approach to design, color has a language and thus can be used to convey meaning" (Patton, 2004, p. 70).

Often, Graves used colors that referenced the natural environment and applied hues in a way that echoed the landscape. For example, earth colors such as brown and terracotta were used to "root a building on its site." As in the landscape, Graves used green tones above the dark earth colors, and "sky" blues were at the highest level of a building. Frequently, Graves used these colors in his designs to "convey meaning" in interiors as well as in furniture, light fixtures, and numerous household objects. For example, a dressing table designed for the initial Memphis collection, Plaza (1981), had a blending of earth and blue colors. The bases of the pedestals were an earth color, and the drawers were bands of blue. The backboard of the dressing table that supported the mirror was also an earth color, but with touches of blue toward the top. Other references to nature included the yellow "sun" circle around the mirror and the "stars" that appeared when light emitted through randomly placed pierced openings. Designed for Alessi, an Italian manufacturer, Graves's whistling bird teakettle (1985) with a blue handle has been enormously successful, with more than two million sold.

Designers and architects in the Memphis Group encouraged the general public to embrace bold colors and forms, but the group conceived this to be a "fad," which like all fads would quickly end. Memphis only lasted until the late 1980s. Sottsass *closed* the group in 1988. However, Sottsass's designs have been featured in recent exhibitions at the Design Museum in London in 2007, and the Philadelphia Museum of Art and at the Los Angeles County Museum of Art in 2006. The

Figure 10.20 Designed by Michael Graves, the Portland Building in Portland, Oregon, exemplified many of the characteristics of Postmodern architecture as well as Memphis by exaggerating classical elements including the podium, columns, "fluting," capitals, and the repetitive application of small square windows.

Source: Wikimedia Commons.

Memphis Group has inspired contemporary architects and interior designers, such as Philippe Starck. Memphis influences are notable in Starck's designs for several hotels for Ian Schrager, including Hotel Mondrian (1996) in Los Angeles, and Hotel St. Martins Lane (1999) and Hotel Sanderson (2000) in London.

GLOBAL BUSINESS AND ECONOMICS

A mere four decades after World War II, nations that had been nearly destroyed during the war were among the world's economic powers. Germany and Japan became prosperous by addressing the escalating global focus on consumerism. The Sony Corporation is an outstanding example of the entrepreneurial spirit that revolutionized Japan. To serve the needs of global corporations, the areas of international banking and financial services came to the fore, which required new innovative buildings in worldwide locations. As a reflection of globalization in the banking industry in 1988, the Basel Committee on Banking Supervision established the Basel Capital Accord (Basel I), a credit risk framework for international banks that became the global accepted standard. The Basel Committee is associated with the Bank of International Settlements (BIS), an international organization headquartered in Basel, Switzerland, created in 1930 to facilitate global banking transactions. A revised standard, Basel II, was completed in 2004, and further changes were implemented in 2009.

The intermingled events between the Japanese Sony Corporation and the U.S. AT&T Corporation illustrate how globalization affected people, products, commerce, and buildings in the 1980s. As Sony was achieving success, AT&T was being dismantled after losing antitrust lawsuits brought by the U.S. Department of Justice. These two opposing paths crossed in 1992 when the significantly weakened AT&T sold their corporate headquarters (AT&T Building; modern Sony Tower) to the up-and-coming Sony Corporation.

Broad-reaching forms of communication were launched in the 1980s, such as the 24-hour news channel Cable News Network (CNN) in 1980. However, progress was accompanied by setbacks. The United States experienced a serious recession from 1980 to 1982 that resulted in the highest unemployment rate—10.8 percent—since the beginning of World War II. The repercussions of this situation were felt around the globe, with extremely high unemployment in Australia, Hong Kong, and the United Kingdom.

International Commerce: Residential Consumer Electronics and the AT&T Building (1978–1984) (Modern Sony Tower) by Philip Johnson and John Burgee

Defeated in World War II, Japan was a nation that required considerable rebuilding and recovery; businesses had to reanalyze the world of international commerce. In the days following defeat, the Japanese emperor addressed his people and encouraged them: "Unite your total strength to be devoted to the construction for the future, [and to] keep pace with the progress of the world" (Morita, 1986, p. 35). Many Japanese heeded those words. Transformational business strategies, such as TQM (Total Quality Management), resulted in tremendous success in several Japanese corporations, such as Toyota, Honda, Mitsubishi, Sanyo, Hitachi, and Sony. In addition to building energy-efficient automobiles, many of the corporations focused on consumer electronics. Electronic "targets" focused on innovative products that were reliable, reasonably priced, and increasingly smaller. Eventually, extraordinary vision and the high level of competitiveness in the consumer electronics industry worldwide resulted in a series of new products that radically affected interior

environments and architecture. Among the products invented that affected the built environment were video recorders, all-transistor "micro" televisions, compact disc (CD) players, personal stereos, and color video projection systems (Figure 10.21).

Sony is an excellent example of a corporation that emerged after World War II and within a relatively short period became one of the most successful companies in the world. Sony was founded in 1946 by a partnership between Akio Morita and Masaru Ibuka. Morita's family brewed sake for nearly 400 years, but his interest was in physics. Ibuka was an engineer and began his career working for Photo-Chemical Laboratory, a company involved with processing motion picture film. The original business, Tokyo Tsushin Kogyo, manufactured telecommunications and measuring equipment.

The corporation's original 1946 "Purpose of Incorporation" had eight overall goals. The company's purposes were to establish an ideal factory, and to assist in the reconstruction of Japan and the war-damaged communications network. The tenets also included promoting "the education of science among the general public" and applying technologies to "common households." References to technologies for "common households" suggest the corporation's immediate interest in pursuing consumer electronics. *Three* of their eight goals focused on residences: (1) "To promptly apply highly advanced technologies which were developed in various sectors during the war to common households"; (2) "To rapidly commercialize superior technological findings in universities and research institutions that are worthy of application in common households"; and (3) "To bring radio communications and similar devices into common households and to promote the use of home electric appliances" (www.sony.net). "High-quality radios" and "radio services" were technologies indentified in the founding prospectus; however, a magnetic tape recorder was the company's first successful product.

Sony's first connection to AT&T occurred in 1952 while Ibuka was in the United States for the purpose of understanding how Americans were using tape recorders. The Western Electric Company, in which AT&T had a majority interest, was searching for a company interested in receiving royalties for manufacturing transistors. Sony signed the contract with Western Electric in 1953. During these early years, researchers believed transistors could be used only for hearing aids, which could explain why Western Electric was willing to share profits from a seemingly low profitable product with another company. Eventually Ibuka and the engineers and scientists who worked for Sony developed the first Japanese transistor radio, the TR-55, in 1955.

Radios made by Sony came to the forefront in 1957 when it launched the "pocketable TR-63," known as the "world's smallest radio." Through most of the 1950s, Sony's sales were primarily in Japan. Sony continued to invent and produce other "common household" technologies, including enhanced "Trinitron" color televisions, a "micro TV," video recorders, CD players, and the Walkman portable music system. In the 1960s, Morita and Ibuka developed their export market, and in 1970 Sony was the first Japanese firm listed on the New York Stock Exchange. During the 1970s the corporation became involved with importing foreign goods, joint ventures, and offshore production facilities.

For AT&T the 1970s was the start of its breakup when the U.S. Department of Justice filed two antitrust lawsuits against the company in 1974. However, during the same time period AT&T launched its computerization of the network (1975–1976), and in 1977 it installed the first fiberoptic cable in a commercial communications system. AT&T's innovative technological developments were accompanied by an invitation to architects in 1975 to submit plans for a new modern headquarters. AT&T executives hired Philip Johnson and John Burgee to design the new building in a thriving area of New York City. Executives indicated to Johnson and Burgee that they wanted a building that reflected "dignity and solidity," and that their structure could not be "another glass box," a common design for office buildings.

Johnson and Burgee's sleek Postmodern design for the building was topped with a supersized broken pediment, which resembled a Chippendale highboy (Figure 10.22). The building's façades were clad in pink

Figure 10.21 As Sony, as well as other manufacturers, was inventing new and improved electronics for consumers, designers and architects were creating new approaches to the design of residences, such as media rooms.

Source: BUILT Images/Alamy.

granite, and the gray-tinted glass had bronze window mullions. In echoing the architecture of respected British architect Edwin Lutyen's Viceroy House (1912–1931) (modern Rashtrapati Bhavan) in India, granite projections and moldings were added to enhance the sculptural appearance of the building (see Chapter 4). Johnson contended that Edwin Lutyen along with Frank Lloyd Wright, Le Corbusier, and Mies contributed to the Western world's "artistic heritage."

A connection to AT&T's heritage occurred when AT&T decided to move the 23-foot-high (7-meter) bronze statue located on the roof of their previous New York headquarters (1916–1984) to a prominent position in the lobby of the new Postmodern building. The statue by Evelyn B. Longman has had several names, including *Genius of Telegraphy, Genius of Electricity, Spirit of Communication,* and *Golden Boy.* AT&T also moved two bronze medallions of Mercury (messenger of the gods) that were recessed in the floor of the lobby of its old headquarters.

AT&T moved into the new $200 million building in 1984, the same year as the conclusion of the illegal monopoly battles between AT&T and the U.S. Department of Justice (known as the breakup of Ma Bell). On the day of the breakup, AT&T's assets of $150 billion were reduced to $34 billion. AT&T was forced to relinquish local telephone services but was able to retain long-distance services, manufacturing, and R&D (research and development). Changes to AT&T after the breakup took a toll on the corporation. By the early 1990s, AT&T was looking for a buyer for their Postmodern headquarters, a building with low occupancy due to the situation that many employees never moved into the new headquarters. Contrary to public reports, AT&T had relocated these employees to facilities in Basking Ridge, New Jersey.

Throughout all of Sony's rapid and successful ventures, the corporation was always focused on the importance of protecting the image of its "brand." As with other corporations discussed in this textbook, to help promote its image, Sony carefully selected the location of its headquarters and the style of architecture. For example, in 1966, the modern Sony Building was completed on the Ginza, a prominent location in Tokyo. When Sony wanted to consolidate its New York City offices into one building, executives purchased the iconic AT&T Building, sometimes called the "Chippendale building," from AT&T in 1992 for $200 million (see Figure 10.22). Johnson's building had a formidable international reputation for transforming attitudes toward the Postmodern movement, which coincided with Sony's image. The AT&T building had exemplified the concept that Postmodern architecture had an important role in the 1970s and 1980s.

When Sony purchased the 36-story building, $80 million was spent to renovate the building. The lower levels and spaces were reconfigured to accommodate more employees. Sony commissioned Gwathmey Siegel, an architectural and interior design firm in New York City, to redesign the facilities by creating space for 1,000 more employees and developing two new Sony retail spaces from the previously open arcades. The renovation included a 75-seat private screening room and an interactive multimedia museum (Sony Wonder Technology Lab) at the plaza level. AT&T's sumptuous executive penthouse and the main corporate dining room were used as designed by Johnson, but Sony added a private restaurant for its international executives. The renovation was completed in 1994.

As Sony and other manufacturers were inventing new and improved electronics for consumers, designers and architects were creating new approaches to integrate these new consumer electronics with the interior environment of residential and commercial buildings (see Figure 10.21). Quality electronics that were also reasonably priced resulted in demands for home entertainment. People wanted entire rooms created for entertainment. **Media rooms** were dedicated to the enjoyment of watching television and films and listening to music. The rooms often featured a large screen and a unit that housed the color video projection system. Comfortable chairs faced the screen, and often the unit that contained the projection system had additional storage compartments for drinks and controls. Stereo sound systems were built into cabinetry, and the materials used for walls, ceilings, and floors were selected for their acoustic properties. To enable people to watch the screen during the day required window treatments that blocked sunlight. Adjustable lighting was installed that could accommodate a variety of desired effects and activities. Furniture was designed to accommodate the new sizes and functions of media equipment; pieces that had been ideal for the antiquated

turntable and similar technology were replaced with small cabinets that housed a front-loading CD player. Video-projection systems were especially challenging. A unit placed on the floor needed an attractive-looking cabinet, and systems mounted on a ceiling required appropriate structural support. Inexpensive and quality consumer electronics also affected other rooms of a residence. Kitchens, bathrooms, "family rooms," and bedrooms were designed to accommodate the newest television and other electronics. These demands also transferred to the hotel industry, as guests expected these modern systems in their rooms.

In less than four decades, Sony had become one of the most successful multinational corporations on the planet and had demonstrated its accomplishments and the effects of globalization by having the company's U.S. headquarters in a building designed by one of the world's most prominent architects. In 2009, AT&T moved the *Golden Boy* statue to their newest headquarters in Dallas, Texas.

Figure 10.22 When Sony wanted to consolidate their New York City offices into one building, executives purchased the iconic Postmodern "Chippendale" building from AT&T, designed by Philip Johnson and John Burgee.

Source: © Alan Schein Photography/Corbis.

The Banking Industry: National Commercial Bank (البنك الأهلي التجاري) (1981–1983) Headquarters in Jeddah, Saudi Arabia, by SOM—Gordon Bunshaft and Bank of China (1988) in Hong Kong by I. M. Pei

To respond to the rapidly rising number of successful corporations, financial institutions had to expand their operations and facilities to adequately serve their clients and grow their own businesses. To invest in research, build factories, purchase equipment, and hire employees, businesses required loans from banks. After World War II, the banking industry expanded from primarily domestic transactions to international financial affairs. By 1988, banking executives had established international standards (Basel Capital Accord) that governed deposits, capital, and liabilities. Global expansions during the 1980s were evident in Foster's Hongkong and Shanghai Bank Corporation Headquarters, as well as new bank buildings in Jeddah, Saudi Arabia, and another skyscraper in Hong Kong.

The basis of modern banks started in Italy during the 13th century; the earliest facilities were merely benches (*bancos*) along the streets. Over the centuries, benches became buildings that had to project a solid and impenetrable image to depositors. To demonstrate that a person's or organization's money was secure and would be available upon withdrawal, banks showcased their massive vault next to the tellers' windows. Some of the doors of vaults were constructed with glass to expose the complicated locking systems. Money in banks also appeared to be protected by the use of tall iron grills that separated tellers from their customers. Interior materials had to reflect permanence—marble was ideal for communicating this idea. Thus, many bank interiors included marble walls, floors, columns, and financial transaction desks.

Marble was also the material of choice for the interior of the 27-story National Commercial Bank (NCB) (1981–1983) Headquarters in Jeddah, Saudi Arabia. However, in an era of electronic banking services, the bank's lobby does not feature a massive vault or iron grills at the teller stations (Figure 10.23). NCB's non-threatening elegant lobby had clear-glass low wall dividers that separated customers from the tellers, and a large skylight centered over a circular white marble unit that contained check-writing stations.

To accommodate Saudi Arabia's rapidly escalating role in international commerce, American architect Gordon Bunshaft of SOM was commissioned to design the new building for NCB. Bunshaft explained the motives of NCB executives, saying, "They wanted a great building. They wanted a unique building. They wanted a tall building. They also wanted a certain amount of working space, which was very little compared to what they wanted in the way of the size" (Krinsky, 1988, p. 270). The desire to have a "great," "unique," and "tall building" for a financial institution reflects Saudi Arabia's newly found wealth and rise as a world power.

Figure 10.23 Marble was the material of choice for the interior of a modern building, the National Commercial Bank (NCB) in Jeddah, Saudi Arabia.
Source: © Ezra Stoller/Esto.

Oil was not discovered in Saudi Arabia until the 1930s. Prior to this, the country was fundamentally undeveloped, with a high percentage of the population living in nomadic tribes. Saudi Arabia comprises four-fifths of the Arabian Peninsula and is bordered by the Red Sea and the Persian Gulf. It is in the center of the Middle East, and nine-tenths of the country's 830,000 square miles (2,149,690 square kilometers) is desert. Oil was discovered both on land and offshore in the Persian Gulf. The Arabian American Oil Company, a company affiliated with Standard Oil of California, was involved with exploration and drillings. In just a few decades, Saudi Arabia's rich petroleum reserves enabled the country to become the largest oil producer in the world. The increasing worldwide demand for oil resulted in it becoming one of the richest nations. Symbolically, an impressive bank building was a commanding way to announce success and power to the world.

Bunshaft responded to the client's vision by designing what he claimed as "his best work." Given Bunshaft's long and illustrious career, which included the Lever Building (1950–1952) in New York City with Mies van der Rohe, his proclamation was profound. During an oral history interview with a historian, Betty

J. Blum, in April 1989, Bunshaft explained his views on NCB and the Lever Building: "The only building that I think has a major concept that's unique and my own is the [National Commercial Bank] in Jeddah. It is a totally new approach to solving an office building in an extremely hot and dry climate. I didn't think there was anything unique in Lever House. We just did the best we could. You didn't think about it. We weren't inventing any new things out of it. The U.N. was being built—the same glass wall. We improved a little on it" (Blum, 2000, p. 3).

Based on his experience designing the Hajj Terminal (see previous section in this chapter), also in Jeddah, Bunshaft was able to apply knowledge of Saudi Arabia's climate and traditional values to the NCB project. He designed the plan of the NCB in the shape of an equilateral triangle (Figure 10.24). A cylindrical-shaped six-story 400-car parking garage was connected to the main building. The triangular shape was a unique approach to traditional skyscrapers, and the form became an integral component to shielding office workers from Saudi Arabia's intense desert sunlight. The solid façades prevented sunlight penetration, but the large openings allowed daylight to illuminate the offices. Direct sunlight was filtered through tinted glazing and deep recesses sheltered windows of the top floor executive offices.

The contrasting solid façades and the large openings illuminated by the interior light fixtures creates an illusive effect at night. The façades surrounding the voids tend to blend into the dark evening sky, and the brightly lit openings appear to be illuminated cubes floating above the city.

To create oases within the courtyard of the building, Bunshaft incorporated rooftop gardens at three different levels. The pinkish color of the travertine marble used on the interior and the exterior reflected local coral that existed in the offshore reefs of Jeddah (see Figures 10.23 and 10.24). References to Islamic art are evident in the geometric pattern of the bank's marble floor, coffered ceilings, and plaza pavement (see Figure 10.23). On the

executive floor, Western influences are present in the traditional Chippendale dining room chairs and the modern **tuxedo-style** cream-colored sofas.

In the 1980s, NCB was (and still is) the largest commercial bank in the oil-wealthy Middle East, but international financial affairs were also on the rise in Asia. The three major banking cities in Asia at the time were Hong Kong, Singapore, and Tokyo. As discussed earlier in this chapter, Hong Kong was rapidly growing, as evidenced by the new Hongkong and Shanghai Bank Corporation Headquarters. Three years after the completion of British architect Norman Foster's Hongkong Bank and just two blocks away, another major bank building was completed in that city. The Bank of China commissioned the Chinese-born American architect I. M. Pei to design a new building for its branch in Hong Kong (Figure 10.25). In anticipation of China regaining control of Hong Kong from Britain in 1997, communist

Figure 10.24 Gordon Bunshaft designed the plan of the NCB in the shape of an equilateral triangle. A cylindrical-shaped parking garage was connected to the main building.
Source: © Ezra Stoller/Esto.

authorities proposed to celebrate the reunion with the construction of a new building—a building that was dedicated to the banking industry and demonstrated to the world that communist China was emerging as an international financial center. Ironically, it was communist authorities who asked Pei to design the new branch building for the same bank that Pei's father, Tsuyee Pei, had been a founder of in 1912 and had eventually left in order to join forces against the communists. Prior to committing to the project, Pei discussed the proposal with his father and declared that the new bank should reflect "the aspirations of the Chinese people."

Executives of the Bank of China identified what was considered an inauspicious site in Hong Kong, but the city's exorbitant land prices and the lack of available sites limited their options. In contrast to the auspicious harbor location of Foster's Hongkong Bank, the Bank of China was constructed on a site that intersected with three highway overpasses. Perceived dissonance with the location persisted and was further enflamed by the common knowledge that Japanese military police used a structure previously on the site to torture Chinese prisoners during World War II.

Pei had to design a skyscraper within the constraints of the site and also had to surpass the renown that accompanied the modern Hongkong Bank. Inspiration for the eventual 70-story tower was derived from four sticks that Pei manipulated into shifting heights (see Figure 10.25). The tower's multiple levels with angled roofs created a novel approach to traditional "boxy" skyscrapers and helped counter the strong winds from frequently occurring seasonal typhoons. To help mask the traffic from the surrounding highways, gardens and water fountains were incorporated into the towers.

Originally, Pei had designed an X-shape for the exterior cross-bracing, but after consultation with feng shui masters, the shape was changed to a diamond. Another choice in response to feng shui was to open the building on August 8, 1988. The repetition of the number 8 meant the date was considered to be the most fortunate day in the century. Unfortunately, not long after the opening of the Bank of China branch in Hong Kong, in June 1989, Deng Xiaoping, the leader of China (1978–1997), ordered military troops with tanks to arrest and shoot thousands of pro-democracy demonstrators in Tiananmen Square. After the tragedy, workers at the Bank of China erected a banner at the top of what was then the tallest building in the world outside of the United States that read, "Blood must be paid with Blood." Pei made a statement denouncing the massacre: "It hurt me very deeply, because doing this building was an expression of confidence in this country. When Tiananmen happened, I looked at the building and I felt terrible" (Cannell, 1995, p. 339).

Figure 10.25 The tallest building is the Bank of China in Hong Kong by I. M. Pei. Hongkong and Shanghai Bank Corporation Headquarters in Hong Kong designed by Norman Foster is on the right.

Source: Inspiration Images/Alamy.

SUMMARY

The decade of the 1980s was affected and influenced by numerous events and situations, one of which was the end of Communist control in Hungary in 1989. Hungary's architectural evolution from the postwar years until the end of Communist control provides for an interesting analysis of how both the presence and withdrawal of communism impacted the design of buildings. Stalinist architecture continued until after the Hungarian Revolution in 1956. The work of the Hungarian architect Imre Makovecz provides an excellent example of organic architecture in the 1980s. One of the outcomes of World War II was a "temporary" division of Germany into four zones and the military occupation of Berlin by France, the United Kingdom, the Soviet Union, and the United States. In 1961, East German military and police forces installed a fence structure, which became the Berlin Wall. The East German army constructed the Berlin Wall without regard for families, ownership of businesses, place of employment, location of buildings, or street patterns. In the late 1980s, as a result of better relations between the superpowers, the Berlin Wall was torn down and the process of reuniting Germany began.

The 1980s also revealed the complexities associated with balancing the needs of people, the natural environment, and the economy. The world's quickly escalating population reached a total of five billion by 1987. Extremely dense living conditions were part of life in several of the world's major cities, including Hong Kong, where land prices have been a major issue for decades. Norman Foster's design for the Hongkong Bank maximized usable space and was constructed quickly. Foster and his associates researched the site, studied the movements of people, and incorporated the principles of feng shui into the building's design. In the United States, the city of Las Vegas continued to experience dramatic and rapid development since the opening of its first hotel in the 1940s. In 1980, Las Vegas was attracting international tourists, with almost 12 million people visiting per year; by 1990 that number would reach 21 million. A fire at the city's MGM Grand Hotel in 1980 resulted in the deaths of 85 people and prompted architects, interior designers, and city officials to reexamine fire factors in hotels, including combustible interior finishes, evacuation systems, and locations of fatalities.

In 1986, a reactor at the Chernobyl Nuclear Power Station exploded and sent radioactive isotopes into the atmosphere. More than 20 years after the disaster, scientists and engineers are still studying the long-term global effects on people, plants, and animals. Understanding causes and effects provides interior designers and architects with the background to design buildings that will help protect people and sustain the planet. More than a decade earlier, the Orsay Station in Paris was abandoned and the formerly grand railroad station was scheduled for demolition. Orsay was saved and the building was listed as a Historical Monument in 1978. During the 1980s, Orsay was transformed into the Musée d'Orsay with a collection of paintings, sculpture, decorative arts, and architecture from 1848 until 1914.

Another type of renovation was occurring at other transportation sites for very different reasons during the decade. The alarmingly rapid increase in hijackings and terrorist attacks around the world prompted a serious analysis of security systems, most notably in airports and other international landmarks. Changi Airport in Singapore, which opened in 1981, has received awards for its security, efficiency, service, air cargo facilities, amenities, eco-friendliness, and aesthetics. Changi Airport's early date for implementing airport security systems helped provide other international airports with valuable information.

Religious architecture was advanced during the decade with the building of the Hassan II Mosque in Casablanca, commissioned by the king of Morocco to reinforce his country's dedication to Islam. Hassan II Mosque is a magnificent religious house that is the largest mosque outside of Mecca and Medina.

The world of visual and performing arts influenced the built environment during the 1980s with the reconstruction of the Globe Theatre in London, the result of Sam Wanamaker's interest in creating a structure that was as close to the original design as possible. Theater, with references to the stage, scenes, acts, and players, became elements in the philosophy of the group of architects and designers who created the Memphis Group. Memphis designs had unexpected combinations of forms, colors, and materials. Michael Graves, a member of the group, challenged traditional expectations in his designs of buildings, interiors, furniture, light fixtures, and accessories. The Portland Building in Portland, Oregon, exemplified many of the characteristics of Postmodern architecture as well as Memphis.

In the business and economic world, Japan began to rise to a place of world prominence after decades of rebuilding after World War II. One example of a Japanese business success was Sony. This company, along with other manufacturers, was inventing new and improved electronics for consumers during the 1980s, with an impressive degree of success. Designers and architects were creating new approaches to the design of residences and commercial buildings in this period as well. When Sony wanted to consolidate its New York City offices into a single building, executives purchased the Postmodern "Chippendale" Building from AT&T. To respond to the rapidly rising number of successful corporations, financial institutions had to expand their operations and facilities. Global expansions during this decade were exemplified by Foster's Hongkong and Shanghai Bank Corporation Headquarters, as well as new bank buildings in Jeddah, Saudi Arabia, and the Hong Kong branch of the Bank of China.

KEY TERMS

adaptive reuse

fauwara

majolica ceramics

means of egress

media rooms

Memphis

mihrab

minbar

museography

Postmodern architecture

qibla

riwaqs

sahn

seismic joints

tuxedo-style

zellij (zellige) tilework

EXERCISES

1. Research Design Project. Take a virtual tour of the interior and exterior of three hotels on different continents. Record a summary of the tours and analyze the differences between the presentations, interiors, and exteriors. Sketch some of the best examples. Discuss your results with several other students and prepare a presentation of your sketches and analyses.

2. Human Factors Research Project. Identify research studies that focus on the relationship between the built environment and human factors. Specifically, examine crisis and panic situations. To begin the research process, an excellent website to study is www.informedesign. umn.edu. The InformeDesign site provides a synopsis of design research studies. In a written report, summarize your findings and provide suggestions for an oral presentation. In a team with other students, prepare a presentation that is supported with visual materials.

3. Philosophy and Design Project. This chapter provided several examples of designs that reflected the philosophies of feng shui. Research the concept and conduct an analysis of a downtown district that focuses on its adherence to feng shui. Sketch some of the best and worst examples. Identify a project in a studio and apply the principles of feng shui to the interior and exterior. Write a report that summarizes your observations and include recommendations for future practice. The report could include sketches, drawings, or photographs.

CHAPTER 11

EMPHASIS: THE 1990S TO THE PRESENT

OBJECTIVES

After reading this chapter, you should be able to describe and analyze:

■ How selected global political events in the 1990s and 21st century, such as the Persian Gulf War and civil wars in Yugoslavia and Slovenia, affected interior environments and architecture.

■ How the natural environment influenced sustainable designs in Finland and Africa in the 1990s and 21st century.

■ How selected global technologies in the 1990s and 21st century affected global interior environments and architecture as evident by projects in New Caledonia, Bilbao, and the 2008 Olympics.

■ How selected global work styles and lifestyles in the 1990s and 21st century, such as the destruction of the World Trade Center and disability legislation, affected interior environments and architecture.

■ How selected global visual arts and performing arts in the 1990s and 21st century affected global interior environments and architecture as evident by innovative textiles and new art museums.

■ How selected global business developments and economics in the 1990s and 21st century, such as the petroleum industry and the economics of housing and land, affected interior environments and architecture.

■ How to compare and contrast selected interior environments and architecture of the Americas, Asia/Oceania, Europe, and the Middle East/Africa in the 1990s and 21st century.

The world has changed dramatically during the past 200 years. In 1800, Spain had many possessions in the Americas, the Russian Empire covered a substantial amount of the northern hemisphere, most of Africa was independent, and the Qing Empire controlled a large region in Asia. By 1900, Spain had few possessions, Britain had many colonies all over the world, Africa was divided into colonial states that were controlled by several Western nations, and the Russian and Qing empires maintained control of their provinces. Today's world map illustrates the fact of independence: Nations have few if any possessions, and any colonial states are small territories. Independence frequently created new borders and names for countries. For example, the Russian and Qing empires became the Russian Federation and the People's Republic of China, respectively.

During the 1990s and into the 21st century, globalization has affected innumerable aspects of daily life for a large portion of the world's population. Globalization could be considered the most central development that has been affecting interior environments and architecture during this time period. The effects of a globally interdependent planet on the built environment were very evident with the worldwide financial crisis that started in October 2008 and continued well into 2009. The crisis included a collapse of the global banking system and rapid devaluation of home prices. Globalization is also apparent with the escalating problems associated with the environment, including global warming, pollution, and overflowing landfills. Fortunately, several nations have initiated green certification programs to help sustain the planet.

Building the world's tallest skyscraper has still attracted the interest of corporations in the 1990s and the 21st century. Construction on the world's tallest building, the 1,474-foot (449-meter) multi-use structure Taipei 101 in Taipei, Taiwan, began in 1998 and was completed in 2004. Technological advances of the past two decades, most notably computer-related, have provided interior designers and architects with enormous flexibility in the form of structures with endless innovation in shapes and use of materials. High-speed Internet access continues to transform architecture, interior environments, lifestyles, and work styles by providing a quick and efficient means to internationally communicate, work, purchase, and sell. Various disciplines, including computer programmers, artists, scientists, interior designers, and architects, are developing new approaches to textiles that incorporate smart technologies (responsive to a stimulus), photonic (controlling light or energy) characteristics, and interactive protocols (stimulus/response capabilities). Regardless of technological advances, millions of people continue to live below the poverty level, are homeless, and die every day at very young ages. To meet the demands of the 21st century, affordable housing, quality health care, and healthy environments are imperative.

To create a unified political and commercial entity, the European Union (EU) organization was formally established in 1993. As reviewed in Chapter 7, the EU's founding organization was the European Coal and Steel Community (ECSC) in 1951, which was followed by the Common Market or European Economic Community (EEC) in 1957. The purpose of the organization has been to advance political and economic initiatives by fostering partnerships between European nations. One outcome of the EU has been the establishment of one currency. Euros were phased in on January 1, 1999, as the new European currency for the member countries. Currently, there are 27 democratic European members, and their Web site identifies their results: "Frontier-free travel and trade, the euro (the single European currency), safer food and a greener environment, better living standards in poorer regions, joint action on crime and terror, cheaper phone calls, millions of opportunities to study abroad . . . and much more besides" (http://europa.eu).

GLOBAL POLITICS AND GOVERNMENT

As is the case throughout the history of humankind, battles continued to be waged through the 1990s and into the 21st century. The Arab-Israeli conflicts continued and resulted in the construction of another wall that separated two nations. Israel began building a barrier wall on the West Bank in 2002 that is currently scheduled to be completed in 2010. There has been significant unrest in Cambodia, Libya, Kashmir, Sri Lanka, and North Korea, and fighting continued between India and Pakistan. A common underlying reason for the unrest has been the desire to establish a separate state. For example, in Sri Lanka, to have a separate Tamil state, thousands of people have been killed in battles between the government and groups, such as the Liberation Tigers of Tamil Eelam (LTTE). Due to political unrest in Afghanistan, an Islamic organization, the Taliban, took control of Afghanistan from 1996 until 2001. The Taliban's control of Afghanistan resulted in a strict imposition of Islamic rules, which included the prohibition of modern technologies, movie theaters, and television and imposed stringent dress and grooming laws. For example, women were required to cover their entire body in public and men had to wear beards.

Nelson Mandela's release from prison in 1990 was cause for celebration in South Africa, a nation that had been torn apart by an official government policy of segregation for decades (see Chapter 9). The country's first democratic elections *open to all races* were held in 1994, and Nelson Mandela became the President of South Africa. In dramatic contrast to the end of apartheid, in 1994 there was a massacre of over 500,000 people in Rwanda.

The demise of communism in the 1980s contributed to the dissolution of the Union of Soviet Socialist Republics (USSR) in 1991. Iraq invaded the small, oil-wealthy nation of Kuwait in 1990; the United States and several other countries then fought and were victorious over Iraq in the Persian Gulf War. Although the war itself lasted only a few months, the environmental damage to Kuwait was significant after retreating Iraqi troops set fire to most of that country's oil wells and dumped millions of barrels of oil into the Persian Gulf. In Europe, the country of Yugoslavia ceased to exist in the 1990s after a series of small wars resulted in the dissolution of the country and independence for several states, creating several smaller countries, including Slovenia and Croatia. After terrorist attacks in the United States in September 2001, America invaded Afghanistan later that year and then Iraq in 2003. The U.S. military continues its efforts to stabilize both nations.

War: The Built Environment in Kuwait

Kuwait is a very small country located on the Arabian Peninsula in the Persian Gulf. The entire country is a desert without any lakes or rivers. Iraq is its neighbor to the north, and Saudi Arabia lies along its southern border. Civilizations have existed in Kuwait for thousands of years, but rich oil reserves discovered in the 1930s attracted global attention to the country. A nation with land that stretches only 90 miles (145 kilometers) from north to south and 95 miles (153 kilometers) from east to west has approximately 10 percent of the world's oil reserves (Casey, 2007).

After World War II, American, Arabian, and Japanese corporations started producing petroleum, and within a few years Kuwait became one of the wealthiest nations in the world. In the 1970s and 1980s, the ruler of Kuwait, Sheikh Jabir al-Ahmad al-Sabah (1977–2006), diverted funds from oil sales and the interest earned from foreign investments into the development of the country's infrastructure, education, health care, social programs, and government entities. Several modern buildings primarily commissioned by the government were constructed during this period, such as the

National Assembly Building (1985) designed by Danish architect Jørn Utzon, three Kuwait needle-shaped towers (1979) by Sune Lindström and Malene Björn, the State Mosque (1984) by Makiya Associates, the Stock Exchange Building (1984) by John S. Bonnington, the Kuwait Ministry of Foreign Affairs (1973–1983) by Raili & Reima Pietilä, as well as an expansion of the National Museum (1983) by Michel Ecochard (Figure 11.1).

In addition to investing in the country's current needs, the government of Kuwait created a foreign account, the Reserve Fund for Future Generations (RFFG), for the purpose of sustaining the country after the eventual depletion of its oil fields. Created in 1976, the foreign account had investments in the United States, Western Europe, and Japan. The account totaled seven billion dollars and generated millions of dollars in interest. For these and other reasons, Kuwait was a valuable property, and on August 2, 1990, the military of Iraq invaded Kuwait.

An 8-year war (1980–1988) between Iraq and Iran over control of the Shatt al-Arab River concluded without resolution, but both countries suffered severe economic hardship and widespread devastation over the course of the fighting. Iraq was attracted to Kuwait's rich oil reserves, billions invested in the RFFG, and its proximity to Saudi Arabia and the Persian Gulf. Capturing Kuwait offered Iraq the potential to invade Saudi Arabia and control that country's oil reserves. This conquest would have given Iraq approximately 50 percent of the world's oil reserves.

The Persian Gulf (also called the Arabian Gulf) bordered by Iran, the United Arab Emirates, Oman, Saudi Arabia, Qatar, Kuwait, and Iraq, is a strategically key spot—in addition to offshore oil wells located there, it is the major waterway for shipping petroleum abroad. Iraq's harbor in the gulf had been damaged during the war with Iran and was inadequate in comparison to Kuwait's multiple ports. As he was in the process of mobilizing Iraqi troops along the Kuwaiti border in 1990, Iraqi President Saddam Hussein (1979–2003) contended that Kuwait was actually a province of Iraq and that Kuwait had violated Organization of the Petroleum Exporting Countries (OPEC) (see Chapter 9) regulations regarding oil production quotas. He claimed that Kuwait's excessive production of oil caused the per-barrel price to decline, which reduced Iraq's income. Iraq had the largest army in the Middle East and thus it was able to conquer Kuwait in 1 day. Iraqi troops killed civilians, destroyed cities, looted communities, and buried countless land mines.

The United Nations (UN) Security Council denounced the Iraqi invasion and declared an economic embargo against the country. In addition, Iraq and Kuwait assets in foreign banks were frozen, including the accounts that created the RFFG. The UN passed a resolution that stated Iraq was to withdraw

Figure 11.1 The Liberation Tower in the center of the photograph. Kuwait's needle-shaped towers that define the nation.

Source: Jon Arnold Images Ltd./Alamy.

from Kuwait by January 15, 1991. The country did not comply. The United States and 39 allied countries attacked Iraq, starting in January 17, 1991. Known as Operation Desert Storm, the televised war used advanced weaponry, such as stealth bombers and "smart bombs," which are designed to precisely hit a specific target and thereby minimize damage to things other than the target. After the air war, troops began the ground battles, which ended when Kuwait City was liberated at the end of February 1991.

The UN Security Council declared the end of the war on April 11, 1991. Although relatively brief, the occupation, bombings, and battles had a devastating effect on the Kuwaiti people, their cities, farms, and roads, and the environment. Thousands of Kuwaitis were executed during the Iraqi occupation, and most buildings throughout Kuwait were either destroyed or looted by Iraqi troops. Factories, power plants, roads, and even desalination plants were badly damaged, destroyed, and burned.

In addition to the damage from bombs, trenches, and the still-unidentified locations of land mines, Iraqi troops inflicted on Kuwait what is considered to be the world's worst ecological disaster. Prior to the war's ending on February 27, 1991, Iraqi soldiers set fire to approximately 800 of Kuwait's 1,000 oil wells. Raging oil fires burned close to 200 million gallons (757.82 million liters) of oil each day, and caused long-term and widespread environmental damage. As the fires burned, the dense, dark smoke blackened the sky so severely that the sun could not be seen from the ground. The wind carried smoke-filled oil droplets and soot for hundreds of miles. Oil lakes were created in the desert, and a thick layer of oil that turned into a tar-like substance covered the landscape. Vegetation and wildlife were immersed in oil, and petroleum seeped into Kuwait's very limited supply of groundwater.

Immediately after the war, to determine the extent of damage and to identify recommendations to contain and rectify the problems, the United Nations Environment Programme (UNEP) initiated several assessment studies. Scientists estimated that the cleanup would take decades and that a great deal of damage was irreversible. Unfortunately, remediation efforts were halted when forces invaded Iraq on March 20, 2003.

These were the conditions that the Kuwaitis had to face in the 1990s, in the aftermath of the Persian Gulf War. Within the context of an ecological disaster, Kuwaitis had to reconstruct their homes, schools, hospitals, stores, government buildings, and infrastructure. Buildings constructed prior to the discovery of the country's vast oil reserves were typically small and simple and had Islamic ornamentation, such as carved and molded plaster designed with floral arabesques and inscriptions (see Chapter 1). Wealth from oil enabled Kuwaitis to construct tall skyscrapers.

Many structures were rebuilt or restored after the war in their original style. For example, Kuwait's first museum, the National Museum, was severely damaged and looted during the war, and has been undergoing a restoration. The museum had an extensive collection of Islamic art and archeological artifacts from excavations on Failaka Island, located in the Persian Gulf approximately 20 miles (32.1 kilometers) from Kuwait. Housed in the former residence of Sheikh Ahmed Al Jaber Al Sabah, the restoration of the museum is still "in process," but some exhibits have opened to the public.

The Kuwait Towers were also vandalized during the 1991 Gulf War and have been restored to their original condition. As a "symbol of resurgent Kuwait," the new Liberation Tower (1996) was dedicated to the "multinational coalition that liberated the nation from seven months of Iraqi occupation during the Gulf War" (see Figure 11.1). Resembling the three traditional Kuwait Towers, the Liberation Tower was built as a telecommunications tower that included a restaurant, a revolving observation level, and a public communications center. Echoing the prominent Kuwait Towers as well as Islamic architecture, the shape of the Liberation Tower resembles a minaret. The smooth concrete used on the

Figure 11.2 The Tareq Rajab Museum, one of the world's largest collections of Islamic art in Kuwait. A separate museum houses an extensive collection of calligraphy, including an early dated Qur'an written on parchment.

Source: Tareq Rajab Museum of Islamic Calligraphy, Kuwait.

façades of the Kuwait Towers *and* the Liberation Tower resembles stone that was used to construct historical buildings, such as the tomb towers (mausoleums) in the 13th century. Both towers have modern interpretations of traditional Islamic decorative arts, such as traditional mosaic faience (glazed earthenware) with intricate floral and geometric patterns. From a distance, mosaic faience appears to cover the large balls on the concrete needles of the Kuwait Towers. However, in reality, the balls are covered with thousands of round steel plates that are painted in eight colors; the dominant color is blue, a predominant color used on the façades of traditional mosques. References to mosaic faience appear on the lower section of the Liberation Tower's façade, which is covered with bluish-colored ceramic tiles in a geometric pattern.

Fortunately, an extensive collection of Islamic decorative arts was saved during the Gulf War. The Tareq Rajab Museum, one of the world's largest collections (over 30,000 pieces) of Islamic arts, would not exist today if the Rajab family had not secured the artwork when Iraqi troops occupied the country. Tareq Sayed Rajab was an art collector and the first Director of the Department of Antiquities and Museums of Kuwait during the 1950s and 1960s. After retiring in 1969,

Rajab and his wife traveled the world to collect materials for the museum and then opened the museum in 1980. The museum has an extensive and valuable historic collection of pottery, glass, manuscripts, textiles, embroideries, and metalwork. A separate museum houses an extensive collection of calligraphy (Figure 11.2), including an early dated Qur'an written on parchment. In 2007, The Tareq Rajab Museum of Islamic Calligraphy was opened with a collection of Arabic script dating from the 7th century to the present.

The U.S. invasion of Iraq in 2003 compounded the environmental as well as other problems stemming from the 1991 Gulf War. When the UN was able to enter Iraq and assess the damage, the UNEP initiated a project titled Assessment of Environmental "Hot Spots" in Iraq. UNEP's 2005 postconflict report provided a summary of the most hazardous sites and recommendations for remediation. UNEP (2005, p. 123) estimated "that there are at least 20 and potentially up to 100 contaminated sites in Iraq where rapid corrective action is required to remove or secure highly hazardous wastes." One of the priority sites was the Al Qadissiya metal-plating facility. UNEP concluded that "this demolished site represents a severe risk to human health, due to cyanide containing hazardous waste" (2005, p. 136). The UN continues to monitor Iraq's environmental problems and advocates for remediating highly hazardous sites.

War: The Built Environment in Slovenia

Slovenia and Kuwait are both very small countries, but geographically, they are dramatically different. In contrast to Kuwait's deserts and lack of waterways, the landscape of Slovenia features green forests, rolling hills, mountain ranges, and numerous rivers, waterfalls, thermal mineral springs, and natural lakes.

Slovenia gained independence in 1991 from the former Yugoslavia. Prior to this, Slovenia did not exist as a nation but as a state within the former Yugoslavia (1918–2003). Located on the Balkan Peninsula in Eastern Europe, Yugoslavia was surrounded by the Adriatic Sea, Italy, Austria, and Hungary to the north, as well as Romania, Bulgaria, Greece, and Albania. First known as the Kingdom of the Serbs, Croats, and Slovenes, Yugoslavia had been formed after World War I by Serbian, Croatian, and Slovenian leaders. In 1929 it became known as the Kingdom of Yugoslavia. Following World War II, it became a communist nation under dictator Josip Tito. Known as the Federal People's Republic of Yugoslavia, the socialist state included six republics—Slovenia, Serbia, Croatia, Bosnia and Herzegovina, Macedonia, and Montenegro—as well as two provinces, Kosovo and Vojvodina. When Tito died in 1980, many republics initiated movements to gain independence. The collapse of the Soviet communist party in Eastern Europe at the end of the 1980s and beginning of the 1990s provided the opening to break ties with communist control. These political changes as well as ethnic conflicts within Yugoslavia prompted independence movements throughout the country.

In 1991, the republics of Slovenia, Croatia, and Macedonia won their independence from Yugoslavia. Bosnia followed the breakup of Yugoslavia by declaring its independence in 1992, but the action precipitated war between Bosnian Muslims, Serbs, and Croats. Ideological differences between three religious faiths and their respective cultural customs played roles in the fighting. The most practiced religion in Bosnia is Islam. Serbians and Croatians practice Orthodox Christianity and Catholicism, respectively. A peace treaty signed in 1995 divided Bosnia into two regions, the Serb Republic and Croat-Muslim Bosnia. In 1992, Montenegro and Serbia joined alliances to create a newly formed Yugoslavia (this union lasted only until 2006, when both countries declared their independence).

The extent of fighting to win independence and acquire territory varied with each republic. Initially, the Yugoslav army fought to quell uprisings by sending troops and tanks into the rebellious regions. People in the republics of Serbia, Croatia, and Bosnia suffered horrendously as "ethnic cleansing" involved hundreds of thousands of individuals and millions became refugees. To have a "homogeneous" ethnic population, Croatian and Serbian military troops fought to eliminate Bosnian Muslims, and concurrently Serbs and Muslims battled together to force Croats out of Bosnia. As a consequence, beginning with trials in 1999, the United Nations International Criminal Tribunal charged military leaders with crimes against humanity.

In contrast, republics, such as Slovenia, combated Yugoslav forces and were able to win their independence with few casualties because of the strength of the Slovene police force and citizens. Slovenia's relatively easy 10-day war for independence saved many lives and reduced the extent of damage to their buildings, towns, and cities. The 19th-century spa Rogaška Slatina, however, had sustained considerable damage during the civil wars in the 1990s. The health resort had been used by the ancient Romans but did not become an international destination for the wealthy until the 19th century. Beautiful classical buildings were constructed at the spa followed by facilities in the Art Nouveau and Art Deco styles (see Chapters 1 and 4, respectively). In addition to notoriety for the therapeutic qualities of its thermal mineral springs, Rogaška Slatina is famous for its architecture and artwork. After the fighting ended,

Slovenia began the historical restoration process that continues today.

Restoring Slovenia's reputation as a destination for curative springs is one example of initiatives that were developed to advance the young nation. Currently, Ljubljana, capital of Slovenia, has numerous cultural, scientific, economic, and political events each year. Slovenia has more than 200 museums, numerous theaters, and more than 100 art galleries. One of the museums is the former residence and studio of Slovenian architect Jože Plečnik (1872–1957). A student of Austrian architect Otto Wagner (1841–1918), Plečnik designed many building in Ljubljana during the 1920s and 1930s, including churches, private residences, public buildings, chapels, and many restorations.

Slovenia's pride in gaining its independence also was reflected in the construction of new public buildings that have received international awards for their innovation. For example, the Chamber of Commerce and Industry of Slovenia (1996–1999) commissioned the architectural firm Sadar Vuga Arhitekti (SVA) to renovate the organization's offices in what was a "strictly rationalist lowrise building" in Ljubljana and to provide additional space for restaurants, lecture halls, and a library (Figure 11.3). SVA has a unique classification system for their projects.

SVA's "formula" for the Chamber of Commerce and Industry Building was classified as "Vertical Hall." SVA considered "formula" a "user-friendly tool," and the firm used the term to communicate a design concept to their client and the public. "Formula" could be applied to a variety of building types. SVA explained the idea in the following way: "A formula is articulated such that it captures both the character of an architectural product and its effect on the observer and user" (www.sadarvuga.com). Examples of SVA's "formula" also included "Acting Light," "Blown-Up Window," "Matrix Volume," and "Landscaper."

SVA's definition for "Vertical Hall" was as follows: "Contrary to the traditional hall that organizes activities horizontally across a vast ground floor level, the programme is distributed among several smaller units inside a vertical volume. According to activity, each level can have a unique ambience and still maintain a visual connection with the other levels and their respective ambiences. The compact space of the Vertical Hall stimulates the connection between activities and interaction between people in the building" (www.sadarvuga.com). As illustrated in Figure 11.3, spaces within the Chamber of Commerce and Industry Building are divided into "several smaller units inside a vast ground

Figure 11.3 In Ljubljana, the Chamber of Commerce and Industry of Slovenia commissioned Sadar Vuga Arhitekti (SVA) to renovate the organization's offices in what was a "strictly rationalist lowrise building."

Source: Hisao Suzuki/Sadarvuga.

Figure 11.4 SVA was also commissioned to design a structure that would link two Slovenian National Gallery Buildings in Ljubljana.
Source: Hisao Suzuki/Sadarvuga.

floor." Various colors tend to reinforce the levels and reflect (to some degree) the organization's activities. An interior photograph reveals a gravity-defying free-form yellow desk that is suspended by cables several levels high. To promote interaction with the local and global community, the chamber also requested additional facilities, such as restaurants and meeting rooms.

SVA was also commissioned to design a structure that would link two Slovenian National Gallery Buildings (1996–2001) in Ljubljana (Figure 11.4). The project illustrates a unique example of Slovenia's intent to sustain ties between the country's heritages despite changes that occurred in the 20th century. SVA's project symbolically creates a link between two museums with national collections, one built before Slovenia's independence and the other after.

To exhibit Slovene fine art, the National Gallery opened in the Kresija building in 1918. After acquiring numerous collections from private as well as public sources, including the National Museum of Slovenia, the National Gallery opened in the renovated Narodni dom Building in 1933. As the gallery received more collections, the Narodni dom Building became too small. After Slovenia's independence, a new gallery was constructed close to the Narodni dom Building. SVA's project, Central Part of the National Gallery,

connected the Narodni dom Building with the new wing. The Central Part also provided a new entrance for the National Gallery and other facilities for museum events. SVA's "formula" for the Museum was "Cinematic Structure," the definition of which was "Within an open volume, the repetition of a single structural element that follows a changing rhythmic or dimensional sequence defines a certain spatial configuration and provides dynamic views inside and outside the building. The Cinematic Structure modifies the volume into micro-ambiences depending on one's position and movement through the building: low, high, dark, bright, shallow, deep" (www.sadarvuga.com).

EFFECTS AND CONDITIONS OF THE NATURAL ENVIRONMENT

Global environmental conditions continued to worsen in the 1990s and during the beginning of the

21st century, but international focus on the problems within the context of the growing population and economic conditions provided hope that the planet could be sustained for future generations.

In 2001, the Ecuadorian oil tanker *Jessica*, owned by Acotramar, ran aground in the Galapagos Islands, spilling nearly 250,000 gallons (approximately 946,353 liters) of oil into the waters. Destruction of the rainforests continued during this time at a rate of approximately 1 percent per year. Beginning in 1986, scientists at the World Glacier Monitoring Service initiated a program to collect data on ongoing glacier changes and reported that the polar ice cap in the Arctic Circle has been shrinking, which has serious ramifications. The rising ocean levels caused by the melting ice caps could cause massive flooding throughout the world. Excessive water had a deadly effect on the people of Indonesia and South Asia on December 26, 2004. The massive rush of water (tsunami) that resulted from the 9.1-magnitude earthquake in the Indian Ocean resulted in the deaths of nearly 300,000 people from drowning, injuries, and dehydration due to the lack of clean water. Hurricane Katrina brought devastation to the Gulf Coast of the United States when it struck in August of 2005, leaving hundreds of people dead and thousands displaced and causing millions of dollars in damage.

As the Earth never stops turning, it never stops shaking. There were many other deadly earthquakes throughout the 1990s and early 21st century, including temblors in Iran, the Philippines, Italy, Pakistan, Afghanistan, Russia, Turkey, Japan, India, Papua New Guinea, Greece, Taiwan, Algeria, and Kashmir. How buildings are constructed plays an important role in the extent of damage, injuries, and deaths. For example, on October 19, 1991, a 6.1-magnitude earthquake occurred in northern India. Faulty construction and other factors contributed to the region's devastation and the deaths of 1,600 people. Due to deforestation occurring in northern India, wood, a traditional building material,

has been scarce. Thus, new buildings were constructed with heavy and inflexible materials, such as stone. When the earthquake struck, it triggered landslides, which were able to move quickly and with great force due to the lack of trees. Landslides, tremors, and the aftershocks easily destroyed stone buildings because they were unable to withstand the strong forces or the movement. People were killed and trapped when the heavy stone walls tumbled on top of them.

Throughout the years, engineers and architects have been working to design buildings that can withstand the forces of earthquakes as well as other natural disasters. Seismic codes focus on a building's site, structure, and nonstructural components. Earthquake protection involves selecting a site with low seismicity and designing the building to reduce vulnerability based on the characteristics of the specific site, such as soil type and fault lines. Reducing damage to a structure requires following seismic codes, which includes appropriate frames, shapes, and connections between structural members and proper maintenance. To reduce damage to nonstructural components, such as mechanical, electrical, plumbing, and furnishings, requires proper bracing and support.

Other natural disasters included a cyclone in Bangladesh that killed 200,000 people in 1991, and the eruption of Mount Nyiragongo in the Democratic Republic of the Congo on January 17, 2002, which left more than 400,000 people homeless. The first known case of severe acute respiratory syndrome (SARS) was identified in China in late 2002. By early 2003, thousands of people worldwide contracted the SARS virus. As has been discussed throughout this book, advances in technology (such as the ability to travel thousands of miles in a single day) have contributed to globalization but have also been significant contributors to the spread of diseases and pollution throughout the world. To respond to these conditions requires global communication and knowledge of best practices.

The Principles of Sustainability and Nature: Contemporary Built Environments in Lahti, Helsinki, and Inari, Finland

Sustainable development and design have been common elements in many of the topics presented in this book. The Industrial Revolution precipitated the extraordinary consumption of natural resources and energy, and the pollution of air, land, and waterways. Subsequent increases in industrial production contributed to the consumption of more resources, more products manufactured and purchased, and more waste in the landfills. As new technologies were invented, new problems arose that affected the natural environment, the lives of people, and the economic stability of nations. The Chernobyl nuclear catastrophe is an example of the extent of damage that can occur when a volatile technology is uncontrollable. Chernobyl also demonstrates the global interdependency between *people*, the *environment*, and the *economy*, elements that form the basis of sustainable development. The dramatic increase in the world's population during the 20th century—from 1.7 billion in 1900 to 6 billion in 1999, on pace to pass 7 billion in 2013—and the consequences to the planet prompted international organizations to begin developing sustainability strategies introduced in the 1970s (see Chapter 9).

As mentioned in Chapter 10, the specific concept of sustainable development was identified in the 1987 UN report of the World Commission on Environment and Development (WCED), entitled Our Common Future, also known as the Brundtland Report. According to the Brundtland Report, "Humanity has the ability to make development sustainable to ensure that it meets the needs of the present without compromising the ability of future generations to meet their own needs. The concept of sustainable development does imply limits—not absolute limits but limitations imposed by the present state of technology and social organization on environmental resources and by the ability of the biosphere to absorb the effects of human activities.

But technology and social organization can be both managed and improved to make way for a new era of economic growth" (WCED, 1987, p. 24).

At the UN's 2002 World Summit on Sustainable Development in Johannesburg, South Africa, 104 representatives from states and governments appeared on behalf of 191 countries. At the conclusion of the summit, participants identified an "Implementation Plan" with a completion target date of 2015. The plan focused on improving the overall quality of life for the world's population by increasing daily incomes, providing safe drinking water and basic sanitation, and reducing mortality rates for infants and children under age 5. World leaders included their concerns regarding climate change and energy in the plan. A substantial increase in the consumption of renewable sources of energy was determined to be an "urgent" issue.

Due to the global nature of the report and its recommendations, the document does not specify consumption quantities. As explained in the report, to implement energy recommendations, governments and organizations should consider "national and regional specificities and circumstances" and should bear "in mind that in view of the different contributions to global environmental degradation, States have common but differentiated responsibilities" (UN, 2002, p. 9). For the protection of human health and the environment, leaders also developed a new, global system for classification and labeling of hazardous chemicals.

Global concerns identified at various international summits, including environmental protection and social and economic development, have dramatically altered the work of interior designers and architects and have imposed the expectation of socially responsible solutions. Interior designers and architects must broaden their view of the built environment by examining designs within the context of sustainable development. Data provided in *The Phaidon Atlas of Contemporary World Architecture* (2004) demonstrate human development factors that affect the design of the built environment, including population, land area, economic indicators based on per capita gross domestic product, environmental sustainability indices, and literacy. Demographic data included population in 2003, projected population in 2050, urban habitants, and the number of people younger than 15 and older than 65.

The Phaidon Atlas is an illustrated collection of exemplary contemporary architecture. To be included in the list of contemporary architecture, a project had to be completed after January 1998. An initial list of more than 4,000 projects was generated by historians, academics, journalists, and practitioners and included an extensive review of international architectural journals. Ultimately, an editorial panel selected 1,100 projects from 75 countries for inclusion. The numbers of projects for each region of the world are as follows: 64 projects in Oceania, 184 in Asia, 588 in Europe, 24 in Africa, 147 in North America, and 45 in South America. The panel reviewed each nominated project within "the context of its contribution to the art and science of architecture, regardless of differences in material, structure, budget, size, location of client" (Phaidon, 2004, p. 5). The two projects by SVA in Slovenia, discussed earlier, are included. A compilation of international

contemporary projects that have been peer-reviewed by architectural experts as the "very best" in the world is an excellent resource for the design profession. It is seen by many as a credible source for innovative designs, as well as providing an awareness of the built environment within the context of social, economic, and environmental concerns in every region of the world.

One of the human development factors identified in *The Phaidon Atlas* was the Environmental Sustainability Index (ESI). The source of this data was the Yale Center for Environmental Law & Policy, which in 2002 defined the ESI as "a composite index that tracks a diverse set of socio-economic, environmental, and institutional indicators that characterize and influence environmental sustainability at the national scale" (http://research .yale.edu/envirocenter). The center also ranked 146 countries according to "the environmental sustainability of their past, current, and projected socio-economic and institutional development trajectories." Finland, Norway, and Sweden were ranked as the top three countries; numerous projects from these three Nordic nations were mentioned in the *Phaidon Atlas*.

Several examples of sustainable design practice were provided by Finnish projects (Figure 11.5). To

Figure 11.5 Finland has many examples of architecture that reflect sustainable design practices such as the Sámi Museum and Northern Lapland Nature Center in Inari, designed by Juhani Pallasmaa.
Source: Sámi Museum Siida.

understand how the Finnish projects incorporated the principles of sustainability requires an awareness of the country's climate, geography, and natural resources. Finland is located in northern Europe on the Scandinavian Peninsula. Approximately one-third of the country is located above the Arctic Circle, which has a significant impact on its climate, temperatures, and hours of daylight. Finland is in a cold climate, but due in part to its long north-south orientation, southern Finland has milder winters than the northern region. The country experiences significant snowfalls that can occur during most of the year in Lapland, the region above the Arctic Circle. Lapland, known as "Land of the Midnight Sun," has sunlight 24 hours a day at summer solstice and barely any daylight during the winter months.

Pine, spruce, and birch forests cover most of the country, which also includes numerous lakes, rivers, and creeks. The Finnish people have a great deal of respect for the natural environment, which is evident by laws that have been enacted to protect forests and wildlife; another indicator is the extensive outdoor activities residents take part in throughout the year, including skiing, skating, cross-country skiing, ski jumping, biking, and hiking. Finnish environmental protection laws have been in place for more than 100 years, and many of the country's conservation laws encourage responsible management of its natural resources. Additional laws and environmental protection programs were created after Finland suffered the spread of toxins from the Chernobyl nuclear accident in 1986 (see Chapter 10). The airborne radioactive fallout from Chernobyl polluted waterways, farmland, forests, and animal grazing land. Reindeer, a source of meat and dairy products, were especially affected after eating one of their favorite foods, lichen. The sponge-like texture of lichen harbored radioactive materials. Hundreds of contaminated reindeer had to be slaughtered.

Many of the Finnish projects in *The Phaidon Atlas* reflect solutions that were derived from the unique characteristics of the Nordic country. For example, to conserve resources and reduce waste in the landfills, the Sibelius Concert and Congress Hall (1998–2000) in Lahti and the Lume Mediacenter (1995–2000) in Helsinki were adaptive reuse (buildings adapted for a new use) projects. Designed by the Finnish architectural firm APRT (Arkkitehtityöhuone Artto Palo Rossi Tikka Architects), a former carpentry factory was renovated to create one of the four main buildings for the Concert Hall complex. The carpentry factory was converted into a restaurant, meeting rooms, and offices. Adjoining the carpentry factory was a space that connected the factory to the main hall, and was used for banquets and exhibitions. In reflecting Finland's extensive forests, the ceiling of the hall had a network of wooden beams, which resembled the branches in a canopy of trees. The Lume Mediacenter, designed by architectural firm Heikkinen-Komonen, is another example of converting old industrial buildings into new uses. Lume Mediacenter was created for the audiovisual department of the University of Art and Design within a former ceramic factory.

Finland's lack of daylight during the winter months poses a unique challenge. To maximize the amount of daylight in the Kiasma Museum of Contemporary Art (1992–1998) in Helsinki, Steven Holl Architects designed the interior with multiple planes (Figure 11.6). The large skylights wash the white surfaces with daylight and pour diffused daylight into the gallery. Additional illumination was derived from daylight that is reflected by the various vertical surfaces.

Maximizing daylight was exceedingly important to the design of the Sámi Museum and the Northern Lapland Nature Centre (1998) in Inari, Finland (see Figure 11.5). Located in one of the northernmost sites in Finland, the museum had a skylight that extended the entire length of the museum. Designed by Finnish architect Juhani Pallasmaa, the museum was created to preserve the cultural heritage of the nomadic Sámi. The Sámi are an ethnic group with origins in northern Finland, Sweden, Norway, and Russia more than 6,000 years ago. They lived in the harsh conditions north of the Arctic Circle by herding wild reindeer. Reindeer were an important source for food, clothing, and shelter—the Sámi used reindeer skins for the covering on their conical-shaped tents. To reflect the Sámi's close relationship to nature, in addition to an abundance of daylight, Pallasmaa incorporated other references to the Finnish landscape. For example, timber was used to clad the façades of the building, and the interior was detailed with wood. To echo the profile of the landscape, Pallasmaa designed the roofline to resemble the surrounding hillside. The curved metal roof also helps to shed heavy snowfalls during the very long winter months. Removal of heavy snowfalls is critical to maintaining a sound structure, increasing the

Figure 11.6 To maximize the amount of daylight in the Kiasma Museum of Contemporary Art in Helsinki, Steven Holl designed the interior with multiple planes.

Source: Petri Virtanen/Contemporary Art Museum, Kiasma.

life of the roof, and helps to eliminate leaks. In the long term, well-maintained structures are important to sustainable development because fewer resources will be used to replace damaged or worn elements. A roof is particularly important because it protects the structure as well as its contents.

The Principles of Sustainability and Nature: Contemporary Examples in Ethiopia, Senegal, Guinea, and the Republic of South Africa

In dramatic contrast to Finland's cold climate is that of Ethiopia, a country close to the equator in east central Africa. Ethiopia is landlocked and includes Dallol, an area of the Danakil Depression that is considered to be the hottest spot on the planet, with temperatures reaching 145 degrees Fahrenheit (approximately 63 degrees Celsius). In the 13th century, to contend with the heat, Ethiopian King Lalibela ordered the construction of 11 medieval churches that were rock-hewn from subterranean stone to create the spatial interior cavities and façades. A series of underground passages connected the churches. The subterranean location maintains a consistent and moderate temperature. The churches, located in what became the city of Lalibela, were inscribed on UNESCO's World Heritage List in 1978.

A long dry season from September until February often results in severe droughts. Therefore, the country, with its more than 64 million people, is very dependent on the country's two rainy seasons. The first rainy season is in March and April, followed by the second phase during the summer months. With a population that the UN estimates will reach 93,845,000 by the year 2015, optimum climatic conditions are essential for agricultural production. More than 85 percent of Ethiopians live in the country and are farmers. Therefore, in a nation whose population has doubled since the 1980s and currently has 80 million people, crop failures, such as maize (corn), teff (cereal grass), and

Figure 11.7 To help improve Ethiopia's severe housing shortage, Ahadu Abaineh designed an experimental Tree House in Adis Abeda that was inexpensive and could be constructed with local resources in a very timely manner.

Source: © Aga Khan Trust for Culture.

wheat, create devastating famine and economic disasters. According to a 2003 World Health Organization study, 472,000 Ethiopian children die each year, and undernutrition was the cause for a substantial proportion of the deaths.

Droughts, food shortages, and poverty result in limited resources for shelter. To help improve Ethiopia's severe housing shortage, Ahadu Abaineh designed an experimental Tree House (2002) in Adis Abeda (also known as Addis Ababa) that was inexpensive and could be constructed with local resources in a very timely manner (Figure 11.7). Included in *The Phaidon Atlas*, the Tree House was constructed for U.S. $3,000 in just 6 weeks. Readily available local materials were used to construct the Tree House. Four live trees native to Ethiopia were the load-bearing structure for the three-story house. Timbers and wooden poles were used for other structural elements, such as floors, the staircase, and screens. Walls were formed using the traditional adobe mud technique. A corrugated metal roof protects the house, and its wavy ridges channel rainwater away from the façades to the roots of the trees. The trees help provide shade for the metal roof, and since the house has three stories, only the top floor is directly exposed to the heat from the roof. The interior has white-colored adobe walls and wood floors, beams, and stairs. In 2002, the AR Awards for Emerging Architecture gave Ahadu Abaineh an award for the Tree House and provided a summary of the design: "All members of the jury were delighted by the notion of making a building out of living trees, and by the idea that it may be possible to make replicable houses with appropriate technology that could last for a very long time and be in harmony with nature" (Architectural Review Awards, 2002, p. 1).

The Tree House in Ethiopia is just one example of many other African buildings that reflect the principles of sustainable design. Several recent projects featured in *The Phaidon Atlas* were constructed with minimal costs and offered solutions for controlling intense sunlight, moderating extreme heat, and conserving water and energy. Furthermore, to help reduce costs and conserve natural resources, many projects used recycled materials and had efficiently planned spaces. Examples of recycled materials are wheel hubs, bottles, and metal frames from abandoned buildings. The projects include the Women's Centre (2001) by Hollmén-Reuter-Sandman Architects, Kaheré Eila Poultry Farming School (1998) by Heikkinen-Komonen Architects, the National Food Technology Research Centre (2000) by Rik Leus, and the Medical Research Facilities for the Africa Centre (2002) by East Coast Architects. Interestingly, the list includes projects that were commissioned to help improve the health and well-being of the people of Africa. Furthermore, to accommodate local traditions, public buildings often included space for crafts and courtyards that are used as social gathering areas.

In the tradition of African settlements, Hollmén-Reuter-Sandman Architects designed the Women's Centre (2001) in the African country of Senegal. As with traditional African settlements, the Women's Centre was designed with a perimeter wall and a "communal courtyard." Other similarities include buildings linked together with walls, brightly painted walls, earthen walls with molded corners, grass roofs, and rooms for everyday activities, such as crafts and laundry. The purpose of the Women's Centre is to provide a place for women in the community to socialize, engage in crafts, and enjoy entertainment. A complex with a shared communal courtyard is an ideal layout for encouraging people to congregate to one area and participate in the activities. To provide shade, one of the entrances is positioned close to an enormous baobab tree. The other entrance is protected by a verandah. During the day, thick concrete walls help moderate the temperatures by absorbing radiant heat. In the evening, rooms are heated by the stored warmth emitted from the concrete walls. Laundry facilities included an outdoors area for drying clothes. In echoing materials used in traditional settlements, ceilings are lined with panels of woven grasses, a local rapidly renewable material. One reason grasses are a common material used in Ethiopian buildings is due to the deforestation that had to occur throughout the country to grow more crops for the rapidly escalating population. The total cost for the complex, which includes three major buildings, was only U.S. $76,000.

Designed by Finnish architects Heikkinen-Komonen, the Kaheré Eila Poultry Farming School also had a central courtyard that was surrounded by three buildings. The buildings were constructed with unfired blocks that were made with local clay. The cement roof tiles were embedded with local grasses, including sisal and woven cane. In another example the passive solar-powered National Food Technology Research Centre was oriented along an east-west axis to maximize heat gain. Architect Rik Leus designed the building with barrel vaults that helped to remove heat from the interior spaces. Several solar chimneys were installed to cool the facilities by drawing the air from the earth through floor grilles and exhausting the room's hot air through ceiling plenums. The system works through natural convection. Rainwater collected on the roof, and a parking area was used for the gardens. The site included a system to treat wastewater.

East Coast Architects based in South Africa also used water-management systems for the Medical Research Facilities for the Africa Centre in the Republic of South Africa. Rainwater and **graywater**—wastewater from sources such as showers and laundry—were used for gardens. Additional technologies that were incorporated into the Medical Research Facilities project to conserve more water were low-flow lavatory fixtures and a wastewater-treatment system. Indigenous eucalyptus was used for balustrades and to provide shade.

The open-air Nelson Mandela Museum (2000) in Mvezo by Cohen & Judin is another African example in *The Phaidon Atlas* that has sustainable design features (Figure 11.8). The museum in Mvezo is one of three sites in South Africa that comprise the Nelson Mandela Museum. The other sites are in Mandela's home

Figure 11.8 The open-air Nelson Mandela Museum (2000) in Mvezo, South Africa, by Cohen & Judin.
Source: Nelson Mandela Museum.

village, Qunu, and the Bhunga building in Mthatha. The open-air museum in Mvezo was built on top of a hill overlooking the African countryside. Indigenous materials were used to construct the museum, such as stonewalls, poles made from gum trees (a eucalyptus species) to support the roof, and reed for the ceiling and fences. Cohen and Judin also involved the skills of local people in the design of the museum by hiring them to weave the grass ceilings and fences. Without using any energy, protection from the hot sun is provided with a simple steel sheet roof and people enjoy cool breezes due to the museum's hilltop location.

GLOBAL TECHNOLOGICAL DEVELOPMENTS

Technological advances and materials, such as steam engines and cast iron introduced during the Industrial Revolution (see Chapter 1), started to become obsolete during the last decades of the 20th century as subsequent industries changed how people lived and worked. Previous industrial sites were demolished and replaced with contemporary architecture, such as the Jean-Marie Tjibaou Cultural Centre in Nouméa (1991–1998), New Caledonia, and the Guggenheim Museum in Bilbao, Spain (1991–1997). Ironically, in order to sustain ethnic heritages, many nations created new cultural centers. The title of "World's Tallest Building" changed hands in 2004 with the completion of Taipei 101 at 1,474 feet (449 meters).

The Olympic Games continued to be seen as an important event to showcase the host nation's technological advances, and one of the best vehicles for this was the spectacular architecture designed for the competition venues. Sophisticated software programs were required to create these types of free-formed sculpted structures. Computer technology and capability has made dramatic strides since 1990, most notably in the areas of power, speed, costs, and the rapid growth of the World Wide Web.

Computers: Jean-Marie Tjibaou Cultural Centre (1991–1998) in Nouméa, New Caledonia, by Renzo Piano Building Workshop and Guggenheim Museum Bilbao (1991–1997) in Bilbao, Spain, by Frank O. Gehry

Another complex was designed to preserve the heritage of an ethnic group: the Jean-Marie Tjibaou Cultural Centre on New Caledonia, a French possession in the South Pacific Ocean. The island of New Caledonia has been a French colony since 1853. In the late 1980s, New Caledonians rallied for their independence, but due to France's interest in the island's significant nickel deposits, the protests were unsuccessful. However, to quell the violence, an agreement signed by the French and New Caledonians included a provision to have an independence referendum around 2015. To preserve the heritage of the indigenous Kanak people, the agreement also included a provision for the establishment of the Agency for the Development of Kanak Culture (ADCK) and facilities for its headquarters. The center was named in honor of Jean-Marie Tjibaou, a leader in the New Caledonian independence movement who was assassinated in 1989. French President Mitterrand added the ADCK facilities to his list of "Presidential Building Projects" (see Chapter 10). In 1991, Italian architectural firm Renzo Piano Building Workshop (RPBW) won the competition to design a complex of buildings in New Caledonia's capital city, Nouméa (Figure 11.9). The architecture's seemingly simple composition is in reality extraordinarily complex and would have been extremely difficult to accomplish without computers.

To construct RPBW's design required computer simulation studies conducted by the Centre

Scientifique et Technique du Bâtiment (CSTB). Computer simulations were created to study the effects of wind on the center's structural components. Simulations included using smoke to follow the path of wind through the structure at varying velocities. The wind tunnel tests provided data that was needed to maximize natural ventilation and to minimize damage from the frequently occurring cyclones in the South Pacific Ocean. Based on the results of the simulation studies, RPBW built two full-size prototypes in France. The final design was determined by the computer simulation results and new details that were discovered during the prototype tests. Inspired by the Kanak huts ("cases") made from local grasses, RPBW designed ten cases in three different sizes. In a traditional Kanak village, huts are grouped into three

Figure 11.9 Jean-Marie Tjibaou Cultural Centre, the Headquarters of the Agency for the Development of Kanak Culture (ADCK). RPBW won the competition for designing the structure in New Caledonia's capital city, Nouméa. The design required complex computer simulations.
Source: John Gollings/© RPBW.

sub-villages; this is the way RPBW designed the new center. The plan also included an outdoor amphitheater for traditional ceremonies. The first village had audio-visual facilities, a cafeteria, and an exhibit of sculptures from the Pacific Region and Kanak. The second village had three cases for the multimedia library. Two lecture theaters and a classroom were housed in the cases in the third village.

Cases were made from vertical ribs and rows of horizontal slats (see Figure 11.9). In resembling materials used to build Kanak huts, the cases' ribs and slats were made from iroko, a termite-resistant hardwood from Africa. A close inspection of the ribbed structures reveals variances in the distances between the slats, and that some slats are fixed and others are adjustable louvers. These subtle differences facilitate natural ventilation. Based on the results of computer simulations, some louvers are open and others are closed, depending upon the wind velocity. The structures were designed to withstand cyclone-strength winds. A combination of open and closed slats also helps to move warm air to the outdoors. During a cyclone, only the louvers at the top of the cases are open. Thus, the structure is protected as the strong winds pass through the tallest section of the case.

Maximizing and controlling the South Pacific trade winds was one environmental example that RPBW incorporated into the design of the center. Located on a promontory next to a lagoon (see Figure 11.9), the cases were sited to blend with the locale's natural vegetation, such as the indigenous Norfolk pines. At a time when a preliterate culture existed on the island, certain vegetation and stones were used as a means of communication. For example, a kaori tree and a Norfolk Island pine planted next to a dwelling communicated to people that the structure was forbidden space. RPBW incorporated this cultural heritage into the design of the center by creating an outdoor garden walk, the Kanak path, which communicates a story told by the vegetation and rocks. As described by RPBW, the beginning and ending of the narrative are marked by large rocks, and the five chapters are *Creation, Agriculture, Habitat, Death,* and *Rebirth*. For each chapter, traditional vegetation has been planted for its symbolic associations. For example, the *Creation* garden has a pond that represents the origin of life. In the *Habitat* garden, there are plants used for traditional medicine and eating, including cabbage, bananas, and yams.

Computer software programs and the natural environment also were essential to the design of the billowy Guggenheim Museum in Bilbao, Spain (Figure 11.10). Canadian-born architect Frank O. Gehry's modern Expressionist design resembles clouds, flower petals, and the scales on fish, but to reproduce these complex moving forms required an extremely sophisticated software program originally developed for the aeronautical industry. **CATIA (Computer-Aided Three Dimensional Interactive Application)**, with excellent virtual design and manufacturing capabilities, was invented by Dassault Systèmes and had been used by Gehry for some parts in other buildings prior to the Guggenheim. Dassault Systèmes is an international company that specializes in three-dimensional products that are able to perform structural and material calculations on sculptural shapes and then transfer the information to the manufacturing process.

The mathematical complexity of the Guggenheim Museum necessitated the full capabilities of CATIA.

Gehry used CATIA to create hundreds of working drawings of the Guggenheim and to provide exact specifications to manufacturers. After a physical model was built, CATIA was used to digitize the shapes of the structure. CATIA translated the form of the buildings into a three-dimensional model complete with shading, shadows, and highlights. The computer model was then used to analyze and test the structural aspects of the design. CATIA generated working drawings, which were used by the manufacturers of the materials for the project. The computer-aided manufacturing component of CATIA enabled the materials to be produced using the exact specifications that were derived from the computer model. Translating working drawings into computerized mechanical instructions enabled the complex geometries of the Guggenheim to become a reality. Without these capabilities, Gehry's curvaceous design would have been impossible or at the very least cost prohibitive.

The origins of Guggenheim Museum Bilbao are traced back to a very difficult time period in the history of the city due to a series of destructive and deadly floods in 1983. To recover from the devastation and revitalize the economy, government officials sponsored a major redevelopment project. In collaboration with the Guggenheim Foundation, the museum was one of the initiatives, as well as the Sondica Airport Terminal and

Figure 11.10 Computer software programs and the natural environment were essential to the design of the billowy Guggenheim Museum in Bilbao, Spain, by Frank O. Gehry.

Source: Wikimedia Commons.

Control Tower (1990–2000) by Santiago Calatrava and the Bilbao Metro (1988–1995) by Foster + Partners.

In referencing its original site, Gehry's design for the Guggenheim contemporizes Bilbao's industrial history. Bilbao's steel industry was referenced in the titanium cladding, and its shipbuilding enterprise was translated into the central "boat gallery" and other exterior forms. Gehry created a link between the new art museum and the historical city by inserting the La Salve Bridge between the main building and its V-shaped observation tower. Located close to the street, an enormous topiary sculpture in the shape of a dog, *Puppy* (1992) by Jeff Koons, presents a playful introduction to the imposing titanium panels that shimmer in the wind. The Guggenheim Bilbao has become an iconic symbol of the city and has provided a new image to the Basque region in northern Spain.

The Internet and Technologies: The Beijing Olympic Green National Stadium (The Bird's Nest) and The National Aquatics Center (The Water Cube) for the 2008 Beijing Olympics

As the opening ceremonies of the 2008 Beijing Olympics were being broadcast, details and illustrations of the new structure designed for the event, the Beijing Olympic Green National Stadium, or the "The Bird's Nest," were made available (Figure 11.11). Simultaneously, online descriptions were available for the event's other innovative structure, the National Aquatics Center, or "The Water Cube." The Internet provided the means to immediately access news of the Olympics, including these new facilities. The ability to see photographs and engage in virtual visits of buildings throughout the world is just one of the ways the Internet has dramatically changed the design profession in a very short period of time.

The origins of the Internet trace back to the Cold War decades (late 1940s to early 1990s) and the Soviet Union's launch of its Sputnik spacecraft. To successfully

Figure 11.11 The 2008 Beijing Olympic Green National Stadium or the "The Bird's Nest." The design consortium for the project was Herzog & de Meuron Architekten AG, Arup, and the China Architectural Design and Research Group.
Source: An Qi/Alamy.

compete technologically with the USSR, President Eisenhower established the Advanced Research Projects Agency (ARPA) within the Department of Defense in 1958. By 1969, the agency initiated the Advanced Research Projects Agency Network (ARPANET) project, the world's first computer network. ARPANET was accessible only to scientists and researchers; very few nodes existed in the system. In 1972, ARPANET had 37 machines, including a node at NASA, and the first e-mail program. International connections were established in 1973, and by 1983 ARPANET had Transmission Control Protocol/Internet Protocol (TCP/IP), a set of rules for transferring information between computers. These rules were necessary to make the Internet a possibility.

In 1989, a British computer scientist, Tim Berners-Lee, invented the World Wide Web (WWW), a vast array of documents (more than one trillion pages) that are connected to each other by means of hypertext or hyperlinks. The WWW revolutionized the Internet by making it relatively easy to navigate the extraordinary amount of information stored on computers throughout the world. ARPANET was decommissioned in 1990 and was replaced by NSFnet, a computer network created by the National Science Foundation (NSF) for research activities.

Using the Internet exclusively for scientific research changed in 1992 when the NSF opened the network to commercial enterprises. The Internet was then available for communication purposes and as a means to create "websites," collections of web pages and related files (such as graphics files and other resources) that share a set of similar addresses. The Internet radically transformed the design profession—along with thousands of other professions—by making it easy to communicate with clients, suppliers, and other professionals throughout the world. The Internet made it realistic for a firm to have multiple international offices and to engage the services of professionals regardless of their location. For example, Arup is a London-based architectural and engineering firm with 92 offices scattered over the continents of Africa, Asia, Australia, Europe, and North America.

The ability to share design files and documents also makes it possible to collaborate with individuals who have the most appropriate expertise required for a project regardless of their location. The ability to search the globe for the best qualified individual or the ideal product results in designs that can be more innovative and code compliant, incorporate the newest cost-effective technologies, and reflect best practices. The Internet is critical for the coordination that is required for project management activities.

The Internet has also affected the design profession by facilitating access to international suppliers, materials, museum collections, libraries, virtual architectural visits, and research studies. Created by the University of Minnesota, InformeDesign (www.informedesign .umn.edu) is an excellent example of a website that presents valuable information to the design profession that would not be easily feasible without the Internet. The InformeDesign Web site provides concise summaries of the results of current research related to types of buildings, design specialization, design issues, occupants, and user types, and is accessible to anyone with an Internet connection.

The projects designed for the 2008 Beijing Olympics are an excellent example of how the Internet made it possible for several firms to work together and maximize knowledge of innovative technologies and materials. The Water Cube project, or what the international design team referred to as their "common child," was awarded to a consortium including Arup, the Australian firm PTW Architects, the China State Construction and Engineering Corporation (CSCEC), and the CSCEC Shenzhen Design Institute (CSCEC+DESIGN) (Figure 11.12). The international design consortium for the Bird's Nest included the Swiss firm Herzog & de Meuron Architekten AG, Arup, and the China Architectural Design and Research Group.

To replicate the seemingly simple forms of soap bubbles and a bird's nest, respectively, required extremely sophisticated technology and specialized expertise. The projects became even more complicated when these familiar shapes also had to accommodate thousands of people, withstand seismic conditions, incorporate the principles of sustainability, and adhere to Chinese building codes. Arup reported that the "four key concerns" in the Development Design Report were the successful integration of "economic, social, environmental and issues relating to natural resources." Remarkably, the collaborative efforts of the two international design teams were able to address the requirements and create innovative architecture that responded to the purposes of the facilities.

"Bubbles" covering the walls and ceiling of the Water Cube were a perfect connection to the facility that was needed for Olympic water sports. Watching the events under a canopy of bubbles gave the 17,000 spectators the simulated experience of swimming underwater. From the exterior, the translucent "bubbles" were used as screens to project images of swimmers racing in the pool and schools of fish swimming in the ocean. To recreate the geometrically complex bubbles required sophisticated technologies and expertise. As explained by Arup (2008), bubbles have either

12 or 14 sides, but they always touch each other. The unique way that bubbles adhere to each other enabled the design team to create a structurally sound and strong cube, but the arrangement required more than a hundred different configurations. Rapid prototyping technology was required to model the structure. To facilitate the structural analysis and design, Arup developed a "structure optimisation [*sic*] program." To ensure the accuracy of the structural model, within a reasonable length of time, Arup developed a conversion program for its three-dimensional AutoCAD system. The firm reported that "The program modeled the entire structure in 25 minutes rather than months" (www.arup.com).

The translucent bubbles were made from **ETFE (ethylene tetrafluoroethylene) film,** a high-tech material manufactured by Vector Foiltec that has excellent insulating properties, is lightweight, is self-cleaning, transmits more daylight than glass, and is recyclable. In combination with an acoustical membrane, ETFE was also used in the Bird's Nest (see Figure 11.11). Arup estimated that the transmittal qualities of ETFE would conserve 30 percent of the energy used to heat the

pools and the interior of the Water Cube. In addition, Arup predicted a 55 percent savings of the electricity required to illuminate the Leisure Pool Hall.

Conserving water was another sustainability goal for the project. To conserve local water resources and reduce waste flowing to the sewer system, the Water Cube was designed to **harvest** water from the roof and pool backwash systems. Safety aspects were also carefully considered and incorporated: The fire design plan for the Water Cube was created using a computer modeling program that simulated the movement of smoke and people. Marianne Foley, the project's fire engineer, explained the plan in the following way: "People prefer to enter and exit from the same place, so the fire design favours [*sic*] open circulation routes, and incorporates fire safety systems like sprinklers and smoke exhaust— making the building safe for longer periods of time and allowing the more familiar circulation routes to be used for exit" (www.arup.com).

Within the context of planning for sustainability and safety, the innovative designs of the Water Cube and the Bird's Nest prompt a reassessment of conventional

Figure 11.12 The Water Cube for the 2008 Beijing Olympics was designed by Arup, PTW Architects, the CSCEC, and the CSCEC Shenzhen Design Institute. Bird's Nest is in the background.

Source: An Qi/Alamy.

functions of a structure, walls, floors, and ceilings. As illustrated in the Olympic opening ceremonies, the Bird's Nest structure and its planes became part of the performance as multimedia images were projected around the circular form. The light-emitting diodes (LEDs) scrolling on the floor of the stadium became the source for the narrative as well as the canvas for the painting created by the performance of the 17,000 Chinese dancers as they demonstrated flawless precision and form while wearing spectacular costumes.

GLOBAL LIFE AND WORK STYLES

Approximately seven billion people live on the planet as of 2009. Population growth worldwide has been due to better health care, vaccinations, and increased longevity. Worldwide, the average life expectancy is almost 68 years and estimated to reach almost 69 by 2015; in the United States, the average life expectancy is nearly 80 years. The escalating population growth has environmental and economical consequences. The UN-sponsored UNICEF estimates that more than 26,500 children die each day due to poverty and hunger. Problems in developing countries are exacerbated by the increasing numbers of people who have been infected with HIV/AIDS. The World Health Organization (WHO) determined that more than 33 million people have HIV/AIDS and nearly 3 million are infected every year. The rising numbers of people living with disease or disability require environments that can accommodate their needs as well as the needs of the general population. Universal Design—design for buildings, products, and services intended to be barrier free and usable and appropriate for everyone, not just people with disabilities—will continue to be a major concern for those designing the built environments of the future.

Designing for security is also a concern for those designing built environments. The use of violence for political purposes continued during the 1990s and into the 21st century. In 1993, a car bomb planted by a radical Islamic group exploded in the parking garage underneath the World Trade Center, killing six people and injuring 100. American Timothy McVeigh was convicted for the truck bombing of the Alfred P. Murrah Federal Building in Oklahoma City, Oklahoma, in 1995. The explosion and its aftermath killed 168 people, including 19 children who were in the building's daycare center. U.S. government property overseas was subsequently attacked on June 25, 1996. Terrorists bombed a residential unit for U.S. Air Force personnel in Khobar, Saudi Arabia. Nearly 400 people were injured and 19 people died in the explosion.

On August 7, 1998, there were two terrorist truck bombings of U.S. Embassies in Africa. The attacks, linked to Osama bin Laden, occurred in the cities of Nairobi, Kenya, and Dar es Salaam in Tanzania. The bombings killed 250 people and injured over 6,000. In 2001, almost 3,000 people were killed and thousands more injured when Islamic extremists, part of the al-Qaeda organization, hijacked four commercial jet airplanes and flew two into the World Trade Center (WTC) in New York City and one into the Pentagon in Arlington, Virginia. The fourth plane crashed in a field in Pennsylvania after passengers fought for control with the hijackers.

Terrorism: World Trade Center (WTC) (1966–1973) in New York City, by Minoru Yamasaki and WTC Plan (2002–present) by Studio Daniel Libeskind

Many people associate one image with September 11, 2001: two 110-story buildings burning and collapsing. Skyscrapers, an icon of America, became targets for unprecedented acts of terrorism. Aircraft, another American invention of the 20th century, were used as weapons. On the morning of September 11, 2001,

American Airlines Flight 11 crashed into the north tower at 1 World Trade Center, followed minutes later by United Airlines Flight 175 striking the south tower at 2 World Trade Center. The Pentagon, the U.S. military headquarters located just outside Washington, D.C., in Arlington, Virginia, was struck by American Airlines Flight 77 and shortly after that, United Airlines 93 was the last plane to crash, in Shanksville, Pennsylvania. The collapse of 2 WTC was followed by 1 WTC a half-hour later; another building in the complex, 7 WTC (a 47-story office building built in 1987) collapsed several hours after that. In addition to the thousands of people who were at the sites already, hundreds of rescue workers were killed. The destructive forces also caused severe damage to several buildings in the World Trade Center complex, including 4 WTC, 5 WTC, 6 WTC, and a Marriott Hotel. Surrounding buildings suffered considerable structural and façade damage. The damage to the Pentagon was contained to a relatively small area on one side of the building, between corridors four and five, but approximately one-third of the building sustained smoke and fire damage. The aftermath of the catastrophes resembled the destructive forces of warfare (Figure 11.13).

The quick and complete destruction of two enormous buildings had a ripple effect on the psyche of people, architecture, and interior environments. Any pending project for a super-skyscraper was reconsidered and often was changed to a shorter structure with less visibility. The devastation reinforced difficulties associated with evacuating people in tall buildings during an emergency. Safe evacuation becomes a greater challenge for people with disabilities, the elderly, children, the injured, and individuals who become frightened or disoriented in panic situations. Many occupants of tall buildings refused or were reluctant to renew their leases.

Large unsightly barricades were installed around historical landmarks, and high-tech security checkpoint systems designed for airports were installed in lobbies. Airport security was heightened and was expanded to include more guards, x-ray machines, bomb-sniffing dogs, security screening areas, and checkpoint units. Building managers, interior designers, and architects had to identify space and amenities for additional people, animals, and new equipment. Some buildings perceived as associated with the ethnic background of the hijackers were ostracized and vandalized.

Soon after September 11, 2001, a movement began to start the process of reconstructing the World Trade Center. However, the rebuilding of the WTC and the lower Manhattan area has been a process unlike any other construction project. Countless individuals, including families who lost loved ones in the attack,

Figure 11.13 The aftermath of the September 11, 2001, terrorist attacks resembled the destructive forces of the Chernobyl nuclear disaster and the bombing of Japan during World War II.

Source: © Aristede Economopoulos/Star Ledger/Corbis.

desired input in the reconstruction process. The multiple public and private entities involved with the project added to the complexity of reconstructing the site.

The vision for the World Trade Center began in the 1950s when the Downtown–Lower Manhattan Development Association and its founder, David Rockefeller, wanted to redevelop lower Manhattan into a thriving area by creating a premier center for finance and trade. This required a partnership with the owner of the land, the Port Authority of New York and New Jersey. Anticipated tenants of the buildings included export-import firms, custom-house brokers, international bankers, the New York Stock Exchange, the New York–New Jersey Port Authority, and New York State agencies. Hundreds of retail establishments in the area had to be demolished prior to construction.

The Port Authority selected American architect Minoru Yamasaki (see Chapter 9) as the architect for the project, and Emery Roth and Sons of New York was hired as associate architect. In 1964, Yamasaki described his feelings about the project: "World trade means world peace and consequently the World Trade Center building in New York signifies something missed and very important which is world peace" (Ruchelman, 1977, p. 48). The original plans featured the two twin towers, a U.S. Customs Building (6 WTC), Northeast Plaza Building (5 WTC), Southeast Plaza Building (4 WTC), Electrical Substation and Access Ramps (7 WTC), and a hotel "under study" (WTC Marriott Hotel) covering 16 acres (6.5 hectares).

Groundbreaking occurred in August 1966, and the North Tower was ready for its first tenants in late 1970 (the upper stories were completed in 1972). The new PATH subway station opened in 1971 and the World Trade Center was formally dedicated on April 4, 1973. Three years later was the opening of the elegant restaurant, Windows on the World, on the 106th and 107th floors of the North Tower.

On July 24, 2001, Silverstein Properties, a New York real estate development firm, obtained a 99-year lease for the WTC from the Port Authority. To reconstruct WTC after the 2001 attack required the involvement of Silverstein Properties, the Port Authority, and the Lower Manhattan Development Corporation, as well as countless other individuals, agencies, and organizations.

Numerous concepts, plans, and schemes have been proposed for the WTC. Architectural Record documented the official and unofficial proposals for the WTC in the book *Imagining Ground Zero* (2004). After reviewing thousands of entries, a planning committee for the "Innovative Design Study" competition identified seven finalists who presented their proposals on December 18, 2002. By February, Studio Daniel Libeskind was selected as the winning proposal and THINK was the second-place entry (Figure 11.14). In writing about his proposal, "Memory Foundations," Libeskind explained:

> *I envisioned five towers—tall but not too tall—arranged by increasing height, from south to north, so that they rose in a spiral with the same shape as the flame in Lady Liberty's torch. And the tallest, I had decided should rise to 1,776 feet, to commemorate the Declaration of Independence, which brought democracy to the world. I would fill the upper floors of the tower with botanical gardens, as a confirmation of life. There would be a memorial site sinking into the bedrock of Manhattan and exposing the foundations of the World Trade Center, and a walkway along the slurry wall. Sheltering it, in an embrace, would be a museum and other cultural buildings. (Libeskind, 2004, pp. 47–48)*

Libeskind also described "The Wedge of Light," a public space that was "inspired by the ray of sunlight." Two lines would define the plaza: "The first would be a line of light that strikes on September 11 of every year at precisely 8:46 a.m.—the moment when the first jet smashed into the North Tower. The second line would

Figure 11.14 Studio Daniel Libeskind's "Memory Foundations" was selected as the winning proposal for the reconstruction of the WTC.

Source: AP Photo/Lower Manhattan Development Corporation.

Figure 11.15 The winning entry for the WTC Memorial, "Reflecting Absence," was designed by architect, Michael Arad and landscape architect, Peter Walker.

Source: AP Photo/Lower Manhattan Development Corporation.

mark the spot where, at 10:28 a.m., the second tower bucked into dust and debris" (Libeskind, 2004, p. 48).

There were separate competitions for the WTC Transportation Hub and the Memorial. Santiago Calatrava, DMJM + Harris, and STV Group won the competition for the Transportation Hub. The winning entry for the memorial, "Reflecting Absence," was submitted by architect Michael Arad and landscape architect Peter Walker (Figure 11.15).

Since the initial presentation, Libeskind's proposal has undergone numerous revisions and Silverstein Properties has hired several architects and engineers to design the new WTC buildings. Libeskind is responsible for the master plan of the WTC, which as of 2009, included six office towers (Freedom Tower, Tower 2, Tower 3, Tower 4, Tower 5, and 7 WTC), Memorial and Museum, the Transportation Hub, Retail, and a Performing Arts Center. The Freedom Tower and 7 WTC were designed by David M. Childs of Skidmore, Owings, & Merrill. Silverstein Properties commissioned Norman + Foster to design Tower 2. Towers 3 and 4 were designed by Sir Richard Rogers and Fumihiko Maki, respectively. Frank O. Gehry was hired as the architect for the WTC Performing Arts Center.

Nearly 5 years after the attacks, visible progress with the reconstruction was evident. In 2006, groundbreaking ceremonies occurred for the construction of Freedom Tower, and the first completed building was 7 WTC. The building was also New York City's first **Leadership in Energy and Environmental Design (LEED)**-certified office building. 7 WTC was awarded the gold rating, the second-highest level in the program. Sponsored by the U.S. Green Building Council, LEED is a voluntary certification program that was created to verify "that a building project meets the highest green building and performance measures" (www.usgbc.org). Certification indicates that "a building is environmentally responsible, profitable and a healthy place to live and work."

Most conceptual design deadlines for the other projects were in 2006, with expected completion dates of 2011–2012. However, as of August 5, 2009, the Web site (www.wtc.com) that provides information and updates regarding the construction process, reported "With the eighth anniversary of the 9/11 attacks just a few short weeks away, New Yorkers face the unfortunate prospect of yet another anniversary where work at the site has ground to a halt. For months, the Port Authority and the site's developer, Larry Silverstein, have been locked in an endless negotiation over financing the remaining towers."

Physical Characteristics of People: Disability Legislation, Universal Design, Inclusive Design, and Mainstream Technologies

The WHO estimated in 2009 that "650 million people live with disabilities around the world," and the numbers are predicted to rapidly increase in the future primarily due to increased longevity. According to the U.S. Census Bureau, the world's senior (aged 65 and older) population is expected to triple by the year 2050. Essential elements to designing successful built environments include an understanding of physical attributes and individuals' wide range of abilities (Figure 11.16). Basic physical functions related to design include seeing, hearing, touching, reaching, holding, lifting, pushing, pulling, climbing, walking, and sitting. Every individual performs these functions differently. For decades, various international organizations and governments have attempted to create a world that enables most people to live independently regardless of individual abilities. Unfortunately, by creating policies and publishing books and guidelines for "disabilities," solutions often focused on accommodating requirements for people with "disabilities," rather than reconceptualizing designs by identifying new approaches to addressing the needs of most people; principles of Universal Design.

"Disability" policies have been around for at least 300 years. Great Britain initiated disability policies in

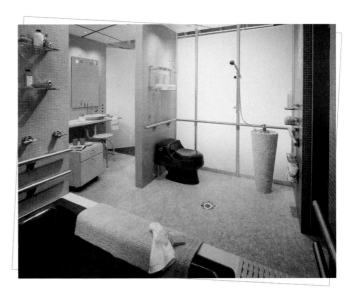

Figure 11.16 A bathroom designed according to the principles of Universal Design.
Source: Kohler Co.

the middle of the 1700s by establishing "workhouses," which were institutions for "impotent" poor people. During the Industrial Revolution, a number of institutions were created for people with disabilities, including St. Luke's Hospital for Lunatics, London; the General Institution for the Relief of Persons laboring under Bodily Deformity, Birmingham; the Cambrian Institution for the Deaf and Dumb, Aberystwyth; and the National Asylum for Idiots in London.

In the early 20th century, several government reports were published that delineated the status of disabled persons. Examples include the *Report of the Inter-Departmental Committee on Physical Deterioration* (1904) and the *Report of the Royal Commission on Lunacy and Mental Disorder* (1926). Topics included "physical deterioration," "lunacy and mental disorder," and "mental deficiency." After World War II, the topics of the *Reports* changed to rehabilitation, training, resettlement, mental illness, and mental deficiency. *The Last Refuge* (1960) was a publication written by Professor Peter Townsend that reported the results of a national research study on the living conditions of the elderly in Great Britain. Progress in designing accessible facilities occurred when the Royal Institution of British Architects published *Designing for the Disabled*, a guide that was based on the research studies of J. Anderson in 1963.

The issue received greater international attention in 1971 when the UN passed the Declaration on the Rights of Mentally Retarded Persons, followed by the Declaration on the Rights of Disabled Persons in 1975. The UN began advocating for people with disabilities in 1945 and increasingly expanded its international efforts with substantial activities occurring after 1980. The UN focused on the "rights and dignity of persons with disabilities." An example of a major initiative is the establishment of the World Programme of Action (WPA) in 1982. As described by the UN, WPA "is a global strategy to enhance disability prevention, rehabilitation and equalization of opportunities, which pertains to full participation of persons with disabilities in social life and national development. The WPA also emphasizes the need to approach disability from a human rights perspective" (United Nations, 1982, p. 1).

To end discrimination experienced by people with disabilities, in 1995 the United Kingdom passed the Disability Discrimination Act (DDA). Expanded in 2005, the act protects the rights of disabled individuals in several areas, including employment, education, access to goods, facilities, and services, and buying or renting land or property.

The United Kingdom's disability policies and legislation during the 20th century somewhat parallel the events in the United States. Involvement with World War I prompted the establishment of a new program for veterans' benefits, which included disability compensation and vocational rehabilitation for the disabled. The GI Bill, signed into law after World War II, provided home loan and educational benefits to veterans. Unfortunately, the thousands of veterans who became disabled serving in the war were unable to take advantage of the benefits due to inaccessible educational facilities. Solutions focused on creating "barrier-free" environments.

The Architectural Barrier Act (ABA) of 1968 was one of the first laws to provide access to facilities, but the legislation was restricted to buildings that were "designed, built, altered, or leased with Federal funds" (U.S. Federal Government, 1968, p. 1). Subsumed under the Office of Civil Rights, in 1973 Section 504 of the Rehabilitation Act was enacted to "protect qualified individuals from discrimination based on their disability." The national law applied to any employers and organizations that received federal financial assistance. At this time, in addition to the many groups who were advocating for rights for people with disabilities, another minority group was beginning to rally for accessibility standards. The rapidly increasing numbers of elderly in highly developed nations precipitated demands for accessible facilities, products, and services.

In 1990, civil rights legislation was passed to address many of these concerns and issues. The **Americans with Disabilities Act (ADA)** dramatically changed the design of public facilities. The ADA "prohibits discrimination against people with disabilities in employment (Title I), in public services (Title II), in public accommodations (Title III) and in telecommunications (Title IV)." Enacted in 1992, the laws imposed numerous requirements for the built environment, which were delineated in the ADA Accessibility Guidelines (ADAAG) and are available at www.access-board.gov/adaag/html/adaag.htm. ADAAG specified the requirements that must be "applied during the design, construction, and alteration of buildings and facilities covered by titles II and III of the ADA."

Since 1992, many projects have been completed by complying with the minimum standards prescribed in the ADAAG rather than closely examining the problems associated with accessibility and developing innovative solutions that could be far more effective than the limited scope that can be achieved with federal legislation. Alarmingly, in a recent report on *The Future of Disability in America* (2007), the Institute of Medicine reported that health-care facilities, the primary institution for people who are temporarily or permanently disabled, must be improved to promote accessibility. The institute's research study found "inaccessible equipment, deficits in communication, and burdensome and inaccessible health care physical plants remain commonplace and create significant barriers to the receipt of timely, high-quality health care by people with disabilities" (Institute of Medicine, 2007, p. 179). The institute's recommendations focused on the involvement of federal agencies and private health-care organizations that are not bound to federal legislation. The institute advocated for the awareness and enforcement of ADA laws as well as the development of standards for accessible medical equipment.

As a wheelchair-bound person, architect and product designer Ronald L. Mace understood the differences between barriers and accessibility. Mace, founder of the Center for Universal Design at North Carolina State University in 1989, created the term "Universal Design" (Figure 11.17). Universal Design is "the design of products and environments to be usable by all people, to the greatest extent possible, without the need for adaptation or specialized design" (www.design.ncsu .edu). To implement the concept, the center developed seven principles of Universal Design (Table 11.1). Internationally, other terms are used that reflect the essence of Universal Design, such as "people-centered design," "**inclusive design,**" and "accessible-design."

The importance and complexity of the topic necessitates a close examination of global solutions. Some useful websites that provide information on global solutions include the WHO, the United Nations Enable organization, international centers, and professional organizations. For example, in Asia and the Pacific region, Self-Help Organizations of People with Disabilities (SHOPs) were created to assist people with disabilities at the local, national, and international levels. Members of SHOPs have a variety of disabilities, and their activities focus on promoting mutual help and self-help, and empowering members to become community leaders. The Royal College of Art Helen Hamlyn Centre in London was established in 1999 for

Figure 11.17 Essential elements to designing successful built environments are to understand physical attributes and individuals' wide range of abilities. This kitchen is an example of an interior that was designed according to some of the principles of Universal Design.

Source: Courtesy of Masco Retail Cabinet Group, manufacturer of KraftMaid Cabinetry.

the purpose of examining "how a people-centred [*sic*] and socially inclusive approach to design can support independent living and working for ageing and diverse populations, improved standards of healthcare and patient safety, and a flow of innovative ideas for business" (www.hhc.rca.ac.uk).

To describe inclusive design, the Centre uses British Standard 7000-6 (2005), "Design of mainstream products and/or services that are accessible to, and usable by, people with the widest range of abilities within the widest range of situations without the need for special adaptation or design" (www.hhc.rca.ac.uk). **Mainstream technologies** should be differentiated from **assistive technologies.** Both terms are discussed in the disability literature, but they fulfill different functions. Mainstream technologies refer to objects that are designed for people with or without disabilities.

Table 11.1 Principles of Universal Design

EQUITABLE USE: The design is useful and marketable to people with diverse abilities.
FLEXIBILITY IN USE: The design accommodates a wide range of individual preferences and abilities.
SIMPLE AND INTUITIVE USE: Use of the design is easy to understand, regardless of the user's experience, knowledge, language skills, or current concentration level.
PERCEPTIBLE INFORMATION: The design communicates necessary information effectively to the user, regardless of ambient conditions or the user's sensory abilities.
TOLERANCE FOR ERROR: The design minimizes hazards and the adverse consequences of accidental or unintended actions.
LOW PHYSICAL EFFORT: The design can be used efficiently and comfortably, and with a minimum of fatigue.
SIZE AND SPACE FOR APPROACH AND USE: Appropriate size and space is provided for approach, reach, manipulation, and use regardless of user's body size, posture, or mobility.

Source: Compiled by advocates of Universal Design, listed in alphabetical order: Bettye Rose Connell, Mike Jones, Ron Mace, Jim Mueller, Abir Mullick, Elaine Ostroff, Jon Sanford, Ed Steinfeld, Molly Story, and Gregg Vanderheiden. North Carolina State University, *The Center for Universal Design,* 1997 (www.design.ncsu .edu/cud/about_ud/udprinciplestext.htm, retrieved August 13, 2008).

Examples of mainstream technologies include Velcro, elevators, and kitchen utensils with ergonomically designed hand grips.

Assistive technologies are specific devices that are designed to help the functional capabilities of a disabled individual. Hearing aids, eyeglasses, and stair-climbing wheelchairs are examples of assistive technologies. Regardless of the terms, designers must create solutions for the built environment that enable all people to easily access facilities, and conveniently use products and technologies. From a community perspective, all citizens should be able to access services and have the ability to participate fully in local activities.

GLOBAL VISUAL AND PERFORMING ARTS

Just as the power loom and the spinning jenny revolutionized textiles and helped launch the Industrial Revolution, fabrics may again stimulate new industries and developments in the 21st century. The opening of Atlanta's Georgia Superdome and its cable-supported, Teflon-coated fiberglass fabric dome is an excellent example of newfound uses for textiles. Various disciplines are developing new approaches to textiles that incorporate smart technologies, photonic characteristics, and interactive protocols. Artists through the 1990s and into the 21st century have also been engaged in artwork that requires interactivity and the newest technologies, including computer animation, computer generations, digital art, and virtual reality.

In the late 20th and early 21st centuries, people from a variety of interests and ages have visited art museums in part due to new initiatives, including family-oriented activities and special exhibitions, or what became known as "blockbusters." Successful programs helped justify and provided some of the financial means to renovate or build new facilities. This spurred a rapid new construction and renovation of art museums throughout the world. New buildings helped to create even more interest in architecture, paintings, sculpture, and the decorative arts. Some of the new structures featured spectacular architectural innovations, such as the Milwaukee Art Museum's moving brise-soleil by Santiago Calatrava, and many of them became masterpieces of architecture that attracted world attention.

The Art and Science of Textiles: Smart Textiles, Photonic Textiles, Textile Shelters, and Interactive Textiles

To design built environments that are accessible to diverse populations and incorporate the principles of sustainability requires professionals to scan the globe for products, materials, and services. This exploration must include nontraditional disciplines as well as unconventional sources. Truly innovative concepts have been stimulated by the visual arts, science, technology, and nature. For example, textile artists are in an enviable position to experiment with a variety of materials and technologies. One example of this can be seen in the 2008 installation exhibition of Japanese fibers artist Akio Hamatani, "Fiber and Space," at the Art Life Mitsuhashi Gallery. The exhibition included works of thousands of suspended threads in various forms and configurations. Textile art may not be feasible for the mass production of interior fabrics, but elements of the creativity may be transferable to interior furnishings.

Other global sources of inspiration related to textiles can be found in the apparel industry, medical field, lighting, aerospace industry, sports, security organizations, **nanotechnology,** microelectronics, wireless technologies, and nature. The multidisciplinary nanotechnology field, or molecular manufacturing, has the potential to revolutionize textiles through controlling materials at the extremely small nanometer scale, one-billionth of a meter. Collaboratively, the art and science of global textiles requires the expertise of artists, designers, architects, engineers, scientists, chemists, computer scientists, mathematicians, physicists, anthropologists, weavers, and fashion designers. As discussed earlier in this chapter, the ETFE membrane used for

the Water Cube and the Bird's Nest is an excellent example of how interdisciplinary design teams explored the innovative potential of textiles. Fortunately, many of the new textile developments have been created to assist people with disabilities, provide shelter for the homeless, and help sustain the planet.

A fundamental awareness of the rapid developments in textiles can be achieved by examining innovations through the lens of traditional characteristics of fabrics. Every aspect related to how textiles have been produced for thousands of years is undergoing revolutionary change. Multidisciplinary teams are inventing new approaches to fibers, yarns, spinning, dyeing, patterns, weaving, and uses. However, some contemporary solutions blend a traditional handicraft, such as embroidery and crocheting, with fibers made from new polymers. For example, Danish textile artist Astrid Krogh created an innovative material for a private commission by combining a traditional brocade weave with a lighting system. Krogh substituted the brocade's customary gold yarns with fiber optics. The high-tech brocade made for Mr. Stefano Gabbanas's seaside resort in Portofino, Italy, has an array of multicolor illuminated patterns.

Because textile developments are constantly evolving, the discussion in this section is intended to provide an awareness of textile research studies and their sources. The information can serve as a means to envision how textiles will impact the design of the built environment in the future and provide an inspiration for monitoring advances on a regular basis.

Conceptually, textile research is developing materials that perform functions delegated to traditional equipment and materials, such as HVAC systems and electricity. For example, textiles are available today that can provide ventilation, warmth, coolness, and illumination. Many of these products were developed by the aerospace and apparel industries. To protect astronauts from extreme heat and cold temperatures in space, NASA developed **phase-changing materials.** Outlast

Technologies and Schoeller Textiles have adapted NASA's technologies to their apparel products. Known as **smart textiles,** the materials continuously interact with the physiological conditions of the human body and react to provide optimum thermal conditions. Depending on the environment and how an individual reacts to climatic conditions, smart textiles can dissipate moisture and phase out temperatures that are too hot or cold. Smart textiles also include consumer products that utilize wireless technologies to monitor an individual's physiological and biomechanical status. For example, sensors in smart textiles made by the Zephyr Company (founded 2003) can detect and report the wearer's physiological data, such as heart rate, breathing rate, body temperature, and posture.

Various manufacturers and research centers have focused on developing textiles that can provide illumination through a variety of technologies. In 1995, a Swiss manufacturer, Schoeller, developed *Schoeller-reflex*, a textile woven with reflective yarns that can be seen at a distance of up to 328 feet (100 meters). The textile reflects "millions of minute glass spheres," and is resistant to abrasion and tears and is washable. Philips, an international company known for their professional and consumer lighting, has developed **photonic textiles** by blending lighting systems with textiles. For example, drapable fabrics are illuminated by integrating yarns with flexible arrays of multicolored LEDs (Figure 11.18). Philips has expanded the concept of photonic textiles by adding sensors and wireless technologies to the fibers. As an **interactive textile,** the material can present animations and scrolling text and is sensitive to touch and pressure. For example, a person's arm moving on a pillow prompts a moving array of colors across the fabric.

The Rocky Mountain Institute (RMI) and Kennedy & Violich Architecture (KVA) have been researching textiles designed to provide illumination for homes in regions of the world that are without electricity. Nanotechnologies have enabled RMI to create textiles

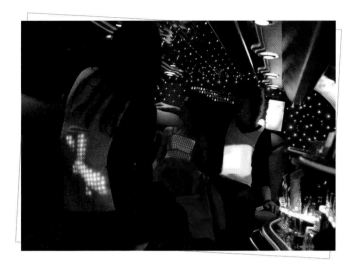

Figure 11.18 An example of phototonic textiles: Drapable fabrics are illuminated by integrating yarns with flexible arrays of multicolored LEDs.

Source: Philips/LumaLive.

Figure 11.19 Nanotechnologies have enabled the development of textiles that are combined with lightweight photovoltaic cells and LEDs. Known as the "Portable Light Project," residents in Mexico's Sierra Madre have apparel and fabric bags made with the innovative textile.

Source: Kennedy & Violich Architecture, Ltd.

that are combined with lightweight photovoltaic cells and LEDs. Known as the "Portable Light Project," residents in Mexico's Sierra Madre Mountains have apparel and fabric bags made with the innovative textile (Figure 11.19). During the day, garments worn or bags carried by the residents store solar energy. In the evening, the solar power is used to generate the energy needed to illuminate the LEDs. RMI reports that "a single portable light unit can also provide enough power to charge a cell phone and provide bright, white light to support community-based education and household economic development" (www.rmi.org).

The high-tech textile industry has also included new products that can substitute for traditional building materials, such as steel, glass, wood, asphalt shingles, and stone. Many of these developments are adapted from industries that manufacture products that require superior strength and endurance, such as automobiles and aerospace. For example, Oxeon developed a woven textile with high-performance carbon reinforcements that are used for racecars, airplanes, and various industrial applications. Researchers are working to identify other applications for these strong, yet lightweight materials. Based on these technologies, American architect Peter Testa developed a model of a skyscraper, Carbon Tower, which substituted woven carbon fibers and composite materials for traditional steel. A lightweight and flexible high-tech woven textile spiraled around the exterior of the structure, creating tubular corridors of interior space.

The U.S. Army's "Fabric Structures Team" developed technology to improve the properties of "soft-wall shelters." These quickly deployable shelters are made with textiles that include "chemical, biological, radiological, [and] nuclear (CBRN) collective protection" (U.S. Army, 2007, p. 1). In addition, the textiles are embedded with flexible photovoltaic cells, high-efficiency insulation, lighting systems, and ballistic protection. Flexible shelters also have been explored by designers creating **textile shelters.** As with Buckminster

Fuller's vision decades ago (see Chapter 6), these shelters are transportable due to their light weight, compactness, and tensile strength. To provide greater versatility, textile architecture is often multifunctional. Apparel and other objects can be converted into shelter.

High-tech textile developments have included products that attempt to replicate the properties and characteristics found in nature. Referred to as **biomimetics,** many of the studies have examined the complexity of a spider's web, bird bones, starch, worms' skin, penguins' scales, and insects. For example, Schoeller developed a textile based on the opening and closing of pine cones. Their waterproof apparel, C-Change, was derived from researching the elements that caused a pine cone to open and close during various climatic conditions.

One of the most innovative textile research organizations is the DESIGN studio of the Interactive Institute in Göteborg, Sweden. In collaboration with Newmad Technologies in Sweden, IT + TEXTILES is one of the Studio's research themes. IT + TEXTILES had nine projects that primarily focused on creating dynamic and interactive textiles. By integrating textiles with information technology and lighting systems, IT + TEXTILES created products that enhance communication and improve the acoustical properties of interior environments. For example, the Fabrication project utilized mobile phones and personal digital assistants (PDAs) to create patterns in textiles. The Interactive Pillows project used information technology to activate dynamic textile patterns. When an individual embraced a pillow, the touch activated the dynamic textile patterns of a pillow located at another location, which illuminated the fabric.

Mute and Sound Hiders are two studies that are examining the absorbing and reflecting properties of textiles. The intent of Sound Hiders was "to catch and hide sound" by using sensors and computer technologies. Dynamic and interactive textiles are elements of Tic Tac Textiles. Square-shaped tables with embedded heating elements were covered in a woven thermochromic fabric. When someone placed a hot beverage on the table, the fabric illuminated an "X" or an "O." People can play tic-tac-toe by moving their beverage to other locations in the 9- by 9-inch (23- by 23-centimeter) grid.

Fine Arts and Culture: Milwaukee Art Museum (1994–2001) by Santiago Calatrava and Shiba Ryōtarō Memorial Museum (2001) in Osaka, Japan, by Tadao Ando

Art museums have been experiencing an amazing revolution beginning in the late 20th century and continuing into the 21st century. International interest in special collections, such as the Impressionist art movement and the treasures of Tutankhamen's tomb (see Chapter 4), have resulted in long lines waiting for tickets, timed admissions to avoid unmanageable crowds, and, at times, ticket purchases through scalpers. These "blockbuster" exhibitions have provided considerable revenues for museums through ticket sales, new memberships, and special exhibition merchandise. Consequently, blockbuster exhibitions and other factors have stimulated museums to re-evaluate the mission of their organizations and the design of their facilities. Museums have become far more than a building used to display art collections. Contemporary museums have auditoriums, restaurants, meeting rooms, gift shops, bookstores, classrooms, libraries, and children's "discovery" areas.

The new addition to the Chicago Art Institute, the Modern Wing (2009), by Italian architect Renzo Piano (see Chapter 9) is an excellent example of how museums have been designed to attract new patrons and provide facilities for multiple functions (Figure 11.20).

Figure 11.20 The new addition to the Chicago Art Institute, the Modern Wing (2009) by Renzo Piano.

Source: Photograph by James Iska, The Art Institute of Chicago. Photography © The Art Institute of Chicago.

First and foremost, to attract the public to the Modern Wing required a spectacular design, which appears to be very successful based on attendance records and architectural reviews. Despite the recession and a recent admission price increase of 50 percent, museum officials reported impressive attendance figures. Compared to 2008, attendance increased more than 80 percent. Features of the Modern Wing lauded by architectural critics, such as Blair Kamin of the *Chicago Tribune*, are the use of natural light through the rooftop's louvered sunshade in the atrium and third-floor galleries, and the beautiful views of Millennium Park.

Located across the street from the Modern Wing, Millennium Park (opened July 16, 2004) is a very popular public destination that has a band shell designed by Frank Gehry, a double tower fountain by Jaume Plensa, a reflective sculpture titled "Cloud Gate" by Anish Kapoor, gardens, a restaurant, a bike facility, an indoor music and dance theater, and an outdoor café that converts into an ice-skating rink in the winter. The interactive nature of the tower fountains and "Cloud Gate," and the free open-air concerts have attracted millions of people to the park every year.

To connect people who were enjoying Millennium Park with the Modern Wing, a 620-foot-long (189-meter) pedestrian bridge was built over the busy street that separated the park from the museum. According to museum officials, in the opening first month, approximately 100,000 people walked over the bridge to the Modern Wing. Beyond the architectural and gallery experiences, the Modern Wing has facilities and programs that promote participation, including an education center, family-orientation room, family workshops, story time, performances, parent workshops, gallery games, a balcony café, the Terzo Piano restaurant, and "Curious Corner," an area that has interactive computer games based on the Art Institute's art collection.

The explosion of new art museums throughout the world includes new and cultural centers that also exhibit paintings, sculpture, and decorative arts. As demonstrated in *The Phaidon Atlas*, the growing interest in the visual arts precipitated the construction of 39 art galleries, 4 art centers, 27 cultural centers, and 69 museums in a variety of themes. Approximately half of these buildings were constructed in Europe, followed by an almost equal number of buildings in Asia and the Americas. These numbers are just for buildings that were completed after 1998. Moreover, this list only includes architecture included in *The Phaidon Atlas*, entries considered after an extensive peer-review process to be some of the best examples of contemporary architecture in the world. Innovative museum architecture has become more commonplace today because many museums receive a substantial amount of their funding from private sources. Generally, public funds are not available for expensive professional fees and high construction costs. As demonstrated by the renown architecture in Columbus, Indiana (see Chapter 9), private donations enable executives to hire the world's most creative architects and interior designers.

An excellent example of this is the Milwaukee Art Museum (MAM) (Figure 11.21). To construct an addition to the former Milwaukee Art Center, designed by Eero Saarinen in 1957, the museum's Board of Trustees launched a capital campaign in 1996 to raise $35 million. The response was so overwhelming that the board was able to increase the goal to $50 million and include other amenities that originally were believed to be cost prohibitive, such as the underground parking garage, additional meeting rooms, and a landscaping program. Ultimately, the completed project was $100 million, and the gardens were an additional $20 million.

The MAM illustrates the success of private fundraising, and the new addition reflects changes in the design of museums. As with Bilbao, Spain, Milwaukee was an industrial city that needed to revitalize its image. As business and community leaders, members

Figure 11.21 The Milwaukee Art Museum (MAM) designed by Santiago Calatrava. View looking eastward is of the Quadracci Pavilion and the brise-soleil. The footbridge is on the left.

Source: Kim Karpeles/Alamy.

of the MAM's Board of Trustees were interested in stimulating the local economy and interest in the museum. Saarinen's building, located on the edge of Lake Michigan, served as an art museum and the Milwaukee County War Memorial. The location presented beautiful views of the lake, but the site was isolated from Milwaukee's downtown business district. The Trustees postulated that by building a spectacular addition and connecting it to the business district, the city of Milwaukee could be revitalized and the museum would draw more visitors. Remarkably, due to Santiago Calatrava's design, both of these goals were realized, as well as other unexpected positive outcomes. Calatrava's transformational design attained international acclaim, presented a modern image of the city, influenced new contemporary structures, and stimulated Milwaukee's tourism. Calatrava noted the connection between the museum's addition and Milwaukee, saying, "in the crowning element of the brise soleil, the building's form is at once formal (completing the composition), functional (controlling the level of light), symbolic (opening to welcome visitors), and iconic (creating a memorable image for the Museum and the city)"

(www.mam.org). By providing people access over a busy highway, Calatrava's pedestrian bridge that links the downtown business district with the museum has stimulated development along the lakefront and along the river. The museum received a substantial collection of more than 450 German Expressionist prints that was donated by a couple in Chicago. The museum has experienced record attendance figures, significant increases in sales of museum-related merchandise, and renewed interests in memberships.

To design the amazing addition to the MAM, Spanish-born architect Calatrava incorporated his experiences and education in the arts, engineering, and architecture. In addition, the complex project required the commitment of locally owned firms and manufacturing companies. The managing architectural and interior design firm was Kahler Slater Architects in Milwaukee. The structural, civil, mechanical, and electrical engineers were all based in Milwaukee. The general contractor was C. G. Schmidt in Milwaukee, and most of the materials and fabrication were supplied by Milwaukee- or Wisconsin-based manufacturers. To accommodate the needs of a contemporary museum,

Calatrava's addition included an entrance approached by the footbridge, an auditorium, offices, meeting rooms, and the Quadracci Pavilion, which can be rented for weddings, meetings, and other special events.

Extremely complex elements of the MAM included the moving brise-soleil, the design of the Quadracci Pavilion, and the elegant cabled footbridge (see Figure 11.21). Hovering over the new addition like the wings of a bird, the steel louvers of the brise-soleil open and close at various times during the

Figure 11.22 The proliferation of new museums is apparent when examining the designs executed by just one architect, Tadao Ando. The Shiba Ryōtarō Memorial Museum is an outstanding example of the blending of a nontraditional museum collection and the design of the interior environment and architecture.

Source: Shiba Ryotaro Memorial Museum.

day. To announce the opening of the museum, music is played, followed by the slow raising of the "wings." At noon, the wings close and reopen, and remain elevated until closing (unless winds become excessive). From the interior, the skylights in the Windhover Hall (located in the Quadracci Pavilion) enable visitors to see the "wings" as well as an unimpeded view of Lake Michigan. The floor of the Windhover Hall appears to be an extension of the lake. The illusion is created by the highly polished marble floor, which reflects the lake and the sky. To connect the addition to Saarinen's building, Calatrava created a long north-south hallway with glass walls facing the lake. The length of the hallway is psychologically reduced by the series of elegant white arches with compound curves. To fabricate the complicated concrete curves of the arches required forms that were filed by hand. Along the hallway, Calatrava designed a museum store with curved cantilevered display cases. The space also has an auditorium, a café, and temporary exhibition galleries. The museum's art collections are located in Saarinen's building and in an addition completed in 1975 by the Milwaukee architect David Kahler.

The proliferation of new museums is apparent when examining the designs executed by just one architect, Tadao Ando (Figure 11.22). Ando has designed more than 30 museums in locations that include Japan, France, Germany, and the United States. Most of these museums were built in the 1990s. Ando's museums were designed for a variety of themes and disciplines—in addition to several art museums, he designed museums for wood, daylight, literature, history, philosophy, children, tombs, memorials, Gojo culture, world cultures, Alexander Calder, cameras, and picture books for children.

Ando's museums are located in highly congested urban settings as well as remote country locations and on hillsides along beaches. Many of the museums have submerged open-air circular structures. Water in a variety of forms is also a recurring element in

Ando's designs. Some of the museums were built close to bodies of water, and Ando often integrated water with the architecture through reflective pools, fountains, and cascading waterfalls. Four of Ando's museums were included in *The Phaidon Atlas*: Aomori Contemporary Art Centre (2001) in Yamazaki, Japan; Shiba Ryōtarō Memorial Museum (2001) in Osaka, Japan; Sayamike Historical Museum (2001) in Osaka, Japan; and Modern Art Museum of Fort Worth (2002) in Fort Worth, Texas. The Shiba Ryōtarō Memorial Museum is an outstanding example of the blending of a nontraditional museum collection and the design of the architecture and interior environment (see Figure 11.22). The museum was built to memorialize Japanese novelist Shiba Ryōtarō (1924–1996), who authored approximately 500 historical novels and essays. The wooded site of the museum was shared with the author's home. Ryōtarō had a collection of more than 20,000 books. These are the books that created the museum's collection and are displayed along the crescent-shaped walls of the library (see Figure 11.22). The rows of oak book shelves are accessed by a tall library staircase and a catwalk at the upper level. As shown in Figure 11.22, to softly illuminate the space, Ando designed a large, stained-glass window with clear glass in a variety of textures. The museum invites visitors to "Please sit on the chair looking up at the wall of books and spend time feeling the author's spirit" (www.shibazaidan.or.jp).

GLOBAL BUSINESS AND ECONOMICS

Globalization has had an enormous impact on business and the economic status of nations and corporations. For example, a slight disruption in the stock market in Japan can have a ripple effect in every other major city in the world. This became apparent when the U.S. stock market faltered in 1987 and when London's Barings Bank collapsed in 1995 due to a loss of U.S. $1.4 billion at the Tokyo Stock Exchange. The effects of a globally interdependent planet were also evident with the worldwide financial crisis that reached a peak in October 2008 when the global banking system collapsed. Fortunately, for the Modern Wing, most of the funding for the $294-million addition was secured prior to the recession. However, as evidenced by the subsequent housing crisis, the interior design and architectural professions and related product-manufacturing industries have been profoundly affected by the recession. As reported by the U.S. Department of Commerce, new home sales dropped from 500,000 in May 2008 to 342,000 in May 2009. Decreases in new home sales were compounded by rising unemployment and record-level defaults on commercial and residential mortgages.

The 1990s and early 21st century witnessed several large corporations filing for bankruptcy, including Enron, General Motors, Chrysler, TWA, United Airlines, WorldCom, and Pacific Gas & Electric Company. Other global initiatives from American-founded companies during this time included the opening of Tokyo Disney Resorts, Euro Disney, and a McDonald's in Beijing. To facilitate trade, industry, agriculture, and commerce between their countries, Canada, Mexico, and the United States signed the North American Free Trade Agreement (NAFTA), which took effect on January 1, 1994. The world's relentless demand for oil as the decades progressed provided the petroleum industry with multibillion-dollar profits, and previously developing countries became very wealthy. But petroleum is not the only valuable nonrenewable resource. Land and the need for affordable housing continue to pose challenges throughout the world, including in highly developed nations. The homeless live in every city in the world.

The Petroleum Industry: Petronas Towers (1993–1998) in Kuala Lumpur, Malaysia, by Cesar Pelli and Burj al Arab Hotel (1994–1999) in Dubai, United Arab Emirates, by Tom Wright

As had been the situation in Kuwait, other nations with rich petroleum and natural gas resources prospered as the price of oil escalated along with the rates of consumption. Petroleum and natural gas were discovered in Malaysia in the 1970s. At the end of the 20th century, Malaysia, a small nation in Southeast Asia, had one of the world's most robust economies. The country is divided into two regions that are separated by the South China Sea. Eastern Malaysia is located along the northern coast of the island of Borneo. Western Malaysia, or Peninsular Malaysia, is located on the Malay Peninsula south of Thailand. Kuala Lumpur, the capital, is located along the western coast of Peninsular Malaysia.

To demonstrate Malaysia's newly found economic success and to attract international attention to the country, in 1990 the government initiated an international competition to develop a master plan that would revitalize Kuala Lumpur's commercial and financial district. In an area known as the Golden Triangle, the master plan was to include buildings for Petronas, the Malaysian petroleum company. A firm from Costa Mesa, California, Klages, Carter, Vail and Partners won the competition, which was followed by another international design competition in 1991 for the Petronas Towers as well as public spaces and retail establishments. The prospectus for the Petronas Towers competition stated that the design should "create a place that people can identify as unique to Kuala Lumpur and Malaysia." In responding to this vision, Argentine-born Cesar Pelli created the winning design (Figure 11.23). Pelli's design has resulted in international acclaim and became an instantly recognizable symbol of Malaysia.

To associate a skyscraper, a typically Western architectural symbol, with an Eastern culture required unique features that are not readily apparent when looking at the Petronas Towers (1993–1998). Pelli explained the regional characteristics of the contemporary towers in the following manner:

> *The national religion of Malaysia is Islam and it permeates the culture. This led us to base the geometry of the towers on Islamic geometric traditions; geometric underlays [sic] to forms are much more important in Islamic countries than in the West and are perceived and appreciated by most people in their societies. In the competition, we proposed a twelve-pointed star*

Figure 11.23 Cesar Pelli's design for the Petronas Towers has resulted in international acclaim and is an instant recognizable symbol of Malaysia.
Source: © David Gee 5/Alamy.

plan because it made for a graceful building and an efficient floor plan. . . . After being selected, we researched traditional Islamic patterns and it became apparent that the eight-sided star obtained by superimposing two rotated squares was the most commonly encountered base for Islamic designs. (Pelli & Crosbie, 2000, p. 10)

Ultimately, the plan for the symmetrical towers was "a form with eight semi-circles superimposed in the inner angles of the eight-pointed star creating a sixteen-lobed form." The Islamic-patterned plan creates a subtle silhouette of traditional Southeast Asian temples, such as the lotus-bud spires at Wat Mahathat in Sukhothai, Thailand (see Chapter 7) and the Kek-Lok-Si monastery and temple on Penang Island in Malaysia. The towers' "bustle tops" and pinnacles resemble the temple's top tier. The 16-lobed form created an interesting space-planning challenge. For example, some of Pelli's conceptual layouts included furniture arrangements that followed the shapes of the semi-circles, and the corner rooms had square-shaped tables. To accommodate the round conference-center facilities on level 40, each of the eight rooms had circular tables with four or six chairs.

Although not the goal in the original plans, the 1,483-foot high (452-meter) Petronas Towers displaced the Sears Tower as the tallest building in the world until the construction of Taipei 101 in 2004. The 88-story twin towers included facilities for a petroleum museum, offices, retail, entertainment, conference center, concert hall, prayer rooms for Muslims, and parking. They were connected by a double-decked sky bridge at levels 41 and 42 (see Figure 11.23). For the exterior cladding of the towers, Pelli specified stainless steel and glass. To unify the exterior's metal appearance, window treatments were stainless steel louvers. Stainless steel is another subtle reference to the history of Malaysia. Malaysia's mining operations supplied the world with tin before the discovery of petroleum, and tin is still being mined there today.

Likewise, discoveries of petroleum and natural gas in the 1950s and 1960s radically altered the United Arab Emirates (UAE). The small nation, located on the Arabian peninsula along the Persian Gulf and bordered by Saudi Arabia and Oman, is geographically and ethnically different from Malaysia, but the two countries share similar histories. Malaysia has lush rainforests and record rainfalls, and is one of the most ethnically diverse nations in the world. UAE is in the Arabian Desert with some of the hottest temperatures in the world, and most of the Emiratis are from Arab nations. Historically, both small countries were controlled by the Portuguese in the 1500s, followed by the Netherlands and then Britain. Malaysia and UAE won their independence from Britain in 1957 and 1971, respectively. The two countries share the same official religion, Islam, and both were transformed by the petroleum industry. UAE had been a poor country that relied on fishing, agriculture, and pearls for income until the 1960s. Today the country is one of the wealthiest in the world and communities have been revolutionized by the construction of roads, schools, hospitals, skyscrapers, shopping malls, hotels, restaurants, nightclubs, museums, theaters, airports, and theme parks.

These developments, as well as the warm climate and beautiful Persian Gulf, have spurred UAE's tourism industry. The income generated from oil and tourism has enabled developers to create new property in the Persian Gulf. At the beginning of the 21st century, Nakheel Properties initiated a project that includes the construction of hundreds of artificial islands. Three projects in Dubai include islands that create the shape of palm trees. Palm Jumeirah was the first project and features luxury hotels, restaurants, residences, retail stores, entertainment, and miles of white sand beaches. The other two palm tree projects are Palm Jebel Ali and Palm Deira. The World project will include 300 artificial islands in the shape of the continents.

The three Palm projects and The World are all designed to entertain and house the planet's

Figure 11.24 The three Palm projects and The World are all designed to entertain and house the wealthiest people in the world. An example of the level of extravagance is the Burj al Arab Hotel on Jumeirah beach in Dubai designed by Tom Wright.

Source: © City Image/Alamy.

wealthiest people. An example of the level of extravagance is the Burj al Arab Hotel (1994–1999) on Jumeirah beach in Dubai (Figure 11.24). Designed by British architect Tom Wright, the unique design of the five-star hotel has become synonymous with UAE. As with the Petronas Towers, the contemporary Burj al Arab Hotel promotes a powerful economic image to the world while subtly referencing the country's recent history. The sailboat shape of the Burj al Arab Hotel recalls the wooden boats (dhows) fishermen

sailed for their livelihood, and the palm fronds used to fabricate the dhows have been transformed into the artificial islands.

Unfortunately, the creation of artificial islands does not reflect principles of sustainable design and development. Unsustainable aspects of the project are exemplified by the announcement from its founder that he was considering the construction of an air-conditioned outdoor beach at the Palazzo Versace Hotel. However, the worldwide financial crisis that started in 2008 has affected people who would have had the financial means to purchase real estate on the islands. The developer of The World project has initiated layoffs and delays, and they have reported mortgage defaults and fewer sales.

The Economy of Land and Housing: Multi-Dwelling Residences in the Netherlands

It was not until recently that the UAE had the resources to build artificial islands for luxury properties; the process involved mounding sand on the floor of the Persian Gulf until land was above the water level. In dramatic contrast, the Netherlands has been reclaiming land for thousands of years by building dikes and pumping the water out of the area. Known as **polders,** these drained areas are currently farms, forests, and communities. Both examples illustrate the value of land and ingenious approaches to manufacturing a limited natural commodity. However, from the perspective of the Netherlands, land reclamation is a matter of survival—and has been throughout the small country's history.

The Netherlands is located in northwestern Europe on the coast of the North Sea. Belgium is located on the country's southern border, and Germany is to the east. Water and the Netherlands are nearly synonymous. Over half of the country is below sea level, and the nation has numerous rivers, lakes, canals, dams, and dikes. To maintain dry land requires the constant operation of electrical pumps. If a dike breaks, which happened in 1953, the resulting flooding can kill thousands of people and destroy entire communities. In 1953, nearly 2,000 people died in the catastrophe and more than 50,000 homes were underwater. After this severe flooding, the government initiated the Deltaplan, an extremely sophisticated engineering system of gates, barriers, and dams that controlled the flow of several rivers and improved the quality of fresh water. Living under these conditions has stimulated extraordinarily creative engineering solutions and a significant appreciation for the value of land. The existence of the Netherlands depends on the success of its engineering projects, something that becomes even more critical in one of the most densely populated countries in the world and in an era of global warming.

Resolving the issue of a finite natural land area and a large population has inspired innovative architectural designs, most notably in the residential sector.

The Dutch interest in superlative contemporary architecture is apparent in the number of projects that were included in *The Phaidon Atlas*. The extraordinarily small country had 59 projects in the book, a number that exceeded most nations, the entire continents of Africa and South America, and was close to Australia's total of 64 projects. Nearly half of the projects in the Netherlands were in the residential category, and most of these buildings were multidwelling units. An analysis of the residential projects reveals many creative solutions that reflect principles of sustainable design as well as modern lifestyles in a densely populated country. In 2000, the Netherlands had 958 people per square mile (369 per square kilometer).

To preserve as much of the nation's limited land as possible, some of the projects were constructed on sites that in most communities would have been abandoned and forgotten. For example, four high-density housing projects in *The Phaidon Atlas* were constructed on the Borneo and Sporenburg quays on the IJ River

Figure 11.25 The redevelopment of the former dock area in the Netherlands included de Architekten Cie's Whale (in the center) with 124 apartments, commercial space, and underground parking.

Source: Rene de Wit/de Architekten Cie.

in Amsterdam (Figure 11.25). Created by West 8 (an international urban design and landscape architecture firm based in the Netherlands) the master plan for the project was to "combine the density of an inner-city area with a suburban feel and programme" (Phaidon Press, 2004, p. 328).

The Borneo Sporenburg project (2000) by West 8 involved 2,500 new dwellings along the quays, which were divided into blocks. To vary the design of the dwellings, each block was designed by a different architect. The unifying stipulations in the program were that each dwelling had to include a garage to reduce parking problems, and 30 to 50 percent of the plot remained open for highly desirable green space. Many of the dwellings had courtyard gardens, and the façades varied by color and type of cladding as well as their angle to the waterfront. To connect people to the quays, the project included three red fanciful wavy pedestrian bridges.

The redevelopment of the former dock area included de Architekten Cie's Whale (2000) with 124 apartments, commercial space, and underground parking (see Figure 11.25). The seemingly sinking whale reflects a humorous perspective of the Dutch; however, functionally the angled rooflines enable sunlight to strike lower windows in the central courtyard garden.

Other entries in *The Phaidon Atlas* for the Borneo and Sporenburg quays were the Borneo Dock Housing (2000) by MAP Arquitectos, and Plots 12 and 18 (2000) by MVRDV. The Dock Housing project was designed as a low-rise with high-density units. The 26 narrow units have separate entrances and a rooftop communal area. The individual houses on Plots 12 and 18 illustrate one of the Netherlands' solutions for limited land area. The very narrow and small dwellings require steep stairways. Each unit is 861 square feet (80 square meters).

There are other examples of reclaiming land in the Netherlands. The Hooikae Housing project (1998)

designed by the architectural and planning firm, KCAP-Kees Christiaanse was constructed on a former industrial site and next to railway lines. Located in Delft, the project provided 140 affordable housing units and is distributed over four blocks. Timber cladding creates a warm appearance to the five-story units.

To conserve land, an amazingly creative approach was used to integrate housing units with the embankment of a street (Figure 11.26). The Sound Wall Houses (2001) in Hilversum were designed by Dutch architectural consulting and engineering firm VHP stedebouwkundigen + Architekten + Landschapsarchitekten. A portion of the single housing units were constructed under the street, which utilizes typically unused land area, and the ground became an acoustical barrier. To maximize green space, the ground level of the two-story units were small and were planned for functions that do not require large spaces—a single-car garage and bedrooms. To provide sufficient space for rooms with shared activities, the second level was larger than the ground level but was cantilevered to preserve green space. The second level had the living room, kitchen, master bedroom, and a small terrace.

Silodam (2002) illustrates an innovative design solution for a former shipping site and unique approaches to customizing high-density housing projects. Dutch architectural firm MVRDV designed a multiple-housing unit next to silos and along the river in Amsterdam. The Silodam (2002) mixed-use project included 157 apartments, offices, and green public space. Within the single unit, MVRDV created "mini-neighborhoods" that were identified by a specific graphic treatment. The sizes of apartments varied, and people had the ability to determine the placement of interior walls. Various configurations within the apartments included different numbers of levels (1–3), which could be vertical or horizontally staggered. Different types of outdoor space included balconies, patios, and rooftop terraces.

Figure 11.26 An amazingly creative approach was used to integrate housing units with the embankment of a street. The *Sound Wall Houses* in Hilversum were designed by VHP stedebouwkundigen. A portion of the single housing units were constructed under the street, which utilizes typically unused land area, and the ground became an acoustical barrier.

Source: Hans Pattist/VHP stedebouwkundigen + architekten + landschapsarchitekten, www.vhp.nl.

Other Netherlands projects in *The Phaidon Atlas* demonstrate creative solutions for a densely populated country. In 2001, the purpose of the Het Wilde Wonen (wild living) Exhibition in Almere was to present prototypes of standard housing units that could be customized by their owners. Two of these projects were selected for the *Atlas* publication. The UN Studio designed housing units (2001) that could be customized by the addition of "plug-in" units in a variety of configurations. The standard units were gray brick and the "plug-in" components, made in a variety of sizes, were clad in red-painted timber. Staggering the stacking created unique profiles, and the cantilevered component created roof terraces, balconies, and patios. Dutch architect Marlies Rohmer's design for the flexible housing exhibition was a row of 18 affordable units (2001). Each unit had a standardized core and a second metallic box that could be customized by varying its location, size, and number of rooms. In addition, to provide for

people who wanted to travel, Rohmer conceived that a camper shell could connect to the standardized core.

Providing variety within standardization was also applied to MVRDV's Hagen Island Housing (2001). Each single-family dwelling had a steep pitched roof but varied in the type of cladding, façade color, and arrangement of the fenestration. The large green communal areas helped provide space to people living in the small, 1,400-square-foot (130-square-meter) dwellings. Rooms were designed with wide windows and sliding glass doors to appear larger.

Interestingly, approximately one-third of the projects in *The Phaidon Atlas* were in the residential category, which included apartments, multiple housing, single housing, and social housing. As the world's population continues to increase, affordable housing will remain a significant issue and the design profession is continuously challenged to address the needs of future generations.

SUMMARY

As in other decades, the driving force for interior environments and architecture during the past two decades has been political, technological, sociological, and economic change. This can be seen on innumerable fronts throughout history. One example is the country of Kuwait, where civilizations have lived for thousands of years. Rich oil reserves discovered there in the 1930s attracted global attention to the country. The small desert country was attacked by neighboring Iraq in 1990, which led to the Persian Gulf War. In addition to the damage from bombs, trenches, and the still-unidentified locations of land mines, Iraqi troops inflicted on Kuwait what is considered to be the world's worst ecological disaster as they set fire to most of the country's oil wells and dumped barrels of oil in the Persian Gulf in early 1991. The country has begun the rebuilding process, including the construction of the Liberation Tower (1996), a telecommunications tower with a restaurant, revolving observation level, and public communications center.

Another country that has experienced war-driven change is Slovenia, a country created through the dissolution of another due to war. Slovenia's relatively easy fight for independence saved many lives and reduced the extent of damage to cities, towns, and buildings. Slovenia began the historical restoration process that continues today. Pride in gaining independence also has been reflected in the construction of new public buildings in Slovenia that have received international awards for innovation.

The Industrial Revolution precipitated the extraordinary consumption of natural resources, energy, and air, land, and water pollution. Increases in industrial production contributed to increased consumption of resources, purchases, and waste in the landfills. The concept of sustainable development was identified in the 1987 report of the World Commission on Environment and Development entitled *Our Common Future*, or the Brundtland Report.

The Phaidon Atlas is an illustrated peer-reviewed collection of exemplary contemporary architecture. One of the human development factors identified in the book was the Environmental Sustainability Index. Finland, Norway, and Sweden were ranked as the top three nations in the world on this index, and the publication included many of their projects. Also included were several projects in Africa. In Adis Abeda, Ethiopia, to help improve a severe housing shortage, Ahadu Abaineh designed an experimental Tree House. Other projects on the continent were the Women's Centre, Kaheré Eila Poultry Farming School, the National Food Technology Research Centre, the Medical Research Facilities for the Africa Centre, and the open-air Nelson Mandela Museum.

Another complex, the Jean-Marie Tjibaou Cultural Centre, was designed to preserve the heritage of an ethnic group on New Caledonia, a French possession in the South Pacific Ocean. To construct Renzo Piano's design required numerous computer-simulation studies conducted by the Centre Scientifique et Technique du Bâtiment. Computer simulations were created to study the effects of wind on the center's structural components. Computer software programs and the natural environment also were essential to the design of the billowy Guggenheim Museum in Bilbao, Spain. Frank O. Gehry's modern Expressionist design resembles clouds, flower petals, and fish scales, but to reproduce these complex moving forms required extremely sophisticated software.

As the opening ceremonies of the 2008 Beijing Olympics were being broadcast, details and illustrations of the structures that had been designed for the event, the Beijing Olympic Green National Stadium and the National Aquatics Center, were available. The Internet provided the means to access instant news of the Olympics, including these new facilities.

But technological advances do have a dark side, as many examples throughout this text have shown. On September 11, 2001, skyscrapers, an American icon, became a target for terrorists, and aircraft, another American invention of the 20th century, were the weapons of choice. After the terrorist attacks that destroyed the World Trade Center in New York City, thousands of concepts, plans, and schemes were proposed for rebuilding the site; Studio Daniel Libeskind's proposal "Memory Foundations" was selected for development.

The WHO estimated in 2009 that 650 million people around the world live with disabilities, a number that is predicted to rapidly increase in the future due to increased longevity. Essential to designing successful built environments is to understand physical attributes and individuals' wide range of abilities. Britain passed the Disability Discrimination Act in 1995 to end discrimination experienced by people with disabilities (the act was expanded in 2005). In the United States, the Americans with Disabilities Act dramatically changed the design of public facilities.

Textiles have undergone a revolution in the last 20 years. Sources of inspiration for textiles can be found in the apparel industry, medical field, lighting, aerospace industry, sports, security organizations, nanotechnology, microelectronics, wireless technologies, and nature. The multidisciplinary nanotechnology field, or molecular manufacturing, has the potential to revolutionize textiles through controlling materials at the extremely small nanometer scale.

On a far larger scale, art museums have also been experiencing an amazing revolution since 1990. An excellent example of this is the Milwaukee Art Museum by Santiago Calatrava. The proliferation of new museums is apparent when examining the work executed by just one architect, Tadao Ando, who has designed more than 30 museums in locations that include Japan, France, Germany, and the United States.

As had been the situation in Kuwait, nations with rich petroleum and natural gas resources prospered as the price for oil escalated along with the rates of consumption. Malaysia experienced a building boom as a result of its success. The master plan for the capital, Kuala Lumpur, included buildings designed by Cesar Pelli for Petronas, the Malaysian petroleum company. The United Arab Emirates (UAE) also experienced phenomenal oil-based economic success. Nakheel Properties initiated a project that includes the construction of hundreds of artificial islands in Dubai, UAE.

Land is also a precious resource in the densely populated European country of the Netherlands, which has been reclaiming land for thousands of years by building dikes and pumping water out of the area. Dutch respect for land has inspired innovative architectural and engineering designs. To preserve as much of the limited land as possible, some projects have been constructed on sites that in most communities would have been abandoned and forgotten. The continually increasing world population will require designers to focus attention and skill on ways to accommodate humans at the least expense to the environment.

KEY TERMS

Americans with Disabilities Act (ADA)

assistive technologies

biomimetics

CATIA (Computer-Aided Three Dimensional Interactive Application)

ETFE (ethylene tetrafluoroethylene) film

graywater

harvest

inclusive design

interactive textiles

Leadership in Energy and Environmental Design (LEED)

mainstream technologies

nanotechnology

phase-changing materials

photonic textiles

polders

smart textiles

textile shelters

EXERCISES

1. Research Design Project. Select two republics that were part of Yugoslavia, and research how they were affected by the civil wars. Identify contemporary design/architectural firms in the two selected nations and analyze their projects. Write a report that includes drawings, sketches, and photographs. The report should include a description of each country's geography, climate, history, economy, people, lifestyle, and arts. The report also should provide your analyses of the architectural projects.

2. Philosophy and Design Project. *The Phaidon Atlas* identified several human development statistics that are critical to analyze within the context of architecture. Identify other nontraditional variables, conditions, and philosophies that are important to consider when planning a sustainable built environment. Select a project in a studio and apply the results to the program. Discuss your results with a team that includes people from multiple disciplines. The team should prepare a presentation of their discussions and recommendations.

3. Human Factors Research Project. Research articles on the InformeDesign website related to the topics of disabilities, ADA, and Universal Design. Visit a health-care facility and evaluate the effectiveness of the medical equipment, accessibility to restrooms, elevators, and so forth. If possible, interview users of the space and conduct observations at various times of the day and week. Record activities, characteristics of people, and interior elements related to Universal Design that are effective, as well as any design features that are hindrances. Write a report that summarizes your observations and include recommendations for future practice. The report could include sketches, drawings, or photographs.

BIBLIOGRAPHY

Aav, M. (Ed.). (2003). *Marimekko: Fabrics, fashion, architecture.* New Haven, CT: Yale University Press.

Abate, M. (Ed.). (2003). *Treasury of world culture: Monumental sites UNESCO World Heritage.* Milano: Skira.

Abercrombie, S. (2003). *A century of interior design 1900–2000: A timetable of the design, the designers, the products, and the profession.* New York: Rizzoli.

Abercrombie, S. (1995). *George Nelson: The design of modern design.* Cambridge, MA: MIT Press.

Aga Khan Award (1983). *Hajj Terminal.* Retrieved June 30, 2009, from www.archnet.com (retrieved June 30, 2009)

Alarcon, N. I. (1991). *Philippine architecture during the pre-Spanish and Spanish periods.* Manila, Philippines: Santo Tomas University Press.

Albers, A. (1959). *Pictorial weavings.* Cambridge, MA: MIT Press.

Albers, A. (1977). *Anni Albers.* Brooklyn, NY: Brooklyn Museum, Division of Publications and Marketing Services.

Albers, A. (2000). *Anni Albers: Selected writings on design.* Middletown, CT: Wesleyan University Press.

Alexander, D. (2000). *Confronting catastrophe.* Oxford: Oxford University Press.

Allen, C. (1997). *Art in Australia: From colonization to postmodernism.* London: Thames and Hudson.

Altherr, A. (1968). *Three Japanese architects: Mayekawa, Tange, Sakakura.* New York: Architectural Book Publishing.

Altotsson, S. (2000). *African style down to the details.* New York: Clarkson Potter.

Altshuler, B. (1994). *Isamu Noguchi.* New York: Abbeville Press.

Altshuler, B. (1994). *Modern masters: Isamu Noguchi.* New York: Abbeville Press.

Ambasz, E. (1972). *Italy: The new domestic landscape.* New York: The Museum of Modern Art.

Ambasz, E. (1976). *The architecture of Luis Barragán.* New York: The Museum of Modern Art.

Anderson, D. (2006). *War: A photo history.* New York: Collins.

Anderson, J. (1965). *The encyclopedia of furniture.* New York: Crown.

Anderson, J. (2006). *The encyclopedia of North American architecture.* Stevenage, Hertfordshire, UK: Chartwell Books.

Anderson, S. (Ed.). (2004). *Eladio Dieste: Innovation in structural art.* New York: Princeton Architectural Press.

Ando, T. (1990). *Architectural monographs 14: Tadao Ando.* New York: St. Martin's Press.

Ando, T. (2003). *Tadao Ando.* Barcelona, Spain: teNeues.

Andreoli, E., & Forty, A. (2004). *Brazil's modern architecture.* London: Phaidon Press.

The Architects' Journal. (1970). *Principles of hotel design.* London: The Architectural Press.

Arima, K. (Ed.). (2007). *Design Japan: 50 creative years with the good design awards.* Berkeley, CA: Stone Bridge Press.

Ashton, D. (1992). *Noguchi east and west.* New York: Knopf.

Ashwood, T. (1987). *Terror in the skies.* New York: Stein and Day.

Avery, D. (2003). *Modern architecture.* London: Chaucer Press.

Avery, D. (2004). *Antoni Gaudí.* London: Chaucer Press.

Aynsley, J., & Grant, C. (2006). *Imagined interiors: Representing the domestic interior since the Renaissance.* London: V & A Publications.

Baal-Teshuva, J. (1993). *Christo: The Reichstag and urban projects.* Munich, Germany: Prestel.

Bahamon, A. (Ed.). (2005). *Shanghai: Architecture & design.* Cologne, Germany: Daab Gmbh.

Balfour, A. (1978). *Rockefeller Center: Architecture as theater.* New York: McGraw-Hill.

Balfour, A., & Shiling, Z. (2002). *World cities: Shanghai.* New York: Wiley-Academy.

Ban, S. (2001). *Shigeru Ban.* New York: Princeton Architectural Press.

Banasiewicz, C. Z. (Ed.). (1968). *The Warsaw ghetto: Drawings by Józef Kaliszan.* New York: Toseloff.

Barnes, I., & Hudson, R. (1998). *The history atlas of Europe.* New York: Macmillan.

Barry, J. M. (2004). *The great influenza: The epic story of the deadliest plague in history*. New York: Viking Press.

Bartolucci, M. (2003). *Gaetano Pesce*. San Francisco: Chronicle Books.

Bartolucci, M. (2004). *Karim Rashid*. San Francisco: Chronicle Books.

Bassegoda-Nonell, J. (2000). *Antonio Gaudí: Master architect*. New York: Abbeville Press.

Bastea, E. (Ed.). (2004). *Memory and architecture*. Albuquerque: University of New Mexico Press.

Battersby, M. (1988). *The decorative thirties*. New York: Whitney Library of Design.

Baudot, F. (1999). *Fashion: The twentieth century*. New York: Universe Publishing.

Baudot, F. (2003). *Eileen Gray*. New York: Assouline.

Baudot, F. (2006). *Fashion: The twentieth century* (Rev. ed.). New York: Universe Publishing.

Baume, M. (1967). *The Sydney Opera House affair*. Melbourne: Thomas Nelson.

Bayer, H., Gropius, W., & Gropius, I. (Eds.). (1938). *Bauhaus 1919–1928*. New York: The Museum of Modern Art.

Bellini, M. (2003). *Mario Bellini*. Melbourne: National Gallery of Victoria.

Ben-Amos, P. G. (1995). *The art of Benin*. Washington, DC: Smithsonian Institution Press.

Bender, M. (1975). *At the top*. Garden City, NY: Doubleday & Company.

Benert, A. (2007). *The architectural imagination of Edith Wharton*. Cranbury, NJ: Associated University Presses.

Bennett, M. (1996). *TV sets: Fantasy blueprints of classic TV homes*. New York: TV Books (distributed by Penguin USA).

Berry, J. R. (2004). *Herman Miller: The purpose of design*. New York: Rizzoli.

Besset, M. (1976). *Le Corbusier*. New York: Rizzoli International.

Best, R. (1982). *Investigation report on the MGM Grand Hotel fire, Las Vegas, Nevada, November 21, 1980: Report revised January 15, 1982*. Boston: National Fire Protection Association (NFPA).

Betsky, A. (2007). *Unstudio*. Hong Kong: Taschen.

Bharadwaj, M. (1998). *India style*. San Francisco: SOMA Books.

Bhirasri, S. (1962). *An appreciation of Sukhothai art*. Bangkok: The Fine Arts Department.

Blaser, W. (1981). *Mies van der Rohe, continuing the Chicago school of architecture*. Boston: Birkhauser Verlag.

Blaser, W. (1982). *Mies van der Rohe, furniture and interiors*. Woodbury, NY: Barron's.

Blauer, E., & Laure, J. (2006). *South Africa*. New York: Scholastic.

Bleecker, I., & Monfried, A. E. (1992). *Of the architecture of Luis Barragán*. New York: Rizzoli.

Blum, B. J. (2000). *Oral history of Gordan Bunshaft*. Retrieved June 30, 2009, from www.som.com

Boesiger, W. (Ed.). (1953). *Le Corbusier: Oeuvre complète 1946–1952*. Zurich, Switzerland: Girsberger.

Boesiger, W. (Ed.). (1970). *Le Corbusier: Last works*. New York: Praeger.

Bonta, J. P. (1963). *Eladio Dieste*. Buenos Aires: Universidad de Buenos Aires.

Booth, B. (Ed.). (2004). *Treasures of China*. New York: Barnes & Noble.

Borsay, A. (2005). *Disability and social policies in Britain since 1750*. New York: Palgrave-Macmillan.

Borsi, F. (1986). *Vienna 1900: Architecture and design*. New York: Rizzoli.

Boyd, A. (1998). *Atlas of world affairs*. London: Routledge.

Boyd, J. (2002). *September 11: A testimony*. New York: Reuters.

Boyd, R. (1962). *Kenzo Tange*. New York: George Braziller.

Brandstätter, C. (2003). *Wiener Werkstätte: Design in Vienna 1903–1932*. New York: Abrams.

Braynard, F. O. (1987). *Picture history of the Normandie*. New York: Dover.

Braziller, G. (1960). *Oscar Niemeyer*. New York: George Braziller.

Brooks, H. A. (Ed.). (1987). *Le Corbusier: The Garland essays*. New York: Garland.

Brownlee, D. B., & De Long, D. G. (1991). *Louis I. Kahn: In the realm of architecture*. New York: Rizzoli.

Brumfield, W. C. (1993). *A history of Russian architecture*. New York: Cambridge University Press.

Bryan, J. L. (1983). *An examination and analysis of the dynamics of the human behavior in the MGM Grand Hotel fire, Clark County, Nevada, November 21, 1980*. Quincy, MA: NFPA.

Buchanan, P. (1993). *Renzo Piano building workshop*. London: Phaidon Press.

Bullock, A. (1971). *The twentieth century*. New York: McGraw-Hill.

Burden, E. (2002). *Illustrated dictionary of architecture, second edition*. New York: McGraw-Hill.

Burney, J. (1991). *Ettore Sottsass*. New York: Taplinger.

Burri, R. (2000). *Luis Barragán*. London: Phaidon Press.

Bussagli, M. (2004). *Understanding architecture, volumes I and II*. Firenze, Milano: Sharpe Reference.

Byars, M. (2005). *The best tables, chairs, lights: Innovation and invention in design products for the home*. Crans-Près-Céligny, Hove, England: RotoVision.

Caattaneo, M., & Trifoni, J. (2005). *The great book of world heritage sites*. Vercelli, Italy: VMB.

Calatrava, S. (1990). *Engineering architecture*. Berlin: Birkhäuser Verlag.

Caldenby, C. (1998). *Sweden*. New York: Prestel.

Camard, F. (1983). *Ruhlmann: Master of Art Deco*. New York: Harry N. Abrams.

Cannell, M. (1995). *I. M. Pei: Mandarin of modernism*. New York: Carol Southern Books.

Caplan, R. (1976). *The design of Herman Miller*. New York: Whitney Library of Design.

Cappellato, G. (Ed.). (2004). *Mario Botta: Light and gravity architecture 1993–2003*. Munich, Germany: Prestel.

Carson, R. (1962). *Silent spring*. Boston: Houghton Mifflin.

Caruncho, E. S. (2003). *Designing Filipino: The architecture of Francisco Mañosa*. Manila, Philippines: Tukod Foundation.

Casey, M. S. (2007). *The history of Kuwait*. Westport, CT: Greenwood Press.

Cathers, D., & Vertikoff, A. (1999). *Stickley style: Arts and crafts homes in the craftsman tradition*. New York: Simon & Schuster.

Cavalcanti, L. (2003). *When Brazil was modern: Guide to architecture 1928–1960*. New York: Princeton Architectural Press.

Cetto, M. L. (1961). *Modern architecture in Mexico*. New York: Praeger.

Champion, J. (2006). *Venice and the Islamic world 828–1797*. New Haven, CT: Yale University Press.

Chang, P., & Swenson, A. (1980). *Architectural education at IIT*. Chicago: Illinois Institute of Technology.

Charlesworth, E. (2006). *Architects without frontiers: War, reconstruction and design responsibility*. New York: Elsevier Architectural Press.

Chernousenko, V. M. (1991). *Chernobyl: Insight from the inside*. Berlin, Germany: Springer-Verlag.

Ching, F. D. K., Jarzombek, M. M., & Prakash, V. (2007). *A global history of architecture*. New York: John Wiley & Sons.

Choay, F. (1960). *Le Corbusier*. New York: G. Braziller.

Christ-Janer, A. (1979). *Eliel Saarinen: Finnish-American architect and educator*. Chicago: University of Chicago Press.

Christo. (1977). *The running fence project*. New York: Harry N. Abrams.

Christo. (1985). *Christo*. New York: Pantheon Books.

Christo & Jeanne-Claude. (2005). *The gates central park, New York City*. London: Taschen.

Christopher, A. J. (2001). *The atlas of changing South Africa*. London: Routledge.

Cianchetta, A., & Molteni, E. (2004). *Alvaro Siza: Private houses 1954–2004*. Milano: Skira.

Clark, R. J. (1972). *The arts and crafts movement in America, 1876–1916*. Princeton, NJ: Princeton University Press.

Clark, R. J. (1983). *Design in America: The Cranbrook vision, 1925–1950*. New York: Abrams, in association with the Detroit Institute of Arts and the Metropolitan Museum of Arts.

Coakley, D. (1982). *The day the MGM Grand Hotel burned*. Secaucus, NJ: Lyle Stuart.

Cole, E. (Ed.). (2002). *The grammar of architecture*. New York: Bullfinch Press.

Coleman, B. D. (2004). *Scalamandré: Luxurious home interiors*. Salt Lake City, UT: Gibbs Smith.

Collins, G. R. (1960). *Antonio Gaudí*. New York: G. Braziller.

Collins, M., & Papakakis, A. (1989). *Post-modern design*. New York: Rizzoli.

Columbus Area Chamber of Commerce. (1984). *Columbus Indiana: A look at architecture*. Columbus, IN: Visitors Center.

Comstock, G. (1978). *Television and human behavior*. New York: Columbia University Press.

Conran, T. (1996). *Terence Conran on design*. Wookstock, NY: Overlook Press.

Cooke, L. (Ed.) (2006). *200 of the world's most beautiful places.* New York: Barnes & Noble.

Cooper, I., & Gillow, J. (1996). *Arts and crafts of India.* New York: Thames & Hudson.

Cracraft, J. (1988). *The Petrine revolution in Russian architecture.* Chicago: University of Chicago Press.

Cresti, C. (1970). *Le Corbusier.* London: Hamlyn.

Crochet, T. (2004). *Designer's guide to furniture styles, second edition.* Upper Saddle River, NJ: Prentice Hall.

Cross, R. (Ed.). (2006). *The encyclopedia of warfare.* New York: Barnes & Noble.

Cruikshank, J. L., & Sicilia, D. B. (1997). *The engine that could.* Boston: Harvard Business School Press.

Curtis, W. J. R. (1996). *Modern architecture since 1900.* Upper Saddle River, NJ: Prentice Hall.

Cussans, T. (Ed.). (1994). *The Times atlas of European history.* New York: Harper Collins.

D'Alleva, A. (1998). *Arts of the Pacific islands.* New York: Harry N. Abrams.

Daftari, F. (2006). *Without boundary: Seventeen ways of looking.* New York: The Museum of Modern Art.

Darwell, J. (2001). *Legacy: Photographs inside the Chernobyl exclusion zone.* Stockport, England: Dewi Lewis.

Dawson, B., & Gillow, J. (1994). *The traditional architecture of Indonesia.* London: Thames and Hudson.

De Leon, F. M. (1982). *The Filipino nation: Philippine art and literature.* Philippines: Grolier International.

De Wit, W. (Ed.). (1986). *Louis Sullivan: The function of ornament.* New York: W. W. Norton & Company.

De Wolfe, E. (1913). *The house in good taste.* New York: The Century Co.

Deamer, P. (2001). *The millennium house.* New York: The Monacelli Press.

Dearstyne, H. (1986). *Inside the Bauhaus.* New York: Rizzoli.

Demetrios, E. (2001). *An Eames primer.* New York: Universe.

Descharnes, R. (1982). *Gaudí, the visionary.* New York: Viking Press.

The Detroit Institute of Arts (1949). *An exhibition for modern living.* Detroit, MI: The Detroit Institute of Arts.

Dewar, D., & Ellis, G. (1979). *Low income housing policy in South Africa with particular reference to the Western Cape.* Cape Town, South Africa: Urban Problems Research Unit, University of Cape Town.

Dini, M. (1984). *Renzo Piano: Projects and buildings 1964–1983.* New York: Rizzoli.

Donald, S., & Benewick, D. (2005). *State of China atlas.* Berkeley: University of California Press.

Donin, G. (Ed.). (1982). *Renzo Piano: Piece by piece.* Rome: Casa del Libro Editrice.

Doordan, D. P. (2002). *Twentieth-century architecture.* Upper Saddle River, NJ: Prentice Hall.

Dossey, B. M., Selanders, L. C., Beck, D., & Attewell, A. (2005). *Florence Nightingale today: Healing, leadership, global action.* Silver Spring, MD: American Nurses Association.

Douglas, G. H. (1996). *Skyscrapers: A social history in America.* Jefferson, NC: McFarland & Company.

Downer, M. (1963). *The story of design.* New York: Lothrop, Lee, and Shepard.

Dowswell, P. (2002). *The Vietnam war.* Milwaukee, WI: World Almanac Library.

Drew, P. (1995). *Sydney Opera House: Jørn Utzon.* London: Phaidon Press.

Drexler, A. (1973). *Charles Eames: Furniture from the design collection.* New York: The Museum of Modern Art.

Drexler, A. (1974). *Architecture of Skidmore, Owings & Merrill, 1963–1973.* New York: Architectural Book Publishing.

Drexler, A., & Daniel, G. (1959). *Introduction to twentieth century design.* Garden City, NY: Doubleday.

Duncan, A. (1998). *Modernism: Modernist design 1880–1940.* Suffolk, UK: Antique Collectors' Club.

Durant, S. (1993). *Christopher Dresser.* London: Academy Editions.

Eames, C., & Entenza, J. (1944). What is a house? *Arts and Architecture.* pp. 22–39.

Eidelberg, M. (Ed.). (1991). *Design 1935–1965: What modern was.* New York: Musée des Arts Décoratifs de Montréal in association with Harry N. Abrams.

Encyclopedia Britannica. (1937). *The Encyclopædia britannica : A new survey of universal knowledge* (14th ed.). New York: Author.

Engel, H. (1964). *The Japanese house: A tradition for contemporary architecture.* Rutland, VT: C. E. Tuttle.

English, B. (2007). *A cultural history of fashion in the 20th century: From the catwalk to the sidewalk.* New York: Berg.

Environmental Literacy Council. (2009). *Plastics.* Retrieved June 8, 2009, from www.enviroliteracy.org

Epstein, D. (1999). *20th century pop culture*. New York: Quadrillion.

Eubank, T. (2005). *Survey of historic costume, fourth edition*. New York: Fairchild.

Evenson, N. (1973). *Two Brazilian capitals: Architecture and urbanism in Rio de Janeiro and Brasilia*. New Haven, CT: Yale University Press.

Faber, T. (1964). *Arne Jacobsen*. Stuttgart, Germany: Verlag Gerd Hatje.

Faber, T. (1965). *A history of Danish architecture*. Copenhagen, Denmark: The American-Scandinavian Foundation.

Faber, T. (1968). *New Danish architecture*. New York: Praeger.

Fachard, S. (1987). *Paris 1979–1989*. New York: Rizzoli.

Farrington, K. (2000). *Historical atlas of expeditions*. New York: Checkmark Books.

Farrington, K. (2002). *Historical atlas of empires*. New York: Checkmark Books.

Fauchereau, S. (1988). *Moscow, 1900–1930*. New York: Rizzoli.

Favata, I. (1988). *Joe Colombo and Italian design of the sixties*. Cambridge, MA: MIT Press.

Federal Emergency Management Agency (FEMA). (2003). *Primer for design of commercial buildings to mitigate terrorist attacks*. Washington, DC: Author.

Fergusson, J. (1971). *Tree and serpent worship: Illustration of mythology and art in India in the first and fourth centuries after Christ*. Delhi, India: Oriental.

Fiell, C., & Fiell, P. (1999). *William Morris*. London: Taschen.

Fiell, C., & Fiell, P. (2001). *Design of the 20th century*. London: Taschen.

Fiell, C., & Fiell, P. (2001). *Modern furniture classics: Postwar to post-modernism*. London: Thames & Hudson.

Fiell, C., & Fiell, P. (2003). *Industrial design A–Z*. London: Taschen.

Fiell, C., & Fiell, P. (2005). *Designing the 21st century*. London: Taschen.

Fiell, C., & Fiell, P. (2006). *Design handbook: Concepts, materials, styles*. London: Taschen.

Filler, M. (2007). *Makers of modern architecture*. New York: The New York Review of Books.

Fisher, R. M. (2004). *National geographic historical atlas of the United States*. Washington, DC: National Geographic Society.

Fleck, B. (1995). *Alvaro Siza*. London: E & FN Spon.

Fleck, G. (Ed.). (1973). *A computer perspective*. Cambridge, MA: Harvard University Press.

Flon, C. (Ed.). (1984). *The world atlas of architecture*. Boston: G. K. Hall & Co.

Fong, W. (Ed.). (1980). *The great bronze age of China: An exhibition from the People's Republic of China*. New York: The Metropolitan Museum of Art.

Ford, J., & Ford, K. M. (1940). *The modern house in America*. New York: Architectural Book.

Ford, K. M., & Creighton, T. H. (1954). *Quality budget houses: A treasury of 100 architect-designed houses from $5,000 to $20,000*. New York: Reinhold.

Forty, A. (1986). *Objects of desire: Design and society 1750–1980*. London: Thames and Hudson.

Frampton, K. (1991). *Tadao Ando*. New York: The Museum of Modern Art.

Frampton, K. (2002). *Le Corbusier: Architect of the twentieth century*. New York: H. N. Abrams.

Freedman, L. (1969). *Public housing: The politics of poverty*. New York: Holt, Rinehart and Winston.

Friedman, M. L. (1978). *Noguchi's imaginary landscapes: An exhibition*. Minneapolis: The Center.

Friedman, W. (Ed.). (1959). *20th century design: U.S.A. A survey exhibition during 1959–1960 co-sponsored by eight museums*. Buffalo, NY: Albright Art Gallery.

Furuyama, M. (2006). *Tadao Ando*. Hong Kong: Taschen.

Futagawa, Y. (Ed.). (1972). *Jorn Utzon Sydney Opera House, Sydney, Australia. 1957–73*. Tokyo: A. D. A. Edita.

Futagawa, Y. (Ed.). (1972). *Louis I. Kahn: Indian institute of management and Exeter library*. Tokyo: A. D. A. Edita.

Futagawa, Y. (Ed.). (1975). *Philip Johnson: Johnson house, New Canaan, Connecticut*. Tokyo: A. D. A. Edita.

Gabra-Liddell, M. (1994). *Alessi: The design factory*. London: Academy Group.

Gallery MA Books 07. (1997). *Oscar Niemeyer 1937–1997*. Tokyo: TOTO Shuppan.

Gardiner, S. (1975). *Le Corbusier*. New York: Viking Press.

Gast, K. (2001). *Louis I. Kahn: Complete works*. Stuttgart, Germany: Deutsche Verlags-Anstalt.

Georgel, P. (2006). *The Musée de l'Orangie*. Paris: Gallimard.

Getlein, M. (2005). *Gilbert's living with art, second edition*. New York: McGraw-Hill.

Gilbert, M. (2002). *Routledge atlas of Russian history*. New York: Routledge.

Gilbert, M. (2006). *Routledge atlas of the Arab-Israeli conflict*. New York: Routledge.

Girard, A. H., & Laurie, W. D. (Eds.). (1949). *An exhibition for modern living, September eleventh to November twentieth, nineteen forty-nine*. Detroit: Detroit Institute of Arts.

Giurgola, R., & Mehta, J. (1975). *Louis I. Kahn*. Boulder, CO: Westview Press.

Glassie, H. H. (1989). *The spirit of folk art: The Girard collection at the museum of international folk art*. New York: Abrams in association with the Museum of New Mexico, Santa Fe.

Goetsch, D. L. (1985). *Computer-aided drafting*. Englewood Cliffs, NJ: Prentice-Hall.

Goldberger, P. (1989). *Renzo Piano and building workshop*. New York: Rizzoli.

Gonzalez, D. (2004). *Great spaces small houses*. Barcelona, Spain: Carles Broto.

Gowing, L. (1983). *A history of art*. New York: Barnes & Noble.

Graham, B. (1989). *Bruce Graham of SOM*. New York: Rizzoli.

Gray, S. K. (2004). *Designers on designers: The inspiration behind great interiors*. New York: McGraw-Hill.

Gresleri, G. (1985). *Josef Hoffmann*. New York: Rizzoli.

Guaitoli, M. T., & Rambaldi, S. (2002). *Lost cities from the ancient worlds*. New York: Barnes & Noble.

Guasch, A. M., & Zulaika, J. (2005). *Learning from the Bilbao Guggenheim*. Reno: Center for Basque Studies, University of Nevada.

Hall, C., Perez, D., & Brignoli, H. (2003). *Historical atlas of Central America*. Norman: University of Oklahoma Press.

Hall, E. T. (1966). *The hidden dimension*. Garden City, NY: Doubleday & Company.

Hall, M., & Hall, E. (1975). *The fourth dimension in architecture: The impact of building on man's behavior*. Santa Fe, NM: The Sunstone Press.

Hamilton, G. H. (1975). *The art and architecture of Russia*. Baltimore, MD: Penguin Books.

Hamilton, G. H. (1983). *The art and architecture of Russia* (2nd ed.). New York: Penguin Books.

Hampton, M. (1992). *Legendary decorators of the twentieth century*. New York: Doubleday.

Hanks, D. (2000). *Design for living: Furniture and lighting 1950–2000*. Montreal: Montreal Museum of Decorative Arts, Montreal Museum of Fine Arts.

Hansen, G. (1996). Relocation of Chinatown. *Virtual Museum of the City of San Francisco*. Retrieved April 16, 2009, from www.sfmuseum.net

Hanson, A., & Hanson, L. (Eds.). (1990). *Art and identity in Oceania*. Honolulu: University of Hawaii Press.

Harle, J. C. (1994). *The art and architecture of the Indian subcontinent*. New Haven, CT: Yale University Press.

Harriman, E. H. (1906, May). San Francisco. *Sunset Magazine*. 1–3.

Harris, C. M. (Ed.). (1975). *Dictionary of architecture and construction*. New York: McGraw-Hill.

Harris, C. M. (Ed.). (1977). *Historic architecture sourcebook*. New York: McGraw-Hill.

Harris, J. (Ed.). (2004). *5,000 years of textiles*. Washington, DC: Smithsonian Books.

Hart, S. (2005). *The Wright space*. New York: Barnes & Noble.

Harwood, B., May, B., & Sherman, C. (2002). *Architecture and interior design through the 18th century*. Upper Saddle River, NJ: Prentice Hall.

Haskin, F. J. (1913). *The Panama Canal*. Garden City, NY: Doubleday, Page.

Hatch, A. (1974). *Buckminster Fuller: At home in the universe*. New York: Crown.

Hawass, Z. (2005). *Tutankhamen and the golden age of the pharaohs*. Washington, DC: National Geographic.

Hayes, D. (2007). *Historical atlas of the United States: With original maps*. Berkeley: University of California Press.

Hemming, J. (Ed.). (1997). *Atlas of exploration*. New York: Oxford University Press.

The Herman Miller Furniture Co. (1948). *The Herman Miller furniture collection*. Zeeland, MI: Author.

Herman Miller, Inc. (1952). *The Herman Miller collection*. Zeeland, MI: Herman Miller Furniture Co.

Herman Miller Research Corporation. (1985). *Everybody's business: A fund of retrievable ideas for humanizing life in the office*. Zeeland, MI: Author.

Hill, A. (Ed.). (1974). *A visual dictionary of art*. Greenwich, CT: New York Graphic Society.

Hilmes, M. (2003). *The television history book*. London: British Film Institute.

Hoffmann, D. (1986). *Frank Lloyd Wright, architecture and nature*. New York: Dover.

Hoffmann, D. (1993). *Frank Lloyd Wright's Fallingwater: The house and its history*. New York: Dover.

Hoffmann, J. F. M. (1981). *Josef Hoffmann: Architect and designer, 1870–1956*. New York: Galerie Metropol.

Hoffmann, J. F. M. (1992). *Josef Hoffmann designs: MAK-Austrian museum of applied arts, Vienna*. Munich, Germany: Prestel.

Hohl, R. (1968). *Office buildings: An international survey*. New York: Praeger.

Horm, R. (1986). *Memphis: Objects, furniture and patterns*. New York: Quarto Book.

Horwitz, S. L. (1981). *The find of a lifetime: Sir Arthur Evans and the discovery of Knossos*. New York: Viking Press.

Howells, T. (Ed.). (1996). *The world's greatest buildings*. San Francisco: Fog City Press.

Iezzoni, L. I. (2006). *More than ramps: A guide to improving health care quality and access for people with disabilities*. New York: Oxford University Press.

Institute of Medicine. (2007). *The future of disability in America*. Washington, DC: The National Academies Press.

Iovine, J. (2002). *Michael Graves*. San Francisco: Chronicle Books.

Irving, R. (1981). *Indian summer: Lutyens, Baker, and imperial Delhi*. London: Yale University.

Ishida, S., & Garbato, C. (1989). *Renzo Piano and building workshop*. New York: Rizzoli.

Issa, R. (Ed.). (2001). *Iranian contemporary art*. London: Booth-Clibborn.

JFK Library. (2009). *Message to the Congress on Urgent National Needs (Excerpt), May 25, 1961*. Retrieved June 8, 2009, from www .jfklibrary.org

Jacobsen, A. (1987). *Arne Jacobsen*. Paris: Union des Arts Decoratifs.

Jacobson, C. (Ed.). (1998). *Takasaki Masaharu: An architecture of cosmology*. New York: Princeton Architectural Press.

Jacobus, J. M. (1962). *Philip Johnson*. New York: G. Braziller.

Jaeger, P. T. (2005). *Understanding disability*. Westport, CT: Praeger.

Jahn, G. (1994). *Contemporary Australian architecture*. Sydney, Australia: Craftsman House.

James, C. (1986). *The Imperial Hotel: Frank Lloyd Wright and the architecture of unity*. Rutland, VT: C. E. Tuttle.

Jencks, C. (Ed.). (1995). *Frank O. Gehry: Individual imagination and cultural conservatism*. London: Academy Editions.

Jodidio, P. (1999). *Mario Botta*. Hong Kong: Taschen.

Jodidio, P. (2006). *Architecture in Japan*. Hong Kong: Taschen.

Jodidio, P. (2007). *Ando: Complete works*. Hong Kong: Taschen.

Joedicke, J. (1962). *Office buildings*. New York: Frederick A. Praeger.

Johnson, J. (2003). *Art: A new history*. New York: Harper Collins.

Johnson, K. R. (1992). *The AUSMAP atlas of Australia: Atlas production, AUSLIG*. Cambridge, UK: Cambridge University Press.

Johnson, P. (1972). *Johnson house, New Canaan, Connecticut, 1949*. Tokyo: A. D. A. Edita.

Johnson, P. (1978). *Mies van der Rohe*. New York: The Museum of Modern Art.

Johnson, P. C. (1947). *Mies van der Rohe*. New York: The Museum of Modern Art.

Jones, O. (2006). *Decorative ornament: Over 2,350 historic patterns*. New York: Tess Press.

Kagan, N. (Ed.). (2006). *National Geographic concise history of the world*. Washington, DC: National Geographic.

Kaliszan, J. (1968). *The Warsaw ghetto*. New York: T. Yoseloff.

Kallir, J. (1986). *Viennese design and the Wiener Werkstaette*. New York: G. Braziller, in association with Galerie St. Etienne.

Kastholm, J. (1968). *Arne Jacobsen*. Copenhagen, Denmark: Andr. Fred. Host & Son's Forlog.

Kasule, S., Dr. (1998). *History atlas of Africa*. New York: Macmillan.

Kenner, H. (1973). *Bucky: A guided tour of Buckminster Fuller*. New York: Morrow.

Kent, C. (2005). *Santiago Calatrava: Milwaukee Art Museum Quadracci Pavilion*. New York: Rizzoli.

Kersten, A. E. (2004). *Greenwood encyclopedia of daily life*. Westport, CT: Greenwood Press.

Kicherer, S. (1990). *Olivetti*. New York: Rizzoli.

Kirkham, P. (1995). *Charles and Ray Eames: Designers of the twentieth century*. Cambridge, MA: MIT Press.

Klassen, W. (1986). *Architecture in the Philippines*. Cebu City, Philippines: University of San Carlos.

Kleiner, F. S., & Mamiya, C. J. (2005). *Gardner's art through the ages, twelfth edition, volume I*. Belmont, CA: Wadsworth/
 Thomson Learning.

Kleiner, F. S., & Mamiya, C. J. (2005). *Gardner's art through the ages, twelfth edition, volume II*. Belmont, CA: Wadsworth/
 Thomson Learning.

Klimt, G. (2001). *Gustav Klimt: Modernism in the making*. New York: H. N. Abrams, in association with National Gallery of
 Canada, Ottawa.

Klotz, H. (1989). *20th century architecture: Drawings-models-furniture*. New York: Rizzoli.

Knight, C. (1985). *Philip Johnson/John Burgee architecture 1979–1985*. New York: Rizzoli.

Koch, R. (1982). *Louis Comfort Tiffany: Rebel in glass*. New York: Crown.

Koda, H., & Bolton, A. (2007). *Poiret*. New York: Metropolitan Museum of Art.

Koe, F. T. (2007). *Fabric for the designed interior*. New York: Fairchild.

Komendant, A. E. (1975). *18 years with architect Louis I. Kahn*. Englewood, NJ: Aloray.

Korea Foundation. (1994). *Korean cultural heritage. Fine arts: painting/handicrafts/architecture*. Seoul: Korea Foundation.

Korean National Commission for UNESCO. (1983). *Traditional Korean art*. Seoul: The Si-sa-yong-o-sa Publishers.

Korean Overseas Information Service. (1986). *Korea arts and culture*. Seoul: Seoul International Publishing House.

Kries, M., & von Vegesack, A. (2005). *Joe Colombo: Inventing the future*. Weil am Rhein, Germany: Vitra Design Museum.

Krinsky, C. H. (1988). *Gordon Bunshaft of Skidmore, Owings, and Merrill*. New York: The Architectural History Foundation.

Kroc, R. (1977, 1987). *Grinding it out: The making of McDonald's*. New York: St. Martin's Press.

Kuan, S., & Rowe, P. G. (Eds.). (2004). *Shanghai: Architecture & urbanism for modern China*. Munich, Germany: Prestel.

Kudriavtsev, A., & Cooke, C. (Eds.). (1988). *Uses of tradition in Russian & Soviet architecture*. New York: St. Martin's Press.

Kultermann, U. (Ed.). (1970). *Kenzo Tange: 1946–1969 architecture and urban design*. New York: Praeger.

Kwok, J. K. F., Chan, R. K. H., & Chan, W. T. (2002). *Self-help organizations of people with disabilities in Asia*. Westport, CT:
 Auburn House.

Lagerfeld, K. (1998). *Tadao Ando-Vitra house*. Göttingen, Germany: Steidl.

Landau, S. B., & Condit, C. W. (1996). *Rise of the New York skyscraper*. New Haven, CT: Yale University Press.

Langley, A. (1999). *Shakespeare's theatre*. Oxford, UK: Oxford University Press.

LaRosa, M., & Mejia, G. (2007). *Atlas and survey of Latin American history*. Armonk, NY: M. E. Sharpe.

Larsen, J. L., & Weeks, J. (1975). *Fabrics for interiors: A guide for architects, designers, and consumers*. New York: Van Nostrand
 Reinhold.

Lasdun, D. (1984). *Architecture in an age of skepticism*. New York: Oxford University Press.

Le Corbusier. (1947). *L'Unité d'habitation à Marseille*. Paris: Le Corbusier.

Le Corbusier. (1964). *When the cathedrals were white*. New York: McGraw-Hill.

Le Corbusier. (1965). *Oeuvre complète*. Zurich: Les Éditions d'Architecture.

Le Corbusier. (1967). *Le Corbusier, 1919–65*. New York: Praeger.

Le Corbusier. (1968). *The nursery schools*. New York: Orion Press.

Le Corbusier. (1970). *Le Corbusier: Last works*. New York: Praeger.

Lebo, H. (1990). *Citizen Kane: The fiftieth anniversary album*. New York: Doubleday.

Leffingwell, W. H. (1925). *Office management principles and practices*. Chicago: A. W. Shaw.

Leffingwell, W. H., & Robinson, E. M. (1950). *Textbook of office management*. New York: McGraw-Hill.

Lepik, A. (2004). *Skyscrapers*. Munich, Germany: Prestel.

Levine, N. (1996). *The architecture of Frank Lloyd Wright*. Princeton, NJ: Princeton University Press.

Libeskind, D. (2004). *Breaking ground*. New York: Riverhead Books.

Lico, G. (2003). *Edifice complex: Power, myth, and Marcos state architecture*. Manila, Philippines: Ateneo de Manila University Press.

Lipman, J. (1986). *Frank Lloyd Wright and the Johnson Wax building*. New York: Rizzoli.

Littleton, C. S. (2002). *Mythology: The illustrated anthology of world myth & storytelling*. New York: Barnes & Noble.

Loewy, R. (1979). *Industrial design*. Woodstock, NY: Overlook Press.

London, E. (2004). *Bangladesh*. Milwaukee, WI: Gareth Stevens.

Longhena, M. (1998). *Ancient Mexico: The history and culture of the Maya, Aztecs, and other pre-Columbian peoples*. New York: Barnes & Noble.

Longhena, M., & Alva, W. (2007). *The Incas and other ancient Andean civilizations*. New York: Barnes & Noble.

Lukach, J. M. (1983). *Hilla Rebay: In search of the spirit of art*. New York: George Braziller.

Lyons, H. (2005). *Christopher Dresser: The peoples' designer*. Easthampton, MA: Antique Collectors' Club.

Lyons, N. (1976). *The Sony vision*. New York: Crown.

Ma, D. (1996). The modern silk road: The global raw silk market, 1850–1930s. *The Journal of Economic History, 56*(2), 330–355.

Maddex, D. (2000). *50 favorite houses by Frank Lloyd Wright*. New York: Smithmark.

Magnum Photographers. (2001). *New York September 11*. New York: Powerhouse Books.

Magocsi, P. (1993). *Historical atlas of Central Europe*. Seattle: University of Washington Press.

Maher, T. J. (1906). *Early work for earthquake research in California*. Virtual Museum of the City of San Francisco. Retrieved April 16, 2009, from www.sfmuseum.net

Maliszewski-Pickart, M. (1998). *Architecture and ornament: An illustrated dictionary*. Jefferson, NC: McFarland & Co.

Mandelker, D. R., & Montgomery, R. (Eds.). (1973). *Housing in America: Problems and perspectives*. Indianapolis, IN: Bobbs-Merrill.

Mander, J. (1978). *Four arguments for the elimination of television*. New York: Morrow.

Manieri-Elia, M. (1996). *Louis Henry Sullivan*. New York: Princeton Architectural Press.

Mankiewicz, F., & Swerdlow, J. (1977). *Remote control: Television and the manipulation of American life*. New York: Times Books.

Manske, B. (Ed.). (2000). *Wilhelm Wagenfeld (1900–1990)*. Ostfildern, Germany: Hatje Cantz.

Manson, G. C. (1958). *Frank Lloyd Wright to 1910: The first golden age*. New York: Reinhold.

Marberry, S. O. (1994). *Color in the office*. New York: Van Nostrand Reinhold.

Marcus, G. H. (2000). *Inside Le Corbusier: The machine for living*. New York: The Monacelli Press.

Marks, R.W. (1960). *The dymaxion world of Buckminster Fuller*. New York: Reinhold.

Marschall, R. (1986). *History of television*. New York: Gallery Books.

Marshall, D. C. (1987). *Australian architects volume 3*. Melbourne: Australian Architects.

Mason, L. E. (2002). *Asian art*. Suffolk, UK: Antique Collectors' Club.

Mazor, M. (1993). *The vanished city*. New York: Marsilio.

McArthur, M. (2005). *The arts of Asia: Materials, techniques, styles*. New York: Thames and Hudson.

McCarty, C. (1987). *Mario Bellini: Designer*. New York: The Museum of Modern Art.

McClay, M. (1995). *The complete picture history of the most popular TV show ever: I Love Lucy*. New York: Warner Books.

McClellan, G. S. (Ed.). (1974). *Crisis in urban housing*. New York: The H. W. Wilson Company.

McDermott, C. (1998). *Design Museum book of 20th century design*. Woodstock, NY: Overlook Press, Peter Mayer.

McEvedy, C. (2002). *The new Penguin atlas of recent history: Europe since 1815*. New York: Penguin.

McIntrye, L. (1975). *The incredible Incas and their timeless land*. Washington, DC: National Geographic Society.

McShine, K. (Ed.). (1989). *Andy Warhol: A retrospective*. New York: The Museum of Modern Art.

Meehan, P. J. (1984). *The master architect: Conversations with Frank Lloyd Wright*. New York: Wiley-Interscience Publication.

Megaw, M. R. & Megaw, V. (2001). *Celtic Art: From its beginnings to the book of Kells*. London: Thames and Hudson.

Mehler, C. (2003). *Atlas of the Middle East*. Washington, DC: National Geographic Society.

Meikle, J. L. (2005). *Design in the USA*. Oxford, UK: Oxford University Press.

Merkel, J. (2005). *Eero Saarinen*. London: Phaidon.

Messler, N. (1986). *The Art Deco skyscraper in New York*. New York: Peter Lang.

Metcalf, V. H. (1906). *Secretary Metcalf's 1906 earthquake report to President Roosevelt*. Virtual Museum of the City of San Francisco. Retrieved April 16, 2009, from www.sfmuseum.net

Michelson, W. (1977). *Environmental choice, human behavior, and residential satisfaction*. New York: Oxford University Press.

Michener, J. A. (1996). *This noble land: My vision for America*. New York: Random House.

Miller, J. (2005). *Furniture: World styles from classical to contemporary*. New York: DK.

Miller, M. (2006). *The art of Mesoamerica from Olmec to Aztec*. London: Thames and Hudson.

Miller, R. C. (1990). *Modern design in the Metropolitan Museum of Art 1890–1990*. New York: Harry N. Abrams.

Miller, W. H., Jr. (1985). *The fabulous interiors of the great ocean liners in historic photographs*. New York: Dover.

Mitchell, J. P. (Ed.). (1985). *Federal housing policy & programs*. New Brunswick, NJ: Center for Urban Policy and Research.

Moes, R. J. (1987). *Korean art*. New York: Universe Books.

Moes, R. J. (1995). *Mingei: Japanese folk art from the Montgomery collection*. Alexandria, VA: Art Services International.

Moos, S. (1979). *Le Corbusier, elements of a synthesis*. Cambridge, MA: MIT Press.

Morgan, C. L. (2000). *20th century design: A reader's guide*. Boston: Architectural Press.

Morita, A. (1986). *Made in Japan: Akio Morita and Sony*. New York: E. P. Dutton.

Morozzi, C., & Pietro, S. S. (1996). *Contemporary Italian furniture*. Milano: Edizioni L'Archivolto.

Moudry, R. (Ed.). (2005). *The American skyscraper: Cultural histories*. Cambridge, UK: Cambridge University Press.

Mount, C. (2004). *Arne Jacobsen*. San Francisco: Chronicle Books.

Mulryne, J. R., & Shewring, M. (Eds.) (1997). *Shakespeare's Globe rebuilt*. Cambridge, UK: Cambridge University Press.

The Museum of Modern Art. (2009). *MoMA revisits what "good design" was over 50 years later*. Retrieved July 22, 2009, from http://press.moma.org/images/press/gooddesign/GoodDesign_Release.pdf

Myers, I. E. (1952). *Mexico's modern architecture*. New York: Architectural Book.

Nash, E. P. (2005). *Manhattan skyscrapers*. New York: Princeton Architectural Press.

Nathan, J. (1999). *Sony: The private life*. Boston: Houghton Mifflin.

National Fire Protection Association (NFPA). (1982). *Investigation report on the MGM Grand Hotel fire*. Washington, DC: Author.

National Fire Protection Association (NFPA). (1983). *An examination and analysis of the dynamics of the human behavior in the MGM Grand Hotel fire*. Washington, DC: Author.

National Fire Protection Association (NFPA). (1983). *Hotel fires: Behind the headlines*. Quincy, MA: Author.

National Geographic Society. (2006). *National Geographic collegiate atlas of the world*. Washington, DC: Author.

National Research Council (2001). *Protecting people and buildings from terrorism: Technology transfer for blast-effects mitigation*. Washington, DC: National Academy Press.

National Research Council. (2005). *Reopening public facilities after a biological attack: A decision making framework*. Washington, DC: The National Academies Press.

Nelson, G., & Wright, H. (Eds.). (1946). *Tomorrow's house: A complete guide for the home-builder*. New York: Simon and Schuster.

Nelson, J. K. (1970). *Harry Bertoia, sculptor*. Detroit, MI: Wayne State University Press.

Nelson, J. K. (1988). *Harry Bertoia, printmaker*. Detroit, MI: Wayne State University Press.

Neuhart, J. (1989). *Eames Design: The work of the office of Charles and Ray Eames*. New York: H. N. Abrams.

Neuwirth, W. (1984). *Wiener Werkstätte: Avantgarde, Art Deco, industrial design*. Wien, Austria: Neuwirth.

Never, R., & Libertson, H. (1978). *Ukiyo-E 250 years of Japanese art*. New York: Mayflower Books.

Nguyet, T. (Ed.). (1983). *Arts of Asia*. 13–2. Hong Kong, China: Hong Kong Arts of Asia.

Nichols, K. (Ed.). (2003). *Michael Graves: Buildings and projects 1995–2003*. New York: Rizzoli.

Nicolle, D. (2003). *Historical atlas of the Islamic world*. New York: Checkmark Books.

Nightingale, F. (1871). *Introductory notes on lying-in institutions*. London: Author.

Noble, C. (1972). *Philip Johnson*. New York: Simon and Schuster.

Noguchi, I. (1986). *Isamu Noguchi, space of akari & stone*. San Francisco: Chronicle Books.

Noguchi, I. (1987). *The Isamu Noguchi garden museum*. New York: H. N. Abrams.

Noguchi, I. (1994). *Isamu Noguchi: Essays and conversations*. New York: H. N. Abrams, in association with the Isamu Noguchi Foundation.

Noyes, E. F. (1969). *Organic design in home furnishings*. New York: Arno Press.

Nute, K. (1993). *Frank Lloyd Wright and Japan: The role of traditional Japanese art and architecture in the work of Frank Lloyd Wright*. New York: Chapman & Hall.

Nuttgens, P. (Ed.). (1988). *Mackintosh and his contemporaries in Europe and America*. London: J. Murray.

O'Brien, P. (Ed.). (1999). *Oxford atlas of world history*. New York: Oxford University Press.

O'Gorman, T. J. (2004). *Frank Lloyd Wright's Chicago*. London: Thunder Bay Press.

O'Riley, M. K. (2006). *Art beyond the west, second edition*. Upper Saddle River, NJ: Prentice Hall.

Office of the Prime Minister. (1979). *Thailand into the 80's*. Bangkok: Office of the Prime Minister, Kingdom of Thailand.

Oliver, P. (1987). *Dwellings: The house across the world*. Oxford, UK: Phaidon.

Overy, P., Büller, L., den Oudsten, F., & Mulder, B. (1988). *The Rietveld Schröder House*. Boston: The Massachusetts Institute of Technology.

Overy, R. J. (2006). *Collins atlas of 20th century history*. New York: Collins.

Pancaroglu, O. (2007). *Perpetual glory: Medieval Islamic ceramics from the Harvey B. Plotnick collection*. New Haven, CT: Yale University Press.

Papadakis, A. C. (Ed.). (1992). *Foster associates: Recent works*. London: St. Martin's Press.

Papadakis, A. C., Cooke, C., & Ageros, J. (Eds.). (1991). *The avant-garde: Russian architecture in the twenties*. New York: St. Martin's Press.

Pare, R. (2007). *The lost vanguard: Russian modernist architecture 1922–1932*. New York: The Monacelli Press.

Parsons, F. A. (1931). *Interior decoration: Its principles and practice*. Garden City, NY: Doubleday.

Pasca, V. (1991). *Vico Magistretti*. New York: Rizzoli.

Patton, P. (2004). *Michael Graves designs the art of the everyday object*. New York: Melcher Media.

Pauly, D. (1997). *Le Corbusier: La Chapelle de Ronchamp*. Boston: Birkhäuser.

Pauly, D. (2002). *Barragán: Space and shadow, walls, and colour*. Basel, Switzerland: Biekhäuser.

Pawley, M. (1999). *Norman Foster*. New York: Universe.

Pegler, M. M. (2006). *The Fairchild dictionary of interior design* (2nd ed.). New York: Fairchild.

Pelli, C., & Crosbie, M. J. (2001). *Petronas Towers*. New York: Wiley-Academy.

Petranzan, M. (1997). *Gae Aulenti*. New York: Universe.

Petranzan, M. (Ed.) (2001). *Alvaro Siza Vieira: Chiesa di Santa Maria de Canavezes, Porto, Portogallo, 1990–1997*. Padova, Italy: Il Poligrafo.

Petranzan, M. (2003). *Gae Aulenti*. New York: Universe.

Pfeiffer, B. B. (1986). *Frank Lloyd Wright: The Guggenheim correspondence*. Fresno: The Press at California State University.

Phaidon Press Limited. (2004). *On tour with Renzo Piano*. London: Author.

Phaidon Press Limited. (2004). *The Phaidon atlas of contemporary world architecture*. London: Author.

Philips, B. (1991). *Fabrics and wallpapers: Sources, design and inspiration*. Boston: Bulfinch Press Book, Little, Brown and Company.

Piña, L. (2002). *Furniture in history 3000 B.C.–2000 A.D.* Upper Saddle River, NJ: Prentice Hall.

Portal, J. (2007). *The first emperor: China's terracotta army*. Cambridge, MA: Harvard University Press.

Portugal, A. S. (1992). *Of the architecture of Luis Barragán*. New York: Rizzoli.

Postell, J. (2007). *Furniture design*. New York: John Wiley & Sons.

Pothorn, H. (1971). *Architectural styles*. New York: Viking Press.

Powelle, K. (2006). *30 St Mary AXE: A tower for London*. London: Merrell.

Pynoos, J., Schafer, R., & Hartman, C. W. (Eds.). (1980). *Housing urban America: Updated second edition*. New York: Aldine.

Quinan, J. (1987). *Frank Lloyd Wright's Larkin building: Myth and fact*. New York: Architectural History Foundation; Cambridge, MA: MIT Press.

Radice, B. (1993). *Ettore Sottsass: A critical biography*. New York: Rizzoli.

Raftery, B. (Ed.). (1990). *Celtic art*. Paris: UNESCO: Flammarion.

Ragheb, J. F. (2001). *Frank Gehry, architect*. New York: The Solomon R. Guggenheim Foundation.

Ranzani, E. (Ed.). (1996). *Mario Bellini architecture 1984–1995*. Basel, Switzerland: Birkhäuser.

Ratcliff, C. (1983) *Andy Warhol*. New York: Abbeville Press.

Reyes, E. V. (2000). *Tropical living: Contemporary dream houses in the Philippines*. Singapore, Singapore: Periplus.

Riabushin, A. V., & Smolina, N. (1992). *Landmarks of Soviet architecture, 1917–1991*. New York: Rizzoli.

Riemschneider, B. & Grosenick, U. (Eds.) (1999). *Art at the turn of the millennium*. London: Taschen.

Riley, T. (2003). *Tall buildings*. New York: The Museum of Modern Art.

Ringelblum, E. (1974). *Notes from the Warsaw ghetto*. New York: Schocken Books.

Risom, J. (1955). *The answer is Risom*. New York: Jens Risom Design.

Rivers, V. (1999). *Shining cloth: Dress and adornment that glitter*. London: Thames and Hudson.

Rosen, S. (1969). *Wizard of the dome: R. Buckminster Fuller, designer for the future*. Boston: Little, Brown.

Rossbach, S. (1987). *Interior design with Feng Shui*. New York: E. P. Dutton.

Roth, L. M. (2007). *Understanding architecture: Its elements, history, and meaning*. Cambridge, MA: Westview Press.

Rowland, B. (1953). *The art and architecture of India: Buddhist, Hindu, Jain*. Baltimore: Penguin Books.

Roy, R. (1994). *The complete book of underground houses*. New York: Sterling.

Ruchelman, L. I. (1977). *The World Trade Center: Politics and policies of skyscraper development*. Syracuse, NY: Syracuse University Press.

Rui, H. (Ed.) (2004). *Reflections on art, architecture and society in China: Beijing 798*. Beijing, China: Timezone 8.

Ruthven, M., Nanji, A. (2004). *Historical atlas of Islam*. Cambridge, MA: Harvard University Press.

Ryabushin, A., & Smolina, N. (1992). *Landmarks of Soviet architecture 1917–1991*. New York: Rizzoli.

Saarinen, E. (1968). *Eero Saarinen on his work: A selection of buildings dating from 1947 to 1964 with statements by the architect*. New Haven, CT: Yale University Press.

Saarinen, E. (1971). *Eero Saarinen*. New York: Simon and Schuster.

Saarinen, E. (1971). *Eero Saarinen: Bell Telephone Corporation Research Laboratories, New Jersey 1957–62: Deere & Company headquarters building, Illinois, 1957–63*. Tokyo: A. D. A. Edita.

Saarinen, E. (1984). *Eero Saarinen*. Tokyo: A + U.

Saint-Gilles, A. (1983). *Mingei: Japan's enduring folk arts*. Tokyo: A. Saint-Gilles.

Sakr, T. M. R. (1993). *Early twentieth-century Islamic architecture in Cairo*. Cairo, Egypt: The American University in Cairo Press.

Sayers, A. (2001). *Australian art*. Oxford: Oxford University Press.

Sbriglio, J. (2004). *Le Corbusier: L'Unité d'habitation de Marseille*. Boston: Birkhäuser.

Scarpari, M. (2000). *Ancient China: Chinese civilization from the origins to the Tang dynasty*. New York: Barnes & Noble.

Schezen, R. (1992). *Vienna 1850–1930, architecture*. New York: Rizzoli.

Schiffer, N. N., & Bertoia, V. O. (2003). *The world of Bertoia*. Atglen, PA: Schiffer.

Schmidt, A. (Ed.). (2003). *A day-by-day review of world events: Today in history*. San Diego, CA: Tehabi Books.

Schoenauer, N. (1981). *6,000 years of housing*. New York: Garland STPM Press.

Schönberger, A. (Ed.) (1990). *Raymond Loewy: Pioneer of American industrial design*. New York: te Neues.

Schulze, F. (1994). *Philip Johnson: Life and work*. New York: A. A. Knopf.

Schulze, F. (2005). *Illinois Institute of Technology: An architectural tour by Franz Schulze*. New York: Princeton Architectural Press.

Schwartz, R. A. (1998). *Cold war culture: Media and the arts, 1945–1990*. New York: Facts On File.

Schwartz-Clauss, M., & von Vegesack, A. (2002). *Living in motion: Design and architecture for flexible dwellings*. Weil am Rhein, Germany: Vitra Design Museum.

Schweiger, W. J. (1984). *Wiener Werkstätte: Design in Vienna, 1903–1932*. New York: Abbeville Press.

Shanes, E. (2004). *Warhol: The life and masterworks*. New York: Parkstone Press Ltd.

Shapira, N. H. (1979). *Design process Olivetti 1908–1978*. Cambridge, MA: Harvard School of Design.

Sharp, D. (Ed.). (1972). *Glass architecture by Paul Scheerbart and Alpine architecture by Bruno Taut*. New York: Praeger.

Shihata, I. F. I. (1975). *The case for the Arab oil embargo*. Beirut, Lebanon: The Institute for Palestine Studies.

Shoshkes, L. (1976). *Space planning: Designing the office environment*. New York: Architectural Record Books.

Shwadren, B. (1986). *Middle East oil crises since 1973*. Boulder, CO: Westview Press.

Singer, R. T. (1998). *Edo: Art in Japan 1615–1868*. Washington, DC: National Gallery of Art.

Sklar, R. (2002). *A world history of film*. New York: Harry N. Abrams.

Smith, B. (1968). *Mexico: A history in art*. New York: Gemini-Smith.

Smith, C. (Ed.). (1895). *Journals and correspondence of Lady Eastlake*. London: John Murray.

Smithsonian. (2009). *Imagery in African Art*. Retrieved July 22, 2009, from http://africa.si.edu/collections/imgrypg.asp

Smithsonian Institution. (1975). *Designs of Raymond Loewy: An exhibition at the Renwick Gallery of the National Collection of Fine Arts, Smithsonian Institution, Washington, D.C., August 1–November 16, 1975*. Washington, DC: Smithsonian Institution Press.

Snyder, R. (1980). *Buckminster Fuller: An autobiographical monologue/scenario*. New York: St. Martin's Press.

Solaguren-Beascoa de Corral, F. (1989). *Arne Jacobsen*. Barcelona: G. Gili.

Solomon R., Guggenheim Foundation. (1960). *The Solomon R. Guggenheim Foundation: Architect: Frank Lloyd Wright*. New York: Solomon R. Guggenheim Foundation and Horizon Press.

Solomon R., Guggenheim Foundation. (1966). *The Solomon R. Guggenheim*. New York: Solomon R. Guggenheim Foundation and Horizon Press.

Sommer, R. L. (1997). *Frank Lloyd Wright: A gatefold portfolio*. New York: Barnes & Noble.

Spade, R. (1971). *Eero Saarinen*. New York: Simon and Schuster.

Spade, R. (1971). *Oscar Niemeyer*. New York: Simon and Schuster.

Sparke, P. (1987). *Design in context*. London: Bloomsbury.

Sparke, P. (1998). *A century of design: Design pioneers of the 20th century*. Hauppauge, NY: Barron's Educational Series.

Sparke, P. (2004). *An introduction to design and culture: 1900 to the present*. London: Routledge.

Spencer, D. D. (1999). *Great men & women of computing* (2nd ed.). Ormond Beach, FL: Camelot.

St. John, P. (1991). *Air piracy, airport security, and international terrorism: Winning the war against hijackers*. New York: Quorum Books.

Stanley, T. (2004). *Palace and mosque: Islamic art from the Middle East*. London: V & A.

Stearns, P. N., & Hinshaw, J. H. (1996). *The ABC-CLIO world history companion to the industrial revolution*. Santa Barbara, CA: ABC-CLIO.

Steele, J. (1992). *Architecture for a changing world*. New York: St. Martin's Press.

Steele, J. (1994). *Architecture for Islamic societies today*. London: Academy Editions.

Steer, J., & White, A. (1994). *Atlas of western art history: Artists, sites, and movements from ancient Greece to the modern age*. New York: Oxford University Press.

Steinhardt, N. S. (2002). *Chinese architecture*. New Haven, CT: Yale University Press.

Stephens, S. (2004). *Imagining ground zero: Official and unofficial proposals for the World Trade Center site*. New York: Rizzoli.

Stewart, D. B. (1987). *The making of a modern Japanese architecture*. Tokyo: Kodansha International.

Stierlin, H. (1984). *Art of the Incas and its origins*. New York: Rizzoli.

Stone-Miller, R. (2002). *Art of the Andes: From Chavin to Inca*. London: Thames and Hudson.

Storrer, W. A. (1993). *The Frank Lloyd Wright companion*. Chicago: University of Chicago Press.

Stratton, C., & Scott, M. M. (1987). *The art of Sukhothai*. New York: Oxford University Press.

Sturgis, R. (1901–02). *A dictionary of architecture and building: Biographical, historical, and descriptive*. New York: Macmillan.

Sudjic, D. (1991). *Australian embassy Tokyo*. London: Blueprint Extra.

Sullivan, L. H. (1979). *National Farmers' Bank, Owatonna, Minnesota, 1907–08: Merchants' National Bank, Grinnell, Iowa, 1914: Farmers' & Merchants' Union Bank, Columbus, Wisconsin, 1919*. Tokyo: A. D. A. Edita.

Sullivan, R. (Ed.). (2001). *One nation remembers September 11, 2001*. New York: Time.

Suzuki, H. (2002). *Paramodern architecture: Shuhei Endo*. London: Phaidon Press.

Swedin, E. G., & Ferro, D. L. (2005). *Computers: The life story of a technology*. Westport, CT: Greenwood Press.

Sweeney, J. J. (1970). *Antoni Gaudí*. New York: Praeger.

Sweet, F. (2003). *Scandimodern*. London: Mitchell Beazley.

Szarkowski, J. (1956). *The idea of Louis Sullivan*. Minneapolis: University of Minnesota Press.

Tange, K. (1972). *Katsura: Tradition and creation in Japanese architecture*. New Haven, CT: Yale University Press.

Tange, K. (1978). *Kenzo Tange*. Barcelona, Spain: Gustavo Gili, S.A.

Tange, K., & Kawazoe, N. (1965). *ISE prototype of Japanese architecture*. Cambridge, MA: MIT Press.

Tarkhanov, A., & Kavtaradze, S. (1992). *Architecture of the Stalin era*. New York: Rizzoli.

Taschen, A. (Ed.) *African style*. London: Taschen.

Teeple, J. (2006). *Timelines of world history*. New York: DK.

Teicholz, E. (Ed.). (1985). *CAD/CAM handbook*. New York: McGraw-Hill.

Teige, K. (2000). *Modern architecture in Czechoslovakia*. Los Angeles: Getty Research Institute.

Temko, A. (1962). *Eero Saarinen*. New York: G. Braziller.

Temple, K. (2004). *Top architects of the world*. Barcelona, Spain: Atrium Group.

Teunissen, B. (2007). *A portrait of Europeans at home*. London: Aperture.

Thau, C., & Vindum, K. (2001). *Arne Jacobsen*. Copenhagen, Denmark: Arkitektens Forlag/Danish Architectural Press.

Thomas, A., & Crow, B. (1994). *Third world atlas*. Bristol, PA: Taylor & Francis.

Thomas, M, Mainguy, C., & Pommier, S. (1985). *Textile art*. New York: Rizzoli.

Thorne, M. (Ed.). (1999). *The Pritzker architecture prize: The first twenty years*. New York: Rizzoli.

Time-Life Books (Eds.). (1990). *The nuclear age: TimeFrame AD 1950–1990*. New York: Author.

Too, L. (1996). *The complete illustrated guide to Feng Shui*. Boston: Element.

Tömöry, E. (1982). *A history of fine arts in India and the west*. Bombay, India: Orient Longman.

Topham, J. (2005). *Traditional crafts of Saudi Arabia: Weaving, jewelry, costume, leatherwork, basketry, woodwork, pottery, metalwork*. London: Stacey International; Riyadh, Saudi Arabia: in association with Al-Turath.

Torres, A. M. (2000). *Isamu Noguchi: A study of space*. New York: Monacelli Press.

Trencher, M. (1996). *The Alvar Aalto guide*. New York: Princeton Architectural Press.

Trulove, J. G. (2004). *Sustainable homes*. New York: Collins Designs.

Tyng, A. (1984). *Beginnings: Louis I. Kahn's philosophy of architecture*. New York: John Wiley & Sons.

Tzonis, A. (2004). *Santiago Calatrava: The complete works*. New York: Rizzoli.

U.S. Army. (2007). *Shelters Technology, Engineering & Fabrication Directorate (STEFD)*. Retrieved June 18, 2009, from www.natick.army.mil

U.S. Federal Government. (1968). *Architectural Barrier Act (ABA) of 1968*. Retrieved June 18, 2009, from www.access-board.gov/about/laws/aba.htm

Ulack, R., & Pauer, G. (1988). *Atlas of Southeast Asia*. New York: Macmillan.

Underwood, D. (1984). *Oscar Niemeyer and Brazilian free-form modernism*. New York: G. Braziller.

UNESCO. (1981). *World Heritage List Old Havana and its Fortificaitons No. 204*. Retrieved August 24, 2009, from http://whc.unesco.org/en/list/204

UNESCO. (1982). *World Heritage List Historic Sanctuary of Machu Picchu No. 274*. Retrieved August 24, 2009, from http://whc .unesco.org/en/list/274

UNESCO. (1986). *World Heritage List The Imperial Palace of the Ming and Qing Dynasties No. 439*. Retrieved August 24, 2009, from http://whc.unesco.org/en/list/439

UNESCO. (1987). *World Heritage List The Pre-Hispanic city of Chichén Itzá No. 483*. Retrieved August 24, 2009, from http://whc .unesco.org/en/list/483

UNESCO. (1989). *World Heritage List Buddhist Monuments at Sanchi No. 524*. Retrieved August 24, 2009, from http://whc .unesco.org/en/list/524

UNESCO. (1997). *World Heritage List Borobudor Temple Compound No. 592*. Retrieved August 24, 2009, from http://whc.unesco .org/en/list/592

UNESCO. (1997). *World Heritage List Guadalajara (Mexico) No. 815*. Retrieved August 24, 2009, from http://whc.unesco.org/ en/list/815

UNESCO. (1997). *World Heritage List Temple of Heaven (China) No. 881*. Retrieved August 24, 2009, from http://whc.unesco .org/en/list/881

UNESCO. (1999). *World Heritage List Horta Houses (Belgium) No. 1005*. Retrieved August 24, 2009, from http://whc.unesco .org/en/list/1005

UNESCO. (2004). *World Heritage List Barrágan House and Studio (Mexico) no. 1136*. Retrieved August 24, 2009, from http://whc .unesco.org/en/list/1136

UNESCO. (2004). *World Heritage List Works of Gaudí (Spain) no. 320*. Retrieved August 24, 2009, from http://whc.unesco.org/ en/list/320

UNESCO. (2009). *The criteria for selection*. Retrieved August 24, 2009, from http://whc.unesco.org/en/criteria/

UNESCO. (2009). *Success stories*. Retrieved August 24, 2009, from http://whc.unesco.org/en/107/

United Nations. (1945). *Atomic energy*. Retrieved June 1, 2009, from www.un.org

United Nations. (1982). *World programme of action concerning disabled persons*. Retrieved June 18, 2009, from www.un.org

United Nations. (2002). *Plan of implementation of the world summit on sustainable development*. Retrieved June 17, 2009, from www.un.org

University of Wisconsin–Madison. (2007). *Visual Culture*. Retrieved July 3, 2009, from www.visualculture.wisc.edu.

Vaizey, M. (1990). *Christo*. New York: Rizzoli.

van Egeraat, E. (2005). *Erick van Egeraat*. Victoria, Australia: The Image Publishing Group.

van Vynckt, R. J. (1993). *International dictionary of architects and architecture*. Detroit: St. James Press.

Van Zanten, D. (1986). *Louis Sullivan: The function of ornament*. New York: W. W. Norton, in association with Chicago Historical Society and the Saint Louis Art Museum.

Varnedoe, K. (1986). *Vienna 1900: Art, architecture and design*. New York: Museum of Modern Art.

Vassilakis, A. (1994). *Knossos: Mythology, history, guide to the archaeological site*. Athens, Greece: Adam Editions.

Vercelloni, V. (1989). *The adventure of design: Gavina*. New York: Rizzoli.

Voyce, A. (1948). *Russian architecture, trends in nationalism and modernism*. New York: Philosophical Library.

Waggoner, L. S. (1996). *Fallingwater: Frank Lloyd Wright's romance with nature*. New York: Universe.

Wallis, R. (1993). *Combating air terrorism*. Washington, DC: Brassey's.

Wallis, R. (2003). *How safe are our skies? Assessing the airlines' response to terrorism*. Westport, CT: Praeger.

Wampler, C. (1949). *Dr. Willis H. Carrier, father of air conditioning*. New York: Newcomen Society of England, American Branch.

Wangpaichitr, S., & Siriwan, J. (2000). *Sukhothai: World heritage*. Bangkok: G. A. Merit.

Watanabe, H. (1991). *Amazing architecture from Japan*. New York: Weatherhill.

Weber, N. F. (1985). *The woven and graphic art of Anni Albers*. Washington, DC: Smithsonian Institution Press.

Weber, N. F. (1999). *Anni Albers*. New York: Guggenheim Museum.

Weisskamp, H. (1968). *Hotels: An international survey*. New York: Praeger Publishers.

Westbrook, A., & Yarowsky, A. (Eds.) (1983). *Design in America: The Cranbrook vision 1925–1950*. New York: Harry N. Abrams.

Westcott, R. (1965). *The Sydney Opera House*. Sydney, Australia: URE Smith.

Weston, R. (2004). *Key buildings of the twentieth century: Plans, sections, and elevations*. New York: W. W. Norton.

Westwell, I. (2007). *Timeless India*. Edison, NJ: Chartwell Books.

White, D. M. (1970). *Pop culture in America*. Chicago: Quadrangle Books.

Whitfield, P. (2005). *Cities of the world: A history in maps*. Berkeley: University of California Press.

Whittick, A. (1974). *European architecture in the twentieth century*. Aylebury, England: Leonard Hill Books.

Whyte, A. (2000). *Skidmore, Owings & Merrill LLP: Architecture and urbanism 1995–2000*. Mulgrave, Australia: The Images Publishing Group.

Whyte, I. B. (1982). *Bruno Taut and the architecture of activism*. Cambridge: Cambridge University Press.

Wiebenson, D., & Sisa, J. (1998). *The architecture of historic Hungary*. Cambridge, MA: MIT Press.

Wilk, C. (Ed.). (1996). *Western furniture 1350 to the present day*. London: Victoria & Albert.

Williams, H. (2005). *Cassell's chronology of world history*. London: Weidenfeld & Nicolson.

Williams, S. (1989). *Hongkong Bank: The building of Norman Foster's masterpiece*. Boston: Little, Brown and Company.

Willis, T. (2002). *Vietnam*. New York: Scholastic.

Wilson, P. R. (1976). *Public housing for Australia*. St. Lucia, Queensland, Australia: University of Queensland Press.

Winchip, S. M. (2005). *Designing a quality lighting environment*. New York: Fairchild.

Winchip, S. M. (2007). *Fundamentals of lighting*. New York: Fairchild.

Winchip, S. M. (2007). *Sustainable design for interior environments*. New York: Fairchild.

Winship, M. (1988). *Television*. New York: Random House.

Wintle, J. (2005). *The timeline history of Islam*. New York: Barnes & Noble.

Wiseman, C. (2001). *I. M. Pei*. New York: Harry N. Abrams.

Wisnik, G. *Lucio Costa*. Sao Paolo, Brazil: Cosac & Naify.

Wittkopp, G. (1995). *Saarinen house and garden: A total work of art*. New York: H. N. Abrams; Bloomfield Hills, MI: Cranbrook Academy of Art Museum.

Wolfensohn, J. D. (2004). *World Bank atlas*. Washington, DC: World Bank.

Woodham, J. M. (1990). *Twentieth-century ornament*. New York: Rizzoli.

Woodham, J. M. (1997). *Twentieth century design*. Oxford, UK: Oxford University Press.

Woodward, C. (1970). *Skidmore, Owings & Merrill*. New York: Simon & Schuster.

Wright, E. R., & Pai, M. S. (2000). *Traditional Korean furniture*. Tokyo: Kodansha International.

Wright, F. L. (1984). *The master architect: Conversations with Frank Lloyd Wright*. New York: Wiley.

Wright, K. R., & Zegarra, A. V. (2000). *Machu Picchu: A civil engineering marvel*. Reston, VA: ASCE Press.

Wurman, R. S. (1986). *What will be has always been: The words of Louis I. Kahn*. New York: Rizzoli.

Yasinskaya, I. (1983). *Revolutionary textile design: Russia in the 1920s and 1930s*. New York: The Viking Press.

Yoshida, K. (2005). *Beijing Shanghai architecture guide*. Tokyo: A + U.

Yoshizaka, T. (1974). *Chandigarh: The new capital of Punjab, India, 1951– /Le Corbusier*. Tokyo: A. D. A. Edita.

Zabalbeascoa, A. (1992). *The new Spanish architecture*. New York: Rizzoli.

Zabalbeascoa, A., & Marcos, J. R. (1988). *Architecture monograph: Renzo Piano*. Corte Madera, CA: Gingko Press.

Zukowsky, J. (Ed.). (2000). *Skyscrapers: The new millennium*. Munich, Germany: Prestel.

GLOSSARY

ABS (acrylonitrile-butadiene-styrene) A strong, long-lasting thermoplastic used for pipes, furniture, and small appliances.

Abstract Art An early 20th-century style with geometrical forms in random arrangements.

Abstract Expressionist A mid-20th-century art movement that is also known as the *New York School*. Abstract designs had elements that provoked emotions in viewers.

Acrylic A transparent thermoplastic that can be used in light fixtures, textile fibers, and paint substances.

Adaptive reuse Renovating a structure for a new purpose.

Aestheticism movement A late 19th-century style in Great Britain emphasizing "art for art's sake" and sharing some of the characteristics associated with the Arts and Crafts movement, such as quality craftsmanship and integrity of materials.

Al-Sadu Loom weavings of the Bedouin nomadic people. The designs are simple and geometric and are often woven with red, black, and white fibers.

Americans with Disabilities Act (ADA) A 1990 civil rights legislation that "prohibits discrimination against people with disabilities in employment (Title I), in public services (Title II), in public accommodations (Title III) and in telecommunications (Title IV)." Enacted in 1992, the laws imposed numerous requirements for the built environment, which were delineated in the ADA Accessibility Guidelines (ADAAG).

Anglo-Japanese style A late 19th-century movement in Great Britain that was influenced by the fine and decorative arts from Japan. Characteristics of the style were simple geometric forms, ebony wood, and Japanese lacquer.

Anthropometric Physiological measurements of a human body that are used to determine the sizes of objects and garments.

Arabesque A decorative surface ornamentation with intertwining vines, flowers, and geometric forms.

Architrave A classical architectural horizontal element below the frieze in the entablature.

Art Deco A mid-20th-century international style that was inspired from a variety of sources, including transportation, the discovery of King Tutankhamen's tomb, and Africa.

Art Nouveau A late 19th- and early 20th-century international style that was applied to architecture, furniture, fashion, decorative arts, fine arts, and graphic arts. Designs were inspired by organic forms, flowing curves, and flora.

Arts and Crafts movement A late 19th- and early 20th-century style in Great Britain and the United States that was stimulated by the writings of the English philosopher and critic John Ruskin. Advocating social reform, Ruskin and William Morris examined the effects of mechanization on the lives and morality of people and society. The style was associated with integrity of materials, craftsmanship, and quality.

Assistive technology Specific devices designed to help the functional capabilities of a disabled person. Examples include hearing aids, eyeglasses, and stair-climbing wheelchairs.

Bakelite The first synthetic resin, developed in 1909 by Leo Baekeland.

Ballast An electrical device used to control the electrical current in electric-discharge lamps.

Barkcloth A crepe-weave fabric with a slightly nubby appearance.

Bas-relief A nearly flat sculpture on a surface.

Batik With origins in Java batik, a resist-dyeing process that involves applying wax in a pattern on cloth. After the application of dyes, the wax is removed and a crackle pattern emerges. Common colors of batik textiles are blue, brown, and red.

Bauhaus School A German program founded by Walter Gropius in 1913 that focused on modern industrial manufacturing processes and materials. The school influenced every aspect of design, including architecture, furniture, textiles, photography, ceramics, film, graphics, and painting.

Bentwood Developed by Michael Thonet, a furniture-manufacturing process that uses heated steam to bend wooden rods into various shapes.

Béton brut A French term for unfinished concrete.

Biomimetics Technologies that replicate the properties, characteristics, and processes found in nature.

Biomorphic Free-form shapes that resemble organic materials.

Bochka A curved roof used for traditional Russian wooden structures.

Bogolan Known as mud cloth. The dark brown color of the textile is derived from minerals in mud and is often emphasized by a geometric pattern in a contrasting color.

Bot A Buddhist ordination hall. Also known as an *ubosot*.

Brazilian Modern An architectural style that blends Brazil's local traditions and international avant-garde. Also known as *Modernismo*.

Brise-soleil (sun breakers) A French term for fixed or movable louvers that help control sunlight.

Building footprint The measure of a structure's area on the ground.

Bullion fringe A decorative trim with a heading and looped cords or ropes in a variety of lengths.

Bundled tube A structural system that uses open space units or tubes that are supported by massive columns and girders around its perimeter.

Bungalow A small single-story residence with a low-pitched roof, deep eaves, and a front veranda.

Calendaring A processing method that involves adhering plastic sheets to a material, such as fabric or paper. The rollers might include a design that is then embossed on the surface.

Calico A small all-over patterned (often floral) cotton textile from India.

Case goods A term for furniture that is used for storage, such as dressers, bookcases, and chests.

Casting A processing method that involves pouring a synthetic resin into a mold. A solid object is formed when the material hardens.

CATIA (Computer Aided Three Dimensional Interactive Application) A sophisticated software program originally developed for the aeronautical industry. Invented by Dassault Systèmes, the program has excellent virtual design and manufacturing capabilities.

Celadon porcelain A hard ceramic ware with a semitransparent bluish-green glaze.

Cellophane A thin transparent sheet of plastic that is moisture proof.

Cellulose acetate A thermoplastic used for decorative objects, packaging, and photographic film.

Chattri A Mughal-inspired small pavilion.

Chedi A Buddhist stupa or reliquary.

Chenille A thick, soft yarn that can be woven into a textile.

Chicago School Founded by William Le Baron Jenney, a group of U.S. architects in the late 19th and early 20th centuries who designed tall buildings using steel framing, masonry cladding (often white terra-cotta), and windows divided into three components (two double-hung windows on each side of the centered large fixed-glass window).

Chiffonier A French term for a tall furniture piece designed for garments.

Chinoiserie Designs that have decorative ornamentation influenced by the Chinese style.

Chintz A printed cotton textile, usually with a glazed finish.

Chofa A decorative element in the shape of a horn that is placed on the end points of roofs. Common in Thai architecture.

Chujja A very thin ledge of stone used on the façades of Indian architecture.

CIAM (Congrès International d'Architecture Moderne) A professional organization founded by several architects, including Le Corbusier. One of the purposes of the organization was to help address the desperate need for low-cost housing and urban planning.

Coffered ceiling A ceiling with recessed panels, often in a square or rectangular shape.

Computer graphics Images, including drawings and photographs, that are created by using technologies.

Computer-aided design/computer-aided manufacturing (CAD/CAM) A computer system with origins in the 1970s that was primarily used by large manufacturing industries. A computer-aided technology that executes drawings, specifications, and structural calculations and facilitates manufacturing processes.

Conical dome An arched architectural element in the shape of a cone.

Constructivism An abstract architectural style developed in Russia during the 1920s and 1930s. Vladimir Tatlin was a leader in the modern movement.

Contract A term for commercial interior design. The concept was reinforced by the first *Contract* magazine publication in 1960.

Corbelled vault An arch formation made from a series of stone units.

Cord A decorative trim made from plied yarns twisted together.

Cove lighting A type of illumination technique mounted on a wall or ceiling that directs light up toward the ceiling.

Cradle-to-grave Buckminster Fuller's housing philosophy for "comprehensive design responsibility" that included nine areas: mass production, package distribution, quick erection, low cost, flexible orientation, fire resistance, concussion resistance, air protection, and demountability.

Crow-stepped gable A stair-stepped formation at the ends of a pitched roof.

Cubism An early 20th-century art movement developed by Pablo Picasso and George Braque. By deconstructing objects and figures, paintings had multiple angular forms and views.

Cupola A substructure on the top of a dome or a roof that may have openings for ventilation.

Curtain wall A construction method that enables a façade to be non–load bearing. The transfer in building loads allowed for new designs on the interiors and exteriors, such as the extensive use of glass.

De Stijl (The Style) A style founded in 1917 by several architects in the Netherlands. Initiators contended that simple abstraction equated to a "universal" style that was constant. This philosophy was translated into two dimensions through paintings and into three dimensions via architecture, interior environments, furniture, and light fixtures.

Dentil Rectangular-shaped protrusions placed under a ledge, molding, or cornice.

Deutscher Werkbund (DWB) (German Work Federation) An organization formed in 1907 by Hermann Muthesius and Henry Van de Velde. The purpose was to provide an appropriate structure that would encourage artists and industrialists to communicate with each other.

Discharge lamp An electrical lamp that operates with gases at a low or high pressure.

Divan A French term for a daybed.

Dovetail joint A woodworking joinery technique with wedge-shaped units that interlock with each other.

Drum An architectural element that has the shape of the musical instrument.

Dutch gambrel A roof with two flat surfaces on either side of the ridge.

Dymaxion Deployment Unit (DDU) A shelter designed by Buckminster Fuller that was based on a grain bin. The product was accompanied by a list of the "design responsibilities" associated with his cradle-to-grave philosophy.

Earth-sheltered housing A bermed dwelling or a structure underground.

Ebéniste A French term for a master cabinetmaker.

Egg-shaped dome An arched architectural element in the shape of an egg.

Epoxy A thermoset plastic resistant to chemicals and weather.

Ergonomics Applying science to equipment designs to blend smoothly with a person's body or actions. Began with the work of Kaare Klint at the Royal Danish Academy of Fine Arts.

ETFE (ethylene tetrafluoroethylene) film A high-tech material that has excellent insulating properties, is lightweight, is self-cleaning, transmits more daylight than glass, and is recyclable.

Expressionist movement As in the fine and performing arts, the Expressionist movement is associated with challenging classical perspectives and distorting objects to create a response. New materials, such as glass, were often used to prompt emotions.

Extrusion A processing method that involves forcing resins through a heated form.

Faience A glazed earthenware popular in ancient Egypt.

Fast-tracking A building method that enables construction to begin prior to the completion of all the working drawings.

Fauwara (fountain) A term used in the context of Islamic architecture.

Favrile A decorative iridescent glass associated with Louis C. Tiffany and the Art Nouveau movement.

Feng shui (wind water) An ancient Chinese philosophy that prescribes auspicious arrangements for buildings and interior environments.

Fiberglass A material consisting of very thin glass fibers that can be woven into textiles.

Fillet A narrow, flat vertical molding.

Finial A decorative object at the end of a unit, such as a pole.

Fluorescent lamp An electric discharge lamp that utilizes electrodes, phosphors, low-pressure mercury, and other gases.

Fluting A narrow concave vertical molding often used on columns.

Foaming A processing method that blends gas-producing chemicals with resins to create polystyrene or polyurethane.

Formica A composite material invented by Daniel O'Conor and Herbert Faber in 1913.

Fossil fuel A natural, nonrenewable resource made from decomposing plant materials and animals over millions of years. Examples are oil, coal, and natural gas.

Fresco A wall painting made by adding paint pigments to wet plaster.

Fretwork A carved geometric decoration with intersecting lines separated by open areas.

Frieze A decorative horizontal area below a crown molding or cornice.

Fringe A decorative trim that has a heading with an attached decorative treatment, such as loops or tassels.

Furniture system An office system comprised of changeable panels, work surfaces, shelves, and components.

Fuseau A conical-shaped furniture leg.

Gasolier A suspended fixture that burns natural gas for illumination.

Gateleg table A furniture piece that has a fixed center section with hinged tabletops. Legs and stretchers support the end tabletops by pivoting back and forth.

Geodesic dome A spherical structure of triangular units invented by Buckminster Fuller in 1949.

Geothermal energy The natural heat in the earth, which can be used to heat buildings. The energy from steam can be used to produce electricity.

Gesamtkunstwerk (total artwork) A concept used by the Wiener Werkstätte (defined below) to create unified interiors and architecture.

Gestural abstraction A form of the Abstract Expressionist movement. Paint was splattered, splashed, poured, and dripped on canvases.

Gimp A decorative narrow, flat trim.

Globalization A concept that describes the worldwide interchange of ideas, goods, services, and capital.

Gothic revival A style popular in the 19th century that reflected medieval architecture of the Gothic period.

Graywater A conservation technology that reverts wastewater from sources such as showers and laundry to alternative uses.

Greenhouse effect A phenomenon associated with global warming that is caused by gases that absorb and retain solar radiation. Carbon dioxide and methane are two gases that contribute to the greenhouse effect by trapping the sun's heat in the atmosphere.

Hang hongse (swan's tail) A common form of decoration along the edges of eave boards.

Hanok A traditional Korean house that has a thatched roof, wood beams, and the ancient ondol method of heating.

Harmika A square-shaped railing on the top of a stupa's dome.

Harvest A sustainability term used to describe the "gathering" of natural resources, such as daylight and water, for productive uses.

Ikat A textile-weaving process that creates a pattern with a water-stained appearance. The complex weaving and resist-dyeing process involves tying threads prior to their being dyed and woven.

Inclusive design An international term synonymous with universal design, people-centered design, or accessible design.

Indoor environmental quality (IEQ) A sustainability term that encompasses many attributes of an interior, including a room's temperature, humidity, ventilation, air quality, and noise levels.

Inrōs A Japanese small nested boxed unit that was used to hold small items, such as medications.

Interactive textile A technology incorporated into fabrics that creates responses from an input.

International Style An architectural style that was a precursor to the Modern movement. Coined by Henry-Russell Hitchcock and Philip Johnson at an exhibition at the Museum of Modern Art in New York City in 1932.

Islamic design Fine arts, architecture, and decorative arts derived from the religious faith of the Muslim Empire. Most notable are Islamic mosques and palaces. The style evolved by blending the native traditions of the countries ruled by the Muslims with specific decorative themes, such as calligraphy, stylized figures, plant motifs, arabesque, and geometric patterns.

Japan work A shellac or varnish finish that became popular in the 17th and 18th centuries when there was a great demand for Japanese lacquered objects d'art. Also known as *Japanning*.

Japanning A shellac or varnish finish that became popular in the 17th and 18th centuries when there was a great demand for Japanese lacquered objects d'art. Also known as *Japan work*.

Japonisme A term used to describe designs that were inspired by Japanese styles and motifs.

Jute A fiber from a tropical woody herb that can be woven into floorcoverings and other products.

Kala A decorative element in the form of a demon's head with pointed ears, sharp teeth, and claws for fingers.

Kinnara A decorative element in the form of a half human and half bird.

Lacquer A specialized finish that is applied to a surface. Applying a very thin layer of lacquer numerous times creates a lacquered piece. After each application, the lacquer must dry and harden in a climate-controlled room with high humidity.

Ladder-back A chair back that has open horizontal slats that resemble the rungs on a ladder.

Laminating A processing method that involves layering sheets of a material, such as paper or wood, with thermosetting resins.

Laterite A clay-like substance that hardens when exposed to air.

Lava lamp A decorative luminaire with illuminated flowing bubbles made from a waxy substance.

Leadership in Energy and Environmental Design (LEED) A voluntary certification program sponsored by the U.S. Green Building Council. The program verifies that a building project "meets the highest green building and performance measures" (www.usgbc.org).

LEDs (light-emitting diodes) As a semiconductor device, LEDs have a chemical chip embedded in a plastic capsule. The light is focused or scattered by using lenses or diffusers (Winchip, 2005).

Leno weave A textile with an open weave and twisted warp yarns.

Linoleum A resilient, sustainable floor covering invented in 1860. Linoleum is made from a mixture of linseed oil derived from flaxseed and other natural substances.

Luminaire An electrical light fixture.

Magnesite A mineral made of magnesium carbonate that can be sculpted.

Mainstream technology Objects and features that help people to perform a task. Examples include Velcro, elevators, and kitchen utensils with ergonomically designed hand grips.

Majolica ceramics With origins in Italy, a highly decorated soft earthenware with tin and lead glazes.

Makara A decorative element in the form of a reptile spewing objects.

Maki-e A decorative technique that involves sprinkling gold or silver particles over wet lacquer.

Means of egress The path for exiting a building.

Mecate A sisal-like fiber that can be woven into strips or other products.

Media room A room dedicated to watching television or movies and listening to music.

Melamine A thermoset plastic resistant to heat and most chemicals.

Memphis A movement (1980–1988) using unexpected combinations of forms, colors, and materials created by a group of architects and designers.

Mihrab A niche in a mosque indicating the direction of prayer, which is always toward the holy city of Mecca.

Minbar A stepped pulpit next to a mihrab in a mosque.

Modern movement An early 20th-century style based on scientific and technological developments.

Modernismo An architectural style that blends Brazil's traditions and international avant-garde. Also known as *Brazilian Modern*.

Modulor system A mathematical system created by Le Corbusier that uses human dimensions as the guide for the sizes of objects and the built environment.

Molding A processing method that involves intense heat and pressure.

Molten plastic Heated plastic poured into a mold and hardened during the cooling process.

Mordant A substance used to set dyes in textiles.

Mortise and tenon joint A woodworking joinery technique with a unit (tenon) that is inserted into a hole (mortise).

Museography A museum's collection program.

Nagas A decorative element in the form of a mythical serpent-like creature.

Nanotechnology (molecular manufacturing) A multidisciplinary field that involves controlling materials at the extremely small nanometer scale, one billionth of a meter.

Neoclassical A mid-18th-century style that was a reaction against the Baroque and Rococo periods. Classical Greek and Roman architecture were the sources of inspiration.

Nonrenewable resource A natural element that cannot be replenished, such as oil, coal, natural gas, and minerals.

Nuclear energy An alternative energy source that utilizes uranium, a nonrenewable and radioactive resource. The nuclear reaction process creates deadly radioactive waste with the potential to be lethal for thousands of years.

Ogive-shaped projections Curved-shaped protrusions often used in traditional Russian wooden architecture.

Ondol (warm stone) A heating system that dates back to the Koguryŏ (Three Kingdoms) (37 BCE–668). The underfloor heating system uses ducts beneath the clay or stone floor to heat the rooms of a structure.

Onion dome An arched architectural element in a bulbous shape.

Open office layout An office space without partition walls.

Organic design As defined by the Museum of Modern Art, "a harmonious organization of the parts within the whole, according to structure, material, and purpose" (Noyes, 1969 reprint edition, p. 1).

Orientalist paintings Middle Eastern scenes painted by Western artists.

Paisley An Islamic-inspired motif used in Indian textiles. The shape resembles an apostrophe and was based on the outline of an elongated floral bouquet.

Palampore A pattern derived from India with a design consisting of a tree of life filled with intertwining vines, flowers, and blooms.

Palladian style A style based on the work of 16th-century Italian Renaissance architect Andrea Palladio. In using the classical orders and harmonic proportions, the Palladian style is similar to the neoclassical style.

Parapet A low wall at the edge of a roof, balcony, or other structure.

Parasol A term used to describe a second roof on a structure.

Passementerie A French term for decorative trims that include gimp, cords, ropes, fringes, tiebacks, and rosettes. The trims can be made by hand, using a handloom or a mechanical loom.

Passive solar energy A technology that uses the sun's energy to heat materials.

Phase-changing material A technology that responds to variations in an environment or an individual, such as temperature fluctuations.

Photonic textile A technology that integrates fabrics with lighting systems.

Pinnacle A pointed decorative element frequently used at the end of a buttress or turret on Gothic architecture.

Plexiglas A privately owned name for a light and transparent acrylic sheet that is weather resistant.

Plywood A construction material that is made by gluing together thin sheets of wood.

Podium An elevated platform that supports a building; often Roman temples were placed on this structure.

Polder Drained areas that were once under water.

Polycarbonate A thermoplastic with high impact resistance.

Polypropylene A thermoplastic that can be extruded and is resistant to heat and chemicals.

Polystyrene (Styrofoam) A lightweight thermoplastic used for packaging and flotation equipment.

Polyurethane A foaming thermoset plastic suitable for padding, seat cushions, insulation, and stretch fabrics.

Polyvinyl chloride (PVC) A thermoplastic that is strong and resistant to sunlight and abrasion. Uses include flooring, imitation leather, textiles, electrical insulation, and pipes.

Pop Art Art movement in the mid-20th century that focused on popular consumerism, celebrities, and politicians.

Postmodern architecture An international style that reacted against the formality of Modernist designs.

Prairie House An architectural style with low horizontal lines that reflected the Midwestern landscape in the United States. The conceptual origins of the Prairie House can be traced to articles written by architect Frank Lloyd Wright for the *Ladies' Home Journal* in February and July of 1901.

Primavera wood A blond-colored wood with graining that resembles mahogany.

Primitive Art A movement based on drawings, paintings, and sculptures created by what are viewed as "untrained" artists. Also known as *tribal art.*

Public housing projects Residences that are owned and managed by a government for low-income people.

Qibla A wall in a mosque that has the mihrab.

Rattan The stems from tropical palms that can be used to make furniture.

Reinforced concrete A building material consisting of cement, sand, gravel, aggregates, and water that is embedded with steel rods for additional tensile strength.

Renewable resource A natural element that can be replenished, such as sunlight and wind.

Resin lacquer A lacquer made from a substance excreted from female insects.

Resist-dyeing A textile dye process that creates a design by using substances that prevent the penetration of a dye. The process is used to create batik, tie-dyeing, and ikat.

Riwaq (covered arcades) A term used in the context of Islamic architecture.

Roof-comb A characteristic of the Puuc-style, a unit on the top of a building decorated in pierced stone.

Rope A decorative trim made from plied yarns that are twisted together. A cord becomes a rope when the thickness exceeds 1 inch (2.54 centimeters).

Rosette A decorative trim made in the shape of a rose.

Ruff A decorative pleated trim that can be used at the top of fringes and bullions.

R-value A designation that indicates a material's resistance to the flow of heat.

Sabot A French term for wooden shoe. Used at the ends of furniture legs.

Sahn (courtyard) A term used in the context of Islamic architecture.

Scandinavian modernism An architectural style that blends Scandinavian's traditions and international avant-garde.

Seismic joint Opening in a structure that is designed to minimize damage to a building during an earthquake.

Settle A wide seating unit made from wood with a high back and arms. Often the seat has a hinged top that accesses a storage area.

Shagreen A rough leather, often dyed green.

Shoji Japanese sliding panels originally made from rice paper.

Sideboard A dining room furniture piece that has cabinets and drawers for storage.

Singha A decorative element in the form of a guardian lion.

Slip decoration A porcelain design that is applied by painting with liquid clay.

Slip inlay decoration A porcelain design that is applied by inlaying clay into its surface.

Smart textile A technology that enables a material to continuously interact and react to physiological conditions of the human body.

Solar energy A technology that uses sunlight for heat and the production of electricity.

Stupa A reliquary containing ashes of Buddhist religious figures.

Supergraphics Large-scale patterns.

Sustainable design An international concept that focuses on creating designs that address the needs of people, the natural environment, and economic development for both immediate and future generations.

Swag and cascade A fabric window treatment with soft horizontal folds and side elements that gradually ripple toward the floor.

Tassel A decorative element of trim made with numerous threads that may be looped or cut.

Tatami mat A Japanese floor covering made in panels from woven grassy materials and bound with a cloth tape.

Tenement A term for high-density apartment buildings.

Tent roof A structural unit in a conical shape that protects a building.

Terrazo A floor covering that is comprised of marble and other stones, set in mortar.

Textile shelter A dwelling that is transportable because it is lightweight and compact and has tensile strength.

Thermoforming (vacuum forming) A processing method that uses heat to adhere plastic sheets over a form. A vacuum pump removes air from the surfaces. A common method used in the fabrication of shower stalls, boats, and parts of aircraft.

Thermoplastic A major classification of plastic materials that can become soft if reheated.

Thermosetting plastics A major classification of plastic materials that will not become soft if reheated.

Tie-dyeing A resist process that involves gathering and tying various areas of a cloth followed by immersion in a dye bath. The tied areas do not absorb the dye, thus creating the pattern.

Tieback A decorative trim used to hold a drapery treatment.

Toranas A gateway used for Buddhist structures.

Transom A fixed or operable window above a doorway.

Travertine A beige-colored stone that can be used for floor and wallcoverings.

Trefoils A three-part clover design often used in Gothic architecture.

True lacquer The most traditional lacquer form. Made from the sap of the *rhus vernicifera* tree, which is indigenous to China. The sap is extracted by collecting the substance as it oozes from numerous horizontal cuts made in the bark.

Tuxedo-style sofa An upholstered seating unit with upholstered arms that are the same height as the back of the sofa.

Ubosot A Buddhist ordination hall. Also known as a *bot*.

Universal Design A concept that focuses on creating designs that are accessible and convenient for all people.

Vedikás Balustrades used on a stupa.

Vihãra A religious assembly hall. Also known as a *wihan*.

Visual acuity The eye's function related to discerning details.

Visual culture An academic discipline that studies everything people see, including paintings, sculpture, movies, television, photographs, furniture, buildings, artifacts, jewelry, apparel, and light. The discipline considers "institutional, economic, political, social, ideological, and market factors" (University of Wisconsin–Madison, 2007, p. 1).

Wat A Buddhist temple.

Water power (hydroelectric power) A technology that utilizes the energy in falling or running water to generate electricity.

Wiener Werkstätte (Vienna Workshops) An organization founded by Josef Hoffmann and Koloman in the early 20th century. To create a unified interior, the workshops produced textiles, furniture, ceramics, glass, and metalwork.

Wihan A religious assembly hall. Also known as a *vihãra*.

Wind power A technology that creates electricity by using the kinetic energy from wind to operate generators.

Zellij (Zellige) tilework A specialized ceramic tile made from intricate mosaic pieces that are set in plaster.

INDEX